Dynamic Web Programming

ISBN 0-13-086184-7

9 780130 861849

90000

Inform*ix* Press

ADMINISTERING INFORMIX DYNAMIC SERVER ON WINDOWS NT
Carlton Doe

DATA WAREHOUSING WITH INFORMIX: BEST PRACTICES
Angela Sanchez, Editor

DYNAMIC WEB PROGRAMMING: USING JAVA, JAVASCRIPT AND INFORMIX
Graham Harrison

INFORMIX BASICS
Glenn Miller

INFORMIX DBA SURVIVAL GUIDE, 2/E
Joe Lumbley

INFORMIX DYNAMIC SERVER.2000: SERVER-SIDE PROGRAMMING IN C
Jacques Roy

INFORMIX DYNAMIC SERVER WITH UNIVERSAL DATA OPTION:
BEST PRACTICES
Angela Sanchez, Editor

INFORMIX GUIDE TO DESIGNING DATABASES AND DATA WAREHOUSES
Informix Software

INFORMIX GUIDE TO SQL: REFERENCE & SYNTAX, 2/E
Informix Software

INFORMIX GUIDE TO SQL: TUTORIAL, 2/E
Informix Software

THE INFORMIX HANDBOOK
Ron Flannery

INFORMIX-ONLINE DYNAMIC SERVER HANDBOOK
Carlton Doe

INFORMIX: POWER REFERENCE
Art Taylor

INFORMIX SQL REFERENCE LIBRARY
Informix Software

JDBC DEVELOPER'S RESOURCE, 2/E
Art Taylor

PROGRAMMING INFORMIX SQL/4GL: A STEP-BY-STEP APPROACH, 2/E
Cathy Kipp

SAP R/3 FOR THE INFORMIX DBA
Sari Nathans

For a complete list of Informix Press titles, please visit
www.phptr.com or www.informix.com/ipress

Dynamic Web Programming

Using Java™,
JavaScript™,
and Informix®

Graham Harrison

Prentice Hall PTR
Upper Saddle River, New Jersey 07458
www.phptr.com

Library of Congress Cataloging-in-Publication Data

Harrison, Graham Paul.
  Dynamic web programming: using Java, JavaScript, and Informix / Graham Paul Harrison.
     p. cm.
  ISBN 0-13-086184-7
  1. Internet programming. 2. Java (Computer program language) 3. JavaScript
(Computer program language) 4. INFORMIX Dynamic server. I. Title.
QA76.625 .H37 2000
005.7'2—dc21   99-055467

Acquisitions Editor: *Miles Williams*
Editorial/Production Supervision: *Precision Graphics*
Cover Design Director: *Jerry Votta*
Cover Design: *Anthony Gemmellaro*
Manufacturing Manager: *Alexis R. Heydt*
Editorial Assistant: *Noreen Regina*
Marketing Manager: *Kate Hargett*
Manager, Informix Press: *Judy Bowman*

Inform*i*x· Press

Informix Press
Informix Software, Inc.
4100 Bohannon Drive
Menlo Park, CA 94025
http://www.informix.com/ipress
ipress@informix.com

 © 2000 by Prentice Hall PTR
Prentice-Hall, Inc.
Upper Saddle River, New Jersey 07458

To Lily, Jack, Sue and Dad, with love

Contents

Preface

The Informix Web DataBlade is one of the most versatile products on the market today for connecting the web to the database. Creating and managing dynamic web content across the enterprise is crucial to web-enabling databases for business—but information on how to do this, how to make the right design decisions and then make it all perform well, is sparse and scattered across multiple volumes of formal documentation. Information on how to integrate all this with Java and JavaScript is nonexistent. This book integrates all the relevant material, including some of the unpublished tips that hard experience brings.

While working with customers to deploy this technology, it became clear that a conceptual Rubicon was crossed in almost every case, and that integrating the different technologies required a simple but clear understanding of the position of each in the overall web systems architecture.

One day in the early 1990s, I, then knowing nothing about the Internet, dialed in to it. I was unprepared for what followed. The concentrated excitement of being able to download tons of information, about almost any subject I was interested in, was impossible to resist. As a professional programmer working with database management systems, I knew I had to master the technology and link it to a database. That excitement, what Shaw called "the seventh degree of concentration," persisted into many long nights of coding, uploading, and downloading.

When I began to use the Informix Web DataBlade, I felt the same excitement at how simple it was to manage the world of rich content and enterprise data. One of the great contributions that Informix makes to the Internet community is the ability to manage this content and deliver it over the Internet; with rich content and mission-critical data merging into information, Informix' technical brilliance is well positioned to leverage that information and deliver it to the growing world of the e-customer.

Developers come to the web wanting to use JavaScript and Java, and the next step is integrating the database. This book will synthesize all three for novice web developers, database administrators, consultants, and experienced developers wanting to understand the wider issues involved. Non–database programmers will have the power to access the database from the web with little or no SQL knowledge.

Acknowledgments

First, very special thanks go to my family, and especially to my partner, Sue Marples, whose support, tolerance and perseverance over many months enabled me to complete the book, and for which I am deeply grateful.

Next, a special "gold star" thank you is given to Randy Willard, a principal engineer with Informix. Randy's outstanding enthusiasm and expertise made a pivotal contribution to the review process that enabled me to complete the book on time; without Randy on board, the book almost certainly would not appear in its present form. Thanks, Randy.

A special thank you is also offered to David Pippin, a former associate of Informix in the United Kingdom, who reviewed the sections on Java and made some valuable suggestions that were incorporated in the final copy.

I would also like to thank Chris Jenkins of the Advanced Technology Group at Informix for his important review of the chapter on performance tuning.

Special thanks must be given to Colin Tucker of Omensoft (omenmedia@ozemail.com.au), who wrote the superb Omentree software described in Chap. 6, and who allowed me to reproduce the software in its original and customized forms in the book and on the CD-ROM.

Special thanks are also given to Fuat A. Kircaali and SYS-CON Publications for permission to reproduce and rework parts of my article in *Java Developer's Journal*, "Browsing the JDBC API" (volume 3, issue 4), which appear in Chap. 11.

A gracious thank you is given to Todd Katz and the Informix By Example team for allowing me to reproduce and develop the complete examples on RMI and some examples for JDBC, and for permission to reuse some of the figures and step-by-step guides from the Informix By Example site in Chaps. 7, 8, and 10. Todd's cooperation has significantly enhanced the book.

A special thank you is given to Andy Stephenson and Tim Clark of Informix Professional Services in the United Kingdom, for allowing me to reorganize my schedule on very short notice to meet the demands of publication.

Thanks are also given to Andrew Hopkinson and Thom Fortunato of Informix Professional Services in the United Kingdom, for making constructive suggestions and comments.

Special thanks are due to my acquisition editor at Prentice Hall, Miles Williams, for courtesy and patience, and for obtaining valuable permissions on short notice. Thanks also to the production team of Anne Trowbridge and Precision Graphics for a great job in creating the final form of the book.

Thanks also to Judy Bowman and Informix Press for allowing me to reproduce useful presentation material throughout the book, especially Parts 1 and 4, and for permission to reproduce text from the Web DataBlade manual and related material, in particular, sections of Part 3, and Appendices A and B.

Finally, thanks are due to the world of logic, for allowing me to be its guest.

The Importance of Dynamic Web Applications

Introduction

This book shows you how to create high-performance database-driven websites using Java, JavaScript, and Informix Dynamic Server with the Web DataBlade.

The Web DataBlade allows you to create web page templates that you can expand to include references to multimedia content and business information stored inside (or outside) of the Informix database.

Even if you just want to query the database from a Java applet, this book is for you. It can, however, also be used as a tutorial for learning how to create distributed applications using remote method invocation (RMI) and Java database connectivity (JDBC). If you want to connect a Java applet to a Java server program that can connect to a database, this book is for you, as well.

Specifically, this book will teach you the following:

- how to create web page templates using Web DataBlade AppPage scripting tags and functions

- how to hide SQL complexity from the web developer by using Web DataBlade dynamic tags
- how to write Java applets and applications that connect to the database using JDBC
- how to write multitier RMI (Remote Method Invocation) Java applets and applications that access different types of objects in the database using JDBC
- how to leverage the power of JavaScript to work with information in the Informix database
- how to integrate Java, JavaScript, and Web DataBlade AppPage Scripting to leverage the power of each language
- how to configure, secure, and tune these applications for performance

The Web DataBlade eases the development, management, and deployment of database applications for the Web. Optimized for both publishing and transaction-based environments, the Web DataBlade combined with Informix Dynamic Server.2000 or Informix Dynamic Server with the Universal Data Option enables organizations to create intelligent web applications that incorporate all types of data, including HTML files and multimedia content such as text, images, maps, and photos—all retrieved dynamically from the Informix database.

The Web DataBlade allows users to construct anything from a simple query front-end web page to an interactive website that retrieves and updates any data stored in the Informix database. Using Web DataBlade tags, developers don't have to write low-level gateway interface code, allowing them to focus instead on application flow and design.

There is another fundamental reason for using this product: Creating dynamic web pages with the Web DataBlade is much simpler than using products from rival vendors to do a similar job.

Who Should Use This Book

This book covers several major topics important to various types of users.

Web application developers, novice to experienced, who use Informix Dynamic Server on UNIX or NT, will find this book extremely useful. In particular, you can learn how to integrate Java and JavaScript with Informix AppPage Script and how to use the Type 4 JDBC driver with the Informix database. Developers interested in web enabling large Informix Databases will find this book especially useful in a hands-on context.

Website administrators can learn to understand why managing dynamic content is crucial to website performance.

Windows NT and Unix system administrators, while in some cases not as directly responsible for website performance as website administrators, still need working knowledge of how to administer mission-critical web-based systems and familiarity with the performance implications for underlying operating systems and hardware. This book covers material essential for Informix Dynamic Server and the Web DataBlade, as well as other important concepts that are applicable regardless of product.

Database administrators who have to administer web-enabled Informix databases will find performance tips in context.

Systems architects and, more generally, those responsible for putting together the components for a commercial web presence, will be able to explore the Informix options involved. Systems architects will learn the benefits of using the Informix Web DataBlade to develop database-driven web applications, particularly important for those who have to implement enterprise-wide Internet commerce or media asset management systems. Making design decisions involving multiple platforms which use Java, JavaScript, and Informix AppPage Script are also discussed.

Anyone interested in the wider performance issues of web-enabling mission-critical Informix applications in particular and database applications in general will benefit from the book. Non-database programmers will have the power to write database access without SQL knowledge.

What You Should Be Familiar With

You need only a basic working knowledge of HTML (hypertext markup language), JavaScript, and Java to cover the chapters that use this material. An elementary level of knowledge should allow you to pick up the Java and JavaScript code samples fairly quickly.

Ideally, you should also have an elementary grasp of SQL (structured query language) or at least understand the concept of a relational database—a level of knowledge that you can pick up by using any relational database product, however small. The aim isn't to teach SQL but to show you how it is used to extract smart information from the database and present it in a web page. You don't need to be an SQL guru to do this. One of the advantages of using the Web DataBlade is that special tags (dynamic tags) can be implemented that hide SQL complexity from you.

How To Use This Book

The key theme of this book is how to use Java, JavaScript, and the Informix Web DataBlade to create dynamic, database-driven websites. This book will provide the relevant tutorial and reference material to help you do this. The book doesn't teach you everything there is to know about the Web DataBlade—or Java and JavaScript for that matter; rather, it shows you how to be effective with all three, primarily focusing on working with the Web DataBlade and integrating Java, JDBC, and JavaScript around this important technology.

You can use this book in a number of ways:

1. as a tutorial on the essentials of JDBC and RMI programming
2. as an example of how to use database-driven JavaScript
3. as a tutorial and reference for the essentials of the Web DataBlade
4. as a reference for configuring, securing, and performance tuning your Informix web application
5. as a compendium of issues that group themselves into related areas

The book is split into four parts that group related information into separate chapters to facilitate the fifth use above. The four parts of the book correspond to the first four uses.

Part One, "The Importance of Dynamic Web Applications," describes the context of database-driven websites and introduces the key technologies used throughout the book.

Part Two, "Dynamic Web Programming with Java, JDBC, and JavaScript," contains all the material essential to a tutorial for learning how to program Java applets and applications with Java database connectivity (JDBC), especially when those applications use the Informix Type 4 JDBC driver. This part of the book also shows how to create distributed Java applets and applications using RMI and JDBC.

Part Three, "Dynamic Web DataBlade Programming," contains all the material relevant to creating Web DataBlade applications using Versions 3 and 4 of the Informix Web DataBlade. Web

DataBlade tags and variable-processing functions are illustrated. Separate chapters are devoted to Informix products, such as Data Director for Web and AppPage Builder, that rely on the Web DataBlade. This part of the book also shows how to manage dynamic forms in the browser, upload and retrieve documents to and from the Informix database, reuse code via dynamic tags, and work with large objects, such as GIF images and audio files, as well as providing a useful reference for Web DataBlade tags and functions.

Part Four, "Advanced Configuration and Performance," shows how to configure the Web DataBlade for Versions 3 and 4 of the product, how to configure web servers from Netscape, Microsoft, and the Apache web server to work with Web DataBlade applications, and, importantly, how to optimize Web DataBlade applications for performance. In addition, separate chapters are devoted to security issues and debugging.

There are many working examples of Java, JavaScript, and Web DataBlade template code. Some chapters are devoted to a particular application example, such as a JavaScript SQL Explorer, Java SQL Editor, Database Browser and a Customer Maintenance Application, although the flavor of most chapters is practical. You can extend the examples as you require.

Chapter Breakdown

The chapters in the book can be summarized as follows:

Chapter 2, "Web Applications: The Generation Gap," explains how web architectures have evolved through well-defined generations from simple flat-file-based systems to complex, dynamic, database-driven, content-rich web architectures.

Chapter 3, "Dynamic Web Solutions: Managing the Digital Value Chain," describes the digital value chain and the customer solution cycle and shows why they are important concepts, especially when the Informix Web DataBlade can be used to manage the whole digital value chain: providing a gateway to talk to credit card authorization, billing, and inventory systems, while managing all the content.

Chapter 4, "Introduction to Dynamic Web Application Development," introduces and places in context the key technologies used in the book, from the browser using JavaScript and Java to the database server using Informix AppPage Script.

Chapter 5, "Create Dynamic Web Pages Using JavaScript," illustrates how to use JavaScript in isolation, with Java (using

LiveConnect), and with the Web DataBlade to create sophisticated, client-based, dynamic web pages. In particular, the chapter contains novel ways of working with database content driven by JavaScript in the browser.

Chapter 6, "A JavaScript SQL Explorer," describes a JavaScript hierarchical tree similar to Windows Explorer that you can use to manage all kinds of web content. Aside from being a great utility function, the tree uses Web DataBlade dynamic tags to manage JavaScript complexity, and so is an interesting example of how to use the power of JavaScript on the client as well as how to generate JavaScript on the web or database server.

Chapter 7, "Informix Java Database Connectivity," introduces key JDBC topics in a practical way so that you can start to connect to an Informix database on your laptop or remote machine very quickly. What you learn in this chapter can be applied in general to other database servers, not just Informix.

Chapter 8, "Essential JDBC Programming," describes the essentials of JDBC programming and how to work with different kinds of web content, including relational data and object content such as GIF images. Tracing JDBC activity and performance tuning of the Informix Type 4 JDBC driver is also covered.

Chapter 9, "Integrating Java Applets with the Database," shows how to serve Java applets from the Informix database and how to parameterize and personalize those applets using Web DataBlade tags.

Chapter 10, "Creating Distributed Applications Using RMI and JDBC," introduces the essentials of creating distributed database applications using remote method invocation (RMI) with the Informix Type 4 JDBC Driver. In particular, you are shown how to create a multitier database application using RMI and how to use RMI in Java applets.

Chapter 11, "A Simple Java SQL Editor," describes an SQL editor written in Java that provides an SQL interface to any database for which there is a JDBC or ODBC driver. The Java SQL Editor provides a basic, useful GUI interface for a database. The aim of this chapter is to use a simple application to pull together some of the key themes from the preceding chapters on Java.

Chapter 12, "Web DataBlade Architecture," illustrates the different components that make up a Web DataBlade application and shows how they all work.

Chapter 13, "Creating and Managing Websites with Data Director for Web," describes the essential features of the Informix Data Director for Web product that you use to build and deploy websites, and shows where Data Director for Web fits into the development lifecycle model.

Chapter 14, "Creating Web Applications with AppPage Builder," shows you how to use the Informix AppPage Builder Application, which ships with the Web DataBlade, to store web content in the Informix database and deliver it using AppPage templates.

Chapter 15, "Working with AppPage Tags and Functions," covers all the fundamental components in AppPage scripting, including AppPage tags, variable processing functions, AppPage variables, and Website navigation. You can use this chapter as a reference to look up the AppPage tags and functions that you require.

Chapter 16, "Web Database Programming with AppPages," shows how to use Informix AppPage Script to create dynamic web pages that maintain data in the Informix database. Using the simple examples in this part of the book, you can learn to create a dynamic database-driven website.

Chapter 17, "Dynamic Web Forms Programming," shows how to use Informix AppPage Script, JavaScript, and HTML to create interactive forms that maintain data in the Informix database.

Chapter 18, "Managing Documents in the Information Repository," shows how to upload desktop and other documents into the Informix database and then retrieve them, using the browser to do both. The chapter contains an example that you can extend to meet your own specific requirements.

Chapter 19, "Creating and Using Dynamic Tags," shows how to reduce the maintenance requirements of your website by using Informix Dynamic Tags to create a common code repository.

Chapter 20, "Working with Large Objects," shows why large objects, such as blobs, are important and how to access these objects in the Informix database for web delivery to the client browser. This knowledge will help you grasp some of the essentials of delivering sophisticated multimedia content over the Web from a database.

Chapter 21, "A Customer Maintenance Application," presents a complete example of a browser application that maintains customer details in the Informix database using HTML forms, AppPage Script, and JavaScript, and it represents a complete end-to-end development exercise.

Chapter 22, "Understanding `webdriver` Configuration," describes the configuration of the `webdriver` program for Versions 3 and 4 of the Informix Web DataBlade, tells why the `webdriver` configuration is important, and explains how to set `webdriver` configuration parameters for AppPage Builder and Data Director for Web applications.

Chapter 23, "Web Server Integration," shows how to configure the Netscape, Microsoft, and Apache web servers for CGI (common gateway interface) and API (application programming interface) `webdrivers`, such as NSAPI, ISAPI, and Apache API.

Chapter 24, "Securing your Web Applications," shows how to secure your Web DataBlade applications at the application and web-server level, including SSL (secure sockets layer).

Chapter 25, "Performance-tuning Essentials," is a guide to performance tuning for the different components in a Web DataBlade application.

Chapter 26, "Debugging Web DataBlade Applications," is concerned with debugging Web applications as well as tracking down problems in an end-to-end context.

Appendix A, "Variable Mappings," lists the `webdriver` variables whose names have changed between Versions 3 and 4 of the Web DataBlade. If you want to check the names of variables between versions, use this Appendix as a quick reference.

Appendix B, "`webdriver` Variables," lists the `webdriver` variables that you can use according to function.

Using the `stores` Database

When you obtain Informix Dynamic Server, you are provided with a test database, `stores7` or `stores9`, depending on whether you are using Version 7.x or Version 9.x of the engine. In order to avoid overcomplicating the examples in this book, the `stores7` database schema was used as the basis for the example data. This schema does not use some of the advanced features of the Universal Data Option schema, such as row types. The aim is to make the essential points as simply as possible without getting sidetracked into advanced schema-related features. In addition, readers who use Version 7 of the Informix Dynamic Server should be able to develop some of the examples without redesigning the schema.

The `stores7` database schema is used as the starting point. Several tables were added to the schema as the examples were developed—in particular, tables that manage smart large objects for an online catalog. The complete schema is contained on the accompanying CD, called `stores.sql`.

Informix Web Products Overview

In this book, we are dealing strictly with the Informix Web DataBlade—specifically, Versions 3 and 4 of the Web DataBlade. The Web DataBlade is designed for Informix Dynamic Server with

the Universal Data Option, which is Version 9.x. Version 4 of the
Web DataBlade is designed for Informix Dynamic Server.2000.

The Web DataBlade and Informix Dynamic Server

The Web DataBlade was formerly positioned as one component in a
product that was known as the *Web Integration Option.* Historically,
the Web Integration Option existed as an umbrella term for two
components; the first was called Universal Web Connect and the
second was called Web DataBlade. You could use only one component for your Informix server, and this depended on the Informix
server you were using.

Table 1-1 shows the product dependencies for the the Web
Integration Option and Web DataBlade.

Informix Dynamic Server.2000 sits within a product offering from
Informix called Informix Internet Foundation.2000 that together
with Informix Dynamic Server.2000, is described briefly in the next
section.

The Web DataBlade

The Web DataBlade is the product that is used in this book,
because it effectively supercedes Universal Web Connect. Version 3
and Version 4 are the two major versions of the Web Datablade.

Table 1-1. **Web Integration Option and Web DataBlade product
dependencies.**

Product	Informix Server version	Description
Web DataBlade Version 4	Informix Dynamic Server.2000	Dynamic pages are created in the database by DataBlade functions under the control of `webdriver` middleware.
Web DataBlade Version 3.x	Informix Dynamic Server/Universal Data Option (Version 9.x)	Same as Web DataBlade Version 4.
Universal Web Connect	Informix Dynamic Server Version 7 (including Workgroup Edition)	Dynamic web pages are created by the `webdriver` middleware component.

Version 4 is a functional enhancement of Version 3, which also enhances the configuration of the product. If you are using Informix Dynamic Server Version 7.x, however, you can only use the Universal Web Connect product with that engine. If you are using Informix Dynamic Server with the Universal Data Option, or Informix Dynamic Server.2000, then you should use the Web DataBlade product, as shown in Table 1-1.

Universal Web Connect

Universal Web Connect for Informix Dynamic Server Version 7 is a different product architecture than the Web DataBlade, since Informix Dynamic Server Version 7 does not have the Universal Data Option to register and use the DataBlade functions that generate dynamic web pages.

If you are using Version 7 of the engine with Universal Web Connect, examples in this book that use Version 4 enhancements to the Web DataBlade will not work. However, sufficient parity exists between earlier versions of Universal Web Connect and the Web DataBlade to implement a reasonable amount of the AppPage Scripting tags and functions described in this book. Bear in mind, though, that Informix Dynamic Server with the Universal Data Option and Informix Dynamic Server.2000 are better suited than IDS Version 7 for content-rich, data-driven web applications.

Informix Internet Foundation.2000

Informix Dynamic Server.2000 sits within a product offering called Informix Internet Foundation.2000. This product contains the following components:

- Informix Dynamic Server.2000
- Informix J/Foundation
- Informix COM Developer's Kit
- Informix Web DataBlade Module
- Informix Excalibur Text DataBlade Module
- Informix Office Connect

You don't need the full Informix Internet Foundation.2000 product to use the Web DataBlade Version 4 product. You can use Informix Dynamic Server.2000 with Web DataBlade Version 4 in isolation.

Informix Dynamic Server.2000

The database server at the heart of Informix Internet Foundation.2000 is Informix Dynamic Server.2000, which combines transaction processing, Internet data management, and content extensibility. Informix Dynamic Server.2000 is a combination of Informix's IDS 7.x and IDS/Universal Data Option 9.1x code lines, that offers enhanced performance and functionality.

Informix J/Foundation

This is a standard Java environment within the Informix database that is created by embedding the best-of-breed Java Virtual Machines (JVMs) into the server process. J/Foundation enables user-defined routines (UDRs) and DataBlade modules to be developed in Java, and it provides an environment for the migration of data-intensive Java logic into the server for greater performance.

Informix COM Developer's Kit

This module offers developers the power to run COM business logic in the Informix server along with Java, allowing organizations to integrate existing COM libraries with business content.

Informix Web DataBlade Module

The Web DataBlade module allows organizations to transform their business data into dynamic data-driven web pages.

Informix Excalibur Text DataBlade Module

This module provides full-text searching inside the database engine for documents in virtually any format that contains ASCII and ISO characters.

Informix Office Connect

This module simplifies the task of retrieving data and visualizing it in office products such as Microsoft Excel Spreadsheets or work-books, regardless of the data types behind the data.

Summary

This introduction has described how the book is structured so that you can make best use of the material within it. Additionally, the products that made up the original Web Integration Option were listed, and the Informix Internet Foundation.2000 and Informix Dynamic Server.2000 products were briefly described. You are now less than one book away from creating dynamic database-driven and media-rich websites.

Web Applications: The Generation Gap

In this chapter:

- Introduction
- First-generation web applications
- Second-generation web applications
- Informix third-generation web applications
- The next generation

Web applications conveniently group themselves into recognizable generations. Each generation is broadly defined by the application architecture, not by age or functional complexity. This chapter will explain how generations of web applications have evolved from simple hypertext document repositories to business-critical, media-asset-based, content management applications. Each generation can present a set of problems that the next generation's architecture tries to solve. The importance of this chapter, however, lies in positioning the Informix web platform within the latest architectural model. Dynamic web content can be more than an exciting technology for adding spice to a website; it should be a design thread for implementing mission-critical business solutions across the intranet, Internet, and extranet surfaces.

Introduction

Classifying web applications into generations allows the features and drawbacks of each generation to be easily identified. If you classify your own or your company's web applications into one of the three categories that follow, you will be able to identify the limitations in your systems and how to overcome them.

In reality, of course, websites can be a combination of generations: Some web content is stored in the database, and some in the file system. What may have begun as a static file-based website that concentrated on listing corporate products and services may become an interactive OLTP (Online transaction processing) site with a database that stores transaction data and customer profiles.

What needs to be remembered is why the website is there in the first place. Some of the questions that drive the technical options in web application development are:

- What information should the website contain?
- How can I manage my corporate assets in such a way that they talk and yield information?
- How can I allow my web surfers to mine the information in my corporate assets to their own, and to my, advantage?
- How can I personalize their service the way my visitors want it?
- How can I use the information they provide to tell me more about themselves and their kind in such a way that I can stop customer churn and keep them coming back?
- How can I leverage my corporate assets such that each and every member of the enterprise is a potential contributor and disseminator of information?

First-generation Web Applications

Early adopters of the Web were technical and academic. The initial business presence covered both external and internal sites. External sites were static pages of products and services, with a company

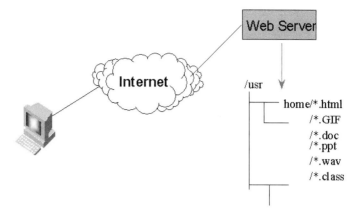

Figure 2-1. First-generation website architecture.

profile. The internal site contained items like the employee hand-book, an organizational chart, and the address of the webmaster to receive suggestions; sometimes there was a bulletin board. There was no real vision of empowerment—what could be made available, how the evolving technology could leverage the knowledge base of the enterprise.

Characteristics of the First Generation

Typically, as Figure 2-1 shows, the architecture of the first-generation website comprises a browser, a web server, and a set of flat files stored in the host file system.

The flat files are not just static HTML pages; they can include audio and video data, as well as MS-Excel, MS-PowerPoint, or Zip files; any file that needs to be downloaded to the browser is stored in a file system folder. The website is itself file based; it lives in the file system and is maintained along with the other files in the file system, even those that do not belong to the website. The website has an identity only in the web server (or web *servers,* if the file system is shared across a network) that contains the file system path of the document directory that contains the files.

The business drivers of the first-generation website tend to be sales and marketing departments who need a "shop font" on the web to advertise products and services. This is often the initial reason a company will create a website: to market its services. In addition, a company may want to allow registered users access to a first-cut knowledge base of information, such as press cuttings, business partners, and business contacts; this can be loosely described as an extranet context. Whatever the web application functionality, though, if the website content is stored as a flat file system, it belongs to the first generation.

The developers of this generation website tend to be ad hoc webmasters, enthusiasts, anyone who wants to get involved. The skills base of this contribution is therefore limited.

One of the advantages of this kind of website is that it is easy to build and deploy static sites. Using website-building tools, a static, corporate presence can be prototyped, built, and deployed in a matter of days. Importing the resulting site to an Informix database is also easy, as we shall see in Chap. 13, "Data Director for Web."

Problems with Static Websites

Content Stored in Multiple Places

The problem with the first-generation web application is that content is stored in multiple places. A website may reference multiple hosts, with website content distributed across a variety of computers. For example, if the website contains thumbnails of item information for a clothing catalog, the full images may be scanned in at one source, downloaded to another box where the thumbnails are produced, and the thumbnails exported to yet another box, perhaps even to a legacy database that supports blobs. This is how it is in the real world, where organization is imposed, not inherited. Organizing and controlling all of these items starts to take too much of the webmaster's time; and this is before considering that website content contains information, not just files and that this information needs as much control as the medium of delivery.

Security Considerations

File systems get hacked. An IT manager charged with securing her multimedia corporate assets may feel that she would like her enterprise database to store this information. As will be described in the chapter on performance tuning, it is extremely difficult to penetrate the database.

Difficult Backup, Recovery, and Search Mechanisms

Static websites are difficult to back up, recover, and query. The backup tends to be part of the overall file system backup of the host. The recovery is therefore open to perhaps gigabytes of information that must be traversed; the redundancy is enormous. The search capability is also limited. What if you want to find information on your websites? How many websites have you gone to where the first thing you jump for is the search mechanism? On a corporate website with perhaps 10,000 pages of static information, users will not leaf through the pages or navigate complicated fastpath indexes.

High Maintenance Cost

Static webpages refer to other webpages in the file system. If a page moves, the link in the referring page has to change: otherwise it will be broken. Most users only have to click one broken link to move on to another site; user interface ergonomics are crucial to site success—not just how the site looks and feels, but how it behaves. A website based on file system references depends on the manageability of the file system itself, and any single change may have multiple effects. For example, if you have a site with 100 pages, each with a feedback link, and the feedback page is moved, that's 100 changes, once you have made the backup of the files you will change. You are slightly better off if you are using UNIX and you can `grep` and `sed`; if you are a corporate user who is interested only in publishing website content as efficiently as possible, `grep` and `sed` are best ignored.

No Persistence of State

The HTTP protocol itself cannot maintain persistence of state. Accordingly, transactions cannot span multiple pages and forms. If you're doing an e-commerce site, this is a problem; you can't really maintain state and you can't use traditional application approaches. So, if you want to replicate a client server application but use the Web as your new way of doing it, a first-generation application will not help, because the design will not support what you want to do. For mission-critical systems to leverage the architecture of the Web, the Web application architecture needs to support the complexity and sophistication of multitiered transaction-based systems.

Content is Static

Of course, the content of the website is static, that is, the webpages— HTML, images, and videos—do not change. For example, a company that sells hardware and software through an online catalog will continually have to maintain the web pages that have product information hardcoded into them. A handful of pages may track your username in cookies, but the web content, the information, does not change. To change the product details, a HTML programmer has to edit the web page in the relevant folder. That's a lot of pages to edit for a lot of products and services.

In contrast to static content, dynamic content doesn't just mean that web pages change according to events in the sponsoring company, such as new products and services, or events in the user profile, such as searching for a certain type of product over another one. Dynamic content has an impact on almost every facet of website creation, maintenance, and use, as you will see.

Second-generation Web Applications: From Static to Dynamic

The second-generation site attempts to rectify some of the problems created with the static first-generation site by adding a programming layer to handle some of the required complexity and allow access to the database and legacy systems.

This programming layer is typically CGI (common gateway interface). It could also be a technology such as Netscape LiveWire, which, although it uses JavaScript and Java to access the database, is still based on the traditional ODBC and client communications API to access the database.

Figure 2-2 shows the components of a basic second-generation architecture. A program is called by the web server to perform some function on the web server host.

Figure 2-3 shows the components of a CGI architecture, and Fig. 2-4 shows the CGI components where the CGI program accesses the database.

In Figs. 2-3 and 2-4, the CGI program `a_program.exe` is recognized as a CGI program by the web server and is executed by the web server. Any parameters passed by the browser to the web server are passed to the CGI program. The output from the CGI program is redirected to the web browser. The CGI program may be a C or 4GL program, which ultimately invokes calls to the connectivity layer between the CGI program, which is a database client, and the database server. For database client programs running without a web server parent call, the same connectivity layer needs to be present, regardless of the web server. For multiple calls to this URL (uniform resource locator), multiple client processes will be spawned by the host operating system, and a connection made for each spawned process.

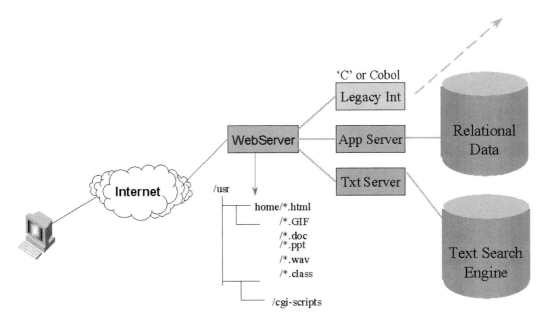

Figure 2-2. *Second-generation website architecture.*

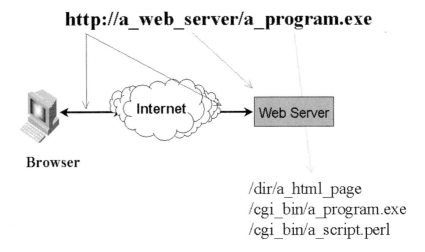

Figure 2-3. *The common gateway interface (CGI).*

It is possible to integrate the middle component (the CGI component in the last example) with some web servers. This allows what
was formerly a CGI program to run, not as a separate process for
each invocation, but as a multithreaded component integrated with
the web server runtime model.

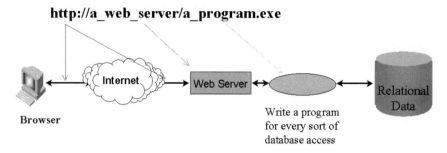

http://a_web_server/a_program.exe

Write a program
for every sort of
database access

Figure 2-4. *CGI access to the database.*

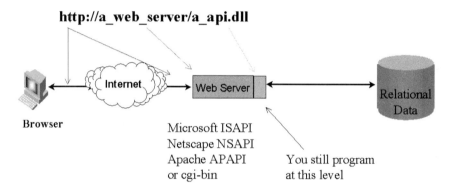

http://a_web_server/a_api.dll

Microsoft ISAPI
Netscape NSAPI
Apache APAPI
or cgi-bin

You still program
at this level

Figure 2-5. *Using the web server API.*

An example of this architecture is the Netscape NSAPI interface, which allows the developer to write a program that is invoked as a dynamic shared object by the Netscape web server.

Another example is LiveWire. This model allows the web server to interpret precompiled JavaScript that can, among other things, access an Informix database.

Figure 2-5 shows the basic architecture of the web server API (application interface).

The drawback with the basic web server API model is that you are restricted to programming in the middle layer, and if the LiveWire program, for example, is being used to dynamically create a web page (by listing the results of a master-detail query) then you have to do all this work yourself, manage the connections, and manage the performance. And the source code and the shared object are all located in filestore.

Characteristics of the Second Generation

User Registration and Profiling

By adding an application tier, information can be stored either in flat files or in a relational database. This application tier can include CGI programs written in C, Shell Script or batch files, AWK, Perl, or Java. It is relatively easy to store information in a flat file database, where each row is a delimited set of fields. User information can be stored in the database to enable user profiling, for example.

Applications Server

Technologies such as CGI, Perl, and LiveWire are used to manage the application semantics against the persistent data storage (for example, flat files or relational data). A CGI script may invoke a C or 4GL program to select data from the database, reformat the results, and send the output to the browser. Additionally, the web server can send queries to the database by invoking a LiveWire program written in JavaScript or Java.

Full-content Search

Site content can be searched using a text search engine. This may or may not include a search against the contents of the database, but it typically involves searching the HTML pages. Some LiveWire scripts may issue queries to the database based on the contents of a submitted form and may format the results for the browser.

Legacy Integration

The web server can use a CGI call to invoke a C or COBOL program to access data in legacy databases, such as indexed-sequential or even hierarchical databases and flat files.

Problems with the Second Generation

Complex Integration with Operational Systems

Developers have tried to integrate a database into their web applications. Developers with experience in Perl and CGI scripts realized that the Web would make an ideal front end. Everyone's got a browser installed on their desktop, and as a result, the possibilities of the Web started to mesmerize programmers who wanted to use the tools with which they were familiar. The first step was to write CGI scripts to link the browser client, the web server, and the database together. The problem is that Perl and CGI were never designed to be transaction monitors or to scale up for multiple connections to a database.

Performance Complexity

The overall problem with the CGI approach is that it is a single-process model: Every time you call a CGI script to start a process, you talk to the database, get the data out, reformat it, hand it to the web server, and then shut the process down. This is problematic because a lot of people are going to hit your database and you have to start up and shut down processes for each hit. Startup and shut-down would probably constitute two-thirds to three-quarters of the work done on the website. This may be an unacceptably high over-head. Also, even if multiple people want to do the same thing against the database, each has to start up a new process, which tends to drag resources to the ground. Finally, because it's a startup-shutdown environment, CGI doesn't really address the persistent state model.

Skills Complexity

Organizations know HTML because they have a web server, and they know SQL because they have a database. The problem is that organizations don't typically know CGI languages such as Perl, C, and Shell Scripting. In general, MIS departments don't have a lot of bandwidth to learn and support new technology in a fasttrack context.

RDBMS Limitations

A RDBMS does not understand HTML by itself. The web server uses a URL, but a database uses SQL. Can a RDBMS keep up with the Web's rate of change?

Version Control and Deployment

Version control of web pages in the second-generation environment is fundamentally a manual process, with the webmaster taking the hit if it goes wrong. Some development environments may have a user interface on top of the version control mechanism to check items in and out of the content repository. In an intranet context where a publishing workflow model exists, managing web content versions can be a major overhead. To move a web page from unpublished to published can be as simple as an FTP (file transfer protocol) call, but the content authors don't know FTP. The webmaster has to do it—for every document, every time.

Enhancement Limitations

The second-generation architecture can only be enhanced within the limitations of the CGI model. Because there is no integration with the database, there is no integrated content search, backup, and recovery, and there is no leverage of the database server characteristics, such as performance tuning. Web applications need complex data and have complicated logic, and HTML is not a programming language.

The Informix Generation: Third-generation Web Applications

While the rest of the industry was discussing the relative merits of second-generation websites, Informix introduced the third-generation architecture. This architecture was based on an innovative ORDBMS (object-relational database management system) and Web DataBlade developed by Illustra Technologies. The third-generation architecture addresses not only the issues of dynamic content and integration with existing operational systems, but also the issues of full single-site administration and full single-site search.

Think about why you bought a database in the first place: centralization of data, data security, query ability, backup, and recovery. Think about how a database really applies to our problems of building a web application: We have a website; it needs to be secured, centrally managed, backed up and restored. It also needs to be queried. Why not just put the website inside the database? Databases give you that functionality for free. Until now the reason no one thought about it was that web pages are not your usual datatype. What kind of datatypes does a database store? Name, address, phone number, date, time, and money. Full text and structured objects are not really what databases do. Enter Informix, whose later versions are object-relational databases that actually allow you to store and manage content other than name, address, date, time, and money. And that's what a web page is.

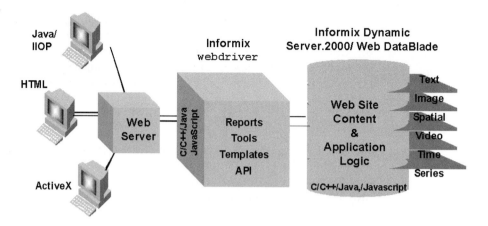

Figure 2-6. *The Informix-generation website architecture.*

Figure 2-6 shows the architecture of what can now be described as the Informix-generation website: the third generation.

Lets go through Fig. 2-6 to understand what the architectural components are.

Browser. *This is the Netscape or Microsoft browser platform: PCs or UNIX terminals connecting to a web server.*

Web Server. *This can be any HTTP-compliant web server. The web server will invoke middleware to access the database.*

`webdriver`. *This is an Informix executable that manages the access and creation of dynamic content for browser delivery. This software can be executed as a CGI program or integrated into Netscape and Microsoft web servers as a dynamically loaded shared object.*

Informix Database. *This can be Informix 9.x or Informix Dynamic Server.2000 databases. These databases are object relational, which allows a greater semantic rendering of the database content.*

Database Content. *HTML pages, images, Office documents, video, audio, Java applets. These objects are stored in the database in an enhanced form of the row/column relational model, except that the column storing the object can have a datatype that is given mean-ing by an installed DataBlade. For example, the column that stores a HTML page is itself of type HTML.*

DataBlades. *A DataBlade is basically a software library that is directly linked into the Informix server. The software has a specific application, such as text or video. The software defines a schema for enhanced datatypes, as well as the methods to operate on the enhanced datatypes. Put together, these components allow intelli-gent content query.*

The Informix architectural model still allows you to use the properties of the first- and second-generation sites. In this case, though, you use them where they are relevant, not because you have to. An application server layer may still exist; for example, you may still use Netscape LiveWire or CGI to access other databases or older versions of the Informix database product. But to enhance website functionality and website performance, the Web DataBlade implementation is the choice you must make, since this option allows you to create dynamic web pages, capture and render the website content across the enteprise, while managing the performance of the site in intranet, Internet, and Extranet contexts without compromising security, reliability, and cost.

The Next Generation

With the explosion of business on the Internet, which needs to be supported by enterprise data and interoperating components, Informix has introduced two products (Informix Dynamic Server.2000 and Informix Internet Foundation.2000) that extend the third-generation model into an inclusive, open platform for supporting OLTP (online transaction processing) applications as well as applications that require Internet content. These products were discussed in Chap. 1.

The third-generation model has been extended to incorporate an open platform that supports inclusion of a best-of-breed Java Virtual Machine *inside* the database server and the ability to run COM business logic, also in the database server. This extension can be called *the open generation.*

A key feature is the ability to run data-intensive Java business logic directly in the database. Java is the language of the Internet, and, in a business context, the Internet is fundamentally a database-driven phenomenon, so it makes sense to fully utilize Java within the engine.

To some extent, the third-generation model has been extended in the open generation model to recast the Informix Database Server as a component in a larger, disparate technology framework, with the ability to deliver traditional data within an OLTP setting, as well as run Internet-aware applications. The latest extension to the Informix database server family, Informix Dynamic Server.2000, allows the server to act as a network-aware application server close to the Internet data that it can understand. Essentially, the database server is woven into the fabric of an open Internet platform.

Summary

This chapter has identified the key characteristics of each generation of web application, from flat-file web applications to database-driven, smart-data-based web applications that use Informix technology. We have seen that data management is essential for web applications. The benefits of a RDBMS are needed, but without the associated limitations. The database must understand the Web and must be extensible by third parties, so that the customer can best exploit the data and application surface he understands. We have also seen how Informix has extended the third-generation model to include the ability to run network-aware, database- and smart-content-intensive applications inside the database server. You are now in a position to put this understanding into practice by creating dynamic websites using the Web DataBlade.

Dynamic Web Solutions: Managing the Digital Value Chain

In this chapter:

- The customer solution cycle
- How to web enable installed applications
- Intranet information repositories
- E-commerce and online catalogs
- Total web systems integration

Most real world environments operate within a complicated set of technological dependencies that can limit a company's ability to integrate and streamline business processes. The Informix Web DataBlade can be used to manage the whole digital value chain by providing a gateway to talk to credit card authorization, billing, and inventory systems, while managing all the content. Most legacy and newer applications can be integrated beneath it, whether the specific goal is marketing products, capturing orders, billing the customer, or tracking product delivery. This chapter describes the digital value chain and the customer solution cycle and demonstrates their importance. Understanding what defines the phases in the customer solution cycle will help you recognize the characteristics, and possibly the limitations, of your own web platform.

The Customer Solution Cycle

The *digital value chain* is realized via implementation of what is called the *customer solution cycle*. This cycle is divided into discrete steps that eventually allow most of the relevant business processes, certainly the mission-critical processes, to become web enabled. Figure 3-1 illustrates the four steps of the customer solution cycle as four modules. The steps are

1. Web enabling the installed application base,
2. Implementing intranet information repositories to store and manage the corporate asset base,
3. Developing the e-commerce catalogs, followed ultimately by
4. Total web systems integration with legacy business applications and data.

Using Informix, what you learn in Step 1 helps you in Steps 2, 3, and 4. Real world corporate IT platforms can be mesmerizingly complicated: Business data generated by legacy applications on mainframes are aggregated into data marts for export to the web platform, where users of the intranet query the information generated; and the company directors want all this information by 7:30 tomorrow morning! The processes of web enabling data in legacy systems and adding value via e-commerce solutions can seem cumbersome and at cross purposes, with each business department obstructing the initiative by defining its own understanding of the business service it provides, and hence confusing the service interfaces. Using the Informix Web DataBlade, however, we will clarify each of the four steps in the customer solution cycle.

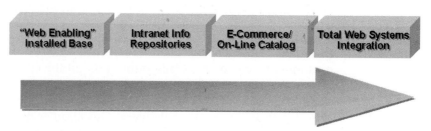

Figure 3-1. The customer solution cycle.

How to Web Enable the Installed Applications

You can web enable your installed base of Informix applications. For example, your installed base of browser clients may include Internet, intranet, or extranet users. You also have a web server and a database that may not be communicating with each other directly, if at all; if they are, they may be using Perl, C, or Shell script to communicate. Adding the Web DataBlade on top gives you the ability to take data already in your database, queries you've already written, and present the query output to a web browser by embedding those queries inside HTML.

To start the customer solution cycle and web enable an installed applications base, you must learn how to use AppPages. AppPages are standard HTML pages that include commands written in Informix AppPage Script. AppPage Script is a set of pseudo-HTML tags that allow you to embed SQL and variable-processing functions inside an HTML page. When the Web DataBlade software interprets these tags, the HTML page is dynamically created to allow sending a variable amount of formatted data as a web page to the browser. Part of the power of using AppPage Script is that you can define a standard web page look and feel by creating tags of your own, called *dynamic tags*. Dynamic tags are defined once but can be reused across all your web applications. This allows you to construct powerful template web pages. Dynamic tags can comprise anything you can put in an AppPage, including other dynamic tags and AppPage Script commands. Those AppPages can then be leveraged for the next step in the customer solution cycle: developing the intranet information repository.

Intranet Information Repositories

At this point, you're just putting more of your corporate asset base inside the database—MS-Word, MS-Excel and MS-PowerPoint documents, for example, or contact and partner details, including press cuttings, which can now be stored inside the database. Using text DataBlades, you can actually search on MS-Word, MS-Excel, and MS-PowerPoint documents. This benefits the people actually in charge of maintaining the website. Why not also make all the people who develop the website content maintain their own content?

Content management applications allow the content authors, owners, and approvers to maintain their own content. Fortunately, content authors, owners, and approvers don't mind bypassing the IT services organization. In some organizations, the IT services department is too slow, and the staff within it have too many technical problems in hand to worry about the outsider coming in with yet another request. The content management application spreads the workload and lets the webmaster and the web application developer maintain the website, while the content authors, owners, and approvers maintain the content.

Content management is achieved by moving the page-building engine, which dynamically generates the data and the web pages from templates, inside the database. You also move to the database most of the web files—HTML templates, Microsoft Word documents, or any of the documents you might publish on a corporate intranet. You can then store a content management application in the database. This way, the same architecture that maintains all your web pages and corporate data also allows you or others to use a browser to maintain the content that supplies that data. In a nutshell, this is how *publishing services* use an intranet information repository.

The *corporate asset base* comprises a set of *media assets.* A single media asset can be any item of information: a press release, a report, a handbook, a database of contact details or partner details, even an image. Creating, editing, publishing, and managing the asset base can take considerable time, effort, and money.

In particular, the asset capture and modification process is often extremely inefficient. For example, a retailer of hardware and software products has a second-generation website. Users can view thumbnails of peripherals and software packages; users can also query on price and availability. A department that has access to the advertising material scans the images in. They are then downloaded to a UNIX box that acts as a corporate file server, and the batch manager is called to set off the batch job that converts the images to thumbnails. Both the full and thumbnail images are then exported to a separate NT box, where they are imported into a database used for elementary catalog management information, such as product attribute maintenance. Every night, a batch job collects all the data from the various sources and creates a compressed set of files, which are then exported to a website.

This is a real world situation where any one corporate asset—images, web pages, product item information—has a cost in some form. The capture and modification process above has several kinks, any one of which could stop the system from delivering a day-old website at start of day.

On the other hand, the company may have an intranet space that could be utilized to streamline its call center services along the lines of its website in order to avoid duplication of data and

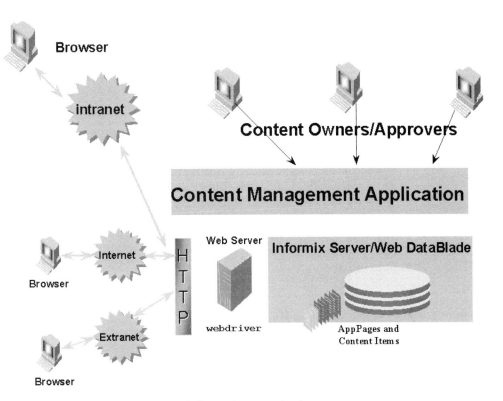

Figure 3-2. Intranet information repositories.

business logic. Of course an intranet information repository (see Fig. 3-2) demands an application to manage the requirements of authoring, maintaining, securing, and publishing information; the application could be called *dynamic content management services.*

There are content owners and content approvers in the intranet dynamic content management services model, but we may also want to publish these catalogs of information on the extranet or the Internet. The content management model lets you dynamically publish information to your users internally as well as to your external customers for e-commerce applications.

In the diagram above, the dynamic content management offering is a content management application written with a combination of HTML, JavaScript, Java, and Informix AppPage Script. It is a web application with rules of engagement for managing rich content.

A content management application usually has an authoring view and a published user view. The user view is the intranet and/or Internet view of the published material. The authoring view is the content administration view, where content authors submit website content such as MS Word documents, PDF files, press reports, Zip files, anything that can be stored in the database and ascribed a set of attributes that identify it. The application itself is stored in the database as a set of AppPage templates.

A content author submits a document to the repository for approval. An authorizer approves the document and asks the application to make the document public. The document then appears on the website.

The benefit of this type of application is that the website content is managed in the database. Using database replication, selected data can be replicated across database servers, making information internally distributed as well as public. Additionally, using an object-relational database allows rich content to be stored in the database and intelligently searched for in context.

These applications usually contain document attribute (metadata) and text search capabilities. All this functionality cannot be realized without a sophisticated document repository application integrated with an object-relational database.

What Is Metadata?

Metadata is data about data. It is a list of attributes that describe other data. For example, a text document (created using Notepad, for example) will contain text typed in by an author. The text document is the data. Example metadata could include "Document Author," "Date Created," and even "Document Type(text)." A database schema is another example of metadata. A database table comprises a table name, column names and column data types. This schema is the metadata for the table; it is separate from the actual data stored in every row. Sophisticated content management applications use metadata to define all content items in a content repository, as well as to catalog the documents and parameterize attribute searches.

Cleverly enough, the catalogs you develop and the processes you put in place to maintain the website can be leveraged into your e-commerce solutions—the next step in the customer solution cycle. This is because you can use the same methodologies and tools to manage your e-commerce website's merchandising, catalog, customer information, and self-help aspects, but now you can add transactions.

E-Commerce and Online Catalogs

As described in the introduction to this chapter, the Web DataBlade adds to the application platform the gateway to talk to credit card authorization systems, as well as billing and inventory systems, while managing all the content along the whole digital value chain.

E-commerce can be called a value chain. E-commerce is not just about credit cards and securing transactions. For successful e-commerce on the web, you have to convince people that you have the right products, services, information, and customer service.

Key parts of that digital value chain—preselling, merchandising, postselling, and customer support—depend on the content. A serious customer will ask of the website:

- Is the catalog up to date?
- Is the database up to date?
- Is the website recommending products to me that I want to buy?
- Are they making my shopping experience unique?
- After I buy the product, are they providing me customer service?
- Are they providing online help, online instructions, online manuals?

Your e-commerce application is worthless unless you provide the information people want, because the transaction will go away. So e-commerce systems can also be described as dynamic content management offerings.

If you have a legacy system already installed and working, you probably don't want to replace that system, but you may want to layer the Informix web application architecture on top because of the value it adds to the organization managing the whole digital value chain.

So that you can recognize key elements of an e-commerce application, here are some brief definitions of the characteristics of an e-commerce solution:

Advertising and marketing: demand-creation activities such as banner ads and brochures. One-to-one marketing.

Merchandising: how the product is presented, priced, and sold. E-commerce sites should support a large number of merchandising methods: coupons, membership discounts, purchase incentives, and demo products, for example. A website with a mature merchandising model must be able to integrate new merchandising methods.

Payment processing: credit card payments and purchase orders.

Price calculation: taxes and shipping charges for the user at the time of purchase.

Order fulfillment: Is a product in stock? When will it arrive? A comprehensive web solution will require a high level of integration with the host company's conventional order fulfillment systems.

Tracking: *Tracks user activity (e.g., click paths).*
Profiling: *market segmentation analysis leading to one-to-one marketing.*
Customer Service: *Converts a one-time buyer into a loyal customer using FAQs, e-mail, and interactivity.*

For a platform to support e-commerce, it must be able to bring these elements together in a scalable and manageable way.

Total Web Systems Integration

Web enable your installed applications base by using the Web DataBlade on top of the existing architecture. This will allow you not only to render application data to the web user, you can also begin to manage your corporate asset base. You can also apply your e-commerce systems on the Web without a fundamental change in your web applications architecture. You want to tie everything in your organization together: your billing systems, inventory, and legacy platform. The same logic that applies to managing e-commerce systems applies here, where the Web DataBlade becomes the front end to all of the applications. And those applications can all integrate around the Web DataBlade on top of this architecture.

You might want to go one step further and web enable all your systems. A unified approach to web applications ties everything in your organization together, completing the customer solution cycle. Figure 3-3 shows the major components in this unified set of web-enabled applications. Note, however, that this simplified architectural model does not reflect the complexity of the physical processes that are sometimes required to yield the information from the external systems.

The incremental approach to web enabling existing applications, through to corporate asset management and e-commerce applications, may seem artificial, but it is based on how the real world operates. The central message is that at each stage the fundamental enabling architecture does not change, and what you learn at one stage is useful for the next.

Summary

In this chapter we have seen how we can web enable an installed application base and extend it until we finally have total integra-

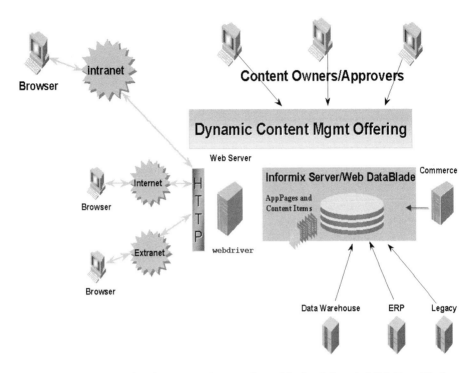

Figure 3-3. *Total web systems integration with the Informix Web DataBlade.*

tion of the corporate application platform with the Web DataBlade at the core. We have seen the importance of the digital value chain and how implementing the customer solution cycle as described can reuse the benefits implemented at the last stage in the cycle. Most real world environments operate within a complicated set of technological dependencies that often impact the ability to integrate and streamline business processes. Using technology such as the Web DataBlade with the Informix database server can allow you to explore the intranet space and reuse a significant amount of business logic across what formerly would be separate applications—one for the web, and one for the internal users.

Chapter

4

Introduction to Dynamic Web Application Development

In this chapter:

- Basic terminology
- Web DataBlade application components
- What is the Web DataBlade?
- What is JavaScript?
- How does JavaScript differ from AppPage Script?
- What is Java?
- How does Java differ from JavaScript?

When you build a dynamic website, you cover a lot of exciting ground, from the client to the web server to the database server. This so-called multitier architecture is the context within which this chapter introduces the key technologies used in this book.

Basic Terminology

This section introduces the basic terms used throughout the book.

HTML (hypertext markup language). *Simple, document markup language that works in a manner similar to the way word processors worked years ago. Programs such as Microsoft Word and Hot Metal can produce HTML automatically for you.*

CGI Program. *The common gateway interface (CGI) is a standard for interfacing external applications with information servers, such as HTTP or web servers. A CGI program is executed on demand in real time, so that it can output dynamic information.*

URL (uniform resource locator). *A URL uniquely identifies a resource that can be accessed on the Internet. The URL tells the web browser where to find the information you want displayed to you. The structure of a URL is usually something like http://www.informix.com:80/demos/welcome.htm. The default port is "80" if no port number is specified in the URL.*

HTTP (hypertext transfer protocol). *This is the protocol that is used to talk to a web server. The HTTP is a stateless protocol that sits on top of TCP/IP. Every request must connect to the web server, do its work, and disconnect from the web server. It is designed for rapid turnaround. It is not like a client server database because the connection is not maintained.*

MIME Types. *Multipurpose Internet mail extensions (MIME) are a standardized method for organizing divergent file formats. The method defines the MIME type according to the file format. For example, when an Internet browser retrieves a file from a server, the server provides the MIME type of the file. The browser uses the MIME type to establish whether the browser's built-in software (or plug-ins) can read the file format or, if not, whether a suitable helper application is available to read the file.*

DTD (document type definition). *A DTD defines the structure of the document, much like a database schema describes the types of information it handles. A DTD provides a framework for the types of elements (chapters, chapter headings, sections) that constitute a document, as well as the rules for relationships between the elements of the document. HTML is a specialized DTD designed to facilitate the storage and retrieval of documents to be displayed by web browsers.*

SGML (standard generalized markup language). *SGML is used to separate the content and structure of the document from the formatting of the document so that the rendering of the document is software and hardware independent.*

Web Components. *A web browser, such as Netscape Navigator, knows how to display HTML pages, play audio, and display images as specified on the page. The web server process is known as HTTPD, and runs as a daemon on the web server machine.*

Web DataBlade Application Components

A Web DataBlade application is typically composed of the elements listed in Table 4-1.

The difference between a HTML page and an AppPage is the presence of AppPage Script tags.

Table 4-1. Web DataBlade application elements.

Element	Description
HTML	The web page as rendered by the browser. Any special tags in the AppPage source have been processed by the Web DataBlade into standard HTML content format.
AppPage	HTML page with special AppPage Scripting tags to interface with the Informix database. The AppPage is stored in the database.
AppPage Scripting Tags	Database-aware tags that allow database content to be rendered dynamically in a HTML page using SQL.
SQL	Structured query language statements that allow you to maintain data in the database.
Java	Object-oriented, network-aware language that can run in the browser as an applet or as an application on the client and server.
JavaScript	Programming language mainly contained in the HTML page, although some server-side JavaScript can be written in a technology called LiveWire.
Web DataBlade	A DataBlade plug-in for Informix Dynamic Server.2000 and Informix Dynamic Server with the Universal Data Option. This DataBlade allows an AppPage to be served from the Informix database using SQL statements, with the AppPage Scripting tags processed and the resulting HTML sent to the browser.

In this book we will be using all of the technologies listed in Table 4-1. We will also be covering Data Director for Web and, to a lesser extent, AppPage Builder. All of the AppPage examples in this book have been created and managed under Data Director for Web.

 The examples in this book that use dynamic tags specific to Data Director for Web can be changed to run under AppPage Builder. You need to understand what the dynamic tag does and use the equivalent tag (or create your own) in AppPage Builder.

Data Director for Web

Data Director for Web is a Windows product that allows full website management for websites that are stored in the Informix database. It allows you to import and export file-based websites to and from the database and to deploy a website to remote machines and databases. It contains a webpage editor and wizards that allow you to construct a database-aware webpage.

AppPage Builder

AppPage Builder is the default browser-based application for storing AppPages and web content in the database. AppPage Builder is delivered with the Web DataBlade. If you don't have Data Director for Web, you can use AppPage Builder. AppPage Builder is much less functional than Data Director for Web and is used as a basic repository for AppPages and multimedia objects. You can still create highly functional, content-rich applications with AppPage Builder, but Data Director for Web is the more intuitive and functional tool.

What Is the Web DataBlade?

The Web DataBlade is used for building dynamic, scalable, media-rich web applications. The Web DataBlade provides a complete set of tools, functions, and examples for developing complex database-driven websites. The Web DataBlade enables the user to create web applications that incorporate data retrieved dynamically from the Informix Dynamic Server.2000 and Universal Data Option databases.

The Web DataBlade is designed to leverage the unique architecture of the Informix Dynamic Server.2000 and 9.x servers to provide the tools and solutions for all phases in the customer solution cycle described in Chap. 3. The Web DataBlade will help you leverage the value of the corporate asset base so that you can store and deliver most if not all of your media formats to a broad user base on the intranet or Internet platform.

You can use the Web DataBlade with Informix Dynamic Server.2000 and Informix 9.x servers to manage multimedia web content dynamically.

What Is a Corporate Asset Base?

The phrase **corporate asset base** *refers to the complete set of documents that have value to your organization. Example documents are marketing bulletins, press cuttings, contact and partner documents, company brochures, and personnel forms. Typically, these documents need to be managed: new ones added, existing ones updated. Often, these documents need to be disseminated in some form within the organization and also externally, to the customer. The word* **asset** *is a useful description of the document; the Web DataBlade is said to leverage the corporate asset base by, for example, offloading internal administrative overhead to the intranet, allowing rapid deployment of new documents to the target audience over the Web.*

The Web DataBlade essentially consists of a middleware component and a database component. The middleware component sits between the web server and the database. The database component is a DataBlade that consists of data types and functions that allow you to manipulate web content inside the database.

The middleware component is a program called `webdriver`. This is the program that sends SQL to the page creation engine, which constructs a web page from a definition of the web page contents and SQL: the page template, or AppPage. `Webdriver` runs on the web server and connects directly to the Informix database server, which may be hosted on another machine. You can run `webdriver` as a CGI program or as a dynamic link library integrated with the web server via the web server API.

Informix Server Versions and the Web DataBlade

The Web DataBlade is a successful product that has been used in the Informix Dynamic Server 9.x product and now the Informix Dynamic Server.2000 product. Informix Dynamic Server.2000 uses Version 4 of the Web DataBlade.

Version 4 of the Web DataBlade differs from Version 3 in some aspects of configuration and some feature additions and

Table 4-2. Informix server and web product.

Informix server	Web product
Informix Dynamic Server.2000	Web DataBlade Version 4+
Informix Dynamic Server 9.1x/ Universal Data Option	up to Web DataBlade 3.32
Informix Dynamic Server 7.x	Universal Web Connect

enhancements. However, most of the examples in this book will run on both Version 3.32 and Version 4 of the Web DataBlade.

The user base of the Web DataBlade spans different versions of the Informix database server. Table 4-2 summarizes the website product for each Informix Dynamic Server.

The *Universal Data Option* allows you to install DataBlades on version 9.x of the Informix Dynamic Server. A DataBlade (or "blade") allows you to define new data types and the operations on those data types. For example, the Web DataBlade defines a data type called HTML. It also defines an operation called `FileToHTML`, which imports a webpage (e.g., `HelloWorld.html`) and stores it in a column of a table that has a data type of HTML.

You cannot install a DataBlade against Version 7.x of Informix Dynamic Server. To do this, you need to upgrade to Informix Dynamic Server.2000 or Informix Internet Foundation.2000.

You can build your own DataBlade using the DataBlade Developers Kit (DBDK) or buy one from specialist vendors. An example of the former would be a blade that interpreted a special file format for a complex database schema. An example of the latter would be a text- or image-searching blade.

The Universal Web Connect product allows you to connect Version 7.x of the Informix server to the web server to serve dynamic web pages. The architecture of this product is different from the Web DataBlade and is not covered in this book, except by comparison in some areas. However, most AppPage Scripting tags and functions are available with this product, although the Web DataBlade implementation of these functions is enhanced and further developed in Versions 3.32 and 4 of the Web DataBlade.

Simplifying Web Application Development

Using the Informix Web DataBlade, a website can be reworked to yield substantial time and cost benefits in running a company website. For example, a site with 400,000 webpages can be reworked to use a few hundred templates. These templates are used to capture the look and feel of the site and can be reused by other webpages. Since the Web DataBlade dynamically generates the formatted data and HTML in a webpage, the page content does not have to be hard coded in the page itself. The look and feel of the website is stored in one place (the template), instead of being defined in every webpage that must render it.

What Is a Web Template?

A web template is a webpage that contains the essential HTML tags and SQL statements to allow dynamic page generation by the Web DataBlade. A datablade function called `webexplode()` *processes the template. This involves interpreting the AppPage scripting tags to render a variable amount of information within the template page structure.*

What Is Web Content?

Put simply, web content is any type of file that can be stored on a website. These file types include word-processing documents, spreadsheet documents, images (e.g., GIF, JPEG), HTML pages, video (e.g., AVI), audio (e.g., WAV) and Java applets. If a program exists to interpret the document type, then that program can use the document when the program is installed as either a plug-in or helper application in the browser. The Informix database can store these documents regardless of type. However, not all types of document should be stored in a database. Later chapters will identify which types of document are best suited for database storage.

Benefits of the Web DataBlade

Optimal for Large-scale Web Management

The web application and content is centrally managed in the database. Server-side page generation is fast. AppPage templates reduce the number of website pages. Also, the scalability of Informix Dynamic Server allows you to manage rapidly growing content.

Rapidly Creates Dynamic and Targeted Web Pages

Database-aware page templates, called AppPages, allow you to reuse common application elements, such as HTML headers and footers, including SQL statements to access the database. For example, a website could be rendered with a common look and feel, with the company logo displayed in the header and e-mail details displayed in the footer. Two AppPage templates, or dynamic tags, could be used to do this.

Provides High-speed Database Connection with Low Overhead

Application server solutions often rely on an ODBC connection to access the database from the page-building engine. The Web DataBlade `webdriver` program does not use ODBC; the connectivity layer is built into the product, removing the need for a middle layer and thus improving performance. In addition, the page-building function is a DataBlade function and runs *inside* the database server, close to the data.

Improves Web Content Administration

Webpages are managed inside the database. As the database is managed so, too, is the website. Informix has client tools, such as Data Director for Web, to provide a fine level of control over the website.

Increases Performance and Scalability

The Web DataBlade `webdriver` program provides session and connection management. Also, cache management of static web content can be implemented. The Web DataBlade `webdriver` program can also be integrated with your web server to allow further performance enhancements. Because the Informix server is a scalable platform for enterprise, database-driven business solutions, and because the Web DataBlade is integrated with the database, dynamic and database-driven websites created with the Web DataBlade will scale along with the database server platform.

Leverages Your Existing Infrastructure and Experience

With the Web DataBlade, you can use your existing Informix databases and web servers. AppPage Script is also very easy to learn, so the migration path from HTML to the Web DataBlade extended tags is minimal. In addition, the webmaster can still use Java, JavaScript, HTML, XML, and the skills base he currently has. Other users who may wish to submit content to the website, such as administrative users who need to submit word-processing documents to the website, continue to use their word-processing and spreadsheet packages as before. The Web DataBlade allows the web applications developed on top of it to maintain this content.

Integrates with Industry-leading Tools and Technologies

You can use your favorite webpage-authoring tools with the Web DataBlade. Instead of publishing to the file system, you can publish to the Informix database. Using Data Director for Web, you can also drag and drop websites from the file system into the database.

Provides an Open/Extensible Platform that Grows with Your Needs and Global Innovation

Informix Dynamic Server.2000 and Informix Dynamic Server/ Universal Data Option allow the database to extend along with innovations in the area of business information. A DataBlade can be developed for new and complex information. Informix and Informix customers do this. That's why the DataBlade API is an open interface that allows you to have your control. Large organizations have a lot of proprietary code that constitutes competitive advantage. You can leverage that code very easily into DataBlade applications.

What Is a DataBlade?

A DataBlade module is a collection of database objects and code that extends Informix Dynamic Server by adding new functionality. A DataBlade module can enable Informix Dynamic Server to provide the same level of support for new data types that it provides for built-in data types (such as VARCHAR).

A DataBlade is always problem specific because it typically supports a specific application domain, such as spatial data management or document indexing and retrieval. Several DataBlade modules can be used to support a single application. For example, a media records application that stores information from many different hospitals might use the Spatial DataBlade module to record and query hospital location, and the Lab DataBlade module to index and query results from tests performed on hospital patients.

Developing a DataBlade module involves defining data types and the routines that operate on them, writing support code for the data types and client applications, as well as testing, documenting, and packaging the module.

Chapter 12 contains the detail necessary to understand DataBlades in general and the Web DataBlade module in particular.

How Is the Web DataBlade Different?

Typically, web database applications require a common gateway interface (CGI) application written in Perl or C to access data. You can even run 4GL procedures using CGI. However, by using the Web DataBlade module, the development of a bespoke CGI interface is not needed. The Web DataBlade module contains client code in the `Webdriver` executable. This is a client application that runs on the web server machine. When using the Web DataBlade module, you create HTML pages (called AppPages) that include database-aware Web DataBlade module tags (called AppPage Script tags) that dynamically execute the SQL statements you specify and format the results. You can retrieve traditional data types, as well as HTML, image, audio, and video data from the Informix Dynamic Server database.

Web DataBlade module tags enable you to

- embed SQL statements directly within AppPages,
- handle errors within AppPages,
- execute statements conditionally within AppPages,
- manipulate variables within AppPages using variable-processing functions, and
- use other advanced query-processing and formatting techniques.

Web DataBlade *dynamic tags* allow you to reuse existing HTML to simplify the construction and maintenance of your Web applications.

The Web DataBlade module provides *system* dynamic tags, but you can also create your own *user* dynamic tags.

The Web DataBlade `webdriver` program allows you to customize web applications by using information from its configuration file, the web server environment, URLs, HTML forms, and your own web application variables, without additional CGI programming.

The web server API implementation of `webdriver` allows you to use Netscape, Microsoft and Apache web server security features, and, it eliminates CGI process overhead.

What Is `webdriver`?

`webdriver` is a program that enables the web server to communicate with the Informix database server to extract AppPages that are stored in the database. `webdriver` replaces the need to write a custom CGI program to enable the web server to interact with the database. `webdriver` has different implementations, depending on the web server in use, as shown in Table 4-3. `webdriver` is one of a small number of programs that is delivered as part of the Web DataBlade package.

As an application, `webdriver` (or the web server API versions) builds the SQL queries that execute the `webexplode()` function inside the database server to retrieve AppPages from the Informix database. The Universal Web Connect version of this software has no DataBlade function to use; the Universal Web Connect software builds the HTML page itself *outside* the database.

What Is `webexplode()`?

The `webexplode()` DataBlade function is installed by Blade Manager when you install the Web DataBlade on an Informix Dynamic Server.2000 or Informix 9.x database. This is the core function that processes an AppPage and interprets the AppPage tags, which in most cases will involve sending SQL queries to the database server and processing the results.

Table 4-3. The `webdriver` implementations.

Implementation	Component used
CGI	`webdriver` (UNIX) or `webdriver.exe` (NT). Will run with any web server that supports CGI.
Netscape Server API (NSAPI)	Shared-object (UNIX) or DLL (NT) version of `webdriver` that is used to interface directly with the Netscape web server for user authentication and performance.
Microsoft IIS API (ISAPI)	DLL version of `webdriver` that is used to interface directly with the IIS web server for user authentication and performance.
Apache API (APAPI)	Shared-object or DLL version of `webdriver` that is used to interface directly with the Apache web server for user authentication and performance.

The `webdriver` program builds an SQL statement that includes a call to `webexplode()`. Parameters passed to `webexplode()` include the name of the AppPage and a set of variables passed from the web server environment and the `webdriver` configuration that may subsequently be used in the AppPage to change the behavior and output of the final HTML page.

What Is an AppPage?

An AppPage is a template webpage that is stored in the Informix database. In typical web database applications, most of the logic is in gateway application code written in Perl or C. This common gateway interface (CGI) application connects to a database, builds and executes SQL statements, and formats the results. Using the Web DataBlade module, you need not develop a CGI application to dynamically access database data. Instead, you create HTML pages that include Web DataBlade module tags and functions that dynamically execute the SQL statements you specify and format the results. These pages are called application pages (AppPages). The types of data you retrieve can include traditional data types, as well as HTML, image, audio, and video data.

What Is AppPage Script?

Informix developed AppPage Script as an extension to HTML. The extension consists of a set of prebuilt *tags* to format and manipulate variable data, mainly retrieved from the database using SQL. AppPage Scripting tags are the interface between the HTML webpage and the Informix database. You can think of AppPage Script as a scripting language, but a very simple one. It is easy to migrate from creating webpages with HTML to working with both HTML and AppPage Script. In fact, AppPage Script and HTML are complementary. The scripting tags are used to initiate SQL commands and work with the results of those commands.

The browser never sees AppPage Script. It is only seen by the Web DataBlade `webexplode()` function, which interprets and executes the AppPage Script tags and variables, and then formats the result. In most cases, this involves a query to the database. The browser sees only the final result.

In contrast, *dynamic tags* allow you to reuse existing AppPage segments to simplify the construction and maintenance of your web applications. The Web DataBlade module provides *system* dynamic tags that you can use. You can also create *user* dynamic tags.

What Is JavaScript?

JavaScript is the ideal technology with which to start web programming. It is easy to learn, although it is object based; the benefits are immediately seen in the web page. JavaScript was originally developed by Netscape as a web-page-scripting language and is probably the most versatile and widely used web-page-scripting language. It is generally used for the following:

- *Interacting with the user.* JavaScript can respond to user events, such as the pressing of an HTML forms button.
- *Interacting with HTML documents.* JavaScript can work with the document objects created for a webpage.
- *Controlling the browser.* JavaScript can open new browser windows, popup windows, and dialog boxes.
- *Managing document appearance.* JavaScript can dynamically format one or more webpages *on the client.*

All of these features are illustrated in this book.

There are two distinct but overlapping systems: client-side JavaScript, which is run in web browsers, and server-side JavaScript, which is run by web servers. This book deals with client-side JavaScript.

Syntactically, the JavaScript language resembles C++ and Java, containing programming constructs such as an `if` statement, a `while` loop and the "`&&`" operator.

Client-side JavaScript

Client-side JavaScript is included inside the webpage or sent as a separate file (with a `.js` suffix). JavaScript is interpreted by the browser and is tightly coupled with HTML inside the browser. The HTML tags are created as internal objects by the browser, and JavaScript can access them. Using JavaScript, you can associate events with browser objects such as HTML forms and links. The power of client-side JavaScript is that you have access to a hierarchy of objects that are based on the content of the web-page.

Client-side JavaScript can also interact with Java applets on the client. Probably the easiest implementation of this is a technology called LiveConnect, described later in the book.

What Is an Applet?

An applet can be defined as mobile application code. An applet is a self-contained application, or code fragment, to perform a specific function. A JavaScript applet is a code fragment that is coded in line between the `<SCRIPT>` and `</SCRIPT>` tags in a webpage. Similarly, a Java applet consists of one or more Java class files that are defined via the `<APPLET>` tag in a webpage. One or more class files are downloaded with the webpage.

JavaScript can access the client objects that are created by the browser to represent the HTML document content. For example, a `Form` *object is created for every form on the webpage. In contrast, JavaScript cannot access any objects for the scripting tags that the Web DataBlade interprets. This is because the AppPage Script tags are not sent to the browser, so there are no objects to access on the client.*

Server-side JavaScript

Server-side JavaScript provides an alternative to CGI programming. Server-side JavaScript is embedded in HTML pages and allows executable server-side JavaScript to run when the container page is requested. Server-side JavaScript contains objects that allow access to the server file system and a database. Database access is via ODBC.

Note that server-side JavaScript solutions to accessing a database belong to the second-generation category introduced in Chap. 2, rather than the third generation. It is the third generation, however, that offers the best platform for e-commerce and totally integrated web solutions.

Although you can access an Informix database via ODBC using server-side JavaScript, the Web DataBlade is a more scalable alternative because the database connection is direct, rather than going through the ODBC layer. Additionally, if you are using server-side JavaScript to format webpages dynamically on the server, the Web DataBlade contains the software to do just that; all you need to concentrate on is the application, instead of reinventing the wheel as part of the application.

JavaScript Components Summary

JavaScript is *object based,* not *object oriented.* JavaScript creates and uses objects in browser memory, but object-oriented concepts, such as inheritance and polymorphism, are not really possible with

Table 4-4. JavaScript technology components.

Component	Description
Client-side JavaScript	JavaScript code is executed by the JavaScript interpreter inside the browser.
LiveWire (Server-side JavaScript)	Server-based, precompiled JavaScript code that is executed on the server under web server control. You can use server-side JavaScript to access the Informix database via ODBC.
LiveConnect	Client-based. Allows Java to access JavaScript data and methods, and vice versa.

JavaScript. Additionally, JavaScript is really alive only when run inside the browser or a LiveWire application, which is controlled by the web server. Nevertheless, JavaScript is a full and beautifully expressive programming language.

To summarize this section, Table 4-4 lists the relevant components. Client-side JavaScript and LiveConnect are described in Chap. 5.

How Does JavaScript Differ from AppPage Script?

Although both have the word *script* in their names, JavaScript is fundamentally different from AppPage Script. AppPage Script is one of the most powerful extensions to HTML for working with a database, as well as the easiest to learn; you could call it HTML script, since standard HTML is static and describes document structure rather than content. In contrast, AppPage Script articulates both document structure and the rendering of document content *dynamically* within that structure.

The migration path from HTML to JavaScript requires an understanding of programming languages and objects to make the effort worthwhile. Also, to access a database using JavaScript *without* AppPage Script you may need to use a technology called LiveWire on the web server.

The migration path from HTML to AppPage Script is minimal. AppPage Script looks like HTML. It is a set of extended tags that are derived from SGML in the same way that HTML is derived from

JavaScript	AppPage Script
Executed in the browser (and in some cases on the web server using LiveWire).	Processed on the web server only.
Object based.	Does not use objects.
Cannot access the database (except through LiveWire and ODBC).	Can access the database without extra coding.
Cannot easily format the results of database queries.	Can easily format the results of SQL queries.
Is a programming language, and looks like C or C++.	Is a scripting language, and looks like HTML.
Can dynamically render a webpage on the client (and in some cases on the server, using LiveWire).	Dynamically formats a webpage on the server using the `webexplode()` component of the Informix Web DataBlade. Can generate JavaScript-based code to render a webpage on the client dynamically, if required.

SGML. You can code the SQL to access the database within the AppPage itself, and you can format the results of an SQL query within the HTML page dynamically.

JavaScript is used to create dynamic webpages on the client. AppPage Script is used to create dynamic webpages on the database server.

Table 4-5 summarizes the differences between JavaScript and AppPage Script.

What Is Java?

There is a misconception about Java. Java is said to be the language that brings the webpage to life; this is only partly true. More importantly, Java is the most significant application and network platform around today.

Fundamentally, Java is a platform for running distributed application components anywhere, and you can include legacy applications within that framework. Historically, distributed applications have had a fairly fixed point of reference. One component in the application would run on one box, and another component would run on another box. Data would be transferred to each application across a network from a variety of databases.

With Java, not only the data travels the network; the *application code* does too. Code that formerly ran on one box can now be sent to any box that needs it. In addition, you can interface to Java functions (or methods) remotely. The Java platform also has built-in networking features. Java application interfaces (called APIs) include APIs for smart cards, embedded operating systems, multimedia, and directory services, to name a few.

Because the networking features of Java are built in, to some extent Java has made the network invisible to applications built with it. Because the APIs define a collection of interoperable services at many levels, they hide the implementation from the developer, and provide a uniform and industry-wide development platform.

JavaBeans is the client component model. Enterprise JavaBeans is the server component model, which is able to encapsulate legacy applications and present them to the Java development platform as a service.

Because Informix recognizes the importance of Java, J/Foundation is used with the Informix Internet Foundation.2000 product set to allow you to run Java modules inside the database server, using the best-of-breed Java Virtual Machine.

This book will show you how to use JDBC and RMI to create distributed database-driven applications.

How Does Java Differ from JavaScript?

It is important to understand the fundamental differences between Java and JavaScript. As a web developer, you need to appreciate the architectural differences between them in order to size, scale, and position your individual web components correctly.

Using LiveConnect (covered later in this book), Java has access to browser objects through JavaScript. Similarly, JavaScript has access to Java methods. Nevertheless, there are significant differences between the two languages. In particular they can be contrasted according to three criteria:

- **Static typing.** JavaScript variables are loosely typed. Java requires that all variables be declared with a type at compile time. This removes some flexibility, but it achieves gains in performance and robustness.

- **Static binding.** With JavaScript, you can refer to objects that do not exist in your script when the script is first loaded and checked by the browser. In contrast, a Java program will not compile unless all objects have been defined.
- **Object models.** JavaScript is object based, with a limited object model. In contrast, Java is a fully object-oriented programming language.

JavaScript does not rely on Java, and vice versa. Nevertheless, they do complement each other. This book will show how to interface Java and JavaScript using LiveConnect.

Summary

This chapter has introduced the main components of Web DataBlade applications and the Web DataBlade. Java and JavaScript were introduced and scoped as complementary technologies for interacting with each other, with AppPages, and with the database. The key technologies in this book were described, contrasted, and placed in context. The implementation of these technologies will be described in the remainder of the book.

Dynamic Web Programming with Java, JDBC, and JavaScript

Create Dynamic Web Pages Using JavaScript

In this chapter:

- "Hello World" using JavaScript
- Create dynamic web pages with frames and JavaScript
- A JavaScript summary
- Mixing JavaScript with AppPage Scripting variables
- Using JavaScript to display the results of a database query
- Integrating JavaScript with Java: the basics of LiveConnect
- Scrolling images from the database
- Creating dynamic selection lists
- Submitting queries without reloading the page
- Performing a JavaScript text search of the HTML page

Throughout this book, and especially in the chapters devoted to Web DataBlade examples, you will find JavaScript closely integrated with AppPage Script. This chapter concentrates on JavaScript—using JavaScript in isolation, using JavaScript with Java, and using JavaScript with AppPage Script to create some wonderful techniques for presenting data to the user that are not obvious. There are several examples of using JavaScript inside the browser to add functionality to the result of a database query. Some of the best and most interesting examples are those that use JavaScript in AppPages to generate queries against the database dynamically.

For details on using JavaScript to create SQL queries dynamically on the client, see Chap. 21, "A Customer Maintenance Application." For details on using JavaScript with forms, see Chap. 17, "Dynamic Web Forms Programming."

For an example of how to create an Explorer-like, database-driven JavaScript menu structure, see Chap. 6, "A JavaScript SQL Explorer." For details on Java applet programming, see Chap. 8, "Essential JDBC Programming," and Chap. 9, "Integrating Java Applets with the Database."

A section on integrating Java with JavaScript in the browser is included, not as a tutorial, but as a pointer to a slightly different way of managing information in the browser. The examples in this chapter effectively position JavaScript within the third-generation web architecture, and what you learn about JavaScript in this chapter can be applied equally well in a variety of contexts, not just on Informix-based systems.

"Hello World" Using JavaScript

The "Hello World" program can be easily written using JavaScript. The HTML page does not have to be stored in the database as an AppPage to do this. The reason this JavaScript example does not have to be stored in the database is that *we are not relying on Informix to execute any special tags.* It is the browser that will execute JavaScript. Even if the web page is stored in the database, it is still the browser that will execute the JavaScript. The Informix webdriver program does not understand JavaScript and will ignore it in the web page it scans.

Conversely, a web page can be stored in the database even if it contains no special Web DataBlade tags, such as <?MIVAR>. The Informix webdriver program will still fetch the web page from the database and pass it through the webexplode() function, but it will emerge *unchanged.*

When the browser displays, or *renders,* the next example in Listing 5-1, it will execute the JavaScript it finds. The JavaScript code will dynamically render the "Hello World" string. You can invoke the web page in Listing 5-1 from the database using a webdriver URL, or from the file system (your own or the web server's).

Listing 5-1. *"Hello World" using JavaScript*
(`HelloJSWorld.html`)

```
<html>
<head>
<title>Hello World: JavaScript and Strings</title>
</head>
<body bgcolor='#DFDFDF'>
<script language=JavaScript>
document.write("<P><CENTER><B>" +
               "Hello World".fontsize(7) +
               "</B></CENTER>");
</script>
</body>
</html>
```

Client and Server Dynamic Web Programming

Server-side dynamic web programming with the Web DataBlade consists of writing AppPages that contain SQL and AppPage Scripting tags and functions. The HTML page is created dynamically on the web server or database server, wherever the Informix database resides. In contrast, client-side dynamic web programming consists of creating HTML pages dynamically on the browser client. You can integrate dynamic page generation on the server and the client to allow client-side JavaScript to work with dynamically generated web page information from the database. A good example of this is described in Chap. 6, "A JavaScript SQL Explorer."

There are a number of interesting points in Listing 5-1.

- Note the use of the `fontsize(7)` method. This is a built-in JavaScript method for strings that outputs a string value delimited by `<FONT SIZE=7>` and `</FONT>`
- Notice how the string "Hello World" is used. Initially, it is coded in-line as a string constant. Then it is used as if it were a string *object*.
- The actual displayed content of the web page is created dynamically by JavaScript using the `document.write()` method call.

Because JavaScript is interpreted as it is read, you can code statements like

```
"Hello World".fontSize(7);
```

The JavaScript interpreter in the browser will create a String object, and initialize it to the "Hello World" string. Because the String object has built-in methods to operate on String data, we can then call one of those methods to operate on the String that we have coded inline—in this case, the fontSize method.

We could have coded the above as follows:

```
Var str = "Hello World";
Str = str.fontsize(7);
document.write(str);
```

By comparing the two alternatives, you get the feel of how elegant and compact JavaScript can be. The browser source output from Listing 5-1 is as follows:

```
<html>
<head>
<title>Hello World: JavaScript and Strings</title>
</head>
<body bgcolor='#DFDFDF'>
<P><CENTER><B><FONT SIZE="7">Hello
 World</FONT></B></CENTER>
</body>
</html>
```

Figure 5-1 shows the output from the code above.

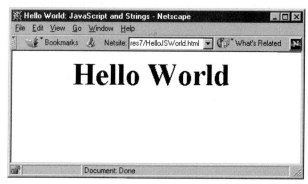

Figure 5-1. *"Hello World" using JavaScript.*

Objects and Methods

Because JavaScript is object based, most data is represented as an object. There are many built-in JavaScript object types that you can use, such as String *or* Array. *Objects can have functions, called methods, associated with them. Built-in objects have a set of predefined methods for operating on object data. These methods contain code to operate on that instance of the object. A method is associated with a single object, not a set of objects. For example, a* String *object with the value "Java" will output a different result when the* fontsize() *method is called than a* String *object with the value "JavaScript".*

Dynamic String Formatting Using JavaScript

The next example shows how to use String methods to format a string dynamically. HTML generated dynamically is shown in uppercase for clarity. Listing 5-2 contains the HelloTime.html

Listing 5-2. *JavaScript Strings and* String *methods AppPage,* HelloTime.html.

```
<html>
<head>
<title>Hello World: JavaScript and Strings</title>
</head>

<body>

<script language=JavaScript>

var now = new Date();

document.write("<P><CENTER><B>" +
               "Hello World".fontsize(7) +
               "<BR>The time is " + new Date() +
               "</B><BR>")

document.write(((now.toString())).bold()) + "<BR>");
document.write(((now.toString())).bold()).
fontsize(5) + "<BR>");
document.write("</B></CENTER>");

</script>
</body>
</html>
```

Listing 5-3.   The HTML output from List. 5-2.

```
<html>
<head>
<title>Hello World: JavaScript and Strings</title>
</head>

<body>
<P><CENTER>
<B><FONT SIZE="7">Hello World</FONT><BR>
The time is Fri Mar 19 10:40:32 GMT+0000 (GMT)
1999</B><BR>
<B>Fri Mar 19 10:40:32 GMT+0000 (GMT) 1999</B><BR>
<FONT SIZE="5">
<B>Fri Mar 19 10:40:32 GMT+0000 (GMT) 1999</B></FONT>
<BR></B></CENTER>

</body>
</html>
```

source, and List. 5-3 contains the HTML page created by JavaScript and displayed by the browser.
   Note that

- a `Date` object is used to capture the current date and time,
- the `Date` object is converted to a `String`, and wrapped inside `<B>` and `</B>` tags, which in turn is wrapped inside `<FONT>` and `</FONT>` tags, and
- a `Date` object is also used inline as part of a `document.write()` statement.

Figure 5-2 shows the browser output of List. 5-3.

Displaying a Popup Box

The next example shows how to use JavaScript to output the "Hello World" string as a popup box. Listing 5-4 contains the AppPage source for `HelloPopupWorld.html`.
   In this example, the `alert()` method is called to output a string in a dialog box. When the JavaScript interpreter in the browser executes the `alert()` method, a dialog box is displayed, as in Fig. 5-3.

Figure 5-2. Listing 5-3 displayed in the browser.

Listing 5-4. *Using a Popup box in JavaScript* (`HelloPopupWorld.html`).

```html
<html>
<head>
<title>Hello World: JavaScript</title>
</head>
<body>
<script language=JavaScript>
    alert("Hello World");
</script>
</body>
</html>
```

*Figure 5-3. JavaScript
Popup box from List. 5-4.*

Built-in methods that belong to the `window` *object (the object created by the browser to represent the browser window) do not need to have the term* window *in front of the method name. For example,* `window.alert()` *and* `alert()` *are synonymous.*

Create Dynamic Web Pages with Frames and JavaScript

JavaScript can be used to powerfully render the contents of the browser display dynamically. Often, a mouse click in one HTML frame will cause the displayed contents in another frame to change, either by downloading a new web page, or by creating the display contents on the client. To do this properly, you need to use *frames*, which enable you to construct a set of HTML documents within the one browser screen. Each document window is called a *frame*, and the sum of these is called a *frameset*.

It is assumed that you have a basic grasp of the practical details of frames and framesets. The next example creates two frames, and the first frame controls the display of the second. When the first frame is downloaded, it writes the "Hello World" string to the second frame. Listing 5-5 contains the AppPage source, called `HelloFramesWorld.html`.

> **Listing 5-5.** *Controlling dynamic page content using frames and JavaScript* (`HelloFramesWorld.html`).

```
<html>
<head>
<title>Hello World: JavaScript</title>

<script language=JavaScript>
function displayHelloWorld() {

   var Header = "<HTML><BODY><CENTER><BR>";
   var Footer = "</CENTER></BODY></HTML>";
   var Message = "Hello Frames World".bold();

   displayFrame = mainPanel.window.document;
   displayFrame.open('text/html');

   displayFrame.write(Header);
   displayFrame.write(Message.fontsize(7));
   displayFrame.write(Footer);

   displayFrame.close();
}
```

Listing 5-5.   (continued)

```
</script>
</head>
<frameset rows="100%,*" onLoad='displayHelloWorld();'>
   <frame name="mainPanel"
          src="<?MIVAL>$WEB_HOME<?/MIVAL>?Mival=blank">
   <noframes>
   <body>
   <p>This page uses frames, but your browser doesn't
      support them.</p>
   </body>
   </noframes>
</frameset>
</html>
```

To summarize this example, there are two documents that the browser is using:

1. The main document is the web page in List. 5-5, which contains the JavaScript code. The second document will contain the dynamically created string.
2. The frameset defines one frame, which is declared to occupy the whole screen. This frame is called `mainPanel`. A blank HTML page is downloaded to it by default. This page is called `blank` and is stored in the database, which is why we are using AppPage tags to identify it.

Once the main document has downloaded, the browser calls a JavaScript function called `displayHelloWorld()`, which then writes to the `mainPanel` frame; this function is bound to the `window` object by default, since it has no other object reference.

The JavaScript code in the `displayHelloWorld()` method in List. 5-5 is really no different than the previous examples. Instead of coding

```
document.write("<HTML>");
```

We are coding

```
displayFrame.write("<HTML>");
```

Here, `displayFrame` is a variable that contains a reference to the HTML document inside the `mainPanel` frame.

Listing 5-6 contains the generated HTML for the main document, which contains the frameset definition, as produced by the Web DataBlade. The only difference between this HTML page and the AppPage source in List. 5-5 is the expanded `<?MIVAR>` tag for the AppPage called `blank`.

Listing 5-7 shows the HTML generated and displayed in the `mainPanel` frame. The generated HTML is in uppercase for clarity as it was defined last in List. 5-6.

Figure 5-4 shows the browser output.

Listing 5-6. HTML output for AppPage source in List. 5-2.

```html
<html>
<head>
<title>Hello World: JavaScript</title>

<script language=JavaScript>
function displayHelloWorld() {
var Header = "<HTML><BODY><CENTER><BR>";
 var Footer = "</CENTER></BODY></HTML>";
 var Message = "Hello Frames World".bold();
 displayFrame = mainPanel.window.document;
 displayFrame.open('text/html');
 displayFrame.write(Header);
 displayFrame.write(Message.fontsize(7));
 displayFrame.write(Footer);
 displayFrame.close();
}
</script>
</head>
<frameset rows="100%,*" onLoad='displayHelloWorld();'>
 <frame name="mainPanel" src="/stores7-
cgi/webdriver.exe?MIval=blank">
 <noframes>
 <body>
 <p>This page uses frames, but your browser doesn't
    support them.</p>
 </body>
 </noframes>
</frameset>
</html>
```

Listing 5-7.   HTML generated by JavaScript
                on the browser client for the
                `mainPanel` *frame.*

```
<HTML>
<BODY>
<CENTER>
<BR
<FONTSIZE="7">
<B>Hello Frames World</B>
</FONT>
</CENTER>
</BODY>
</HTML>
```

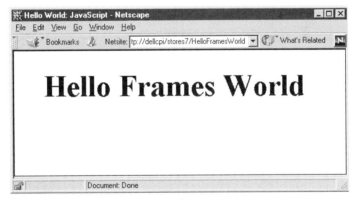

Figure 5-4. Browser output of List. 5-7.

Mixing JavaScript with AppPage Scripting Variables

The next example combines JavaScript with AppPage Script variables to show how to popup a JavaScript alert box to display the name of the user that can connect to the database, as well as the name and type of the web server software. This example works with the CGI version of `webdriver`; some web server variables are not available to the NSAPI, ISAPI, and Apache API versions of `webdriver`.

Listing 5-8 shows the AppPage source that combines JavaScript and AppPage Script to popup a JavaScript alert box.

Listing 5-8. The `mixer.html` *AppPage source.*

```
<html>
<head>
<script language=javascript>
function displayMessage(userName, serverSoftware) {
    alert("Hello " + userName + "\nThank you for using
    " + serverSoftware);
}
</script>
</head>
<?MIVAR>
<body onLoad="displayMessage('$MI_USER', '$SERVER_SOFT-
WARE');">
<?/MIVAR>
</body>
</html>
```

Note that the `<?MIVAR>` AppPage tag is wrapped around the whole `<body>` HTML tag. This allows the Web DataBlade to process the AppPage Script variables without cluttering up the code with too many `<?MIVAR>` tags.

The AppPage variables are expanded at the database server before the generated HTML page is sent to the browser. That is, we are dynamically generating JavaScript method parameters when those parameter values are AppPage Script variable values.

We can see from this example that, when the Web DataBlade processes the AppPage, the AppPage Script variable values will be output in place of the AppPage Script variable names. When the client browser has loaded the HTML page, the `displayMessage()` event handler for the `onload` event will popup an alert box with the values supplied by the Web DataBlade.

Listing 5-9 shows the generated HTML page.

Listing 5-9.   *HTML output of List. 5-8.*

```
<html>
<head>
<script language=javascript>
function displayMessage(userName, serverSoftware) {
    alert("Hello " + userName + "\nThank you for using
    " + serverSoftware);
}
```

Listing 5-9. (continued)

```
</script>
</head>
<body onLoad="displayMessage('Informix','Netscape-
Enterprise/3.6');">
</body>
</html>
```

Figure 5-5. Popup box displayed
after the HTML page in List. 5-9
has loaded.

Figure 5-5 shows the contents of the popup dialog box.

Using JavaScript to Display the Results of a Database Query

You can use JavaScript to display the results of a database query
very easily without complicated string handling in the JavaScript
code.

You may want to display the result set of a query in a JavaScript
window, instead of a HTML table. The AppPage `custAlert.html` in
Listing 5-10 shows how to display a SQL result set in a JavaScript
alert box.

When the AppPage is expanded by `webexplode()`, the SQL
statement is executed, and each row of the result set is formatted.
For each row returned, the customer value has a new-line character
appended (`\n`). The formatted output is written to the AppPage
variable called `$custList`, declared with the `NAME` attribute of the
`MISQL` tag. The contents of this variable are then written as a parameter to the JavaScript `alert()` method, as shown in the snippet
below.

Listing 5-10. *The AppPage* `custAlert.html`.

```
<HTML>
<BODY>
<?MIVAR NAME=custList>OK <?/MIVAR>
<?MISQL NAME=custList SQL="
select trim(fname) || ' ' || trim(lname) from customer
order by 1;">$1\n<?/MISQL>

<?MIVAR>
The list of Customers is as follows:<BR>
<script>

alert ("Selected Customers are:\n\n" + "$custList")
</script>
<?/MIVAR>
</BODY>
</HTML>
```

```
alert ("Ludwig Pauli\nCarole Sadler\nPhilip
Currie\nAnthony Higgins\nRaymond Vector\nGeorge
Watson\nCharles Ream\nDonald Quinn\nJane Miller\nRoy
Jaeger\nFrances Keyes\nMargaret Lawson\nLana
Beatty\nFrank Albertson\nAlfred Grant\nJean
Parmelee\nArnold Sipes\nDick Baxter\nBob Shorter\nFred
Jewell\nJason Wallack\nCathy O'Brian\nMarvin
Hanlon\nChris Putnum\nJames Henry\nEileen Neelie\nKim
Satifer\nFrank Lessor\n")
```

You can use the NAME attribute of the MISQL tag to store the formatted results of a database query into an AppPage variable. You
then use the variable in AppPage Scripting statements. Remember
that the AppPage variable is not "seen" by JavaScript. The AppPage
variable is processed by the `webexplode()` function, which returns
the value of that variable and writes it to the HTML page being
constructed.

When the browser renders the page, the `alert()` method will be
executed as soon as it is encountered, so the list of customers will
appear before the page has been completely rendered in the browser.
Figure 5-6 shows the list of customers displayed in the alert box.

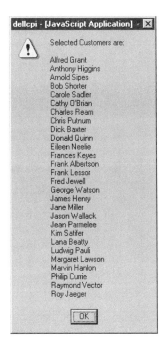

Figure 5-6. *JavaScript customer list.*

If the value of an AppPage variable contains embedded delimiters, using that variable in a JavaScript expression may violate JavaScript syntax.

White space between the MISQL *start and end tags are significant when you are storing the results in a variable using the* NAME *attribute. For example, if you* URLENCODE *the variable and display the result, you will see white space as part of the variable value. The example in List. 5-10 requires that the formatting section of the* MISQL *tag has no white space characters, since these characters will affect the rendering of the AppPage variable value to the* alert() *method. Try it: place the formatting commands on a separate line. If the formatted output was written to the HTML page instead of a variable, the browser ignores white space, so there is no impact.*

If you are having difficulty formatting the results of SQL in JavaScript, use the URLENCODE *function to see precisely which special characters are output. For example, perform the query,* URLENCODE *the result, and pass the variable declared by the* NAME *attribute to the* alert() *method.*

A JavaScript Summary

You have started to create dynamic web content with these relatively simple examples. Table 5-1 lists the summary meaning of the concepts introduced in the sections so far.

Table 5-1. JavaScript summary.

Term	Description
window	The browser window. It acts as a container for other windows, called frames. It is also an object, with built-in methods to manipulate windows, such as `alert()`.
frame	A browser window can be divided into screens. Each screen is a frame. Each frame is treated as a separate window object.
frameset	The definition of a set of frames that exist within a browser window.
document	The HTML document that exists in a browser window. It is addressed as `window.document` or just `document`. This document is an object, with built-in methods to act on the document display, such as `write()`.
Object	A JavaScript object. This can be an HTML object created by the browser or a scripted object created by the programmer. It contains data and methods to operate on the data.
Object instance	A single occurrence of an object. It will have its own address in browser memory. You can create multiple object instances with the same value; each will be unique.
Method	A function that is bound to an object. It contains code that typically operates on the object data, although it is not restricted to this.
Built-in method	Standard methods that are part of the JavaScript language definition. For example, the `window` and `document` objects have methods to open windows and write to documents. You use them; you don't have to create them.

Table 5-1. *(continued)*

Term	Description
function	Another word for method. In JavaScript, all functions are methods because a function created in an HTML document is automatically bound to that window. For example, `window.myFunc()` is the same as `myFunc()` when referenced inside the document that defines `myfunc()`. Functions can also be used as class definitions, which are templates for objects.
string	The name for a String object. In JavaScript, there are standard data types that are created as JavaScript objects in browser memory. These objects have built-in methods that allow you to operate on the data encapsulated in the object.
fontsize	A method of the String object. It takes the String data (for example, "Hello World") and delimits the data with the `<FONT>` tag.
Interpreter	The JavaScript interpreter. JavaScript is an interpreted language. The browser will contain a JavaScript interpreter, which controls the execution of JavaScript under the control of the browser. JavaScript can be executed while a web page is being rendered or after the web page has been displayed; for example, when a user presses a button.

Integrating JavaScript with Java: The Basics of LiveConnect

LiveConnect is a Netscape technology that allows you to connect JavaScript with Java in the browser. Using LiveConnect, Java methods can access JavaScript objects and methods, and vice versa. This interoperability gives each language a portal through which to exploit the strengths of the other.

Note that the ability to interface Java with JavaScript can vary among browser vendors. You will need to test these examples against your own browser version; most of the examples will work with Navigator 4 and Internet Explorer 5, and may work with earlier versions.

You can obtain comprehensive details about LiveConnect from `http://developer.netscape.com`.

Both Java and JavaScript must be enabled in the browser before they can interact with each other.

Object Interfaces

When Java and JavaScript interact, they do so using wrapper objects. The LiveConnect software creates a wrapper object automatically. For example, Java can access JavaScript via a wrapper object called `netscape.JavaScript.JSObject`*; this object allows you to invoke JavaScript methods and work with JavaScript variables.*

Calling Java from JavaScript

Navigator contains an object called `Packages`. The `Packages` object allows JavaScript to call Java methods. You can treat the `Packages` object in the same way that you treat the `Document` or `Window` objects in JavaScript.

Don't confuse the JavaScript `Packages` *object with the Java concept of a* `Package`*; they are totally separate.*

Syntax of Calling Java Methods

The syntax for calling Java methods is as follows:

```
[Packages.]packagename.classname.methodname
```

The `Packages` prefix is optional for some Java Packages, such as `java`, `sun` and `netscape`. Here is a fully qualified example:

```
Packages.java.lang.System.out("Hello World");
```

A Simple Example

This very simple example shows you how to write to Navigator's *Java Console* using JavaScript. The HTML page shown does not have

Listing 5-11.   The HTML page `console.html`.

```
<html>
<body>
<script language=javascript>
   var System=Packages.java.lang.System;
   System.out.println("\nHello Java from JavaScript");
</script>
</body>
</html>
```

to be an AppPage in the Informix database; you can drop the page from the filesystem into the browser. Listing 5-11 shows the HTML page, called `console.html`.

The example writes to Navigator's Java Console using the `println()` method of the `System` object in the Java package called `lang`. The Java Console can be accessed in Navigator using `Window\Java Console`. When the `console.html` page is loaded, the contents of the console should be similar to Figure 5-7.

JavaScript can access Java packages in the browser because the browser will ship with its own set of Java classes that will run in the browser's Java Virtual Machine (JVM). Because different browsers ship with their own version of the Java classes, it is often difficult to rely on a complete implementation of a Java release in

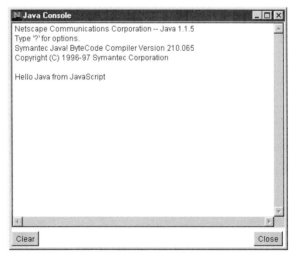

Figure 5-7. *Java Console.*

any browser. For this reason, you can download and install the Java Plug-In from Sun, which will allow you to use the full capabilities of a Java release. This is because when you use the Java Plug-In, you substitute the JVM from the plug-in for the browser JVM. The side effect is that you can't interface JavaScript with an applet running inside the Java Plug-In, although this feature may become enabled in future releases of the Java Plug-In.

You can download the Java Plug-In from Sun at the following URL:

```
http://java.sum.com
```

Controlling Applets from JavaScript

You can control Java Applets from JavaScript. For example, you can stop and start applets by invoking the `stop()` and `start()` applet methods. Any *public* Java method or variable in an applet is accessible from JavaScript; the method or variable must have the Java keyword `public` in front of it.

It is good programming practice to create `public` Java methods in your applet to get and set the variable that you want to make available to JavaScript; you can filter the setting of the variable to avoid unexpected applet results. Similarly, you should implement get and set methods in JavaScript for those properties that are read and written to and from Java.

The `applets` Array

When applets are specified in an HTML page, an applet object is created by the browser, and you can reference the applet by name in an array of applet objects called `applets`. For example:

```
document.appletname.method()
document.appletname.variable
document.applets['appletname'].method()
document.applets[0].variable
```

You can reference the `applet` by name directly or by offset in the `applet` array.

A Simple Example

This example sets the text of a Java `Label` object that exists in an applet in the web page. The `Label` class is a Java AWT (abstract windowing toolkit) class that defines a text label, and you can set the text in this label using the `Label.setText()` Java method. In this case, we will set the label from two events:

1. We set the label text to the `HREF` value when the mouse passes over an anchor in the HTML page.
2. We set the label text to the value of text typed in by the user when prompted by the JavaScript `prompt()` method.

When the mouse passes over the `Enter Text` hyperlink, a JavaScript prompt is displayed; the user can type in some text, and the text is set into the `Label` object in the Java Applet. Figure 5-8 shows the JavaScript prompt:

The text is set into the `Label` object in the applet using the following JavaScript statement:

```
document.urlApplet.setUrlLabel(
    prompt('Enter Text'))">
```

The applet is called `urlApplet`. The `setUrlLabel()` method is a `public` Java method that allows you to set the text of the `Label` object called `urlLabel`, as shown in the following snippet from the `setTextApplet` applet:

```
java.awt.Label urlLabel;
public void setUrlLabel( String txtValue ) {
  urlLabel.setText(txtValue);
}
```

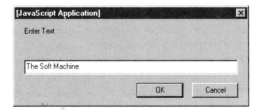

Figure 5-8. *JavaScript prompt when the mouse passes over the* `Enter Text` *hyperlink.*

The HTML source for `stringSet.html` is shown in List. 5-12.

When the text is set into the Java applet using the `setUrlLabel()` method, the applet in the browser displays the text. Figure 5-9 shows the browser display after the prompt shown in Fig. 5-8 previously.

Figure 5-10 shows the browser display after the mouse is passed over the Informix hyperlink.

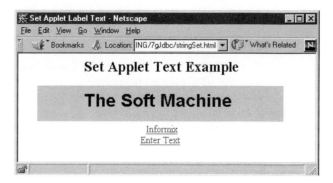

Figure 5-9. *Browser display after the JavaScript prompt is entered.*

Listing 5-12. HTML source for `stringSet.html`***.***

```
<html>
<head>
<title>Set Applet Label Text</title>
</head>
<body>
<center>
<h2>Set Applet Text Example</h2>
<applet NAME="urlApplet" CODE="setTextApplet.class"
        WIDTH="395" HEIGHT="56">
</applet>
<br>
<a href="http://www.informix.com"
 onMouseOver="document.urlApplet.setUrlLabel(this.href)">
Informix</a><br>
<a href="javascript:void"
  onMouseOver="document.urlApplet.setUrlLabel(
                        prompt('Enter Text'))">Enter
                        Text</a>
</body>
</html>
```

Figure 5-10. *Browser display after the mouse passes over the informix hyperlink.*

Calling JavaScript from Java

There are two essential tasks to perform in order to access JavaScript methods and variables from a Java applet.

1. Import the `netscape.JavaScript.JSObject` class into your Java applet and include the `MAYSCRIPT` keyword into the `APPLET` HTML tag.
2. Create Java objects in the applet to hold the different components of the browser window and use these objects to access JavaScript methods and variables.

Import the `JSObject` Class

Java communicates with JavaScript via the `netscape.JavaScript.JSObject` class. The `JSObject` class makes the JavaScript objects inside the HTML document available to Java. You import the class in your applet code. For example:

```
import netscape.javascript.JSObject;
```

In the `APPLET` tag, you need to specify the `MAYSCRIPT` attribute. For example:

```
<applet NAME="urlApplet" CODE="setTextApplet.class"
WIDTH="395" HEIGHT="56" MAYSCRIPT>
</applet>
```

Note that if you are using the Java Plug-In, the `MAYSCRIPT` attribute may not be supported, which means that you cannot access JavaScript from Java if the applet is executed with the Java Plug-In.

Creating JavaScript Objects inside the Applet

To access JavaScript methods and variables, you create objects that represent the different components of the browser window.

These components are created in an *instance hierarchy;* for example, `window.document.myForm.myFormField.value` is an instance hierarchy. Accordingly, you create `JSObject` objects at each level. For example:

```
JSObject win = (JSObject) JSObject.getWindow(this);
JSObject doc = (JSObject) win.getMember("document");
JSObject form = doc.getMember("myForm");
JSObject formfield = form.getMember("myFormField");
String strVal = (String) formField.getMember("value");
```

You can access the properties of all JavaScript objects in this way.

Setting JavaScript from Java

You can assign values to JavaScript properties from Java. A certain amount of data conversion takes place between Java and JavaScript.

There are two basic ways to set JavaScript properties. You can invoke a JavaScript function to assign a value using the `call()` or `eval()` methods of the `JSObject` class, or you can use the `setMember()` method of the `JSObject` class. You may want to implement *get* and *set* methods in JavaScript so that Java can call these methods instead of the `getMember()` and `setMember()` methods.

Calling JavaScript Methods

The `JSObject` class provides two methods for invoking JavaScript methods. The `call()` method accepts two parameters; the *method name,* and an array of arguments. The `call()` method is useful if you want to pass objects to JavaScript methods.

The `eval()` method accepts a string that should evaluate to a method call with or without parameters, as it would be coded in JavaScript. This method is useful if you want to pass literal values to JavaScript methods.

Example: Get and Set JavaScript

This example passes values between Java and JavaScript, and is controlled by a Java Applet. You can enter a string value and check a checkbox. Then, click the `Get JavaScript` button on the applet, and the values will be read and posted to the textbox and checkbox on the Java form. If the JavaScript checkbox is checked, the Java checkbox will be checked also.

In addition, a JavaScript object is created on the HTML page, called `myNumber`. This object has a property called `numberVal` that is read by the Java Applet and posted to the `Number` textbox in the applet.

You can also enter text into the applet textboxes, and check the checkbox; when you click the `Set JavaScript` button, these values will be posted to the HTML form, and the `numberVal` property will be updated. A confirmatory `alert()` is performed to show that the property has been set correctly.

Listing 5-13 shows the `setJavaScript.html` page.

Listing 5-13.   The `setJavaScript.html` page.

```
<HTML>
<HEAD>
<TITLE>Get and Set JavaScript</TITLE>
</HEAD>
<BODY>
<h2>Get and Set JavaScript</h2>
<APPLET CODE="setJavaScript.class" WIDTH=355 HEIGHT=98
        NAME="myApplet" MAYSCRIPT>
</APPLET>
<FORM NAME="myForm" method=post>
<TABLE BORDER=0>
<TR>
<TD ALIGN=RIGHT>String:</TD>
<TD><INPUT TYPE=TEXT SIZE=30 NAME="myString"></TD>
</TR>
<TR>
<TD ALIGN=RIGHT>Boolean:</TD>
<TD><INPUT TYPE=CHECKBOX NAME="myCheck"></TD>
```

Listing 5-13.   (continued)

```
</TR>
</TABLE>
</FORM>
<script>
function fmyNumber( pNumber ) {
this.numberVal = pNumber;
}
myNumber = new fmyNumber("12.99");

function setMyCheck (pValue) {
    document.myForm.myCheck.checked = pValue;
}

function setMyNumber(pValue) {
    myNumber.numberVal = pValue;
    alert(myNumber.numberVal);
}
</script>
</BODY>
</HTML>
```

The individual form elements are accessed via a generic JavaScript handler called `getJavaScriptFormObject()` as shown below:

```
jsString =
getJavaScriptFormObject("myForm","myString");
jsBoolean =
getJavaScriptFormObject("myForm","myCheck");
```

Listing 5-14 shows a snippet from the `getJavaScript FormObject()` method. Note the use of `JSException`. This exception belongs to the `netscape.javascript` package, and is generated if any JavaScript error is encountered when invoking methods in the `JSObject` class.

The `myNumber` JavaScript object is accessed as `window.myNumber`, and the `numberVal` property is accessed as `window.myNumber.numberVal`, as shown in the next snippet:

```
JSObject win = (JSObject) JSObject.getWindow(this);
JSObject myNumO = (JSObject) win.getMember("myNumber");
String myNum = (String) myNumO.getMember("numberVal");
```

Listing 5-14.   Managing the interface to an HTML form element.

```
try {
      win = (JSObject) JSObject.getWindow(this);
      doc = (JSObject) win.getMember("document");
      documentForm = (JSObject) doc.getMember(jForm);
      formField = (JSObject)documentForm.getMember
                  (jFormField);
      return formField;
}
catch (Exception e) {
      if (e instanceof JSException) {
        System.out.println("JavaScript Exception
        Encountered");
      }
      e.printStackTrace();
}
```

To set the `myString` form field, we map the form field as shown in the previous snippet, and use the `setMember()` method (`stringField.getText()` fetches the textbox contents for the applet textbox called `stringField`):

```
jsString =
  getJavaScriptFormObject("myForm","myString");
jsString.setMember("value",stringField.getText());
```

To set the HTML checkbox, we call the `JSObject eval()` method, which invokes the JavaScript `setMyCheck()` method. We also invoke the `setMyNumber()` method to set the property of the `myNumber` JavaScript object, as shown in the next snippet:

```
jsWin = (JSObject) JSObject.getWindow(this);
jsWin.eval("setMyCheck(" + checkbox1.getState()+
");");
jsWin.eval("setMyNumber(" + numberField.getText() +
");");
```

Figure 5-11 shows an example browser display for the "Get and Set" example.

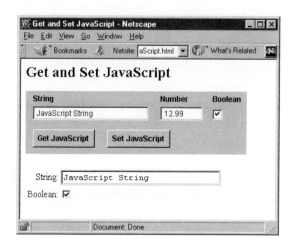

Figure 5-11. Example "Get" and "Set" of variables between Java and JavaScript.

Connecting JavaScript to the Wider Application Network from the Browser

Because you can now invoke applet methods from JavaScript, you can also interface JavaScript with the Informix database using the JDBC Type 4 driver that can be downloaded with the applet. In fact, you can use the Java Applet as a portal through which your JavaScript methods, form objects, and browser events can communicate with the wider application network.

For example, if you have configured applet security correctly, you can manage RMI (remote method invocation) from the browser client (see Chap. 10 for information on how to work with applets and RMI).

For example, to connect your JavaScript methods to the Informix database from the browser:

- Create a hidden frame that contains the applet; ensure that the JDBC Type 4 driver classes are available to the applet.
- The applet should create a JDBC connection with the target database server either in the `init()` method of the applet, or on demand via a `public` method that is visible to JavaScript.
- The applet should close the connection before the applet is destroyed.
- Create JavaScript code that can invoke the appropriate Java methods to perform queries and execute stored procedures.

Scrolling Images from the Database

Most of us have seen the way an image will change when you run the mouse over the image or an associated hyperlink. This section will show you how to accomplish this when the images are extracted from the Informix database. Listing 5-15 shows the AppPage source for the scroller.html AppPage that demonstrates the functionality.

Listing 5-15. *The* scroller.html *AppPage source.*

```
<html>
<head>
<?mierror>
Error in SQL: $MI_ERRORCODE, $MI_ERRORMSG
<?/mierror>

<script language="JavaScript">
<!- Begin
var computer = new Image();
var bag = new Image();
var diskettes = new Image();
var monitor = new Image();
var laptop = new Image();
var scanner = new Image();
var blankimage = new Image();

<?mivar>
// name the source images
computer.src = "$WEB_HOME?MIvalObj=computer&type=
              image/gif";
bag.src = "$WEB_HOME?MIvalObj=computerBag&type=
          image/gif";
diskettes.src = "$WEB_HOME?MIvalObj=diskettes&type=
              image/gif";
monitor.src = "$WEB_HOME?MIvalObj=monitor&type=
              image/gif";
blankimage.src = "$WEB_HOME?MIvalObj=blankimage&type=
                              image/gif";
<?/mivar>
```

Listing 5-15. *(continued)*

```
// select the source images
<?misql sql="select $MInamObj, $MIcolObj
            from $MItabObj
         where $MInamObj in ('laptop','scanner');">
$1.src = "$WEB_HOME?LO=$2&type=image/gif"
<?/misql>

// swap the images
function doImages(picimage) {
    document['picture'].src= picimage.src ;
}


// display the webdriver URL
function showLO() {
   alert(document['picture'].src);
}
// End ->
</script>
</head>

<body>
<center>
<h2>JavaScript Image Rotation</h2>
<h3>Pass the Mouse over the Hyperlink to View the
    Image</h3>
<h4>Click the Hyperlink to View the Webdriver URL</h4>
<table border=5>
 <tr>
   <td>
     <a href = "javascript:showLO()"
        onmouseover = "doImages(computer)"
        onmouseout = "doImages(blankimage)">
                  <b>Computer</a>
  </td>
  <td rowspan=6>
    <img name=picture src="blank.gif" width=285
    height=286 border=0>
  </td>
 </tr>
 <tr><td>
```

Listing 5-15. *(continued)*

```
 <a href = "javascript:showLO()"
    onmouseover = "doImages(bag)"
    onmouseout = "doImages(blankimage)"><b>Bag</a>
</td></tr>
<tr><td>
  <a href = "javascript:showLO()"
     onmouseover = "doImages(diskettes)"
     onmouseout = "doImages(blankimage)">
                  <b>Diskettes</a>
</td></tr>
<tr><td>
 <a href = "javascript:showLO()"
    onmouseover = "doImages(monitor)"
    onmouseout = "doImages(blankimage)"><b>Monitor</a>
</td></tr>
<tr><td>
 <a href = "javascript:showLO()"
    onmouseover = "doImages(laptop)"
    onmouseout = "doImages(blankimage)"><b>Laptop</a>
</td></tr>
<tr><td>
 <a href = "javascript:showLO()"
    onmouseover = "doImages(scanner)"
    onmouseout = "doImages(blankimage)"><b>Scanner</a>
 </td></tr>
</table>
</center>
</body>
</html>
```

Downloading the Images

Two examples of downloading the images are given. In the first, the image is retrieved by name. In the second, the image is retrieved by LO (large object) handle. See Chap. 20, *"Working with Large Objects,"* for more information on capturing and retrieving multimedia objects.

An `Image` object is created for each image. A URL that maps onto an image is then assigned to the `src` property of the `Image` object, and the image is downloaded but not displayed at this point:

```
var computer = new Image();
computer.src =
"$WEB_HOME?MIvalObj=computer&type=image/gif";
```

In the next snippet, an `Image` object has already been created, but the name of the object and the URL are assigned dynamically from the results of the `SELECT` statetement; the `Image` object is nominated using the first column in the result set, and the large object (LO) handle is assigned from the second column. The image is then downloaded, but not displayed.

```
// select the source images
<?misql sql="select $MInamObj, $MIcolObj
            from $MItabObj
          where $MInamObj in ('laptop','scanner');">
$1.src = "$WEB_HOME?LO=$2&type=image/gif"
<?/misql>
```

 You should consider caching large objects for performance. See Chap. 25 for details on how to do this.

Scrolling Images

The images are scrolled using the `doImages()` function, which takes an image object as a parameter, and assigns the `src` attribute value to another `Image` object.

```
// swap the images
function doImages(picimage) {
    document['picture'].src= picimage.src ;
}
```

The `picture Image` object is the `Image` object created by the `IMG` tag, with the `NAME` attribute set to `picture`.

When the mouse passes over a hyperlink, the `onMouseover` event handler is set as in the following example:

```
onmouseover = "doImages(bag)"
```

When the mouse has passed over a hyperlink, the `onMouseOut` event handler is set to display the `blankimage.gif` image:

```
onmouseout = "doButtons(blankimage)">
```

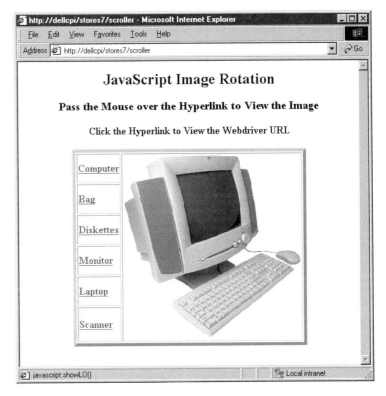

Figure 5-12. *When the mouse passes over "Computer"* `computer.gif` *is displayed.*

When a hyperlink is clicked, the `webdriver` URL is displayed in a JavaScript alert box. The text is taken from the `src` property of the `Image` object.

Figure 5-12 shows the display when the mouse is passed over the "Computer" hyperlink. Figure 5-13 shows the display when the mouse is passed over the "Bag" hyperlink. Figure 5-14 shows the JavaScript alert box displayed when the "Bag" hyperlink is clicked. Figure 5-15 shows the JavaScript alert box displayed when the "Scanner" hyperlink is clicked.

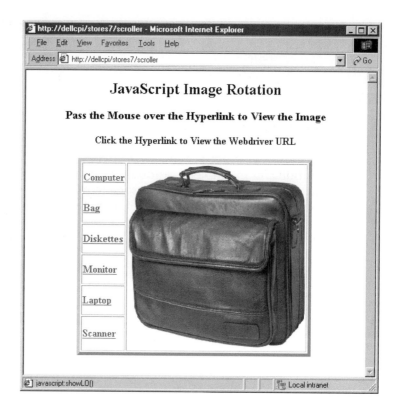

Figure 5-13. When the mouse passes over "Bag" `bag.gif` is displayed.

Figure 5-14. URL displayed when the "Bag" link is clicked.

Figure 5-15. URL displayed when the "Scanner" link is clicked.

Creating Dynamic Selection Lists

You can use JavaScript to create dynamic selection lists in HTML forms (this may not be true for older browsers or browsers that do not implement Version 1.1 of JavaScript). For example, you may want to change the available links from a web page dynamically if those links are stored in a selection list.

The applications of this technique are limited only by your imagination. For example, a database administrator may decide to use a list such as this to send a message to a selection of logged-in users, or even to a selected number of users listed by the `onstat -u` Informix command. The essential point is that you can use Java Script to dynamically update the selection list currently viewed without reloading the page.

The example in this section uses two selection lists to filter the display of order items for selected customers. The essential design of the JavaScript selection list manipulation is taken from the excellent "The JavaScript Source" at `http://javascript.internet.com`. The required functionality for this example is that the system

- selects all the customers from the `customer` table into a selection list,
- allows the user to select one or more customers from the selection list into another list of selected customers, and
- selects all the order items for the selected customers.

What the example will show in detail is

- how to populate selection lists from queries without using dynamic tags,
- how to dynamically refresh one selection list from another,
- how to parameterize a call to an AppPage using the contents of a selection list, and
- how to do all this using frames.

Frameset Specification

The `frameset` specification is basic. The frame called `results` will contain the results of executing an AppPage called `dynamicListOutput.html`. For the initial display, the `frameset` is set to a blank screen, using a blank HTML page. Listing 5-16 shows the `frameset` AppPage.

Listing 5-16.   The controlling frameset
dynamicListExample.html.

```
<html>
<head>
    <title>Dynamic List Example</title>
</head>
<frameset rows="30%,*">
  <frame name="top" src="$WEB_HOME?MIval=dynamicList">
  <frame name="results" src="$WEB_HOME?MIval=blank">
  <noframes>
  <body>
  <p>This page uses frames, but your browser doesn't
     support them.
  </body>
  </noframes>
</frameset>
</html>
```

Table 5-2.   Data movement buttons.

Button	Function
>>	Move customer names to the right-hand list and delete them from the left-hand list.
<<	Move customer names to the left-hand list and delete them from the right-hand list.

Generating the Selection Lists

The example uses two SELECT form fields. You can select which customers you want to view order items for by selecting one or more customers from the left-hand list and moving them to the right-hand list. Table 5-2 lists the buttons to do this.

Populating a SELECT List from a Query

You can populate the contents of a SELECT list without using the SELECTLIST dynamic tag. For example, the following snippet from `dynamicList.html` creates a list of customer names; when one or more customers are selected, the AppPage that processes the form results will receive a variable vector called `fromList` that contains the list of selected customer numbers:

```
<select multiple size="5" name="fromList">
  <?misql sql="select trim(fname) || ' ' ||
                  trim(lname), customer_num
          from customer">
     <option value="$2">$1</option>
  <?/misql>
</select>
```

Creating One Selection List from the Selected Contents of Another

Listing 5-17 shows the JavaScript methods to populate the selection list on the right of the screen (`toList`) with the selected contents of the left-hand selection list, called `fromList`, or vica versa.

> **Listing 5-17.   The AppPage** `dynamicList.html`.

```
<html>
<base target=bottom>
<body bgcolor="#e1e1e1">

<SCRIPT LANGUAGE="JavaScript">
var firstPass=0;
function copy(from,to) {
    if (firstPass==0){ firstPass=1; rollup(to); }
    for(var i=0; i < from.options.length; i++) {
        if(from.options[i].selected
            && from.options[i].value != "") {
            var opt = new Option();
            opt.value = from.options[i].value;
            opt.text = from.options[i].text;
            to.options[to.options.length] = opt;
            from.options[i].value = "";
            from.options[i].text = "";
        }
    }
    rollup(from);
}
```

Listing 5-17. *(continued)*

```
function rollup(box) {
    for(var i=0; i < box.options.length; i++) {
        if(box.options[i].value == "") {
            for(var j=i; j < box.options.length-1; j++)
{
                box.options[j].value =
                box.options[j+1].value;
                box.options[j].text =
                box.options[j+1].text;
            }
            var ln = i;
            break;
        }
    }
    if(ln < box.options.length) {
      box.options.length -= 1;
     rollup(box);
    }
}


// The following function is required because we need to
// pass a variable vector to webExplode()
function doSubmit( toList ) {
    with (toList) {
        for (var i=0; i < options.length; i++) {
            options[i].selected=1;
        }
    }
    return true;
}
</script>

<center>
<h1>Select Customers</h1>
<form ACTION="<?mivar>$WEB_HOME<?/mivar>" METHOD="POST"
>
<input type=hidden name=MIval value="dynamicListOutput">
<input type=hidden name=MI_WEBRAWMODE value="0">
  <table border="0">
  <tr>
    <td>
        <select multiple size="5" name="fromList">
```

Listing 5-17. *(continued)*

```
              <?misql sql="select trim(fname) || ' ' ||
                                 trim(lname), customer_num
                      from customer">
          <option value="$2">$1</option>
          <?/misql>
        </select>
    </td>
    <td>
      <input type="button" value="  >>  "
          onclick="copy(this.form.fromList,this.
                    form.toList)"
          name="copyFrom"><br>
      <input type="button" value="  <<  "
          onclick="copy(this.form.toList,this.form.
                    fromList)"
          name="copyTo"><br>
    <input type="submit" value="Select " name="goButton"
      onclick="return doSubmit(this.form.toList);">
  </td>
  <td>
    <select multiple size="5" name="toList">
    <option value="">This is sizing text</option>
    </select>
  </td>
 </tr>
</table>
</form>
<script>
  // clear out the sizing text
  document.forms[0].toList.options[0].text="";
</script>
</center>
</body>
</html>
```

The JavaScript method `copy()` scrolls the `fromList selection` list to find one or more selected items. If an option has been select-ed, the `option.value` and `option.text` values are written to a new `Option` object, and this object is assigned to the next free element in the `toList selection` list.

Once the assignment is complete, the source SELECT list is rolled up to cover the selected option or options.

You use the copy() method to move a SELECT option from one list to another left to right or right to left.

Listing 5-17 shows the copy() and rollup() methods. The remainder of the listing shows the HTML to render the SELECT lists, including the SQL to create the customer list.

Dummy text is used by dynamicList.html *to pad out the contents of the target* SELECT *list, which initially contains no data. Once the target* SELECT *list has been created using dummy text, the display text is set to spaces. This is required because we need to render the* SELECT *list with an appropriate size.*

Using the WITH *Keyword*

You can use the with *keyword to specify a default scope for your JavaScript variables. For example, a variable that is accessed as* document. forms[0].toList *can have this path shortened by using* with (document.forms[0].toList) *to define the scope of the remaining objects in the path. For example, you could use* options[0] *instead of* document.forms[0].toList.options[0].

In the following screenshots, the top browser frame has been resized for clarity. Figure 5-16 shows the initial state of the lists; the customer names have been listed in the left-hand selection list.

Customer *Ludwig Pauli* is then selected, and the >> button clicked. The customer is moved to the right-hand list box, as shown in Fig. 5-17.

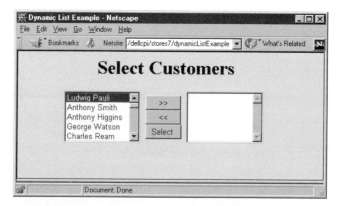

Figure 5-16. Initial customer list.

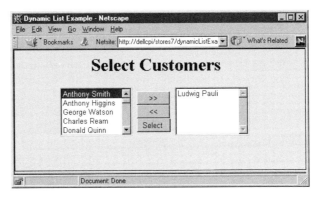

Figure 5-17. *Moving one customer to the other list box.*

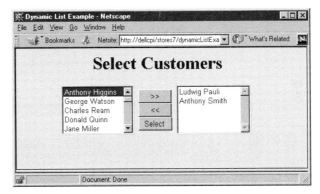

Figure 5-18. *Moving another customer to the other list box.*

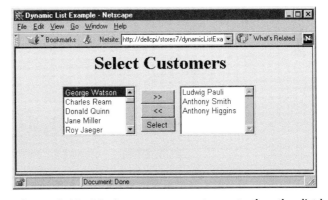

Figure 5-19. *Moving one more customer to the other list box.*

Two more customers are moved to the right-hand list box, as shown in Figs. 5-18 and 5-19.

Parameterising the Results Display and Viewing the Results

When the user clicks the `Select` button, the results frame displays the list of order items for all the selected customers displayed in the `toList selection` list.

The `toList` is a `SELECT` list defined in a form, and as such, is a form field whose values can be accessed by the target AppPage.

The target AppPage that is to process the form field results is called `dynamicListOutput.html`. This is specified in the form via `dynamicList.html` as follows:

```
<input type=hidden name=MIval
       value="dynamicListOutput">
```

The contents of `toList` are passed to `dynamicListOutput.html` as a variable vector; for every selected item in `toList`, a name/value pair is created. The values are the selected option values specified in the `VALUE` clause of the `OPTION` tag.

Listing 5-18 shows the AppPage that selects the order items from the database and displays them in a HTML table.

Listing 5-18. The `dynamicListOutput.html` AppPage.

```
<html>
<body bgcolor="#e1e1e1">

<?mivar name=inClause>$(SEPARATE,$toList,",")<?/mivar>
<?mivar name=MI_NULL>Outstanding<?/mivar>

<center>
<h2>Order Details for Selected Customers</h2>
<table border=1 cellpadding=1 cellspacing=1>
<tr>
<td><b>Customer Number</td>
<td><b>Name</td><td><b>Order Number</td>
<td><b>Order Date</td>
<td><b>Shipping Date</td><td><b>Description</td>
<td><b>Paid Date</td>
</tr>
<?misql err=sqlError
        sql="select c.customer_num, trim(c.fname) || ' '
             || trim(c.lname),
```

Listing 5-18. (continued)

```
                    o.order_num, o.order_date,
                    s.description, o.ship_date, o.paid_date
                    from customer c, orders o, items i, stock s
                    where
                    c.customer_num = o.customer_num and
                    o.order_num = i.order_num and
                    i.stock_num = s.stock_num and
                    i.manu_code = s.manu_code and
                    c.customer_num in ($inClause)
                       order by c.customer_num, o.order_num">
<tr>
<td bgcolor="#ffffff"><b>$1</td>
<td bgcolor="#ffffff"><b>$2</td>
<td bgcolor="#ffffff"><b>$3</td>
<td bgcolor="#ffffff"><b>$4</td>
<td bgcolor="#ffffff"><b>$5</td>
<td bgcolor="#ffffff"><b>$6</td>
<td bgcolor="#ffffff"><b>$7</td>
</tr>
<?/misql>
</table>
</center>
</body>
</html>
```

The incoming variable $toList contains the list of selected values in a variable vector. The $(SEPARATE) AppPage function is used to put a comma between each selected value. The resulting string is assigned to a variable called inClause, which is used in the misql tag as a specification for the IN clause.

```
<?mivar name=inClause>
   $(SEPARATE,$toList,",")
<?/mivar>
```

Figure 5-20 shows the results of selecting three customers, then clicking the Select button to display the orders for the selected customers. Note that in Fig. 5-20, there are no orders for customer "Charles Ream."

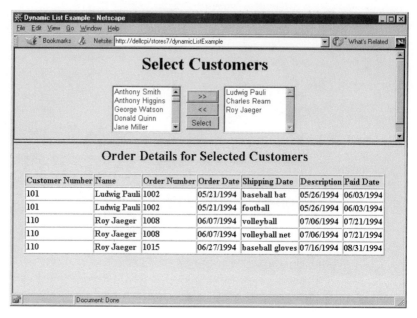

Figure 5-20. *Using dynamic select lists to select customer and order details.*

Submitting Queries without Reloading the Page

We can send queries to the database from an HTML page and display the results in the requesting HTML page *without reloading the requesting page.* Normally, we have to submit a form or click a hyperlink to refresh the current page (or target frame) with the results of the query that was executed. Instead, we can dynamically update the currently displayed HTML page by submitting queries in *secret* and using JavaScript to interrogate the query results.

Perception is everything, and to the user it looks as though the currently active HTML page itself has sent a query to the database and formatted the results of that query.

How Does it Work?

We do all this by using a page in a hidden frame and reloading that frame from the database. The frame source is an AppPage that contains SQL to query the database and assign the results to a set of JavaScript objects. When the resulting page is downloaded to the hidden frame in the browser, the JavaScript is executed and the objects are populated with data. The main viewing page can then use these JavaScript objects.

For example, the query results can be used to dynamically refresh the contents of a selection list, similar to the example above. Instead of the right-hand list being populated from the list on the left, the selected list is populated from the contents of a database result set that has just arrived from the database server. The JavaScript manipulation of the selection lists is taken from "The JavaScript Source" at `http://javascript.internet.com.`

Example Functionality

The example in this section allows the user to select a database table from a list of tables in the `stores7` database, and then view the columns from the selected table in another list on the same page.

When the user selects a table, the selected table name is passed as a parameter to the AppPage that selects the column details from the `syscolumns` table. The resulting page is downloaded to a hidden frame, and the column details are extracted from the hidden page and posted to the "Select Table Columns" list. Figures 5-21 and 5-22 show an example.

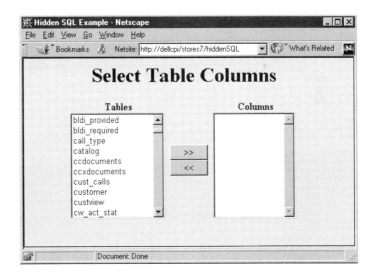

Figure 5-21. Initial state of the selection list screen.

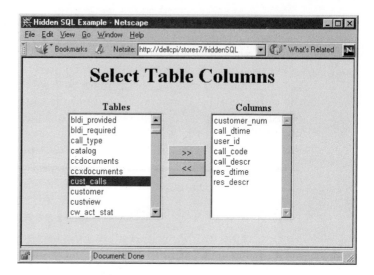

Figure 5-22. *The* `cust_calls` *table is selected and the column list is retrieved from the database.*

Specifying the Frameset and the Hidden Frame

Listing 5-19 shows the frameset `hiddenSQL.html`. There are two frames: The first one, called `selection`, occupies the whole browser window; the second, called `columnData`, is the hidden frame that will contain the query results expressed in JavaScript.

> **Listing 5-19.** *The frameset* `hiddenSQL.html` *AppPage source.*

```
<html>
<head>
<title>Hidden SQL Example</title>
</head>
<?mivar>

<frameset rows="100%,*">
  <frame name="selection" src="$WEB_HOME?MIval=selectionLists">
  <frame name="columnData" src="$WEB_HOME?MIval=listRefresh">

  <noframes>
  <body>
  <p>This page uses frames, but your browser doesn't support
     them.
```

Listing 5-19.   (continued)

```
  </body>
  </noframes>
</frameset>

<?/mivar>
</html>
```

The Main Frame selectionLists.html

The AppPage that displays the SELECT lists and controls the invocation of the hidden AppPage is selectionLists.html, which is shown in List. 5-20. There are two essential JavaScript functions in this AppPage: populateList() and writeList(). The populateList() function invokes the hidden AppPage to select the columns from the chosen table. The writeList() function takes a JavaScript array of OPTION objects created in the hidden AppPage and writes the contents to the column list on the screen.

Listing 5-20.   The AppPage selectionLists.html.

```
<html>
<head>
</head>
<body bgcolor="#e1e1e1">
<SCRIPT LANGUAGE="JavaScript">
var columns=null;
function writeList() {
   with (document.forms[0].toList) {
     if (top.columnData.pageLoaded) {
       columns = top.columnData.getOptionCollection();
       for (var i=0; i < columns.length; i++) {
       // Note: The following assignment is valid in
          Navigator
       // but not Explorer: options[i] = columns[i]
          options[i] = new Option();
          options[i].text = columns[i].text;
          options[i].value = columns[i].value;
          }
```

Listing 5-20.   *(continued)*

```
            length=columns.length
    }
    else {
        setTimeout("writeList()",1000);
    }
  }
}
function populateList( fromList, toList ) {
<?mivar>
    with (toList) {
        top.columnData.document.location=
            "$WEB_HOME?MIval=listRefresh&TABID=" +
            fromList.options.value;
    }
    top.columnData.pageLoaded=null;
    setTimeout("writeList()",1000);
<?/mivar>
}
function clearList( toList ) {
    with (toList) {
        for(var i=0; i < options.length; i++) {
            if(options[i].selected) options[i].value = "";
        if(options[i].value == "") {
            for(var j=i; j < options.length-1; j++) {
                options[j].value = options[j+1].value;
                options[j].text = options[j+1].text;
            }
            var ln = i;
            break;
        }
    }
    if(ln < options.length) {
        options.length -= 1;
        clear(toList);
    }
  }
}
</script>
```

Listing 5-20. *(continued)*

```
<center>
<h1>Select Table Columns</h1>
<form ACTION="<?mivar>$WEB_HOME<?/mivar>"
      METHOD="POST" NAME="listForm">
<input type=hidden name=MIval value="dynamicListOutput">
  <table border="0">
  <tr>
   <td align=center><b>Tables</b><br>
     <select multiple size="10" name="fromList">
        <?misql sql="select tabname, tabid
                     from systables order by 1">
         <option value="$2">$1</option>
       <?/misql>
    </select>
  </td>
  <td>
     <input type="button" value="  >>   "
     onclick="populateList(this.form.fromList,
                           this.form.toList)"
     name="populate"><br>
     <input type="button" value="  <<   "
      onclick="clearList(this.form.toList)" name="clear">
  </td>
  <td align=center><b>Columns</b><br>
     <select size="10" name="toList">
     <option value="">This is sizing text</option>
     </select>
    </td>
  </tr>
</table>
</form>
<script>
  // clear out the sizing text
  document.forms[0].toList.options[0].text="";
</script>
</center>
</body>
</html>
```

Populating the Select List of Tables

The following snippet shows how the select list of tables is created:

```
<select multiple size="10" name="fromList">
    <?misql sql="select tabname, tabid
                 from systables order by 1">
      <option value="$2">$1</option>
    <?/misql>
</select>
```

The table name is displayed in the list; the table ID is used to pass to the hidden AppPage that selects the column data, described next.

Invoking the Hidden AppPage Directly in JavaScript

The following snippet shows how you can invoke an AppPage directly using JavaScript:

```
top.columnData.document.location=
"$WEB_HOME?MIval=listRefresh&TABID=" +
fromList.options[fromList.options.selectIndex].value;
```

The TAB_ID parameter is taken from the selected option in the table's select list.

Executing Secret SQL Using the Hidden Frame listResfresh.html

When a table is selected, the listRefresh.html AppPage is invoked in JavaScript to select all the column names for the selected table. Listing 5-21 shows the listRefresh.html AppPage.

When this AppPage is processed on the database server, a number of JavaScript statements are output to create JavaScript objects and assign values to them. This JavaScript is executed in the client browser.

An array called optionCollection is created. When the MISQL tag processes the result set from the query to select the column names from the syscolumns table, a new Option object is created and assigned to the next element in the array. The Option text and value properties are set to a column name and number, respectively.

Listing 5-21.   The listRefresh.html AppPage.

```
<html>
</head>
<script language="JavaScript">

// optionCollection is refreshed once per page load
var optionCollection= new Array();
var pageloaded=null;
var i=0;

<?miblock cond=$(XST,$TABID)>
    <?misql sql="select colname, colno from syscolumns
where tabid = $TABID;">
        optionCollection[i] = new Option();
        optionCollection[i].text = "$1";
        optionCollection[i].value = "$2";
          i++;
    <?/misql>
<?/miblock>

// getOptionCollection() returns the optionCollection
// array. You could reference the optionCollection array
// by name, but we want a first cust hiding of the
// variable implementation function
   getOptionCollection() {
     return optionCollection;
}
</script>
</head>
<body onLoad="pageLoaded=true;"></body>
</html>
```

What Is an Option *Object?*

An Option *object is a built-in JavaScript object type that represents a single*
OPTION *in a* SELECT *list. For example, the browser will create an* Option
object to represent the value and label text for the following Option clause:
<OPTION VALUE=10>Ten. *In this case,* Option.text *is set to "Ten" and*
Option.value *is set to "10."*

Using the `pageLoaded` Variable

Note the use of the `pageLoaded` variable. When the page has finished loading, the `onLoad` event is fired and the variable is set to the value "true," as shown in the following snippet:

```
<body onLoad="pageLoaded=true;"></body>
```

This variable is used by the `selectionLists.html` page to check whether the hidden page has finished loading from the database server; if so, the `writeLists()` function in `selectionLists.html` can interrogate the `optionCollection` array.

Waiting for AppPages to Load Using JavaScript

When the `selectionLists.html` page invokes the `listRefresh.html` AppPage, the AppPage contains SQL that may take time to execute. Since the `writeList()` function in `selectionLists.html` needs to use the JavaScript data that is created when the `listRefresh` page has been loaded, a *timeout* is set that polls a variable in the hidden frame every second to check whether the hidden page has been loaded.

Using the `setTimeout()` Function

The `populateList()` function in `selectionLists.html` invokes the hidden AppPage and then executes the following code:

```
top.columnData.pageLoaded=null;
setTimeout("writeList()",1000);
```

The expression `top.columnData.pageLoaded` refers to the hidden frame (`columnData`) and the `pageLoaded` variable created by the last document rendition. When the hidden AppPage `listRefresh.html` has loaded, the variable `pageLoaded` is set to "true" using an `onLoad` event handler.

The `setTimeout()` function shown here takes two parameters; some JavaScript to execute, and the interval in seconds before executing the JavaScript. The thread does not loop every second. Once the second is up, the JavaScript is executed and that's it. If you want to keep performing some JavaScript every second, you need to keep performing the `setTimeout()` function, as shown in the following snippet:

```
if (top.columnData.pageLoaded) {
 // code snipped out
} else {
      setTimeout("writeList()",1000);
}
```

Performing a JavaScript Text Search of the HTML Page

It is sometimes useful to be able to search on the *contents* of an
HTML page within the browser window. For example, suppose you
have performed an SQL query against the `catalog` table in an
AppPage and have retrieved a large number of records from the
database. It would be nice to be able to enter another search string,
but this time search *within* the rendered HTML page on the browser
client. This section shows you how to do this. The JavaScript to perform the search is taken from "The JavaScript Source" at
`http://javascript.internet.com`.

Remember that JavaScript and `webexplode()` *are totally separate.*
JavaScript is executed on the browser client, and if JavaScript uses any
AppPage variable values, it does so after they have been exploded.

The following example shows how to search for text inside the
rendered HTML page. The search form is contained in one frame,
and the HTML page to search is rendered in a separate frame.
Separating the search frame from the *results* frame allows us to
repeat the search and scroll the results window.

Creating a Search Frameset

Listing 5-22 shows the AppPage frameset called `find.html` that
contains a search frame and a frame that displays the results of a

Listing 5-22.   AppPage frameset `find.html`.

```
<frameset rows="20%,*">
  <?mivar>
    <frame name=select src=$WEB_HOME?MIval=findInPage>
    <frame name=sql src=$WEB_HOME?MIval=findInPageSQL>
  <?/mivar>
</frameset>
```

database query. The search frame is called `select` and the results frame that contains the results of a database query is called `sql`. Although all the HTML pages are stored in the database, only the `findInPageSQL.html` AppPage needs to be stored in the database, since this AppPage contains SQL to select the `catalog` details, and the resulting search is performed on the client.

The Search Frame

Listing 5-23 shows the `findInPage.html` AppPage source frame, which contains the search form and the JavaScript code to perform the text search of the `sql` results frame.

Listing 5-23. *The AppPage source frame* `findInpage.html`.

```
<html>
<HEAD>
<SCRIPT LANGUAGE="JavaScript">
var NS4 = (top.sql.document.layers);
var IE4 = (top.sql.document.all);

var win = this;
var n   = 0;

function findInPage(str) {
  var txt, i, found;
  if (str == "")
  return false;
if (NS4) {
  if (!top.sql.find(str))
      while(top.sql.find(str, false, true))
      n++;
  else
      n++;
  if (n == 0) alert(str + " was not found on this page.");
}
if (IE4) {
  txt = top.sql.document.body.createTextRange();
  for (i = 0; i <= n && (found = txt.findText(str)) != false; i++) {
      txt.moveStart("character", 1);
      txt.moveEnd("textedit");
  }
```

Listing 5-23.   (continued)

```
  if (found) {
     txt.moveStart("character", -1);
     txt.findText(str);
     txt.select();
     txt.scrollIntoView();
     n++;
  }
  else {
     if (n > 0) {
        n = 0;
        findInPage(str);
     }
     else
        alert(str + " was not found on this page.");
  }
  }
  return false;
}
</script>
<title>Find in Page</title>
</HEAD>

<body>
<h2>Find Text in Page</h2>

<form name=search onSubmit="return findInPage(this.string.value);">
<b>Find in Page:</b>
<input name=string type=text size=15 onChange="n = 0;">
<input type=submit value='Go'>
</form>
</body>
</html>
```

The Searchable Frame

The `sql` frame contains the exploded results of the `findInPageSQL.html` AppPage, which selects the `catalog_num` and `cat_advert` columns from the `catalog` table. Listing 5-24 shows this AppPage.

Listing 5-24. The AppPage findInPageSQL.html.

```
<html>
<body>
<table border=1>
<?misql sql="select catalog_num, cat_advert from catalog
            order by 1">
<tr><td>$1</td><td>$2</td></tr>
<?/misql>
</table>
</body>
</html>
```

Performing a Search

Using `find.html`, `findInPage.html`, and `findInpageSQL.html`, we can perform a search of a HTML page that contains the results of an SQL query without going back to the server to perform another SQL query.

Figure 5-23 shows the initial state of the browser display of the `find.html` frameset.

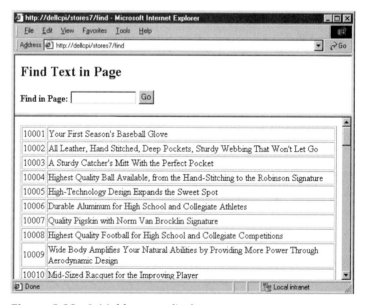

Figure 5-23. Initial browser display.

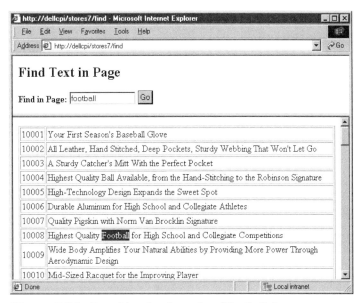

Figure 5-24. *Searching for the string "football."*

Figure 5-24 shows the results of typing in the search string "football" and clicking the `Go` button or hitting the return key. The first case-insensitive occurrence of the string is highlighted in the `sql` frame. If the `Go` button is clicked again, the next occurrence is found.

Summary

This chapter has focused on leveraging the power of JavaScript in a variety of contexts. You should now be able to create web pages that use JavaScript to interact with the user, the database (indirectly using AppPages), and a Java Applet.

In particular, we saw how to scroll images that are retrieved from the Informix database, and how to submit queries to the database server without reloading the requesting page in the browser. In addition, a handful of useful JavaScript utilities were shown, such as how to create dynamic selection lists and how to perform a text search of the HTML page in the browser. In all, we have covered the basics of JavaScript programming by way of some novel and unusual ways of interfacing with the user and the database.

A JavaScript SQL Explorer

In this chapter:

- What is the JavaScript SQL Explorer?
- How the JavaScript SQL Explorer Works
- Managing web content and related information
- Using the JavaScript SQL Explorer
- Putting the tree together—the basics
- Drawing the tree
- Implementing and customizing the JavaScript SQL Explorer

This chapter presents a simple hierarchical menu that works inside the browser using JavaScript with data retrieved from the Informix database. The hierarchical menu is called a JavaScript SQL Explorer.

The JavaScript SQL Explorer is based on a hierarchical tree developed by Colin Tucker of OmenSoft, called OmenTree, which is one of the best implementations of a hierarchical tree in JavaScript. The source code for the OmenTree software is contained on the accompanying CD. This chapter shows how the OmenTree software was implemented in AppPages using dynamic tags and SQL; it also shows how to implement your own database-driven tree.

What Is the JavaScript SQL Explorer?

The JavaScript SQL Explorer is a hierarchical menu tree structure implemented using JavaScript on the client. It is a logically presented menu that runs in a frame on your website.

The design of the tree is taken from the superb OmenTree software. In contrast to the OmenTree software, the JavaScript SQL Explorer implementation

- populates the tree with data from the Informix database,
- uses dynamic tags to encapsulate and reuse the JavaScript code.

Aside from these two features, the working of the tree inside the browser is replicated from the OmenTree design.

Hierarchical menu trees have been around for some time. If you have used Windows Explorer you have used a hierarchical menu tree. The JavaScript SQL Explorer is based on the Windows Explorer interface, so it will be instantly recognizable and usable by regular Explorers.

The three parts to the name describe the components:

- **JavaScript** is used to manage the hierarchical tree on the client.
- **SQL** is processed from AppPages on the database server that retrieve the data from the Informix database to populate the tree and create the tree structure.
- **Explorer**—the tree structure resembles the Windows Explorer tree. The difference is, however, that the JavaScript SQL Explorer is run in a browser and can map information semantically as well as physically, whether the information resides in the database or outside of it.

Although the examples used in this chapter retrieve all the tree icons and documents from the Informix database, you can use a mixture of database and nondatabase content as you think fit.

For more information on dynamic tags, see Chap. 19, "Creating and Using Dynamic Tags." If you don't want to work through Chap. 19, then just think of dynamic tags as macros you can parameterize that contain JavaScript code. The dynamic tag reference is substituted for by the JavaScript code it contains.

Why Use a Hierarchical Tree?

By using the tree, you are giving the users of your website a helping hand, especially if the site is large and difficult to navigate using conventional inline hypertext links.

Hierarchical structures are familiar to us all, since we naturally organize things into categories to help conceive the relations between them. Hierarchy is a logical way to present information; it is very easy to understand and comprehend.

The JavaScript SQL Explorer is like a file structure for the Web, except that the files themselves are replaced by hyperlinks to web-based content such as the following:

- logically related information stored in the Informix database,
- documents in the Informix database (or the file system),
- Web DataBlade and other web applications,
- local files,
- remote servers, newsgroups, and e-mail addresses.

Anything that can be pointed to by a URL can be represented by a node in the tree structure, and these nodes can in turn be categorized and organized logically.

The analogy of the hierarchical tree with the layout of files in the file system is not the most important aspect of the tree. What we are implementing is a view of relationships that do not have to exist in any computer filestore. We can organize and re-organize the "information space" in any convenient way; the tree structure allows us to make sense of the data, whether the data is in the database or comprises a set of web pages on a remote web server.

What the JavaScript SQL Explorer Demonstrates

The JavaScript SQL Explorer demonstrates a great way of organizing information in various ways, and also shows how to integrate JavaScript with AppPages. Briefly, the JavaScript SQL Explorer shows how to

- parameterize JavaScript methods and functions on the database server using AppPage Script,
- create a web page dynamically on the client using JavaScript generated on the database server,
- use dynamic tags with JavaScript to manage some of the coding complexity and enable code reuse,
- use large objects, such as GIF images, with JavaScript, and
- use SQL with JavaScript.

How the JavaScript SQL Explorer Works

AppPage Script is used to manage the generation of JavaScript code on the database server. It is used to extract data from the Informix database and parameterize the JavaScript statements with this data. The generated JavaScript is used to load the tree on the browser client and to manage the opening and closing of folders, together with the rendering of folder contents.

When the user clicks a folder, the folder is expanded or contracted. The top frameset will draw and redraw the tree in the browser to a frame called `treeframe` in order to show the expanded or contracted folders. When a link is clicked in the tree, the results will be displayed in a frame called `pageframe`. Both the `treeframe` and `pageframe` definitions are contained in a frameset page, called `jsqlExplore.html`. The frameset page is the page that contains all the JavaScript SQL Explorer code.

Summary Architecture

Figure 6-1 shows the steps involved in generating a hierarchical tree using data in the Informix database.

The steps can be described as follows:

1. The user requests the URL that contains the top-level frameset for the JavaScript SQL Explorer, called `jsqlExplore`.

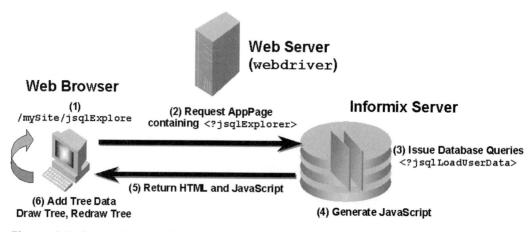

Figure 6-1. *Requesting, populating, and drawing the tree.*

2. The web server invokes `webdriver`, which requests the `jsqlExplore` AppPage; this AppPage contains the `jsqlExplorer` dynamic tag, which is the JavaScript library for the hierarchical tree.

3. The `webexplode()` function expands the `jsqlExplorer` tag, inserts all the JavaScript methods and data, and then processes the `jsqlLoadUserData` dynamic tag, which includes SQL to extract data from the database.

4. As the `jsqlLoadUserData` tag is processed, JavaScript is generated that contains column values from the results of the SQL statements executed; these values will be used to populate the tree on the client.

5. An HTML page, complete with the JavaScript SQL Explorer code and the data to populate the tree, is returned to the browser client.

6. The browser loads the tree data, draws the tree, and redraws the tree as the user navigates it.

Note that the tree data is collected once, when the complete frameset (`jsqlExplore.html`) is requested.

Code ReUse with Dynamic Tags

A handful of dynamic tags are invoked throughout the tree source code to create JavaScript string expressions when processed by the `webexplode()` function. These string expressions are evaluated in the browser to produce IMG tags and hyperlinks. For example:

```
newStructure = newStructure +
    <?jsqlImage image=img-vert-line-
    width=19 height=16 align=TEXTTOP method=no> ;
```

Superficially, it looks as though dynamic tags are used with JavaScript directly as part of the same expression. This is false. The JavaScript expression is evaluated on the client. The dynamic tag is evaluated on the database server; the tag result (JavaScript code) is substituted for the tag reference, and this result is downloaded to the client.

When writing the code to create an HTML page on the client using JavaScript, you can get trapped in a mass of string expressions. Therefore, dynamic tags are useful for breaking up code into functional units. You can go one better and parameterize the tags to make them more generic.

Encapsulation of Tree Design

The JavaScript SQL Explorer code is contained in a set of dynamic tags. These dynamic tags contain the JavaScript objects that the tree uses, as well as the JavaScript methods that work on those objects.

You can reuse the JavaScript SQL Explorer across different applications. You can extend the dynamic tags by parameterization to fully customize the tree from dynamic tags, or use as is and parameterize the JavaScript variables that the tree uses.

You can use the Data Director for Web or AppPage Builder schemas to maintain the JavaScript SQL Explorer.

Managing Web Content and Related Information

You can use the JavaScript SQL Explorer to organize the information space to which you have access. The example described in this chapter pretends that we are using the JavaScript SQL Explorer to organize different levels of information in a corporate intranet. At the top level, this information is grouped into the following areas:

- customers and related customer information, such as customer orders and customer calls;
- web applications, such as customer search, document management, and database browsing;
- documents, with a listing of document content stored in the Informix database repository;
- search engines;
- newsgroups;
- email.

The first three are related to information and content that can be stored in the Informix database. The last three have a general utility function. We will look at the first three.

Managing Customer-Related Information

The JavaScript SQL Explorer is used to visualize the relationships between customers, orders for the customers, and calls made by the customers to the fictional call center. The three tables used to support this information (`customer`, `orders`, and `cust_calls`) are used to populate the tree. The summary functionality is as follows:

- When a customer folder is clicked, customer details are displayed in the `pageframe`, and the folder is expanded or contracted.
- When a customer folder is expanded, an orders folder is displayed.
- If the customer has made any calls, a calls made folder is displayed.
- When the orders folder is expanded, any orders the customer has are displayed as links.
- When an "order" link is clicked, the order details are displayed in the `pageframe`.
- When a "calls made" link is clicked, the list of calls for that customer are displayed in the `pageframe`.
- If the customer has an order for which payment has not been received, a special icon is displayed (a folder with a star in the middle) to alert the user.

When the customer details are displayed, we reuse parts of another application, which selects and drills down into customer details. This application is listed under the applications folder, called *"Customer Lists."*

Managing Web Applications

In contrast to managing a relational view of information, the tree is used to group web applications so that you can invoke and run them in a separate frame.

The web applications are *separate* from the JavaScript SQL Explorer. The JavaScript SQL Explorer is used to manage the *links* to the entry point of these applications.

For example, in a large intranet context many web applications may be under development. As they are completed, you want to publish the URL for the application, in which case you can create an entry in the database to store the URL, and in due course the URL will appear as a link in the tree folder called *"Applications."* When the link is clicked, the application will be displayed in a separate frame.

All of the applications that are grouped under the applications folder are contained in this book in the following chapters:

- Maintain Customer—see Chapter 21, "A Customer Maintenance Application."
- Maintain Documents—see Chapter 18, "Managing Documents in the Information Repository."
- Customer Lists—see Chapter 16, "Web Database Programming with AppPages."
- Database Browser—see Chapter 17, "Dynamic Web Forms Programming."

Listing Documents

The documents folder contains links to some of the document content that is stored in the Informix database. This includes word-processing documents, PDF documents, spreadsheets, HTML, plain text documents, and images.

The application that manages the document content is found under the applications folder, called "Maintain Documents." When you store documents in the Informix database using this application, the document will appear under the documents folder when the frameset containing the tree is refreshed.

Each listed document is displayed with an icon appropriate to the document content-type.

Using the JavaScript SQL Explorer

This section takes you through using the JavaScript SQL Explorer for the example data used in this chapter.

Invoking the JavaScript SQL Explorer

You invoke the top-level frameset for the application, which in this case is called jsqlExplore. Once the AppPage has been processed on the database server and the tree data loaded on the client, the tree is drawn, resulting in a screen such as Fig. 6-2.

Viewing Customers, Orders, and Customer Calls

When you click on the "Customers" folder, the folder expands to reveal a list of individual customer folders. Click on a customer folder, and the "Orders" folder for that customer is displayed, together with an optional link for customer calls made by that customer.

Figure 6-2. *Invoking the JavaScript SQL Explorer.*

Viewing Customer Details

When a customer folder is clicked, the customer details are displayed in the adjacent frame. Figure 6-3 shows an example. Note that some of the customers displayed have a "*" character in the folder. This means that they have one or more unpaid orders.

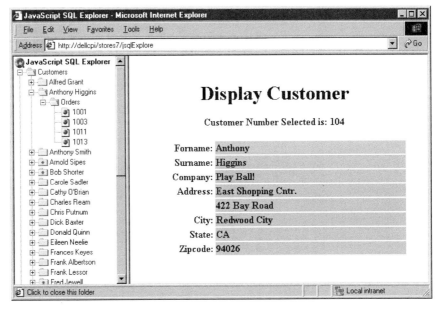

Figure 6-3. *Viewing customer details.*

Viewing Order Details

When the "Orders" folder has been listed, clicking one of the orders will result in the order details being displayed in the adjacent frame, as shown in Figure 6-4.

Viewing Customer Calls Details

When the customer contains a "Customer Calls" link, you can click it to list the call details in the adjacent frame, as shown in Figure 6-5.

Navigating Applications

If you click the "Applications" folder, a list of application links will be displayed. Clicking on one of these links will populate the adjacent frame with the application pages. Figure 6-6 shows one of the "Maintain Customer" application pages after the "Maintain Customer" application has been clicked.

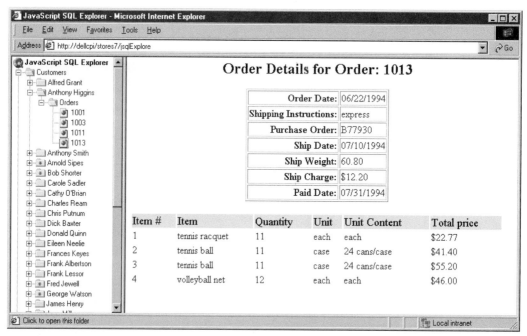

Figure 6-4. Viewing order details.

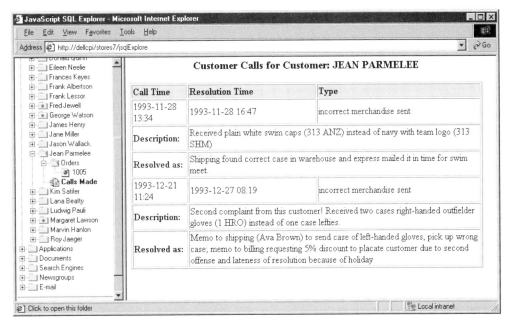

Figure 6-5. Viewing customer calls details.

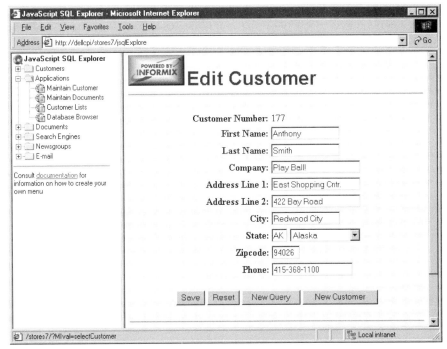

Figure 6-6. Working with the "Maintain Customer" application from the tree.

Viewing Documents

When you click the "Documents" folder, a list of document links is displayed. With each document, an icon describing the document is also displayed. Both the document and the icon are stored in the Informix database.

When a document is clicked, the document is retrieved from the database. The document will be handled by the browser, a browser plug-in, or a helper application, depending on the MIME types that are configured in your browser (see Chap. 18 for more details on this topic).

Figure 6-7 shows the contents of the "Documents" folder, and the `pageframe` shows the contents of a PDF document after the "DDW User Guide" PDF link has been clicked; in this example, MS-Internet Explorer handles the PDF document in the `pageframe`.

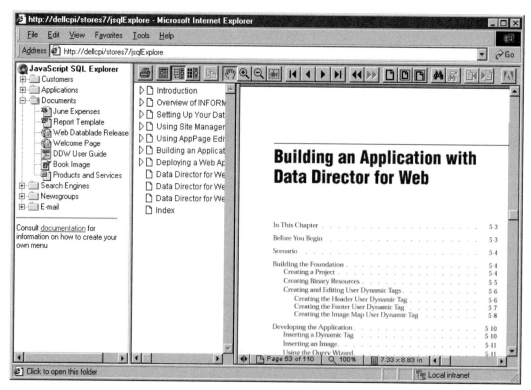

Figure 6-7. Viewing a PDF document after selection from the tree.

tip See Chap. 25 for information on caching large objects, such as MS-Office documents, for performance.

Navigating Multiple Folders

You can view multiple open folders simultaneously. When you open a folder, any subfolders are displayed open or closed, depending on how they were when you closed the parent folder.

Figure 6-8 shows all the visible folders open (and Order 1008 displayed, from the "Order" link at the top of the screen). Figure 6-9 shows multiple open customer folders, with the "Calls Made" link in the middle of the tree displayed in the `pageframe`.

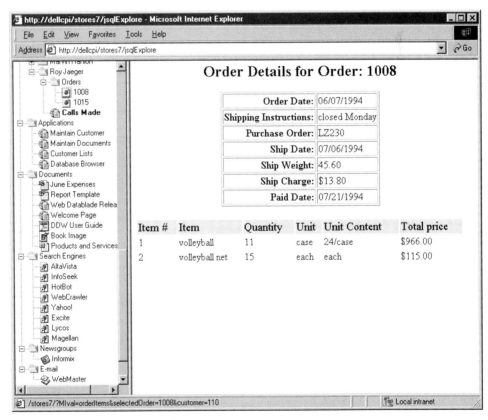

Figure 6-8. *Multiple open folders.*

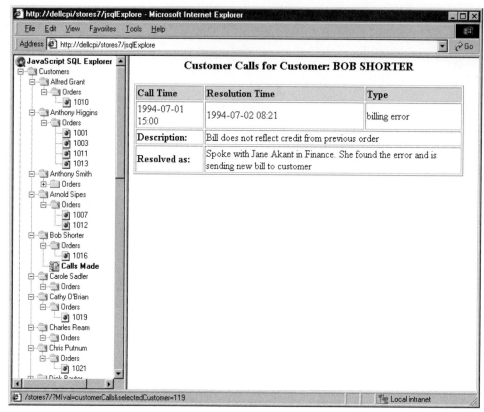

Figure 6-9. *Multiple open customer folders.*

Putting the Tree Together—The Basics

This section describes how the tree is put together using JavaScript, dynamic tags and SQL, starting with the main page, `jsqlExplore.html`, then working through the most important tags in sequence.

Nodes and Collections

The JavaScript SQL Explorer tree is a *collection* of objects of specific types, called *nodes*. A node is an object that contains data and references to one or more other objects. A collection object is similar to an array; you can add objects to a collection dynamically. The hierarchical tree is a collection of nodes.

There are three basic types of node—root, folder and link—and one type of collection. None of these objects are built-in JavaScript types, such as `Array()`; they are created solely for this application.

The Root Node

The tree has one root node, which contains properties that describe the icon for the root node, and the URL that will populate a target frame when the root node is clicked. The root node is defined in the dynamic tag `jsqlRootNode`, as shown in List. 6-1.

Listing 6-1.   The root node using the `jsqlRootNode` dynamic tag.

```
// RootNode() - OBJECT - represents the top-most node of
// the hierarchial tree.

function RootNode(id,name,url,target,icon) {
        this.id = id;
        this.name = name;
        this.url = url;
        this.target = target;
        this.icon = icon;
        this.type = 'root';
        return this;
}
```

The root node takes the parameters described in Table 6-1.

Table 6-1.   Root node parameters.

Name	Description
ID	Internal name of the root folder
Name	Display name of the folder
URL	Optional; the URL to display in the `pageframe` if the root folder is clicked
target	The target frame for the URL
Icon	Optional; nondefault image for the root folder

The Folder Node

The tree can contain objects that are called *folder nodes*. A folder node is a JavaScript object with a predefined number of properties that describe the folder. A dynamic tag is used to encapsulate the JavaScript definition of a folder, which is described in List. 6-2.

When the folder is clicked, the `link` property is used to populate the `pageframe` with the contents of the `folderURL` parameter. In the example, this is set to the display of customer details.

> **Listing 6-2. The folder node using the `jsqlFolderNode` dynamic tag.**

```
// FolderNode() - OBJECT - represents a node which
// branches to contain other nodes.
function FolderNode(id,parent,name,iconClosed,iconOpen,
folderURL) {
        this.id = id;
        this.parent = parent;
        this.name = name;
        this.iconClosed = iconClosed;
        this.iconOpen = iconOpen;
        this.type = 'folder';
        this.open = 0;
         this.link = folderURL;
return this;
}
```

The folder node takes the parameters described in Table 6-2.

> **Table 6-2. Folder node parameters.**

Name	Description
ID	Internal name of the folder
Parent ID	Name of the folder that is the parent of this folder
Name	Display name of the folder
Icon Closed	Optional; nondefault image for the closed folder
Icon Open	Optional; nondefault image for the open folder
folder URL	Optional; the URL to display in the `pageframe` if the folder is clicked

The Link Node

A link node describes the properties that are used to form a leaf of the tree. The Link node is the last item in the hierarchy and represents a URL that can map onto the delivery of web content, whether that is an HTML page, an application, or a document.

Listing 6-3 shows the link node as contained in the `jsqlLinkNode` dynamic tag.

Listing 6-3.   *The link node using the* `jsqlLinkNode` *dynamic tag.*

```
// LinkNode() - OBJECT - a node that represents a link
// using a URL.
function LinkNode(parent,name,url,target,icon) {
      this.parent = parent;
      this.name = name;
      this.url = url;
      this.target = target;
      this.icon = icon;
      this.type = 'link';
      return this;
}
```

The link node takes the parameters described in Table 6-3.

Table 6-3.   *Link node parameters.*

Name	Description
Parent ID	Name of the folder that is the parent of this link
Name	Display name of the link
URL	URL to display in the page frame when the link node is clicked
target	Target frame for the URL when clicked
Icon	Optional; nondefault image for the link

The Collection Object

The collection object as implemented with the `jsqlCollection` dynamic tag, which is shown in List. 6-4. The tree is formed from entries in a collection object called `treeData`.

The `Collection` object is defined with the `Collection()` function. An `add()` method is also defined in the `jsqlCollection` tag. A reference to the `add()` function is stored in the `add` property in the `Collection` object, so that the `Collection.add()` method call can be used to add a node to the collection.

> **Listing 6-4.** *JavaScript collection object in the* `jsqlCollection` *dynamic tag.*

```
// Collection() - OBJECT - a dynamic storage structure
// similar to an Array.
function Collection() {
        this.length = 0;
        this.add = add;
        return this;
}

// add() - METHOD of Collection - adds an object to a
// Collection.
function add(object) {
        this.length++;
        this = object;
}
```

The Main Page: `jsqlExplore.html`

When we were using the tree in the previous section, we invoked the `jsqlExplore` AppPage in the URL. When this page is still an unexploded AppPage in the database, it contains the references to the `jsqlExplorer` application code in the form of dynamic tag references. When the page reaches the browser, it contains the complete JavaScript SQL Explorer application, and a frameset to display it.

Listing 6-5 shows the `jsqlExplore` AppPage.

Listing 6-5. *The* `jsqlExplore.html` *AppPage Source.*

```
<HTML>
<HEAD>
<TITLE>JavaScript SQL Explorer</TITLE>

<!- include the JSQL Explorer JavaScript Library ->
<?jsqlExplorer>

<!- include the JSQL Explorer User Initializations ->
<?jsqlLoadUserData>

</HEAD>
<FRAMESET COLS="180,*" onLoad="start()">
    <FRAME SRC=<?MIVAR>$WEB_HOME<?/MIVAR>?MIval=preload
           NAME=treeFrame
           MARGINWIDTH=2 MARGINHEIGHT=2 SCROLLING=Auto>
    <FRAME SRC=<?MIVAR>$WEB_HOME<?/MIVAR>?MIval=welcome
           NAME=pageFrame
           MARGINWIDTH=8 MARGINHEIGHT=4 SCROLLING=Auto>
</FRAMESET>
</HTML>
```

This page defines the frameset that we will use. The left-hand
frame will contain the tree as drawn on the client using JavaScript,
and the right-hand frame contains the results of clicking the various
folders and links in the tree. The left-hand frame is called
`treeframe`, and the right-hand frame is called `pageframe`.
There are two references to dynamic tags in this AppPage.

- The `jsqlExplorer` dynamic tag encapsulates the JavaScript
  methods used to operate the JavaScript SQL Explorer.
- The `jsqlLoadUserData` dynamic tag contains the tree content
  initializations. This tag contains the SQL to populate the tree
  definition using information from the database. This is the tag
  that we will look at in most detail.

The `jsqlExplorer` *dynamic tag must be placed in the frameset
AppPage because only the* `top` *document in the frameset can contain
the code to control the drawing of the tree in the* `treeframe`*.*

If you implement the tree, then most of your customizations will be focused on the `jsqlLoadUserData` tag.

The `welcome` page is a banner type of page that is loaded while the tree is being created; it is very simple, as shown below.

```
<HTML><BODY BGCOLOR='#FFFFFF'>
<FONT FACE='Verdana,Arial,Helvetica' SIZE=5
  COLOR='#000000'>
Welcome to the <B>JavaScript SQL Explorer</B>!
</FONT>
</BODY></HTML>
```

You can click on the globe at the top of the tree to show the `welcome` page again.

The tree is created only once on the client. Expanding or contracting folders does not change the data in the tree, nor does reloading the `treeframe`. If you want to refresh the contents of the tree (the tree data), you need to reload the entire frameset, `jsqlExplore.html`, which will enable the SQL to be processed, which will in turn extract the data for the tree. You may want to do this if the underlying data changes frequently and you want frequent updates.

The `jsqlExplorer` JavaScript Library

The JavaScript SQL Explorer code is wrapped up in a library of dynamic tags. The main reason for implementing the original OmenTree JavaScript functions in this way was to take advantage of code reuse by parameterizing some of the lengthy JavaScript that writes HTML to the `treeframe`.

The essential point is that you can use dynamic tags to provide a simple and easy way to understand the interface to functionality that is implemented using JavaScript. You can create a dynamic tag library that hides the underlying complexity of the implementation from the user.

Listing 6-6 shows the `jsqlExplorer` dynamic tag.

Populating the Tree with the `jsqlLoadUserData` Tag

This tag contains all the SQL to populate the tree. The `jsqlExplorer` tag references all the JavaScript that is used to manipulate the tree, but the `jsqlLoadUserData` tag contains the

Listing 6-6. **The** `jsqlExplorer` *dynamic tag.*

```
<SCRIPT LANGUAGE="JavaScript">
<!- Begin Hiding

// JavaScript method to load user data and draw the tree
<?jsqlStart>

// JavaScript method to draw tree
<?jsqlDrawTree>

// JavaScript method to draw branch of tree
<?jsqlDrawBranch>

// JavaScript method to open and close folder nodes
<?jsqlToggleNode>

// JavaScript method to find a folder node
<?jsqlIndexofNode>

// JavaScript method to extract the children of a
// parent folder
<?jsqlExtractChildren>

// JavaScript objects and methods for Collections
<?jsqlCollection>

// JavaScript Root node object definition
<?jsqlRootNode>

// JavaScript Folder node object definition
<?jsqlFolderNode>

// JavaScript Link node object definition>
<?jsqlLinkNode>

// end hiding -->
</SCRIPT>
```

AppPage Script that populates the tree. Listing 6-7 shows the `jsqlLoadUserData` dynamic tag as customized for the example application in this chapter.

 *Although the JavaScript used to populate the tree is generated in this dynamic tag, the JavaScript is only executed in the browser on the client. What we are generating dynamically are JavaScript statements that are parameterized with data from the* Stores *database.*

Listing 6-7. *The* `jsqlLoaduserData` *dynamic tag.*

```
<SCRIPT language=JavaScript>
<!- begin hiding
//
// loadData() - GENERAL FUNCTION - user defined data and variables
// exist in this function.

function loadData() {
      treeData = new Collection();
      // Root Node MUST be first!
      treeData.add(new RootNode('root',
        'JavaScript SQL Explorer','welcome','',''));

      // add folders for main groupings
      treeData.add(new FolderNode('Customers',
                 'root','Customers','','',' '));
      treeData.add(new FolderNode('Applications',
                 'root','Applications','','',' '));
      treeData.add(new FolderNode('Documents',
                 'root','Documents','','',' '));

      // add customer folder heirarchy
      <?misql sql="select distinct trim(a.fname) || ' '
                 || trim(a.lname), a.customer_num
                 from customer a
                 order by 1">
          // add customer folder
          treeData.add(new FolderNode('C$2',
                 'Customers',"$1",'','',
                 '?MIval=HelloWorld6&selectedCustomer=$2'));
```

Listing 6-7. *(continued)*

```
        // add an order folder to the customer folder
        treeData.add(new FolderNode('O$2','C$2',
                'Orders','','',' '));
<?/misql>

// add an Order link for each customer with an order
<?misql sql="select distinct a.customer_num, b.order_num
            from customer a, orders b
            where a.customer_num = b.customer_num
            order by 1">
        treeData.add(new LinkNode('O$1','$2',
          '?MIval=orderItems&selectedOrder=$2&customer=$1',
          '','img-page'));
<?/misql>

// flag customers with unpaid orders
<?misql sql="select customer_num
            from orders
            where paid_date is null">
        with (treeData) {
          iconClosed='img-folder-closed-fav';
          iconOpen=  'img-folder-open-fav';
        }
<?/misql>

// add a customer call link for each customer with a c
// customer call
<?misql sql="select distinct customer_num from cust_calls">
        // add a customer calls link to the customer folder
        treeData.add(new LinkNode('C$1',
          '<b>Calls Made</b>',
          '?MIval=customerCalls&selectedCustomer=$1','',''));
<?/misql>

// add a list of documents
<?misql sql="select a.id, a.object, a.mime_type, b.icon_name
            from appdocuments a, iconmap b
            where a.mime_type=b.mime_type">
        treeData.add(new LinkNode('Documents',
                        '$1','?LO=$2&type=$3','','$4'));
<?/misql>
```

Listing 6-7.   (continued)

```
      // add a list of applications
      <?misql sql="select appname, appURL from applications">
        treeData.add(new LinkNode('Applications',"$1","$2",
                            '',''));
      <?/misql>

      // insert any other initialisations
      <?jsqlother>

      // insert user default properties for the tree
      <?jsqlDefaults>
}
// End Hiding ->
</SCRIPT>
```

The tag is used as a wrapper around the JavaScript `loadData()` function. This is the function that is called by the `start()` method when the frameset is loaded.

Creating the Tree

The following snippet from List. 6-7 above shows how the tree creation begins.

```
treeData = new Collection();
// Root Node MUST be first!
treeData.add(new RootNode('root',
        'JavaScript SQL Explorer',
        '<?mivar>$WEB_HOME?MIval=welcome<?/mivar>',
        '',''));
```

After the tree is instantiated with the `new Collection()` statement, the root node is added. All top-level folders will be added to this root folder.

Adding the Top-Level Folders

The following snippet shows the addition of three of the main top-level groupings to the tree: "Customers," "Applications," and "Documents."

```
// add folders for main groupings
  treeData.add(new FolderNode(
      'Customers','root','Customers','','',' '));
  treeData.add(new FolderNode(
      'Applications','root','Applications','','',' '));
  treeData.add(new FolderNode(
      'Documents','root','Documents','','',' '));
```

See the earlier subsection "Nodes and Collections" to understand the actual parameters passed to the node instances.

The `jsqlOther` dynamic tag contains the tree data that is not derived from the database. The following snippet shows the "newsgroups" folder being added to the tree, followed by the addition of a link node to the newsgroups folder.

```
treeData.add(new FolderNode(
            'newsg','root','Newsgroups','','',' '));
  treeData.add(new LinkNode(
            'newsg','Informix',
            'news:comp.databases.informix','',
            'img-newsgroup'));
```

Once these top-level groupings are in place, we are ready to use AppPage Script to generate the JavaScript to populate the tree with data from the Informix database.

You don't have to add nodes to the tree in the tree sequence. For example, you don't have to populate a complete folder before moving on to the next one. You can add the top-level folders, then add data to any folder in any order, as long as you specify the folder name. The parent/ child references are resolved to yield the hierarchical structure when the tree is drawn.

Adding Customer Folders

We add a list of customers to the customer folder. Each customer will contain an orders folder, and optionally, a calls-made link node if they have made any calls to the call center. The orders folder will contain links to display order details for each order under the folder.

We don't add the orders and calls-made links immediately; we add the entire customers and orders folders first and then list the orders, followed by all the calls-made links. Listing 6-8 shows the SQL and JavaScript to do this.

Listing 6-8. *Add the customer folder hierarchy.*

```
// add customer folder hierarchy
<?misql sql="select distinct trim(a.fname) || ' ' ||
                    trim(a.lname), a.customer_num
          from customer a
          order by 1">
      // add customer folder
      treeData.add(new FolderNode(
            'C$2','Customers',"$1",'','',
            '$WEB_HOME?MIval=customerDetail&selectedCustomer=$2')
      );
      // add an order folder to the customer folder
      treeData.add(new FolderNode(
            'O$2','C$2','Orders','','',' '));
<?/misql>
```

The JavaScript contained within the `<?misql>` and `<?/misql>` tags will be written to the output HTML page once *for each record retrieved* by the SQL statement.

When adding the customer folders, we use the `customer_num` value appended to the letter `c` as the identity of the node; for example, `C115`. We will use this identity later to find specific customer folders to insert nodes under.

Note that we also store a `webdriver` URL with the customer folder. This is the AppPage that will display details for the customer when the folder is clicked. The `customer_num` is passed as a parameter for the customer detail selection in the `customerDetail` AppPage.

We also create an empty orders folder under the customer folder. We name the parent folder for the orders folder using the `C$2` (`customer_num`) string, and identify the orders folder as `O$2`; `O115`, for example. We can then add order links to a named orders folder later.

Adding Orders to the Orders Folder

Once an empty orders folder has been created for each customer in the tree, we add any orders that exist for each customer to the orders folder for that customer. Listing 6-9 shows the SQL and JavaScript to do this.

Listing 6-9.   Add orders to the orders folder.

```
// add an Order link for each customer with an order
<?misql sql="select distinct a.customer_num, b.order_num
            from customer a, orders b
            where a.customer_num = b.customer_num
            order by 1">
        treeData.add(new LinkNode('O$1','$2',
        '$WEB_HOME?MIval=orderItems&selectedOrder=$2&customer=$1',
        '','img-page'));
<?/misql>
```

What we are adding is a link node for each customer order to the orders folder for a specific customer. We identify the orders folder using the O$1 string—for example, O115—where $1 is the customer_num column from the query.

Note that when the JavaScript is executed in the browser, the tree data is not automatically sorted as nodes are entered.

When the link for a particular order is clicked, the orderItems AppPage is invoked to display the order details with all the items listed for that order. Listing 6-10 shows the orderItems AppPage.

Listing 6-10.   The orderItems AppPage source.

```
<html>
<head>
<title>Order Items</title>
</head>

<!— handle nulls —>
<?mivar name=MI_NULL><b>None</b><?/mivar>

<body>
<center>
<strong><big><big>Order Details for Order:
<?mivar>$selectedOrder<?/mivar></big></big></strong>
```

Listing 6-10. (continued)

```
<br><br>
<table border="1">

<?misql sql="select order_date, ship_instruct,
                    po_num, ship_date,
                    ship_weight, ship_charge, paid_date
             from orders
             where order_num=$selectedOrder">
  <tr>
    <td align="right"><strong>Order Date:</strong></td>
    <td>$1</td>
  </tr>
  <tr>
    <td align="right"><strong>Shipping Instructions:</strong></td>
    <td>$2</td>
  </tr>
  <tr>
    <td align="right"><strong>Purchase Order:</strong></td>
    <td>$3</td>
  </tr>
  <tr>
    <td align="right"><strong>Ship Date:</strong></td>
    <td>$4</td>
  </tr>
  <tr>
    <td align="right"><strong>Ship Weight:</strong></td>
    <td>$5</td>
  </tr>
  <tr>
    <td align="right"><strong>Ship Charge:</strong></td>
    <td>$6</td>
  </tr>
  <tr>
    <td align="right"><strong>Paid Date:</strong></td>
    <td>$7</td>
  </tr>
<?/misql>
</table>
</center>
<br>
```

Listing 6-10. (continued)

```
<table border="0" width="100%">
  <tr>
    <td bgcolor="#E0E0E0"><big>Item #</big></td>
    <td bgcolor="#E0E0E0"><big>Item</big></td>
    <td bgcolor="#E0E0E0"><big>Quantity</big></td>
    <td bgcolor="#E0E0E0"><big>Unit</big></td>
    <td bgcolor="#E0E0E0"><big>Unit Content</big></td>
    <td bgcolor="#E0E0E0"><big>Total price</big></td>
  </tr>
<?misql sql="select a.item_num, b.description,
                    a.quantity, b.unit, b.unit_descr, a.total_price
             from items a, stock b
             where a.order_num=$selectedOrder and
                   a.stock_num=b.stock_num and
                   a.manu_code=b.manu_code">
  <tr>
    <td>$1</td><td>$2</td>
    <td>$3</td><td>$4</td>
    <td>$5</td><td>$6</td>
  </tr>
<?/misql>
</table>
</body>
</html>
```

Marking Customers with Unpaid Orders

In the `jsqlDefaults` dynamic tag, we specify the default icons that
the JavaScript SQL Explorer will use for the tree nodes. However, in
some instances we want to specify a nondefault icon for a node. For
example, customers who have unpaid orders are flagged with a "*"
in the folder icon.

The JavaScript code to do this differs from the examples shown
so far. We use SQL to extract customers with unpaid orders, but we
need to change the default icon in the *existing* customer folder node
to specify the new flag-based icon.

The jsqlIndexofNode dynamic tag contains a JavaScript utility function called indexOfNode(). When you pass a value to this function, the function returns a reference to the JavaScript object that has the identity to match the value.

In our case, we pass the customer_num to the function, and the customer folder node object for that customer is returned. We can then set the icon reference accordingly. Listing 6-11 shows the AppPage code to mark customers with unpaid orders; it uses the indexOfNode() function. Listing 6-12 shows the jsqlIndexofNode dynamic tag.

Listing 6-11. AppPage code to mark customers with unpaid orders.

```
// flag customers with unpaid orders
<?misql sql="select customer_num from orders where
        paid_date is null">
        with (treeData) {
            iconClosed='img-folder-closed-fav';
            iconOpen=  'img-folder-open-fav';
        }
<?/misql>
```

Listing 6-12. The jsqlIndexofNode dynamic tag.

```
// indexOfNode() - GENERAL FUNCTION - finds the index
// in the treeData Collection of the node with
// the given id.
function indexOfNode(id) {
    var currentIndex = 1;
    while (currentIndex <= treeData.length) {
       if ((treeData[current Index].type == 'root') ||
           (treeData[current Index].type == 'folder')) {
       if (treeData[current Index].id == id) {
            return currentIndex
         }
       }
       currentIndex++}
       return -1;
}
```

Adding Customer Call Links

To add customer call links for customers who have registered a call with the fictional call center, we perform a query to add a link node to the customer folder. In the link node, we set the webdriver URL for the customer calls page. Listing 6-13 shows the AppPage source to achieve this.

The link description is set to HTML, Calls Made, which will render bold when drawn in the tree.

When the "Calls Made" link is clicked, the customerCalls AppPage is invoked, and the customer_num passed to it. Listing 6-14 shows the simple customerCalls AppPage source, which uses the customer_num value set into the $selectedCustomer variable.

Listing 6-13.   Adding customer call links.

```
// add a customer call link for each customer with a customer call
<?misql sql="select distinct customer_num from cust_calls">
        // add a customer calls link to the customer folder
        treeData.add(new LinkNode(
                'C$1','<b>Calls Made</b>',
                '$WEB_HOME?MIval=customerCalls&selectedCustomer=$1',
                '',''));
<?/misql>
```

Listing 6-14.   The customerCalls AppPage source.

```
<html>
<head>
<title>Customer Calls</title>
</head>
<body>

<?misql sql="select trim(fname) || ' ' || trim(lname)
        from customer
        where customer_num = $selectedCustomer">
<p align="center"><strong><big>Customer Calls for Customer:
$(UPPER,$1)</big></strong></p>
<?/misql>
```

Listing 6-14. *(continued)*

```
<center>

<table border="1">
  <tr>
    <td  bgcolor="#DDDDDD"><strong>Call Time</strong></td>
    <td  bgcolor="#DDDDDD"><strong>Resolution Time</strong></td>
    <td  bgcolor="#DDDDDD"><strong>Type</strong></td>
  </tr>
<?mivar name=MI_NULL><strong>Unresolved</strong><?/mivar>
<?misql sql="select a.call_dtime, a.res_dtime, b.code_descr,
a.call_descr, a.res_descr
              from cust_calls a, call_type b
              where a.call_code = b.call_code
              and a.customer_num = $selectedCustomer;">
  <tr>
    <td>$1</td>
    <td>$2</td>
    <td>$3</td>
  </tr>
  <tr>
    <td><strong>Description:</strong></td>
    <td colspan=2>$4</td>
  </tr>
  <tr>
    <td><strong>Resolved as:</strong></td>
    <td colspan=2>$5</td>
  </tr>
<?/misql>
</table>

</center>
</body>
</html>
```

Creating a List of Documents

The documents folder contains a list of documents that, in this
example, are stored in the Informix database, together with
the metadata for the document. These documents are maintained
by the "Maintain Documents" application, which is listed under

Listing 6-15.   Add document links to the documents folder.

```
// add a list of documents
<?misql sql="select a.id, a.object, a.mime_type,
                   b.icon_name
           from appdocuments a, iconmap b
           where a.mime_type=b.mime_type">
       treeData.add(new LinkNode(
           'Documents','$1',
           '$WEB_HOME?LO=$2&type=$3','','$4'));
<?/misql>
```

the applications folder and described in Chap. 18. Listing 6-15 shows the AppPage source to add document links to the documents folder.

The `appdocuments` table is described in Chap. 18; essentially, it stores the reference to the document object and the metadata for it, such as the name of the document and a MIME type.

The `MISQL` query in List. 6-15 links the `appdocuments` table with the `iconmap` table. The `iconmap` table maps the MIME type of the document to the name of a GIF image that represents the icon for the document. For example, if the document is an MS-Word document, the MS-Word icon is displayed instead of a default link icon; if the document is a PDF document, the PDF icon is displayed.

When we add a link node for a document, we specify the `webdriver` URL for the document, which in this example uses the large object (LO) handle to retrieve the document. We also specify the MIME type and the icon to use in place of the normal link icon (see Chap. 20, "Working with Large Objects," for more information on large objects).

The following snippet shows the structure of the `iconmap` table:

```
create table iconmap (
    mime_type varchar(40),
    icon_name varchar(20)
  )
```

The `mime_type` column in the `iconmap` table is used to link the `mime_type` column in the `appdocuments` table. The `icon_name` column is the name of a GIF image stored in the `wbBinaries` or `webimages` table (depending whether you are using Data Director for Web or AppPage Builder).

Listing 6-16 shows the `dbaccess` output from the query:

```
select * from iconmap;
```

```
mime_type                 icon_name

application/xls           xls
application/msword        word
image/gif                 imageicon
text/plain                img-page-globe
text/html                 img-page-globe
application/ppt           ppt
application/pdf           pdf
```

Creating a List of Web Applications

In order to store a list of web application links under the applications folder, we need to find some way of storing the information about those applications. Storing the information in a table is a good idea; we can add, remove, or change the application links as required. The following snippet shows the structure of the `applications` table:

```
create table applications (
    appname varchar(40,10) not null,
    appurl varchar(40,20) not null
);
```

The `appname` column is the display name of the application link in the tree. The `appurl` column is the `webdriver` URL of the application. In this example, we store `webdriver` URLs for the applications that are described in full in this book.

To create the application links, we read the `applications` table and create link nodes under the applications folder. We set the link URL to the contents of the `appurl` column. Listing 6-17 shows the AppPage source to achieve this.

Note that we use the AppPage variable-processing function EVAL to transform any AppPage variable expressions in the `appurl` column. For example, if the `appurl` column contains the

```
// add a list of applications
<?misql sql="select appname, appURL
          from applications">
      treeData.add(new LinkNode(
            'Applications',"$1","$(EVAL,$2)",'',''));
<?/misql>
```

variable $WEB_HOME, then we need to substitute the variable name with the value of $WEB_HOME at this point in the AppPage.

Figure 6-10 shows the "Applications" folder expanded after the contents of the applications table have been used to populate the applications folder. In Fig. 6-10, the "Database Browser" application has been selected from the folder link, and the contents of the

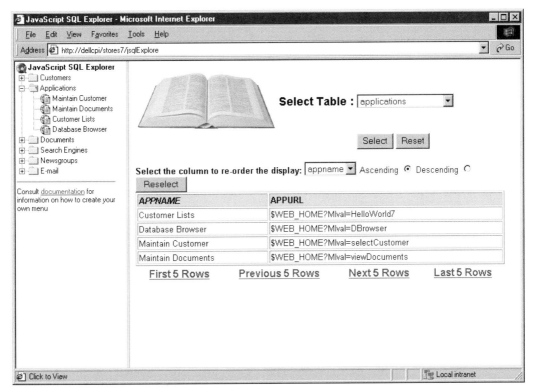

Figure 6-10. Using the database browser application to list the applications table.

`applications` table displayed. You can see the `webdriver` URL that is used to invoke the "Database Browser" application under the `appurl` column.

Setting Tree Defaults

The `jsqlDefaults` tag contains the JavaScript that initializes variables to values that set default tree characteristics, such as the

- default target frame,
- default image URL,
- default link icon,
- text and link colour,
- fonts, and
- prefix and suffix HTML for the tree.

You can change these variables to suit your own requirements. For example, all the icons in the tree are retrieved from the Informix database by name. The default image URL is set as follows:

```
defaultImageURL = '<?mivar>$WEB_HOME?MIvalObj=<?/mivar>';
```

When the tree is drawn, the `IMG` tag for the icons will reference the `webdriver` URL for the icon. Similarly, the default link icon and default image type are set as follows:

```
defaultLinkIcon = 'img-page-globe';
defaultImageType = '&MItypeObj=image/gif'
```

These variables are used to form the `webdriver` URL when the tree is drawn on the client.

Drawing the Tree

JavaScript is used to write HTML to the document in the `treeframe` dynamically. Every time a folder is expanded or contracted, the `treeframe` document is redrawn.

The actual logic to do this is written in fairly complex JavaScript, so you can look at the actual code that is contained on the CD that accompanies this book if you want to know the raw detail of how the tree is managed. However, the Web DataBlade implementation of the tree has included some dynamic tags that allow you to parameterize some of the JavaScript that writes HTML, as well as toggle folders open and closed when they are clicked. These are the topics we will cover in this section.

If you want to see the complete end-to-end JavaScript listing for the JavaScript SQL Explorer, you can implement the dynamic tags in your own copy of AppPage Builder or Data Director for Web, and then invoke the main page, `jsqlExplore`. *You can then view the HTML source for the top page in the frameset. For example, with Microsoft Internet Explorer 5, select* `View\Source` *from the menu bar. If you don't want to implement the tree using dynamic tags, then you can use the original OmenTree source code contained on the accompanying CD.*

Starting the Drawing Process

The tree is redrawn when the user expands or contracts a folder, or if the `jsqlExplore` page is refreshed. When the `jsqlExplore.html` page is loaded by the browser, the `start()` method is invoked to load the data and draw the tree.

```
<FRAMESET COLS="180,*" onLoad="start()">
```

The data generated on the database server by the expansion of the `jsqlLoadUserData` dynamic tag is now contained in a series of JavaScript statements that load the tree when executed. The start method is contained in the `jsqlStart` tag:

```
function start() {
   loadData();
   drawTree();
}
```

The `loadData()` method is contained in the `jsqlLoadUserData` dynamic tag, which we have already covered in the subsection "Populating the Tree with the `jsqlLoadUserData` Tag."

The `drawTree()` method is contained in the `jsqlDrawTree` dynamic tag and calls the `drawBranch()` method to recursively draw the nodes in the tree using the identities in each node to map out the tree hierarchy. The `drawBranch()` method is contained in the `jsqlDrawBranch` dynamic tag, and it is this method that performs most of the work.

Two dynamic tags are used to parameterize the JavaScript that writes the HTML tags for images and folders; `jsqlImage` and `jsqlToggleFolder`.

Using the `jsqlImage` Tag

The `drawBranch()` method contains a number of references to the `jsqlImage` dynamic tag, such as the following:

```
<?jsqlImage image=img-branch-cont- width=19
            height=16 align=TEXTTOP method=yes>
```

The `jsqlImage` tag allows common JavaScript code that formats the HTML `IMG` tag to be parameterized and reused. For example, the `image` parameter specifies the image name to use; in the dynamic tag, a style is appended to the name to identify the specific image. The tree is drawn using images that vary in style within a theme such as "image branch." The style is controlled by the tree logic.

The `width`, `height`, and `align` parameters are used directly in the `IMG` tag that is being written. The `method` parameter specifies whether the `IMG` tag is being written by the JavaScript `output()` method or is being placed directly in the HTML source.

Three other parameters exist for the `jsqlImage` dynamic tag: `alt`, `border`, and `toggle`. These are defaulted to spaces, `0` and `off` in the dynamic tag declaration:

```
&alt=&border=0&toggle=off
```

The `alt` and `border` parameters are attributes of the `IMG` tag. The `toggle` parameter is used to manage the switching of folder icons in JavaScript, and it is set by the `jsqlToggleFolder` dynamic tag (see the next subsection for details).

Listing 6-18 shows the `jsqlImage` tag.

Listing 6-18. *The* `jsqlImage` *dynamic tag.*

```
<?mivar cond=$(EQ,@method@,yes)>outputFrame.write(<?/mivar>
"<IMG SRC='" + defaultImageURL
<?mivar cond=$(EQ,@toggle@,off)>
+ "@IMAGE@"
+ structureStyle
+ defaultImageType
<?/mivar>
<?mivar cond=$(NE,@toggle@,off)>+ @IMAGE@ <?/mivar>
+ "' WIDTH=@width@ HEIGHT=@height@ ALIGN=@align@ ALT='@alt@'
BORDER=@border@>"
<?mivar cond=$(EQ,@method@,yes)>);<?/mivar>
```

An example of using the `jsqlImage` tag in a JavaScript expression is as follows:

```
newStructure = newStructure +
        <?jsqlImage image=img-vert-line-
                    width=19 height=16
                    align=TEXTTOP method=no> ;
```

In this snippet, the `jsqlImage` tag is used to generate a string that is appended to the string value contained in the JavaScript `newStructure` variable.

Remember, however, that the `jsqlImage` tag is evaluated by the `webexplode()` Web DataBlade function on the database server, which results in a JavaScript string expression. It is the browser on the client that executes the JavaScript statement.

The `jsqlImage` tag is also used in the `jsqlToggleFolder` dynamic tag, described next.

Using the `jsqlToggleFolder` Tag

When a folder is clicked, it either expands or contracts (opens or closes). This means that separate sets of images are required for the open and closed state of the folder.

The `jsqlToggleFolder` dynamic tag contains the JavaScript that is used to manage the toggling of folders between open and closed. Listing 6-19 is an example from the `drawBranch()` method.

Listing 6-19.   Using the `jsqlToggleFolder` dynamic tag.

```
if (children.open == 0) {
    <?jsqlToggleFolder
        toggle=open
        image=img-plus-end-
        icon=iconClosed
        level=1>
}
else {
    <?jsqlToggleFolder
        toggle=close
        image=img-minus-end-
        icon=iconOpen level=0>;
    { .. extra code .. }
}
```

When `jsqlToggleFolder` is processed, the resulting JavaScript will be used to switch the folders and icons around when processed in the browser. The JavaScript is a set of `write()` methods to write to the `treeFrame` HTML document. Listing 6-20 shows the `jsqlToggleFolder` dynamic tag source.

Listing 6-20.   The `jsqlToggleFolder` dynamic tag.

```
outputFrame.write("<A HREF=\"javascript:top.toggleFolder('"
  + children.id +
  "',@LEVEL@);\" onMouseOver=\"window.status='Click to @TOGGLE@
  this folder'; return true\">" +
  <?jsqlImage image=@IMAGE@
              width=19 height=16 method=no
              align=TEXTTOP border=0
              alt="Click to @TOGGLE@ this folder">);

outputFrame.write(
    <?jsqlImage image=@ICON@
              width=16 height=16 method=no
              align=TEXTTOP border=0 toggle=on
              alt="Click to @TOGGLE@ this folder"> +
    "</A> "   + children.name + "<BR>\n");
```

To manage the JavaScript even further, we include the use of the `jsqlImage` dynamic tag within `jsqlToggleFolder`.

tip

You can have one central repository of JavaScript for the operation of the tree but still customize your own tree contents using a different `jsqlLoadUserData` dynamic tag. By using dynamic tags to manage the workings of the tree, you can change a dynamic tag so that the changes are exported to each implementation.

Dynamic Tags Used

Table 6-4 lists the dynamic tags used by the JavaScript SQL Explorer. Most of the tags are simple containers of JavaScript that split the code up according to function, and some of the tags are parameterized to allow reuse of common JavaScript methods whose parameters and behavior can vary in a well-defined manner.

You can customize these tags further to fully parameterize the JavaScript they contain.

Table 6-4. *Dynamic tags used by the JavaScript SQL Explorer.*

Dynamic tag	Description
jsqlCollection	Defines a collection object and the methods to add objects to a collection
jsqlDefaults	Initializes the variables used by the tree software to generate URLs, links, and HTML to prefix and suffix the tree
jsqlDrawBranch	Recursively draws all visible nodes in the tree structure
jsqlDrawTree	Draws the root node, and then recursively draws the branches
jsqlExplorer	Contains references to all the supporting dynamic tags that contain the tree code
jsqlExtractChildren	Returns a collection that contains all the immediate children of a tree node
jsqlFolderNode	Object definition of a folder node
jsqlImage	Generates an IMG tag based on the format of the tree and the icons associated with the tree content; parameters are: METHOD—yes or no, if IMG tag is within a JavaScript write() method call TOGGLE—on or off, on if controlled by jsqlToggleFolder IMAGE—the image to place in the IMG tag WIDTH,HEIGHT,ALIGN,BORDER—IMG tag attributes
jsqlIndexofNode	Finds a node in the tree, and returns the index of the node
jsqlLinkNode	A node that represents a link using a URL
jsqlLoadUserData	Uses SQL to extract the relevant data from the database to define the folders, subfolders, and links to content items
jsqlRootNode	Object definition of a root node, the top of the tree
jsqlStart	Called by the HTML page directly once loaded; loads the user data into the tree, then draws the tree
jsqlToggleFolder	Generates the HTML to render the opening and closing of a folder; parameters are: IMAGE—the plus or minus sign ICON—open or closed folder icon TOGGLE—open or close the folder LEVEL—tree depth indicator
jsqlToggleNode	Controls the opening and closing of folders
jsqlTreeFooter	Draws the tree footer HTML
jsqlTreeHeader	Draws the tree header HTML

Implementing and Customizing the JavaScript SQL Explorer

When you want to implement the tree, your folders and content will differ from the example in this chapter. What will not vary is the operation of the tree (e.g., expanding and contracting folders) and the method of populating the tree.

Using OmenTree Directly

You can use Colin Tucker's OmenTree JavaScript application to add folders and links to the tree manually by editing the HTML directly. You can do this even if the content referenced by the folders and links is in the database; in this case, any hyperlink or reference to an image or icon is a `webdriver` reference. Really, if the tree structure is based on content that may change (that is, added, changed, or deleted), then the tree should be implemented using the methods described in this chapter; by using Dynamic Tags and AppPages with SQL. You then don't have to worry about changing any HTML or JavaScript; you let the Web DataBlade do the work for you.

You can create a new set of table relations that map the root folder onto a set of subject areas, such as customers, applications, and documents, and use the MISQL *tag to generate the tree folders. In this chapter, the immediate children of the root folder are assigned manually to show how manual assignment is performed.*

How Do You Implement a New Tree?

There is a quick checklist that you can follow to work out what you need to do to implement a new database-driven tree.

You can take the OmenTree code and edit the loadData() *function to include the SQL to map the web content to the tree structure if you don't want to use dynamic tags. In this case, you still need to store the OmenTree code in the database so that the SQL can be processed.*

- Map out your content base; decide how you want to structure the tree and what links you want to put into the tree.

- Create a new project in Data Director for Web or AppPage Builder, called `myTree`, for example.
- Store the JavaScript SQL Explorer Dynamic Tags in the `myTree` project.
- Create a frameset AppPage (`jsqlExplore`, for example) to include the dynamic tags that operate the tree, and add to the `myTree` project.
- Customize the `jsqlDefaults` dynamic tag, which sets the tree defaults, such as colors and icons.
- Customize the `jsqlLoadUserData` dynamic tag. This is the tag that will contain SQL to retrieve data and parameterize the JavaScript code to populate the tree and create the tree structure.
- Create a URL prefix in the web server so that you can invoke the `jsqlExplore` AppPage, if such a prefix has not been created already (you can use the CGI or API `webdriver`).

You can customize the `jsqlExplore` AppPage and the dynamic tags from the accompanying CD, if required. The important point is that you need a frameset, a tree frame, and a page frame. You also need the dynamic tags that contain the JavaScript code to operate the tree.

Really, the customization is in the `jsqlLoadUserData` dynamic tag. This tag contains the SQL to create the tree structure based on the content base that we are grouping, such as customer information, documents, and applications.

It is worth taking the existing code as a template and customizing the `jsqlDefaults` *and* `jsqlLoadUserData` *dynamic tags for your own site.*

Summary

This chapter has shown you how to use server-side AppPage Script and client-side JavaScript to create a database-driven hierarchical tree, as well as how to approach your own implementation of the tree. The mapping of relational views was contrasted to mapping object content in order to show how the same tree can be used to view the relationships between data as well as manage objects in the same information space.

Dynamic tags were used to implement common JavaScript code, and some of these dynamic tags were parameterized to allow code reuse. The difference between server-side AppPage processing and client-side JavaScript processing was highlighted, and these two separate processes were shown to complement each other in a well-defined application context. You can take the example application in this chapter or the original OmenTree source code and create cyberspace menus for yourself, the use of which is limited only by your own imagination.

Chapter

7

Informix Java Database Connectivity

In this chapter:

- What is JDBC?
- Types of JDBC driver
- The Informix Type 4 Driver
- Browsing the JDBC API
- Configuring the JDBC driver
- Informix client/server connectivity
- Database environment properties for the JDBC API
- Connecting to the database
- Testing your JDBC connection using JLogin
- Using the JDBC/ODBC Bridge

This chapter will show by example how to configure the JDBC Type 4 driver and then how to connect to the database using JDBC method calls. It is important to have an understanding of the components that make a JDBC connection work. What you learn in this chapter can be applied in general to other database servers, not just Informix. The chapter will introduce key topics such as JDBC URLs, protocols, and connection parameters in a practical way so that you can start to connect to an Informix database from your laptop or remote machine.

What Is JDBC?

Put simply, JDBC means *Java Database Connectivity.* It is an API developed by Sun to allow Java applications to connect to a database server. A JDBC driver is therefore required in order to connect to the database server; this is provided by the database vendor or a third party. In any event, a driver is JDBC compliant if it implements the set of JDBC methods for the target database the driver is to support. These methods allow the client application to connect to a database server or a database, create SQL statements, execute those statements, and interrogate the results. There is a library of methods to interrogate the metadata of the database and query results. The same methods are used whatever the source database, whether Informix, DB2, or Oracle. In reality, some of the JDBC methods return slightly different results depending on whose driver you use, and some drivers do not implemement all of the published JDBC methods. The Informix Type 4 Driver is no exception to this rule.

JDBC is not a substitute for ODBC (Open Database Connectivity). JDBC works only for Java applications. It is not an extension for ODBC, either, but it can work with ODBC. There is a special type of JDBC driver, called the JDBC/ODBC Bridge, that translates JDBC method calls into ODBC method calls.

Types of JDBC Driver

In this book, we are using two types of JDBC driver, the Informix Type 4 JDBC Driver, and the Type 1 JDBC/ODBC Bridge Driver. For most of the examples, however, we will be using the Informix Type 4 Driver, which is a pure Java driver that connects directly to the database server.

It is useful to know what the different types of JDBC driver are. To some extent, they reflect the evolution of vendor support for the JDBC API, which started as a portable interface to ODBC and ended as a direct, pure Java connection to the database. Table 7-1 lists the types of JDBC driver.

Table 7-1.   Types of JDBC driver.

Type of Driver	Description
1. JDBC/ODBC Bridge	Translates JDBC calls into ODBC calls on the client
2. Native API, Partly Java	Translates JDBC calls into DBMS API calls on the client
3. JDBC-Net, Pure Java	JDBC API calls are sent to a middle tier, which converts them to a specific DBMS network API call.
4. Native Protocol, Pure Java	Translates JDBC API calls directly into DBMS networking calls, connecting directly to the database server

Type 1—JDBC/ODBC Bridge

The JDBC/ODBC Bridge driver is provided free with the JDK (Java Developers Kit), and is called `sun.jdbc.odbc.JdbcOdbcDriver`. This JDBC driver is called a bridge because it translates the JDBC method calls into ODBC method calls. The ODBC driver then handles the connection to the database.

You need to place the ODBC binaries on all the clients that will use the JDBC/ODBC Bridge. Note if the Java client is an applet: Untrusted applets cannot load the ODBC driver from the client that has downloaded the applet.

This type of connection is typically used to access data sources for which there is no other JDBC driver.

However, the JDBC/ODBC Bridge is portable in that it should work with most ODBC drivers.

Type 2—Native-API, Partly Java Driver

This driver will be written for a specific DBMS API, so it is not portable between DBMS vendors. The driver translates JDBC method calls into calls to vendor-specific DBMS networking software on the client, which takes the database request and then connects to the database server. The driver is called "partly Java" because it relies on the DBMS API binaries being installed on every client that will use this JDBC driver. This JDBC driver depends on the underlying networking API of the DBMS.

Type 3—JDBC-net, Pure Java Driver

This driver sends JDBC API calls to a middle-tier net server, which translates the JDBC request into a DBMS-specific network API call. The translated call is then sent on to the appropriate DBMS. This JDBC driver is not dependent on the networking API of the DBMS.

The difference between this type of JDBC driver and Types 1 and 2 is that, when the JDBC driver sends a request to the middle tier, the request is in a vendor-independent protocol, not ODBC or DBMS specific. The middle-tier net server understands this protocol and translates it into the DBMS-specific protocol. It is not the JDBC driver that performs the API translation.

This type of driver is useful when your enterprise platform consists of multiple database servers from different suppliers and you need to manage the different DBMS connections.

Type 4—Native Protocol, Pure Java Driver

This driver converts the JDBC method calls into DBMS-specific networking calls. It is called "pure Java" because the DBMS-specific networking protocol is implemented in the JDBC driver itself without relying on any client API libraries or a middle-tier translator. For Informix, the protocol implemented is `jdbc` and the subprotocol is called `informix-sqli`. The `sqli` is the protocol Informix clients use to connect to Informix servers.

Because a Type 4 driver implements the DBMS networking protocol in Java, this type of driver is proprietary to the DBMS. For example, you could not use the Informix Type 4 Driver to access another vendor's database server.

There are two advantages with this type of driver: portability and performance.

Portability and Performance Advantages

Because the driver is not reliant on client libraries, the JDBC driver can be deployed across the network. For example, you can send the JDBC driver with applet code so that the applet can access the database from the browser.

Since the driver implements the DBMS networking protocol, there is no translation to ODBC or to a DBMS networking API, which should improve connection throughput.

The Informix JDBC Type 4 Driver

The Informix Type 4 Driver can only connect to the Informix database and uses the `jdbc:informix-sqli` protocol. The Informix JDBC Driver is a Type 4 JDBC driver. This means that it is pure Java and does not require any client libraries to be installed on any host that will use it. All you need is the Java Virtual Machine on the appropriate host that is to run the Java application or applet that will load the JDBC driver.

The JDBC driver allows you to develop and deploy Java applications running against the Informix database. The JDBC driver implements the JDBC Type 4 driver specification and runs on any standard Java platform. Figure 7-1 provides an architectural view of JDBC and, in particular, the Informix database interface.

Obtaining the Informix JDBC Driver

You can obtain the Informix Type 4 JDBC Driver either separately or as part of the Client SDK (Software Development Kit) bundle.

The Informix Client SDK is a package of several application programming interfaces (APIs) that you use to develop client applications for Informix servers. These interfaces allow you to write applications in Java, C, and ESQL.

For example, if you host the `webdriver` program on an NT web server machine, and the Informix database on another machine, you will need the connection libraries from the Client SDK installed on the web server machine so that `webdriver` can make a connection to the

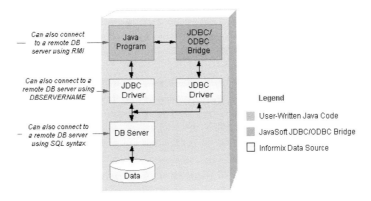

Figure 7-1. *JDBC architecture.*

remote Informix database. The Informix server contains these connection libraries, so you don't have to install the connectivity components from the Client SDK on the Informix server machine.

Browsing the JDBC API

The JDBC API is the JDK package called `java.sql`, and consists of a set of interfaces, classes, and exception handlers that allow the Java developer to access data in the database in a portable way. Table 7-2 lists the essential JDBC interfaces, classes, and exceptions.

Table 7-2. Interfaces, classes, and exceptions in the `java.sql` package.

Interface	Description
Connection	Establishes a connection to a database
DatabaseMetaData	Returns metadata information about a database
Statement	Sends static SQL statements to the database server
CallableStatement	Executes stored procedures.
PreparedStatement	Sends precompiled SQL statements to the database server
ResultSet	Examines the results of executing a query
ResultSetMetaData	Extracts information about the columns in the result set
Driver	Locates the driver for a particular DBMS

Class	Description
DriverManager	Manages a set of drivers
DriverPropertyInfo	Discovers and supplies properties to a driver
Types	Defines constants that are used to identify standard SQL datatypes
Date	Used for the SQL DATE datatype
Time	Used for the SQL TIME datatype
TimeStamp	Used for the SQL TIMESTAMP datatype

Exception	Description
DataTruncation	Exception or warning thrown if data has been truncated
SQLException	Provides information about a database error
SQLWarning	Warning that provides information about a database warning

Interfaces and Classes

An interface is a template for methods and constants. It specifies the methods and constants that must be implemented in a Java class if the Java class wishes to use the interface. The methods in an interface have no code. It is the responsibility of the class to implement the code. A Java class must implement all of the methods in an interface in order be instantiated. Interfaces are used to manage a consistent design thread in an application. Generally, the output from a design phase, such as a database design, would be a set of interfaces. In this way, Java classes can maintain the design signature of one or more cooperating applications that have different implementations in code. Java allows you to declare a variable of an interface type. The method that creates the object will return a concrete class that implements the methods in the interface.

Configuring the JDBC Driver

Setting the CLASSPATH Variable

The CLASSPATH environment variable tells the Java Virtual Machine (JVM) and other applications where to find the Java class libraries used in a Java program. Since we need to make the JDBC driver available to our Java programs, we need to add the location of the driver to the CLASSPATH variable.

Using the Driver in an Application

To use a JDBC driver in your applications, you must set your CLASSPATH environment variable to point to the driver files. You can make the JDBC driver visible by including the jar archive in the CLASSPATH or by including the directory containing the classes that have been unpacked from the jar archive.

Using the jar file

You need to add the full pathname of ifxjdbc.jar to the CLASS-PATH variable. For example, on UNIX:

```
setenv CLASSPATH
   /usr/informix/jdbc/lib/ifxjdbc.jar:$CLASSPATH
```

or, under Windows:

```
set CLASSPATH=C:\informix\jdbc\lib\ifxjdbc.jar;%CLASSPATH%
```

Using a Directory

If you do not specify the `jar` archive as shown above, then you need to unpack the `jar` archive and place the contents in a directory. You include this directory in the `CLASSPATH`. For example, on UNIX:

```
cd /usr/informix/jdbc/lib
jar -xvf ifxjdbc.jar
setenv CLASSPATH /usr/informix/jdbc/lib:$CLASSPATH
```

or, under Windows:

```
cd C:\informix\jdbc\lib
jar -xvf ifxjdbc.jar
set CLASSPATH=C:\informix\jdbc\lib;%CLASSPATH%
```

Using the Driver in an Applet

You can use the JDBC driver in an applet to connect to the database directly from the applet. You need to make sure that the `jar` archive is specified as follows:

- Ensure that `ifxjdbc.jar` is placed in the same directory as the applet class
- Specify `ifxjdbc.jar` in the `archive` attribute of the `applet` tag

For example,

```
<html>
<body>
<applet archive=ifxjdbc.jar
      code=commerce_applet.class
      codebase=http://theale2.eu.informix.com
      width=110 height=36>
</applet>
</body>
</html>
```

If you have more than one `jar` archive, then you define them as follows:

```
<applet
      archive=ifxjdbc.jar,commerce.jar
      code=commerce_applet.jar
```

```
            codebase=http://theale2.eu.informix.com
            width=110 height=36>
</applet>
```

If the HTML page is generated from a Web DataBlade AppPage, then you can parameterize the `applet` components in the AppPage as follows:

```
<?mivar>
<applet
 archive=$JARFILE_HOME/ifxjdbc.jar,$JARFILE_HOME/
 commerce.jar
 code=$COMMERCE_START width=$COMMERCE_HEIGHT
 height=$COMMERCE_WIDTH>
</applet>
<?/mivar>
```

The AppPage variables are set as follows:

- `$JARFILE_HOME` is set to `http://theale2.eu.informix.com`
- `$COMMERCE_START` is set to `commerce_applet.class`
- `$COMMERCE_HEIGHT` is set to 110
- `$COMMERCE_WIDTH` is set to 136

Note that the JDBC URL in the Java applet should connect to `http://theale2.eu.informix.com` (and not a shortened version that may be resolved on your network); otherwise, the applet security manager may think that the driver is not connecting back to its source web server host. You may also find this problem if the URL you use to download the web page differs from the URL in `$JARFILE_HOME`.

If you anticipate more than a small number of connection requests against a live production database, it may be worth locating the JDBC driver on the web server or other visible host in the network. This allows you to manage a pool of connections to the database in a controlled manner.

If any client browser does not support the archive *attribute of the* applet *tag, then unpack the* ifxjdbc.jar *file into a document directory on the web server. If the browser's JVM does not support the JDBC API, then you need to place the classes in* java.sql *with the driver also.*

note

If you wish to use the driver that supports debugging, then use ifxjdbc-g.jar *instead of* ifxjdbc.jar.

Informix Client/Server Connectivity

A client program, such as a Java application or applet, can connect to most valid Informix database environments over the network. Once connected, a client program can access any of the databases managed by the Informix database server defined for that environment.

Three different Informix APIs enable client programs to make connections to Informix database environments. Table 7-3 lists them.

What Is the Native Network Protocol?

For Informix, this protocol is called sqli. *It is specific to Informix and is a protocol understood by both the client and server programs, including the JDBC driver. The client will request a service and parameterize the request with data, sending the full request as a message formatted according to the* sqli*protocol. The database server understands this request and will respond to it. The server replies to the client by sending the response as a message formatted according to the* sqli*protocol.*

Table 7-3.   Client/server APIs.

API	Description
JDBC	Translates JDBC requests into the native network protocol used by the Informix database servers
ODBC	Translates ODBC requests into the native network protocol used by the Informix database servers
ESQL/C	Translates ESQLC requests into the native network protocol used by the Informix database servers

Database Environment Properties for the JDBC API

You must specify in your Java client program the properties for at least the database server and its host machine. Using a JDBC URL string, a client program must specify the properties of the database environment (at least those for the database server) to which the client wants to connect.

What Is the Database Environment?

To connect to a particular database server running on a particular host machine, a client program must identify a specific database environment to use, regardless of the API used to implement the connection.

A database environment consists of the properties listed in Table 7-4. Depending on the API used, the client may specify one or more of these properties at runtime.

Informix Java APIs, such as the JDBC driver, do not use the system registry or system files to determine database environment properties. Instead, they use the properties passed to them by the Java client

Table 7-4.   Properties of the database environment.

Property	Description
Database server host	Hostname or IP address of the machine that runs the Informix server
Informix server	The name of the Informix server on the database server host
Network port or service name	The port number that the client will connect to on the database server host. The service name is the name of the remote database server process used to listen to all incoming requests. It maps down to the port number.
Network protocol	The network protocol to use (e.g., `olsoctcp`, `olsocspx`). The JDBC driver uses `informix-sqli`.

program. You can either set these properties via parameters to the Java application or applet, or use a properties file. You use a properties file to store the equivalent of environment variables and other parameters to the Java program.

Setting Connection Parameters in JDBC URLs.

For a Java program to connect to a database, it must specify a URL that maps directly to a port on the machine that hosts the database server. The format of the URL is similar to HTTP and FTP URLs. We call it the JDBC URL. The connection parameters specify the database environment properties.

The JDBC URL contains all the information required to make a connection to a database server (see Table 7-5). The database server can be local or remote. The connection can be made from a stand-alone Java program or a Java applet (there are restrictions for applets, see subsection "Using the Driver in an Applet").

When connecting to an Informix database environment, a JDBC URL has the form:

```
jdbc:informix-sqli://{<ip-address>|<host-name>}
  :<port-number>[/<dbname>]
  :INFORMIXSERVER=<servername>
  ;user=<username>
  ;password=<password>
```

Table 7-5. JDBC URL parameters.

Parameter	Description
ip-address	IP address of the machine that hosts the Informix server
host-name	Name of the machine that hosts the Informix server; you can use this instead of the IP address
port-number	The port number on the server machine that listens for incoming requests
dbname	Optional; the name of the database we wish to use
servername	The name of the Informix server to which you wish to connect
user	A valid username that can connect to the target database
password	The password for the user

Table 7-6.	Parameter mapping.	
Parameter	**Value**	**Description**
host-name	`theale2`	IRIX machine that runs an Informix server
port-number	`1526`	Listen port for the `sqlexec` service on `theale2`
dbname	`stores7`	The `stores7` database
servername	`online_tcp`	The name of the Informix server specified in the `sqlhosts` file on `theale2`. Always prefix this parameter value with `INFORMIXSERVER`.
user	`joe`	The name of the account on `theale2` that can access `stores7`
password	`myPassword`	The password for the account on `theale2`

To illustrate the JDBC URL specification, here is an example URL that allows a Java application or applet to connect to the `stores7` database on the machine called `theale2` using the Informix JDBC driver:

```
jdbc:informix-
sqli://theale2:1526/stores7:INFORMIXSERVER=online_tcp;
user=joe;password=myPassword
```

Table 7-6 maps the connection parameters to the values in this example.

You can store the complete URL specification in a properties file, which the Java application can read. Similarly, if you are using an applet in an HTML page generated by webdriver, *then you can store the JDBC URL, or any part of the URL, in variables in* web.cnf *and use these variables in the AppPage to parameterize the applet. See Chapters 8 and 9 for more information on this topic.*

Connecting to the Database

To summarize the content of the previous sections, we will now connect to an Informix database.

1. *Import the network and SQL packages in your Java module:*

```
import java.net
import java.sql
```

2. *Specify the JDBC driver class in your Java code.* To support Netscape Navigator, you load the class:

```
// Load the Informix-specific Type 4 JDBC driver
Class.forName ( "com.informix.jdbc.IfxDriver" );
```

To support both Navigator and Internet Explorer, you might need to register the driver explicitly in your applet:

```
DriverManager.registerDriver(
(Driver) Class.forName(
"com.informix.jdbc.IfxDriver" ).newInstance());
```

3. *Open the database connection:*

```
// Specify the database URL
Connection conn = DriverManger.getConnection (
   "jdbc:informix-sqli://hostname:portnumber/
   database:" +
   "INFORMIXSERVER=servername;" +
   "user=username;" +
   "password=password");
```

You must pass environment settings needed for the driver as namevalue pairs separated by semicolons (;). Alternatively, you can use the put() method of the Properties class, as in the following code fragment:

```
String urlConnection =
    "jdbc:informix-sqli://123.45.67.89:1526"  +
    "/stores7:";
Properties params = new Properties();
params.put ("informixserver","online_tcp");
params.put ("user","joe");
params.put ("password","myPassword");
// Create Connection Object to manage the connec-
tion to the database server
conn = (Connection) DriverManager.getConnection (
        urlConnection,
        params
          );
```

When the `getConnection` method is executed, the JDBC driver manager loads the Informix JDBC driver and passes the connection request to that driver.

Testing Your JDBC Connection Using `JLogin`

Informix provides a utility called `JLogin` that allows you to test your JDBC URL in advance of coding it. The `JLogin` utilty is the Java equivalent of `ILogin`, which ships with the Client SDK. You can use `JLogin` to test only the Type 4 JDBC driver. You can't use `JLogin` to test the JDBC/ODBC bridge. You can, however, change the source code to implement this feature (Hint: Implement another radio button, with a textbox to accept the ODBC data source name.).

Running `JLogin` as an Application

If you run `JLogin` as a standalone application, set your `CLASSPATH` environment variable to include the full, absolute pathname of `jlogin.jar` and `ifxjdbc.jar`. Assuming that the file `jlogin.jar` is in the `C:\Informix\JDBC` directory, then set `CLASSPATH` as follows:

```
SET CLASSPATH=C:\Informix\JDBC\jlogin.jar;%CLASSPATH%
```

Then enter the following on the command line:

```
java JLogin
```

The JVM should locate the `JLogin.class` file in the `jlogin.jar` archive.

Running `JLogin` as an Applet

If you run `JLogin` as an applet, the archive containing the Informix JDBC Driver, `ifxjdbc.jar`, must be available to the browser's class loader on the client host. To do this, follow one of these two procedures:

Place `JLogin` on the Web Server

Specify an `archive` attribute in the `applet` tag to locate `ifxjdbc.jar` on the web server. This will allow the driver to be downloaded over the network, as needed.

Place `JLogin` on the Client

Install `ifxjdbc.jar` on each client host and then set the `CLASSPATH` environment variable on the client to point to the location of `ifxjdbc.jar` before launching the browser.

Changing the `JLogin` Code

If you want to change the source code for `JLogin`, *then use the command* `jar -xf jlogin.jar Jlogin.java` *to extract the Java source code into a standalone directory. Change, compile, and rebuild the* `jlogin.jar` *file using* `jar -cf jlogin.jar *.class`.

When `JLogin` *is run as an applet, the* `Host` *parameters are fixed because the database server to which a JDBC-based applet can connect can only reside on the machine hosting the web server that delivered the applet.*

Testing the JDBC URL

Assuming that you have set `CLASSPATH` correctly after placing the `jlogin.jar` archive on the relevant platform, perform the following steps in order to test your JDBC URL.

1. Identify the host to which you want to connect. If you run `JLogin` as an applet, you cannot change the host-name or IP Address; if you run `JLogin` as a standalone application, you can use any valid name or address for the host. Use either name or IP Address.
2. Enter the port-number on which the database server is listening.
3. Enter a username and password that is valid for the host machine to which you are connecting.
4. Enter the name of a database server running on the host machine.
5. Optionally, enter the name of a database managed by the nominated database server.
6. Click one of the "Ping" buttons.

Depending on which "Ping" button you push, `JLogin` attempts to establish a connection with the specified database server or database. In the `Status` textbox, `JLogin` displays the JDBC URL being used for the connection and various progress messages that indicate whether the connection was successful.

tip

You can easily change the default properties that JLogin *displays by editing the* JLogin.java *source file and recompiling it. You can also look at the code to see how* JLogin *creates a frame (window), populates it, and tests the JDBC connection.*

Figure 7-2 shows an example test. We are trying to connect to the dellcpi machine, to the database server called ol_dellcpi listening on port 1526, and we want to connect to the stores7 database managed by this server. We can ping the database server and the database connection separately.

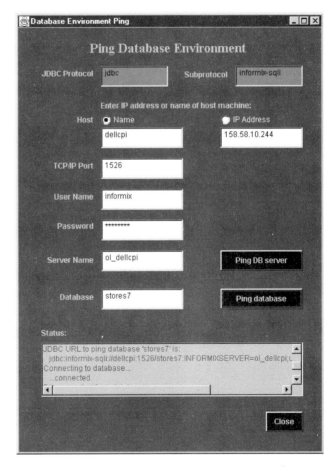

Figure 7-2. Using JLogin *to test a JDBC URL by pinging it.*

Using the JDBC/ODBC Bridge

The JDBC package lets you access an Informix database through a bridge that translates JDBC requests, coming from the JDBC Driver Manager, into ODBC requests, which are sent on to an ODBC driver.

You can use the JDBC/ODBC bridge to connect to any data source that has an ODBC driver available for it.

This type of JDBC connection is a Type 1 connection. We rely on client software (the ODBC driver) being available.

In summary, the steps involved in using the JDBC/ODBC bridge to make a connection to an Informix data source are as follows:

- Configure the Informix client software.
- Define an ODBC data source.
- Write Java code to use the ODBC data source.

These steps are described in the ensuing subsections.

You can use the JDBC/ODBC bridge to connect to any data source that has an ODBC driver, not just the Informix database server. You can use these steps as a guideline to configuring a JDBC/ODBC data source for non-Informix servers. However, you will need to successfully configure the client software libraries for your particular ODBC driver.

Configuring the Informix Client Software

There are two basic configurations, Windows and UNIX. Both are described here.

Windows (`win32`) Configuration

You must set the properties for at least the database server and its host machine through a utility called `Setnet32`. This utility is included in the Informix Client Software Development Kit (SDK).

To set and test your database environment properties when using an ODBC API on Windows platforms, follow these steps:

1. *Download the client SDK (if you have not already done so).* Informix client software contains ODBC drivers that you'll need. (For Windows platforms, this client software also includes `Setnet32`.) Make sure you define a database server that you can use.

2. *Define a network service that the ODBC driver can use.* Using a predefined network service, the ODBC API sends and receives database requests to and from the database server running on the server host. Each network service communicates over a specific, unique port-number on the network. The database driver is therefore assured of communicating with a specific server on the network. When you define a database server on a client host using `Setnet32`, you should ensure that an appropriate network service is defined on that host in the network services file. You can also save the port-number in the services box of the `Setnet32` utility. Consult the subsection on "Defining a Network Service" later in this chapter.

3. *Use `Setnet32` to define database environment properties.* You use `Setnet32` to define a database server.

   The example in Fig. 7-3 shows the definition of a server called `online_tcp`. The settings are stored in the registry.

   In this example:

   - The Informix server `online_tcp` resides on the `theale2` machine.
   - The Informix server uses TCP/IP protocols over network sockets.

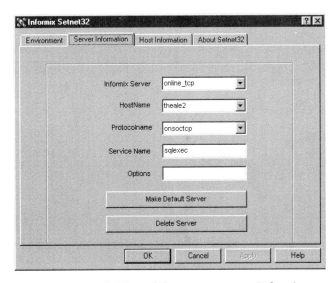

Figure 7-3. *Definition of the* `online_tcp` *Informix server.*

- The network service called `sqlexec` can be found in the local services file, and it lists the port on which the database server listens for connections.

4. *Use* `Ilogin` *to test the database environment properties.* You create an Informix login profile through `Setnet32`. After creating a login profile, you should test it. An easy way to demonstrate the validity of your settings and to test your connection is to run the Informix utility `ILogin`, which is shipped with the Informix Client deliverables such as the Client SDK.

   This utility attempts to connect to a specified database server and, if successful, performs a simple query on a database.

Figure 7-4 shows the default dialog for making a connection, and Fig. 7-5 shows the results displayed on making a successful connection.

To test the default settings that you established through `Setnet32`, leave all fields blank. Whatever database you choose, for `ILogin` to succeed, that database must contain a table called `customer`.

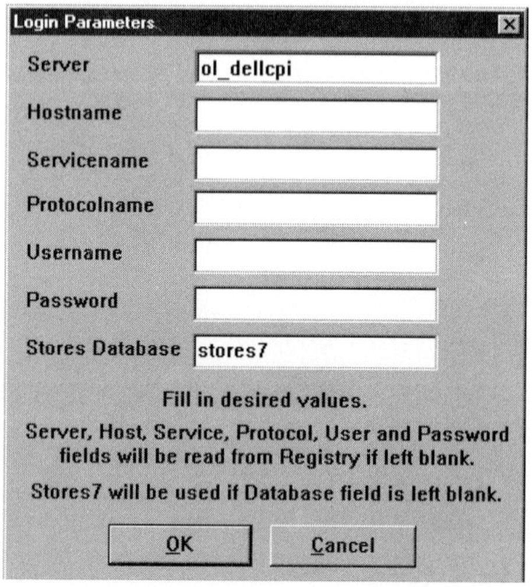

Figure 7-4. Default `ILogin` *dialog to test your connection settings.*

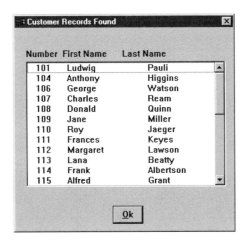

Figure 7-5. Successful connection.

The equivalent Java connectivity test is JLogin, described earlier in this chapter. The JDBC Type 4 driver does not use the registry settings, so ILogin does not prove that your JDBC Type 4 connections will work.

UNIX Installation

You need to define your data source in the odbc.ini file and your database server in the $INFORMIXDIR/etc/sqlhosts file. You may also need to modify the odbcinst.ini file.

At runtime, through a connection string defined in the client program, the client can override one or more properties of the database environment to which the client wants to connect.

Defining a Network Service

Network services are defined in a file called services. The location of this file depends on the client platform.

Platform	Location
Windows 95	c:\windows
Windows NT	c:\winnt40\system32\drivers\etc
UNIX	/etc

A service is defined by two parameters, and an optional third parameter:

servicename	port#/protocol	alias (optional)
turbo	1526/tcp	myServer

Clients wanting to use this service refer to the name you assign to the service. For example, using `Setnet32` under Windows, you would enter `turbo` into the service name box. The port-number you assign to this service must match the corresponding port-number on the server host.

For example, under Windows, to connect to a database server, you specify the Informix server in the client program. The `Setnet32` registry would map this name onto a service name on a host. The service name maps onto the entry in the `services` file that contains the target port-number. Then the connection is attempted.

The protocol must also match that being used by the database server on the server host. Where this protocol is defined depends on the platform where the server is running:

Platform	Location
Windows NT	HKEY_LOCAL_MACHINE\SOFTWARE\Informix\SqlHosts
UNIX	$INFORMIXDIR/etc/sqlhosts

Use the database server name as your lookup key to determine the protocol being used by the server.

Defining an ODBC Data Source

On Windows platforms, you define an ODBC data source through the ODBC data source administrator, which can be launched from the control panel.

For example, Figs. 7-6 and 7-7 show the configuration of an ODBC data source on a Windows NT 4.0 server machine. The Informix server is identical to the server accessed by `JLogin` previously.

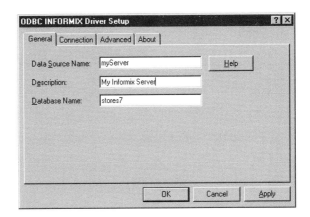

Figure 7-6. *Defining the ODBC data source name called* `myServer`.

 You may need to check your requirements against the required compliance level of the ODBC driver. For example, the Informix 2.80 ODBC driver is ODBC 2.5 compliant. The Intersolv 3.01 driver is ODBC 3.0 compliant.

Write Java Code to Use the JDBC/ODBC Driver

We now use the ODBC data source created in the previous step as the ODBC component in the JDBC/ODBC bridge.

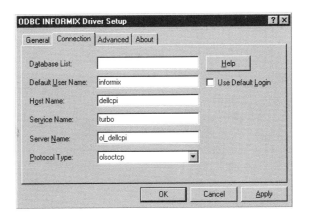

Figure 7-7. *ODBC Informix driver setup.*

Registering the JDBC/ODBC Driver

You can register the driver using the following statement:

```
Driver d = (Driver)Class.forName("sun.jdbc.odbc.
   JdbcOdbcDriver").newInstance();
```

The class `sun.jdbc.odbc.JdbcOdbcDriver` is the JDBC bridge provided for free by JavaSoft.

Connecting to the ODBC Data Source

We created the Informix ODBC data source called `myServer` in Step 2. We now wish to connect to that Informix server, and the `stores7` database defined for it. Therefore, we create a `Connection` object to manage the connection detail. The user name is `informix` and the password is `in4mix`.

```
Connection con = DriverManager.getConnection
("jdbc:odbc:myServer","informix","in4mix");
```

From this point on, we can create a statement object and use it to submit SQL to the Informix database.

Listing 7-1 contains the full details of the code. Note the use of `try` and `catch` to manage exceptions that may be thrown by the JDBC methods. We also scroll through any warnings encountered when connecting to the target server and database, and we write these to standard output.

Listing 7-1.   Connecting to the Informix database using the JDBC/ODBC bridge.

```
// REGISTER DRIVER
try {
    Driver d =
      (Driver)Class.forName("sun.jdbc.odbc.JdbcOdbcDriver").
      newInstance();
} catch (Exception e) {
    System.out.println(e)
}
```

Listing 7-1. *(continued)*

```
// GET CONNECTION
Connection con;
try{
    con = DriverManager.getConnection
            ("jdbc:odbc:myServer","informix","in4mix");
}catch(Exception e){
    System.out.println(e);
}

// GET CONNECTION WARNINGS
SQLWarning warning = null;
try {
    warning = con.getWarnings();

    if (warning == null){
        System.out.println("No Warnings");
        return;
    }

    while (warning != null) {
        System.out.println("Warning: "+warning);
        warning = warning.getNextWarning();
    }
} catch (Exception e){
    System.out.println(e);
}
```

Summary

In this chapter we have learned what JDBC is, what the different types of JDBC driver are, and how to connect to a data source using JDBC method calls for both the Type 1 and Type 4 JDBC drivers. What you have learned in this chapter can be applied throughout the rest of this book and will help you connect to non-Informix data sources.

Essential JDBC Programming

In this chapter:

- Setting variables in the JDBC environment
- Mapping DBMS datatypes to JDBC datatypes
- Executing SQL statements and retrieving data
- Error handling
- Managing transactions
- Calling stored procedures
- Working with large objects
- Managing large objects using Java forms
- Debugging JDBC
- Performance tuning the Informix JDBC Driver
- JDBC API methods not supported by the Informix Type 4 Driver

This chapter describes the essentials of Java programming using JDBC. In particular, its shows you how to use web content such as GIF images in a Java program, especially when those GIF images are stored in the database. By the end of this chapter, you will have working examples of Java programs to maintain data in a database over a web connection, and this data includes objects such as GIF images for applications such as online shopping catalogs. In addition, you will also learn how to tune to the performance of the JDBC driver and how to trace the JDBC methods executed by a running client program.

To use JDBC effectively, we need to understand how to configure the JDBC driver and how to maintain data in the database in an optimum manner. The following sections describe the major elements of configuring and implementing Java programs that use the Informix JDBC Driver to maintain database content.

Setting Variables in the JDBC Environment

The JDBC driver does not read the user's environment to obtain the values of environment variables. Instead, these variables must be declared and assigned a value in the JDBC URL or in a connection *properties list*. Whichever method you choose, you set an environment variable using a name/value pair.

Using the JDBC URL

You specify name/value pairs in the URL string. The following example shows how to set `user`, `password`, and `OPTOFC` environment variables:

```
String newUrl =

"jdbc:informix-sqli://theale2:1526/"  + "
stores7:INFORMIXSERVER=online_tcp;" +
"user=informix;password=in4mix;OPTOFC=1";
```

Using a Connection Properties List

You can also specify environment variables via a property list. Use the `java.util.Properties` class to build the list of properties. A property list is an array of name/value pairs. By specifying the name of a variable, you can look up the value in this list. The JDBC driver will appropriate this list as the set of environment variables that it uses.

Listing 8-1 sets the `user`, `password`, and `OPTOFC` variables in the properties list, in contrast to specifying them in the URL.

Listing 8-1. *Using properties to set variables.*

```
try {
        String newUrl ="jdbc:informix-
sqli://theale2:1526/stores7:INFORMIXSERVER=online_tcp"
        Properties pr = new Properties();
        pr.put("OPTOFC","1");
        pr.put("user","informix");
        pr.put("password","in4mix");
        conn = DriverManager.getConnection(newUrl, pr);
}
catch (SQLException e) {
        System.out.println("ERROR: failed to
        connect!");
  }
```

Informix Environment Variables

Table 8-1 lists the environment variables that you can set for the JDBC driver.

Table 8-1. *Environment variables supported by the Informix JDBC Driver.*

Environment variable	Description
DBANSIWARN	Checks for Informix extensions to ANSI standard syntax at runtime
DBSPACETEMP	The dbspaces in which temporary tables will be built.
DBUPSPACE	The amount of system disk space that the UPDATE STATISTICS statement can use when constructing multiple-column distributions simultaneously.
DELIMIDENT	Strings set off by double quotes are delimited identifiers.
FET_BUF_SIZE	This value overrides the default setting for the size of the fetch buffer for all data except large objects.

Table 8-1. *(continued)*

Environment variable	Description
IFX_AUTOFREE	The `Statement.close()` method does not require a network round-trip to free the server cursor resources if the cursor has already been closed in the database server.
INFORMIXCONRETRY	The maximum number of additional connection attempts that should be made to each database server by the client during the time limit specified by the default value of the `INFORMIXCONTIME` environment variable (15 seconds).
INFORMIXOPCACHE	The size of the memory cache for the staging-area `BLOB` space of the client application.
INFORMIXSERVER	The default database server to which a connection is made by a client application.
INFORMIXSTACKSIZE	The stack size in Kbytes that the database server uses for a specific client session.
NODEFDAC	Prevents default table and routine privileges from being granted to the public user when a new table or routine is created in a database that is not ANSI compliant (default is NO).
OPTCOMPIND	The preferred `join` method that the query optimizer should use.
OPTOFC	Closing a `ResultSet` does not require a network round-trip if all the rows have been retrieved in the client's buffer. The database server automatically closes the cursor after all the rows have been retrieved if this variable is set to 1.
PATH	The directories that should be searched for executable programs.
PDQPRIORITY	The degree of parallelism used by the database server.
PLCONFIG	The name of the configuration file used by the high-performance loader.

Table 8-1. *(continued)*

Environment variable	Description
PSORT_DBTEMP	Directories to which the database server writes the temporary files it uses when performing a sort.
PSORT_NPROCS	Allows the database server to improve the performance of the parallel-process sorting package by allocating more threads for sorting.
USEV5SERVER	This environment variable is mandatory if you are connecting to an informix Online 5.x Database Server, in which case set the property to YES

Mapping DBMS Datatypes to JDBC Datatypes

This section shows how to map an Informix datatype to a JDBC datatype, and recommends the method for extracting the `ResultSet` data for that datatype.

Mapping Informix Datatypes

`java.sql.Types` defines a set of generic SQL datatypes that map onto the different implementations of these datatypes by DBMS vendors. The Informix JDBC Driver maps these datatypes onto the corresponding Informix datatype. When you write Java programs that access the Informix database, you use the JDBC datatype. Table 8-2 lists these mappings.

Transferring Data from the Database to the Java Program

When you perform a query (using the `Statement.executeQuery()` method, for example), the `Statement` object that submits the query may return a `ResultSet` object. This object contains a reference to one or more rows of data (called *tuples*) returned by the query.

Table 8-2. *Corresponding datatypes between Informix and JDBC.*

Informix datatype	JDBC datatype	ResultSet.getxxx()
BOOLEAN	OTHER	getBoolean()
BYTE	BINARY	getBytes()
BYTE	LONGVARBINARY	getBinaryStream()
BYTE	VARBINARY	getBytes()
BLOB	LONGVARBINARY	getBinaryStream()
CHAR(n)	CHAR	getString()
CLOB	LONGVARCHAR	getAsciiStream()
DATE	DATE	getDate()
DATETIME	TIME	getTime()
DATETIME	TIMESTAMP	getTimestamp()
DECIMAL	DECIMAL	getBigDecimal()
DECIMAL	NUMERIC	getBigDecimal()
FLOAT	DOUBLE	getDouble()
INT8	BIGINT	getLong()
INTEGER	INTEGER	getInt()
LVARCHAR	LONGVARCHAR	getAsciiStream()
SERIAL	Not implemented	getSerial()
SERIAL8	Not implemented	getSerial8()
SMALLFLOAT	FLOAT	getDouble()
SMALLFLOAT	REAL	getFloat()
SMALLINT	SMALLINT	getShort()
SMALLINT	TINYINT	getByte()
TEXT	LONGVARCHAR	getAsciiStream()
VARCHAR(max,start)	VARCHAR	getString()
Not supported	BIT	Not supported

In order to extract the data for a column from the ResultSet, we use ResultSet.getxxx(), where xxx is replaced by the JDBC type you wish to return from the column data.

For example, ResultSet.getInt() will return an integer, ResultSet.getString() will return a String object, and

`ResultSet.getBytes()` will return a byte array, which can be a GIF image.

To map an Informix datatype to a JDBC `ResultSet.getxxx()` method:

1. Identify the Informix datatype.
2. Map the Informix datatype onto the JDBC datatype.
3. Map the JDBC datatype onto the recommended `ResultSet.getxxx()` method.

The `ResultSet.getxxx()` methods can be applied to a variety of JDBC datatypes, but the *recommended* methods are shown in Table 8-2.

Using `SERIAL` and `SERIAL8`

The Informix types `SERIAL` and `SERIAL8` do not have any obvious mapping to JDBC datatypes. Therefore, you need to import Informix specific classes into your Java program, and cast the `Statement` object to `IfxStatement`, which is an Informix extension to the JDBC `Statement` class:

```
import com.informix.jdbc.*;

PreparedStatement pStmt = conn.prepareStatement
("insert into customer ... ");

pStmt.executeUpdate()

Integer serial_number =
((IfxStatement)pStmt).getSerial();
```

In the code snippet above, the `serial` value assigned to the column of the table will be returned to the `serial_number` variable, unless the table does not have a `SERIAL` or `SERIAL8` column, in which case zero is returned. To assign consecutive `SERIAL` values, set the `SERIAL` column to zero in the `INSERT` query.

You can use the `getString()` method on most datatypes to return the value as a string.

If the retrieved column value is NULL, *the* `getxxx()` *methods return* NULL.

Executing SQL Statements and Retrieving Data

In order to send SQL queries to the database server for execution, you need to

- register the JDBC driver,
- connect to the database server,
- create a `Statement` object and submit the query via this object,
- interrogate the `ResultSet`, if any.

Register the JDBC Driver

You need to register the JDBC driver with the JDBC driver manager. The following snippet registers the Informix Type 4 Driver.

```
try {
    Driver d =
(Driver)Class.forName("com.informix.jdbc.IfxDriver").
newInstance();
} catch (Exception e) {
    System.out.println(e)
}
```

You can register more than one JDBC driver with the driver manager. You can register the Informix Type 4 JDBC Driver to make a direct connection to an Informix data source, and you can also register the JDBC/ODBC bridge in order to connect to an ODBC data source. You can use the static method `DriverManager.getDrivers()` *to return an enumerated list of drivers. The driver manager will select the appropriate driver based on the JDBC URL that you supply. For example, if you connect to a data source with a URL starting as* `jdbc:informix-sqli`, *the Informix driver will be selected. If the URL begins with* `jdbc:odbc`, *then the JDBC/ODBC bridge will be selected.*

You can ensure that the Java Virtual Machine will find your driver, if you set `CLASSPATH` *correctly. For the Informix Type 4 Driver, you need to specify the* `ifxjdbc.jar` *archive explicitly in the* `CLASSPATH`, *unless you have unzipped the archive to a folder, in which case you can use the folder specification.*

Connect to the Database Server

Once you have registered the appropriate JDBC driver, you can connect to the target database server using the `Connection` object, which is produced by the `DriverManager`. You can connect to the database server without specifying a database, or you can connect to a database server *and* a database. This does not stop you from switching databases later on, using the `DATABASE` statement. Similarly, the Informix database server will not stop you from using the staple synonyms and server networking that Informix database programmers are used to.

```
Connection con;
try{
    con = DriverManager.getConnection("jdbc:
        informixsqli://dellcpi:1526/stores7:informix
        server=ol_dellcpi;user=informix;password=inf
        ormix",userName,password);
}catch(Exception e){
    System.out.println(e);
}
```

For details on the format and content of the JDBC URL, see Chap. 7, "Informix Java Database Connectivity."

Once connected, you can prepare and submit SQL statements to the database server.

Create a `Statement` Object

A `Statement` object allows you to send SQL statements to the database server. For example:

```
Statement stmt;
try {
    stmt = con.createStatement();
} catch (Exception e){
    System.out.println(e);
}
```

There are three basic kinds of statement: `Statement`, `PreparedStatement`, and `CallableStatement`. These are summarised in Table 8-3.

Table 8-3. The varieties of JDBC Statement.

Statement	Allows SQL statements to be submitted, including calls to stored procedures.
PreparedStatement	Specifies a parameterised query string. The SQL statement is precompiled to the query plan stage.
CallableStatement	Allows stored procedures to be called.

Statement

The Statement object allows you to submit SQL statements to the database server, and is best suited to those SQL statements that will be executed *once*. The database server will check the syntax of the SQL statement and generate a query plan as soon as the statement is received. Once the statement is executed, the query plan is discarded. Table 8-4 lists the most important methods.

These methods take a String as an argument. The string is an SQL statement. The executeQuery() method passes the SQL statement to the data source via the JDBC driver, and returns a ResultSet, which consists of one or more rows of results, each row consisting of columns. You can use the execute() or executeQuery() methods to run most types of query, but you should use execute() to run queries that may return more than

Table 8-4. *Important methods of the* Statement *class.*

Method	Description
executeQuery	Executes a query that will return a result set (e.g., SELECT).
executeUpdate	Executes a query that does not return a result set (e.g., INSERT).
execute	Executes a query that may return more than one result set (the Informix JDBC Driver returns one ResultSet).

one `ResultSet` object; note, however, that the Informix implementation of this API behaves differently in that `execute()` will return one `ResultSet`.

important

The Informix JDBC Driver implementation of the `Statement.execute()` *method returns a single* `ResultSet` *object. This differs from the JDBC API specification, which states that the method can return multiple* `ResultSet` *objects.*

note

Always be sure to explicitly close a `Statement`, `PreparedStatement`, *or* `CallableStatement` *object by calling the appropriate* `close()` *method in your Java program when you have finished processing the results of an SQL statement. This releases the resources that have been allocated to execute your SQL statement.*

The `executeUpdate()` method is used for queries that do not return a `ResultSet`, such as UPDATE, DELETE, and DDL (Data Definition Language) statements. This method returns an `Integer`, which indicates the number of rows affected by the SQL statement.

PreparedStatement

The `PreparedStatement` allows you to reuse an SQL query. The database server will generate and store the query plan for the query once. In the Java program, you can parameterize the query by filling in the runtime values of the query before the query is executed.

You use the `executeQuery()`, `executeUpdate()`, and `execute()` methods as you do for the `Statement` object, but you don't pass any parameters in the method call. Instead, you use one of the `PreparedStatement.setxxx()` methods to substitute a parameter marker in the `PreparedStatement` with an actual value.

With the `PreparedStatement`, the JDBC driver sends only the *execution plan ID* and the *parameters* to the database server. This results in less network traffic; it is well-suited for Internet-based applications if you need to execute a query many times. Note that the query execution plan is stored for the duration of the program and is discarded once the Java program terminates. Listing 8-2 illustrates the use of `PreparedStatement`.

In List. 8-2, we set the first (and only) parameter marker to the integer value 1000 and then execute the query. We then interrogate the `ResultSet`.

Listing 8-2. **Using the** PreparedStatement *object.*

```
String forename;
String surname;
String company;
try {
    pstmt =
    con.prepareStatement(
      "select fname, lname, company from customer where
      customer_num > ?");
}
catch (Exception e) {
    System.out.println(e);
}

try {
    pstmt.setInt(1,1000);
    ResultSet rs = pstmt.executeQuery();
    while (rs.next()) {
        forename = rs.getString(1);
        surname = rs.getString(2);
        company = rs.getString(3);
        ......
    }
}
catch (Exception e) {
    System.out.println(e)
}
```

CallableStatement

Java allows you to call stored procedures using the
CallableStatement class and with a string called an *escape clause.*
A CallableStatement object is created by the prepareCall()
method in the Connection object, which takes an escape clause as
the parameter. The escape clause can take two forms:

```
"{ ? = call procedureName [ ? ? . . . . ] }"
"{ call procedureName [ ? ? . . . .]}"
```

The "?" characters are parameters, and identified by position left to right, starting from 1. Parameters can either be variables or literals. If you use the first escape clause definition, then you must register the parameter on the left-hand side of the assignment as an *output* parameter. The `CallableStatement` is shown in detail later in this chapter in the section, "Calling Stored Procedures."

Interrogate the `ResultSet`

A `ResultSet` object is returned from an `executeQuery()` or `execute()` method. If the query returned no rows, the value returned instead of a `ResultSet` object is `NULL`.

Retrieving Rows

A `ResultSet` consists of one or more rows of data. Each row is formatted into columns. Each column has a JDBC-mapped datatype. You use one of the `getxxx()` methods to extract the column value. You can extract large objects such as `TEXT`, `BYTE`, `BLOB`, and `CLOB` from a `ResultSet` column, as well as simpler datatypes such as `VARCHAR`, `INTEGER`, `DATE`, and `TIME`.

Using JDBC, you can only see one row of data at a time, and you do this by retrieving the resulting rows in sequence, one at a time. The Java program uses the `ResultSet.next()` method to fetch the next row. With JDBC you cannot move backward in the `ResultSet` or bookmark a row.

Retrieving Columns

You identify columns by *position* or by *name*. Positions start at 1. You should identify the JDBC datatype for the column before extracting the column value. You extract the column value using the appropriate `ResultSet.getxxx()` methods. You can use `ResultSet.getString()` on most columns, including integer columns.

You can find the name of a column by using the `ResultSetMetaData` object returned from the `ResultSet` as follows:

```
ResultSetMetaData rsmd = rs.getMetaData();
String colHeader = rsmd.getColumnLabel(1);
String forName = rs.getString(colHeader);
// alternatively
String forName = rs.getString(1);
```

You can use `ResultSetMetaData` to extract an astonishing amount of information about the `ResultSet` and the columns of data within it. The *Java SQL Editor* shown later in the book uses this information to format the display of query results, which can be arbitrarily complex.

tip

If you use an alias name in your projections (e.g., `select fname as Firstname, lname as Lastname from customer`*), where* `Firstname` *and* `Lastname` *are the aliases, then the* `ResultSetMetaData.getColumnLabel()` *method will return the alias. Similarly, if you cast any extended object type to another type (for example,* HTML *to* LVARCHAR *as in* `select object:: lvarchar from wbpages`*), then the column type returned will be the target of the cast (i.e.,* LVARCHAR *in this example). You can use* `ResultSetMetaData.getColumnType()` *to extract the value of the JDBC datatype.*

Interpreting Datatypes in the `ResultSet`

To extract the data for a `ResultSet` column from the `ResultSet`, you need to know the JDBC datatype of that column before you extract it, unless you want to extract the `String` equivalent of that value, which will not work for all JDBC datatypes.

You can use the `ResultSetMetaData.getColumnType()` method to extract the `java.sql.Type` for the column. Listing 8-3 illustrates how to identify the datatypes of `ResultSet` columns and extract the values from the `ResultSet`. For simplicity, the column values are appended to a `String`.

The `ResultSet.wasNull()` method is used to check if the *last column read* was NULL.

Listing 8-3. *Interpreting datatypes in the* `ResultSet`.

```
// retrieve resultset metadata.
ResultSetMetaData rsmd = rs.getMetaData();

// get query results, row by row.
String s = null;
while ( rs.next() ) {
      String st = new String();
```

Listing 8-3. *(continued)*

```
        // Build the next row, column by column.
        for (int numcol = 1; numcol <= ncols; numcol++) {
          switch(rsmd.getColumnType(numcol)) {
                case Types.CHAR:
                case Types.VARCHAR:
                case Types.LONGVARCHAR:
                        s = rs.getString(numcol);
                        break;
                case Types.SMALLINT:
                        if (!rs.wasNull() )
                                s = "" + rs.getShort(numcol);
                        break;
                case Types.INTEGER:
                        if (!rs.wasNull() )
                                s = "" + rs.getInt(numcol);
                        break;
                case Types.BIGINT:
                        if (!rs.wasNull() )
                                s = "" + rs.getLong(numcol);
                        break;
                case Types.FLOAT:
                        if (!rs.wasNull() )
                                s = "" + rs.getFloat(numcol);
                        break;
                case Types.DOUBLE:
                        if (!rs.wasNull() )
                                s = "" + rs.getDouble(numcol);
                        break;
                case Types.DECIMAL:
                case Types.NUMERIC:
                        if (!rs.wasNull() )
                                s = "" + rs.getBigDecimal(numcol, 4);
                        break;
                case Types.BIT:
                        if (!rs.wasNull() )
                                s = "" + rs.getBoolean(numcol);
                        break;
                case Types.DATE:
                        if (!rs.wasNull() )
```

Listing 8-3.   (continued)

```
                          s = "" + rs.getDate(numcol);
                  break;
          case Types.TIME:
                  if (!rs.wasNull() )
                          s = "" + rs.getTime(numcol);
                  break;
          case Types.TIMESTAMP:
                  if (!rs.wasNull() )
                          s = "" + rs.getTimestamp(numcol);
                  break;
          case Types.BINARY:
                  if (!rs.wasNull() )
                          s = "" + rs.getByte(numcol);
                  break;
          case Types.VARBINARY:
          case Types.LONGVARBINARY:
                  if (!rs.wasNull() )
                          s = "" + rs.getBytes(numcol);
                  break;
          default:
                  break;
      } // switch

      if (rs.wasNull() ) s = "<null> ";
  } // end for
} // end while
```

Sharing `Statement` and `ResultSet` Objects

If your `Statement` and `ResultSet` objects are visible to other objects
that may want to use them, such as threads running concurrently,
you should be mindful of unexpected results that may arise if the
same object is accessed by more than one other object (e.g., two
threads) at the same time.

Essentially, this is a situation you should avoid. Remember that
the `ResultSet` object allows you to process one row at a time.
Suppose thread A performs the `next()` method, and then thread B
performs the `next()` method on the same `ResultSet`: The next time
thread A calls `next()`, the row pointer for that `ResultSet` will not
be as expected, since thread B has moved it to row 3.

Similarly, if a `Statement` object is accessed by more than one thread, and each thread then performs a query, the results can be undefined—since the `Statement` object will return a `ResultSet` for `executeQuery()` and `executeUpdate()`—and the thread that expects a `ResultSet` for a specific query may end up with the `ResultSet` for another. You need to remove these interdependencies from your program.

Error Handling

Errors can occur in the JDBC driver or the database server. In either case, use the `java.sql.SQLException` class to handle the error. The `SQLException` class has three methods that you may want to use to report on the error you encounter.

Method	Description
getMessage	Returns a description of the error.
getErrorCode	Returns an `integer` value that corresponds to the Informix database server *or* Informix JDBC Driver error code.
getSqlState	Returns a `String` that described the `SQLState` value.

All Informix JDBC Driver errors return error codes of the form `-79xxx`.

Using `SQLException`

The following snippet shows how to catch `SQLException`.

```
try {
    ResultSet r = stmt.executeQuery(
            "select lname, company" +
            " from customer");
    while(r.next()) {
            short i = r.getShort(1);
            System.out.println("Select: fname = " + i);
    }
```

```
        r.close();
        stmt.close();
    }
    catch (SQLException e) {
        System.out.println("ERROR: statement failed: " +
                e.getMessage() + " CODE: " +
                e.getErrorCode());
    }
```

Looking Up Error Messages

The class `com.informix.jdbc.Message` can be used to display the text for an error message, like the Informix `finderr` utility. You may want to wrap the command in a script to save typing it all in. For example, the following is a Windows command file, called `jerror.bat`:

```
echo off
java com.informix.jdbc.Message %1
```

You invoke the command file as follows:

```
jerror 100
```

The following message should be displayed:

```
-100: ISAM error: duplicate value for a record with
unique key.
```

Remember to set your CLASSPATH to find the Message class.

Managing Transactions

With JDBC you have control over the database transactions you wish to implement, unlike the Informix Web DataBlade, where transactions exist only as long as the AppPage is exploded.

Transactions are managed at the connection level, via the Connection object.

Default Transaction Behavior

The default behavior for a `Connection` is to *autocommit* every statement executed. To start a transaction , you need to turn autocommit off.

Starting a Transaction

You initially start a transaction by invoking `Connection.setAutoCommit(false)`. The Informix JDBC Driver automatically starts a transaction with the next statement executed. Issuing `setAutoCommit(false)` after the method has already been called has no effect on the transaction. Once a transaction has been committed or rolled back, the next statement starts another transaction.

Ending a Transaction

Assuming that autocommit is off, you invoke either `Connection.commit()`, `Connection.rollback()`, or—via an explicit SQL statement—COMMIT or ROLLBACK.

Switching Autocommit On

If you switch autocommit on within a transaction using `Connection.setAutoCommit(true)`, then the transaction is rolled back before autocommit is switched back on.

Table 8-5 lists the important `Connection` methods for transaction handling.

You can use the BEGIN WORK statement when the autocommit mode is ON (true). If you switch autocommit on, then you can explicitly start a transaction using BEGIN WORK. The result is that, even though autocommit mode is ON, no updates will be made permanent until you execute the COMMIT WORK statement or call the `Connection.commit()` method. If you want to discard the changes, use ROLLBACK or `Connection.rollback()`.

The methods described in the example—`Connection.rollback()`, *for one—are not static methods. They are* instance *methods, which means that you need to create an instance of the* `Connection` *class to call the method. In contrast, static methods do not need an object to*

be created; to use a static method, you only need to load the class. The examples appear in the text as `Connection.rollback()` *for simplicity, to bind the method with the class.*

Tables 8-6 and 8-7 show the results of using SQL statements when autocommit is switched on and off.

If you turn autocommit off and use the `BEGIN WORK` statement, you will receive an error from the database server (similar to "already in transaction"). This is because an SQL statement automatically starts a new transaction if autocommit is off.

Example: Updating the `Stores7.items` Table

The example in List. 8-4 (`updateItems.java`) updates the stock position and price of stock in the `stores7.items` table.

Table 8-5. The `Connection` *methods for handling transactions.*

Method	Description
`commit()`	Makes all changes for this transaction permanent and releases all database locks for the requesting connection.
`rollback()`	Discards all changes for this transaction and releases all database locks for the requesting connection.
`getAutoCommit()`	Returns the connection autocommit state, true (ON) or false (OFF).
`setAutoCommit()`	If a connection is in autocommit mode, then all its SQL statements will be executed and committed as individual transactions.
`getTransactionIsolation()`	Returns the transaction isolation mode for the current connection.
`setTransactionIsolation()`	Changes the transaction isolation level.

Table 8-6. **Using autocommit set to false (OFF).**

Statement	Result
`conn.setAutoCommit(false);`	Autocommit switched off
`perform INSERT`	START next transaction (1)
`perform UPDATE`	in transaction (1)
`conn.commit(), "commit work"`	commit or rollback transaction
`conn.rollback(), "rollback work"`	(1)
`perform next INSERT`	START next transaction (2)
`perform next UPDATE`	in next transaction (2)
`conn.commit(), "commit work"`	commit or rollback transaction
`conn.rollback(), "rollback work"`	(2)
`perform next INSERT`	START next transaction (3)
`peform next UPDATE`	in next transaction (3)
`conn.setAutoCommit(true)`	rollback transaction (3), switch autocommit on.

Table 8-7. **Using autocommit set to true(ON).**

Statement	Result
`conn.setAutoCommit(true)`	true by default
`perform INSERT`	START and COMMIT transaction (1)
`perform UPDATE`	START and COMMIT transaction (2)
`stmt.execute("BEGIN WORK")`	START transaction (3)
`perform INSERT`	in transaction (3)
`perform UPDATE`	in transaction (3)
`conn.commit(), "commit work"`	commit or rollback transaction (3)
`conn.rollback(), "rollback work"`	

Listing 8-4. **Using** `updateItems.java` **to manage a transaction.**

```
import java.sql.*;
import java.io.*;

public class updateItems
{

  static String connURL;
  Connection conn;
  ResultSet queryResults;

  public static void main(String args[]) {
    if (args.length != 0) {
      connURL = args[0];
    }
    else {
      System.out.println("Usage: java txn <jdbc:url>");
      return;
    }

    updateItems thisDemo = new updateItems();
    thisDemo.run();
  } //end of main method

  public void run()   {
    try {
        connectToDBServer();
        executeUpdates();
    }
    catch (Exception e) {
    }
  } // end of run


  private void connectToDBServer() throws Exception {
    try {
      String ifxDriver = "com.informix.jdbc.IfxDriver";
      Driver IfmxDrv =
(Driver)Class.forName(ifxDriver).newInstance();
      conn = DriverManager.getConnection(connURL);
      System.out.println("Connected");
    }
```

Listing 8-4. *(continued)*

```
  catch (Exception e) {
    System.out.println("Could not connect to database server at " +
    connURL);
    System.out.println(e.toString());
    throw e;
  }
} // end of connectToDBServer method


private void executeUpdates() throws Exception {
  String unitPriceUpdateStmt = "UPDATE items SET total_price =
  total_price*1.15";
  String stockUpdateStmt = "UPDATE items SET quantity =quantity
  +10";

  BufferedReader prompt = new BufferedReader(new
  InputStreamReader(System.in));
  String answer;

  try {
    // Begin Work
    conn.setAutoCommit(false);
      Statement stmt = conn.createStatement();
      stmt.executeUpdate(unitPriceUpdateStmt);
      stmt.executeUpdate(stockUpdateStmt);
    // Commit Work


    System.out.print("Commit or Rollback [CR]?: ");
    answer = prompt.readLine();
    if (answer.equals("C")) {
       conn.commit();
      System.out.println("Updates executed...transaction
      committed");
    }
    else {
       System.out.println("Proceeding to ROLLBACK");
      conn.rollback();
       conn.commit();
      System.out.println("Transaction rolled back");
    }
  }
```

Listing 8-4. (continued)

```
  catch (Exception e) {

    System.out.println("Could not commit the transaction....rolling
    back!!");
    System.out.println(e.toString());

    try {
      conn.rollback();
    }
    catch (Exception ex) {
      System.out.println("Could not rollback....");
      System.out.println(ex.toString());
    }
  }
} //end of executeUpdates method
} // end of class updateItems
```

Once the records have been updated, the user is prompted to confirm the commit or rollback of the changes. Any value entered other than "c" will rollback the transaction.

Listing 8-5 shows the example output when run in a Windows console.

Listing 8-5. Sample output from running updateItems.

```
C:\PENDING>java updateItems jdbc:informix-
sqli://dellcpi:1526/stores7:INFORMIXSERVER=ol_dellcpi;user=informix;
password=informix
Connected
Commit or Rollback [CR]?: R
Proceeding to ROLLBACK
Transaction rolled back

C:\PENDING>java updateItems jdbc:informix-
sqli://dellcpi:1526/stores7:INFORMIXSERVER=ol_dellcpi;user=in
formix;password=informix
Connected
Commit or Rollback [CR]?: C
Updates executed...transaction committed
```

Calling Stored Procedures

Stored Procedures are used to implement application business rules in the database, and to enforce dependencies between tables. You can use stored procedures to thin out the client and separate the application logic from the client code.

This section shows how to execute stored procedures with JDBC calls. Informix allows your stored procedure to return multiple values, in addition to returning with a *resume* state. If you return multiple values from a stored procedure, then your ResultSet will contain one column for each return value, which you interrogate using the getxxx() methods.

You would return with resume if you wanted to break out of a loop in the stored procedure and return where you left off the next time you executed the procedure. For example, you may be selecting multiple rows from the customer table. For each row, you may want to return to the calling program to use the customer values, and then resume at the next row in the customer table in the stored procedure.

Using the CallableStatement

Setting Input Parameters

A CallableStatement is an extended form of PreparedStatement, so you use the setxxx() methods to set the values of parameters by position. For example, to set the actual parameters to a String, Int, and String using a combination of literals and variables, use the following example:

```
String str = "Pauli";
CallableStatement CSmt = conn.prepareCall("{call
custCount (?,?,?)}");
CSmt.setString(1,"Lugwig");
CSmt.setInt(2,100);
CSmt.setString(3,str);
```

The CallableStatement extends PreparedStatement, so you can use the PreparedStatement methods to set values into the escape clause.

Registering and Retrieving Single Output Parameters

You register output parameters so that the JDBC driver knows how to handle them. The `registerOutParameter()` method of the `CallableStatement` object is used to register the datatype of the output parameter. For example:

```
CallableStatement CSmt = conn.prepareCall("{?=call
custCount ()}");

CSmt.registerOutParameter(1,java.sql.Types.INTEGER);
```

To extract the return value from the procedure, you first call the procedure and then extract the return value from the `CallableStatement` object using the appropriate `getxxx()` method:

```
int retStatus = CSmt.executeUpdate();

int custCount = CSmt.getInt(1);
```

If your output JDBC type is NUMERIC *or* DECIMAL, *use the second form of the* `registerOutputParameter(int position, int type, int scale)` *method.*

When reading the value of an output parameter, you must use the `getxxx()` *method whose datatype corresponds to the SQL datatype of the parameters registered.*

Executing the Procedure

You use the `CallableStatement.executeUpdate()` method to execute a stored procedure. Table 8-8 lists the `execute` methods based on the Informix procedure return types. For example:

```
int retStatus = CSmt.executeUpdate();
```

You can also use the EXECUTE PROCEDURE call in a `CallableStatement.executeQuery()` method call.

Table 8-8. *The* `execute` *Methods to call based on procedure return types.*

Procedure returns	CallableStatement *Method*
single value	`executeUpdate`
multiple values	`executeQuery`
return with resume	`executeQuery`
return multiple values with resume	`executeQuery`

Returning Multiple Values from a Procedure

If your procedure returns multiple values, then you can use the `CallableStatement.executeQuery()` method, which returns a `ResultSet`. Each return value is specified as a column value in the `ResultSet`. You can then use the `getxxx()` methods to extract the return values.

If your procedure uses `RETURN WITH RESUME` then you can use `CallableStatement.executeQuery()`. You can also use this method if your procedure returns *multiple* values with resume.

Calling Procedures That Return with Resume

The following example shows how to process the results from a procedure that uses the `RETURN WITH RESUME` clause. Listing 8-6 shows the procedure.

This procedure takes an input parameter and uses it to multiply the values 1 through 5, returning each value to the caller.

The Java application that uses this procedure is shown in List. 8-7. This application calls the stored procedure `multipleReturns`, passing in the value 2. The outputs from the procedure are presented to the client in a `ResultSet`, which the Java application examines in sequence.

The application is called `callableSPL` and can be run as follows:

```
java callableSPL jdbc:informix-
sqli://dellcpi:1526/stores7:INFORMIXSERVER
=ol_dellcpi;user=informix;password=informix
```

Listing 8-6. **The** multipleReturns **Stored Procedure.**

```
CREATE PROCEDURE multipleReturns (i integer)
             RETURNING integer;
     define j integer;
     for j in (1 to 5)
         return i*j with resume;
     end for;
END PROCEDURE;
```

```java
import java.sql.*;
import java.io.PrintWriter;

public class callableSPL
{
  static String connURL;
  Connection conn;
  ResultSet procResults;

  public static void main(String args[])
  {
    if (args.length != 0) {
      connURL = args[0];
    }
    else {
    System.out.println("Usage: java callableSPL <jdbc:url>");
    return;
    }

    callableSPL thisDemo = new callableSPL();
    thisDemo.run();
  } //end of main method

  public void run() {
    try {
```

Listing 8-7. *(continued)*

```
        connectToDBServer();
        createProcedure();
        executeProcedure();
        displayResults();
        dropProcedure();
    }
    catch ( Exception e ) {
    System.out.println("Error encountered: " +
        e.getMessage());
    }
} // end of run

  private void connectToDBServer() throws Exception {
    try {
        String ifxDriver = "com.informix.jdbc.IfxDriver";
        Driver IfmxDrv = (Driver)
Class.forName(ifxDriver).newInstance();
        conn = DriverManager.getConnection(connURL);
        System.out.println("Connection Successfull");
    }
    catch (Exception e) {
        System.out.println("Could not connect to database server at " +
        connURL);
        throw e;
    }
  } // end of connectToDBServer method

  private void createProcedure() throws Exception {

    String createProcStmt =
      "CREATE PROCEDURE multipleReturns (i integer)" +
                          "RETURNING integer;" +
                          "   define j integer;" +
                          "   for j in (1 to 5)" +
                          "       return i*j with resume;" +
                          "   end for;" +
                          "END PROCEDURE;";

    try {
        Statement stmt = conn.createStatement();
        stmt.executeUpdate(createProcStmt);
```

Listing 8-7. *(continued)*

```java
      System.out.println("Procedure multipleReturns Created");
    }
    catch (SQLException e) {
      System.out.println("Error creating procedure multipleReturns: "
      + e.getErrorCode());
      throw e;
    }
  } //end of createProcedure method

  private void executeProcedure() throws Exception {
    String procCallStmt = "{call multipleReturns(?)}";
    try {
      CallableStatement cstmt = conn.prepareCall(procCallStmt);
      cstmt.setInt(1,2);

      procResults = cstmt.executeQuery();
      System.out.println("Procedure executed...");
    }
    catch (Exception e) {
      System.out.println("Could not execute procedure
      multipleReturns");
      throw e;
    }
  } //end of executeProcedure method

  private void displayResults() throws Exception {
    try
    {
      while (procResults.next())
      {
        Integer procRetVal =
          new Integer(procResults.getInt(1));
        System.out.println("Procedure iteration returned: " +
            procRetVal.toString());
      }
      procResults.close();
    }
    catch (Exception e) {
      System.out.println("Could not display procedure return
      values");
```

Listing 8-7. *(continued)*

```
      throw e;
   }
 } // end of displayResults method

 private void dropProcedure() throws Exception {

   String dropProcStmt = "DROP PROCEDURE multipleReturns";
   try {
     Statement stmt = conn.createStatement();
     stmt.executeUpdate(dropProcStmt);
     System.out.println("Procedure dropped");
   }
   catch (Exception e) {
     System.out.println("Could not drop procedure multipleReturns");
     throw e;
   }
 } //end of dropProcedure method
} // end of class callableSPL
```

Defining the Query

The escape clause for this example is set as follows:

```
String procCallStmt = "{call multipleReturns(?)}";
```

A `CallableStatement` is then created using the escape clause:

```
CallableStatement cstmt =
conn.prepareCall(procCallStmt);
```

The first parameter marker is set to the value 2:

```
cstmt.setInt(1,2);
```

The procedure is then executed, and the results are returned to a `ResultSet`:

```
ResultSet procResults;
procResults = cstmt.executeQuery();
```

Processing the Results

Each return from the procedure is stored as a column in the
`ResultSet` row. Each return with resume results in one `ResultSet`
row. We iterate around the `ResultSet` rows to extract the values of
each return from the procedure:

```
while (procResults.next()) {
Integer procRetVal =
     new Integer(procResults.getInt(1));
System.out.println("Procedure iteration returned: " +
procRetVal.toString());
}
procResults.close();
```

Working with Large Objects

This section shows how to work with large objects such as BLOBs via
JDBC methods. The section concludes with an example that shows
in detail how to insert and select large objects into the database
from a Java form.

The Informix datatypes BYTE, TEXT, BLOB, and CLOB can be
maintained via JDBC. Table 8-9 summarizes the object types.

The BLOB *and* CLOB *datatypes are only supported with Informix
servers from Version 9.x, including Informix Dynamic Server.2000.*

Maintaing Large Object Columns

Informix BYTE and BLOB datatypes are managed using the same
methods in JDBC. Informix TEXT and CLOB datatypes are also managed in the same way. Table 8-10 summarizes the large object
retrieval methods for these large object types.

Table 8-9. Large object types.	
LO type	**Description**
BYTE, BLOB	Stores binary data, such as spreadsheets, audio, video; no maximum size.
TEXT, CLOB	Stores any kind of large text object, no maximum size.

| Table 8-10. | Retrieval methods for Informix large object types. | |

Informix datatype	JDBC datatype	Retrieval method
BYTE, BLOB	BINARY, LONGVARBINARY	getBytes(), getBinaryStream()
TEXT, CLOB	LONGVARCHAR	getBytes(),getAsciiStream()

The SQL LONGVARBINARY and LONGVARCHAR datatypes can be of arbitrary size. The getBytes() and getString() methods can read these types up to the limits imposed by the JDBC driver. These limits can be read using the Statement.getMaxFieldSize() method. For larger blocks of data, JDBC allows developers to use the java.io.InputStream methods to return the data in chunks.

Inserting and Updating Large Objects

Use the PreparedStatement object to insert or update large objects. The PreparedStatement object has methods for inserting objects of various sizes. Depending on the limits of your JDBC driver, you can use either setBytes() or setBinaryStream(). Table 8-11 describes these set methods.

When a very large binary value needs to be sent to the database server, it may be more efficient to send the object via an InputStream, since JDBC will read from the input stream as required until the end of the stream.

Selecting Large Objects

When you select a record that contains a large object, the method you use to retrieve the data from the appropriate column in the

| Table 8-11. | The set methods for large objects. | |

Method	Description
setBinaryStream	Converts a very large binary value to LONGVARBINARY.
setBytes	Converts a byte array to a BINARY or LONGVARBINARY, depending on the size of the argument.
setAsciiStream	Converts a very large binary value to LONGVARCHAR.

Table 8-12. Methods for retrieving large objects.

Retrieval method	Description
getBinaryStream	Extracts a very large binary value from a `LONGVARBINARY ResultSet` column
getBytes	Extracts a byte array from a `BINARY` or `LONGVARBINARY` column
getAsciiStream	Extracts a very large binary value to `LONGVARCHAR`

`ResultSet` depends on the JDBC datatype of the object. You can use `getBytes()` to extract large objects, or one of the byte or ASCII input stream methods. You should use `getAsciiStream()` and `getBinaryStream()` for very large objects. Table 8-12 summarizes the relevant methods for retrieving large objects from the `ResultSet`.

Where Does the JDBC Driver Store Large Objects?

With the Informix Type 4 JDBC Driver, if the object exceeds the size of the memory buffer, the object is either stored in memory on the client or stored in a temporary file on the client filesystem. If you use an applet to select a large object, you may run into a security violation if the applet attempts to create a temporary file. The Informix JDBC driver uses a variable called LOBCACHE to manage large objects on the client.

Configuring Memory for Large Objects

Table 8-13 summarizes the settings of the LOBCACHE variable.
Table 8-14 summarizes what happens if a security violation occurs when the driver tries to create a temporary file on the client to store the large object.

Setting LOBCACHE

You can set LOBCACHE as a name/value pair in the JDBC URL, or in a properties list. For example:

```
jdbc:informix-
sqli://theale2:1526/stores7:informixserver=online_tcp;
user=informix;password=in4mix;lobcache=8192
```

Table 8-13. *Setting the* LOBCACHE *variable.*

LOBCACHE *value*	**What happens**
0	Large object is always stored in a temporary file.
Negative number (e.g., –1)	Large object is always stored in memory; if no memory is available to store the large object, an SQLException is thrown.
Number of bytes (e.g., 4096)	Maximum number of bytes (e.g., 4096) is allocated in memory to hold large objects.

Table 8-14. *Results of security violations using* LOBCACHE.

LOBCACHE *value*	**What happens**
0	Object is not stored in memory or file
Negative number	An SQLException is thrown
Positive number	Object is stored in memory regardless of LOBCACHE maximum specification.

Managing Large Objects Using Java Forms

It is important to know how to manage objects, such as images, in a Java application, especially when the application domain is e-commerce and online shopping, and the web content (such as the GIF images) is stored in the database.

This example shows how to use a Java form to maintain the contents of a simple online catalog. The example represents a simple online catalog browsing and administration interface.

A catalog item consists of text attributes plus an image of the item. The form will allow you to select files from the visible filesystem and save the file contents to the database. For example, you can select GIF and JPEG images to accompany the item text.

The functionality is as follows:

- Allows the user to scroll through the catalog items, viewing the catalog item text and a picture of the item.
- Allows the user to add catalog items by adding the corresponding textual information, and a picture for the item (for example, a GIF file).
- Allows the user to select a picture from the visible filesystem.
- Once the picture is selected, allows the user to view the picture before the catalog item is saved to the database.
- Allows the user to remove the catalog item.

At the JDBC level, the example demonstrates how to

- select columns of different datatypes from the database and display the column values in a form, including BLOB and CLOB;
- scroll through the ResultSet and populate the form with the next record;
- insert columns of different datatypes in the database, including BLOB and CLOB
- make basic use of Java AWT forms combined with JDBC.

The form display is based on the AWT, which is a core deliverable with Version 1 of the JDK. This means that you don't need any special classes or source code from a supplier of advanced form tools to understand the example.

The AWT

The abstract windowing toolkit (AWT) is a set of classes that form part of the JDK Version 1. The package name is java.awt. *The package consists of a set of user interface classes to create windows, form fields (such as a list box), form events, and graphical objects.*

The focus of this book is not the user interface, which is considered the most disposable part of an application. There are lots of Java IDEs (integrated development environments) that contain a screen painter to render a Java form the way you want it. The important issue in this example is how we read and write columns of data, including large objects such as BLOB and CLOB, to the Informix database via the JDBC driver.

However, it will be useful to see how we capture the images in the user interface so that they can be saved on approval.

A Note on Design

When designing applications, you need to separate the user interface (the pre-sentation layer) from the application or business logic. In traditional systems, a system was built from a set of applications, and the user interface was built into that application, This meant that, if either the user interface or the application logic changed, the whole application needed to be rebuilt. In a distributed Java application, the Java objects should not mix user interface code with code that implements business rules. Observing this rule allows you to make the user interface disposable and allows both types of components to be reused.

Java Classes Used in the Example

Table 8-15 lists the Java classes used in this example.

The classes we are concerned with are `Catalog`, `dataBase`, and `ImgCanvas`.

The `Catalog` Class

This class creates and manages the Java form for selecting and inserting rows to the `myCatalog` table. The class creates and positions all the form elements, such as the text fields, buttons, and a canvas for the display of images. This class also instantiates

Table 8-15. *Example Java classes for managing large objects.*

Class	Defined in	Description
Catalog	Catalog.java	Creates the Java form and associated dialogs; instantiates the database object.
dataBase	dataBase.java	Performs the interface to the database, creating the connection and passing the SQL to the database server. Also extracts the data from the ResultSet and writes the data to the Java form.
ImgCanvas	Catalog.java	An Inner class that extends the Canvas class. It is used to manage Image objects for display. The class is defined within Catalog.java.
AboutDialog	AboutDialog.java	Popup dialog box to display application information.
QuitDialog	QuitDialog.java	Popup dialog box to request confirmation when Exit is requested or when the main browsing window is closed.

| Table 8-16. | Application functions. |

Function	Description
Select	Selects the rows from the `myCatalog` table and populate the form, starting with the first row in the `ResultSet`.
Next	Reads the next row in the `ResultSet` and populates the form.
Picture	Uses a `FileDialog` object to select an image file from the client filesystem, for example, a GIF image.
Save	Inserts a new catalog item into the `myCatalog` table.

the `dataBase` object, which provides the interface to the database.

This class is the main entry point to the application, so it contains the `main()` method, creating both the `Catalog` object and the `dataBase` object: :

```
public static void main(String args[])
{
        Catalog f1 = new Catalog();
        f1.show();
        f1.db = new dataBase(f1);
}
```

The constructor method for `Catalog` creates the entire set of user interface controls, including the `ImgCanvas`, discussed later. Once the form is displayed, the application waits for the `Select` button to be clicked. The functions available are described in Table 8-16.

The main form implements a menu bar that performs some of the functions that are also implemented through buttons, but it includes the `Remove` menu item, as well. The menu items are described in Table 8-17.

The `Catalog` class also implements a set of get and set methods for each field that is populated from a column in the `myCatalog` table. The `dataBase` object calls these methods when inserting a new `myCatalog` record, and when posting a row from the `ResultSet` to the form. Listing 8-8 shows these methods. Note that these methods would be required if the form were to be deployed as a Java Bean.

In a multitier system, the `dataBase` *object could be relocated to the database server host, and the higher-level database methods that are callable from the user interface could be made remote methods invoked*

Table 8-17. Application menu items.

Menu	Menu item	Description
File	Open Picture/	Selects an image from the filesystem.
	Save	Saves a new catalog item to the database, including the image.
	Exit	Closes the database connection, and exits the application.
Edit	Remove	Deletes the catalog item.
Help	About	Gives brief description of the application.

through RMI. The current design uses a basic `get` *and* `set` *model, where the user interface presents public methods to get and set data in the user interface form without revealing the implementation details of the form fields. Similarly, the* `get` *methods could be* `public` `dataBase` *object methods that have their implementation detail in the* `getxxx()` *methods of the* `ResultSet`.

Listing 8-8. The GET and SET methods for the main "Browse Catalog" form.

```
// GET methods
public String getCatalogNum() {
    return catalogNum.getText();
}
public String getUnit() {
    return unit.getText();
}
public String getCatalogDescr() {
        return catalogDescr.getText();
}
public String getCatAdvert() {
    return catAdvert.getText();
}
public String getProductType(){
    return productType.getText();
}
public String getSelectedFile() {
    return selectedFile;
}
```

Listing 8-8. (continued)

```
      // SET methods
   public void setCatalogNum( String s ) {
      catalogNum.setText(s);
   }
   public void setUnit( String s ) {
      unit.setText(s);
   }
   public void setCatalogDescr( String s ) {
      catalogDescr.setText(s);
   }
   public void setCatAdvert( String s ) {
      catAdvert.setText(s);
   }
   public void setProductType( String s ){
      productType.setText(s);
   }
   public void setCatalogPictureCanvas( byte []
   imageSourceBytes ) {
      Image img = Toolkit.getDefaultToolkit().
      createImage(imageSourceBytes);
         catalogPictureCanvas.setImage(img);
         catalogPictureCanvas.repaint();
   }
```

The dataBase Class

The dataBase class manages the interface to the database via JDBC.
This class creates a connection to the database server, submits SQL,
and processes the ResultSet.

When the class is first instantiated, the dataBase object makes a
connection to the database server. The constructor for this class
must accept a reference to a user interface object that contains the
get and set methods used to initialize and display data from the
database. Listing 8-9 shows this sequence.

*The user interface component addressed by this example may be any
kind of user interface object for any platform. Because the* dataBase
*object uses get and set in that object, the target interface is hidden
from view.*

The `ImgCanvas` Class

We want to be able to control the writing of images to the screen. Because the get and set of an image is slightly more complicated than the text field get and set, we subclass the `Canvas` class into an `ImgCanvas`, which stores a reference to the `Image` object and manages the display of the image on the `canvas` object in the screen display. Listing 8-10 shows the `ImgCanvas` class.

Listing 8-9. Instantiate the `dataBase` object and connect to the database server.

```
public class dataBase
{

  Connection conn;
  ResultSet  queryResults;
  Catalog ui  = null;

  public dataBase ( Catalog ui ) {
     this.ui = ui;
     connectToDBServer();
  }

  private void connectToDBServer()
  {
    try
    {
      String ifxDriver = "com.informix.jdbc.IfxDriver";
      Driver IfmxDrv = (Driver)
Class.forName(ifxDriver).newInstance();
      conn = DriverManager.getConnection("jdbc:informix-sqli://
dellcpi:1526/teacher:informixserver=ol_dellcpi;
user=informix;password=informix");
      System.out.println("Connected");
    }
    catch (Exception e)
    {
      System.out.println("Could not connect to database server");
      System.out.println(e.toString());
    }
  } // end of connectToDBServer method
```

*Listing 8-10. **The** ImgCanvas **class in** Catalog.java.*

```
public class ImgCanvas extends Canvas {
    private Image myImage;

    ImgCanvas()
    {
      super();
      myImage = null;
    } // end of ImgCanvas constructor

    public void setImage(Image img)
    {
      myImage = img;
    } // end of setImage method

    public Image getImage()
    {
      return myImage;
    } // end of getImage method

    public void paint(Graphics g)
    {
      if(myImage == null)
        return;
      else
        g.drawImage(myImage, 0, 0, this);
    } // end of paint method
} // end of inner class ImgCanvas
```

The setImage() method is called from the dataBase object to initialize the ImgCanvas object. The paint() method is called to render the image in the top left-hand corner of the ImgCanvas.

Catalog Schema

The table that stores the catalog data is called myCatalog. The schema contains a description of the item, which is defined as a clob, and a picture of the item, stored as a blob.

```
create table mycatalog (
    catalog_num integer,
```

```
      unit char(4),
      cat_descr clob,
      cat_picture blob,
      cat_advert varchar(255,65),
      prod_type char(10),
      primary key (catalog_num)
   );
```

The emphasis of this example is on working with the `clob` and `blob` columns.

Selecting and Browsing the Catalog Items

When the `Select` button is clicked, all the rows in the `myCatalog` table are selected for display, including the images. The following code snippet shows the event handler for the `Select` button, and List. 8-11 shows the called methods in the `dataBase` object.

Listing 8-11. *Using* `dataBase.java` *to select the catalog records from the* `myCatalog` *table.*

```
public void executeSelectQuery() {

    String str = "select catalog_num, unit, cat_descr, cat_picture,
cat_advert, prod_type " +
               "from myCatalog";

    try
    {

      Statement stmt = conn.createStatement();
      queryResults = stmt.executeQuery(str);
      System.out.println("Query executed");
      nextRow();
    }
    catch (Exception e)
    {
      System.out.println("Could not execute query");
      System.out.println(e.toString());
    }
```

The `database.executeSelectQuery()` method creates a SELECT statement, executes the query, and then calls a method called `nextRow()` to move the `ResultSet` to the first row and extract the column data from the first row.

```
void selectButton_Action(java.awt.event.ActionEvent
event) {
  db.executeSelectQuery();
}
```

The `nextRow()` method is used to move to the next `ResultSet` row and post the data to the form, as shown in List. 8-12.

Listing 8-12. Using `dataBase.java` to implement the `nextRow()` method.

```
public void nextRow()
  {
     try
     {
       if (queryResults.next())
       {

         ui.setCatalogNum(queryResults.getString(1));
         ui.setUnit(queryResults.getString(2));
         ui.setCatalogDescr(new String(queryResults.getBytes(3)));
         ui.setCatAdvert(new String(queryResults.getString(5)));
         ui.setProductType(queryResults.getString(6));

         byte[] catalogPictureArray = null;
         try {
            catalogPictureArray = queryResults.getBytes(4);
         }
         catch (SQLException e)
         {
            if ( ! queryResults.wasNull() ) throw e;
         }
         if (catalogPictureArray != null)
         {
           ui.setCatalogPictureCanvas(catalogPictureArray);
         }
       }
     else
```

Listing 8-12. *(continued)*

```
    {
        System.out.println("No more rows!!");
    }
}
catch (Exception e)
{
    System.out.println("Could not display next row...");
    System.out.println(e.toString());
}
} // end of nextRow method
```

Populating the Catalog Description Field (CLOB)

The Catalog Description form field is a CLOB column in the database table myCatalog. We have a choice of using the getAsciiStream() or getBytes() methods of the ResultSet. For simplicity, we use the getBytes() method and convert the resulting bytes into the 2-byte UNICODE String for the platform. The resulting String is posted to the description field on the form.

```
ui.setCatalogDescr(new
String(queryResults.getBytes(3)));
```

Populating the Catalog Picture Field (BLOB)

The ImgCanvas form field is used to render the image onto the screen. We could use getBinaryStream(), but for simplicity (since we know we are using small GIF images) we use the getBytes() method:

```
byte[] catalogPictureArray = null;
try {
    catalogPictureArray = queryResults.getBytes(4);
}
catch (SQLException e) {
}
```

The ImgCanvas form field is populated as follows:

```
ui.setCatalogPictureCanvas(catalogPictureArray);
```

The Catalog method setCatalogPictureCanvas() contains the method shown in List. 8-13 to render the image into an AWT canvas.

Listing 8-13. **Write the BLOB *image to the form Canvas.***

```
public void setCatalogPictureCanvas(
    byte [] imageSourceBytes )
{
    Image img =
    Toolkit.getDefaultToolkit().createImage(imageSourceBytes);
    catalogPictureCanvas.setImage(img);
    catalogPictureCanvas.repaint();
}
```

Remember that we have extended the Canvas class to create an ImgCanvas class, which contains the setImage() and repaint() methods.

Selecting the Next Row

When the user clicks the Next button, the form invokes the nextRow() method of the database object (see above) to move to the next row of the ResultSet (which is still open) and post the row data to the form:

```
void forwardButton_Action(java.awt.event.ActionEvent
event) {
        db.nextRow();
    }
```

Inserting a Catalog Item: Choose a Picture for Approval

When the user wishes to create a new catalog item, the user must select an appropriate image. The image is displayed on the screen *before* the user saves the image to the catalog, which enables the user to change the image if required.

The main form has two options that allow you to do this. You can either click the Picture button, or select File/Open Picture from the menu bar. Whichever one you choose, a FileDialog window is opened so that you can select the GIF or JPEG image that you require.

Once the image has been selected, the image is painted onto the ImgCanvas so that the user can see what has been selected.

Listing 8-14 shows the code that performs the capture of the *filesystem path* for the image file, and the painting of the image to

Listing 8-14. *Choose an image file and see it displayed on the screen.*

```
void chooseButton_Action(java.awt.event.ActionEvent event) {
    // Show the OpenFileDialog
    openFileDialog1.show();
    selectedFile=openFileDialog1.getDirectory() +
openFileDialog1.getFile();
    selectedItem.setText(selectedFile);

    try {
        // display the image in the window
        File f = new File(selectedFile);
        FileInputStream fs = new FileInputStream(f);
        byte [] b = new byte [ (int)f.length() ];
        int junk = fs.read(b);
        Image img =
            Toolkit.getDefaultToolkit().createImage(b);
        catalogPictureCanvas.setImage(img);
        catalogPictureCanvas.repaint();
    } catch (Exception e) {
        System.out.println("Could not render Image: "
            + e.toString());
    }
}
```

the screen. The image file is opened, and a stream of bytes is read as
a byte array. This stream of bytes is used to construct an `Image`
object, which is posted to the `ImgCanvas` object, which is then used
to paint the image onto the `ImgCanvas`.

Inserting a Catalog Item: Save to the Database

The catalog item text and the catalog picture are saved to the database when the user clicks the `Save` button or selects `File/Save` from
the menu bar. The following snippet shows the event handler for the
`Save` and `File/Save` objects, and List. 8-15 shows the `dataBase`
method that performs the SQL `insert`.

```
void saveButton_Action(java.awt.event.ActionEvent
event) {
    db.executeQuery();
}
```

```java
public void executeQuery() {

    PreparedStatement pstmt;

    String insertStatement =
            "insert into myCatalog ( " +
            " catalog_num, unit, cat_descr, cat_picture, cat_advert,
prod_type ) " +
            "values ( " +
            " ?, ?, ?, ?, ?, ? )";

    try {

       pstmt = conn.prepareStatement(insertStatement);
       pstmt.setInt(1, (new Integer(ui.getCatalogNum())).intValue() );
       pstmt.setString(2, ui.getUnit());
       pstmt.setBytes(3,ui.getCatalogDescr().getBytes());
       pstmt.setString(5, ui.getCatAdvert());
       pstmt.setString(6, ui.getProductType());
    }
    catch (Exception e)
    {
       System.out.println("Could not prepare statement");
       System.out.println(e.toString());
       return;
    }

    File pictureFile = new File(ui.getSelectedFile());
    int fileLength = (int)pictureFile.length();

    // this is the input stream for the setBinaryStream method.
    InputStream inp = null;
    // this is the file input stream that the above input stream will
use
    FileInputStream finp = null;


    int row = 0;
    String str = null;
```

Listing 8-15. *(continued)*

```
    int rc = 0;
    ResultSet rs = null;

    System.out.println("Inserting picture file " +
ui.getSelectedFile());
    try {
        finp =  new FileInputStream(pictureFile);
        inp = (InputStream)finp;
    }
    catch (Exception e) {
        System.out.println("Could not create file input streams");
        System.out.println(e.toString());
    }

    try {
        pstmt.setBinaryStream(4,inp,fileLength);
    }
    catch (SQLException e) {
        System.out.println("Unable to set parameter");
        e.getMessage();
        return;
    }

    try {
        pstmt.executeUpdate();
    }
    catch (SQLException e)  {
        System.out.println("Failed to insert Catalog record: " +
e.toString());
        e.printStackTrace();
    }
} // end of executeQuery method
```

The insert statement is a PreparedStatement to allow us to set the parameter markers with the form values, including the selected image. The getxxx() methods of the Catalog object are used to extract the contents of the form fields.

Inserting the CLOB Description

The catDescr column of the myCatalog table is a CLOB type in order to store a large volume of ASCII text. The form field is called `catalogDescr`. The method `ui.getCatalogDescr()` returns a UNICODE `String` object (two bytes per character), which in turn is converted into an array of bytes where a character is represented by one byte, not two. The array of bytes is used to parameterize the query string in the `PreparedStatement`. This is shown below:

```
pstmt.setBytes(3,ui.getCatalogDescr().getBytes());
```

We could have used `pstmt.setAsciiStream()` for this column to allow the JDBC driver to handle a large amount of text as an input stream in contrast to setting the `PreparedStatement` to a fixed parameter value.

Inserting the BLOB Image

The catalog item picture is rendered as an image on the `ImgCanvas` canvas, which is just another object on the screen. When we insert this image into the database, we use an `InputStream` object to read the image source file that the user selected from the file dialog (alternatively, we could have created a `ByteArrayInputStream` using the original byte array that was implemented to create the image). The `getSelectedFile()` method returns the absolute path of the image file on the filesystem (e.g., `D:\images\laptop.gif`):

```
File pictureFile = new File(ui.getSelectedFile());
int fileLength = (int)pictureFile.length();
```

A `FileInputStream` is opened on the file and is cast to its *superclass*, `InputStream`, which is the required class of the `setBinarySream()` method:

```
finp =  new FileInputStream(pictureFile);
inp = (InputStream)finp;
```

The `InputStream` for the image file is then posted as a parameter to the `PreparedStatement`:

```
pstmt.setBinaryStream(4,inp,fileLength);
```

The `PreparedStatement` containing the `insert` is then executed:

```
pstmt.executeUpdate();
```

Removing a Catalog Item

The user can remove a catalog item in one of two ways:

1. Scroll through the catalog until the catalog item is displayed and then select Edit/Remove from the Menu bar.
2. Enter a catalog number into the catalog_num field, and select Edit/Remove from the Menu bar.

Whichever method is chosen, the delete method in the dataBase object requires only the key value: the catalog_num. Listing 8-16 shows the method that performs the delete of the catalog item.

Because the SQL contains a variable parameter, it is easier to use a PreparedStatement than to format a String with the appropriate SQL and parameter values. Using PreparedStatement allows the formatting specifics to be hidden from the application.

In an industrial-strength application, you would also use a PreparedStatement to precompile the SQL in the database and produce a query plan in advance that can be reused for each invocation of the query.

The delete statement is executed using the executeUpdate() method, which returns the number of rows affected.

Listing 8-16.   Using dataBase.java to delete a catalog item.

```
public void executeDeleteQuery() {

    String str =
            "delete from myCatalog where catalog_num = ?";
    int numRows;

    try {
      PreparedStatement pstmt = conn.prepareStatement(str);
      pstmt.setInt(1,
         (new Integer(ui.getCatalogNum())).intValue() );
      numRows = pstmt.executeUpdate();
    }
    catch (Exception e) {
      System.out.println("Could not execute query");
      System.out.println(e.toString());
    }
}
```

Execute the Catalog Browser

To run the catalog browser, type `java Catalog` on the command line. Figure 8-1 is displayed:

From this point on, you can type in the catalog number of the item you wish to delete, or click the `Select` button to begin scrolling through the records in the `myCatalog` table.

If you click `Select`, the first catalog item is displayed, as shown in Fig. 8-2.

To display the next catalog item, click the `Next` button, and the next row from the `ResultSet` is read and displayed on the screen. The following figures (Figs. 8-3 through 8-6) show the successive displays of catalog items when the `Next` button is clicked four times.

To insert a new catalog item, just overwrite the text fields. To select a new image, click the `Picture` button or select `File/Open Picture`. Whichever you select, a `FileDialog` is displayed, as shown in Fig. 8-7. Note that the `FileDialog` has a title set by the Java application ("Select a Picture").

A `FileDialog` is a standard Java AWT class that invokes the native windowing system to display a dialog that allows you to select a file or save a file. You will encounter security violations if you use this dialog from an untrusted *applet.*

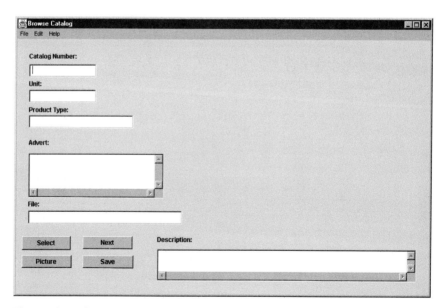

Figure 8-1. *"Browse Catalog" Screen.*

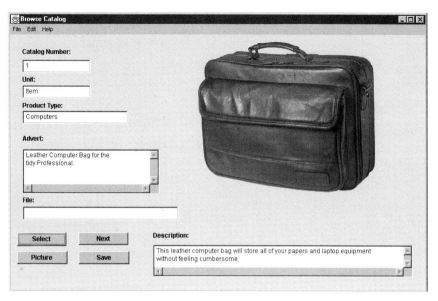

Figure 8-2. *"Browse Catalog" item.*

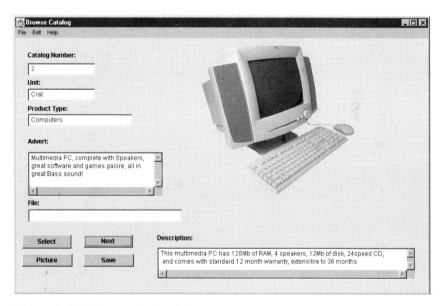

Figure 8-3. *"Browse Catalog" item.*

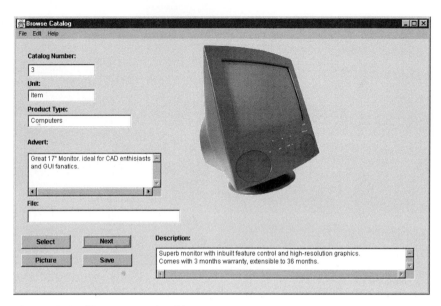

Figure 8-4. *"Browse Catalog" item.*

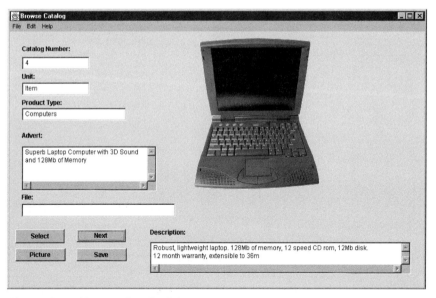

Figure 8-5. *"Browse Catalog" item.*

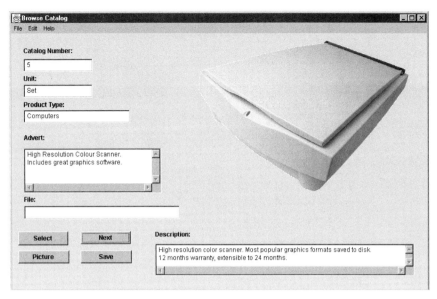

Figure 8-6. *"Browse Catalog" item.*

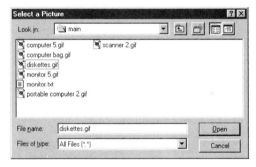

Figure 8-7. *Select a picture.*

Once the picture has been selected, the picture is displayed on the screen so that the user can see what the final result will look like. Additionally, the path to the image file for the picture is displayed in the file textbox. Figure 8-8 shows the form after the new text has been entered and the picture selected.

To view the catalog from the start, click the `Select` button, and the catalog will scroll from the first record. If you scroll to the end by clicking the `Next` button, you will see the catalog item you inserted.

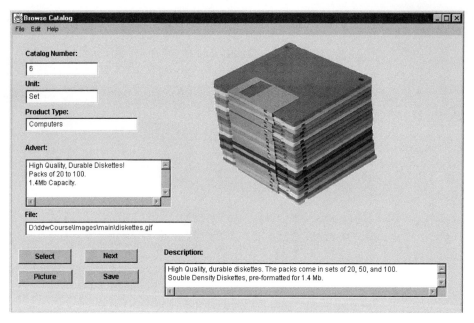

Figure 8-8. *Display the picture in the form.*

 The "Description" field of the form is a CLOB *column in the* myCatalog *table. If you enter linebreaks, these linebreaks will be stored as you see them. Similarly, the "Advert" form field is a text area stored as a* VARCHAR. *Linebreaks are also stored as you see them to the database column.*

Debugging JDBC

This section briefly describes the debugging and tracing options you can use with the Informix JDBC Driver.

There are two basic deliverables with the Informix JDBC Driver package:

ifxjdbc.jar—*the optimized version of the JDBC driver classes.*
ifxjdbc-g.jar—*the debug version of the JDBC driver classes.*

Tracing JDBC Activity

You can trace driver activity by switching on trace variables, which set the granularity of tracing, and by setting trace files to capture the output from the trace. The files are created on the client that is using the JDBC driver.

General Activity Tracing

Use the variables shown in Table 8-18 to trace general activity from the JDBC driver.

The TRACE variable can be set to one of a number of values depending on how much information you need for debugging purposes. These values are listed in Table 8-19 as levels of granularity. The default value for the TRACE variable is set to zero, which indicates no tracing.

Informix Protocol Message Tracing

You use the variables shown in Table 8-20 to trace protocol messages and protocol data passed between the JDBC driver and the Informix database server.

Table 8-18.   Trace variables.

Variable	Description
TRACE	When set, traces general information from the driver.
TRACEFILE	Full pathname of the client file to hold trace output.

Table 8-19.   Granularity of the TRACE variables.

Level	Granularity
1	Traces the entry and exit of methods.
2	Performs level 1, plus generic error messages.
3	Performs level 2, plus trace driver variables.

Table 8-20.	Protocol-tracing variables.

Variable	Description
PROTOCOLTRACE	Traces SQLI protocol messages between the driver and the database server.
PROTOCOLTRACEFILE	Full pathname of the client file to hold trace output.

Table 8-21.	Protocol-tracing granularity.

Level	Granularity
1	Traces the message IDs.
2	Performs level 1 plus generic message data.

The PROTOCOLTRACE variable can be set to one of a number of values, as shown in Table 8-21. PROTOCOLTRACE is set to zero by default, which means no tracing.

Setting TRACE Variables

You can set the values of these TRACE variables in the JDBC URL or in a properties list passed to the JDBC URL. For example:

```
jdbc:informix-
sqli://theale2:1526/stores7:informixserver=online_tcp;
user=informix;password=inf4mix;TRACE=2;TRACEFILE=d:\in
formix\jdbc.out
```

Remember to set CLASSPATH *to include the* ifxjdbc-g.jar *archive before the* ifxjdbc.jar *archive if you want to trace driver activity.*

The following code snippet is a level 2 general trace of the JDBC driver when a SELECT query was executed, and the columns in the ResultSet extracted:

```
IfxValue.makeInstance:
  ColInfo.SQLType = 0
  ColInfo.ExtendedId = 0
  This instance is com.informix.jdbc.IfxChar
```

```
IfxResultSet.getValue() exited
IfxResultSet.getString(int) called. ColumnIndex: 2
IfxResultSet.getString() exited.
IfxResultSet.getValue(int) called
IfxValue.makeInstance:
  ColInfo.SQLType = 44
  ColInfo.ExtendedId = 11
  This instance is com.informix.jdbc.IfxSmBlob
IfxBaseType: fromIfx.length = 72
IfxBaseType: fromIfx.index = 5
IfxSqli: constructor() exited
IfxSqli: receiveMessage() called
IfxSqli: flip() called
IfxSqli: flip() exited
IfxSqli: receiveMessage() exited
IfxSqli: sendBind(Vector) called
```

Always close the Statement, PreparedStatement,
CallableStatement, *and* ResultSet *objects when you have finished
processing the results. To do this, invoke the* close() *method of the
statement object; for example,* PreparedStatement.close().
Closing the statement *object releases the resources allocated to that*
statement *object; if you close the* ResultSet *on its own using*
ResultSet.close(), *then the resources allocated to the statement
are not released.*

Performance Tuning the Informix JDBC Driver

While it is true that a significant amount of performance gain can
be delivered by a well-designed database and a well-written application, there is still more that you can do to optimize the specific
implementations of software across the application platform. In
particular, there are at least two ways to address performance issues
when using JDBC. This section shows how to manage the fetch
buffers for a ResultSet and optimize network traffic.

Managing the SELECT Buffer Size Using FET_BUF_SIZE

When a SELECT statement is sent from a Java program to an
Informix server, the returned rows (called *tuples*) are stored in a *tuple
buffer* in the Informix JDBC Driver memory. The default size of the

tuple buffer is the larger of the complete returned tuple size or 4096 bytes. You can override the size of this buffer, which in other languages may be termed the *fetch buffer*.

What we are trying to do is to ensure that we are making best use of *network resources* and *locality*. We make best use of network resources if we submit less network requests. We are making best use of locality if the data we require is already present on the client. Increasing the size of the fetch buffer will result in less requests to the database server to send the remaining tuples, and it will enable us to scroll through more rows locally, since more rows have been returned in a single fetch.

Configuring FET_BUF_SIZE

You can use the FET_BUF_SIZE environment variable to override the default size of the tuple buffer. The FET_BUF_SIZE value can be less than or equal to 32,767 (bytes). If this variable is set and is larger than the default tuple size, then FET_BUF_SIZE is used to define the tuple buffer size.

Limitations of FET_BUF_SIZE

Because FET_BUF_SIZE can be configured to use more memory, you may degrade performance by using too much memory and thereby forcing other applications or data segments out of memory; in other words, you will force the *swapping out* of memory. If the swap space on your machine is limited, you need to be mindful of this possibility.

If you have many simultaneous open connections to the database, then each connection will use up FET_BUF_SIZE memory units. This will also eat unto memory and may degrade performance if your machine has limited memory resources. You should evaluate the practicalities of using FET_BUF_SIZE in your application for the target platform you will be using.

Reducing Network Traffic

Reducing network traffic should help increase the visible performance of your Java program, since we are reducing the dependence on the network bandwidth. Informix provides two environment variables that you can set to help reduce this network dependency. These variables are named OPTOFC and IFX_AUTOFREE.

Configuring `OPTOFC` for the `ResultSet` Object

The `OPTOFC` variable is short for *optimize open fetch close*, and is used to reduce network traffic when you close `Statement` and `ResultSet` objects.

You set `OPTOFC` to 1 to specify that the `ResultSet.close()` method does not require a network dialog with the database server to close the `ResultSet` if all the qualifying rows have already been retrieved in the driver's tuple buffer. This is because the Informix database server automatically closes the cursor after all the rows have been retrieved.

When the `ResultSet.next()` method is called, the JDBC driver may or may not already have additional rows in the tuple buffer. Unless the JDBC driver has received all rows from the database server, the `ResultSet.close()` method may still require a network dialog with the database server when `OPTOFC` is set to 1.

Configuring `IFX_AUTOFREE` for the `Statement` Object

You set `IFX_AUTOFREE` to 1 to specify that the `Statement.close()` method does not require a network dialog with the database server to free the server cursor resources if the cursor has already been closed. The database server automatically frees the cursor resources after the cursor is closed. You close the cursor *explicitly* by invoking the `ResultSet.close()` method. You can also close the cursor *implicitly* by using the `OPTOFC` environment variable. When the cursor resources have been freed, the cursor can no longer be referenced.

Setting Performance-tuning Variables

As with all other environment variables, you can set `FET_BUF_SIZE`, `OPTOFC`, and `IFX_AUTOFREE` in the JDBC URL or in a properties list. For example:

```
jdbc:informix-
sqli://theale2:1526/stores7:informixserver=online_tcp;
user=informix;password=in4mix;OPTOFC=1;IFX_AUT-
OFREE=1;FET_BUF_SIZE=8192
```

JDBC API Methods Not Supported by the Informix Type 4 Driver

Table 8-22 lists the JDBC methods that are not implemented by the Type 4 Driver from Informix.

For the Informix Type 4 Driver, the behavior of the methods in Table 8-23 differs from the behavior specified by the JDBC API.

Table 8-22. JDBC API methods not implemented by the Informix Type 4 Driver.

Method	Description
Connection.setCatalog()	Selects a subset of the database catalogs.
Connection.setReadOnly()	Sets connection to read-only mode to enable database optimizations.
Connection.isReadOnly()	True if connection is read-only.
Statement.setMaxFieldSize()	Sets the max field size for a column; discards the excess.
Statement,setQueryTimeout()	Specifies the number of seconds to wait for a Statement to execute.
Statement.cancel()	One thread cancels a Statement being executed by another thread.
PreparedStatement.setUnicodeStream()	Sends a large UNICODE value as an InputStream.
CallableStatement.registerOutParameter()	Registers the java.sql.Type of each OUT parameter.
ResultSet.getUnicodeStream()	Retrieves a large UNICODE value from an InputStream.

Method	Return value
Statement.execute()	Returns a single ResultSet
PreparedStatement.execute()	Returns a single ResultSet
CallableStatement.execute()	Returns a single ResultSet
ResultSetMetaData.getTableName()	Returns " "
ResultSetMetaData.getSchemaName()	Returns " "
ResultSetMetaData.getCatalogName()	Returns " "
ResultSetMetaData.isReadOnly()	Returns FALSE
ResultSetMetaData.isWritable()	Returns TRUE
ResultSetMetaData.isDefinitelyWritable()	Returns TRUE

Summary

This chapter has focused on the nuts and bolts of practical JDBC programming in Java. All the major issues with using the Informix JDBC driver were covered. In particular, we mapped an Informix datatype to a JDBC datatype and used this information to maintain the data in the database. We also showed how to set JDBC tracing information and how to tune the performance of the JDBC driver.

The basics of an online shopping catalog administration interface were described; more specifically, you learned how to maintain large objects, such as GIF images, in the database by implementing JDBC methods.

Using the examples in this chapter, you are now ready to manage multiple datatypes in your database from a Java applet or application and then capture and render that data in a Java client program.

Integrating Java Applets with the Database

In this chapter:

- Serving Java applets from the database: managing a Java applet as *web content*, where the applet is stored in and retrieved from the database.
- Integrating dynamic web pages with Java applets: A Java applet can be parameterized using AppPage variables that are specific to a browser client.

It is important to understand how to integrate a Java applet with dynamic web pages, because successful integration allows us to change the behaviour of a Java applet dynamically without changing the Java applet code or the AppPage that contains it. This is important when the data and behavior of the Java applet need to be *personalized* for a specific intranet or Internet client. For example, a user may be able to see only a subset of the available data on the database. Rather than code all the permissions in Java or SQL, you can instead manage this complexity dynamically by using AppPages to parameterize the Java applet. By extension, this dynamic parameterization of applets allows you to connect to a variety of databases using simple JDBC and RMI.

Serving Java Applets from the Database

Overview

The source code of a Java applet is stored in a file with the suffix `.java`. The source code is compiled into bytecode and stored in a file with the suffix `.class`. The `.class` file is included in the HTML document using the APPLET tag. Here is an example of the APPLET tag used by a demo applet:

```
<APPLET CODE="Demo.class" WIDTH=170 HEIGHT=150>
```

A Java applet is executed by a web browser when the browser loads an HTML document that contains an APPLET tag. The APPLET tag specifies a Java applet that will run in a web page.

Using the Data Director for Web Schema

Java applets can be served from an Informix database via the Web DataBlade and Data Director for Web. The Data Director for Web schema stores binary objects in the wbBinaries table. Each object stored in wbBinaries has an associated extension that is used to look up the MIME type of the object in the wbExtensions table. The MIME type is required for the web server to successfully serve the AppPage to the client.

Adding Applet Content Types Via Site Manager

The Site Manager tool facilitates the development, management, and deployment of websites. It enables users to easily create, edit, and maintain application pages and associated content. For the purpose of supporting Java applets, the following tasks must be performed.

Specify New Content Types for Java Class Files and JAR Archives

The Data Director for Web schema needs to understand the content types that it manages. Example content types include HTML pages,

AppPages, GIF and JPEG images, office documents, as well as video and audio files. These objects are stored in the database, usually in the `wbBinaries` table. The metadata for each object describes what the object is and will generally reflect what we want to do with it. A Java applet is a set of compiled classes. A `JAR` archive is a set of compiled Java classes and other objects, such as GIF images, stored in one archive file.

So, we need to describe a class file and a `JAR` archive to Data Director for Web and then store the classes or `JAR` archives in the database, ready to be served in an HTML page. We do this by adding file extension information to Data Director for Web. When we add a resource (a new file, for example) to Data Director for Web, the file extension (and the associated extension information) will determine how the resource is rendered in the HTML page.

Add the `.class` and `.jar` Extensions

After selecting a database server and database, select the `Tools/Extensions` menu option from Site Manager. A dialog similar to Fig. 9-1 will be displayed that shows all the mappings of file suffixes (e.g., `.PDF`) to an object MIME type, and hence to the target application that reads the object.

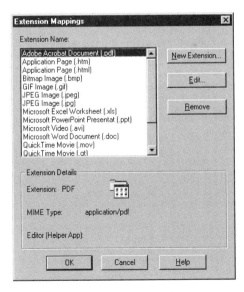

Figure 9-1. Extension mappings.

note

Although we are storing objects in a database, we need to take the data for an object from a file on the filesystem, and the file extension describes the data in some way. The file suffix is the most basic metadata; from the suffix .PDF, *for example, we know that a PDF reader is required and we can understand the basic characteristics of the file contents. If we store a PDF file in the database, it is stored as a large object, and we store the contents of the whole file, not just the text. We use the original file extension as metadata for the object; when the PDF file is delivered to the browser from the database, we know how to define the MIME type for the object so that the client browser can invoke the appropriate plug-in or helper application for the object. If we use Data Director for Web to export the contents of the website (which are stored in the database) to flat files, the* PDF *object is created as a file with the name and extension it was given when it was registered.*

Now, click on the New Extension button. We will add a mapping for a class file and a mapping for a JAR archive.

A "Create Extension" dialog appears (see Fig. 9-2). This dialog consists of three tab panels that capture information about the type of object we want to register in the database. Table 9-1 lists the functions of these tab panels.

Set the extension attributes to the values specified in Table 9-2 (screen shots follow), and click OK. The new extension mapping will be created.

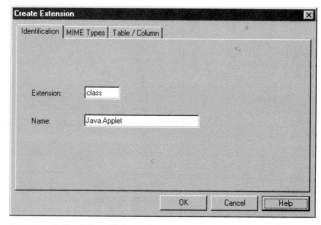

Figure 9-2. *Identifying the extension in the "Create Extension" dialog (.class).*

Table 9-1. Meaning of the "Create Extension" dialog tab panels.

Tab panel	Description
Identification	Names a specific file extension to which we add properties that describe how to use the object that is sourced from a file.
MIME Types	The MIME type is the definition of the object that is sent to the client browser, which then invokes a plug-in or helper application on the client. The helper application in this dialog is for Data Director for Web.
Table/Column	Identifies the table and table columns in the Data Director for Web schema, or in a schema not controlled by Data Director for Web. We also define the retrieval method for the object and thereby state whether it is transformed (exploded), delivered as a large object, or rendered unchanged.

Table 9-2. Extension values for `.class` and `.jar` files.

Property	Value for `.class` files	Value for `.jar` files
Extension	class	jar
Name	Java Applet	Java Archive
Super Type	application	application
Sub-Type	x-java	x-jar
Source Table	wbBinaries	wbBinaries
Name Column	id	id
Content Column	object	object
Path Column	path	path
Retrieval Method	Blob	Blob

For class files, Figs. 9-2, 9-3, and 9-4 show the completed tab panels. Figure 9-5 shows the completed mapping in the "Extension Mappings" dialog.

For JAR archive files, Figs. 9-6, 9-7, and 9-8 show the completed tab panels. Figure 9-9 shows the completed mapping in the "Extension Mappings" dialog.

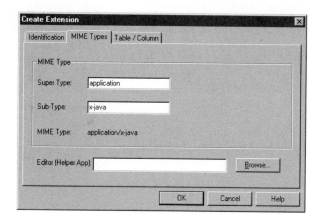

Figure 9-3. *Identifying the MIME type in the "Create Extension" dialog (.class).*

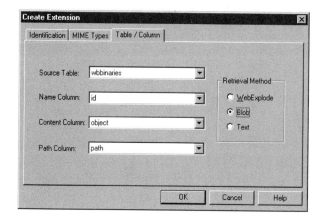

Figure 9-4. *Identifying the source tables and retrieval method (class).*

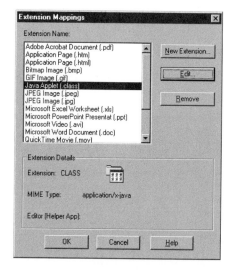

Figure 9-5. *Viewing the completed extension mapping (class).*

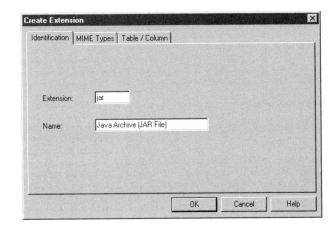

Figure 9-6. *Identifying the extension in the "Create Extension" dialog (JAR).*

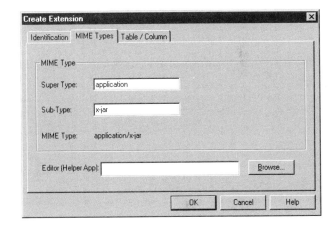

Figure 9-7. *Identifying the MIME type in the "Create Extension" dialog (JAR).*

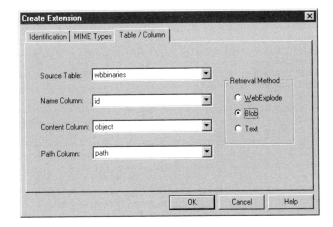

Figure 9-8. *Identifying the source tables and retrieval method (JAR).*

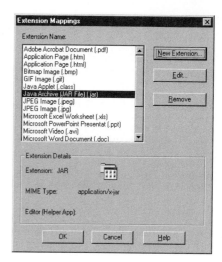

Figure 9-9. *Viewing the completed extension mapping (JAR).*

Adding the Java Applet Resources to the Web Project

This can be achieved by dragging the resource from the filesystem and dropping it into the desired project, or by using the `File/New/Resource` menu option. The Java `.class` and `.jar` files are added to the application folder of the project you dropped them onto, or to the application folder of the "Not in Projects" folder.

Creating the AppPage that Contains the Java Applet

AppPage Editor allows the creation and editing of AppPages. Java applets can be displayed in an AppPage by using the `APPLET` tag.

The `CODE` attribute specifies the name of the Java applet to run.

The `CODEBASE` attribute specifies the NSAPI-mapped URL that is to be used to direct an NSAPI `webdriver` to extract the applet (specified by the `CODE` attribute) from the database.

The `CODEBASE` *URL must be an NSAPI URL, which maps onto an Informix NSAPI* `webdriver` *request.*

You can use the `PARAM` attribute between the `<APPLET>` and `</APPLET>` tags to provide information about parameters or arguments to be used by the Java applet.

Listing 9-1 shows a simple AppPage that contains an applet retrieved from the database, and Fig. 9-10 shows the browser output of the AppPage.

The Java class file `dbMessage.class` is stored in the `wbBinaries` table.

```
<HTML>
<HEAD>
<TITLE>Messages</TITLE>
</HEAD>
<BODY>
<center>
<APPLET
      CODE="dbMessage.class"
      CODEBASE="/stores7"
      WIDTH=426 HEIGHT=266 IGNORE="" >
  <PARAM NAME=User VALUE="Web">
  <PARAM NAME=Message VALUE="This text is an applet parameter">
 </APPLET>
</center>
</BODY>
</HTML>
```

Figure 9-10. *Browser output of List. 9-1.*

How it Works in Summary

When the HTML page is loaded by the browser, the browser uses the CODEBASE URL to fetch the Java class specified by the CODE attribute:

```
CODE="dbMessage.class"
CODEBASE="/stores7"
```

The URL `/stores7` must be an NSAPI-mapped URL that the web server resolves to point to the NSAPI `webdriver`. The web server will receive a request of the form:

```
/stores7/dbMessage.class
```

The NSAPI `webdriver` is invoked, and the Java class is retrieved from the `wbBinaries` table and sent to the browser client. Once the browser has the class file, the applet can be instantiated.

If the `APPLET` tag specifies one or more `JAR` archives that are stored in the database, then the `JAR` archives are retrieved in exactly the same way. For example, the following `APPLET` attributes nominate two `JAR` archives and the initial class that extends `java.applet.Applet`, that is, `dbMessage.class`:

```
CODE="dbMessage.class"
ARCHIVE="ifxjdbc.jar, viewCustomerJdbc.jar"
CODEBASE="/stores7"
```

In this example, both of the `JAR` archives are stored in the database and are retrieved using the `CODEBASE` URL. The web server will receive requests of the form:

```
/stores7/ifxjdbc.jar
/stores7/viewCustomerJdbc.jar
```

The `ifxjdbc.jar` archive contains the Informix JDBC Driver. The `viewCustomerJdbc.jar` archive contains all the associated classes that are required by the applet, plus objects such as GIF images and audio files.

If possible, use `JAR` *archives to store your Java classes and associated objects, such as GIF images. The advantage of using a* `JAR` *archive is that the archive is downloaded only once, involving one HTTP request; if the classes and images were stored separately on the webserver machine, there would be a separate HTTP request to fetch each class and image.*

Configuring `CODEBASE` in `web.cnf`

Making the whole thing work from end to end can be slightly tricky, but as long as you pay attention to the detail, it will work.

Assuming that the URL prefix `/stores7` is an NSAPI-mapped URL (a URL that directs the Netscape web server to invoke a method in the NSAPI `webdriver` shared-object to connect to the database), then the following entries are required in the `webdriver` configuration file, `web.cnf`:

```
WEB_HOME /stores7/
MI_WEBNSNAMETRANS /stores7
```

When using the Data Director for Web schema, the variable `MI_WEBNSNAMETRANS` is required. This is set to the NSAPI URL, which is also used by the `WEB_HOME` variable. Note, however, that the `MI_WEBNSNAMETRANS` URL does not have the slash ("/") character appended to it, which is a restriction imposed by the NSAPI `webdriver` (`/stores7` is the URL defined in the Netscape configuration file, `obj.conf`).

Mapping `CODEBASE` in the `APPLET` tag

To successfully direct the browser to retrieve the `class` or `JAR` objects from the database, you need to set the `CODEBASE` attribute of the `APPLET` tag correctly.

You must set `CODEBASE` to the value of `MI_WEBNSNAMETRANS`. For example, given the setting of `MI_WEBNSNAMETRANS`:

```
MI_WEBNSNAMETRANS /stores7
```

then set `CODEBASE` to

```
CODEBASE="/stores7"
```

Tracing HTTP Requests Using the Web Server Access Log

If you have problems extracting an applet from the database (for example, the browser says that it cannot find or load the class specified in the `CODE` attribute of the `APPLET` tag), then you can trace what the HTTP web server is trying to fetch by looking at the Netscape web server *access log* and *error log*. You can find these logs in the web server administration screens for your Netscape web server.

For example, when requesting the AppPage in Listing 9-1, which contains a reference to one `class` file, the Netscape access log shows the AppPage request, followed by the subsequent applet request:

```
127.0.0.1 - - [18/Jun/1999:23:47:06 +0100] "GET
/stores7/message1 HTTP/1.0" 200 280
127.0.0.1 - - [18/Jun/1999:23:47:11 +0100] "GET
/stores7/dbMessage.class HTTP/1.0" 200 1685
```

When retrieving an AppPage called `viewCustomer1`, which contains two JAR archive references in the APPLET tag, the following HTTP requests are logged:

```
134.168.237.55 - - [18/Jun/1999:12:53:11 +0100] "GET
/stores7/viewCustomer1 HTTP/1.0" 200 459
134.168.237.55 - - [18/Jun/1999:12:53:12 +0100] "GET
/stores7/ifxjdbc.jar HTTP/1.0" 200 297665
134.168.237.55 - - [18/Jun/1999:12:53:13 +0100] "GET
/stores7/viewCustomerJdbc.jar HTTP/1.0" 200 6077
```

If you do encounter an error when trying to load the `class` files or JAR archives from the database, look at the error log. For example, if the CODEBASE is not configured correctly, an error similar to the following should be found in the error log:

```
[17/Jun/1999:17:06:28] failure ( 364): for host
134.168.237.55 trying to GET /stores7/dbMessage.class,
informix_explode reports: HTTP/1.0 404 Asset not found
```

This error message states that the NSAPI `webdriver` function `informix_explode` can't find the object in the Data Director for Web schema. Provided the `class` file is actually in the `wbBinaries` table, this suggests that the CODEBASE URL `/stores7` does not match `MI_WEBNSNAMETRANS`.

You don't have to use an AppPage, which is stored in the database, to use applets and JAR files that are stored in the database. You can use an HTML file that is stored in the filesystem, but you still need to configure CODEBASE correctly.

Integrating Dynamic Web Pages with Java Applets

One of the advantages of using AppPages to contain Java applets, whether they are delivered from the database or otherwise, is that you can parameterize the behavior of the applet. You can do this using AppPage variables. These variables can be set inside the AppPage or initialized inside the `webdriver` configuration file, `web.cnf`. The next section will extend the AppPage called `message1`, shown in List. 9-1, and use AppPage variables to display database content without using JDBC.

note

You don't have to store Java applets in the database to parameterize them in the AppPage.

Parameterising Java Applets Dynamically

To illustrate how to parameterize a Java applet using AppPage variables, we will extend the message1 AppPage. This time, instead of hardcoding the parameter values to the APPLET tag, we will perform an SQL query, format the results, and pass these results to the Java applet.

The SQL query selects the most recent call that a customer has placed with your call center, which is stored in the cust_calls table in the stores7 database. The call is formatted and passed to the applet for display, together with the name of the user who has logged into the site.

The AppPage is shown in Listing 9-2.

Listing 9-2. *Using AppPage Variables to parameterize a Java applet in* message2.html.

```
<HTML>
<HEAD>
<TITLE>Parameterised Messages</TITLE>
</HEAD>
<BODY>
<CENTER>
<?misql
  sql="select customer_num, call_descr, trim(user_id),
         call_dtime
    from cust_calls
    where call_dtime = (
      select max(call_dtime) from cust_calls
    );">
  $(SETVAR,$MESSAGE,Customer $3 called at $4: $2)
<?/misql>
<?mivar>
 <APPLET
     CODE="dbMessage.class"
     CODEBASE="/stores7"
     WIDTH=426 HEIGHT=266>
  <PARAM NAME=User VALUE="$REMOTE_USER">
  <PARAM NAME=Message VALUE="$MESSAGE">
 </APPLET>
<?/mivar>
</CENTER>
</BODY>
</HTML>
```

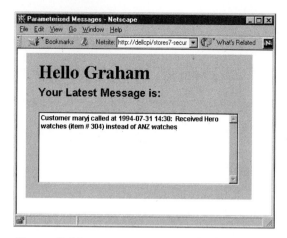

Figure 9-11. `message2.html` *displayed in the browser.*

In Listing 9-2, the variable `$REMOTE_USER` is set to the value defined in `web.cnf`, which is usually set to the default value. If the user accesses the AppPage through a secure URL (using NSAPI or ISAPI, for example), then `$REMOTE_USER` is set to the user ID that the user authenticated with.

The `$MESSAGE` variable is set from the results of the SQL query using the `SETVAR` AppPage variable-processing function.

Note that the `APPLET` tag is enclosed by the `<?mivar>` and `<?/mivar>` tags. This ensures that the AppPage variables used to parameterize the applet will be expanded when the AppPage is processed by the `webexplode` function.

Assuming that the secure URL prefix `/stores7-secure` is used and the authenticated user is called Graham, then the browser will display a message like the one shown in Fig. 9-11.

Finally, the complete source code for the `dbMessage` applet is shown in List. 9-3.

The applet parameter values are retrieved using the `getParameter()` method of the `Applet` class, as shown below:

```
userName.setText("Hello " + getParameter("User"));
messageArea.setText(getParameter("Message"));
```

The string passed to `getParameter()` is expected to match one of the `PARAM` attributes of the `APPLET` tag. For example, to extract the value of the `User` parameter, which has been declared as

Listing 9-3. Complete source code for dbMessage.java.

```
import java.awt.*;
import java.applet.*;

public class dbMessage extends Applet
{

          java.awt.Label userName;
          java.awt.TextArea messageArea;
          java.awt.Label label1;

          public void init()
          {
             setLayout(null);
             setSize(426,266);
             setBackground(new Color(12632256));
             userName = new java.awt.Label("Hello ");
             userName.setBounds(24,12,396,44);
             userName.setFont(new Font("TimesRoman", Font.BOLD, 34));
             userName.setBackground(new Color(12632256));
             add(userName);
             messageArea =
new java.awt.TextArea("",0,0,TextArea.SCROLLBARS_VERTICAL_ONLY);
             messageArea.setEditable(false);
             messageArea.setText("No Message");
             messageArea.setBounds(24,108,377,131);
             messageArea.setFont(new Font("Dialog", Font.BOLD, 12));
             messageArea.setBackground(new Color(16777215));
             add(messageArea);
             label1 = new java.awt.Label("Your Latest Message is:");
             label1.setBounds(24,60,313,24);
             label1.setFont(new Font("Dialog", Font.BOLD, 20));
             add(label1);

             userName.setText("Hello " + getParameter("User"));
             messageArea.setText(getParameter("Message"));
          }
}
```

```
<PARAM NAME="User" VALUE="$REMOTE_USER">
```

the call to getParameter() is:

```
getParameter("User");
```

Dynamic JDBC Connections and SQL Queries

We can pass JDBC information to an applet using AppPage variables. In this example, we want to connect to the `stores7` database *from an applet* in order to view customer records. To make it simple, we want to download the viewing application *and* the Type 4 JDBC Driver to the browser so that the applet can make a direct connection to the database from the browser. Rather than hard code the reference to the JDBC driver that we need or to the JDBC URL that we use to connect to the database, we want to pass these values into the applet dynamically from variables. These variables are initialized in the `web.cnf` file.

Parameterising the JDBC information like this allows us to target specific databases for particular URLs. For example, we may want secure users to access one database, and nonsecure users to access another database. Users connecting via the URL prefix `/stores7-secure` may receive a different JDBC URL than users connecting via the `/stores7` URL. This is because the JDBC variables are stored in the `web.cnf` file, and the two URLs point to different `web.cnf` configurations.

It is also useful to demonstrate how to pass SQL queries into an applet. This is not important in itself, but it may be used to dynamically bind a *permissions filter* to a query, based on the URL that a user can request. For example, a filter may specify that a broker can only query prices for a certain type of stock. The permissions filter would express this rule as part of an SQL `WHERE` clause, and pass this string to the applet. The `WHERE` clause would be defined in a variable inside `web.cnf`.

It is always useful to have examples of connecting to the database, performing a query and scrolling through the `ResultSet`. This is a fairly small example, so the connectivity functionality is listed as code.

`customerView` Applet Functionality

The user can enter a customer number into the "Customer Number" screen field. When the `Select` button is clicked, all customer records with a `customer_num` greater than the entered customer number are selected, and the screen is populated with one customer record at a time. The user can scroll through the matching records by clicking the `Next` button.

The `customer` table is joined with the `state` table to expand the `customer.state` column with the description held in the `state` table. Both the code and the description are to be displayed in the Java applet.

Configuration of JDBC Variables

The `web.cnf` file for this application contains variables that are used in the AppPage that contains the `APPLET` tag. These variables are expanded by `webexplode`, and the resulting values are passed into the applet via the `PARAM` attribute of the `APPLET` tag.

Listing 9-4 contains the section of `web.cnf` that contains the variables for the `customerView` applet.

The `JDBCURL` and `QUERYSTRING` variables must have the variable values typed in using one line. Table 9-3 lists the usage of the variables.

Listing 9-4. *AppPage variables declared in* `web.cnf`.

```
#### Application Variables
# applet class
JAVACLASS      viewCustomer.class

# JAR archive containing the applet class and other classes
APPARCHIVE     viewCustomerJdbc.jar

# Informix Type 4 JDBC driver archive
JDBCARCHIVE    ifxjdbc.jar

# Informix Type 4 JDBC driver
JDBCDRIVER     com.informix.jdbc.IfxDriver

# The URL used by the applet to connect to the database
JDBCURL        jdbc:informix-sqli://dellcpi:1526/stores7:
informixserver=ol_dellcpi;user=informix;password=informix

# The query that is passed into the applet in Prepared format
QUERYSTRING    SELECT trim(fname) || ' ' || trim(lname),
company,address1,address2,city,zipcode,phone,state,sname,customer_num
FROM customer,state WHERE customer_num > ? and customer.state =
state.code
```

| Table 9-3. | Using the web.cnf variables to parameterize a JDBC applet. |

Variable	Description
JAVACLASS	The applet class instantiated by the browser.
APPARCHIVE	The JAR archive that contains the applet class and any other classes used by the applet.
JDBCARCHIVE	The Informix JDBC Driver JAR file containing the Type 4 JDBC Driver classes.
JDBCDRIVER	Classname of the Informix Type 4 JDBC Driver as registered by the applet.
JDBCURL	The URL used by the JDBC driver to connect to the database from the Java applet.
QUERYSTRING	The SQL string that will be used to select customer records from the stores7 database. This statement contains parameter markers ("?") that are used by the PreparedStatement class.

The customerView AppPage

Listing 9-5 shows the AppPage that contains the applet.

The applet does not have to be retrieved from the database for this example to work, but the example is based on working code that retrieves the AppPage and the two JAR archives from the database, with MI_WEBNSNAMETRANS set to the NSAPI-mapped URL in the Netscape obj.conf file (e.g., /stores7). If you do not store the applet JAR files in the database, store them in the CLASSPATH on the same web server from which the AppPage is retrieved.

| Listing 9-5. | customerView.html, containing the applet that references the JAR archives to view customer records. |

```
<HTML>
<HEAD>
<TITLE>View Customer</TITLE>
</HEAD>
<BODY>
   <?mivar>
        <APPLET CODE="$JAVACLASS"
```

Listing 9-5.   (continued)

```
                  ARCHIVE="$JDBCARCHIVE, $APPARCHIVE"
                  CODEBASE="$MI_WEBNSNAMETRANS"
                   WIDTH=685
                   HEIGHT=400>
                     <PARAM NAME="JdbcDriver" VALUE="$JDBCDRIVER">
                     <PARAM NAME="JdbcUrl" VALUE="$JDBCURL">
                     <PARAM NAME="QueryString" VALUE="$QUERYSTRING">
                   </APPLET>
            <?/mivar>
        </BODY>
        </HTML>
```

In List. 9-5, we can see that the `<?mivar>` tag delimits a section of the AppPage where AppPage variables are expanded. The AppPage variables (e.g., `$JAVACLASS`, `$JDBCARCHIVE`) are initialized in `web.cnf` and written to the resulting web page. These values are passed to the applet using the `PARAM` attribute of the `APPLET` tag.

Listing 9-6 shows the resulting HTML page sent to the browser after the AppPage has been exploded.

Listing 9-6.   Exploded `customerView` AppPage, sent to the browser.

```
<HTML>
<HEAD>
<TITLE>View Customer</TITLE>
</HEAD>
<BODY>
 <APPLET CODE="viewCustomer.class"
    ARCHIVE="ifxjdbc.jar, viewCustomerJdbc.jar"
    CODEBASE="/stores7"
    WIDTH=685
    HEIGHT=400>
 <PARAM NAME="JdbcDriver" VALUE="com.informix.jdbc.IfxDriver">
 <PARAM NAME="JdbcUrl" VALUE="jdbc:informix-
sqli://dellcpi:1526/stores7:informixserver=ol_dellcpi;user=informix;
password=informix">
 <PARAM NAME="QueryString" VALUE="SELECT trim(fname) || ' ' ||
trim(lname), company, address1, address2, city, zipcode, phone, state,
sname, customer_num FROM customer, state WHERE customer_num > ? and
customer.state = state.code">
</APPLET>
</BODY>
</HTML>
```

Extracting Applet Parameters

The `viewCustomer` applet extracts the parameters passed in via the `PARAM` attribute of the `APPLET` tag as follows:

```
private void getVariableParameters() {

    JdbcDriver = getParameter("JdbcDriver");
    JdbcUrl = getParameter("JdbcUrl");
    QueryString = getParameter("QueryString");
}
```

The parameter values are extracted using the `getParameter()` method of the `Applet` class, and stored in Java `String` variables.

The `viewCustomer.getAppletParameters()` method is called in the `init()` method of the applet:

```
public class viewCustomer extends Applet
{
  public void init()
  {
        // get parameters
        getVariableParameters();
  }
}
```

Connecting to the Database

Once the applet parameters are retrieved, they can be used to connect to the Informix database. Listing 9-7 shows the connection method of the applet.

The first two `try` blocks use the parameter values to register the Informix JDBC Driver and connect to the database. The third `try` block *prepares* the SQL query that was passed in as a parameter. This is the SQL query that contains the "`?`" parameter marker. This query is prepared once but used many times by the applet. Because the query is prepared, the first and subsequent executions of the query do not involve generation of the query plan in the database server, which is ideal for the `viewCustomer` applet because, once the query is prepared, the user can perform multiple selections using the same SQL query (differing only by `customer_num`).

Performing the Query

The user enters a customer number into the "Customer Number" text box on the screen, and then clicks the `Select` button to fetch

```java
private void connectToDB() {
        try {
            // load driver
            System.out.println( "Loading Driver: " + JdbcDriver );
            Class.forName (JdbcDriver);
        } catch (Exception e) {
            System.out.println("Can't load driver: " +
                                                e.getMessage() );
            return;
        }

        try {
            System.out.println("Connecting to " + JdbcUrl);
            // Connect to the database
            con = (Connection) DriverManager.getConnection(
                                                jdbcUrl);
        } catch (Exception e) {
                System.out.println("Can't connect: " +
                                                e.getMessage());
                return;
        }

        try {
            System.out.println("Preparing " + QueryString);
            // Create a prepared statement
            stmt = con.prepareStatement(QueryString);
        } catch (Exception e) {
            System.out.println("Can't create statement: " +
                        e.getMessage());
        }
}
```

all customer records with a customer number greater than the entered value. The following snippet shows the event handler for the Select button:

```java
void goButton_Action( java.awt.event.ActionEvent
event)
{
    performQuery();
}
```

Listing 9-8 shows the applet method that performs the parameterized query.

The first task the method performs is to set the parameter marker in the SQL query to the value of the customer number entered by the user. Then, the `executeQuery()` method of the `PreparedStatement` is performed to select the relevant customer records. Once this has completed successfully, the `results()` method of the applet is invoked. The method scrolls initially to the first, and then the subsequent, records of the `ResultSet` returned from the query. The `results()` method also populates the screen with the column values retrieved for each row.

Scrolling the `ResultSet`

After the query has been executed, the `results()` method is invoked to scroll the query `ResultSet`. Remember that you need to perform the `ResultSet.next()` method to fetch the first row of data. The `results()` method is used to fetch the first and subsequent rows of customer records from the `ResultSet` and write the column values to the screen. Listing 9-9 shows the `results()` method.

Listing 9-8.   *Perform the query passed in as a parameter to the applet.*

```
private void performQuery() {
        try {
            // set the customer number
            stmt.setInt(1,
                Integer.valueOf(customerNum.getText()).intValue() );
        } catch (Exception e) {
            System.out.println("Error in set: " + e.getMessage());
            return;
        }

        try {
            System.out.println("Executing Query");
    // rs is a ResultSet defined at the start of the class
    // definition
            rs = stmt.executeQuery();
        } catch (Exception e) {
            System.out.println("Error in Query: " +
                        e.getMessage());
            return;
        }
        results();
}
```

Listing 9-9.   The `results()` *method.*

```
private void results() {
        try {
            // get first and next result set rows, one by one
            if ( rs.next() ) {
                noMoreRows.setVisible(false);
                name.setText( rs.getString(1) );
                company.setText( rs.getString(2) );
                addressLine1.setText( rs.getString(3) );
                addressLine2.setText( rs.getString(4) );
                city.setText( rs.getString(5) );
                zip.setText( rs.getString(6) );
                phone.setText( rs.getString(7) );
                state.setText( rs.getString(8) );
            stateLabel.setText( rs.getString(9) );
            customerNum.setText( rs.getString(10) );
            }
            else {
            // no more rows, close the ResultSet
            rs.close();
            noMoreRows.setVisible(true);
        }
        } catch (SQLException e) {
            System.out.println("Error using ResultSet: " +
                                            e.getMessage());

        } catch (Exception e) {
            System.out.println("Error in results: " +
                                            e.getMessage() );
        }
}
```

The `ResultSet.next()` method is used to fetch the next row. If the method returns `false`, we assume that either the `ResultSet` is empty (no matches) or the end of the `ResultSet` was reached. In either case, we display the message "No More Rows" to the applet screen.

If a row exists, then we write the column data from the `ResultSet` to the screen fields. Since we are treating all the screen fields as `text` objects, we use the `setText()` method of these objects to populate the screen with the column values.

When the user clicks the `Next` button, the `results()` method is called again to scroll to the next row and populate the screen. The following snippet shows the `event` handler for the `Next` button.

```
void next_Action(java.awt.event.ActionEvent event)
{
```

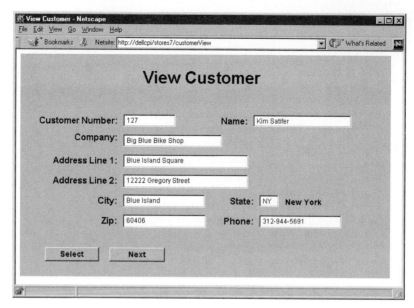

Figure 9-12. *Browser display of the* `customerView` *applet.*

```
        results();
}
```

The `customerView` Applet Display

Figure 9-12 shows the browser display of the `customerView` applet
when the user has entered a "Customer Number" and clicked the
`Select` button. Note that all the screen fields are populated, and
that the state description is written to the display as a `Label` object,
next to the `state` code.

Summary

This chapter has addressed the practical issues of serving Java
applets from the database and provided an illustration how to parameterize Java applets with AppPage variables. In particular, the
chapter also showed how to pass JDBC connection information and
SQL queries to an applet via AppPage variables.

With the material in this chapter, you can integrate the functionality of the Web DataBlade with Java applets and JDBC to create
dynamic database-driven web applications.

Creating Distributed Applications Using RMI and JDBC

In this chapter:

- Understanding remote method invocation (RMI)
- Creating a multitier database application using RMI
- Implementing RMI in applets
- A working RMI applet example
- Connecting to the database from the RMI server host
- Parameterising connection information

This chapter introduces the essentials of creating distributed database applications using remote method invocation (RMI) and JDBC. Together, JDBC and RMI will allow you to implement highly scalable, distributed database applications. By the end of the chapter, you will understand how to connect Java client objects to remote objects using RMI, and how to invoke remote methods that connect to the database using JDBC.

Understanding Remote Method Invocation (RMI)

The RMI technology lets you easily develop networked Java applications that hide the underlying mechanisms for transporting method arguments and return values.

RMI enables programmers to create distributed Java-to-Java programs. Under distributed Java computing, one part of the program—running in one Java Virtual Machine as a client—can invoke the methods of server objects in another virtual machine, often on a different host.

However, client programs do not communicate directly with server objects. When invoking remote methods, clients instead invoke the methods of a remote object's *stub,* which resides on the client host. The local stub does the networking needed to pass remote method invocations to the *skeleton* (another interface to the remote object) that resides on the server host.

Figure 10-1 shows the RMI architecture.

The RMI allows client and server objects to interact as if they were local objects residing in the same Java Virtual Machine. Additionally, server objects can be RMI clients of other remote objects.

Passing Parameters and Return Values

RMI allows Java clients to pass parameter values to remote server methods and accept return values from those methods. It does this by allowing the stubs and skeletons to *marshal* and *unmarshal*

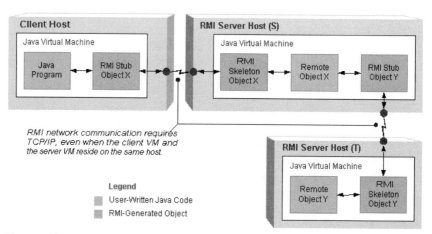

Figure 10-1. *RMI architecture.*

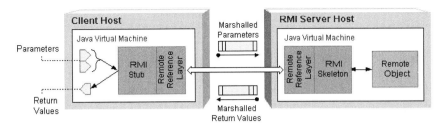

Figure 10-2. *Marshalling parameters and return values.*

method parameters and return values. Figure 10-2 shows the characteristics of object marshalling.

What Is Marshalling?

Marshalling refers to the process of packaging method arguments and return values so that they can be moved across the network. This process involves serialization, which is a way to convert objects so they can be passed over the network. Serializable objects include primitive types, remote Java objects, AWT components, and any other object that implements the serializable interface. Note that, if you declare a Java property as transient, then that property will not be serialized.

Essential RMI Components

The essential RMI components that we will use to create a working RMI application are listed in Table 10-1. The next few sections will show in greater detail how to use these components.

Useful Links

For more information about RMI, you can view the following documentation:

JavaSoft RMI Documentation at:

http://Java.sun.com/products/jdk/1.1/docs/guide/rmi/index.html

Table 10-1.   Essential RMI components.

Component	Function
RMI compiler (rmic)	Generates the stubs and skeletons for the remote server class.
Stubs	A client view of the remote methods.
Skeletons	On the server, connects the stub to the remote server class.
Remote interface	An interface that defines the remote methods that the remote server class will implement in code.
Remote server class	A class that implements the methods defined in the interface file.
Server factory	A program that generates an instance of the remote server class, and registers it with an RMI registry.
RMI registry service	The RMI bootstrap registry program that runs on the server host and registers remote RMI objects by name on the network.

JavaSoft RMI FAQ at:

http://Java.sun.com/products/jdk/1.1/docs/guide/rmi/faq.html

JavaSoft RMI Specification at:

http://Java.sun.com/products/jdk/1.1/docs/guide/rmi/spec/rmiTOC.doc.html

Creating a Multitier Database Application Using RMI

The steps involved in creating a distributed database application are as follows:

1. **Define the remote interfaces.** Create and compile an interface class that extends java.rmi.Remote. This interface defines the methods that the server implements. The client Java program will call these methods as if they were local, when in fact they are remote.

2. **Define the remote classes.** Create and compile a remote server class that extends a RemoteObject such as java.rmi.server.UnicastRemoteObject. This class will implement the interfaces defined in Step 1.

3. **Create stubs and skeletons.** Using the RMI compiler, `rmic`, generate stubs and skeletons for the implementation class you created in Step 2.
4. **Create a server program to generate the remote object.** Create and compile a server program that creates an instance of the remote object you created in Step 2 and then registers the object by name with an RMI registry service.
5. **Start the RMI registry service on the server.** On the server host, start the bootstrap registry service, `rmiregistry`, and start the server program that you created in Step 4.
6. **Create the Java client program.** Create and compile the client Java program that will call the remote methods.

Define the Remote Interfaces

What we are trying to do is run SQL queries using distributed Java objects. To manipulate a remote server object, client code needs to know what it can do with that object. Therefore, an interface is shared between the client and server. It is this interface that exposes the methods of the remote object to the client.

Create the Remote Interface

We create an interface in a file called `JR.java`. To create a remote interface, import the RMI package in your Java code and, if you will use SQL, also import the SQL package. The interface in List. 10-1 declares methods that open and close database connections, execute queries, and retrieve table rows.

In order to expose the remote methods to a client, the interface must extend `java.rmi.Remote`.

Each exposed method must declare `java.rmi.RemoteException` in its `throws` clause, because many things can go wrong when making remote invocations over the network. Calls to remote hosts are inherently less reliable than calls to the local host. For example, the remote host might not be available when you make the remote call.

Note also that, because we are using the SQL package, we also need to declare `java.sql.SQLException` in the `throws` clause of the remote methods.

Try to maintain the design of the remote interfaces. If you are using parameters, try to encapsulate all the related parameters into a single object. If you need to add another parameter, you don't have to change the remote interface, only the parameter class.

Listing 10-1. *Define the remote methods in an interface* (JR.java).

```
import java.rmi.*;
import java.sql.*;

public interface JR extends java.rmi.Remote {

        public int openConnection()
           throws RemoteException,
                SQLException,
                ClassNotFoundException;

        public void closeConnection( int id )
           throws RemoteException,
                SQLException;

        public void performQuery( int id, String searchString )
           throws RemoteException,
                SQLException;

        public String getNextRow( int id )
           throws RemoteException,
                SQLException;
}
```

Compile and Locate the Interface

You compile the interface file using the javac command.

```
javac JR.java
```

This produces a file called JR.class.

For stand-alone Java applications, place the compiled interface on *both* the client host and on the server host.

On both hosts, point the CLASSPATH environment variable to the directory in which you placed the interface. This must be done before starting the client program on the client host and before starting the registry service and server factory on the server host.

For client programs that are Java applets, place the compiled interface into the same directory on the RMI server host in which the applet resides.

Once you've declared and compiled an interface class, your next action is to define the remote server class that implements the remote methods you've declared.

You can place compiled interfaces anywhere on the RMI server. Make sure the CLASSPATH *environment variable used when starting the server program points to the location of these interface classes.*

Define the Remote Classes

This step creates the *remote server class*. The remote server class implements all of the methods defined by the interface we created in Step 1 by creating the actual Java methods to match the interface signatures.

What Does "Remote Server Class" Mean?

This implementation class is a server class because it extends UnicastRemoteObject, *which makes objects remotely accessible. This class inherits the basic technology for communication between the server object and its stubs on the client host, so you don't have to code it.*

Create the Remote Server Class

You can create methods in this class that are not remote. In more complex applications, you can create many interfaces and many remote server classes. This is a design issue; generally, the output of the design phase would be a set of interfaces that have one or more defined as remote.

Because the Java platform handles the marshalling of data and remote invocation, you don't have to code it. Apart from defining the remote nature of the methods, you concentrate on the application functionality you need to code.

In this example, we define the remote server by creating a Java class called JRImpl in a file called JRImpl.java, shown in List. 10-2.

Note that we import the java.rmi.server package into the class.

In order to define the class as containing methods that can be accessed remotely, we define JRImpl as a subclass of UnicastRemoteObject, implementing the interface JR.

Listing 10-2.   Remote server class `JRImpl.java.`

```
import java.rmi.*;
import java.rmi.server.*;
import java.sql.*;

public class JRImpl
        extends UnicastRemoteObject
        implements JR {

//Default constructor
public JRImpl () throws RemoteException { }

        public synchronized int openConnection()
           throws RemoteException,
              SQLException,
           ClassNotFoundException
        {
    . . .
        }

        public void closeConnection( int id )
           throws RemoteException,
              SQLExccption
        {
    . . .
        }

        public void performQuery( int id, String searchString )
           throws RemoteException,
              SQLException
        {
    . . .
        }

        public String getNextRow( int id )
           throws RemoteException,
              SQLException
        {
    . . .
        }
}
```

Why Use `UnicastRemoteObject`*?*

The `UnicastRemoteObject`*, along with other RMI components, takes care of all remote method invocation tasks; you need not take any special action whatsoever, other than to ensure that all remote methods declared in the interface class declare* `java.rmi.RemoteException` *in their respective* `throws` *clauses.*

Compile and Locate the Remote Server Class

Compile the remote server class using `javac`:

```
javac JRImpl.java
```

This produces a file called `JRImpl.class`. You can place compiled remote server classes anywhere on the RMI server host. Make sure the `CLASSPATH` environment variable points to the location of these remote server classes.

Alternatively, place all the supporting classes that you develop for a particular program in the same directory on the RMI server; and point the `java.rmi.server.codebase` property to that directory on the command line when starting the *server factory* (see subsection "Start the Server Factory" later in this chapter).

RMI client and server programs should install a security manager to control the actions of stub and skeleton objects loaded from a network location. For applets, there is a default security manager to ensure that the applet does no harm. For stand-alone applications, there is no default security manager, so you must set one when using RMI.

Remote server objects must already be running on the server host when a service is requested from the client.

Create Stubs and Skeletons

With RMI, client programs and remote objects use proxies, called stubs and skeletons, to handle the necessary networking between them.

You don't need to be concerned in any way with stubs and skeletons other than how to create and locate them.

Stubs and skeletons are Java classes. You place the compiled stub on the client (unless it's an applet, in which case you bundle it with the applet code), and the compiled skeleton on the server. Note that the RMI server host may cooperate as a client for another RMI server host in a highly distributed application. Even so, the steps to follow are the same.

Generate the Stub and Skeleton Classes

You create stubs and skeletons using `rmic` (RMI compiler), which ships with the JDK. Make sure that you have already compiled the remote interface, `JR.java`, and the remote server, `JRImpl.java`, before you generate the stubs and skeletons.

You generate the stub and skeleton for the remote server, `JRImpl.class`, as follows:

```
rmic JRImpl
```

This creates two class files:

```
JRImpl_Stub.class
JRImpl_Skel.class
```

If the compiled class is part of a Java package, give the full package name to `rmic`.

Locate the Stubs and Skeletons

You can place the generated skeletons, `*.Skel`, anywhere on the RMI server. Make sure that the CLASSPATH environment variable used when starting the server program points to the location of the skeleton classes. Typically, you'd place all the supporting classes for the server application in the same directory on the RMI server, and point the CLASSPATH environment variable to that directory when starting the server factory.

For stand-alone Java applications, you need to copy the stub classes to a directory on the client host and point the CLASSPATH environment variable to that directory before starting the client program.

For Java applets, you need to place the stub classes into the same directory on the RMI server host in which the applet resides.

Create a Server Program to Generate the Remote Object

You need to create and compile a server program that creates an instance of the remote object and then registers the object by name with an RMI registry service. When the remote object is registered with the RMI registry service, the clients can access the remote methods in the object.

The server program that we create now is called a *server factory* because it instantiates the remote object.

Creating the Server Factory

For a client program to access a remote object, the client must first have a reference, or *object handle,* to that remote object. To get that reference, the client can invoke a remote method in the server factory running on the RMI server host, which returns a reference to the object that contains the remote methods.

Server programs register remote objects with the *bootstrap registry service.* Once the remote object is registered, server programs can return references to the object.

You register a remote object on the RMI server host by giving a reference to the object (servlet) and some name (rmiExample) to the bootstrap registry. This registration process *binds* the remote object by name to a host (dellcpi) and port (1099). These objects are summarized in the Table 10-2. The JRServer.java is shown in List. 10-3.

The class that contains the remote methods is instantiated in the following line:

```
JRImpl servlet = new JRImpl ();
```

The object is then registered with the RMI registry service:

```
Naming.rebind(
    "//dellcpi.eu.informix.com/rmiExample", servlet );
```

Table 10-2.   Important objects in JRServer.java.

Object	Description
servlet	An instance of the class that implements the remote methods the client will invoke.
Naming.rebind	Naming provides the default registry service. The rebind method adds an object to the RMI registry.
//dellcpi:1099	Host and port on which the RMI registry runs.
rmiExample	A label for the registered object; all clients can use the label.

This is all you need to do to set up the remote factory to instantiate remote objects; RMI does everything else.

Locating the Server Factory

You can place the compiled server factory class anywhere on the RMI server host, but make sure that the CLASSPATH environment variable used when starting the server factory points to the location of this server factory class.

If your Java client is an applet, then the server factory must be running before the applet starts.

Listing 10-3. *The server factory,* `JRServer.java`, *which creates and registers objects with the RMI registry.*

```
import java.rmi.*;
import java.rmi.registry.*;
import java.net.*;

public class JRServer {
  public static void main( String args[] ) {

    String hostName   = null;
    String hostIP     = null;
    try {
        java.net.InetAddress hostInet =
                       java.net.InetAddress.getLocalHost();
      hostName = hostInet.getHostName();
      hostIP   = hostInet.getHostAddress();
      System.out.println(
              "Starting RemoteSQL on " + hostName +
              " ["+hostIP+"]");
      }
      catch (java.net.UnknownHostException e) {
        System.err.println("JRServer.main exception: "
                       + e.getMessage());
        e.printStackTrace();
      }
      if ( System.getSecurityManager() == null ) {
        System.setSecurityManager( new RMISecurityManager() );
      }
```

Listing 10-3. (continued)

```
try {
    JRImpl servlet = new JRImpl ();

            System.out.println( "Binding to the registry" );
    Naming.rebind(
       "//dellcpi.eu.informix.com/rmiExample", servlet );
    System.out.println( "...RemoteSQL is bound and ready." );
    }
catch ( Exception e ) {
        System.err.println("JRServer.main exception: "
                           + e.getMessage());
        e.printStackTrace();
    }
  }
}
```

Start the RMI Registry Service on the Server

The RMI bootstrap registry program runs on the server host and registers remote RMI objects by name on the network. Once registered,
remote objects are in effect exported and can be accessed by RMI
clients.

To access a remote object, a client program first gets a reference
to the object by using the Naming class to look up the object using
its registered name. The client program specifies the name as an
rmi: URL. The registry service then returns an instance of the remote
interface for the remote object—the object's *stub.*

Starting the Registry Naming Service on the RMI Server

Set your environment to point to the location of your Java installation. On UNIX, for example:

```
setenv JAVA_HOME /usr/local/java/jdk1.1.7
setenv PATH $JAVA_HOME/bin:$PATH
```

The Windows equivalent would be

```
set JAVA_HOME=D:\java\jdk1.1.7
set PATH=%JAVA_HOME%\bin;%PATH%
```

You can then start the registry naming service, `rmiregistry`. You start this program on UNIX as follows:

```
unsetenv CLASSPATH
rmiregistry &
```

On Windows:

```
unset CLASSPATH
start rmiregistry
```

In the Windows example, if `unset` doesn't work on your system, use `set CLASSPATH=`.

Before starting the registry, CLASSPATH *should be* unset*; at least, it should not be pointing to any classes. When the* rmiregistry *program starts, if it can find your stub classes, it won't remember that these stubs can be loaded from your server's codebase.*

The registry runs on port 1099 by default. To start the registry on a different port, specify the port number on the command line. For example, start rmiregistry 1090*. The RMI bootstrap registry must remain running so that the registry's naming service is always available.*

Start the Server Factory

Set CLASSPATH as appropriate and start the server program that you created in Step 4, which creates an object that implements the methods accessed remotely by the client. You can start the server program as follows:

```
java JRServer
```

Create the Java Client Program

Client programs use remote objects that have been exported by remote server programs. In order to do this, the client program must look up the remote object in the remote RMI registry. When the remote object is located, the stub of the remote object is sent to the client. The client invokes the methods in this stub as if the stub were the actual remote object in the local Java Virtual Machine. The stub communicates with the remote skeleton associated with that stub, and the skeleton invokes the method that the remote client has requested.

Obtaining a Reference to the Remote Object

The client uses the `Naming.lookup` method to obtain a reference to the remote object. The returned value is actually a reference to a stub object.

```
JR servlet = (JR)Naming.lookup( registryName );
```

The `registryName` variable should define the RMI server host and port that the RMI registry runs on, and it should also state the name of the object.

For example, the applet in List. 10-4 is downloaded from `//dellcpi.eu.informix.com`. The RMI registry on that host is running on the default port, 1099. The required `JRImpl` object is labeled `rmiExample`. Therefore, the URL for the `lookup` method is:

```
//dellcpi.eu.informix.com/rmiExample
```

If the RMI server was started on a different port (`rmiregistry 1090`), then the URL would be:

```
//dellcpi.eu.informix.com:1090/rmiExample
```

Implementing an RMI Security Manager on the Client

Because the Java client will be downloading an untrusted stub object, implement the `RMISecurityManager` object in the client code:

```
System.setSecurityManager( new RMISecurityManager() );
```

Listing 10-4 shows the `init()` method of a Java applet that uses RMI to connect to the remote instance of the `JR` class that is stored in the RMI registry.

Listing 10-4. *The* `TestApplet.java` *client applet.*

```
import java.rmi.*;
import java.awt.*;
import java.awt.event.*;
import java.applet.Applet;

public class TestApplet extends Applet
        implements ActionListener {

        // install security manager
        public void init() {
            if (System.getSecurityManager() == null) {
            System.setSecurityManager(
                    new RMISecurityManager() );
            }

            //get a reference to the remote object
            String registryName;
            try {
                // Get the name of the host machine from where this
                // applet was loaded. The remote object and its
            // interface resides on that host.
                    rcgistryName = "//" +
                getCodeBase().getHost() +
                    "/";

                // Append the predetermined name of the remote
                // object that has been bound to the registry
                // on the server host
                    registryName += "rmiExample";

                // Get a reference to the remote object.
        JR servlet = (JR)Naming.lookup( registryName );
            }
            catch ( Exception e ) {
                showStatus( "Cannot connect to RMI registry." );
            return;
            }

            // invoke the remote methods
            try {
```

Listing 10-4. *(continued)*

```
        connectionId = servlet.openConnection();
    }
    catch (RemoteException e) {
        showStatus("Failed to Open Connection");
    }
}
}
```

Implementing RMI in Applets

Because of applet security restrictions, untrusted applets can make network connections only to the host from which they were loaded. This means that all server objects must reside on the same machine that hosts the web page. These objects include

- the HTML web page that contains the APPLET tag,
- the applet class,
- the compiled stubs,
- the compiled skeletons,
- the compiled server classes and objects,
- the RMI bootstrap registry.

For applets, compiled stubs are bundled with the applet code. You need to place the stub classes into the same directory on the RMI server host in which the applet resides. In addition, place the compiled interfaces (e.g., JR.class) into the same directory.

The remote object that an applet can reference is not prevented from connecting to other machines and objects on the network. For example, the remote object on machine 1 *can implement a method to invoke another remote method in an object on another machine,* machine 2. *If an applet required service from a remote object on* machine 2, *it would call the remote method on* machine 1 *to manage this interface.*

The RMI client and server programs should install a security manager to control the actions of stub and skeleton objects loaded from a network location. For applets, there is a default security manager to ensure that the applet does no harm. For stand-alone applications, there is no default security manager, so you must set one when using RMI.

Registry and server objects must be running before the applet starts.

A Working RMI Applet Example

Once you have the RMI registry running and the server factory has instantiated and registered the remote object, you can invoke the client application.

Listing 10-4 contained the `init()` method of a Java applet that attempted to open a JDBC connection to a database through a remote object. Listing 10-4 is a good summary of the essentials of establishing a connection to a remote object.

This section lists a fully working applet that calls methods in the remote object (`JRImpl.java`) to open a database connection and execute SQL commands entered by the user at the browser.

To run this example, make sure that you follow all the steps in the previous section so that you have a registered instance of the `JRImpl` class in the RMI registry.

To run RMI-based applets, the viewer or browser used to run the applet must support the RMI features of Java 1.1. Browsers not supporting these features may crash.

This section lists the following code:

• `RemoteSQLApplet.java`, which is the applet that requests a remote connection from the browser
• `JR.html`, which contains the `APPLET` tag to download and instantiate the applet.

The `RemoteSQLApplet` Class

This Java class creates and displays a form in the browser so that the user can submit `SELECT` queries to the database and display the results. Listing 10-5 shows the Java source code.

Listing 10-5. *Java source code for* RemoteSQLApplet.java.

```java
import java.awt.*;
import java.awt.event.*;
import java.applet.Applet;
import java.rmi.*;
import java.rmi.registry.*;


public class RemoteSQLApplet
        extends Applet
   implements ActionListener {

   Panel      north, center;
   TextField  searchCriteria;
   Button     searchButton, clearButton;
   List       searchResults;
   extArea    samples;

   int        connectionId;
   JR         servlet;

   //Initializes the applet, displays a GUI
   // for entering SQL queries, and opens a
   // connection to the remote object.
   public void init() {
       String    registryName;

       // Build the applet display.
       setLayout( new BorderLayout() );

       north = new Panel();
       north.setLayout( new FlowLayout() );
       north.add( new Label( "Enter SELECT statement:" ) );
       searchCriteria = new TextField( 40 );
       north.add( searchCriteria );
       searchButton = new Button( "Query" );
       searchButton.addActionListener( this );
       north.add( searchButton );

       clearButton = new Button( "Clear" );
       clearButton.addActionListener( this );
       north.add( clearButton );
       add( "North", north );
```

Listing 10-5. *(continued)*

```
        searchResults = new List( 10, true );
        add( "Center", searchResults );

        Panel notes = new Panel();
        notes.setLayout( new BorderLayout() );
        samples = new TextArea( "", 4,60,
                TextArea.SCROLLBARS_BOTH );
        samples.setFont( new Font( "TimesRoman",
                Font.BOLD, 10 ) );
        samples.setBackground( Color.darkGray );
        samples.setForeground( Color.white );
        samples.setText("");
        notes.add( "North", samples );

        Panel messages = new Panel();
        messages.setFont( new Font( "SansSerif",
                Font.BOLD + Font.ITALIC, 12 ) );
        messages.setBackground( Color.white );
        messages.setForeground( Color.black );
        messages.add(
           new Label( "Check your browser status bar" +
                       " for any SQL messages.", Label.CENTER ) );
        notes.add( "South", messages );

        add( "South", notes );

        validate();
        setVisible( true );

        try {
            // install security manager
                if (System.getSecurityManager() == null) {
                    System.setSecurityManager(
                            new RMISecurityManager() );
            }

            searchResults.addItem("RemoteSQLApplet:init: Preparing
for registry lookup..." );
        registryName = "//" + getCodeBase().getHost() + "/";
        registryName += "rmiExample";
```

Listing 10-5.   (continued)

```
          searchResults.addItem("RemoteSQLApplet:init: Looking up
                                 '"+registryName+"'..." );

      servlet = (JR)Naming.lookup( registryName );
      if ( servlet == null ) {
        searchResults.addItem(
"RemoteSQLApplet:init:Naming.lookup: Lookup failed. Servlet is null."
);
          return;
      }
          searchResults.addItem(
"RemoteSQLApplet:init: Lookup successful..." );
        }
    catch ( Exception e ) {
      showStatus( "Cannot CONNECT to RMI registry
                  for 'RemoteSQL'" );
      e.printStackTrace();
      return;
    }

    try {

      // Open a connection to the remote object.
      // This call causes the remote server
      // to load the JDBC driver on the server host and to
      // use that driver to establish
      //a JDBC connection to the "stores7" database.

          searchResults.addItem(
"RemoteSQLApplet:init: Starting OPEN db connection task..." );
      connectionId = servlet.openConnection();

          searchResults.addItem(
"RemoteSQLApplet:init: Finished OPEN db connection task..." );
      if ( connectionId == -1 ) {
                  searchResults.addItem(
"RemoteSQLApplet:init: Error during OPEN db connection task..." );
                  searchResults.addItem(
"-1: Cannot OPEN DATABASE connection." );
        }
```

Listing 10-5.   (continued)

```
        }
      catch (Exception ex) {
                    searchResults.addItem(
"RemoteSQLApplet:init: Exception during OPEN db connection task..."
);
                    searchResults.addItem(
"Exception: Cannot OPEN DATABASE connection." );
                    ex.printStackTrace();
        }
  }


  // Closes the connection to the remote object.
  // This call causes the remote server to close all
  // server host and database resources that are associated
  // with the JDBC connection. For example, all cursors,
  // result sets, statement objects, and connection objects
  // are freed.

  public void finalize() {
    try {
          servlet.closeConnection( connectionId );
    }
    catch (Exception ex) {}

    super.destroy();
  }


  // Handles the two action events belonging to this applet:
  // Query button and Clear button clicks.

  public void actionPerformed( ActionEvent e ) {
    if ( e.getActionCommand().equals( "Query" ) ) {
    try {
        showStatus( "" );
        performQuery();
      }
      catch (Exception ex) {
            showStatus( ex.toString() + ": Cannot issue Query");
      }
    }
    else {
```

Listing 10-5. *(continued)*

```
      showStatus( "" );
      clearListBox();
   }
   return;
}


public void clearListBox() {
 searchResults.removeAll();
}

// Passes the SQL string that was entered to the
// remote object for execution and retrieves the result set
// row by row from the remote object, displaying
// each row as it's retrieved.

public void performQuery() throws Exception {
    String searchString;
    String result;

    clearListBox();
    searchString = searchCriteria.getText();

    // Execute the query.
    servlet.performQuery( connectionId, searchString );

    // Get and display the result set.
    result = servlet.getNextRow( connectionId );
    if ( result == null ) {
            showStatus( "No rows found using specified
                         search criteria." );
            return;
    }

    while ( result != null ) {
            searchResults.addItem( result );
            result = servlet.getNextRow( connectionId );
    }
  }
}
```

Using `RemoteSQLApplet` in the Browser

Listing 10-6 shows the HTML page, `JR.html`, that references the applet.

Figure 10-3 shows the `RemoteSQLApplet` class instantiated and displayed by the browser. When the applet attempts to open a remote connection to the database, the remote object writes a set of confirmatory messages to the console, which are shown in List. 10-7. The applet also confirms it's own processing state by writing to the List object, which is displayed in the applet window.

Listing 10-7 shows the output from the server factory, `JRServer`, from starting up the factory using `java JRServer`, connecting to

---

Listing 10-6. *The* `JR.html` *page.*

```
<HTML>
<APPLET CODE="RemoteSQLApplet" WIDTH=600 HEIGHT=300></APPLET>
</HTML>
```

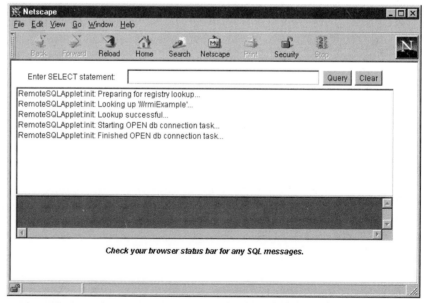

Figure 10-3. *Starting* `RemoteSQLApplet` *in the browser.*

Listing 10-7. **Output from invoking** JRServer *from command line.*

```
Binding to the registry
...RemoteSQL is bound and ready.
JRImpl:openConnection: Starting...
JRImpl:openConnection: Creating connection object...
JRImpl:openConnection: Opening connection to DATABASE...
JRConn:openConnection:  Loading driver...
JRConn:openConnection:urlConnection: jdbc:informix-sqli://
dellcpi:1526/stores7:INFORMIXSERVER=ol_dellcpi;user=
informix;password=informix;
JRConn:openConnection:getConnection: Making connection...
JRImpl:openConnection: Returning connection Id...
JRConn:performQuery:stmt.executeQuery().
```

the database on behalf of the applet running in the client browser, and running an SQL query when requested from the client.

Figure 10-4 shows the browser output when the user enters a query string and clicks the Query button.

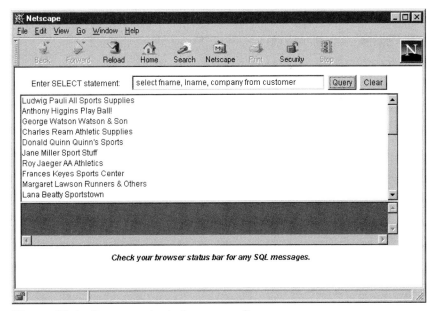

Figure 10-4. *Browser output of query results.*

Connecting to the Database from the RMI Server Host

We can use JDBC to connect to the Informix database from the remote object. This database can reside on the RMI server host, or it may be located on another visible host in the network.

Because we are not connecting to the database from the applet, we are not subject to the restrictions imposed on applets. The applet connects to the remote object on the RMI server that implements the remote methods it requires.

Listing 10-8 shows the `JRImpl` class. The remote object, `JRImpl`, creates an instance of the `JRConn` class for every connection established on behalf of a client. It is the `JRConn` class that implements the JDBC API calls. The remote methods in `JRImpl` are wrappers for calls to the `JRConn` methods. Multiple clients will all connect to the same `JRImpl` object. Collisions are avoided when opening connections by using the `synchronized` keyword as follows:

```
public synchronized int openConnection()
```

Why Use synchronized?

When a synchronised method is called, an object lock is taken at the start of the method. This prevents other objects from invoking the method while the lock is taken. When the method is exited, the lock is released. Because multiple remote client connections wait in turn to obtain object locks, each will occupy a different slot in the connection pool.

Listing 10-8. The `JRImpl.java` class.

```
public class JRImpl
        extends UnicastRemoteObject implements JR {

        // Create a table that can hold
        // connection (JRConn) objects.
        Private JRConn jrc [] = new JRConn [100];

        public JRImpl () throws RemoteException {
        super();
        }
```

Listing 10-8. (continued)

```
        // Implement each of the remote methods
        // specified in the remote interface, JR
        public synchronized int openConnection()
     throws RemoteException,
          SQLException,
          ClassNotFoundException {

          int connectionId;
          System.out.println(
             "JRImpl:openConnection: Starting...");

     // Loop through connection table
     // until an empty slot is found.
     for ( connectionId = 0; connectionId < jrc.length;
                         connectionId++ ) {
          if ( jrc [connectionId] == null )
          break;
        }

     // If no empty slots found, generate an error.
     if ( connectionId >= jrc.length ) {
          System.out.println(
        "WARNING: No more connection objects available"
             + " for RemoteSQL example." );
          return -1;
        }

     // Create a connection for the new process
     // and run it
     System.out.println(
"JRImpl:openConnection: Creating connection object...");
     jrc [connectionId] = new JRConn();

     System.out.println(
"JRImpl:openConnection: Opening connection to DATABASE...");
     jrc [connectionId].openConnection();

     // Return the connection identifier.
     System.out.println(
"JRImpl:openConnection: Returning connection Id...");
```

Listing 10-8. *(continued)*

```
        return connectionId;
      }// end openConnection

  // Executes the SQL query by passing the string
  // on to the connection object for
  // actual execution.
  Public void performQuery( int id,
                            String searchString )
     throws RemoteException,
        SQLException {
          jrc[id].performQuery( searchString );
  }

  // Fetches the next row from the current query result.
     Public String getNextRow( int id )
     throws RemoteException,
        SQLException  {
     return jrc[id].getNextRow();
     }

  // Closes the current database connection
     public void closeConnection( int id )
     throws RemoteException,
        SQLException {
     jrc[id].closeConnection();
     jrc[id] = null;
  }
}
```

The JRImpl object instantiates a JRConn object for every remote client, then slots the object into the array of JRConn objects, which has a limit of 100 remote client connections. In effect, the JRImpl class implements a basic *connection pool,* which is a way of managing multiple connections to one or more data sources. A connection ID is returned to the remote client to identify the database connection to the client. The remote methods implemented in JRImpl map down onto JRConn method calls, which implement the JDBC interface.

Parameterising Connection Information

We may want to specify a different remote host to access a different set of services. In addition, we may want to connect to one or more remote objects—multiple databases, for example. An Informix server can connect to other Informix servers, but we may want to use the JDBC/ODBC Bridge or another JDBC driver to connect to a non-Informix database. This is especially true if the database is a non-Informix legacy database we are in the process of web enabling to participate in a larger application framework.

Parameterising Client Applets Dynamically

If you are using an applet to connect to a remote service, you can use the PARAM attribute of the APPLET tag to nominate the remote host and object name that you use in the Naming.lookup() method call.

In a larger treatment of a distributed database application, you may want your secure users to connect to a different database or a different set of remote objects. In this case, you would implement a secure interface, such as NSAPI authentication, with an NSAPI-bound URL prefix and parameterize the APPLET tag accordingly to nominate the appropriate remote objects.

You can use an AppPage to parameterize the parameter values passed into an applet. For simplicity, assume that you have a secure URL prefix called /catalog. Your users are registered in the webusers table in the database. Each user has a nominated remote interface to one or more remote Informix databases.

```
<APPLET CODE=catalog.class WIDTH=400 HEIGHT=500>
<PARAM NAME=user
    VALUE="<?MIVAR>$REMOTE_USER<?/MIVAR>">
<?MISQL SQL="select host, db1, db2 from rmiUsers">
  <PARAM NAME=remoteHost VALUE="$1">
  <PARAM NAME=remoteObject1 VALUE="$2">
  <PARAM NAME=remoteObject2 VALUE="$3">
<?/MISQL>
</APPLET>
```

Summary

In this chapter, we have learned how to create and deploy a distributed, multitier Java application that connects to a remote database using JDBC, and we have seen how easy it is to do this using RMI. The concept of a connection pool was introduced, and we also learned how to hide away the JDBC detail from the client and server objects by implementing a database handler.

The example presented in this chapter is a clear and simple multitiered, distributed-component application that you can use to scale up to industrial-strength, distributed Java applications.

A Simple Java
SQL Editor

In this chapter:

- What is the Java SQL Editor?
- Java SQL Editor functionality
- Java SQL Editor component summary
- The Java SQL Editor design
- Invoking the Java SQL Editor
- Establishing a database connection
- Listing tables and table information
- Executing queries and displaying results
- How query and display works
- How the Java SQL Editor User Interface works
- Handling SQL Editor events
- Understanding the Protocol Handler
- Managing the JDBC Layer

This chapter describes a simple SQL editor, written in Java, which uses JDBC to connect to the database and run SQL queries. The Java SQL Editor is a Java application that provides an SQL interface to any database for which there is a JDBC or ODBC driver, and it provides a useful basic GUI (graphical user interface) for that database. The essential aim of this chapter is to use a simple application to illustrate and pull together some of the key themes from the preceding chapters on Java. The Java SQL Editor is provided on the accompanying CD with the entire Java source files so that you can extend it any way you want. Because the Editor aims to provide a general browsing interface for a database, you will find the approach to writing the code useful, and the application can be used as a working tutorial that you can play with.

What Is the Java SQL Editor?

The Java SQL Editor is a simple Java application that provides an SQL interface to any database for which there is a JDBC or ODBC driver. If you wish to use a Type 2 driver, than you will need the appropriate vendor client libraries installed. The Editor allows you to submit SQL queries, view the results, look up the tables in a database, and view the column information for a table. The Editor uses Java 1.1 AWT classes to create the look and feel of the application, and it does not rely on third-party class libraries to render the user interface.

tip

If you only have access to an ODBC driver for your data source, you can use the JDBC/ODBC Bridge with the Java SQL Editor to access your data source. The JDBC/ODBC Bridge driver is shipped with the JavaSoft JDK.

Why Is this Example Useful?

The Java SQL Editor is an important example for a variety of reasons.
    You can use the source code to understand how to employ the JDBC API, implement a basic protocol handler, and use basic and advanced AWT features, as well as a host of other Java-language-related features. You can extend the core software to make it do what you want; this includes managing components in an RMI context.
    The Editor shows how to use the Java AWT package to create a GUI form using tab panels and other form fields. You will therefore understand how to create an advanced AWT interface yourself

The JDBC methods are used to submit queries and format the results. You will learn how to use JDBC methods to accept any type of query, and how to use the Java AWT classes and the Java language to format an arbitrarily complex set of results.

Java SQL Editor Functionality

The available functionality is summarized in the next few sections.

Enter and Submit SQL to the Database Server

- Enter SQL as free-format text and submit the SQL for execution.
- Optionally, specify the number of rows to display from the result set.
- Display the SQL results as a tabular display in a separate window.

The user can enter an SQL query into a textbox, which is then sent to the database server for execution. The query can be any SQL that the database server supports (e.g., SELECT, INSERT, UPDATE, DELETE, EXECUTE PROCEDURE).

The user can limit the number of rows displayed from a query by specifying a number in a row count textbox. This number is the number of rows to display.

Queries that are not SELECT statements (e.g., UPDATE, INSERT) will return an update count, and a confirmatory message is appended to the panel display

List Database Metadata

- List the available databases.
- List the tables in a database.
- List the catalogs and schemas in a database.
- List the columns, column datatypes, and other column metadata from a selected table.

JDBC drivers can differ in their implementation of some of the metadata API methods. However, it is useful to query the objects in a database. For example, we may want to list the columns in one or more tables before we query them.

Specify and Query JDBC Connectivity

- Connect and disconnect to a data source using a JDBC driver or JDBC/ODBC Bridge driver, and a JDBC URL.
- Show the JDBC driver information.

The user can select the JDBC driver and JDBC URL to connect with. The default driver is the JDBC/ODBC Bridge supplied in JDK 1.1, to be used with the `jdbc:odbc` protocol. However, any valid driver can be entered, and the database URL can target a remote database server.

Once connected to a data source, the user can display important metadata information about the JDBC driver.

Java SQL Editor Component Summary

The Java components of the SQL Editor consist of a set of interfaces and classes. Each interface enforces a *design thread* that all classes implementing that interface must follow. For example, all classes that implement the `DBProtocol` interface are able to create protocol instructions that bind to the protocol design.

Table 11-1 lists the interfaces. Table 11-2 lists the classes.

Table 11-1.   Interfaces defined for the SQL Editor.

Interfaces	Comments
DBProtocol	Specifies protocol operators and operand offsets. Classes that implement this interface will share protocol constants.
DBConstants	Specifies application constants. Classes that implement this interface will share application-wide constants.
DBHandle	Allows one component to refer to another. Classes that implement this interface will share a reference to an object called a database handler.
LogComponent	Allows one component to write to another. A class that implements this method must supply the code to write to a log device.

Table 11-2. *Classes defined for the SQL Editor.*

Classes	Interfaces	Comments
DataBase	DBConstants DBProtocol	Handles the JDBC interface, including connection and JDBC API.
DataBrowser	DBProtocol DBHandle DBConstants	This is the main user interface client. It manages an interface to the protocol client to ask the server to execute database requests.
ProtocolClient	DBProtocol	Packages a protocol instruction and dispatches it to the protocol server.
ProtocolServer	DBProtocol	Interprets a protocol instruction and sends a message to the DataBase object to execute the instruction operand.
ProtocolData	DBProtocol	Creates and stores a protocol instruction.
LogDevice	LogComponent	Implements the write to a log device provided by the DataBrowser. For this example, the log device is the screen panel where query results are displayed.

The Java SQL Editor Design

The SQL Editor has the following design properties.

- separation of the *presentation* layer from the *database* layer,
- use of interfaces to support component integration,
- protocol handling with the use of a protocol client and server,
- tight coupling of component to event, using *anonymous* classes,
- strict use of core Java 1.1 AWT classes, including a card layout for a tab panel.

Separation of Presentation Layer from Database Layer

The user interface classes, which capture query requests and display output (and can be called *consumers*), are separate from the database classes, which service the requests (and can be called *producers*).

The user interface communicates a service request to the database class via the protocol handler. The database class performs the requested service and obtains a handle to two items; a results component to display query results, and a log device to contain standard error output. For the purposes of the example, the log device is the panel that displays query results. Therefore, the user interface class implements the `LogDevice` interface. Cooperating objects will invoke methods whose signatures are defined in the `LogDevice` interface that, for this example, is implemented in the user interface.

Use of Interfaces to Support Component Integration

A small number of interfaces are used to ensure that a design thread is followed in each relevant component. The interfaces perform two functions:

- specification of constant values so that interacting components can share them (interfaces `DBConstants` and `DBProtocol`)
- allowing method signatures to be specified so that one component can invoke a method whose detail is completed by another component (interface `LogComponent`)

Protocol Handling Using Protocol Client and Server Classes

Most multitier architectures implement some form of protocol handling between the clients and the servers, however informal.

On a protocol-based platform, requests are formalized into a protocol that consists of an instruction with data, or, more formally, an *operator* with *operands*. Client components that interact with a service on a remote host need to understand how to package the instructions, or protocol data, into a suitable form.

The Java SQL Editor uses a *protocol client* class to package a protocol instruction into a *protocol data* class, which forwards the protocol instruction to the *protocol server* class for interpretation—a call to a database method to execute a JDBC method call. The added value of this superficial complexity is that the protocol client should be able to manage the translation of an application service request into a more detailed implementation request.

The protocol client class contains a method to package operand values and send a protocol instruction to the protocol server. The protocol data object is a *singleton* object; that is, one instance of the class is created regardless how many times the constructor is called.

The protocol client and protocol server classes are never instantiated; the relevant variables and methods are declared as static, so they are referenced at class level.

 A distributed multitier treatment of the protocol handling could use RMI. In an RMI treatment, the protocol server request is an RMI call.

Tight Coupling of Component to Event using Anonymous Classes

Java 1.1 introduced both event delegation and anonymous classes.

Event delegation allows events generated from one component (e.g., a button) to be handled by another component.

Anonymous classes allow the event-handling code to be specified when registering the event listener for that component and obviate the need to define and instantiate another class. This reduces design and build complexity. The *anonymous* tag describes a class that has no name; as far as the builder is concerned, it is an inline event-handling code. When the code is compiled, a class file is generated that contains the event-handling code, and the class is named after the enclosing class, with a "$" character and a class number suffixed to it.

Strict Use of Core Java 1.1 AWT Classes

Although many widget libraries exist that support grid and tree controls, the SQL Editor does not use any; instead, it uses the core AWT components and layout managers. This reduces some of the complexity in the user interface and simplifies the design. You can learn how to put basic forms together from this example.

 You can unhook the existing user interface and supply your own. For example, you may want to use a grid control to display the `ResultSet`*. You can retain the existing interface to the database to provide your new interface with the service it requires.*

Good use is made of the `CardLayout` component, which implements tab-like functionality. Here, the user clicks a button (Query, Tables, Connect) and a different card, or *tab*, is displayed. The contents of the tab persist between displays so that, for example, the list of tables is still displayed when entering and returning from the Query tab.

The following sections show you how to use the Java SQL Editor.

Invoking the Java SQL Editor

You invoke the application from the command line as follows:

```
java DataBrowser
```

The main application window is displayed as shown in Fig. 11-1.

The control panel is split into four CardLayout panels, each with its own set of functions. The CardLayout is designed to emulate tab paneling, and from this point on in this chapter, the term *tab* is synonymous with a *panel* in a CardLayout.

The application is displayed with the default Connect tab, and the default JDBC driver is the JDBC/ODBC bridge.

The top window is use to display query results and error messages. The bottom half of the application window is a control panel used to create SQL statements and administer the connection to the database.

Table 11-3 lists the main functions of each control panel tab

Table 11-4 lists the functions of the remaining control panel buttons, which map onto simple actions.

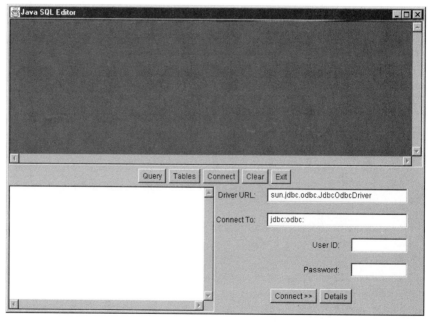

Figure 11-1. *Java SQL Editor application window.*

| Table 11-3. | Control panel tab functions. |

Tab	Function
Query	Executes SQL queries.
Tables	Lists the databases, tables, views, and other entities that are visible to the connected database server. You can interrogate the properties of these items.
Connect	Connects to a database server and lists the JDBC driver details.

| Table 11-4. | Control panel actions. |

Button	Function
Clear	Clears the top display.
Exit	Exits the application

Establishing a Database Connection

You are not restricted to using the Informix Type 4 JDBC Driver. You can use the JDBC/ODBC Bridge to connect to an ODBC data source, or you can use another type of JDBC driver.

Using the JDBC/ODBC Bridge

For example, assume you have an ODBC data source configured to interface with an MS-Access database called `AdvWorks`. Using the Connect tab:

- set Driver URL to `sun.jdbc.odbc.JdbcOdbcDriver` (this is displayed by default when the application starts up),
- set Connect To to `jdbc:odbc:AdvWorks`,
- set User ID to a valid user account that can access the database, if required,
- set Password to the password for that account, if required,
- click Connect.

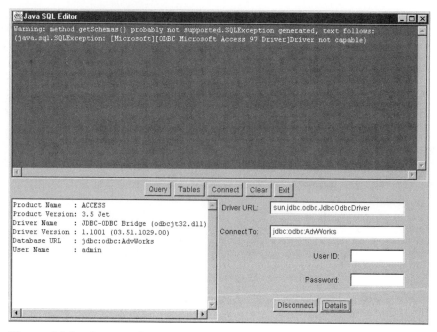

Figure 11-2. *Connected to an ODBC data source.*

The left-hand textbox will display connection status messages. The top window will display any connection warnings and errors. The label of the Connect button will be changed to show "Disconnect."

If you click the Details button, the essential metadata for the current registered driver will be displayed.

Figure 11-2 shows the screen after the steps above have been followed.

Using the Informix Type 4 JDBC Driver

The procedure doesn't change, but the connection values do. The following values assume that you are connecting to the `stores7` database on the `dellcpi` machine, with the server listening on port 1526.

- Set Driver URL to `com.informix.jdbc.IfxDriver`.
- Set Connect To to `jdbc:informix-sqli://dellcpi:1526/stores7:informixserver=ol_dellcpi`.
- Set User ID to a valid user account that can access the database, if required.

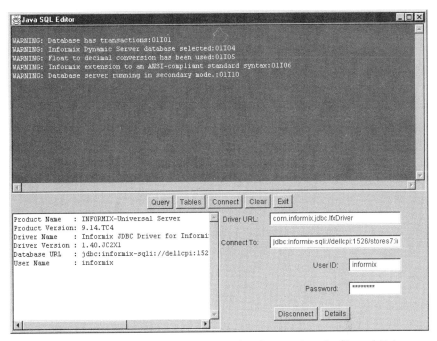

Figure 11-3. Connecting to an Informix database using the Type 4 Driver.

- Set Password to the password for that account, if required.
- Click Connect.

Click Details to see the essential JDBC driver metadata. The final screen looks like Fig. 11-3.

The top window contains the SQL warnings encountered when connecting.

You can register more than one JDBC driver in a program to connect to multiple databases. For example, you can register a Type 4 Driver and the JDBC/ODBC Bridge driver. You can extend the Java SQL Editor to implement this functionality; currently, it works with only one driver.

Listing Tables and Table Information

You select the database you want to connect to in the JDBC URL. You can list the different types of object in the database—such as tables, synonyms, and views—from the Tables tab.

The Tables tab contains four lists that allow you to filter the different types of entities in the database. Each list is populated by a JDBC metadata method call. Different JDBC drivers will interpret the metadata calls in their own way. For example, the Informix Type 4 Driver will display in the Schemas list the owners of tables within the selected database; it will display all the databases managed by the Informix Dynamic Server you are connected to in the Catalogs list. Other drivers may yield different lists depending on the implementation of the JDBC driver. The remainder of this section assumes that you are using the Informix Type 4 Driver.

Listing the Column Information for a Table or View

In the Table Types list box, select either `TABLE` or `VIEW` and click Select. The right-hand list will populate with a list of tables or views in that database. To view the column information for a particular table, click a table in the right-hand list. Figure 11-4 shows the result of selecting the `orders` table.

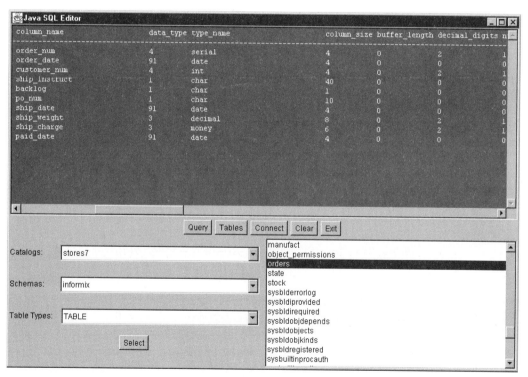

Figure 11-4. Column information for the `orders` table.

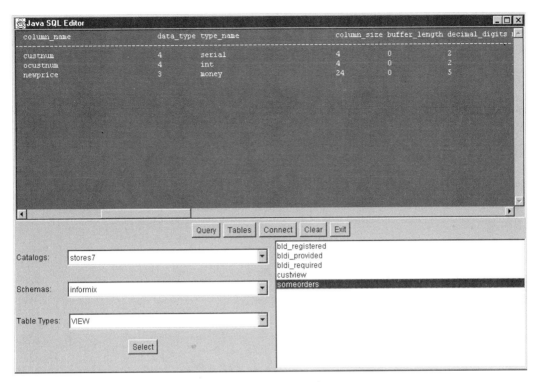

Figure 11-5. *Column metadata for the* `someorders` *view.*

Figure 11-5 shows the results of selecting `VIEW` from the Table Types list, and selecting the `someorders` view. The projected columns for the view are displayed in the top window.

Executing Queries and Displaying Results

The Query tab allows you to submit any SQL commands that your target data source supports. The top window displays the results of the SQL statement.

Generally, you will use the Tables tab to look up table or view columns, and then put an SQL query together in the Query tab.

The Query tab has three features of interest.

- Go button. This button submits the SQL query to the database server.

- Clear button. This button clears the text area where you type SQL commands
- Row Count. This textbox allows you to specify the number of rows to display from the `ResultSet`, starting with the first.

The contents of each tab panel are retained between tabs, so you can move tab panels around without losing any information you have obtained.

Executing Stored Procedures

You can create and execute stored procedures from the Query tab. If the stored procedure returns more than one result, then the `ResultSet` from the query will display each return value as a separate column. For example, assume that you have created a stored procedure as follows:

```
create procedure returnTwo()
returning char(5), char(12);
    return "Hello", " Java World";
end procedure;
```

Then, type in `execute procedure returnTwo()` in the Query tab and click the Go button. The top window should display output similar to the following:

```
(expression) (expression)
--------------------
Hello       Java World
```

Selecting and Displaying HTML Pages

You can display AppPage source and the exploded versions of AppPages in the top panel.

Figure 11-6 shows the query sent to the database server, and the results are shown in the top window. Note that the AppPage displayed has not been exploded.

Figure 11-7 shows the results of submitting a query to explode the AppPage. The top window displays the exploded AppPage returned in the JDBC `ResultSet`.

Figure 11-8 shows the browser display of the exploded AppPage when requested using HTTP.

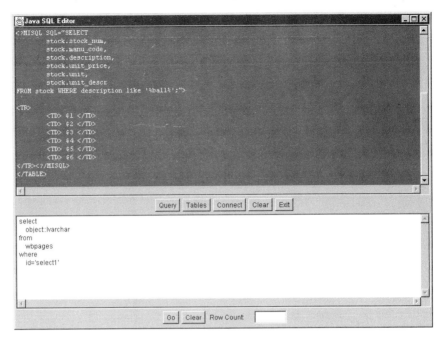

Figure 11-6. *Select and display AppPage source.*

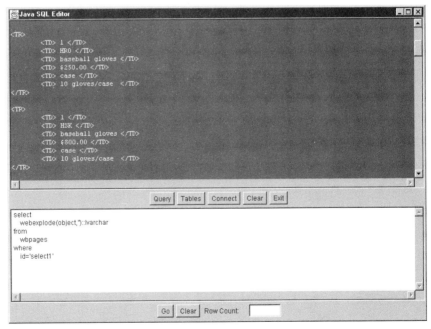

Figure 11-7. *Select an AppPage for* `webexplode` *and display the results.*

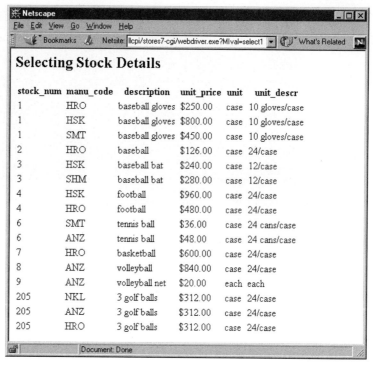

Figure 11-8. Selecting the AppPage via HTTP in the browser.

Note that we *cast* the HTML object column to LVARCHAR using the ":: " operator so that we can extract and display printable text from the ResultSet:

```
select object::lvarchar from wbpages
where id='select1'
```

An example that is simpler to visualize in its entirety is the "HelloWorld" example. Figure 11-9 shows the AppPage source, and Fig. 11-10 shows the exploded AppPage. The display of both is achieved by extracting a String object from the ResultSet of the query.

You can select an alias name for a column (e.g., select fname as FirstName from customer*), and the column heading will be displayed as the alias name in the top panel.*

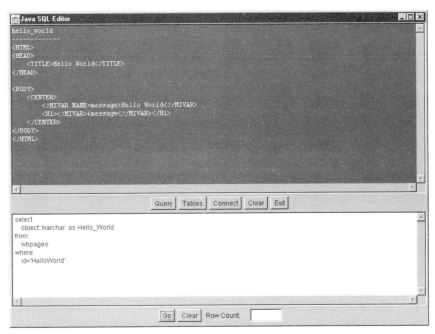

Figure 11-9. *AppPage source for "HelloWorld."*

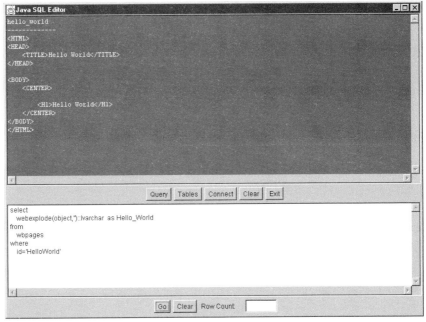

Figure 11-10. *Exploded AppPage source for "HelloWorld."*

Inserting, Updating, and Deleting Data

You can insert, update, and delete data by entering the SQL command in the Query tab, and clicking the Go button. The top window will display the number of `rows` affected by the operation

Using Transactions

Provided your Informix database has logging enabled, you can create explicit transactions. Type BEGIN WORK, and click the Go button. Then enter and submit the appropriate SQL commands, each time clicking the Go button. When you have finished, type COMMIT or ROLLBACK in the Query tab, and click the Go button. Note that the Query tab will accept only one SQL statement at a time for submission.

How Query and Display Works

The key to managing the results of unknown queries is the ability to display results of arbitrary complexity. If you don't know the query, you don't know the `ResultSet` columns. So you need to use `ResultSetMetaData` to interrogate the query results in order to display column names and values in a printable sequence.

Step-by-step Query and Display

- A query is entered into a textbox in the Query tab, and the Go button is clicked.
- The `DataBrowser` object handles the Go button, and asks the protocol client to create an application request to be sent to a database server.
- The protocol client is passed the SQL query text from the Query tab, and formats a protocol instruction, which is a request for the protocol server to perform an operation. The protocol instruction consists of an operator (perform a query) and an operand (the SQL text). The protocol instruction is then sent to the protocol server for execution.
- The protocol server interprets the protocol instruction, extracts the operand values (if any), and calls the `DataBase` class to

execute the appropriate method, which in this case involves performing a JDBC query.

- The query results are returned to the user interface object, `DataBrowser`.

A more advanced treatment of the architecture would return a `ResultSet` *to the user interface as a vector of record objects. For example, a query that returned ten customer records would return a ten-row* `ResultSet` *to the database handler. The database handler would in turn ask an application-specific object to convert the ten, raw* `ResultSet` *records into a vector of customer records that the higher-level tiers of the application can understand. In some cases, having a middle-tier repository of business objects, such as a vector of customer records, may obviate the need to requery the database, since the relevant objects may have already been extracted.*

How the Java SQL Editor User Interface Works

The user interface is created by the `DataBrowser` class. This class is the main entry point to the application, since it contains the `main()` method. In addition, the `DataBrowser` class is a subclass of the `java.awt.Frame` class:

```
class DataBrowser extends Frame
```

Because all the components of the application run in the same virtual machine, this class also instantiates all the other components, such as the protocol objects and the database handler.

Creating the Main Window

The `DataBrowser` class creates the user interface components using a method called `createControls()`.

The user interface is constructed using Java 1.1 AWT containers and components (e.g., Frames, Textareas, Lists, Buttons) and LayoutManagers, such as CardLayout. A container, such as a frame or window, can contain other components. In addition, the container can be enclosed in a higher-level container and therefore can also be described as a component.

The LayoutManager for a container is used to position the components within it.

Listing 11-1 shows the `createControls()` method. The `createStructure()` method creates the actual user interface display; the `createListeners()` method creates and registers event handlers for the user interface components.

Creating Panels and Buttons

The `createStructure()` method creates `Panel` objects and embeds other panels within them. A LayoutManager is assigned to each panel. Once the structure is complete, text areas and buttons are added.

Listing 11-2 shows fragments from the `createStructure()` method. In summary, three panels are created with either `BorderLayout` or `FlowLayout` managers. A `panel4` is created with a `CardLayout` (see next section) to emulate a tab layout. The main results display area is created and assigned to `panel2`.

Creating the Button Bar

Adding buttons to `panel3`, which uses a `FlowLayout` manager, creates the button bar in the center of the screen. The following code snippet is taken from the `createStructure()` method.

```
// add smallest components that are left
panel3.add(queryButton = new Button("Query"));
panel3.add(schemaButton = new Button("Tables"));
panel3.add(connectButton = new Button("Connect"));
panel3.add(clearLogButton = new Button("Clear"));
panel3.add(exitButton = new Button("Exit"));
```

Using the `LogDevice` Class to Create the Main Results Display

The main results display area at the top of the screen is a special type of `TextArea`, called a `LogDevice`. The `LogDevice` class is a simple extension of the `TextArea` class, which is designed to handle messages written to a log device by other components.

Put simply, the results display is used to display query results as well as error messages. Any object that wants to write to the application error log will write to the object that implements the `LogComponent` interface, which in our case is the `LogDevice` class.

Listing 11-1. *Creating user interface components via*
`DataBrowser.createControls()`.

```java
public void createControls() {
        try {
                createStructure();
                createListeners();
        }
        catch (IllegalArgumentException e) {
                e.printStackTrace();
        }
        catch (Exception e) {
                e.printStackTrace();
        }
}
```

Listing 11-2. *Fragments from the* `createStructure()` *method.*

```java
private void createStructure()
                                throws IllegalArgumentException {

    // Create Panels within Panels to format the separate
    // functional areas
    setLayout(new BorderLayout());
    add("Center", panel1 = new Panel(new BorderLayout()));
    panel1.add("Center",
        panel2 = new Panel(new BorderLayout()));
    panel1.add("South",
            panel4 = new Panel(tabOptions = new CardLayout()));

    // create the
    panel2.add("Center", resultList = new LogDevice());
    resultList.setFont(
        new Font( "Monospaced", Font.PLAIN, 12));
    panel2.add("South",panel3 = new Panel());
    resultList.setEditable(false);
    resultList.setBackground(new Color(22,69,218));
    resultList.setForeground(Color.white);
```

The following snippet from the `DataBrowser.createStructure()` method shows the creation and formatting of the main results display.

```
panel2.add("Center", resultList = new LogDevice());
resultList.setFont( new Font( "Monospaced",
Font.PLAIN, 12));
resultList.setEditable(false);
resultList.setBackground(new Color(22,69,218));
resultList.setForeground(Color.white);
```

Listing 11-3 shows the very simple `LogComponent` interface, and List. 11-4 shows the `LogDevice` class.

Listing 11-4 shows that the `LogDevice` class has implemented the `writeLog()` method whose signature is defined in the `LogComponent` interface.

The `LogComponent` *interface and* `LogDevice` *class are simple examples of maintaining a design thread in one or more component-based applications. Generally, the design phase for a Java application will produce a set of interfaces (constants and method signatures) that concrete classes use as templates for implementing real Java methods. For example, if we want to write to an error device, then we pick a class that implements the* `LogComponent` *interface. The object that writes to the error device is not*

Listing 11-3. *Simple* `LogComponent.java` *interface.*

```
public interface LogComponent {
        public void writeLog( String mesg );
}
```

Listing 11-4. `LogDevice.java`.

```
import java.awt.*;

public class LogDevice extends TextArea
                                implements LogComponent {
  public void writeLog( String mesg ) {
        append(mesg);
      }
}
```

concerned with the specifics of writing to the log. We could swap out the `TextArea` *and swap in a class that writes to a log file in the filesystem. The class could be called* `FileDevice`, *but it would still have to implement the* `LogComponent` *interface, which means that the* `FileDevice` *class must implement the* `writeLog()` *method from the* `LogComponent` *interface template. However, instead of writing to the screen, the method would write to a* `FileOutputStream`.

Creating a Tab Panel Using `CardLayout`

There are many component libraries on the market today that contain advanced GUI components such as Tab Panels and Grid Boxes to display tabular data such as the contents of the `ResultSet`. The user interface of the Java SQL Editor uses the Java AWT classes from Version 1 of the JDK. Not only does everything come free, but we can learn something about how the basic Java user interface components actually work.

The closest thing to a Tab Panel in the AWT is the `CardLayout` manager. The `CardLayout` class allows you to create one or more *cards,* which are instances of the `Panel` class, to act as containers for other components. We display the cards on top of each other, so only one is visible at any time. Other than that, we can add other containers and components to the card.

We have three cards to populate:

1. Query: Type in SQL queries.
2. Tables: List tables and query column metadata information.
3. Connect: Connect to database via JDBC.

Let's look at the Query card. The same procedure is followed for the other two.

Creating the Query Card

The `DataBrowser.createStructure()` method creates a panel, called `panel4`, to contain all the cards and assigns the `CardLayout` manager to it.

```
panel1.add("South", panel4 = new Panel(tabOptions =
new CardLayout()));
```

The object reference for the `CardLayout` is stored in the `tabOptions` variable, which is later used to control card sequence. We then create separate panels for each of the cards.

For the Query card, we create `panel5` to contain all the components for the Query card.

```
panel5 = new Panel(new BorderLayout());
```

We then add a `TextArea` to fill the center region of `panel5`, called `queryWindow`. This is the text area where we type SQL commands.

```
panel5.add("Center", queryWindow = new TextArea(10,10));
```

The remainder of the Query panel consists of a Go button, a Clear button, and a Row Count text field, which is used to limit the number of rows *displayed* from a `ResultSet`. The Go button submits the query to the database server. The Clear button clears the `queryWindow`.

To format these components, we create `panel6` and add the remaining components for the Query card to it. The default `LayoutManager` for a panel is `FlowLayout` (components added left to right, centered, eventually wrapping).

```
panel6 = new Panel();
panel6.add(goButton = new Button("Go"));
panel6.add(clearButton = new Button("Clear"));
panel6.add(new Label("Row Count:"));
panel6.add(rowCount = new TextField(5));
```

When `panel6` is complete, we add it to the main panel for the Query card, `panel5`.

```
panel5.add("South",panel6);
```

Adding Cards to the `CardLayout`

Once all three panels for each of the cards have been created, we add them one by one to the panel that contains the `CardLayout` manager, `panel4`, passing in a text label for the panel. We use this label later to identify a card in the `CardLayout`.

```
// Add cards to the card layout
panel4.add(panel5, new String(queryButton.getLabel()));
panel4.add(panel9, new String(schemaButton.getLabel()));
panel4.add(panel13, new String
(connectButton.getLabel()));
```

At this point, we can state which is the first panel to be shown. The `tabOptions` variable is a reference to a `CardLayout` object. We invoke the `show()` method of the `CardLayout` to display the card, passing in the panel with the `CardLayout` manager, and the `text label` of the panel that represents the particular card:

```
// flip to the first card
tabOptions.show(panel4, connectButton.getLabel());
```

Scrolling through the Cards

When one of the Query, Tables, or Connect buttons are clicked, the card for that button is displayed. For example, when the Query button is clicked, the lower panel of the display is refreshed with the Query card. In technical terms, the Query card is *flipped*.

We discuss event handlers and component listeners later. For now, assume that one of the three buttons has been clicked and the delegated event handler for that action is handling it.

If the Query button is clicked, the event handler performs the following:

```
tabOptions.show(panel4,queryButton.getLabel());
```

When the Tables button is clicked:

```
tabOptions.show(panel4,schemaButton.getLabel());
```

When the Connect button is clicked:

```
tabOptions.show(panel4,connectButton.getLabel());
```

Populating Lists

The Tables tab allows the user to display column metadata information by selecting a table from a list of tables in the database. This list can be filtered to select on Table Type, such as View, System Table, and (standard) Table. This section shows how these lists are populated.

To implement the required functionality, the Tables tab contains three Choice components and a List component. The contents of these components are populated with metadata information from the database we are connected to.

note

The implementation of the JDBC API differs between drivers for the Catalogs, Schema, and Table Type API methods.

Populating the Table List

When the connection is first established, the database metadata is queried, and the catalogs, schemas, and table types are written to the screen components using the method `DataBrowser.addChoiceTypes()`. For example,

```
addChoiceTypes( dataBase.getCatalogs(),
catalogChoices );
addChoiceTypes( dataBase.getSchemas(),
schemaChoices );
addChoiceTypes( dataBase.getTableTypes(),
tableTypeChoices );
metaWindow.append("Connected.\n");
connectCardButton.setLabel("Disconnect");
```

The `getxxx()` methods are wrappers for the JDBC database metadata API calls `getSchemas()`, `getCatalogs()`, and `getTableTypes()`. What the user interface sees is a `Vector` of `Strings`, which are used to populate the three `Choice` components.

The `addChoiceTypes()` method is shown in List. 11-5. The first thing the method does is to remove all the items. Because we are

---

Listing 11-5.   *Populate a* Choices *component from a* Vector *of* Strings.

```
private void addChoiceTypes( Vector v, Choice c ) {

        // add first choice item
        c.removeAll();
        c.add("All");
        Enumeration e = v.elements();

        while (e.hasMoreElements()) {
           c.add((String)e.nextElement());
        }
}
```

---

using a `Vector`, we can use an `Enumeration`, which allows us to scroll through all the `elements` using the `hasMoreElements()` method to check if we are at the end of the list.

In the Tables tab, the user can filter the type of table to list (Views, for example), before clicking the Select button to fetch the list of tables from the database metadata. The method `addListTypes()` is used to populate the Tables list box. This differs from `addChoiceTypes()` in signature only, the method detail is the same:

```
private void addListTypes( Vector v, List c )
```

Handling SQL Editor Events

When the user clicks a button, a service is requested. For example, if the user clicks the Tables button, that table's tab is displayed; if the Connect button is clicked, the connect tab is displayed.

Java lets you handle events using a technique called *event delegation*. Put simply, event delegation lets you register an event handler for a component. For example, the Query button is an instance of the `java.awt.Button` class, but you can nominate another class to handle various types of events for that particular button; in other words, you are *delegating* the event handling to another object. An object that is delegated to handle an event is called a *listener* for that event.

There are many types of event that can be handled, but generally they fall into two catagories; item events and semantic events. Item events deal with specific, individual events such as a mouse click. Semantic events deal with a higher-level event. For example, clicking a button involves pressing the mousekey down and then releasing it; all these events can be handled. However, the semantic event is called an ActionEvent—a click of a button.

In brief, the steps involved in handling events are:

- create the component that will generate the event,
- create the event handler, or *listener*, that contains the code to handle the event,
- register the event handler as a listener with the component.

The Java SQL Editor registers *anonymous* classes to handle events, so the final two steps are merged.

Creating Event Handlers Using Anonymous Classes

Most of the listeners in the Java SQL Editor are created as anonymous classes. An anonymous class is a class that is declared without a name in the body of another class, and in our example it is used to create event-handling code for a component without the clutter of using separate source files or maintaining separate object references. However, you don't have to use anonymous classes to handle events.

Although an anonymous class is nameless within the Java source file, it is compiled into a separate class file. This class file has the same name as the enclosing class, but has a "$" and a number suffixed to it for identity.

The `DataBrowser` class contains many anonymous classes for handling events from each of the user interface components. When `DataBrowser.java` is compiled, class files are created for the anonymous classes, as well as for the main `DataBrowser` class. For example, this is a list of some of the class files created:

```
DataBrowser.class
DataBrowser$1.class
DataBrowser$2.class
DataBrowser$3.class
DataBrowser$4.class
```

Creating and Registering Listeners

A component can have many registered listeners. For example, if a button is clicked, several objects may have registered themselves as listeners for that event, all doing something slightly different with the event. More technically, the `Button` object will store a reference to all objects that have registered themselves as listeners, and it will invoke in sequence the appropriate event-handling methods in each object.

A `listener` object will be defined as implementing an interface from the `java.awt.event` package. For example, an object that implements the `java.awt.event.ActionListener` interface will implement the code for the `ActionPerformed()` method defined in that interface.

The `DataBrowser` class contains a method called `createListeners()` that creates and registers various objects as listeners for user interface events such as a button click, or a list selection.

Listing 11-6 shows a fragment from the `createListeners()` method. It shows the creation of an anonymous class that implements the `ItemListener` interface.

```
tableList.addItemListener(
          new ItemListener() {
            public void itemStateChanged( ItemEvent e ) {
                Integer index = (Integer)e.getItem();
                tableName = tableList.getItem(index.intValue());
                try {
                    ProtocolClient.tellProtocolClient( DBP_COLUMNS );
                    }
                catch (Exception ea) {
                    ea.printStackTrace();
                }
            }
          }
);
```

When the code is run, the anonymous class is instantiated, and the object reference is passed to the `addItemListener()` method, which registers the object as a listener for item events, such as selecting a list element. The `tableList` component will send an `ItemEvent` to the anonymous `listener` object when the user selects a database table from the list of displayed tables.

The anonymous class is declared and instantiated by referring to the *interface* that it implements:

```
new ItemListener()
```

From that point on, the class implements the `itemStateChanged()` method. In this example, the selected table name is extracted from the list, and the static method of the protocol client class, `tellProtocolClient()`, is invoked to manage the display of column metadata for the selected table.

Most of the user interface components have anonymous classes registered as listeners. Listing 11-7 shows the listeners for the Tables button, the Query button, and the Go button in the Query tab. Clicking these buttons results in an `ActionEvent` being sent to the anonymous `listener` object, which implements the `actionPerformed()` method of the `java.awt.event.ActionListener` interface.

Listing 11-7.   Event handlers for buttons.

```
schemaButton.addActionListener(
        new ActionListener() {
            public void actionPerformed( ActionEvent e )
            {
                tabOptions.show(panel4,schemaButton.getLabel());
            }
        } );

queryButton.addActionListener(
        new ActionListener() {
            public void actionPerformed( ActionEvent e )
            {
                tabOptions.show(panel4,queryButton.getLabel());
            }
        } );

goButton.addActionListener(
        new ActionListener() {
            public void actionPerformed( ActionEvent e )
            {
                try {
                    ProtocolClient.tellProtocolClient(
                                DBP_EXECUTE_QUERY );
                } catch (Exception x) {
                    x.printStackTrace();
                }
            }
        } );
```

For the Go button, the `actionPerformed()` method results in a request to execute the query that has been entered into the text area of the `Query` tab. This request is sent to the protocol handler, which will manage the request from that point on.

Registering the `DataBrowser` Class as a Listener

The `DataBrowser` class itself handles item events for the `Choices` components displayed in the Tables tab, and registers itself as follows:

```
        catalogChoices.addItemListener(this);
        schemaChoices.addItemListener(this);
        tableTypeChoices.addItemListener(this);
```

When item events occur in those components (such as clicking a
list item), the event-processing code inside the component will call
the `itemStateChanged()` method in the `DataBrowser` object.

The `DataBrowser` class implements the `java.awt.event.`
`ItemListener` interface, which means that it must contain the
implementation of the interface method `itemStateChanged()`.
Part of the class declaration for `DataBrowser` is:

```
class DataBrowser extends Frame implements ItemListener
```

Listing 11-8 shows the `itemStateChanged()` method. This
method sets up the essential parameter values for a JDBC

Listing 11-8.   The `DataBrowser.itemStateChanged()` method.

```
// item listener for choices
// set the parameter values for the JDBC method call here;

public void itemStateChanged( ItemEvent e ) {

        Object csrc = e.getSource();
        String s = (String)e.getItem();

        if (csrc == catalogChoices) {
            catalog = s;
            if (catalog.equals("All"))
            catalog = null;
        }
        else if (csrc == schemaChoices) {
          schema = s;
          if (schema.equals("All"))
            schema = null;
        }
        else if (csrc == tableTypeChoices) {
          tableType = s;
          if (tableType.equals("All"))
            tableType = null;
        }
}
```

DataBaseMetaData API call later, when the user clicks the Select button in the Tables tab. To do this, we need to find out which `Choices` component has generated the event. The `getSource()` method of the `ItemEvent` object is invoked, which returns the object reference for the delegating component. If the item selected is `All`, then the JDBC API call requires `null` as a parameter, rather than the string `All`.

Understanding the Protocol Handler

In any component-based application, components need to communicate through method calls or by raising an event that is intercepted by an event handler.

The messages that are passed between cooperating components can be complicated, consisting of a request and, optionally, some data to accompany the request.

To make applications scalable and reusable, it is useful to create a formal way to structure messages, called a *protocol*. The protocol is understood by client and server components. For example, browsers and web servers understand the HTTP protocol, even though the actual products are different. A browser can send HTTP requests to any HTTP web server.

The Java platform allows you to create a highly sophisticated protocol handler for your protocol. However, the Java SQL Editor does not go that far. The Java SQL Editor implements a protocol so that the user interface of the application can send requests to a database server and not worry about the specifics of the request. The `protocol client` and `protocol server` objects handle the specifics of the request.

In summary, the protocol handler sits between the client and server components as follows:

- The user interface talks to the protocol client.
- The protocol client talks to the protocol server.
- The protocol server talks to the database handler, which in turn connects to the database server using JDBC.

Each layer has its own function, the implementation of which is hidden from the other layers.

In effect, the methods of the protocol handler are considered to be a *service API*. Any client that wanted a service available via a server that understood this protocol would interface to a protocol client to connect to that service, in the same way that we use the JDBC driver to connect to the database server.

Handling Protocol Data

The `ProtocolData` object is used to pass requests from the user interface to the database handler, using the `ProtocolClient` class to create the instruction, the `ProtocolData` class to format the instruction, and the `ProtocolServer` class to execute the instruction.

The `DBProtocol` Interface

The `DBProtocol` interface contains all the constants required by the protocol-handling components and is shown in List. 11-9.

Listing 11-9. *The* `DBProtocol.java` *interface.*

```
public interface DBProtocol {
      // Instruction Operators
      final byte DBP_EXECUTE_QUERY    = 1;
      final byte DBP_TABLES           = 2;
      final byte DBP_COLUMNS          = 3;
      final byte DBP_METADATA         = 4;
      final byte DBP_CONNECT          = 5;
      final byte DBP_DISCONNECT       = 6;

      // Operand descriptors
      final byte DBP_SQLTEXT_ARG      = 0;
      final byte DBP_ROWCOUNT_ARG     = 1;

      final byte DBP_DRIVER_ARG = 0;
      final byte DBP_URL_ARG          = 1;
      final byte DBP_USERID_ARG = 2;
      final byte DBP_PASSWORD_ARG     = 3;

      final byte DBP_CATALOG_ARG      = 1;
      final byte DBP_SCHEMA_ARG = 2;
      final byte DBP_TYPES_ARG  = 3;
      final byte DBP_TABLES_ARG = 3;

      final byte DBP_PROTOCOL_OPERANDS = 10;
}
```

The protocol client will create protocol instructions using these values. The protocol server will interpret protocol messages, also using these values.

Instruction operators define the service that is implemented by the protocol server. For example, the instruction DBP_EXECUTE_QUERY instructs the protocol server to tell the DataBase object to perform an SQL query, using the SQL text operand passed from the Query tab in the user interface.

Operand descriptors are used to describe the instruction operand to the protocol server.

For example, to execute an SQL query that is passed from the user interface component, the protocol instruction can be summarised as follows:

- Instruction: DBP_EXECUTE_QUERY defines the service to execute.
- Operand 1: DBP_SQLTEXT_ARG describes the content of the first operand, an SQL command string.
- Operand 2: DBP_ROWCOUNT_ARG describes the content of the second operand, the number of rows to display from the ResultSet.

The ProtocolData Class

The ProtocolData class encapsulates the specifics of handling a protocol instruction operator and one or more protocol instruction operands. The constants defined in the DBProtocol interface are used to manipulate the instructions. Listing 11-10 shows the ProtocolData class.

Listing 11-10. *The* ProtocolData.java *class source.*

```
public class ProtocolData implements DBProtocol{
      private int opcode;
      private String [] operand =
            new String[DBP_PROTOCOL_OPERANDS];

      private static ProtocolData pd;

      public int getOpcode()
      {
            return opcode;
      }
```

Listing 11-10.   (continued)

```
public String getOperand( int index )
{
      return operand[index];
}
public String [] getOperand()
{
      return operand;
}
public void setOpcode( int opcode )
{
      this.opcode = opcode;
}
public void setOperand( String operand, int index  )
{
      this.operand[index] = operand;
}

public ProtocolData()
{
      if (pd == null)
      {
            pd = this;
      }
}

public static ProtocolData getProtocolData() throws Exception
{
      if (pd == null)
      {
            throw new Exception("No Protocol");
      }
      return pd;
}
}
```

A protocol instruction consists of an instruction, or *opcode,* and one or more operands, up to the maximum number of operands specified by DBP_PROTOCOL_OPERANDS.

The class consists of a collection of get and set methods for protocol instruction. The instruction operands are stored in a String array. The operands can be selected by using the DBProtocol constants to refer to the operand by position.

In this implementation, the `ProtocolData` class is implemented as a singleton object. If a class is instantiated as a singleton, it is instantiated once only. The class constructor, `ProtocolData()`, ensures that only one instance is created.

This design is satisfactory for a single client. Multiple client requests will require separate `ProtocolData` objects for each client. Again, a singleton object could maintain a vector of `ProtocolData` objects, each element representing one client on that machine.

The Protocol Client

The `ProtocolClient` class is responsible for creating protocol instructions to be passed to the `ProtocolServer`. The user interface invokes the `ProtocolClient` to request a service. The `ProtocolClient` selects the appropriate instruction operator and operand values, and stores them in the `ProtocolData` object. The `ProtocolClient` then invokes the `ProtocolServer` to service the instruction.

For example, if the user types an SQL query into the Query tab, and clicks the Go button, the event handler for that button executes the following method:

```
ProtocolClient.tellProtocolClient( DBP_EXECUTE_QUERY );
```

Inside the `tellProtocolClient()` method, a reference to the `ProtocolData` object is obtained, and the instruction created using the `setOpcode()` method. The two arguments (the SQL command and the number of rows to retrieve) are created using the `setOperand()` method. The second parameter to `setOperand()` is the index into the array of operand values. Finally, the `ProtocolServer` is invoked to request the `DataBase` object to perform the query. Listing 11-11 contains a fragment of the `ProtocolClient.tellProtocolClient()` method.

The `ProtocolClient` object contains a reference to the user interface component, `DataBrowser`, so that the operand values can be taken from the screen fields.

The Protocol Server

The `ProtocolServer` class takes the `ProtocolData` object, which contains an instruction, and performs the service defined by its contents.

The `ProtocolServer` class contains a reference to the database-handling object, which performs the detailed JDBC API calls.

Listing 11-11. *The* `tellprotocolClient()` *method fragment.*

```
ProtocolData protocolData = ProtocolData.getProtocolData();
protocolData.setOpcode(opcode);

switch (opcode){

    case DBP_EXECUTE_QUERY: {

    protocolData.setOperand(
        ui.queryWindow.getText(),DBP_SQLTEXT_ARG);
    protocolData.setOperand(
        ui.rowCount.getText(),DBP_ROWCOUNT_ARG);

    ProtocolServer.serviceDBRequest(protocolData);
    break;
}
```

The central method in the `ProtocolServer` is the `serviceDBRequest()` method. This method interprets a protocol instruction. First, it reads the instruction opcode and then extracts the operand values before calling the appropriate service function and passing the operand values to it.

For example, suppose that the `DBP_EXECUTE_QUERY` instruction, shown above, was sent to the `ProtocolServer`. The following code is responsible for interpreting it.

```
public static Object serviceDBRequest( ProtocolData
p ) throws Exception {

switch (p.getOpcode()){
    case DBP_EXECUTE_QUERY:{
            db.execSQL(p.getOperand(DBP_SQLTEXT_ARG),
            p.getOperand(DBP_ROWCOUNT_ARG));
            return db.getResults();
    }
```

The `ProtocolServer` understands the protocol format used, so it knows that the `DBP_EXECUTE_QUERY` instruction has two operands. We are not relying on the `DataBase` method `execSQL()` to understand the protocol, so we extract the operand values before passing them into the `execSQL()` method.

Almost every piece of functionality in the Java SQL Editor is implemented in this way, allowing you to replace the presentation layer of the application without regressing the application architecture.

tip

You could reuse this simple instruction-handling model in a variety of situations, not just for communicating service requests between a presentation layer and a database layer. You could use it to implement service requests between network clients and servers (with or without RMI) or between network-based batch schedulers; in fact, you could use it in any application where a middle-tier program controls service requests that are implemented by other components.

The `ProtocolServer` class is a very small class. The detailed JDBC interface is provided by the `DataBase` class, discussed next.

Managing the JDBC Layer

All the interaction with the database server is contained in one class, called the `DataBase` class. This is the database handler. This class contains methods invoked by the protocol server to perform functions such as connect and disconnect to and from the database, execute a query, retrieve JDBC driver metadata, and fetch column metadata for a database table selected by the user from a list of tables. The `DataBase` class is the class that will register the JDBC driver and connect to the JDBC URL that was entered by the user in the Connect tab.

For the purpose of illustration, we will look at how the `DataBase` object executes an SQL query and returns the results.

Passing an Instruction to the `DataBase` Class

The protocol server will interpret an instruction that is passed to it by the protocol client. In this example, the instruction is to *execute an SQL query*. The protocol server extracts the operands from the `ProtocolData` object and passes them to the `DataBase` class as parameters. There are two operands: the SQL query text, and the number of rows to display from the `ResultSet`, if any.

```
db.execSQL(
    p.getOperand(DBP_SQLTEXT_ARG),
    p.getOperand(DBP_ROWCOUNT_ARG)
);
```

Performing the Query

The SQL text that the user typed into the Query tab has found its way to the `DataBase` object and so, too, has the requested maximum number of rows to display. This number does not affect the number of rows returned in the `ResultSet`.

The query is executed using the `Statement.execute()` method.

```
boolean status=query.execute(queryStmt);
```

Remember that we do not know what the query is, whether it is a `SELECT`, `UPDATE`, `BEGIN WORK` or even `EXECUTE PROCEDURE`. We need to manage the query result accordingly. The `execute()` method returns true if a `ResultSet` is returned from the query. If a `ResultSet` is not returned, the query was probably an `INSERT`, `UPDATE`, or `DELETE` type of query, in which case we can extract the number of rows affected.

We call the `resultsInfo()` method to extract the values from the `ResultSet` and post them into an instance of an application class, `ResultsInfo`. Listing 11-12 shows the complete `execSQL()` method.

Listing 11-12. The `DataBase.execSQL()` method.

```
public void execSQL(String queryStmt, String rowcount)
throws Exception
{
    info.numUpdates=0
    try{
        rowCount=(new Integer)rowcount)).intValue();
    }catch(NumberFormatException ne){
        rowCount=0;
    }
    boolean status=query.execute(queryStmt);
    if(status){
        //query has returned a ResultSet
        rs=query.getResultSet();
        rowspec=rs.getMetaData();
        resultsInfo();
    }
    else{
        //insert, update or delete
        info.numUpdates=query.getUpdateCount();
    }
}
```

Extracting the Results

We need to interrogate the metadata of the `ResultSet` in order to find out information such as the names and sizes of the columns returned, if any. The following line invokes the `getColumnCount()` method of the `ResultSetMetaData` object, `rowspec`, to extract the number of columns returned by the query:

```
numberOfColumns=rowspec.getColumnCount();
```

The following snippet extracts the column name and display size for each column in the `ResultSet`.

```
for(int i=0; i<numberOfColumns; i++){
    names[i]=rowspec.getColumnName(i+1);
    sizes[i]=rowspec.getColumnDisplaySize(i+1);
}
```

If a selected column contained an alias name (for example, `select fname as Forename from customer`), then the alias name is displayed on the screen. We know what to display, since we extract the column label from the metadata for the `ResultSet` column:

```
labels[i]=rowspec.getColumnLabel(i+1);
```

Finally, we need to provide some formatting information that will help the display component to present the query results in some form. Strictly speaking, we should just provide the arrays of objects, but the aim is to deal only once with the metadata properties of the `ResultSet`.

Listing 11-13. *The* `ResultsInfo.java` *class source.*

```
import java.awt.*;

public class ResultInfo{

    List values;                //Row set
    String [] names;            //column names
    String [] labels;           //column labels
    int [] sizes;               //column size
    int [] displaySizes;        //column display size
    int numUpdates;             //insert/update/delete (>=0)
                                            //or select (-1)

    int rowSize;                //size of row in bytes
}
```

```
public void resultsInfo() throws Exception{
   String [] names;
   String [] labels;
   int [] sizes;

   info.rowSize=0;
   numberOfColumns=rowspec.getColumnCount();
   names=new String[numberOfColumns];
   labels=new String[numberOfColumns];
   sizes=new int[numberOfColumns];

   for (int i=0; i<numberOfColumns; i++){
         names[i]=rowspec.getColumnName(i+1);
         sizes[i]=rowspec.getColumnDisplaySize(i+1);
         //some drivers return -1
         //also, metadata column size is big
         if ((sizes[i]==DBC_NO_DISPLAYSIZE)||(sizes[i]>30))
         {
             sizes[i]=30;
         }
         if (sizes[i]<names[i].length()){
             sizes[i]=names[i].length();
         }
         sizes[i]++;
         labels[i]=rowspec.getColumnLabel(i+1);
         info.rowSize+=sizes[i];
   }
   info.names=names;
   info.labels=labels;
   info.sizes=sizes;
}
```

Although the formatting of the results into columns looks complicated, it is made easier with the ability to query column properties,
such as column and label size. Listing 11-14 shows the complete
`DataBase.resultsInfo()` method. The `info` object is a `wrapper`
class for returning the values from a `ResultSet` into a `ResultsInfo`
object, which obviates the need for nondatabase components to
understand how to interrogate the JDBC API. Listing 11-13 shows
the `ResultsInfo` class.

Summary

This simple Java SQL Editor allows you to connect to a data source via JDBC in order to submit queries and query database metadata in a highly flexible way without compromising portability. With the source code provided, this chapter should enable you to use and extend the Editor, learn how to work with layout managers to achieve a reasonably sophisticated effect without third-party widget class calls, and, chiefly, learn how to connect to a database and use JDBC method calls.

If you feel ambitious, you can try to distribute the components over a network using RMI, which involves little modification to the code. For example, you could locate the user interface and protocol client on one host, and the protocol server with the database object on another host. If the presentation layer of an application is more appealing to you, then you can unhook the basic AWT components and replace them with your favourite GUI forms. In summary, you have a lot of code to play with.

Dynamic Web DataBlade Programming

Web DataBlade
Architecture

In this chapter:

- Web DataBlade architecture
- How dynamic page generation works
- Understanding the `webexplode()` DataBlade function
- Understanding the Web DataBlade
- Registering and unregistering the Web DataBlade

The Web DataBlade supports the capture, management, and delivery of very sophisticated and dynamic multimedia-based websites. The purpose of this chapter is to provide a clear illustration of the architectural components involved and how they all work. Because we are using the Web DataBlade, a section is included with enough detail for you to work directly with DataBlades and DataBlade functions. This chapter will show you how the Web DataBlade works without hiding it's importance in a mass of detail. Understanding how it works will help you make important design decisions in your web projects.

Web DataBlade Architecture

Figure 12-1 shows the components of the Web DataBlade.

Figure 12-1 shows three essential platforms, the Web Browser, Web Server and the Informix Database Server. You can regard each of these platforms as a logically separate host, or computer, that performs a specific task. Table 12-1 describes the platforms and how they interact.

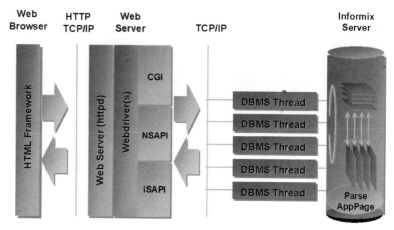

Figure 12-1. Web DataBlade architecture.

Table 12-1. *Web DataBlade architecture: logical platform components.*

Platform	Components
Web Browser	Typically Netscape and Microsoft browsers hosted by UNIX or Windows workstations.
HTTP TCP/IP	The HTTP *protocol* enables the browser client to communicate with the web server application. TCP/IP is used to transport the HTTP requests from the client to the web server.
Web Server	UNIX servers or NT4 Server that host web server products. This platform also hosts the Informix middleware, such as `webdriver`, plus any shared objects that may be required.
TCP/IP	TCP/IP is used to support the network communication between the `webdriver` program and the Informix server. If `webdriver` and the Informix server are on the same host, then shared memory, stream pipes, or named pipes can be used.
Informix Database Server	UNIX or NT4 host for the Informix Dynamic Server.2000 or Informix Dynamic Server with Universal Data Option.

Table 12-2. Architecture software components.

Component	Description
HTML Framework	Web application rendered by the browser software. No direct interaction with any other platform component except the web server.
HTTPD Web Server	Web Server daemon. This can be any CGI-compliant web server. If an API implementation is required, this should be Netscape (Fasttrack/Enterprise), Microsoft (IIS), or Apache.
`webdriver`(s)	The program(s) that connects to the Informix database requesting a web page to be exploded by the `webexplode()` DataBlade function.
CGI	CGI implementation of `webdriver`. It is invoked once for each and every CGI request.
NSAPI	`webdriver` is implemented as a shared object for integration with web servers, such as Netscape Fasttrack and Enterprise.
ISAPI	`webdriver` is implemented as a shared object for integration with IIS.
DBMS Thread	When `webdriver` connects to the Informix server, a DBMS thread is started. For NSAPI/ISAPI connections, the thread is maintained. For CGI connections, the thread is closed once the page build has finished.
Parse AppPage	This is the `webexplode()` DataBlade function that builds the resulting HTML page from the AppPage template.

Architecture Software Components

Table 12-2 lists the software components of each platform in more detail then shown in Figure 12-1.

Distributed-Component Architecture

You can have all three logical platforms on one physical platform. For example, NT4 Server could host the Netscape Browser, a Netscape Web Server and the Informix Database Server.

In contrast, the Netscape Web Server and `webdriver` could be hosted under NT4, and the Informix database hosted under UNIX on another computer. Table 12-3 lists an example.

The decision to relocate cooperating objects such as `webdriver` to a different machine can be taken on many grounds, depending on wider issues in the customer installation:

- The current architecture is heterogeneous and the requirement is to keep it so for financial reasons or otherwise.
- Performance requirements dictate that the database server platform be dedicated to the Informix database and client applications (such as 4GL reports and batch jobs), so one or more other machines are dedicated to handling client HTTP web server requests (large-volume sites, for example).
- For security reasons the web server is outside the firewall, but the database is behind the firewall.

Figure 12-2 shows the default positioning of the components. The web server, `webdriver`, and the Informix Database Server (with the Web DataBlade installed) are on the same host computer (NT or UNIX) in an intranet context.

Figure 12-3 shows an advanced implementation of the Web DataBlade across different servers. Note that the `webdriver` middleware is hosted with the web server software. The `webdriver` middleware can communicate across a network to an Informix database server on another machine. as long as the dependencies in Table 12-4 are met.

Table 12-3. Distributing Web DataBlade components.

NT4 components	UNIX components
Web Server	Informix Dynamic Server.2000, Informix Dynamic Server/Universal Data Option
Web DataBlade for NT4 (`webdriver` component)	Web DataBlade for UNIX
Client/SDK for NT. (This distributed architecture principally requires the I-Connect library that implements the SQLI protocol.)	Connectivity is in-built into the Informix server

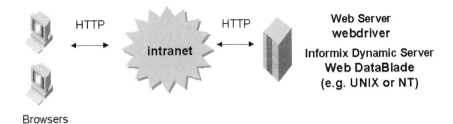

Figure 12-2. *Single-server hosting of database, web server, and Web DataBlade.*

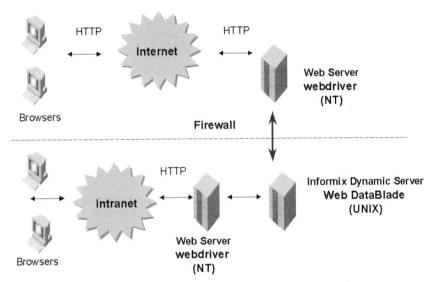

Figure 12-3. *Distributed web component architecture.*

Table 12-4. *Connection dependencies.*	
Web server NT to database UNIX	**Web server UNIX to database NT/UNIX**
Registry entries initialized for the database host and server using `setnet`	`Sqlhosts` entries set up to describe the database host and server

Using Protocols to Communicate

Each component in the architecture must be able to receive and send messages to other components. A protocol is a set of rules defining how computers—and software applications—communicate. A protocol helps different applications on different computers to communicate via a shared language. The HTTP protocol defines the interaction between an HTTP client (a browser) and an HTTP protocol handler (a web server). A protocol handler interprets the protocol instructions and uses the data passed between the client and server to perform the function defined by the protocol instruction.

Types of Protocol

There are different types of protocol for different uses. Your web browser doesn't care whether the web server is on UNIX or NT4 Server, since the web server will understand the HTTP protocol. When you enter `http://` into the browser location bar, this is the start of a protocol dialog with an HTTP server on the targeted host, on port 80 by default. If you type `ftp://`, the browser will attempt an FTP protocol dialog with an FTP server on port 21 on the targeted host.

Protocol Levels

The protocol instructions defined by HTTP are different from those defined by FTP. TCP/IP (transmission control protocol/Internet protocol) is a transport/addressing protocol for communication between computers. The HTTP or FTP protocol instruction is carried by a TCP-defined packet to a computer with an IP address (such as 920.325.123.0). Both HTTP and FTP are application-level protocols. TCP is a transport-level protocol, and IP is an Internet-addressing protocol. Ethernet may be used at the physical level to transport the data. Informix client programs (such as `webdriver`) are called client programs because they connect to the database server. However, communication with the Informix database server is via a protocol that the client and server understand, called SQLI. In this case, the Informix server is the protocol handler. This is transparent to the application developer.

Application Protocols

You can define your own application protocol. Put simply, you define a set of commands and write a protocol handler to accept and interpret these commands. You can use Java to implement a protocol handler that communicates with clients across a network fairly easily (see Chap. 11, "A Simple Java SQL Editor"). An example of this would be a distributed batch-scheduling application, with each computer running a batch job dependent on other batch jobs on other computers. Implementing a protocol so that the controlling programs on each computer could understand what the others were doing would enable you to write components that interact as clients and servers, since they should all interpret the semantics of the language-independent protocol. In this case, the controlling program on each computer is both a protocol client (sends instructions) and a protocol handler (receives and processes instructions).

How Dynamic Page Generation Works

This section will describe how the Web DataBlade works to make a dynamic web page using an HTML template (AppPage), AppPage Scripting tags, `webdriver`, and the Web DataBlade.

Figure 12-4 shows the steps involved in generating a dynamic web page when the browser client requests a URL.

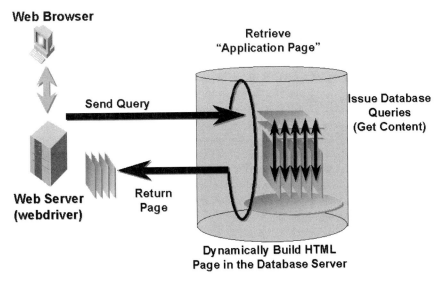

Figure 12-4. *Dynamic page generation.*

Table 12-5. *Dynamic page generation components.*

Component	Description
Web Browser	The client browser that requests the URL from the web server, for example, `http://dellcpi/stores7-cgi/webdriver.exe?Mival=HelloWorld`
Web Server	Processes the URL request. The web server maps the URL to a CGI call to `webdriver.exe` by using information stored in the web server configuration file.
`webdriver`	The CGI program to request the page called "HelloWorld" from the database and return it to the browser via the web server.
Send Query	`webdriver` sends a query to the database to fetch an AppPage, and uses the `webexplode()` function to process it. The parameter `'MIval=HelloWorld'` tells `webdriver` what AppPage to fetch.
Retrieve "Application Page"	The Informix server processes the query by first selecting the requested AppPage from the database.
Get Content	The `webexplode()` function, used in the query, processes the AppPage Script tags, which can include SQL statements to retrieve data, including audio and video.
Dynamically Build HTML	Once the data is retrieved from the database, the data is formatted in the HTML page. For example, a list of customers is formatted in HTML table rows.
Return Page	The query sent by `webdriver` returns the result—an HTML page. This page is sent back to the browser via the web server.

Table 12-5 lists the components actually involved in the Fig. 12-4 diagram.

Step-by-Step Dynamic Page Generation

When a URL contains a `webdriver` request, the web browser makes a request to the web server to invoke `webdriver`. The request may be a CGI or API request. For example, to invoke `webdriver` as a CGI program on UNIX:

```
http://dellcpi/stores7/cgi-bin/webdriver?Mival
=mywebpage
```

To invoke `webdriver` as a CGI program on NT:

```
http://dellcpi/stores7/cgi-bin/webdriver.exe?Mival
=mywebpage
```

To invoke `webdriver` as part of a web server API implementation on both UNIX and NT:

```
http://dellcpi/stores7api?Mival=mywebpage
```

This is what happens next:

- Based on configuration information, `webdriver` composes an SQL statement to retrieve the requested AppPage and then expand it by executing the `webexplode()` function.
- The `webexplode()` function takes the selected AppPage from the web application table (stored in an Informix database), executes the SQL statements within that AppPage, expands the Web DataBlade module tags, and formats the results.
- The `webexplode()` function returns the resulting HTML to `webdriver` and `webdriver` returns the HTML to the web server.
- The web server returns the HTML to be rendered by the web browser.

`webdriver` enables the web server to communicate with the database to extract AppPages that are stored in the database. The `webdriver` replaces the need to write a CGI program to enable the web server to interact with the database.

`webdriver` has three essential implementations up to Version 4 of the Web DataBlade; *Netscape Server API (NSAPI), Microsoft ISAPI,* or *CGI.* From Version 4, an Apache API `webdriver` is provided. As an Informix application, `webdriver` builds the SQL queries that execute the `webexplode()` function to retrieve AppPages from the Informix database. `webdriver` returns the HTML resulting from calls to `webexplode()` to the web server.

A web server calls `webdriver` through a CGI or API interface to retrieve AppPages from the Informix database. The `webdriver` obtains configuration information from the following sources:

- A `webdriver` configuration file—a file on the web server machine called `web.cnf` that contains the name of the target database, database user, user authentication table names, and other important configuration information.
- Web browser—"cookies" information can be passed from the browser to the web server and then to `webdriver`.
- Web server environment—`webdriver` can use the environment variables that the web server uses.

Understanding the webexplode DataBlade Function

webexplode() is a DataBlade function. It uses the Informix DataBlade API to interface with Informix Dynamic Server.

The webexplode() *Function and Informix Dynamic Server*

Because webexplode() *is a DataBlade function, it requires Informix Dynamic Server.2000 or Informix Dynamic Server with the Universal Data Option. These servers allow the DataBlade API to be used to "link in" functions, like* webexplode()*, that have been written by third-party vendors, customers, and consultants. Informix can use these functions in SQL statements as if they were part of the core SQL implementation.*

The webexplode() function builds HTML pages dynamically based on data stored in the Informix database. The webexplode() function performs the following:

- parses AppPages that contain AppPage Script tags within HTML and dynamically builds and executes the SQL statements and processing instructions embedded in the AppPage tags.
- formats the results of these SQL statements and processing instructions, and returns the resulting HTML document to the client application (usually webdriver).

For example, the following query will assign values to Web DataBlade variables specifically for the Web DataBlade webexplode() function. This query can be executed in dbaccess or an AppPage:

```
select webexplode( object,
"MI_DATABASE='stores7'&MI_USER='joe'&HTTP_HOST=
'theale2'&"
||
"REMOTE_HOST='theale2.informix.com'&SERVER_NAME=
'theale2'&"
||
"SERVER_URL='http://theale2'&SERVER_PORT='80'&"
||
"SERVER_PROTOCOL='http://'&SERVER_SOFTWARE='Netscape
FastTrack'&"
||
```

```
"HTTP_USER_AGENT='Netscape Browser'")
from webpages
where ID='HelloWorld1'
```

The AppPage variables that are passed to the webexplode() *function are linked together with syntax similar to URL syntax for parameters to a CGI program. The operator that joins the parameters in sequence is the "&" character.*

This query is the type of query that the webdriver program will send to the Informix server. The query in this example:

- identifies the AppPage in the database called "HelloWorld1,"
- initializes the AppPage Scripting variables that the AppPage requires (e.g., MI_USER),
- invokes the webexplode() function to process the AppPage source with the AppPage Scripting variables set to the values in the webexplode() parameter list.

If you override variable assignments in the second argument of your call to webexplode()*, the new variable assignment will be retained until it is reassigned elsewhere.*

Because webexplode() *is a powerful server function that can be called in an SQL query, you can use* webexplode() *recursively to chain together several AppPages to generate very sophisticated web pages dynamically.*

The first webexplode() parameter is called "object"; this is a column in the webpages table with a datatype of HTML—one of the new datatypes introduced by the Web DataBlade. Only the Web DataBlade understands the HTML datatype, which is why the Web DataBlade installs functions to create, select, and maintain the HTML object column.

Figure 12-5 shows the dbaccess query.

Figure 12-6 shows a selection of the output from the webexplode() query.

What we have done in this example is not very different from the query that the webdriver program constructs. Remember, it is webdriver that puts the query together; it is the webexplode() function that transforms an AppPage into an HTML page for the browser.

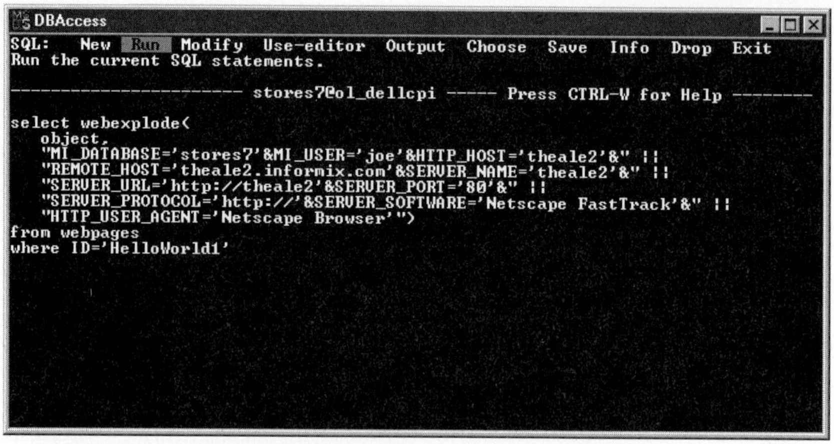

Figure 12-5. *Example* webexplode() *query in* dbaccess.

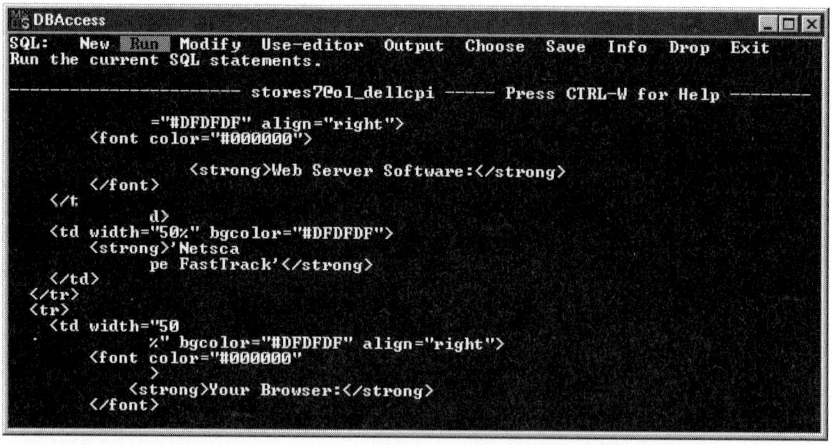

Figure 12-6. *A* webexplode() *query sample output in* dbaccess.

Is webdriver *a Client or Middleware?*

The webdriver *component of the Web DataBlade is a program that connects to the Informix database using the SQLI protocol.* webdriver *can be referred to as middleware, because it operates between the web server and the Informix Dynamic Server, possibly on a middle tier between the browser client and the Informix server. It is also an Informix database client.*

Understanding the Web DataBlade

What Is a DataBlade Module?

A DataBlade module is a collection of database objects and supporting code that extend the database server by adding new datatypes,
functions, casts, aggregates, or access methods; for example, images
or HTML-encoded text. Figure 12-7 shows the typical components of
a DataBlade module.

DataBlade Installation (Server)

*A DataBlade module is installed on a server when the module files are copied
from the distribution media to the filesystem of the host computer.*

important

Unregistering a DataBlade

*You cannot unregister a DataBlade module if tables or indexes in the database
depend on it. For example, if a table exists that has a column of a type defined by
the module, an attempt to unregister the module will fail if the table contains data.*

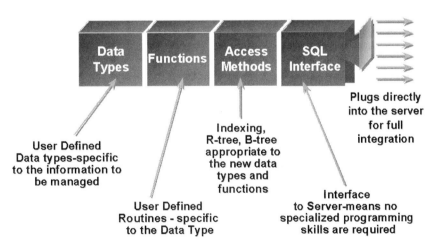

Figure 12-7. Typical DataBlade module components.

User-defined Datatypes

These components are new datatypes that you define to add to the datatypes built into the server. The Web DataBlade HTML datatype is an example. When the Web DataBlade is installed by the BladeManager application, datatypes specific to the Web DataBlade are created.

The keyword *class* is often used to describe a datatype. As in object-oriented programming, a class contains data and the methods to operate on that data. For example, the built-in datatype VARCHAR identifies a string of variable length. Internally, the string is stored with a length attribute. The server will use internal functions to obtain the length of the string when the VARCHAR is used in expressions involving the concatenation operator "||." New datatypes registered with a DataBlade can have functions that are specific to that new datatype. Similarly, an existing function can be *overloaded* to work with the new datatype. Table 12-6 summarizes the meaning of datatypes.

The datatypes relevant to our understanding of the Web DataBlade are row and opaque.

If you use the Informix dbexport utility to dump the contents of a database to disk, you can view the commands that are required to

Table 12-6.   Datatypes.

Datatype	Description
Distinct	A datatype identical to an existing type, but it is treated by the server as being completely distinct from that other type in its behavior.
Collection	A group of elements of the same datatype.
Row	A datatype that contains a group of data fields, of the same or different datatypes, that form a template for data records.
Opaque	A datatype that stores a single value and cannot be divided into components by the server (e.g., HTML, lld_lob).
Built-In	A datatype that is built into the server (e.g., integer, char, date).

create and use the row and opaque types. For example, the opaque
type called html is created as follows:

```
create opaque type 'informix'.html
    (
    internallength=variable,
    maxlen=8192,
    alignment=8
    );
```

This schema defines a variable-length datatype.

The table webpages (installed with the Application Page Builder
application, part of the Web DataBlade deliverable) defines a column called object to store html pages as follows:

```
create table "informix".webpages
  (
    id varchar(40) not null ,
    project varchar(40) not null ,
    object_type varchar(40) not null ,
    mime_type varchar(40) not null ,
    description varchar(250),
    author varchar(40),
    page_version integer,
    last_changed datetime year to second,
    last_changed_by varchar(40),
    write_level integer,
    read_level integer,
    object "informix".html,
    primary key (id)
  ) PUT object in
  (
    sbspace
  )  extent size 32 next size 32 lock mode page;
```

The object column is defined to be of type html, which is
declared as an opaque type. In contrast, read_level is defined to be
of type integer, which is a *built-in* type.

User-defined Routines

These can be C functions or stored procedures. They are callable in
SQL by the database server that supports opaque data. When the

Web DataBlade is registered, the *signatures* of the functions and procedures are defined.

What Is a Signature?

A signature uniquely identifies a procedure. A procedure (routine or function) can be defined more than once with the same name and return type, but the arguments to that procedure must be different in datatype or number. When a routine or function is defined with the same name but different arguments, this is called function overloading. In object-oriented programming, it is called method overloading and is generally used to group related behavior for an object.

For example, the following function is created in the database when the `BladeManager` utility installs the Web DataBlade:

```
create function "informix".filetohtml(lvarchar)
returns html
external name
"$INFORMIXDIR/extend/web.3.32.TC4/web.bld(filetohtml)"
language c;
```

This function converts a file on disk to the HTML datatype, and is usually called using the SQL `INSERT` statement. It is the responsibility of the function to perform any conversion on the source data.

The function definition states that the executable code that does all the work is stored in the `web.bld` object in the directory `$INFORMIXDIR/extend/web.3.32.TC4` and that the source language was C. The `web.bld` object will contain many functions such as this.

When a function is first called from the `web.bld` object, Informix loads `web.bld` as a dynamically linked object library. You can use `onstat` to view the loading of the object. For example, after invoking the `FileToHtml()` function, you can type `onstat-m` to produce the example output below:

```
INFORMIX-Universal Server Version 9.14.TC4    -- On-Line
      -- Up 05:54:47 -- 90560 Kbytes
17:28:07   Logical Log 79 Complete.
17:33:05   Checkpoint Completed:  duration was 0 seconds.
18:17:02   Loading Module
<$INFORMIXDIR/extend/web.3.32.TC4/web.bld>
18:17:06   C Language Module
<D:\informix/extend/web.3.32.TC4/web.bld> loaded
18:53:17   Checkpoint Completed:  duration was 0 seconds.
```

Listing 12-1.   Lengths of AppPages.

name	html_page_size
apb	628
apb_add	478
apb_add_ObjectType	1692
apb_add_Audio	3605
apb_add_Document	3157
apb_add_Image	4027
apb_add_Tag	3505
apb_add_MimeType	2543
apb_add_Page	6941
apb_add_Project	1845
apb_admin	1352

Another Web DataBlade function that operates on HTML is the `length()` function. This is defined as follows:

```
create function "informix".length(html)
returns integer
with
(
    not variant
)
external name
"$INFORMIXDIR/extend/web.3.32.TC4/web.bld(htmlLength)"
language c;
```

The `length()` function can be used in SQL expressions. So, to find out the length in bytes of all the AppPages in the `webpages` table, perform the following query in `dbaccess`:

```
select id as name, length(object) as html_page_size
from webpages;
```

Here, `object` refers to the column of type `html`. Listing 12-1 shows sample output.

Access Methods

An access method is a set of server functions used to access and manipulate an index or table used to support user-defined datatypes.

A *primary* access method is a set of functions used to access a table. These routines perform table operations such as creating, dropping, inserting, deleting, updating, and scanning data in a table. The server calls these routines instead of the built-in table access routines. An example of a primary access method is a gateway to another relational database.

A *secondary* access method is a set of functions used to access and manipulate an index.

SQL Interface

The user-defined datatypes are manipulated by DataBlade functions, and these functions are callable in SQL statements.

In essence, a DataBlade is used to implement a complex datatype, together with the behavior of that datatype. For example, the Web DataBlade implements the HTML datatype. The Web DataBlade provides a function called `FileToHtml()`. This function converts source text into the `HTML` datatype.

A DataBlade typically has other components that are used in conjunction with those mentioned above.

Casts

A cast is a mechanism for converting data from one type to another. Casts allow you to make comparisons between values of different datatypes or to substitute a value of one datatype for a value of another datatype.

If the two datatypes do not have the same binary representation, the database server calls a C function to perform the conversion. If the two types have the same binary representation, a C function might not be needed.

The Informix server provides a built-in cast function and also "::" as a cast operator. Casting values allows the query-processing engine implicitly or explicitly to change the type of a value and use it as an argument to functions that require the destination type.

Table 12-7 summarizes the types of cast that you may encounter when developing DataBlade applications in general.

A cast is defined schematically as follows:

```
create implicit cast (lvarchar as html with
        'informix'.htmlin);
create explicit cast (html as lvarchar with
        'informix'.htmlout);
```

Table 12-7.	Types of cast.

Cast	Description
Explicit	Explicit casts require the use of the cast function or cast operator " : : " to specify the type conversion between two datatypes. Explicit casting is required when the cast is more than one level deep or when ambiguity exists.
Implicit	Implicit casts allow automatic type conversion between two datatypes.
System-defined	A cast that is built into the database server. This cast performs automatic conversions between different built-in datatypes.

The supporting functions are defined as

```
create function "informix".htmlin(lvarchar)
returns html
external name
"$INFORMIXDIR/extend/web.3.32.TC4/web.bld(htmlInput)"
language c;
create function "informix".htmlout(html)
returns lvarchar
external name
"$INFORMIXDIR/extend/web.3.32.TC4/web.bld(htmlOutput)"
language c;
```

An example of an implicit cast would be

```
select weblint("<?MIVAR><?/MIVAR>",1) from webpages
where
id='apb';
```

The first argument to the `weblint` function is converted from characters to HTML. The resulting HTML object is then parsed for AppPage Script syntax errors.

An example of an explicit cast would be:

```
select weblint("<?MIVAR><?/MIVAR>"::HTML,
"3"::integer) from webpages where
id='apb';
```

Web DataBlade Architecture   **367**

The character string containing an AppPage Script tag is converted to HTML. The character string "3" is converted to an `integer`, which is the required signature for the `weblint` function. Note that if the cast was not explicit, the Informix server would cast the character strings to `HTML` and `integer` anyway, since implicit casts have already been defined. You would use an explicit cast if the conversion was not defined as implicit.

Interfaces

Unique IDs are assigned to DataBlade modules or subsets of the types and routines in DataBlade modules. DataBlade modules that depend on other DataBlade modules' interfaces declare the interfaces they require so that BladeManager can ensure that all needed DataBlade modules are registered in a database.

Client Files

Client files are installed on the server with the other DataBlade module files and are be copied to each client workstation that accesses the DataBlade module's objects. Examples include stand-alone client programs, linkable client libraries for use by developers, and `help` and `readme` files. Not all DataBlade modules provide client files.

A client installation is only necessary if the client needs local files to perform actions such as retrieving and verifying data.

The `webdriver` program is a client application, not a DataBlade, although it ships as a component in the Web DataBlade suite of components. It can be installed on the same host as the web server if the web server is on a host computer other than the Informix database server.

Web DataBlade Module Components

The Web DataBlade consists of multiple components, as listed in Table 12-8.

Using the HTML Datatype

You can use the HTML datatype to store AppPages in the Informix database. The external representation of an AppPage is a text string. You can use the standard SQL commands (such as SELECT,

Table 12-8. *Web DataBlade module components.*

Component	Description
HTML datatype	Allows the user to embed SQL statements and use variables within AppPages.
DataBlade functions	Functions implemented in a language such as C to perform operations on the HTML datatype in SQL expressions. Functions exist for the components below, except `webdriver`, which is an application executable.
`webexplode`	Returns the specified AppPage with all the DataBlade module tags expanded and SQL results dynamically retrieved.
`Weblint`	Reports syntax errors in Web DataBlade module tags in the specified AppPage.
`WebUnHtml`	Returns the specified text with special HTML characters replaced for display by a web browser.
`WebURLDecode`	Returns the specified text with hexadecimal values replaced with their nonalphanumeric ASCII characters.
`WebUrlEncode`	Returns the specified text with nonalphanumeric ASCII characters replaced with the hexadecimal values.
`webdriver`	Allows the web application to retrieve data dynamically from the database and to expand the AppPage Script tags.

`INSERT`, `UPDATE`, `DELETE`, and `LOAD`) for AppPages in the Informix database. Since a cast exists from `HTML` to the `CHAR` datatype, you can also execute string functions against the `HTML` objects. When the string function executes, the `HTML` object will be converted to `CHAR`.

Where Is the HTML Object Stored?

The Web DataBlade module supports arbitrarily large AppPages stored as the HTML datatype. Table 12-9 lists the storage strategy.

The implementation of the storage strategy is transparent to the user. Based on the size of the object, the Web DataBlade module determines whether a particular `HTML` object is stored entirely in the

Table 12-9. Storage strategy for HTML objects.

Size of HTML object (AppPage)	Storage strategy
<= 7500 bytes	Store entirely in the table row.
> 7500 bytes	Create smart large object for the remaining portion and store in the nominated sbspace.

row or is extended into a smart large object, and it only retrieves the contents of the smart large object when necessary. Table 12-9 illustrates the concept.

The nominated sbspace is the sbspace in which the HTML column is stored. When the webPages (or, for the Data Director for Web schema, the wbpages) table is created, the column that stores the html object can nominate an sbspace to store the data, For example:

```
CREATE TABLE webPages
(
  object                    html,
) PUT object in (sbspace2);
```

In this example, HTML AppPages larger than 7500 bytes will be stored in the smart BLOB space sbspace2.

Because the AppPage is stored partially or entirely in row, you cannot use smart large object functions against the HTML object.

Because the smart BLOB space for the webTags table is set during Web DataBlade module installation, the default smart BLOB space for the webTags table is the default smart BLOB space for the server. If you wish to change this setting, edit the ONCONFIG file for your server instance, and change the SBSPACENAME parameter.

Memory Management of Large HTML Pages

You can configure an upper limit on the buffer size for the HTML datatype by setting the MI_WEBMAXHTMLSIZE environment variable. Setting this variable allows dynamic memory allocation without causing uncontrollable web server memory growth. The default buffer size is 32KB. For the NSAPI `webdriver`, each thread will initially allocate 8KB, and grow up to `MI_WEBMAXHTMLSIZE`.

Entering HTML Using Applications other than AppPage Builder or Data Director for Web

When using applications other than AppPage Builder (APB) or Data Director for Web (DDW) to create and edit AppPages, you must execute the following procedure for each session. Otherwise, new lines cannot be entered in your AppPages and stored as the HTML datatype. For example, in `dbaccess`:

```
execute procedure ifx_allow_newline('t');
```

To disallow new lines:

```
execute procedure ifx_allow_newline('f');
```

Registering and Unregistering the Web DataBlade

Installing the Web DataBlade

The Web DataBlade installation media will consist of a CD or tape. The command format to copy the files from the installation media to the host filesystem will be described in the media documentation. For a tape archive, `cpio` is usually required to transfer the tape contents to the host filesystem.

The Web DataBlade needs to be installed for each Informix instance that has a database that requires it. This means that if a computer has two Informix instances, then the Web DataBlade needs to be installed twice, once for each instance.

Installing is not the same as registering a DataBlade. Installation copies the DataBlade components to a filesystem directory, once per instance. Registering involves the use of the `BladeManager` utility to register the DataBlade for each database that needs to use the DataBlade functions and datatypes.

For example, a host has one Informix instance. The Web DataBlade is installed once. The instance has six databases, one per application. Three applications need to use the Web DataBlade to be web enabled. The Web DataBlade is registered three times, once for each of the three application databases.

Installed Directories

DataBlades are installed into the `$INFORMIXDIR/extend` directory on both UNIX and NT. The name of the Web DataBlade directory is derived from product version control codes. Put simply, `web.3.32.TC4` denotes the Version 3.32, with patches, for NT.

After installation, the following directory will exist (using the NT example in the last paragraph):

```
D:\informix\extend\web.3.32.TC4
```

Configuring The Web DataBlade

To use the Web DataBlade, you must have created:

- a smart BLOB space to store large binary objects
- a logged database.

The default `sbspace` is defined in the `ONCONFIG` file.

What Is a Smart BLOB Space

One or more chunks form a smart BLOB space, or `sbspace` *(sometimes called a smart large object space). The page size of a smart BLOB space is defined when the* `sbspace` *is created. You can have multiple* `sbspaces` *in an Informix Universal Server instance. This is a storage space for large objects, such as CLOBs, BLOBs, HTML, and other DataBlade object types (such as text DataBlade indexes). The* `sbspace` *has read, write, and seek properties similar to a UNIX file; it is recoverable, obeys transaction isolation modes, and can be retrieved in segments by applications.*

Creating a Smart BLOB Space

You can create an `sbspace` with the `onspaces` command. For example, to create a smart BLOB space called `etxspace`, with the initial cooked `chunk` called `d:\ifmxdata\ol_dellcpi\etx_idx_chunk`, (on NT), perform the following:

```
onspaces -c -S etxspace -g 1 -p D:\
    ifmxdata\ol_dellcpi\etx_idx_chunk -o 0 -s 50000
```

Note that if the `sbspace` `chunk` was on a raw device, the `-o` parameter may be zero or greater. For cooked chunks, the offset is always zero (the start of file).

Table 12-10 lists the parameter semantics.

Table 12-10.   Creating a smart BLOB space.

Parameter	Description
-c	Create a BLOB space
-S sbspacename	Create a smart BLOB Space called sbspacename
-g n	Create the sbspace with a page size of n multiples of the Informix system page size.
-p pathname	The initial chunk for the sbspace is called pathname, where pathname is the absolute path.
-o offset	The chunk offset. For cooked chunks, the offset is zero. For raw devices, the offset can be specified by the systems administrator.
-s size	The initial sbspace size in Kbytes. For example, specify 50000 for an initial chunk (and sbspace) size of 50,000KB, or, 50MB.

Registering the Web DataBlade Module Using BladeManager

The Web DataBlade module needs to be registered in each database that will use the Web DataBlade functions, such as the webexplode() DataBlade function.

You use the BladeManager utility to register DataBlade modules. The BladeManager utility comes in two essential forms, command line and GUI. Generally, you will use the GUI version under windows and the command line version under UNIX, although you can use BladeManager in command line mode under Windows if you are happy to do this, and you can use the GUI version to manage DataBlades on UNIX servers remotely.

Why Register DataBlade Modules?

When you register a DataBlade module with a database, you are basically creating a map between functions that are available to the SQL interface, datatypes that are available to the applications, and the native (or source) functions that will implement the behavior associated with those functions and datatypes.

note

You install a DataBlade once only for each Informix instance. You register the DataBlade with each database that needs to use the DataBlade datatypes and functions. For example, you would install the Web DataBlade once on your host computer. If you created two databases, `stores7Dev` *and* `stores7prod` *(for development and production data), you would register the DataBlade twice, one for each database.*

Important BladeManager Commands

Table 12-11 lists the relevant BladeManager commands that you would use to identify, register, and audit your Web DataBlade installation. These commands are available in the GUI and command line versions of BladeManager. They are listed in command line form.

Table 12-11. BladeManager summary commands.

Command	Purpose
list database	List the registered DataBlades for the named database.
show modules	List the installed DataBlade modules for the current Informix instance.
register module database	Register the DataBlade named by module into the named database.
unregister module database	Unregister the DataBlade named by module from the named database.
info module	Display information about the DataBlade named by module.
show log	Display the contents of a log file created when executing DataBlade commands.
del logs	Delete all logs.
?	Show help on all commands.

Step-By-Step Web DataBlade Registration

This section will show how to register the Web DataBlade in a database, using a database called `onlineorders`.

- Ensure that you have created a database with buffered logging.
- Start BladeManager

```
$ blademgr
online_pln>
```

- List the registered DataBlade modules in the `onlineorders` database

```
online_pln>list onlineorders
There are no modules registered in database
onlineorders.
```

- List the installed DataBlade modules that can be registered.

```
online_pln>show modules
7 DataBlade modules installed on server online_pln:
        web.3.30.UC6        web.3.31.UC2
        TXT.1.10.UC1B1       ETX.1.10.UC1A8
        ifxrltree.1.00       ifxbuiltins.1.1
        LLD.1.20.UC1B1
```

- Register the Web DataBlade Version 3.31.UC2.

```
online_pln>register web.3.31.UC2 onlineorders
Register module web.3.31.UC2 into database
    onlineorders? [Y/n]Y
Registering DataBlade module... (may take a while).
DataBlade web.3.31.UC2 was successfully registered in
database onlineorders.
```

- Relist the registered DataBlade modules for the `onlineorders` database.

```
online_pln>list onlineorders
DataBlade modules registered in database onlineorders:
        web.3.31.UC2
```

If the registration (or unregistration) process fails, you can view the BladeManager diagnostics as follows:

```
online_pln>show log
```

This shows all the `BladeManager` logs. Example output would be:

```
14 1999-04-04 13:24:56 Unregister web.3.31.UC2 Fail
     - Log in /tmp/blademgr/1111g
15 1999-04-04 13:27:38 Prep ifxmngr OK
     - Log in /tmp/blademgr/1111/log015.log
16 1999-04-04 13:28:21 Register web.3.31.UC2 OK
     - Log in /tmp/blademgr/1111/lg
Type 'Enter' for next page, or
     'Q' and 'Enter' to quit. :-
Pick the number of a log or N to cancel :- 16
Nothing to report.
```

In this case, Log 16 is for the registration performed above. Log 14 is for the failed unregistration, described in the next section.

Unregistering DataBlades

Unregistering a DataBlade means that you are removing the new datatypes and functions from the database. You unregister at the database level, not the installation level. If you have six databases with the Web DataBlade and you unregister the DataBlade from one of them, the other five databases will still have the DataBlade registered.

You will not be able to unregister a DataBlade if one of the types implemented by that DataBlade is in use. Similarly, you would not want to unregister the VARCHAR datatype if you had a table that contained a column of that type.

Listing 12-2 shows what happens when you try to unregister the Web DataBlade from the database called web when the webpages table contains AppPages.

You must ask yourself why you want to remove a datatype when that type is in use. If you need to remove a DataBlade, you will have to delete the data from the relevant tables or drop the tables involved; then attempt to unregister.

Listing 12-2.   Unregistering a DataBlade whose datatypes are in use.

```
$ blademgr
online_pln>unregister web.3.31.UC2 web
Unregister module web.3.31.UC2 out of database web? [Y/n]y
blademgr: ERROR: DataBlade web.3.31.UC2 could not be unregistered
      from database.
Use 'show logs' for details of failures in module's scripts.
online_pln>show logs
1 1999-03-19 16:13:41 Prep ifxmngr OK
      - Log in /tmp/blademgr/1111/log001.log
2 1999-03-19 16:14:20 Register ifxbuiltins.1.1 OK
      - Log in /tmp/blademgr/1111g
3 1999-03-19 16:14:43 Register ifxrltree.1.00 OK
      - Log in /tmp/blademgr/1111/g
4 1999-04-04 09:03:32 Prep ifxmngr OK
      - Log in /tmp/blademgr/1111/log004.log
5 1999-04-04 09:04:48 Prep ifxmngr OK
      - Log in /tmp/blademgr/1111/log005.log
6 1999-04-04 09:05:25 Unregister web.3.31.UC2 Fail
      - Log in /tmp/blademgr/1111/g
Pick the number of a log or N to cancel :-  6
  blade: web.3.31.UC2
err expct: unexpected
 SQL stmt: drop type html restrict;
SQL state: XIX000:-9630 : Cannot drop type (html): still in use.

    blade: web.3.31.UC2
err expct: unexpected
 SQL stmt: EXCEPTION
SQL state: Unregistration failed for DataBlade module
      "web.3.31.UC2".
```

The following snippet shows the successful unregistration of the
Web DataBlade from the `onlineOrders` database.

```
$ blademgr
online_pln>unregister web.3.31.UC2 onlineOrders
Unregister module web.3.31.UC2 out of database
      onlineOrders? [Y/n]y
DataBlade web.3.31.UC2 was successfully unregistered
      from Database onlineOrders.
```

Summary

This chapter has outlined the Web DataBlade architecture. DataBlade functions and datatypes were covered in enough detail to get you working directly with DataBlade functions, such as the Web DataBlade `length()` function.

The chapter also showed how an AppPage is constructed and how dynamic page generation can be distributed over multiple computers.

In addition, you successfully used the BladeManager utility to register the Web DataBlade in an Informix database.

Experience navigating these administrative and architectural issues should help you manage your Informix database-driven website better than before and will inform your decisions how to relocate the Web DataBlade components across multiple computers.

Creating and Managing Websites with Data Director for Web

In this chapter:

- What is Data Director for Web?
- Data Director for Web development environment
- Designing and building Websites
- Data Director for Web objects
- An overview of Site Manager
- Storing multimedia content in the database via Site Manager
- An overview of AppPage Editor
- Using AppPage Editor Wizards
- Migrating AppPage Builder resources into Data Director for Web
- Deploying websites
- Multimedia QuickStart Example

Storing web pages in the database is only half the story when creating database-driven websites; if you can store a web page and graphics in the database, why not store the website structure in the database as well? It would also be helpful if the tools we use to build the website could also add value in each phase of the development project lifecycle.

This chapter describes the features of Data Director for Web essential for building and deploying websites. Data Director for Web is referred to throughout the book; the elements of building dynamic web pages are covered in separate chapters. This chapter, however, is primarily concerned with using Data Director for Web to build and manage websites within a project lifecycle model.

Data Director for Web is an Informix GUI tool for Windows clients that allows you to manage your websites inside the database. It is crucial that you understand where Data Director for Web fits into the development lifecycle model, because you will need to manage more than a particular website. You will also need to integrate and deploy website content to and from multiple databases, as well as between intranet and Internet platforms.

This chapter also includes a simple, on-demand multimedia example to demonstrate how easy it is to store all kinds of resources in the database and deliver them over the Web, using Data Director for Web to hide the implementation detail. You should also read Chap. 19, "Creating and Using Dynamic Tags," to learn how implementing dynamic tags can yield the benefits of code reuse, which will have an impact across the whole development project.

What Is Data Director for Web?

Data Director for Web is a suite of graphical user interface tools that enable you to build and manage Informix-based websites and applications throughout the development lifecycle. It allows you to

- create and maintain AppPages and dynamic tags,
- manage website content that is stored in the database,
- use Wizards to add, update, and retrieve data and objects in the database,
- deploy content among databases,
- add and extend content types,
- integrate with other development environments, such as Microsoft FrontPage.

Data Director for Web has more functionality than the APB (Application Page Builder) that is bundled with the Web DataBlade.

You can migrate existing APB applications to the Data Director for Web schema by using the Migrate from APB2 menu option.

Data Director for Web is installed with two essential applications: Site Manager and AppPage Editor.

Site Manager

The Site Manager allows you to maintain database-driven websites. You can create a website on any visible database that has the Web DataBlade registered. Using Site Manager, you can

- create project, file, and resource views,
- edit and preview resources,
- implement resource concurrency and version management,
- deploy websites from the development to the live environment.

AppPage Editor

AppPage Editor allows you to create and maintain AppPages. AppPage Editor comes with a variety of features of which the important ones are summarized below.

- Wizards take you through creating queries, such as INSERT, UPDATE, and DELETE queries.
- You can drag resources from the filesystem and drop them into Data Director for Web, enabling link conversion of the filesystem links.
- Color coding of AppPage tags is implemented.
- Dialogs exist for tags and variable-processing functions.
- You can preview an AppPage without extracting it from the web server if, for example, you want to preview the results before you save the page to the database.

Data Director for Web Development Environment

Figure 13-1 shows a typical Data Director for Web development environment. It shows a website created by third-party tools and imported into the database via Data Director for Web. The website is then deployed from one or more development databases to one or more live, production databases.

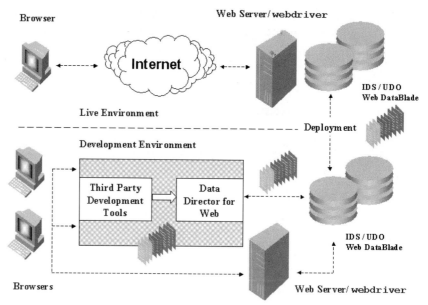

Figure 13-1. Data Director for Web development environment.

You use tools such as FrontPage to create a website look and feel, and the overall website structure in the filesystem. You then drag and drop this website—HTML, images, audio, and video—into the Data Director for Web Site Manager. You then maintain the website within the database.

You can migrate your legacy first- or second-generation websites to the Informix database in order to leverage both the administrative and content management capability of Data Director for Web and Informix Dynamic Server.

Designing and Building Websites

Data Director for Web fits nicely into an inclusive development-lifecycle model, where multiple products are used to take advantage of their particular strengths. This section will show where Data Director for Web fits into a project lifecycle.

The ability to use tools to create a website rapidly doesn't obviate the need to manage the process of creating a website. If you build a website that the customer doesn't want or need, you won't get paid.

Conversely, a site that contains everything the customer wants will be no better unless the customer can understand how to use it.

This failure isn't limited to Internet technology. I have heard customers complaining that an old step-by-step-by-screen application was replaced by a new GUI application using one of the visual development tools with everything on it: They found it totally unusable! This was because the users were not asked how they wanted to use the system—a staggering oversight, since rapid development tools are ideal for prototyping user requirements at an early stage. The phrase *user interface ergonomics* is an important concept for designing and building a website, but it applies as well for any visual interface to business functions that the application is meant to realize.

Every application is different. We saw in Chap. 2, "Web Applications: The Generation Gap," the evaluation of static websites into dynamic ones. On a sliding scale, a customer may initially want to have a simple, browser frontend to his database. He would just want dynamic pages to render an unknown quantity of data according to variable selection filters. Further up the scale, though, a customer might like to manage all her media assets so that she can store and retrieve all the media content, such as pictures and videos. They may already be stored in another database in another department. Think of the roles involved in managing all the content of a newspaper. One person puts a picture into the database, another will use it in a story, after she has located it, of course. These customers will have backend systems that are too expensive to convert to other formats, so they want them to integrate with the web-enabled systems.

As you can see, the presentation layer is not the most critical component. The broader the requirements' scope, the more important the issue of systems integration becomes. It can be argued that the presentation layer is the most disposable part of an application, but this is only true if it has been designed to be disposable. A lot of traditional applications are designed in such a way that throwing away the user interface loses half the application logic as well.

Some larger organizations have developed an approach called a *technical applications framework,* which identifies components and their interaction across departmental and corporate application platforms, including OLTP and data warehousing applications. This doesn't mean that the deployment technology is Java or Enterprise Java Beans, although it could be. It means outlining a set of constraints that each application must adhere to, such as ensuring that an HTML page does not contain any business logic and that in some cases business logic is written using a portable language, such as Java, rather than stored procedures.

What Is Business Logic?

Business logic *comprises rules and procedures for implementing a business function like* Add Customer Order. *In this case, the business logic would create a set of order items related to a particular customer. In addition, an outstanding order total may need to be updated. This logic may be implemented in a stored procedure within the database, or a business object in a middle tier may implement the methods to perform the functionality, perhaps using JDBC to connect to the database. This function is* not *implemented in the client software, for example, in a Java Applet. The point is that we have separated the business logic from the application's user interface so that we can reuse the business component in multiple applications.*

We can define a number of discrete phases of a development project, such as design and discovery, build, integration and functional testing, and live deployment. Data Director for Web has a role in each of these phases.

Design and Discovery

This phase is concerned with capturing the user requirements, which include the website look and feel, business functions, and project constraints. The deliverables are usually a functional specification that contains the detailed user requirements and a design specification that, for a rapid development environment, is a high-level overview of the functions that a builder will implement. For RAD (rapid application development) projects, a system design document (which contains the key links in the overall architecture) is still important, but the prototyping, design, and build is an iterative process. For example, if you need to change the look and feel of the site, you change a *dynamic tag,* not the AppPage.

Functional Prototyping

Functional prototyping is used to emulate the functions that the user will interact with. This usually involves creating mock-ups of the business logic. *Horizontal* and *Vertical* prototyping is used to define the user interface and site structure. Vertical prototyping defines the look and feel of individual screens. Horizontal prototyping creates the site map, with the menu navigation paths defined.

The enabled, or empowered, users are those who can make decisions affecting all aspects of functionality. JAD (joint application development) sessions are usually held as a group comprising the empowered users, a scribe to take notes, and a facilitator who directs the JAD session.

JAD sessions are iterative. The critical functions are prototyped on the client side using dummy business logic. Between JAD sessions, the observations and recommendations of the users are implemented in the prototype. The next session reviews the functions prototyped thus far.

There are lots of iterative RAD environments on the market. It may be useful, for example, to create the look and feel of the site (screens, site map) using a tool such as Microsoft FrontPage.

You can use AppPage Editor to show how a web page can be dynamically created from the contents of the database. Take the page from the page builder software, and import it as a resource. Add the appropriate SQL, and format the result set. You can then demonstrate, using `WINSIZE` and `WINSTART`, for example, how to walk the result set for the selected data.

Once the prototype is in a stable state, the look and feel of the site is extracted from the prototype, and a set of AppPage *dynamic tags* is created in Data Director for Web so that the look and feel is created in one place for reuse across the site.

Nonfunctional Prototyping

This step involves a set of end-to-end prototyping tasks. This is the functionality the user does not see, which is mainly concerned with overall systems architecture. Backend functionality, such as interfaces to external systems, may require the interface prototyping to map out the design constraints.

Database Design

The logical database design is developed during this phase. It will be implemented as an Informix schema for the build. Remember that the website will be database driven, with an OLTP profile in terms of hits, users, and query filters; pay special attention to the physical implementation of the logical design. You don't have to design the schema that contains the website content; this already exists. But you may have to interface to an external database or integrate content from legacy databases. The logical design is mapped onto an Informix schema, and the schema is deployed in the development database.

Build

This phase involves building the AppPages and dynamic tags for the whole website. Note that you should create AppPage templates that will result in different HTML pages, depending on the AppPage Scripting behavior. You should also implement and parameterize dynamic tags that can be deployed across the complete set of AppPage templates (an example would be a header or footer template; see Chap. 19 for more details). This phase also includes creating the supporting stored procedures, batch jobs, and interfaces to external systems to support the underlying requirements.

The design phase should have identified the AppPages that need to be built, as well as the application database design that will support the required queries.

The design should state where the business logic is implemented. For example, business logic may be implemented in stored procedures. Forms validation can be performed in the browser (using JavaScript) or on the server when the next AppPage is exploded.

In this phase, you would use Data Director for Web to create the projects, store the resources in the database (such as the graphics and baseline office content), and create the production-level AppPages and dynamic tags via tools such as the query and update wizards.

Testing the Website

The nature of creating websites is that building and testing go together. You can't really build a set of pages without testing them as you go along. What you may not be able to test is the effect of business logic, which may not have been built at the point you create an HTML form to trigger it.

You can deploy projects incrementally to a test database. Depending on how you manage the projects in Data Director for Web, it may be best to deploy a set of changes in one go, especially if the build and integration test phases overlap, since you don't want to deploy half-finished resources.

You would use Data Director for Web to deploy the resources from the development database to the test database.

You should emulate the production environment in this phase. If the web server and database servers are on separate machines, you should test against this architecture.

Integration and Functional Testing

Integration testing will test that all the different components work together. Functional testing will test that the business requirements defined in the requirements specification have been realized in the application, and this involves testing business scenarios as well as end-to-end testing that includes interfaces to external systems.

Volume Testing

For a site expected to receive a large number of hits, you need to configure the web server and database server to support the maximum number of allowable connections. In addition, a web user firing queries at the database may expect a response in a matter of seconds. Volume testing should simulate the stresses imposed on the web server and database server.

Live Deployment

Data Director for Web will deploy the tested application to the live database from the test database. The database may reside across a network on a machine hosted by an ISP (Internet service provider), or it may be within the corporation, hosted on a machine on the other side of a firewall.

Data Director for Web Objects

Data Director for Web acts on objects stored under the Data Director for Web schema. You can use Data Director for Web to manipulate resources, extensions, dynamic tags, variable-processing functions, and projects.

Creating Resources from Web Content

Website content, such as AppPages, images, and other content types (e.g., PDF documents) are known as *resources*. Data Director for Web contains the built-in resources as shown in Table 13-1.

A resource is an object stored in the Data Director for Web schema for which we know the MIME type. At some point, the

Table 13-1. **Data Director for Web built-in resources.**

Resource	Description
AppPage	Stored in the `wbPages` table.
Binary	An object like an image or an audio clip that is stored as a BLOB in the `wbBinaries` table.
Other	This resource describes all objects not stored in Data Director for Web tables. The resource is stored as a binary or text object in a user table, and the source table information is stored in the `wbExtensions` table.

resource will be delivered over the Web, so we need to know the MIME type of the object. The Data Director for Web table `wbExtensions` maps a file suffix, such as DOC or XLS, to a MIME type. If a file is imported from the filesystem to the database using Site Manager, then the file suffix is used to identify the MIME type, and from there it identifies the folder in the Project View that will contain it. The `wbExtensions` table contains other information for resources, such as the database table to contain the resource.

Extensions

An extension specifies mapping information for web content. You add a new MIME type by defining an extension for it, including the name of the table in which the objects reside. Generally, text objects should reside in the `wbPages` table and binary objects in the `wbBinaries` table, but existing database tables with resource content can also be used. Tables other than `wbPages` and `wbBinaries` can be associated with only a single extension. Extensions are stored in the `wbExtensions` table.

Data Director for Web Dynamic Tags

A dynamic tag is a dynamically expanded AppPage fragment that can be easily shared among multiple AppPages. Dynamic tags are stored in the `wbTags` table. Dynamic tags are another type of resource.

Variable-processing Functions

A variable-processing function is used in a variable expression that enables calculations to be performed using AppPage variables.

Projects

A *project* is a collection of related resources, such as AppPages, images, and dynamic tags, that are associated with a particular web application. A resource can belong to one or more projects, but it is not required to belong to any project. Information specific to a given project is stored in the wbProjects table.

The Data Director for Web Schema

Data Director for Web uses its own set of tables, called the Data Director for Web schema. This schema is different from the AppPage Builder schema. Table 13-2 lists the tables in the schema.

Table 13-2. **Data Director for Web summary schema.**

Table	Description
wbPages	stores AppPages and any other text format resources, such as plain text files or HTML pages.
wbBinaries	stores all nontext resources, such as GIF images, audio, video, Java applets.
wbTags	stores dynamic tags.
wbExtensions	maps a MIME type to the table that stores the object of that type in the database.
wbProjects	stores project information for all projects in the database.
wbResProjects	stores a map of which resources belong to which projects in a many-to-many relationship.
wbPreviews	stores preview information for each project, which allows you to preview an exploded AppPage in AppPage Editor.

tip   You can migrate your AppPage Builder applications to the Data Director for Web schema so that you can manage them using Data Director for Web. Any changes you make to the migrated content are not reflected in the AppPage Builder version.

The schema that you use is stated in the `web.cnf` file. You can't use the AppPage Builder and Data Director for Web schema for the same URL, since this maps onto a `web.cnf` (or a *Mapping* in Version 4 of the Web DataBlade, that nominates a *Configuration*), which supports either AppPage Builder or Data Director for Web.

tip   You can install both Data Director for Web and AppPage Builder in the same database. You create a separate URL for each `web.cnf` that maps the appropriate schema. However, you can't access AppPage Builder objects from Data Director for Web and vice versa, unless you migrate the AppPage Builder application to Data Director for Web or write some customized code. If you need to access AppPage Builder objects from Data Director for Web, you are advised to migrate the AppPage Builder project to a new Data Director for Web project.

Installing the Data Director for Web Schema

Site Manager will install the Data Director for Web schema in the database if the schema has not been installed already.

For example, we would like to use the `restock` database to manage a warehouse intranet site, which monitors the status of stock going in and out of the warehouse. The steps to follow are:

- Select the database `restock` from Site Manager Project View
- Select `Install Schema` from the Install Schema into Database dialog.

When you select the `restock` database from the Project View, a screen similar to Fig. 13-2 is displayed.

The dialog will display which component you are using to manage web content, either Universal Web Connect or the Web DataBlade. The dialog will also provide a list of Smart BLOB Spaces, of which you should select one.

Once the Install Schema button is clicked, the Data Director for Web schema is created in the `restock` database, and a confirmatory message will be displayed similar to Fig. 13-3.

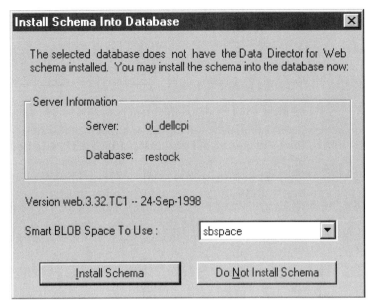

Figure 13-2. Install Schema into Database.

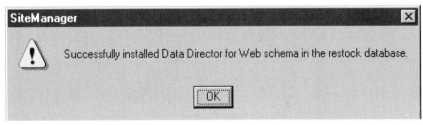

Figure 13-3. Schema installation completed.

An Overview of Site Manager

The Site Manager component helps you develop and manage Informix-based websites and creates new Data Director for Web resources. Using Site Manager, you can view your website using a filesystem model like Microsoft Windows Explorer.

The Site Manager main window consists of two frames. The left frame provides a tree view of the network environment; the right frame provides a resource view. When fully expanded, these views provide you with a list of all the available database servers, databases, and web-related database resources.

The Project View

In the Project View, you view a database as a group of projects. Each project contains folders for each of the different Data Director for Web *supertypes.* When you install the Data Director for Web schema into a new database, two default folders are created: a *Not In Project* folder and an *Other Resources* folder. The *Not In Project* folder contains all resources not associated with any project. The *Other Resources* folder contains all resources that are stored in the database and mapped in the wbExtensions table but are not stored in the Data Director for Web schema.

Figure 13-4 shows the Project View, with the text supertype object selected in the MaintainCustomer project. You can see all of the

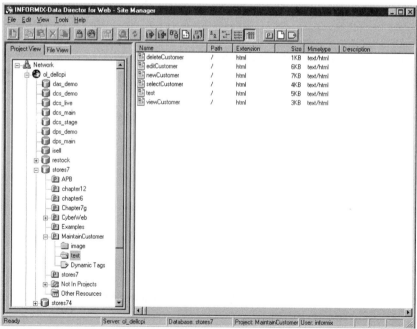

Figure 13-4. *The Data Director for Web Project View.*

databases managed by the `INFORMIXSERVER ol_dellcpi`. Some of these databases do not have the Data Director for Web schema installed. If you clicked on one, the installation dialog would appear.

The File View

In the File View, you view databases as individual filesystems. Clicking a folder displays the next level of subfolders. Figure 13-5 shows the File View for the `myCompany` project, which is shown in the Project View in Fig. 13-6.

When retrieving content such as AppPages from the Data Director for Web schema, you don't specify the project. Project information is not stored in the `wbPages` table. AppPages don't have to belong to a project—in which case, they appear in the Not In Projects *folder.*

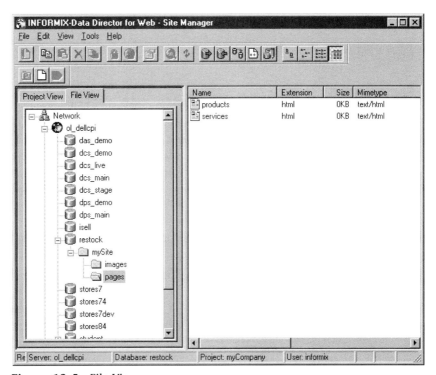

Figure 13-5. File View.

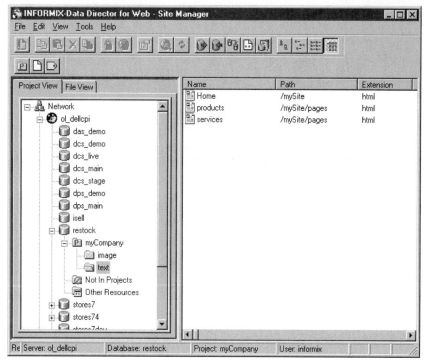

Figure 13-6. *Project View of Fig. 13-5.*

Connecting to the Database Server

You can connect to multiple database servers and databases through a single instance of Site Manager on the Windows client. Connections are maintained at the database level, one per database. Login information is provided at the database server level. You must have login access on the host machine. Database connections are maintained until you exit Site Manager or lose the network connection.

To connect to a database server, click the appropriate server icon in the Project View. Once you are connected to the server, a list of databases in the server is displayed. You select a database by clicking the database icon in the Project View.

Configuring Data Director for Web to Use Dynamic Tags

Data Director for Web uses the `wbTags` table to store dynamic tags. To use dynamic tags, the `web.cnf` file needs to contain a variable called `MI_WEBTAGSSQL`, which is set as follows:

```
MI_WEBTAGSSQL  SELECT parameters, object FROM wbTags
WHERE webupper(ID)=webupper('$MI_WEBTAGSID');
```

This variable should be set in the server side `web.cnf` and in the preview settings for the project on the Data Director for Web client.

If dynamic tags are displayed in the browser as unexpanded text, then check the setting of `MI_WEBTAGSSQL`.

Tracing Connection Problems

In the Data Director for Web installation directory, there is a file called `error.log` that contains tracing information written by the product. It is worth checking this file if you experience problems connecting Site Manager or AppPage Editor to the database server. If the error log says something like "The INFORMIXSERVER value is not listed in the sqlhosts file or the Registry" check the value of the `INFORMIXSERVER` variable in Setnet32. If it is not set, go to the Server Information tab and click "Make Default Server." In addition, if you are connecting to the database from the web server via `webdriver`, make sure that the schema definitions in `web.cnf` exist in the database.

Locking Projects and Resources

Locking a project or resource, such as an AppPage, prevents other users from updating or deleting the resource while you are editing it. Every time a resource is modified, its version number is increased by one.

When you lock a project, you lock all resources within the project. You may not be granted the lock if resources in the project are locked by another user. This can occur when another user has locked resources individually, or when a project lock has been put on a project that contains resources shared by the project that you wish to lock.

Importing and Exporting Projects

You can import an entire project into the database from the filesystem by using the *Import* menu option. On import, the static links can all be converted to dynamic links made valid in the database through a process called *link conversion*. The URL is changed to a `webdriver` URL, using `$WEB_HOME` in the Preview Settings for the project.

In addition, you can export a project from the database to the filesystem. All content stored in the Data Director for Web schema and mapped in the wbExtensions table is exported.

You can also import a website from the filesystem into the database by dragging the root folder from Windows Explorer onto the Data Director for Web project in the Project View.

You cannot export dynamic tags to the filesystem.

Adding Resources

There are two basic ways to add a resource. You can use the *Create Resource* dialog to create a new blank resource (such as an AppPage) or to import an existing resource from the filesystem. Alternatively, you can drag an existing resource from the desktop to Site Manager.

A resource will consist of a name, extension, and path. The extension is used to map the content type onto an extension in the wbExtensions table. This is required so that, when the content is delivered to the Web, webdriver knows the MIME type of the object.

You can drag and drop any resource from the filesystem for which a mapping has been defined in the wbExtensions table. The file extension is used to map the appropriate resource extension.

Table 13-3 shows the default path, ID, and extension metadata created for the filesystem objects added to Site Manager as resources. If you drag and drop a resource, the path is set to "/" and the file extension is used to map the resource type. If you use the Import option to import a folder and subfolders, the folder hierarchy is maintained in the path, and the file extension is used as before. You can change the path later in Site Manager.

Table 13-3.   Example resource metadata.

Filesystem Object	Path	ID	Extension
d:\mySite\pages\home.html	mySite/pages	home	html
d:\mySite\images\logo.gif	mySite/images	logo	gif
d:\mySite\audio\welcome.wav	mySite/audio	welcome	wav

Storing Multimedia Content in the Database via Site Manager

You can store many types of web content in the database. You can store audio, video, VRML objects and behaviors, anything that can be interpreted by a helper application or browser plug-in. What you need to do is make sure that the MIME type is defined as an *extension mapping*. If it isn't, create one. If you want to view the object from within Data Director for Web, create a link to a helper application when you create the extension mapping.

tip

Sometimes it's not practical to store certain types of web objects in the database. For example, you would not store streaming audio or video in the database because the overhead of delivering that content from the database would be excessive. This doesn't stop you from storing the URLs for this content in the database, together with the content metadata. You may want to do this if you intend to publish the latest collection of streaming video samples. In this case, you store the URL that points to the video server in the database, then select and format the URL in the ANCHOR *tag using the* MISQL *AppPage tag. The actual video content resides outside the database.*

MIME Types and Data Director for Web

Every content item maintained by Data Director for Web has a MIME type. These content types can be any object that you store in the database. For example, a Microsoft Word document, a PowerPoint Presentation, a Quick-Time video. The definition of the MIME type is stored in the wbExtensions table. When you create a resource, you use the extension of the resource to identify its MIME type. If you drag and drop resources into Data Director for Web, the file extension is used to identify the MIME type. In any event, the file extension is stored as metadata for the item; it is used if the item is exported to the filesystem from the database and also when the object is delivered via an HTML page.

Installed Extension Mappings

You can view all the registered extensions in the *Extension Mappings* dialog, which you can select from the button bar or from the menu bar using Tools/Extensions. The *Extension Mappings* dialog is then displayed, as shown in Fig. 13-7.

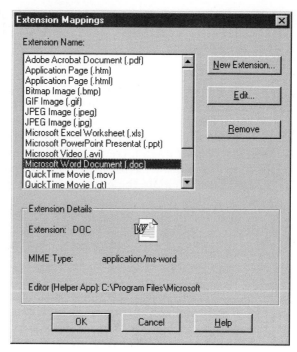

Figure 13-7. Installed extension mappings.

Data Director for Web is installed with lots of MIME types already defined, and you can see this in Fig. 13-7.

Helper application information is not installed with Data Director for Web. You have to set this yourself when you add a new extension, or you can edit the installed extensions in the Extension Mappings dialog.

Understanding Extensions and Project Folders

For every supertype that is defined in the `wbExtensions` table, a corresponding folder will be created in the Project View when an instance of that content type is created in the database.

The folder to which the content item is added depends on the *supertype* defined for the MIME type, which is mapped by the extension of the object (e.g. `DOC`, `PDF`, `GIF`).

For example, if you add a Microsoft Word document to the database, the MIME type defined in the extension mappings for content with a DOC extension is `application/ms-word`. The supertype is `application` and the subtype is `ms-word`. Therefore, the object will be added to the *application* folder.

Table 13-4.   Content supertypes, folders, and examples.

MIME supertype	Folder	Example content
application	application	PDF documents, EXCEL spreadsheets, PowerPoint presentations, WORD documents
text	text	HTML pages
image	image	BMP, JPEG, GIF files
video	video	AVI files

At the point you add resources, if the selected item in the Project View is a project folder, the object will be added to the application folder for that project. Otherwise, it will be added to the application folder in the Not In Projects folder.

There can only be one instance of an object with a particular name in the database. You can have an object with the same name in another database. You can use one object in many projects. You don't have to use a project at all. Projects are a convenient way to group related semantic information for content items. When you import or export content, this is project based. The mapping of content items and projects is stored in the wbResProjects *table.*

Table 13-4 lists some examples of content types and the folders they are assigned to.

Adding a New MIME Type

Chapter 9, "Integrating Java Applets with the Database," contains a complete working example of adding MIME types for Java class files and JAR archives so that we can add Java applets to the database and deliver them over the Web from the database. This example can be applied to any new MIME type that you wish to add.

Configuring Viewers for Data Director for Web Resources

It is useful to be able to view the resources from Data Director for Web using a helper application. For example, you may want to read the Word document that you can see in the Project View. You can invoke the appropriate helper application to view the object as long

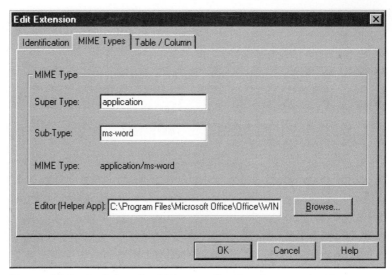

Figure 13-8. *Defining the Helper application for an extension.*

as you have created the mapping for the helper application in the MIME Type tab of the Extension Mappings dialog.

For example, to add Microsoft Word as the helper application that Data Director for Web should call if a Word document is double-clicked from Site Manager, enter the path to the Word application in the MIME Types tab of the Extension Mappings dialog, as shown in Fig. 13-8.

Integrating Web Content from Other Sources

We use extension mappings to name the tables that store MIME types. By default, the `wbBinaries` table stores all objects except `text` supertypes. However, we may be integrating web content from other applications, and these applications may not be using the Data Director for Web schema. So, if we need to deliver web content from a different set of tables, we map the MIME type of the content to the application table that stores it.

The extension information is local to a database. Each database has its own version of the `wbExtensions` table.

The Identification and MIME Type tabs of the Extension Mappings dialog remain the same. The Table/Column tab however must state the source table and table columns that identify and store the objects in the database. You may find that the other schema is incompatible, especially when there is no metadata for the object; for example, if the metadata is stored with information not directly related to the object (e.g., a customer credit report stored in the same table as the customer details). If you find a discrepancy in the schema as in the latter case, then you would be wiser to migrate the objects from the old schema to the wbBinaries table and set the MIME attributes accordingly.

Caching Extension Information

Extension mappings should be cached in the production and system-testing environment in order to avoid repeated querying of static extension information in the wbExtensions table. You do not have to cache this information in the development environment, since it is expected that this information will change.

You should set the webdriver variable MI_WEBEXTENSIONS to the absolute path of a file in the filesystem that will contain the extension mapping information that webdriver will use. The file does not have to exist when you nominate it. You can give the file any name you like.

For example, the following setting in web.cnf instructs webdriver to create a file in the d:\tmp folder called extensions.txt.

```
MI_WEBEXTENSIONS        d:\tmp\extensions.txt
```

Listing 13-1 shows the contents of the file referred to by MI_WEBEXTENSIONS after a URL has been invoked that runs webdriver with the above setting.

Note that you can see the Java class and jar resources defined at the end of the file. These extensions are created in Chap. 9, "Integrating Java Applets with the Database."

The cached mappings reflect what was entered in the Extension Mappings dialog, and they are arranged one row per mapping, with each row split into entries as follows:

- The first entry is the extension.
- The second entry is the table that stores an instance of the resource with that extension.
- The third entry is the MIME type.
- The fourth entry is the name of the column in the nominated table (e.g., wbBinaries) that identifies the resource.
- The fifth entry is the name of the column in the nominated table which stores the actual resource.
- The sixth column is an internal code that tells webdriver how to retrieve the object: 1 (webexplode it), 2 (use it as if it were text), and 3 (BLOB retrieval by name or Large Object handle)

Listing 13-1.   Cached extension mappings.

```
#This file was automatically generated
#Manual editing could cause problems
html    wbPages  text/html ID           object   1
htm     wbPages  text/html ID           object   1
txt     wbPages  text/plain ID          object   2
gif     wbBinaries        image/gif ID  object   3
jpg     wbBinaries        image/jpeg ID object   3
jpeg    wbBinaries        image/jpeg ID object   3
bmp     wbBinaries        image/bmp ID  object   3
doc     wbBinaries        application/ms-word ID object   3
ppt     wbBinaries        application/ms-ppt ID  object   3
xls     wbBinaries        application/ms-excel   ID       object   3
pdf     wbBinaries        application/pdf        ID       object   3
wav     wbBinaries        audio/x-wav    ID      object   3
qt      wbBinaries        video/quicktime        ID       object   3
mov     wbBinaries        video/quicktime        ID       object   3
avi     wbBinaries        video/x-msvideo        ID       object   3
vrml    wbPages  x-world/vrml    ID      object   2
class   wbbinaries        application/x-java     id       object   3
jar     wbbinaries        application/x-jar      id       object   3
```

See Chap. 20, "Working with Large Objects," for a description of retrieving large objects by name or large object (LO) handle.

If you are using NSAPI, ISAPI, or Apache API webdriver, *remember to stop and start the web server when you change the* web.cnf *file (manually in Version 3, or using the Administration tool in Version 4), since the* webdriver *variables are stored in web server memory when the* webdriver *shared object is first loaded.*

An Overview of AppPage Editor

AppPage Editor helps you easily create and edit AppPages, as well as add AppPage tags to existing HTML pages. The AppPage Editor has a single main window where you create, edit, and view AppPages and dynamic tags. You can view the currently open document within this window. You can also connect to a different database entirely.

Invoking AppPage Editor

You can either click on an AppPage in Site Manager or select it from the Programs menu. If you select it from the Programs menu, then you need to connect to the Informix database server and database.

Connecting to the Database

Select `File/Connect to DB` from the File menu. A dialog similar to Fig. 13-9 should be displayed. Select the database server, which will then populate the list of available databases to select. The User Name and Password entries are taken from the registry.

Data Director for Web is a Windows client application, so the settings for the Informix server and remote hosts are located in the registry. Use `setnet32` *to manage the registry settings for your Informix servers and host machines.*

Retrieving an AppPage or Dynamic Tag from the DataBase

Select `File/Open from DB`. You are then presented with a list of projects in the selected database. Select the project if required, and the list of AppPages from that Project is displayed. You can also select a dynamic tag to edit by selecting the Dynamic Tag resource type at the foot of the dialog. Figure 13-10 shows the dialog. Select the resource that you wish to edit, and click OK. The AppPage or dynamic tag is retrieved from the database and displayed in the AppPage Editor main window.

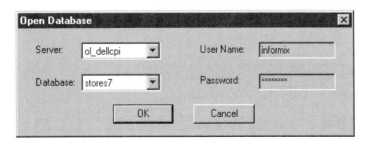

Figure 13-9. Connect to database from AppPage Editor.

Figure 13-10. *Open a resource from the database.*

Setting User Preferences

Select `Tools/Preferences` to set the user preferences when using
AppPage Editor.

You can set the following information from the User Preferences
dialog:

- color coding HTML text and special tags,
- enabling or disabling `META` tag information,
- Enabling or disabling `webexplode()` in page preview.

Once set, these preferences are persistent across all subsequent invocations of AppPage Editor. Figure 13-11 shows the User Preferences
dialog. Probably the most important option is the color coding
option.

*Data Director for web makes a native connection to the Informix data-
base server via the Informix connectivity libraries. Therefore, you must
have* `Informix-Connect` *and the* `Informix-DBA` *kit installed.*

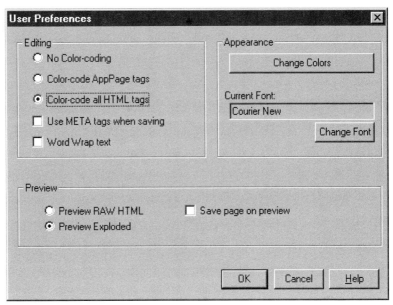

Figure 13-11. Setting user preferences.

Switching Between Edit and Preview Modes

Edit mode allows you to edit the AppPage or dynamic tag. Preview mode allows you to view the exploded AppPage or dynamic tag within AppPage Editor. You can switch between these modes using the Menu bar.

In Preview mode, AppPage editor uses the preview settings to manage the explosion of the AppPage or dynamic tag. Essentially, the explosion of the resource is performed on the client.

Preview Settings

You can edit the preview settings by selecting `Tools/Preview` Settings from the menu bar. Think of preview settings as the `web.cnf` for the client. For example, `WEB_HOME` is defined in the preview settings. If your AppPage needs an AppPage variable, you can define a default value in the preview settings. You can change this default value in the `WebExplode Parameters` textbox in AppPage Editor. If you have no default specified, you must assign a value to the named variable in the `WebExplode Parameters` textbox. You can also import a `web.cnf` from the filesystem as a preview configuration. In this case, the configurations are totally separate but are used to bind the client preview closely with the eventual web browser view.

You can only define one preview for a project. If you want to define multiple previews for a resource, share the resource across multiple test projects.

Associating Preview Settings with Projects

A *Default* preview setting is installed with Data Director for Web. You can use this as the basis for defining project-specific settings by copying the Default preview settings to another setting's file and linking it with the relevant projects. Figure 13-12 shows the Preview Settings for the `stores7` database. You can associate a preview setting with multiple projects.

If your AppPage needs AppPage variables defined for the Preview function to operate, then enter them in the `WebExplode Parameters` box using URL notation. For example, if your AppPage

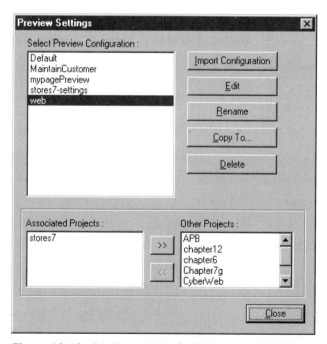

Figure 13-12. Preview settings for the `stores7` *database.*

requires two variables to be set, called `MIval` and `customerId`, enter the following in the `WebExplode Parameters` box:

```
MIval=myPage&customerId=101
```

tip

It may be easier to test your AppPages in the browser, using the web server and the server-side `webdriver`. For example, you can save your AppPage or dynamic tag to the database from AppPage Editor using the Save icon or the File\Save as DB menu option. Then, switch to the browser and enter the URL in the location box. The saved AppPage will be exploded from the database instead of exploded locally at the client. This option is probably the most reliable.

Creating AppPages

The main function of AppPage Editor is to help you build AppPages quickly. Using AppPage Editor you can create AppPages, add resources, and save the AppPage to either the database or filesystem. You define attributes of an AppPage through the properties sheet for the AppPage. Table 13-5 lists the essential properties.

Using AppPage Editor Wizards

AppPage Editor contains wizards to help you quickly build query tags, delete tags, input forms, and update forms. Each wizard allows you to visually create the tag or form and to choose an output format. The wizard dynamically builds the HTML to perform

Table 13-5. *Essential AppPage properties.*

Property	Description
Description	Text description of the AppPage.
Author	Author of the AppPage.
Version	Version number of the AppPage.
Keywords	Keywords that describe the AppPage.
Read level	The user authorization level required at runtime to view the AppPage.

the appropriate actions; you choose either to store the resultant text in the database as a dynamic tag or insert it directly into the AppPage. The advantage of storing the result as a dynamic tag is that you can reuse the form in multiple AppPages.

Using the Query Wizard

The query wizard guides you through creating an MISQL tag to query against underlying tables. You provide the tag name, output format, table names, column names to be retrieved, column names to be displayed, selection criteria, and any necessary hyperlinks.

Using the Delete Wizard

The delete wizard guides you through creating an MISQL tag to delete information from an underlying table. You provide the tag name, table name, selection criteria, and success message.

Using the Input Form Wizard

The input form wizard guides you through creating HTML forms to insert new rows into underlying database tables. You provide the table name, column names, and success message. In addition, you choose the output format.

The input wizard generates two tags. You give a name for the tags, and this name is prefixed to the tag title.

The *Add* tag creates the input form. The *Insert* tag posts the data to the database. The AppPage variable `apb_state_` is used to control which tag is executed. The `apb_state_` variable is set to GET or POST: GET means that we are in input mode; POST means that we are in processing mode after the form has been submitted.

Using the Update Wizard

The update wizard guides you through creating HTML forms to update information in underlying database tables. You provide the tag name, table name, selection criteria, success message, and the output format.

The update wizard generates two tags. You give a name for the tags, and this name is prefixed to the tag title.

The *Edit* tag creates the input form and populates it with current information. The *Update* tag posts the data to the database. The AppPage variable `apb_state_` is used to control which tag is executed. The `apb_state_` variable is set to GET or POST and is used as described above.

Migrating AppPage Builder Resources into Data Director for Web

To take advantage of the Data Director for Web tools, you can transfer all of your AppPage Builder projects into the Data Director for Web schema using Site Manager. The original project is not deleted from the AppPage Builder schema. Any changes you make to the Data Director for Web version are not automatically transferred back to the AppPage Builder project.

Summary Tasks

Using Site Manager, the task list can be summarized as follows:

- Select the database server and database for the project.
- Select *Tools/Migrate APB2 Resources* from the Site Manager menu. The Migrate APB2 Resources dialog should appear, which lists the AppPage Builder projects and Data Director for Web projects held in the different schemas in the selected database.
- If you want to transfer the dynamic tags (AppPage Builder and user tags), check the Copy Dynamic Tags box.
- Select the AppPage Builder project that you wish to transfer from the left-hand panel, and click the >> button.
- The resources from the AppPage Builder project are then transferred to the Data Director for Web schema.
- Change the schema-related variable values in `web.cnf` to reflect the Data Director for Web schema.

If the AppPage Builder project was accessed using NSAPI, you need to set the variable `MI_WEBNSNAMETRANS` in the `web.cnf` file. This variable is set to the value of `WEB_HOME`. For example:

```
# If you are using the NSAPI Webdriver, include the
  following:
# NOTE: The line must end with slash ( / )
WEB_HOME /stores7/
MI_WEBNSNAMETRANS /stores7
```

Once the transfer is complete, a new project is created with the same name as the AppPage Builder project, and the resource extensions are mapped into folder locations for the transferred items.

Remember to change the schema-related variables in `web.cnf`, as well as any other dependency you may have introduced as a customization.

Changing the web.cnf File

This section lists an example web.cnf file for the AppPage Builder configuration, and the equivalent web.cnf file for the Data Director for Web configuration. If you migrate any AppPage Builder projects that use the first configuration, change the web.cnf file to match the second configuration. The number of changes is very small, but it is worth showing two complete examples. Listing 13-2 shows the AppPage Builder configuration, and List. 13-3 shows the Data

Listing 13-2. AppPage Builder version of web.cnf variables.

```
# Connection Specific Variables
        MI_DATABASE                 stores7
        MI_USER                     informix
        MI_PASSWORD                 informix
        REMOTE_USER?                admin
        INFORMIXDIR                 d:\informix
        INFORMIXSERVER              ol_dellcpi

# If you are using the NSAPI Webdriver, include the following:
# NOTE: The line must end with slash ( / )
        WEB_HOME        /stores7/

# Webdriver Specific Variables
        MInam        ID
        MIcol        object
        MItab        webPages

        MInamObj?    ID
        MIcolObj?    object
        MItabObj?    webImages
        MItypeObj?   image/gif

        MIval?       apb

# Security Schema
        MIusertable  webusers
        MIusername   ID
        MIuserpasswd password
        MIuserlevel  security_level
        MIpagelevel  read_level
```

Listing 13-3.   Data Director for Web version of `web.cnf` **variables.**

```
# Connection Specific Variables
      MI_DATABASE          stores7
      MI_USER              informix
      MI_PASSWORD          informix
      REMOTE_USER?         admin
      INFORMIXDIR          d:\informix
      INFORMIXSERVER       ol_dellcpi

# If you are using the NSAPI Webdriver, include the following:
# NOTE: The line must end with slash ( / )
      WEB_HOME             /stores7/
      MI_WEBNSNAMETRANS    /stores7

# Webdriver Specific Variables
      MInam                ID
      MIcol                object
      MItab                wbPages

      MInamObj?            ID
      MIcolObj?            object
      MItabObj?            wbBinaries
      MItypeObj?           image/gif

      MIval?               HomePage

# Security Schema
      MIusertable          webusers
      MIusername           ID
      MIuserpasswd         password
      MIuserlevel          security_level
      MIpagelevel          read_level

# Data Director for Web Schema and Dynamic Tag Variables
      MI_WEBSCHEMADEF      wb
      MI_WEBTAGSSQL        SELECT parameters,object FROM wbTags WHERE
                           webupper(ID)=webupper('$MI_WEBTAGSID');
```

Director for Web configuration after the project has migrated from AppPage Builder to Data Director for Web.

Deploying Websites

Deployment of websites using Data Director for Web is an important topic, because, at the simplest level, we are taking a development version of a web application and "putting it live." Thereafter, you need to maintain one or more live applications with the minimum of disruption, especially when the expected uptime of the website is 24×7.

When a web application goes live for the first time, the application is transferred in bulk, but the subsequent deployment can be incremental.

A physical website in Data Director for Web is the complete collection of resources in the Data Director for Web schema for one database. A web application is a collection of linked resources in that physical site. The live database may contain only a subset of all the entries in the development schema, and these subsets can be managed as projects. So, you can relate a web application to a project. Because you deploy between databases at project level, you can deploy multiple applications discretely if you manage them correctly as projects.

Using URL prefixes and `webdriver` configurations, you can manage basic and authenticated access to the physical site. As a result, the viewable site may differ for different groups of users.

If you wish to deploy a web application to a target machine that is not available on the network, then export *the project from the source installation, and* import *it to the target installation.*

Deployment of a website means copying one Data Director for Web project to another Data Director for Web installation. The target installation can be another database in the same Informix server or another database in a remote Informix server.

Full Deployment

This is the *default* deployment method. All resources are copied to the target database. Note that newer versions of the resource in the target database will be overwritten, so this option should be used to force parity between the source and target projects. Typically, you will use this option the first time the application goes live and thereafter if you have made any major revisions.

The following is a checklist of tasks to perform when deploying an Informix Web DataBlade application from Site Manager:

- Configure the target database server.
- Deploy the website from the Data Director for Web Client to the target database.
- Deploy the Application schema to the target database.
- Configure the web server that will connect via `webdriver`, to the target web application.

Configure the Target Database Server

- Create a logged database on the target Informix instance using `createdb`.
- Create a smart BLOB space for the target instance, if one has not been created already, using `onspaces`.
- Register the Web DataBlade on the target instance using `blademgr`.

Deploy from the Data Director for Web Client

- Install the Data Director for Web schema on the target database by clicking on the database icon in Site Manager; you will be prompted to install the schema.
- Create the target project on the target database using Site Manager.
- Select *Tools/Deployment* from the Site Manager menu.
- Enter the source Informix server (database and project) and the target Informix server (database and project). Select Full Deployment in the Deployment Option box. Click OK.

Figure 13-13 shows an example of deploying the `MaintainCustomer` project from the `stores7dev` database to the `stores7live` database in the Deployment dialog. This example deploys between databases in the same Informix server instance, but the source and target databases can be managed by remote Informix instances on any supported platform.

Figure 13-14 shows the Site Manager Project View after deployment.

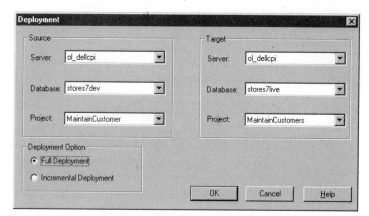

Figure 13-13. *Specifying source and target projects in the Deployment dialog.*

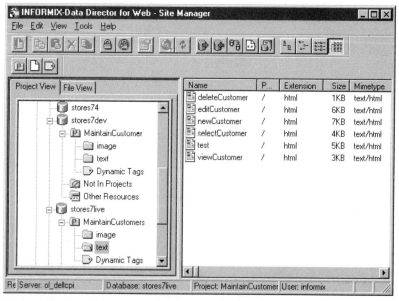

Figure 13-14 *Site Manager Project View after deployment.*

Deploy the Application Tables

When you deploy a Data Director for Web project, it is the resources in the Data Director for Web schema that are deployed. You still need to install the schema for the *application,* which is not maintained by Data Director for Web. For example, you would manually deploy the stores database schema outside of Data Director for Web.

Configure the Web Server

- If the Informix server is on a different machine than the web server, ensure that `webdriver` or a `webdriver` shared object (such as `drvisapi.dll`) is located on the web server machine, and that the `sqlhosts` file (UNIX) or `setnet` registry settings (NT) have been completed correctly.
- Create the appropriate URL prefixes for the target web server.
- Create the appropriate `web.cnf` entries for the target URL prefixes.
- Remember to set `MI_WEBEXTENSIONS` in `web.cnf` to cache extension information.

See Chap. 23, "Web Server Integration," for details of how to perform these four steps.

Incremental Deployment

At intervals, you will want to update the live production site with new AppPages, new applications, and enhancements to the existing site. To deploy new and changed resources, you use the *Incremental Deployment* option in Site Manager.

Incremental Deployment copies the resource to the target database only if the working source version is more recent than the target version.

The tasks can be summarized as follows:

- Select Tools/Deployment from the Site Manager menu.
- Enter the source Informix server, database and project, and the target Informix server, database and project. Select Incremental Deployment in the Deployment Option box. Click OK.

Viewing the Deployment Status of a Project

You can view the deployment status of a project by selecting the target project, and choosing *Edit/Properties* from the Site Manager menu, or right-clicking the project and selecting *Properties*. The *Edit Project* dialog is displayed; it shows the date and time of the last full or incremental deployment, which Informix user performed it, and where the source project is defined. Only information about the most recent deployment is stored, and this is kept in the `wbProjects` table in the target database.

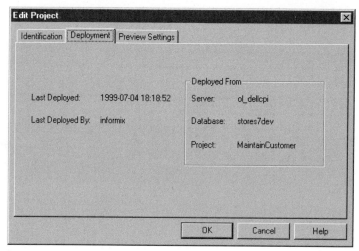

Figure 13-15. *Deployment status.*

Figure 13-15 shows the *Deployment* tab of the *Edit Project* dialog, for the *MaintainCustomer* project in the `stores7live` database.

In some versions of Data Director for Web, the incremental deployment of a project has a bug related to the last changed timestamp and the confirmatory messages displayed. Generally, the last changed date of the resources must differ in the minutes column.

Deployment to Multiple Locations

You may want to deploy your projects to multiple databases from a single development or test database. Figure 13-16 shows an example deployment path with two deployment web servers on the other side of the corporate firewall, each containing the same web content.

In Fig. 13-16, two web servers are connected using third-party hardware or software *failover* support to ensure that, even if one machine is down, the other can function, thus avoiding a single point of failure. In this example, Informix Dynamic Server/ Universal Data Option (or Informix Dynamic Server.2000) resides on each web server; alternatively, it could reside on a different machine altogether, so that the switched web servers can connect to a single instance of the Informix server.

The essential point is that the web content is deployed to multiple locations, with single or multiple projects deployed to multiple locations, as well.

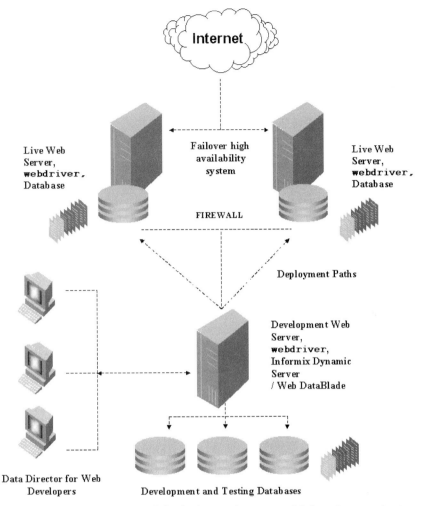

Live Web
Server,
webdriver,
Database

Failover high
availability
system

Live Web
Server,
webdriver,
Database

FIREWALL

Deployment Paths

Development Web
Server,
webdriver,
Informix Dynamic
Server
/ Web DataBlade

Data Director for Web
Developers

Development and Testing Databases

Figure 13-16. *Creating and deploying projects to multiple web server hosts.*

Multimedia QuickStart Example

This example demonstrates how to use Site Manager to store various types of objects in the database, which includes audio, video, image and Office documents such as Microsoft Word documents. We then go on to create an AppPage in AppPage Editor, and use the Resource dialogs to create HTML links to these multimedia resources in the database. When the link is clicked in the browser, the browser will handle the resource natively (or use a plug-in), or will spawn a registered helper application to handle the resource. If the browser can handle the resource, the resource will be displayed in a separate frame. If not, the registered helper application will be invoked.

The essential point is that the multimedia content is delivered on demand from the Informix database. And, we can use the Resource dialogs in AppPage Editor to hide the details of the resource implementation from the web developer.

What we will do is

- import the multimedia resources into the database,
- create an optional preview setting for the new project so that you can preview AppPages in AppPage Editor,
- create AppPages to contain links to the resources,
- create links in the AppPages to retrieve the resources on demand and deliver them to the browser client,
- test the new AppPages.

Import the Multimedia Resources into the Database

Using Site Manager:

- Select a database server and database.
- Create a new Project in the database called QuickStart.
- Select, for example, a Word document, an Excel spreadsheet, a GIF image, an AVI video, and a WAV file.
- Check your extension mappings to ensure that MIME type mappings exist for these content types (the content types listed above should come as default with the Data Director for Web installation).
- Drag the objects that you have selected from the desktop to the Site Manager Project that you have just created.

In the Project View, you should now have one folder for each of the content types that you dropped into the QuickStart project, with the Path set to "/." Project folders should exist for audio, video, image, and application.

If you create a set of folders in Windows Explorer and place your objects in these folders, you can drag the root folder into the Site Manager project you have created. The folder structure is then maintained using the Path column in the content metadata. Use the File View to verify the folder structure.

Create an Optional Preview Setting for the Project

Do this *only if* you want to preview the exploded AppPage inside Data Director for Web. For the *first* attempt, you may be better off using the browser directly and worrying about the preview configuration later.

- Select *Tools/Preview* Settings from the Site Manager menu.
- Select the `Default` preview configuration, click the Copy To button.
- In the Copy To dialog, type `QuickPreview` and click OK. A copy of the `Default` preview configuration for the project will be created, called `QuickPreview`.
- Select the newly created preview configuration `QuickPreview` and click the `Edit` button.
- In the Preview Editor, change `WEB_HOME` to be the same as the `WEB_HOME` setting in the server `web.cnf` for the URL.
- assign the `QuickPreview` configuration to the `QuickStart` project, as shown in Fig. 13-18.

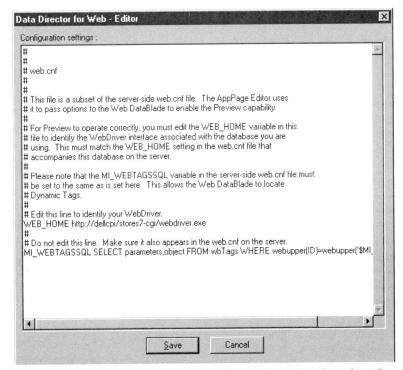

Figure 13-17. The `QuickStart` *preview configuration, based on the* `Default` *configuration.*

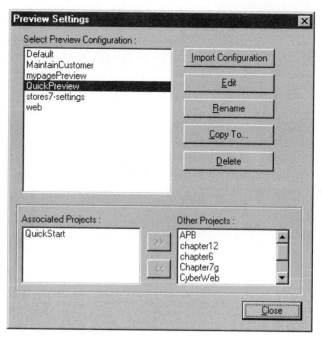

Figure 13-18. *Assign the* `QuickPreview` *configuration to the* `QuickStart` *project.*

Figure 13-17 shows an example `QuickStart` preview configuration, with the `WEB_HOME` variable changed.

In a departmental setting where there are a number of users creating AppPages and submitting content to the database, the best option is for the webmaster or development administrator to set up a number of template preview configurations so that developers can import them. Data Director for Web is geared toward a workgroup environment, so be careful when changing preview configurations, since your change may impact another developer.

If you want to preview AppPages under different preview configurations, create separate preview configurations and assign them to the project when you need them.

Create AppPages to Retrieve the Content Items

Create two new AppPage Resources, called `QuickTest` and `QuickFrames`, by using `File/New Resource` or by clicking the Create Resource button. Make sure that the Extension is `html` or `htm`. Figure 13-19 shows an example. If you wish to import a file from the filesystem, use the Content File textbox in the Create Resource dialog. You may wish to use a text editor to create the AppPages first, and then import them.

A new folder called `text` will be created under the `QuickStart` project. If you did not select the `QuickStart` project before creating the resource, the resource will be added to the `Not In Projects/text` folder.

Create Links to the Content Items in the AppPage

Using AppPage Editor, we are going to add links to the content items we have added to the database. We will use the *Insert Resource* dialogs to add the links. Do not bother too much at the moment about formatting the links; just get the links generated in the AppPage.

- In Site Manager, double-click the `QuickTest` AppPage. The AppPage Editor will be invoked, and the AppPage will be retrieved from the database for editing.

In AppPage Editor:

- add a link for the imported image by selecting *Insert/Link To/Image* from the menu, or by pressing the Insert Image button on the left of the AppPage editor window.

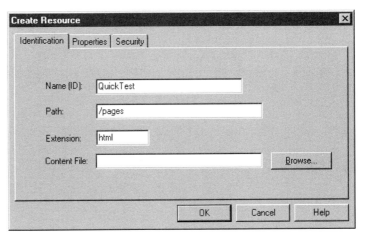

Figure 13-19. Create a new AppPage resource.

- The Choose a Resource dialog will appear. If not already selected, select the QuickStart project and the image type. A list of objects with the image supertype for the QuickStart project will be displayed. Select the appropriate image, and click OK. Figure 13-20 shows an example. The Insert Resource dialog is then displayed.
- In the Insert Resource dialog, select whether you want to link or embed the resource. For either option, you can generate a dynamic tag or in-line HTML. In the Resource box, select Link to Resource. In the Type of Text box, select Dynamic Tag. The Tag Text box is refreshed with each choice you make. You can edit the contents of this box to change the resulting text that is written to the AppPage. Click the Insert Tag button. The tag text is written to the AppPage (see Fig. 13-21 for an example).
- Repeat this process for each of the audio, video, and Word documents that you have imported, using the *Insert/Link To Resource* menu option in AppPage Editor.
- Add some formatting HTML around the generated tags.
- Save the AppPage to the database using the *File/Save* menu option.

Figure 13-22 shows AppPage editor and the generated tags.

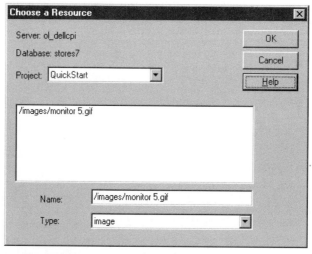

Figure 13-20. *Choose an* image *resource.*

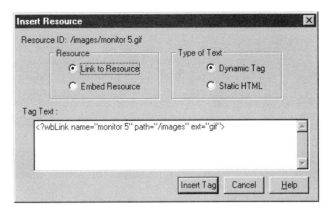

Figure 13-21. Insert a dynamic tag to retrieve an image.

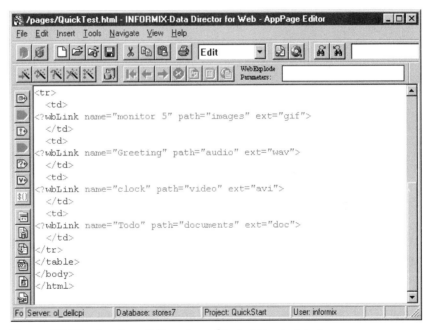

Figure 13-22. AppPage Editor view of `QuickTest.html`.

List. 13-4 shows the formatted source of `QuickTest.html`. Note that the dynamic tag `wbLink` is installed with Data Director for Web.

tip

If you wish to change the behavior of the dynamic tags installed with Data Director for Web, you can edit them in AppPage Editor by selecting the tags from the Dynamic Tags folder in Site Manager. The preferred option is to create another dynamic tag based on the installed tag; that way you retain the original.

Listing 13-4. *Formatted source of* `QuickTest.html`.

```
<html>
<head><title>Multimedia Content Example</title></head>
<body>

<base target=mediaPanel>

<h1>Multimedia Content Delivery</h1>
<h3>Click one of the following </h3>
<table border=1>
<tr>
  <td><b>Image</td>
  <td><b>Audio</td>
  <td><b>Video</td>
  <td><b>Document</td>
</tr>
<tr>
  <td>
    <?wbLink name="monitor 5" path="/images" ext="gif">
  </td>
  <td>
    <?wbLink name="Greeting" path="/audio" ext="wav">
  </td>
  <td>
    <?wbLink name="clock" path="/video" ext="avi">
  </td>
  <td>
    <?wbLink name="Todo" path="/documents" ext="doc">
  </td>
</tr>
</table>
</body>
</html>
```

Create the Frameset Page

- In AppPage Editor, open `QuickFrames.html`.
- Add the code in List. 13-5 to the AppPage.
- Create the AppPage `blank.html`. This is just a blank page that is used to display the results of clicking the links if the browser handles the MIME type or uses a plug-in to do so. For example:

```
<html><body></body></html>
```

Test the AppPages

Select the URL for the `QuickFrames.html` AppPage in the Browser Location bar. For example:

```
http://dellcpi/stores7-cgi/webdriver.exe?MIval=/pages/
QuickFrames.html
http://delcpi/stores7/pages/QuickFrames
```

Select the Image Link

If you click the Image link, the image should be displayed in the `mediaPanel` frame (see Fig. 13-23).

Select the Audio Link

If you click the Audio link, then, depending on your browser setting, a helper application will be invoked separately from the browser, or a plug-in will handle the playing of the object in the `mediaPanel` frame, as Fig. 13-24 shows.

Listing 13-5. `QuickFrames.html` *AppPage source.*

```
<html>
<?MIvar>
  <frameset rows="30%,*">
   <frame src=$WEB_HOME?MIval=/pages/QuickTest>
   <frame name=mediaPanel src=$WEB_HOME?MIval=/pages/blank>
  </frameset>
<?/MIvar>
</html>
```

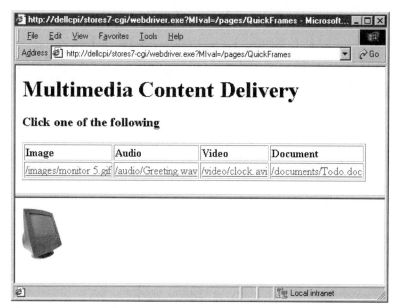

Figure 13-23. *Explorer display after clicking the Image link.*

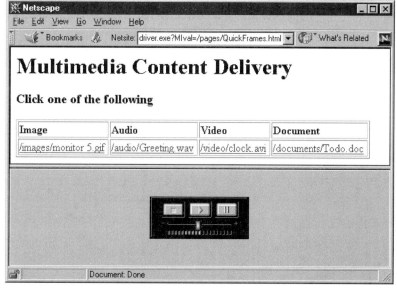

Figure 13-24. *Navigator display after clicking the Image link.*

Select the Video Link

If you click the Video link, either a helper application or a plug-in will handle the resource. For example, if you click the Video link in Explorer, the default setting for the MIME type `video/x-msvideo` may be to spawn the Windows Media Player application.

Select the Document Link

When you click the Document link for the Microsoft Word document, the document will be rendered in the `mediaPanel` if you have a Word plug-in installed, or else Microsoft Word will be invoked, and the Word document passed to it from the browser after it has been downloaded from the database. Note that, if you change the document in Word, you cannot save it back to the database automatically. You must save it to the desktop, and then resubmit the document to Site Manager.

Figure 13-25 shows the dialog displayed by Navigator when you click the Document link and Microsoft Word is installed as a helper application. You have the option of saving it to disk, or using the helper application to view it.

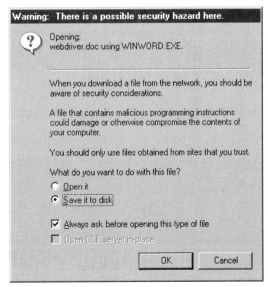

Figure 13-25. *Download the document: Save or Open Dialog in Navigator.*

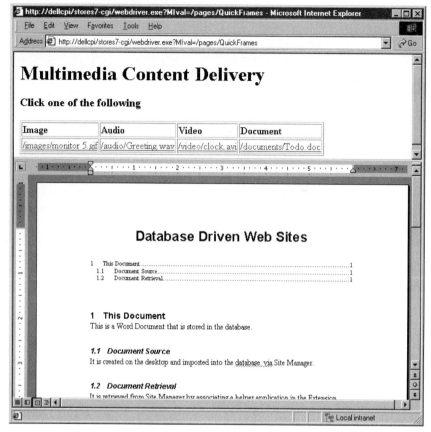

Figure 13-26. *Viewing the document in the* `mediaPanel` *frame in Explorer.*

Figure 13-26 shows the Word document displayed in the `mainPanel` frame in Explorer when the browser handles Word documents.

It may be more convenient to spawn a separate browser window for the Word document. This obviates the need to install Word on the desktop, but requires the Word Plug-In for the browser.

Summary

In this chapter, we have learned where Data Director for Web fits into the web development environment. We have seen how you can create resources, including the import of websites from the filesystem, and use projects to organize them. We have also learned how to selectively deploy projects to target databases.

We have also seen how you can use AppPage Editor resource dialogs and dynamic tags to hide the implementation detail when retrieving multimedia objects from the database. These dialogs and dynamic tags hide the SQL interface to the database when retrieving data and objects, such as audio, video, and Office documents.

Importantly, we have learned the basics of what to look for in designing and building a web project from the Project Manager's perspective, with the emphasis on code reuse with dynamic tags, user interface ergonomics, prototyping, and iterative delivery of core functionality.

Chapter

14

Creating Web Applications with AppPage Builder

In this chapter:

- Using AppPage Script with AppPage Builder
- AppPage Builder components
- Creating web applications with AppPage Builder
- Working with large objects and MIME types
- AppPage Builder Administration
- Maintaining versions of AppPages
- Extending AppPage Builder

AppPage Builder is a browser-based Web DataBlade application that ships with the Web DataBlade. It allows you to create AppPages, dynamic tags, and store large objects separately from Data Director for Web, and works out of the box as the default application for managing web content and Web DataBlade applications in the Informix database.

Chapter 13, "Creating and Maintaining Websites with Data Director for Web," shows how to use the Data Director for Web toolset.

This chapter shows you how to use AppPage Builder to store web content in the Informix database and deliver it using AppPage templates. It is useful to know how to use AppPage Builder because it constitutes a default interface to managing web content and rendering it dynamically. If you have used Data Director for Web, however, you probably won't want to go back to AppPage Builder.

You can use AppPage Builder to create AppPages with any web browser that supports forms and tables, as defined in the HTML 3.0 specification. If you use a browser that supports client file upload, you can also use AppPage Builder to manage multimedia content in the database.

Using AppPage Script with AppPage Builder

The same AppPage Scripting functions are available to both AppPage Builder and web applications created via Data Director for Web. AppPage Builder and Data Director for Web are different functional interfaces for managing web content and websites in the database. If you are serious about managing database-driven websites, you should be using Data Director for Web, but you can create highly sophisticated applications with AppPage Builder.

Typically, if you have used AppPage Builder and then want to use Data Director for Web, you migrate your AppPage Builder projects to the Data Director for Web schema.

See Chap. 13 for details on how you can migrate applications from AppPage Builder to Data Director for Web.

AppPage Builder Components

You install AppPage Builder on every database that will store web content that is managed by AppPage Builder. AppPage builder requires the following components:

- the Web DataBlade installed on the database that will host the AppPage Builder application;
- the AppPage Builder schema installed on the same database; this is the set of tables used to store the web content (such as AppPages) and large objects (such as office documents);

- a `webdriver` configuration for AppPage Builder, nominating the correct schema;
- a URL prefix defined in the web server that maps onto the `web.cnf` defined for AppPage Builder;
- a browser.

AppPage Builder and `webdriver` Configuration

With Version 3 of the Web DataBlade, you create a `webdriver` configuration for AppPage Builder in the `web.cnf` file. This file defines the AppPage Builder tables that store web content. For example, the `webpages` table stores AppPages and the metadata associated with AppPages. From Version 4, you use the `apb` configuration that is installed with the Web DataBlade Module Administration Tool.

If you have applications that are stored in the AppPage Builder schema and want to develop applications that run under Data Director for Web, you need to implement separate `webdriver` configurations (the `web.cnf` file) for the Data Director for Web application. This is because AppPage Builder and Data Director for Web use different tables.

See Chap. 22, "Understanding `webdriver` Configuration," for the details of implementing the `web.cnf` for AppPage Builder.

Version 4 Specific

When you install Version 4 of the Web DataBlade, you can create a mapping for AppPage Builder. You can also create a mapping for AppPage Builder using the Web DataBlade Module Administration Tool. For example:

- Create a mapping for AppPage Builder using the Web DataBlade Module Administration Tool.
- Add a web server URL prefix for the mapping that is added to `web.cnf`

For example, if you wanted to run AppPage Builder on the `catalog` database, an example entry in `web.cnf` for AppPage Builder is as follows:

```
<map path=/apb>
database catalog
user informix
password 7f02d4393b21b02c1a76c321fbcde4f2
```

```
password_key 37bdce41
config_name apb
</map>
```

In this snippet, the configuration is `apb`; this configuration names the AppPage Builder tables that store web content. You then need to create a URL prefix in the web server for the `/apb` mapping.
Example mappings would be:

```
http://dellcpi/apb/webdriver.exe
http://dellcpi/apb/
```

The first is a CGI URL mapping; the second, an NSAPI mapping.

What Types of `webdriver` Can AppPage Builder Use?

AppPage Builder is independent of `webdriver`. You can use the CGI, NSAPI, ISAPI, and (from Version 4) the Apache API `webdriver` with AppPage Builder. Remember that AppPage Builder is the interface to creating web content in the database. Because `webdriver` uses the `web.cnf` file to identify the correct web content schema, you create the AppPage Builder version of `web.cnf` that `webdriver` requires.

Creating Web Applications Using AppPage Builder

When you create a web application with AppPage Builder, you will typically create a new AppPage Builder project and add content to that project, such as AppPage templates and multimedia objects.

This section will create a simple application to list selected customer phone numbers. The user can enter a search string that will be matched against the first and last names of customers in the `customer` table. If a match is found, the name, company, and phone number will be displayed in an HTML table. Dynamic tags will be used for the AppPage header, footer, and query control.

To create a web application and add content to it in AppPage Builder, follow the steps below:

- Invoke AppPage Builder.
- Create a new project (called `shopper`, for example).
- Add dynamic tags to the shopper project.

- Add AppPages to the shopper project.
- Add multimedia content to the shopper project.
- Invoke the application.

You can add dynamic tags, AppPages, and multimedia content in any order that suits you, but this is the order we will follow in the example.

Invoking AppPage Builder

You invoke AppPage Builder using an HTTP URL from the browser. You can invoke AppPage Builder using any of the CGI, NSAPI, ISAPI, or Apache API `webdrivers`.

The webmaster or systems administrator will set up a URL prefix that will map onto a `webdriver` configuration that nominates the AppPage Builder schema. See Chap. 23, "Web Server Integration," for details on how to add CGI and API URL prefixes for `webdriver`.

When you invoke AppPage Builder, a screen similar to Fig. 14-1 is displayed.

Table 14-1 contains the elements listed in Fig. 14-1.

The administration properties can be set on the Admin Menu page. See the section entitled "AppPage Builder Administration" later in this chapter for details on administering AppPage Builder.

Figure 14-1. *Invoking AppPage Builder*

Table 14-1.	AppPage Builder main menu elements.

Element	Description
Add Object	Add a Web Application object
Edit Object	Edit a Web Application object
Admin Menu	Maintain a user account, project, MIME types and object types
Administration Properties	Administration properties for this user

Creating a New Project

We create a project to contain related content items. All web content, except dynamic tags, belongs to a project. Projects are for organization only; the project has no bearing on rendering the content dynamically. To create a new project, follow the steps below:

- From the main menu, choose Admin Menu.
- From the Admin Menu, choose Add Project.

The Add Project screen is displayed. Enter the name of the project and a description. You can leave the owner of the project as the user with which you are connected. For example, if we create the `shopper` project, the resulting screen should look like Fig. 14-2.

When you click the Save button, the project is created and a confirmatory screen is displayed, as shown in Fig. 14-3.

It's easy to see how AppPage Builder (APB) works. Just look at the AppPage source that is stored under the APB project. It is useful to see how AppPage Builder uses AppPage Script to populate forms and upload documents to the database server for inserting into the database.

Add Dynamic Tags to the `shopper` Project

Once we have created a project, we can add AppPages and other web content. Some of this web content can include dynamic tags. This example will create three simple dynamic tags called `header`, `footer`, and `sqlView`, which represent the HTML page header, footer, and some formatting code for an SQL statement.

Figure 14-2. *Add the* shopper *project.*

Figure 14-3. *The* shopper *project has been created.*

See Chap. 19, "Creating and Using Dynamic Tags," for a list of AppPage Builder Dynamic Tags that are part of the core AppPage Builder product that you can use to create hyperlinks and forms.

All the tags in this example are referenced in the example AppPage, Home.html.

Create the header Dynamic Tag

The header dynamic tag accepts two parameters and creates the HTML for an image link and a page title. To create the tag, perform the following in AppPage Builder:

- From the AppPage Builder main menu, select Add Object.
- From the Add Object screen, choose Dynamic Tag, and click Continue; the Add Dynamic Tag screen will be displayed.
- Enter the dynamic tag metadata; ID, class, parameters, and description.
- Enter the dynamic tag source, and click the Save button.

The dynamic tag metadata consists of the Tag ID, which is the name of the tag; the Class, which, unless it is system, is documentary; the tag Parameters, which in the example define two mandatory parameters called title and link; and a Description.

Figure 14-4 shows part of the Add Dynamic Tag page, and Fig. 14-5 shows the text area in which you add the dynamic tag HTML and AppPage Scripting commands.

When you add a dynamic tag, you can base the new tag on any existing dynamic tag, or you can create the new tag from scratch. Enter the AppPage source (see List. 14-1) into the Add Dynamic tag screen.

Listing 14-1.   The header dynamic tag.

```
<html>
<head><title>@title@</title></head>
<body bgcolor="#F7F7F7">
<a href="<?mivar>$WEB_HOME<?/mivar>?MIval=@link@">
<img src="<?mivar>$WEB_HOME<?/mivar>?MIvalObj=directoryImage&
MItypeObj=image/gif" border=0 alt="Home"></a>
<font size=+3 face="arial" color="#003300"><b>@title@</b></font>
<br clear=all>
<hr>
```

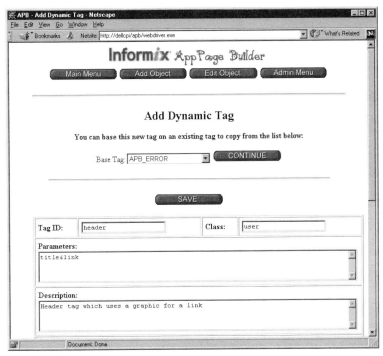

Figure 14-4. Add dynamic tag metadata.

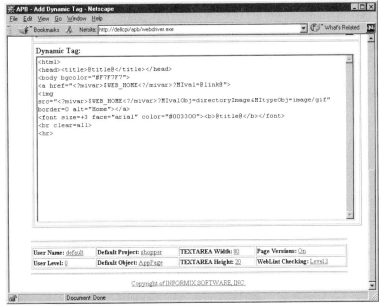

Figure 14-5. Add dynamic tag source.

Create the `footer` Dynamic Tag

The `footer` tag displays the webmaster email and summary HTML, as shown in List. 14-2.

To create this tag, follow the same procedure used to create the `header` tag. The `footer` tag has one parameter, the `ATSIGN` symbol (this is explained in more detail in Chap. 19), which allows the dynamic tag to evaluate the @ symbol without confusing it with the syntax for parameters. Figure 14-6 shows the Add Dynamic Tag screen for this tag.

Create the `sqlView` Dynamic Tag

This dynamic tag contains an `MISQL` tag that accepts the SQL to be executed as a parameter. It then formats the rows and columns from the result set into an HTML table.

Because the `MISQL` tag doesn't know what SQL is being executed, it can't know what the columns are. Therefore, a wildcard expression is implemented as follows:

```
<tr>{<td>$*</td>}</tr>
```

The `$*` variable specification denotes any column in the result set. The expression within the curly braces, `{}`, is executed once for each column that is returned in the result set. As a consequence, the body of the `MISQL` tag will format each column as a separate HTML table cell, and each row as an HTML table row.

Listing 14-3 contains the `sqlView` dynamic tag source. Create this dynamic tag as described for the `header` tag. Figure 14-7 shows the Add Dynamic Tag screen for the `sqlView` dynamic tag.

Listing 14-2. `footer` *dynamic tag.*

```
<hr>
<center>Questions? Email me at
<a href="mailto:webmaster@ATSIGN@mysite.com">
        webmaster@ATSIGN@mysite.com</a><br>
</center>
</body>
</html>
```

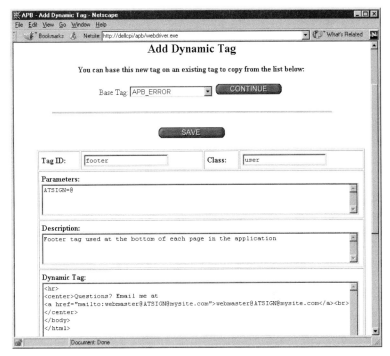

Figure 14-6. Add the `footer` dynamic tag.

Listing 14-3.   The sqlView dynamic tag.

```
<table border=1>
<?misql sql="@SQL@">
<tr>{<td>$*</td>}</tr>
<?/misql>
</table>
```

Add AppPages to the Project

To create an AppPage, follow these steps

- Create the AppPage using your favorite web page authoring tool; include any AppPage Scripting and dynamic tags.
- Choose to add an AppPage from the Add Object screen; the Add AppPage screen will be displayed.

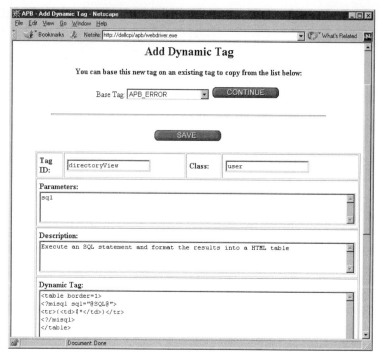

Figure 14-7. *Add the* `sqlView` *dynamic tag.*

- Add the AppPage metadata, such as ID and description.
- Import the AppPage using the Browse button, or type it in directly.

Create the AppPage

You can use any web page authoring tool to generate the HTML page look and feel. For example, you can use an authoring tool to create a site structure, user interface, and one or more forms. You can then add the AppPage Script and AppPage variables to the web pages, including any SQL to manipulate data in the database. The resulting AppPage is still external to AppPage Builder.

Listing 14-4 shows the AppPage that we will enter into AppPage Builder, called `Home.html`. This AppPage creates a simple form and

Listing 14-4. *The* Home.html *AppPage source.*

```
<?header
   title="Online Directory"
   link="$WEB_HOME?MIval=Home">

<?mivar name=shopper default=Guest>$shopper<?/mivar>
<?mivar name=viewstart default=0><?/mivar>
<center>

<h2><?mivar>Hello $shopper<?/mivar></h2>

<form method=post action=<?mivar>$WEB_HOME<?/mivar> >
<input type=hidden name=MIval value=<?mivar>$MIval<?/mivar>>
Enter search string:
<input name=searchString type=text size=20 value="">
<br>
<input type=submit value=Search>
</form>

<?miblock cond=$(XST,$searchString)>
<?sqlView
    sql="select fname,lname,company, phone
         from customer
         where lname matches '$searchString' or
               fname matches '$searchString';"
  >
<?/miblock>
<?footer>
```

uses the `sqlView` dynamic tag to perform a query and format the results. The AppPage also uses the `header` and `footer` dynamic tags previously created.

Add the AppPage to the AppPage Builder Project

The Add Object screen is shown in Fig. 14-8. You use the Add Object screen when you want to add AppPages and other web content to the database. The Add Object screen lists the type of objects that can be stored in the database using AppPage Builder.

Figure 14-8. Add an object to the AppPage Builder repository.

When you choose to add an AppPage object, the Add AppPage screen is displayed as shown in Fig. 14-9.

You can base your new AppPage on an existing page. To do this,

- select the project, and click Continue; the list of base pages will be refreshed;
- select the AppPage from the project, and click Continue.

For this example, we are not reusing any AppPage that exists.

If you are uploading files, upload first and then enter the AppPage metadata. When you upload a file, the Add AppPage screen refreshes to accept the metadata, and any data you had typed in will be lost.

The Project list should contain the newly created `shopper` project. Select it if it is not the default.

Set Page ID to a name such as `Home` or `Home.html`. This is the ID that you will reference in the `MIval` parameter.

You can set the read and write level for the AppPage. When using a secure URL prefix, an authenticated user will have a security level defined in the `webusers` table; this value is assigned to the `MI_WEBACCESSLEVEL` variable. When selecting an AppPage, if the `read_level` of the AppPage is less than or equal to

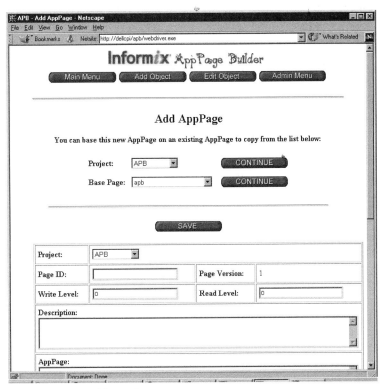

Figure 14-9. Add AppPage screen.

`MI_WEBACCESSLEVEL`, then the page is retrieved, otherwise an error is generated.

When the metadata and the AppPage are displayed in the Add AppPage screen, click the `Save` button. The AppPage will be written to the `webpages` table.

If the `Home.html` AppPage is in a file on the filesystem, use the Browse button on the Add AppPage screen to select the file ready for uploading as form data, and then click the Continue button. Alternatively, you can type the AppPage into the text area by hand, and then click the Save button.

Add Multimedia Content

AppPage Builder is shipped with a default set of object types. These object types allow you to add all kinds of objects to the database. For example, you can use AppPage Builder to add an MS-Word document, a GIF image, or a PDF document. In this case, the object types are `Document` and `Image`.

AppPage Builder maps the object type (for example, `Image`) to one or more MIME types that belong to that object type. For example, AppPage Builder defines the `Document` object type. You can use the Add Document screen to add MS-Word or PDF documents.

This section shows you how to add an Image and an MS-Word document to the database using AppPage Builder.

Adding an Image Object to the Database Using AppPage Builder

We will add a GIF image called `book.gif` to the `shopper` project. This image will be used in the `header` dynamic tag. To add an `Image` object:

- Choose Add Object from the main menu.
- From the Add Object screen, choose Image; the Add Image Object screen will be displayed.
- Select the project; in our case, choose the `shopper` project.
- Enter the image name in the Image ID text field (the image name in the `header` tag is called `directoryImage`).
- Select the MIME type of the image; choose GIF for this example.
- Enter the height and width of the image (optional).
- Enter the description of the image (optional).
- Select the image file from the filesystem using the Browse button.
- Once the above tasks are complete, click the Save button.

When the image is saved to the database, it is stored in the `webimages` table. Figure 14-10 shows the Add Image Object screen for the `book.gif` object. Once the image has been saved to the database, Fig. 14-11 is displayed.

AppPage Builder does not have the drag-and-drop facilities of Data Director for Web, nor the ability to use wizards to create forms and dynamic tags.

Adding an MS-Word Document to the Database Using AppPage Builder

The procedure is the same as adding the `Image` object.

- Choose Add Object from the main menu.
- From the Add Object screen, choose Document; the Add Document Object screen will be displayed.
- Select the project; in our case, choose the `shopper` project.

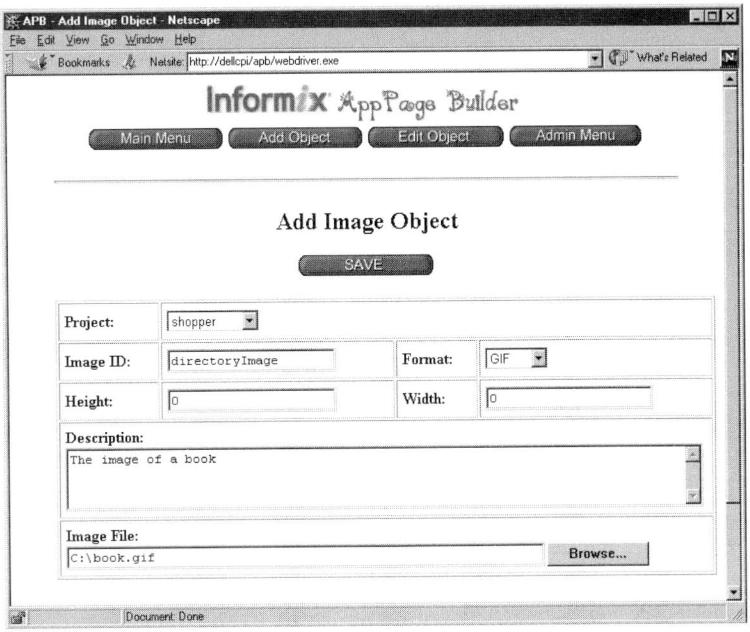

Figure 14-10. Add an `Image` object.

Figure 14-11. The `Image` object stored in the AppPage Builder schema.

- Select the Format of the document; this will map onto the MIME type of the document; choose Microsoft Word.
- Enter the document name in the Document ID text field.
- Enter the description of the document (optional).
- Select the document from the filesystem using the `Browse` button.

Once the tasks above are complete, click the `Save` button. The document will be inserted into the AppPage Builder table, `webdocuments`.

Invoke the Application

At this point, we have

- a project called `shopper`,
- an AppPage called `Home`,
- a GIF image called `directoryImage`,
- three dynamic tags—`header`, `footer` and `sqlView`.

We can invoke the application as follows:

`http://dellcpi/apb/webdriver.exe?MIval=Home`

A screen similar to Fig. 14-12 should be displayed.

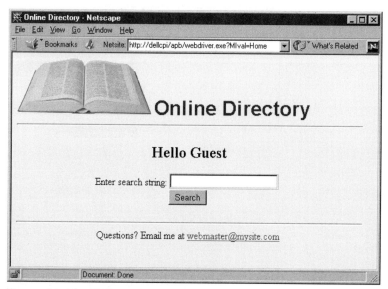

Figure 14-12. Online Directory `Home`.

Selecting Customer Numbers

Enter the * wildcard character in the textbox and click Search. All customers will match the search string, and the browser display should look like Fig. 14-13.

Enter the string M* into the textbox and click Search. Customers whose first or last names start with "M" should be displayed. Figure 14-14 shows the search results for this query.

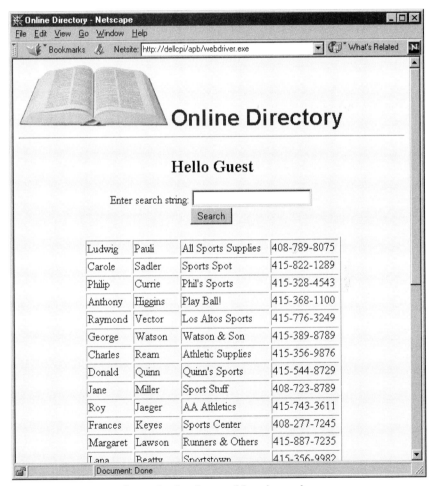

*Figure 14-13. Search results for the * wildcard search.*

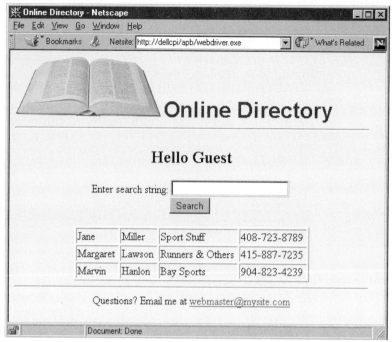

Figure 14-14. Search results for the M* search.

Working with Large Objects and MIME Types

You can use AppPage Builder to store objects such as images, audio, and video in the database. AppPage Builder ships with default definitions of multimedia object types so that you can start to add different object types to the database straight away.

What Is an Object Type?

In AppPage Builder, an object type is used to identify the method of capturing different types of web content and storing this content in the AppPage Builder schema. To do this, AppPage Builder creates a mapping between an AppPage Builder object type, one or more MIME types, and the set of AppPages that are used to capture and maintain objects of a given type. An AppPage Builder object type defines the metadata for a content item and can have objects with different MIME types defined.

For example, AppPage Builder is shipped with the object type `Image`. When you want to add an image to the AppPage Builder repository, you select the Add Image screen. From this screen, you give the image object a name and select the MIME type, which could be `image/gif` or `image/jpeg`. When you save the image to the database, the image metadata and a reference to the image in a blobspace is stored in the `webimages` table.

In practical terms, objects of a particular object type are stored in a particular AppPage Builder table. The mapping of object type to database table is listed in Table 14-2.

Note that the Routine object type is not available before Version 4 of the Web DataBlade.

Mapping MIME Types to Object Types

All objects stored in the AppPage Builder schema have a MIME type, including AppPages.

This MIME type is used by the `webexplode()` function to generate the HTTP `content-type` header for the object when requested by the browser. The `content-type` is interpreted by the browser so that the object is rendered correctly either via a plug-in helper application or natively in the browser.

When you insert an object, first map the object to the appropriate AppPage Builder object type and then select the MIME type from the list of those available for objects of that type.

Table 14-2. Database tables used for object types.

Object type	Table
Images	webimages
Audio	webaudios
Video	webvideos
Documents	webdocments
AppPages	webpages
Dynamic tag	webtags
Routine	webudrs

For example, to insert an MS-Word document,

- select Document from the Add Object screen,
- choose Microsoft Word from the Format list in the Add Document screen.

The list of formats available to an object is the same as the list of MIME types available. The table that stores the mapping of MIME type to object type is called webmimetypes.

AppPage Builder is installed with a default set of object-to-MIME-type mappings. These are listed in Table 14-3. The MIME Name column is used to populate the Format list in the Add Document screen.

For example, if you wanted to add a GIF image called book to the database, you would choose Image (the object type) from the Add Object screen, and then select the GIF format from the Add Image screen. You can refer to this object by name in an AppPage as follows:

```
<?mivar>
<img src=$WEB_HOME?MIvalObj=book&type=image/gif>
<?/mivar>
```

Table 14-3.   MIME Types for Objects in AppPage Builder.

MIME name	MIME type	Extension	Object type
AppPage	text/html	html	AppPage
AU	audio/basic	au	Audio
AIFF	audio/x-aiff	aiff	Audio
WAV	audio/x-wav	wav	Audio
Microsoft Word	application/msword	doc	Document
Microsoft PowerPoint	application/ppt	ppt	Document
Adobe PDF	application/pdf	pdf	Document
GIF	image/gif	gif	Image
JPEG	image/jpeg	jpeg	Image
Dynamic Tag	text/plain	tag	Dynamic tag
Quicktime	video/quicktime	mov	Video
MPEG	video/mpeg	mpeg	Video
AVI	video/x-msvideo	avi	Video

When `webdriver` retrieves the image information from the `webimages` table using `book` as the key, the HTTP `content-type` sent to the browser will be `image/gif`.

You can use the `APB_IMG` dynamic tag to generate a reference to an image stored in the `webimages` table. This tag will extract the object reference for the image, as well as the MIME type, from the `webimages` table. See Chap. 20, "Working with Large Objects," for detailed information on using objects in AppPages.

Mapping Object Types to AppPage Builder Pages

When you create an object, you will invoke an AppPage that is dedicated to adding an object of that type to the database.

Each object type has its own set of AppPages to maintain objects of that type. For example, the `Document` object has the following AppPages created for it in the APB project:

- `apb_add_Document`—add a document to the `webdocuments` table; for example, add PDF or MS-Word documents.
- `apb_edit_Document`—edit the document metadata and/or replace the document by uploading another document.
- `apb_delete_Document`—delete the document from the `webdocuments` table.

When you want to add or edit an object, you select the Add Object or Edit Object screen. From this screen you select the type of object you want to add or edit. Based on this selection, AppPage Builder puts together the name of the AppPage that will service the request by adding the Page Suffix to the `apb_add_` or `apb_edit_` AppPage name.

The table that stores the mapping of object type to page suffix is called `webobjecttypes`. You can maintain the data in this table from the Admin menu by selecting Edit Object Type.

Figure 14-15 shows the Edit Object Type screen for the `Document` object type, which shows that the page suffix for document objects is "Document."

If you change an existing object-type/page-suffix mapping, then AppPage Builder may not work if the derived page name can't be found in the `webpages` table. Generally you will use the Add Object Type and Edit Object Type Admin functions when customizing AppPage Builder to accept web content with different metadata requirements.

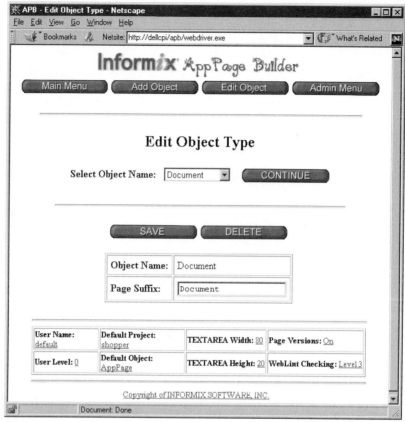

Figure 14-15. The `Document` *object type and page suffix.*

AppPage Builder Administration

You can administer the AppPage Builder properties for the user that you have used to connect to AppPage Builder. You can also set the properties for the AppPage Builder session for this user. Any changes you make apply to the particular user that is displayed in the Administration screen.

Invoking the Administration Screen

There are two ways to invoke the Administration screen:

- click one of the hyperlinks in the administration footer of each AppPage Builder screen, or

- click the Admin Menu button at the top of the AppPage Builder screen, and then select Edit User from the Administration Menu.

Figure 14-16 shows the AppPage Builder Administration screen.

What is the AppPage Builder Username?

The AppPage Builder username is in the administration footer on each AppPage Builder screen and on the Administration screen itself. This is the user under which you are running AppPage Builder.

When you request the AppPage Builder URL in the browser, the web server invokes `webdriver` to retrieve the AppPage Builder application pages.

If you are using the CGI `webdriver` or the basic API version of `webdriver`, the AppPage Builder username will be set to the value of `REMOTE_USER` from the `web.cnf` file.

If you are using a secure URL prefix and hence the API version of `webdriver`, the username will be set to the *authenticating username*. This is the username that is stored in the `webusers` table. This table

Figure 14-16. *AppPage Builder Administration screen.*

is used for authenticating the user at the browser. When requesting a secure URL, the user will be prompted to enter a username and password at the browser. If the user authenticates successfully, the AppPage Builder administration properties are extracted from the `webusers` table and are then used to personalize the AppPage Builder session. All the administration properties for the user are stored in the `webusers` table.

The AppPage Builder username is not the same as the name of the user session that is connected to the database (as shown by `onstat -u`*), unless* `MI_USER_REMOTE` *(*`connect_as_user`* in Version 4) is set to ON.*

Setting the Default Project and Object Type

The first change you may want to perform after you have created a project is to set the default project and object type for the user you are running AppPage Builder under. If you leave the default project set to AppPage Builder, then you will first have to select the correct project and object type every time you need to select an object from a list. For example, in the Edit Object screen, you will have to select the `shopper` project and then click the Continue button before you can select the object you want to edit. This might seem trivial, but it becomes annoying after a short time.

To set the default project, follow these steps:

- Select the project from the Default Project selection list.
- If you want to change the default object type, then select the required object type from the Default Object Type list. For example, you may always want to see a list of Documents instead of AppPages for the `shopper` project when you enter the Edit Object screen.

Changing the Size of the Edit Window for AppPages and Dynamic Tags

You can change the size of the textarea that is displayed when you add or edit AppPages and dynamic tags. You may want to do this if a lot of your editing is peformed in AppPage Builder.

To change the size of this textarea from the Administration screen,

- enter the required TEXTAREA Height value.
- enter the required TEXTAREA Width value.

For example, if you set TEXTAREA Height to 100, and leave TEXTAREA Width at 80 (the default), then the editable textarea contains 100 rows and 80 columns when you choose the Add or Edit AppPage screen.

Page Versioning

You can turn *page versioning* on or off from the Administration screen. See the ensuing section "Maintaining Versions of AppPages," below for details on how to manage page versions.

`weblint` **Parsing**

When you save AppPages to the database using AppPage Builder, you can check for syntax errors using the `weblint` utility. Any errors are displayed to a textarea on the Add or Edit AppPage screen after you have saved the AppPage to the database. You set the level of `weblint` checking in the Administartion screen. See Chap. 26, "Debugging Web DataBlade Applications," for more information on the `weblint` utility.

 You can check the administration settings for a user by looking at the Administration footer on each AppPage Builder screen. This footer is derived from the APB_FOOTER *dynamic tag.*

Maintaining Versions of AppPages

If you turn page versioning on in AppPage Builder, you can store the previous versions of pages. For example, if page versioning is on and you edit an AppPage, when you save the updated version of the AppPage to the database, a new version of the AppPage is created with the version number incremented by one. The previous version remains in the database but will never be used unless activated via a special screen in AppPage Builder.

Page versioning gives you a very basic form of configuration management for your AppPage Builder applications. Alternatively, you can maintain previous versions of the AppPage outside the database.

Note that if you want both a live version and a development version of an AppPage in the same database, then you will have to customize AppPage Builder to do this. You can't edit an AppPage version in the Edit AppPage screen unless you activate the version you require, which is not recommended for a live application.

When Page Versions is turned on, a new button appears on the Edit AppPage screen, called `Versions`. This button appears when the version of the AppPage is greater than one.

What Is an AppPage Version?

A version of an AppPage comprises the AppPage source plus the AppPage metadata, such as description, object type, read and write levels, plus the version number. The table that stores this information is called `webpagesversions`.

This table will store all the versions of an AppPage except the latest version, unless the user activates a previous version of an AppPage, in which case the latest version is stored away in the `webpagesversions` table.

Activating and Deleting Page Versions

Activating an AppPage version means that you are copying it to the `webpages` table. Deleting an AppPage version means that you are deleting the specific AppPage *version* from the `webpagesversions` table. Figure 14-17 shows the AppPage Versions screen.

To activate a version of an AppPage,

- click the Versions button in the Edit AppPage screen; the AppPage Versions screen will be displayed;
- select the version of the AppPage to make current (active), from the Activate list (the currently active AppPage will not be available);
- click the Activate button; the screen will be refreshed and the available page versions will now include the page version that has been deactivated.

To delete a version of an AppPage:

- click the Versions button in the Edit AppPage screen; the AppPage Versions screen will be displayed;
- select the AppPage version to delete from the Delete list; the currently active AppPage will not be available for deletion;
- click the Delete button; the screen will be refreshed and the available versions will no longer include the deleted AppPage version.

Figure 14-17. *AppPage Versions.*

Example Change History

Table 14-4 shows the actions performed on an AppPage called `Home.html`, and the page-versioning results of those actions.

warning

If you delete a versioned AppPage from the Edit AppPage screen, you will delete the AppPage from the webpages *table and all versions of the AppPage from the* webpagesversions *table, even if the active version is not the latest version.*

Extending AppPage Builder

You will typically want to extend AppPage Builder by adding to the database new types of content that are not supported by the out-of-the-box application. This will involve the addition of new MIME

Table 14-4. Page Versioning of an AppPage.

Action	Result
Add version 1 of `Home.html`	Version 1 added to the `webpages` table.
Change version 1 AppPage source or metadata	Version 1 of `Home` stored in the `webpagesversions` table
	Version 2 stored in the `webpages` table
Change version 2 AppPage source or metadata	Version 2 of `Home` stored in the `webpagesversions` table
	Version 3 stored in the `webpages` table
Activate version 2 of `Home`	Version 3 of Home stored in the `webpagesversions` table
	Version 2 stored in the `webpages` table
Delete version 1 of `Home`	Version 1 deleted from the `webpagesversions` table

types and possibly new object types. For example, if you want to be able to store plain text in the database, you add a new MIME type, `text/plain`, to the AppPage Builder schema and associate this MIME type with the `Document` object type.

You may want to create a new object type if you need to store extra metadata about an object stored in the database. You may want to store content-authoring details about the objects in the database; you may also want to link content items in various ways.

For example, you may want to store weekly spreadsheets in the database and deliver them to authorized users over the intranet. To do this, you may want to store the name of the author of the spreadsheet, the department authorized to view the spreadsheet, and an expiration date when the spreadsheet can no longer be viewed. This information can be stored as metadata with the spreadsheet.

The AppPage Builder Add Document screen does not, however, support this metadata. If you add the MIME type for MS-Excel, you still won't have the information stored with the document that you require.

In this case, you would create a new object type, called `SecureDocument`, and also create three AppPages to maintain objects of this type. You would also create a MIME type for the spreadsheets used if one did not already exist.

AppPage Builder supports a one-to-one mapping between object type and MIME type. If you want to associate a MIME type with more than one object type, you need to customize the AppPage Builder schema.

To extend AppPage Builder in this way, perform the following steps:

- Create a new object type (for example, `SecureDocument`).
- Create a new MIME type and map this type onto the new object type.
- Create a table to store the new object type (for example, `websecuredocs`).
- Create three AppPages to maintain objects that are `SecureDocument`s.

Create a New Object Type

You create a new object type as follows:

- From the Admin Menu, choose Add Object Type.
- Enter the object type name and the page suffix in the Add Object Type screen, and click Save.

Figure 14-18 shows an example for the `SecureDocument` object. The page suffix is set to `SecureDoc`. We will need to create AppPages with the `SecureDoc` suffix.

Create a new Mime Type

To add a new MIME type to AppPage Builder, perform the following:

- From the Admin Menu, choose Add MIME Type.
- Enter the MIME type details in the Add MIME Type screen, and associate the MIME type with an object type.

Figure 14-19 shows the example of creating an MS-Excel MIME type, and associating the type with the new `SecureDocument` object type.

Figure 14-18. *Add a new object type.*

Figure 14-19. *Add a new MIME type.*

Create a New Table for the Object Type

You need to create a new table to store the object reference and the object metadata for SecureDocument objects. Listing 14-5 shows an example.

In this example, the webdocuments table has been used as a template for the new websecuredocs table. We have added author, expiry_date, and department to the document object metadata, resulting in the SecureDocument metadata.

The metadata for a SecureDocument will be stored in the websecuredocs table, but the object itself will be stored in the smart BLOB space called sbspace.

Create AppPages

You need to create three new AppPages to maintain the new object type. For example, using the SecureDocument object type, the page suffix is SecureDoc.

Listing 14-5. The websecuredocs table.

```
create table websecuredocs
   (
     id varchar(40) not null,
     project varchar(40) not null,
     object_type varchar(40) not null,
     mime_type varchar(40) not null,
     description varchar(250),
     author varchar(20) not null,
     expiry_date date not null,
     department char(3) not null,
     object blob,
     primary key (id)
   ) PUT object in
   (
     sbspace
   ) extent size 32 next size 32 lock mode page;
```

You should therefore create:

- `apb_add_SecureDoc`—add a `SecureDoc` object;
- `apb_edit_SecureDoc`—edit the metadata and overwrite the `SecureDoc` object;
- `apb_delete_SecureDoc`—delete the `SecureDoc` object.

You should base these AppPages on the existing pages for the Document object type; for example, `apb_add_Document`. Remember to customize the page to include the new metadata and to use the new table.

Add `SecureDocument` Objects

Once you have completed all the steps above, you can add `SecureDocument` objects to the `websecuredocs` table.

When you choose Add Object from the AppPage Builder menu, the list of object types shown in Fig. 14-20 is displayed.

Choose the `SecureDocument` object type, and the `apb_add_SecureDoc` page will be displayed.

Figure 14-20. *Add a SecureDocument object.*

Summary

You can use AppPage Builder out of the box to create Web DataBlade applications using AppPage Script. In this chapter, we have learned how to create web applications using AppPage Builder. In particular, we learned how to add dynamic tags, AppPages, and large objects to the AppPage Builder schema within the context of a working Online Directory application. We also learned how to set user preferences for users of AppPage Builder.

Importantly, we learned how to extend AppPage Builder to accept different MIME types and object types, why each of these is different, and why you would want to extend AppPage Builder in this way.

15

Working with AppPage Tags and Functions

In this chapter:

- Creating the "Hello World" program with the Web DataBlade
- Working with AppPage Tags
- Working with AppPage Script
- Using variable-processing functions
- Variable-processing function summary
- Navigating websites

The Web DataBlade allows you to create sophisticated and dynamic web pages by using HTML and AppPage Scripting tags contained in template web pages, called AppPages. This chapter will cover all the fundamental components in AppPage Scripting, including AppPage tags, variable-processing functions, AppPage variables, and website navigation. You can use this chapter as a reference to look up the AppPage tags and functions that you require.

A web application constructed using the Web DataBlade module and Informix Dynamic Server.2000 or Informix Dynamic Server with the Universal Data Option uses AppPages to both retrieve data from the database and to format that data for presentation as an HTML page to the user at the browser.

In most cases you will use one of the following to store the AppPages in the database:

- Data Director for Web, using AppPage Editor and Site Manager to type in the AppPage or to import the AppPage from the filesystem,
- AppPage Builder, typing or importing the AppPage source into the AppPage Builder schema.

You may be more comfortable using your desktop editor to create the AppPage first and then import it into the Informix database using Data Director for Web or AppPage Builder. You may create a complete website framework using a website creation tool, and then import this website into Data Director for Web so that you can add AppPage Script to provide the dynamic database-driven functionality.

Creating the "Hello World" Program with the Web DataBlade

Before you develop dynamic, database-driven web applications, though, it is important that you understand the fundamentals.

You don't need JavaScript, Java, JDBC, or ODBC to do this. You can use simple HTML and AppPage Scripting to access your data and format it appropriately. Because the AppPage Scripting language is an *extension* to HTML, you don't have to climb another learning curve: AppPage Scripting tags look familiar to you already. If you have an elementary grasp of SQL (Structured Query Language) as well, you can put HTML, AppPage Script, and SQL together to create a dynamic database-driven website.

A dynamic Informix web application can be as simple as a web page with additional scripting commands that are executed on the server; in our case, the scripting language is AppPage Script, which is understood by the Web DataBlade software. This section introduces the method of dynamically creating a web page via simple AppPage Script.

The first example is a rendition of the "Hello World" program. The second example shows how to use AppPage Scripting variables to display information that formerly would require JavaScript coding with objects. Neither example selects data from the database.

"Hello World"—AppPage Script

It is very easy to write the classic "Hello World" program using AppPage Script. Listing 15-1 illustrates this. At first, the HTML page looks like a standard web page. However, there are some tags in the page that are not standard HTML tags. These tags are delimited by "`<?`" and "`<?/`" characters. Note how similar these tags are to standard HTML tags. The only syntactic difference is the presence of a "`?`" character.

This HTML page is actually stored in the Informix database. When the page is requested from the browser, the web server makes a CGI call to an Informix program (called `webdriver`), which submits a query to the database. This query calls the `webexplode()` DataBlade function to take the HTML page from the database and process the tags delimited by "`<?`" and "`<?/`". When this processing is complete, a new HTML page is ready to be passed back to the browser. The `webdriver` takes this HTML page and returns it to the web server for transmission to the browser. Because the `webexplode()` function treats the tags as more than HTML document markup tags, it interprets them as though they were a simple programming language.

The `<?MIVAR>` tag is a special Informix tag that allows you to define and use variables within an HTML page template (or AppPage). The web browser and web server never see these tags and variables. Only the Web DataBlade understands them.

In List. 15-1, a variable is declared (called `message`). This variable contains the string `Hello World`. The next line shows the contents of the variable being output.

Listing 15-1. *The* `HelloWorld.html` *AppPage source.*

```
<html>
<head>
    <title>Hello World</title>
</head>
<body>
    <center>
        <?MIVAR NAME=message>Hello World<?/MIVAR>
        <h1><?MIVAR>$message<?/MIVAR></h1>
    </center>
</body>
</html>
```

As the `webexplode()` program reads the AppPage, it interprets the Informix tags and performs a task relevant for each tag. Whatever the task is, there will usually be an output string although the output string may be blank. It is this output string that the browser will render. In the example above, `webexplode()` will take the contents of the variable `$message` and output `Hello World`. That is, the first Informix tag creates and initializes the `$message` variable; the second will output the contents of the `$message` variable.

The output page sent to the browser is shown in List. 15-2. Figure 15-1 shows HTML rendered in the browser.

Listing 15-2.   *The HTML page sent to the browser after the AppPage in List. 15-1 has been processed by the Web DataBlade.*

```
<html>
<head>
    <title>Hello World</title>
</head>

<body>
    <center>

        <h1>Hello World</h1>
    </center>
</body>
</html>
```

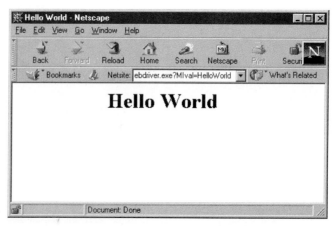

Figure 15-1. *"Hello World"—browser output of List. 15-2.*

Listing Client and Server Information with AppPage Script Tags

The next example shows how to use AppPage Script variables to display client and server information to the user. Unlike the preceding example, the variables are not created in the AppPage. The variables in this example are part of the Web DataBlade and web server configuration, and so are passed to the `webexplode()` function by `webdriver`.

What we want to do is display the following information in the user's browser:

- the user who is going to connect to the Informix database,
- the database that the user can access from that URL,
- the name of the web server host,
- the IP address of the server,
- the name of the web server,
- the URL of the web server,
- the web server host's port on which the the web server is listing,
- the protocol the web server understands,
- the web server software and version,
- the browser from which the user is connecting.

None of this information will be retrieved from the database. The only component retrieved from the database is the AppPage source, shown in List. 15-3.

important

Why Use a Database Here?

The AppPage in List. 15-3 does not contain any scripting tags to work with database content. However, the AppPage itself is stored in the database, and the Web DataBlade function `webexplode()` *"inside" the database processes the AppPage. If the AppPage were not stored in the database, the Web DataBlade could not process the special tags that give the example its power and simplicity.*

Listing 15-3 shows the AppPage source for the example.
The characteristics of this example are as follows:

- The HTML page that is sent to the browser is constructed dynamically from the AppPage source template above.
- All AppPage Scripting variables start with a "$" character, just like user-defined variables.
- The list of AppPage Scripting variables are contained within a single `<?MIVAR>` to `<?/MIVAR>` tag.

```html
<html>
<head>
<title>Hello World: AppScript</title>
</head>

<body bgcolor="#FFFFFF">
<br>
<?MIVAR NAME=message>Welcome, $MI_USER<?/MIVAR>

<?MIVAR>
<center>
    <b><font size=6>$message</font><br>
    You can access the
    <font size=+1>$MI_DATABASE database</font> from this site.<br>
    Your Connection Information is:<br><br>
</center>

<div align="center"><center>

<table border="0" width="73%" cellpadding="2" bgcolor="#FFFFFF">
  <tr>
    <td width="50%" bgcolor="#686868" align=center>
        <font color="#FFFFFF">
          <big><strong>Description</strong></big>
        </font>
    </td>
    <td width="50%" bgcolor="#686868" align=center>
        <font color="#FFFFFF">
            <big><strong>Value</strong></big>
      </font>
    </td>
  </tr>
  <tr>
    <td width="50%" bgcolor="#DFDFDF" align="right">
        <font color="#000000">
            <strong>Web Server Host:</strong>
        </font>
    </td>
    <td width="50%" bgcolor="#DFDFDF">
        <strong>$HTTP_HOST</strong>
```

Listing 15-3. *(continued)*

```
    </td>
 </tr>
 <tr>
   <td width="50%" bgcolor="#DFDFDF" align="right">
       <font color="#000000">
           <strong>Web Server IP:</strong>
       </font>
   </td>
   <td width="50%" bgcolor="#DFDFDF">
       <strong>$REMOTE_HOST</strong>
   </td>
 </tr>
 <tr>
   <td width="50%" bgcolor="#DFDFDF" align="right">
       <font color="#000000">
           <strong>Server Name:</strong>
       </font>
   </td>
   <td width="50%" bgcolor="#DFDFDF">
       <strong>$SERVER_NAME</strong>
   </td>
 </tr>
 <tr>
   <td width="50%" bgcolor="#DFDFDF" align="right">
       <font color="#000000">
           <strong>Web Server URL:</strong>
       </font>
   </td>
   <td width="50%" bgcolor="#DFDFDF">
       <strong>$SERVER_URL</strong>
   </td>
 </tr>
 <tr>
   <td width="50%" bgcolor="#DFDFDF" align="right">
       <font color="#000000">
           <strong>Web Server Port:</strong>
       </font>
   </td>
   <td width="50%" bgcolor="#DFDFDF">
       <strong>$SERVER_PORT</strong>
   </td>
```

Listing 15-3.   (continued)

```
    </tr>
    <tr>
      <td width="50%" bgcolor="#DFDFDF" align="right">
          <font color="#000000">
              <strong>Web Server Protocol:</strong>
          </font>
      </td>
      <td width="50%" bgcolor="#DFDFDF">
          <strong>$SERVER_PROTOCOL</strong>
      </td>
    </tr>
    <tr>
      <td width="50%" bgcolor="#DFDFDF" align="right">
          <font color="#000000">
              <strong>Web Server Software:</strong>
          </font>
      </td>
      <td width="50%" bgcolor="#DFDFDF">
          <strong>$SERVER_SOFTWARE</strong>
      </td>
    </tr>
    <tr>
      <td width="50%" bgcolor="#DFDFDF" align="right">
          <font color="#000000">
              <strong>Your Browser:</strong>
          </font>
      </td>
      <td width="50%" bgcolor="#DFDFDF">
          <strong>$HTTP_USER_AGENT</strong>
      </td>
    </tr>

</table>
</center></div>

<?/MIVAR>

</body>
</html>
```

- Standard HTML can be placed between the AppPage Scripting tags.
- The AppPage Script variables are part of the *web server environment* of the `webdriver` program.
- There is no Java or JavaScript code required to control the rendering of this information.

Why Use AppPage Script instead of JavaScript?

Without AppPage Script, you would have to use a scripting language such as JavaScript to obtain the browser and web server environment information from objects created internally by the browser. However, the JavaScript code would run on the client once the HTML page containing it was downloaded from the web server. Using AppPage Scripting variables, no code is run on the client. Instead, the Web DataBlade software initializes or inherits the variables on the server and outputs the relevant values to the HTML page being constructed.

When the Web DataBlade has processed the AppPage source, the resulting HTML page is sent to the browser that requested it. Listing 15-4 shows this HTML.

Listing 15-4. **List. 15-3 after the Web DataBlade has processed the AppPage Script variables. This HTML page is sent to the browser.**

```
<html>
<head>
<title>Hello World: AppScript</title>
</head>

<body bgcolor="#FFFFFF">
<br>

<center>
    <b><font size=6>Welcome, Informix</font><br>
    You can access the <font size=+1>stores7 database</font> from
this site.<br>
    Your Connection Information is:<br><br>
</center>
<div align="center"><center>
```

Listing 15-4. *(continued)*

```
<table border="0" width="73%" cellpadding="2" bgcolor="#FFFFFF">
  <tr>
    <td width="50%" bgcolor="#686868" align=center>
        <font color="#FFFFFF">
            <big><strong>Description</strong></big>
        </font>
    </td>
    <td width="50%" bgcolor="#686868" align=center>
        <font color="#FFFFFF">
            <big><strong>Value</strong></big>
        </font>
    </td>
  </tr>
  <tr>
    <td width="50%" bgcolor="#DFDFDF" align="right">
        <font color="#000000">
            <strong>Web Server Host:</strong>
        </font>
    </td>
    <td width="50%" bgcolor="#DFDFDF">
        <strong>dellcpi</strong>
    </td>
  </tr>
  <tr>
    <td width="50%" bgcolor="#DFDFDF" align="right">
        <font color="#000000">
            <strong>Web Server IP:</strong>
        </font>
    </td>
    <td width="50%" bgcolor="#DFDFDF">
        <strong>127.0.0.1</strong>
    </td>
  </tr>
  <tr>
    <td width="50%" bgcolor="#DFDFDF" align="right">
        <font color="#000000">
            <strong>Server Name:</strong>
        </font>
    </td>
    <td width="50%" bgcolor="#DFDFDF">
```

Listing 15-4. *(continued)*

```
            <strong>dellcpi.</strong>
      </td>
</tr>
<tr>
      <td width="50%" bgcolor="#DFDFDF" align="right">
            <font color="#000000">
                  <strong>Web Server URL:</strong>
            </font>
      </td>
      <td width="50%" bgcolor="#DFDFDF">
            <strong>http://dellcpi</strong>
      </td>
</tr>
<tr>
      <td width="50%" bgcolor="#DFDFDF" align="right">
            <font color="#000000">
                  <strong>Web Server Port:</strong>
            </font>
      </td>
      <td width="50%" bgcolor="#DFDFDF">
            <strong>80</strong>
      </td>
</tr>
<tr>
      <td width="50%" bgcolor="#DFDFDF" align="right">
            <font color="#000000">
                  <strong>Web Server Protocol:</strong>
            </font>
      </td>
      <td width="50%" bgcolor="#DFDFDF">
            <strong>HTTP/1.0</strong>
      </td>
</tr>
<tr>
      <td width="50%" bgcolor="#DFDFDF" align="right">
            <font color="#000000">
                  <strong>Web Server Software:</strong>
            </font>
      </td>
      <td width="50%" bgcolor="#DFDFDF">
```

Listing 15-4.   (continued)

```
            <strong>Netscape-Enterprise/3.6</strong>
    </td>
  </tr>
  <tr>
    <td width="50%" bgcolor="#DFDFDF" align="right">
        <font color="#000000">
            <strong>Your Browser:</strong>
        </font>
    </td>
    <td width="50%" bgcolor="#DFDFDF">
        <strong>Mozilla/4.08 [en] (WinNT; I ;Nav)</strong>
    </td>
  </tr>

</table>
</center></div>
</body>
</html>
```

In List. 15-4, notice how the AppPage Scripting variables have been replaced by the contents of those variables. Also notice that there is not a single line of JavaScript code in the web page.

Figure 15-2 shows the browser display of the HTML in List. 15-4.

Figure 15-3 shows the variable values when connecting to a different web server host.

Figure 15-4 shows the result of taking out the special "?" character in the `<?MIVAR>` AppPage Script tag. The AppPage is still retrieved from the Informix database; however, the Web DataBlade *ignores* tags that do not begin with the "?" character, so the variable name is output unprocessed.

Figure 15-4 is useful because it also lets you see what AppPage Script variables were used. However, you can employ a special configuration variable, called `MI-WEBRAWMODE`, to list the variables used and their values without changing the AppPage source. This is described in Chap. 26.

The only change required in the AppPage is as follows. Change this:

```
<?MIVAR>
code
<?/MIVAR>
```

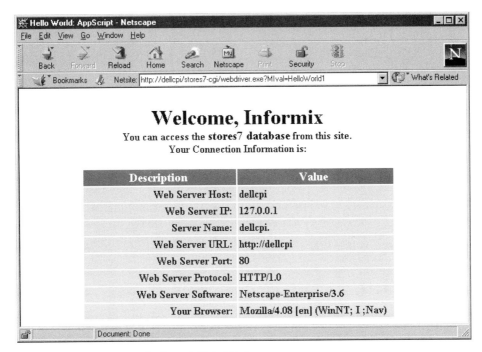

Figure 15-2. Browser display of List. 15-4.

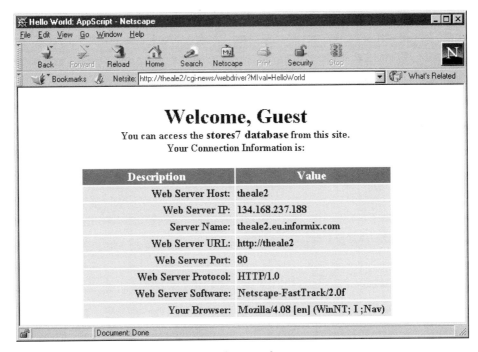

Figure 15-3. Values for a different web server host.

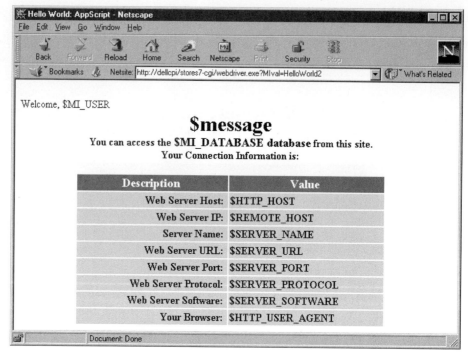

Figure 15-4. *Unprocessed variable references.*

to this:

```
<MIVAR>
code
</MIVAR>
```

The Web DataBlade will ignore tags lacking the "?" character after the "<" character. The browser, too, will ignore tags that it does not understand, such as `<MIVAR>` and `</MIVAR>`.

Working with AppPage Tags

Syntax of AppPage Scripting Tags

The Web DataBlade module tags use the SGML processing-instruction tag format, `<?tag_info>`, `<?/tag_info>`. An SGML processor, such as a browser, ignores tags that it does not recognize. Web

DataBlade module tags are ignored by the browser because they are recognized only by the Web DataBlade module. Web DataBlade module tags and attributes are not case sensitive. Users can also define their own tags.

List of Tags

Table 15-1 lists the tags available with the Web DataBlade.

Nesting Tags

Nesting Tags in Version 4

Only the MIBLOCK and MISQL tags have nesting properties. The MIBLOCK tag allows you to nest all other AppPage Scripting tags, including MIBLOCK. You can also nest an MISQL tag within another MISQL tag.

Nesting Tags up to Version 3.3

In Version 3, only the MIBLOCK tag is allowed to have all other tags nested within it, including MIBLOCK.

Table 15-1.	AppPage tags.

Tag	Description
MISQL	Executes SQL and formats the results.
MIVAR	Creates, assigns, and displays webdriver variables.
MIBLOCK	Defines a logical block of HTML that can be included conditionally.
MIELSE	Used if MIBLOCK is conditional.
MIERROR	Manages SQL error handling.
MIFUNC	Allows NSAPI or ISAPI user-written functions to be called.
MIDEFERRED	Enables caching of parts of a web page.
MIEXEC	Enables invocation of PERL programs from a web page.

Using Special Characters in Tags and Formatting

Special Characters in AppPage Tags

If a special character appears within an AppPage tag (between the angle brackets `<  >`), the character must be replaced by the entity reference for that character. This is because `webdriver` will not interpret the special character if not translated.

For example, to translate the following `insert` statement for use in an `MISQL` tag, you need to insert the `&quot` character. The following snippets show the before and after version.

```
insert into customer (forename, surname) values ('Joe
"Joey"','Smith')
<?MISQL SQL="insert into customer (forename,surname)
values ('Joe &quot;Joey&quot;','Smith')">Customer
inserted<?/MISQL>
```

Special Characters in Dynamic Tags

While you create and use Dynamic AppPage tags as if they were system defined, you need to translate special characters that are meaningful to the dynamic tag parser. In contrast to dynamic tag parameter specification, if the "@" character appears within the dynamic tag *content,* then you must replace it with the entity reference "`&#64`".

Special Characters in Formatting Statements

Formatting statements have special syntax, and if you use the formatting symbols "{", "}", or "$" outside of the formatting context, you need to prefix the symbol. Table 15-2 lists the characters that need special attention.

Table 15-2. *Special character translation.*

Character	Entity reference or replacement
Double quote (")	&quot
@	&#64
{	{{
}	}}
$	$$

What Is an Entity Reference?

An entity reference is used by the browser to identify special characters that must be displayed in the browser. The entity reference is placed in the source HTML page by the page author. Example entity references include &amp (&) and &#153 (™). The browser looks them up and replaces them with equivalent characters.

The `MISQL` Tag

The `MISQL` tag is used to execute SQL statements and format the results of those statements. The SQL statements can include the execution of SPL (stored procedure language) procedures using the `execute procedure` statement.

Attribute	Mandatory?
SQL	Yes
NAME	No
COND	No
ERR	No
WINSTART	No
WINSIZE	No
RESULTS	No
MAXROWS	No

SQL

You specify a single `SQL` statement with this attribute. The `SQL` statement can be parameterized by AppPage variables, or it may be stored inside an AppPage variable. For example:

```
<?MISQL SQL="select fname, company from customer where
lname = '$lastName';">
<?MISQL SQL="select $columns $fromList $whereClause;">
<?MISQL SQL="$selectStatement">
```

NAME

When the SQL statement is executed, the formatted results can be stored in an AppPage variable denoted by NAME. If NAME is not specified, the formatted results are output to the HTML page. You can use the NAME attribute to store the results of SQL statements so that you can pass a single, formatted result set to different AppPages if required. Because the formatting statements are for the browser, the formatting statements can contain HTML and JavaScript.

COND

The MISQL tag will only be interpreted if the expression in COND evaluates to true, which is the same as nonzero. You often use the COND attribute to establish SQL execution as dependant on other query values or AppPage parameters.

ERR

If the SQL statement encounters an error, ERR specifies the MIERROR tag that handles the error in the AppPage. Because you can have multiple MISQL tags on an AppPage, you should name the MIERROR handlers and reference them in the ERR attribute.

WINSTART

The WINSTART attribute indicates the first row in the *current* result set to process. The WINSTART attribute can be assigned a value or can be designated a value by a variable. The value of WINSTART increments to begin with the next consecutive row number following the last row number that was retrieved.

For example, if you have set the WINSIZE attribute to 20, the WINSTART value is 0 for the first iteration through the relevant portion of the AppPage. The second iteration through the AppPage sets the WINSTART value to 20. The third iteration through the AppPage sets the WINSTART value to 40. This continues until webexplode() retrieves all rows.

Using the NAME attribute disables the function of WINSTART and WINSIZE.

WINSIZE

The WINSIZE attribute sets the maximum number of rows that are displayed in the output of the MISQL tag. Use WINSIZE to limit the size of the result set being returned across the network if the queries you are executing might return a very large number of rows. Setting this attribute limits the system resources required to execute the query and return the results to the client.

RESULTS

This attribute is only available from Version 4 onwards. The RESULTS attribute defines a location, or *namespace*, where the SQL result set can be addressed. The MISQL statements can be nested within one another from Version 4 onwards. With RESULTS you specify the name of a container whose attributes are the column values. These values are addressed by position. To access the RESULTS value, type in the column number, dot ("."), and the RESULTS attribute.

You don't need to specify the RESULTS attribute in a nested MISQL tag, since the SQL formatting section will still iterate around the result sets. However, if you want to address columns from different result sets, you must use the namespace defined by the RESULTS attribute to do this.

If you address the column values returned as $1..$n instead of using a namespace, then the scope is limited to the current MISQL tag.

You can nest MISQL statements to perform Master Detail queries and to denormalise tables.

You can use namespace values to parameterize inner, nested SQL queries (see the examples later in this chapter).

MAXROWS

This attribute specifies the maximum number of formatted rows to be displayed. It is not officially supported from Version 4.

The MIVAR Tag

The MIVAR tag enables you to assign and display variables. You can use the MIVAR tag to expand Web DataBlade variables inline. You don't need to use MIVAR when using variables inside a MISQL formatting section.

Attribute	Mandatory?
NAME	No
DEFAULT	No
COND	No
ERR	No

You will also want to use MIVAR to invoke AppPage Scripting functions outside of AppPage tags. With MIVAR, the webexplode() function can identify and expand the variables between the start and end MIVAR tags.

NAME

This attribute declares a variable name, and whatever value appears between the start and end MIVAR tags is assigned to a variable with that name. The snippet below assigns the value "My name is Joe" to a variable called $selectedCustomer, and this value is written to the HTML page (or, expanded) on the next line.

```
<?MIVAR NAME=$selectedCustomer>My name is Joe<?/MIVAR>
<?MIVAR>$selectedCustomer<?/MIVAR>
```

You do not have to specify the "$" character with the variable name when declaring the NAME attribute. If the NAME attribute is not specified, the text between the start and end tags is output.

DEFAULT

Use the DEFAULT attribute to specify a default value for any unassigned variables between the start and end MIVAR tags. This is useful if you want to use a parameter passed to the AppPage but are not sure whether the parameter has been set in the URL or in a form. In the following example, if the variable $optionParameter, is unassigned, it will be set to the value "Bond Option".

```
<?MIVAR DEFAULT="Bond Option">$optionParameter
<?/MIVAR>
<?MIVAR> The Option selected is $optionParameter
<?/MIVAR>
```

COND

The COND attribute specifies a condition that is evaluated before the tag is processed. If the condition is true, the tag is processed. Conditions are variables or variable expressions that are false if zero and true if nonzero.

```
<?MIVAR COND=$(EQ,$optionParameter,"Bond Option")>The
option selected is Bond.<?/MIVAR>
```

ERR

The ERR attribute links an MIVAR tag with an MIERROR tag to be invoked if an error occurs in the processing of that tag.

The MIBLOCK Tag

The MIBLOCK tag enables you to group logically related blocks of HTML to be executed on a variety of conditions. Version 4 has introduced extensions to the MIBLOCK tag to allow for iterations of the statements within the MIBLOCK start and end tags.

The MIBLOCK iteration is a simple but powerful tool and a major improvement over the Version 3 implementation of MIBLOCK. See subsection "Using Loops in AppPage Script," later in this chapter.

Attribute	Mandatory?
COND	No
ERR	No
INDEX	No
FROM	No
TO	No
STEP	No
FOREACH	No
WHILE	No

COND

Execute the MIBLOCK section if COND evaluates to true (nonzero). For example, the following MIBLOCK will be processed only if the variable $option is set to the value "Customer".

```
<?MIBLOCK COND=$(EQ,$option,"Customer")>

You will be presented with a list of Customers to
select from.

<?/MIBLOCK>
```

ERR

This is the label of the MIERROR tag that is to handle errors generated within the COND attribute of the MIBLOCK tag.

INDEX

This attribute defines a variable that is used as a loop counter. It is required if either the FROM or FOREACH attributes are specified. See the subsection on using loops later in this chapter.

FROM

This attribute specifies the initial value of the INDEX attribute in the FOR loop version of MIBLOCK iteration.

TO

Specifies the maximum value of the INDEX in a FROM or FOREACH loop.

STEP

Specifies the increment or decrement value of the INDEX attribute. The default value is "1" if STEP is not specified.

FOREACH

Used in the FOREACH loop, it specifies a variable that may or may not be a variable vector but is used to provide values for iterations of the loop.

Variable Vectors

A variable vector consists of multiple variables with the same name that are passed into the AppPage using checkboxes or the MULTIPLE attribute of selection lists. You can create your own variable vectors in an AppPage by repeated use of the NAME clause with a subscript for the variable name.

If the variable is not a variable vector, the loop is processed once only. If the variable is a vector, then the body is processed once for each value in the vector. You can use this attribute to process an HTML form where each value that has been checked in a checkbox is passed in a variable vector that has the same name as the checkbox in the form.

Vectors and Arrays

In this book, a vector is synonymous with an array. Both contain a list of values, and therefore each has a length. JavaScript has a length property for the `Array` *object that we can read to check the array size, but the AppScript vector has no public length property. However, both are loosely typed. This means that there is no concept of an element type, where every element of the array is the same type (as in Java). AppPage vectors and JavaScript arrays can contain numbers and text in adjacent elements.*

WHILE

Evaluation of this attribute determines if the body is processed. If this attribute is not equal to zero, the body is processed.

The MIELSE Tag

The `MIELSE` tag works with the `MIBLOCK` tag and is only available from Verson 4 onward. It is used to implement a logical structure that mimics the if-then-else conditional structure.

AppPage conditional	Standard conditional
`<?MIBLOCK COND=$()>`	IF (condition) THEN
`<?MIELSE COND=$()>`	ELSE IF (condition) THEN
`<?MIELSE>`	ELSE
`<?/MIBLOCK>`	ENDIF

Listing 15-5 shows the `MIBLOCK` and `MIELSE` structure, which includes the nesting of `MIBLOCK` and `MIELSE` tags. If you understand if-then-else, you can't go wrong.

Listing 15-5. *The* MIELSE *tag with* MIBLOCK *and nested* MIBLOCK *tags.*

```
<HTML>
<BODY>
<?MIVAR NAME=$False>false<?/MIVAR>
<?MIVAR NAME=$True>True<?/MIVAR>
<?MIBLOCK COND=$(EQ,$False,True)>
This will not be displayed.
<?MIELSE COND=$(EQ,$True,True)>
  <?MIBLOCK COND=$(EQ,$True,True)>
   This will  be displayed.<BR>
  <?MIELSE COND=$(EQ,$True,True)>
  Although the condition is true, this line will not be displayed
because the last MIBLOCK condition has been evaluated to true.
  <?MIELSE>
   This will never be displayed.
  <?/MIBLOCK>
This will always be displayed.
<?MIELSE>
This will never be displayed.
<?/MIBLOCK>
</BODY>
</HTML>
```

The MIERROR Tag

The MIERROR tag is used to specify error handling in AppPages. When webexplode() encounters an error within other Web DataBlade tags, those tags can specify an ERR attribute to handle errors arising from the execution of that tag. You associate an ERR attribute with an MIERROR tag.

For example, errors can occur if the database server cannot successfully process an SQL statement, or if you try to access an unassigned variable, or if you use an incorrect tag construct.

When AppPages are exploded in a nested manner (when webexplode() is called within an AppPage by an MISQL tag), then any errors encountered within dynamic tags in the nested AppPage will be handled by any MIERROR tag that has an ERR tag matching the failed tag, even if the MIERROR tag is higher up in the page chain.

Attribute	Mandatory?
TAG	No
COND	No
ERR	No

A well-behaved application will always handle errors gracefully. At the very least, you should specify a generic MIERROR *tag that will catch all errors not directed to a nominated error handler. Consider error handling to be part of user interface ergonomics. Users will move on from a site that behaves in an uncontrolled manner.*

TAG

This attribute specifies the error-handling behavior. If no TAG is specified, the default behavior of MIERROR is to behave like an MIVAR tag; the text between the start and end MIERROR tags is output. You can change this behavior by using the TAG attribute. You need to specify one of the following tags:

MISQL	MIERROR behaves as if it were an instance of an MISQL tag.
Dynamic tag	MIERROR behaves as if it were an instance of the dynamic tag.

If you use MISQL, then the MIERROR tag behaves like the MISQL tag, and the remainder of the error handling follows the rules for MISQL. If you specify a dynamic tag, then the remainder of the error handling follows the rules for the particular dynamic tag used.

If you use dynamic tags, you can create a generic error handler that may be reused throughout your application. You can still include MISQL *and* MIVAR *inside the dynamic tags. Using dynamic tags allows you to specify and parameterize common behavior just once and to implement that behavior application-wide simply by inserting the dynamic tag name where required.*

The placement of MIERROR *tags is significant. You must specify* MIERROR *tags within an AppPage before they are invoked.*

COND

This attribute specifies an error condition that must evaluate to true (nonzero) before the MIERROR tag is processed. Note that COND is evaluated once only, when webexplode() first encounters the MIERROR tag in an AppPage. If COND evaluates to false when first encountered by webexplode(), then the MIERROR tag is ignored.

For example, if the COND attribute relies on the existence or content of variables, then these variables may be declared to have or may already have the appropriate *values at the point of error*. However, if these variables were not set when the COND attribute of the MIERROR tag was evaluated, then the MIERROR tag will be ignored, since COND is not evaluated at the point of error for MIERROR tags.

ERR

The ERR attribute is a label for the MIERROR tag. If an MIERROR tag does not have an ERR attribute, it is called a generic error handler. Errors encountered when processing AppPage tags that do not nominate an MIERROR handler or that nominate a nonexistent handler will be directed to the MIERROR tag with no ERR attribute.

If you define multiple MIERROR *tags with no* ERR *attribute in an AppPage, then the error handler invoked is the last one defined.*

In the following example, errors in the select statement will be handled by the MIERROR tag with the ERR attribute set to selectError. Errors in the insert statement will be handled by the MIERROR tag with the ERR attribute set to insertError.

```
<?MIERROR ERR=selectError>Error in Select<?/MIERROR>
<?MIERROR ERR=insertError>Error on Insert<?/MIERROR>
<?MISQL ERR=selectError SQL="select * from
customer;"><?/MISQL>
<?MISQL ERR=insertError SQL="insert into
customer values (...);"<?/MISQL>
```

The MIFUNC Tag

The MIFUNC tag allows the execution of user-written server modules invoked by the NSAPI or ISAPI webdriver from an AppPage, and it's use is out of scope for this book.

You use the MIFUNC tag in those situations where you need to implement functionality that cannot be easily implemented in AppPages. An example of this would be a C function to perform some detailed calculation or to perform an interface with the host operating system. Although you could access this function via a system call from an SQL procedure called by MISQL, this is the longest and most time-consuming path. Using the compiled C function, you would then create a shared object and declare it to NSAPI or ISAPI. Your AppPage would then invoke the function when required. Integrating the function with NSAPI or ISAPI allows webdriver to identify and address the function identity, because webdriver is also a shared object belonging to the same process in the NSAPI and ISAPI implementations.

Before you use the MIFUNC tag in an AppPage, you must create a shared object or DLL and register it with the web server. When the webexplode() function encounters an MIFUNC tag in an AppPage, webexplode() passes the function name to webdriver, which then executes the user-written function and returns the results back to the webexplode() function. Within the MIFUNC tag, you must include the variables to be imported and exported (passed by reference) as name/value pairs.

Attribute	Mandatory?
FUNCTION	Yes
OPTION	No

FUNCTION

The FUNCTION attribute specifies the location of the webdriver function in the web server and names the routine requested.

OPTION

Specifies a user-defined function that has to provide a usage description of inputs and outputs.

The MIDEFERRED Tag

The MIDEFERRED tag delimits sections of an AppPage that are always exploded, even if the AppPage is cached. The cached AppPage will consist of generated content plus zero or more

AppPage sections delimited by the MIDEFERRED tag. These MIDEFERRED sections have not been exploded, and consist of the original raw AppPage Script. Cached AppPages are stored on the web server. When webexplode() is passed the cached AppPage by webdriver, it will ignore the static sections of the page and explode the MIDEFERRED sections.

webdriver caches the AppPage by creating a file in a directory on the web server machine that is set aside for caching AppPages. The file is suffixed with a .def extension. The first time the AppPage is invoked and cached, webdriver calls webexplode() a second time to complete the explosion of the page.

note

See Chap. 25, "Performance-tuning Essentials," for the details of full and partial AppPage caching.

The MIEXEC Tag

The MIEXEC tag enables you to execute a Perl program in your AppPage, and is available from Version 4. You pass parameters to the Perl program by specifying user-defined attributes to the MIEXEC tag. You pass text to the Perl program by including it between the MIEXEC tags. Use of this tag is beyond the scope of this book.

If the Perl program returns information, the webexplode() function replaces the full MIEXEC tag specification in the AppPage with the returned information before passing the exploded AppPage back to webdriver.

To use MIEXEC, you need to have created a WEB virtual processor (VP) by changing the Informix ONCONFIG file to add the new VP class, WEB, to service MIEXEC requests.

Attribute	Mandatory?
SERVICE	Yes
NAME	No
COND	No
ERR	No
UserAttribute1	No

SERVICE

The SERVICE attribute identifies the commands needed to find and execute the Perl program. Set the SERVICE attribute to the command needed to change to the directory that contains the Perl program you want to execute, and then set it to the command needed to execute the Perl program. Use the full pathname of the perl binary.

NAME

This attribute is the name of the variable to which the formatted results of the MIEXEC tag are assigned. If NAME is not specified, the results are output to the exploding page.

COND

If COND evaluates to true (1), then the MIEXEC tag is evaluated; otherwise it is ignored. You use AppPage functions to evaluate COND expressions to return true or false.

ERR

The ERR attribute identifies the MIERROR tag that handles errors encountered when parsing or processing the MIEXEC tag.

UserAttribute1

This is the name of a user-defined attribute that is passed to the Perl program specified by the SERVICE attribute. You can specify more than one user-defined attribute.

Working with AppPage Script

Creating Variables

You can create AppPage variables in the following ways:

- creating variables in the URL,
- creating variables from form fields,
- creating variables in AppPage Script,

- creating variables using the HTTPHEADER function,
- creating variables by selecting columns from a database table.

Creating Variables in the URL

```
http://theale2/stores-
cgi/webdriver?MIval=myAppPage&var1=10&var2=20
```

Two AppPage variables will be created:

- $var1 will be created and assigned the value 10
- $var2 will be created and assigned the value 20

Creating Variables from Form Fields

When a form is submitted to the web server for processing by webdriver, the HTML form fields are changed into AppPage variables that you can use just like any other variable. For example:

```
<form method=post action=<?mivar>$WEB_HOME<?/mivar>>
<input type=hidden name=var1 value=10>
<input type=text name=var2 value=20>
<input type=hidden name=MIval value=myAppPage>
<input type=submit name=submitButton value=Go>
</form>
```

When this form is submitted, the following variables will be visible:

- $var1 will be created and assigned the value "10" from the form.
- $var2 will be created and assigned the value "20" from the form (or from whatever the user types at the browser).
- $MIval will be used by webdriver to retrieve the AppPage myAppPage from the database.
- $submitButton will be created with the value "Go" from the form.

Creating Variables in AppPage Script

You can create AppPage variables in AppPage Script. In the first example, $myVar is created with the value "My String." In the second example, $myVar2 is created with the value "Value Exists." In the third example, $myVar3 is created with the value in $myVar if $myvar exists, otherwise it is created with the value "New String."

```
<?MIVAR name=myVar>My String<?/MIVAR>
<?MIVAR name=myVar2 default="New String">Value
Exists<?/MIVAR>
<?MIVAR name=myVar3 default="New String">$myVar<?/MIVAR>
```

You can also use the SETVAR function to create and initialize a variable. For example:

```
<?MIVAR>$(SETVAR,$myNewVar,"My New String")<?/MIVAR>
```

Creating Variables Using the HTTPHEADER Function

You can create variables using the HTTPHEADER function to create one or more cookies on the client. For example, if you wanted user information to persist between browser sessions on the same client, then you can create cookies.

```
<?MIVAR>
$(HTTPHEADER,set-cookie,myCookieName="Hello World"")
<?/MIVAR>
```

Any AppPages exploded after the page containing this function is exploded will be able to access an AppPage variable called $myCookieName.

Creating Variables by Selecting Columns from a Database Table

When you use the MISQL tag to select rows and columns from a database table, the columns are numbered $1 through $n. You can reference these values by using the $n notation within the MISQL tags. You can also reference them after the MISQL tag has completed but, strictly speaking, as the values will represent the last row of the table, it would be bad programming practice to do so. If anyone changed the AppPage source, the context of these variables may be corrupted.

Variable Vectors

A variable vector is an AppPage variable that contains one or more elements. Each element is a distinct value.

Typically, a variable vector is created from HTML form fields that can accept multiple values. These include Select boxes and checkboxes (see Chap. 17 for details on dynamic web forms programming using these form fields with AppPage Script).

The following script fragment initializes a variable vector explicitly in AppPage Script and then addresses the second element (from Version 4 of the Web DataBlade):

```
<?MIVAR NAME=myList[1]>10<?/MIVAR>
<?MIVAR NAME=myList[2]>20<?/MIVAR>
<?MIVAR>$myList[2]<?/MIVAR>
```

Using Loops in AppPage Script

Version 4 of the Web DataBlade introduces the concept of loops using the MIBLOCK tag. You can mimic the types of iterating constructs found in other programming languages.

The FOR Loop

You can emulate a FOR loop using the MIBLOCK tag. Table 15-3 lists the attributes of the MIBLOCK tag when using it to emulate a FOR loop.
    Listing 15-6 shows the use of the FOR loop, and the browser display of the result is shown in Fig. 15-5.

You can use the INDEX variable outside the loop, but not before the loop in which it has been declared.

The FOREACH Loop

You can use the MIBLOCK tag to scroll through the elements of a variable vector, which can be returned from an HTML form or may be constructed dynamically in AppPage script. This type of loop is called a FOREACH loop (see Table 15-4). The contents of the MIBLOCK tag will be processed for each element of the variable vector.

Table 15-3. The MIBLOCK *attributes for the* FOR *loop.*

Attribute	Description
INDEX	loop counter variable
FROM	initial value of INDEX
TO	maximum value of INDEX
STEP	increment of INDEX at the start of each loop iteration, defaults to 1 or –1

Listing 15-6.   Using the FOR **loop.**

```
<html>
<body>
<?MIBLOCK index=counter from=1 to=10 step=2>
Value of counter is <?MIVAR>$counter<?/MIVAR><br>
<?/MIBLOCK>

<?MIVAR><br>The value of the counter is currently
$counter<br><br><?/MIVAR>

<?MIBLOCK index=newCounter from=$counter to=1>
Value of counter is <?MIVAR>$newCounter<?/MIVAR><br>
<?/MIBLOCK>

<?MIVAR><br>The value of the counter is now
$newCounter<br><br><?/MIVAR>
</body>
</html>
```

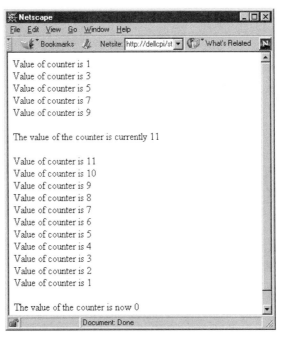

Figure 15-5.   Browser output of List. 15-6.

Table 15-4. *The* MIBLOCK *attributes for the* FOREACH *loop.*

Attribute	Description
INDEX	name of an AppPage variable that will be initialized with an element value at the start of an iteration.
FOREACH	the variable vector used to control the loop.

Listing 15-7. *Using* MIBLOCK *for a* foreach *loop.*

```
<?MIVAR cond=$(NXST,$myList)>
<form method=post action=$WEB_HOME>
<select name=myList multiple size=4>
<option value=one>One
<option value=two>Two
<option value=three>Three
<option value=four>Four
<option value=five>Five
<option value=six>Six
</select>
<input type=hidden name=MIval value=$MIval>
<input type=submit value="Go">
</form>
<?/MIVAR>

<?MIBLOCK cond=$(XST,$myList)>
<?MIBLOCK INDEX=$myElement foreach=$myList>
The following option was selected:
<?MIVAR>$myElement<?/MIVAR><br>
<?/MIBLOCK>
<?/MIBLOCK>
```

Listing 15-7 shows how to use the MIBLOCK tag as a FOREACH loop. An HTML form is created that includes a select list. On submission of the form, the multiple items selected are interpreted by the foreach loop and written to the HTML page for display on the browser. If the user selects the first three options and clicks the Submit button, the AppPage in List. 15-7 is exploded again, and the following HTML is produced:

```
The following option was selected: one
The following option was selected: two
The following option was selected: three
```

If the variable vector does not exist, the MIBLOCK FOREACH construct
is not processed.

The WHILE Loop

You can use the MIBLOCK tag to represent a WHILE loop. When you
specify the WHILE attribute to MIBLOCK, the variable expression it
uses must evaluate to a numeric value. If the value is zero, the
MIBLOCK tag is skipped. If the value is greater than zero, the body of
the MIBLOCK tag is processed once. At the end of the MIBLOCK body,
the condition is evaluated again. Note that it is your responsibility
as the programmer to increment or decrement any values used in
the expression that the WHILE attribute uses.

Table 15-5 lists the attributes for the MIBLOCK tag when used as a
WHILE construct.

Table 15-5.   The MIBLOCK attributes for the WHILE loop.

Attribute	Description
WHILE	an expression that evaluates to a numeric value.

The following snippet shows an example of using the while
attribute.

```
<?MIVAR NAME=counter>10<?/MIVAR>
<?MIBLOCK while=$counter>
The value of counter is:<?MIVAR>$counter<?/MIVAR><br>
<?MIVAR NAME=counter>$(-,$counter,1)<?/MIVAR>
<?/MIBLOCK>
```

The HTML output from this AppPage Script is as follows:

```
The value of counter is:10<br>
The value of counter is:9<br>
The value of counter is:8<br>
The value of counter is:7<br>
The value of counter is:6<br>
```

```
The value of counter is:5<br>
The value of counter is:4<br>
The value of counter is:3<br>
The value of counter is:2<br>
The value of counter is:1<br>
```

Using Variable-processing Functions

A variable processing function is an AppPage Script function that can manipulate AppPage variables or literals to produce a result that can be included in the generated HTML page. Additionally, the function result can be used in the COND attribute of AppPage tags to enable decisions to be made as the web page is built.

AppPage Script functions are executed by the webexplode() function. When webexplode() encounters an AppPage Script function, the function operands are evaluated and the function operator is executed, although not necessarily in this order. For example, some AppPage functions do not evaluate all operands supplied to the function if the operands are evaluated conditionally.

Syntax of Variable-processing Functions

AppPage variables are identified by a dollar sign ($) followed by alphanumeric and underscore characters. Similarly, a variable-processing function is identified by a dollar sign, parentheses, an operator, and one or more operands.

Variable Expressions

A variable expression is a set of AppPage variables and functions nested to an arbitrary depth. Variable expressions yield a single result. Nested variable expressions evaluate the innermost expression first and pass the result to the next higher expression until all expressions have been evaluated.

In AppPages, you must enclose a variable expression in parentheses prefixed by a dollar sign thus: $(). This allows webexplode() to identify it.

Within a variable expression, you use AppPage variables and variable-processing functions to manipulate those variables.

Variable-processing Functions

Variable-processing functions allow you to evaluate and manipulate variables and literals within variable expressions. A variable-processing function has the following characteristics:

- single operator,
- one or more operands,
- function result.

Single Operators

An operator defines the function. It takes one or more operands and performs an action with them to yield a result. Table 15-6 lists some examples. Note that the operands can themselves be the result of variable expressions.

One or More Operands

An operand is considered to be an expression that yields a value. It may be a literal (such as `1.29` or `Customer`) or an AppPage variable (such as `$category`), so the expression evaluates to the value of the literal or AppPage variable, respectively. However, if the operand is an expression such as `$(+,2,2)`, then the expression must first be evaluated to yield a value before this operand value can be used.

Some variable-processing functions do not evaluate all operands if the evaluation is based on a condition. For example, the expression `$(IF,expr,truescript,falsescript)` comprises the three operands `expr`, `truescript`, and `falsescript`. The `falsescript` operand will not be evaluated if `expr` produces a result that yields 1

Table 15-6.   Example operators.

Operator	Description
+	Add operands together
IF	Logical IF
<	Operand 1 less than operand 2
TRUNC	Truncate an operand

(true). For example, the following snippet will result in the string
This is false being output to the HTML page:

```
<?MIVAR>
$(IF,$(EQ,abc,123),"This is True",$(UPPER,"This is
false"))
<?/MIVAR>
```

The function operands are the parameters to the function. An AppPage function can have one or more operands, depending on what the function operator is. An operand can also be an expression that yields a result that must be the same type as the operand expected. In List. 15-8, the EQ function (string equal) requires two string operands. The second operand is written as a function, UPPER, that converts a string to uppercase. This operand is evaluated and the string result returned to the EQ function before the EQ function is processed.

Listing 15-8 contains three IF functions. The condition that must be tested is EQ. The second operand of each EQ function is an expression returning a string. The first IF function will return the string Uppercase. The second IF function will return the string Uppercase delimited by the HTML bold tag. The third IF function will return a JavaScript command string. Each string returned is written to the HTML page that is being constructed by webexplode().

When the listing is processed by webexplode() and returned to the browser, a JavaScript alert box will pop up with the string 'Hello Uppercase' displayed.

Listing 15-9 is the HTML sent to the browser by the AppPage source in List. 15-8.

Function Results

An AppPage function will return a result. This result can either be a string or a boolean (true or false). A string result can be used in a web page directly. If a function result is a boolean, then it is used in a decision path for some related action.

What this means to the web developer is that you have an impressive list of functions to use without the programming overhead of standard procedural languages.

Variables and variable expressions are interpreted only within MISQL, MIVAR, *and* MIERROR *tags, and within the* COND *attribute of tags.*

Listing 15-8.   Operand evaluation.

```
<HTML>
<HEAD><TITLE>Operand Evaluations</TITLE></HEAD>
<BODY>
<?MIVAR>
$(IF,$(EQ,ABC,$(UPPER,abc)),Uppercase,Lowercase)
<?/MIVAR>
<BR>
<?MIVAR>
$(IF,$(EQ,ABC,$(UPPER,abc)),"<B>Uppercase</B>",Lowercase)
<?/MIVAR>

<?MIVAR NAME=displayString>Hello Uppercase<?/MIVAR>
<?MIVAR NAME=htmlString><script>alert('$displayString');
          </script><?/MIVAR>
<?MIVAR>
$(IF,$(EQ,ABC,$(UPPER,abc)),$htmlString,Lowercase)
<?/MIVAR>
</BODY>
</HTML>
```

Listing 15-9.   The HTML output for List. 15-8.

```
<HTML>
<HEAD><TITLE>Operand Evaluations</TITLE></HEAD>
<BODY>
Uppercase
<BR>
<B>Uppercase</B>
<script>alert('Hello Uppercase');</script>
</BODY>
</HTML>
```

Handling Errors from Variable-processing Functions

If the variable-processing function fails, then `webexplode()` generates an exception, and an exception message is returned to the
browser. You can trap and handle these exceptions by using the ERR
attribute of the tag containing the function.

An error may occur unexpectedly because an AppPage variable was not recognized or because a syntax error has occurred, for example. A well-behaved application, however, catches these errors and recovers gracefully from them.

Because variable-processing functions are bound to MISQL, MIVAR, MIERROR, and the COND attribute of tags, you can handle errors using the MIERROR tag associated with these tags.

You do not have to use the ERR attribute in every instance of the relevant tags. If you define a generic error handler in the AppPage (using MIERROR, with no NAME attribute), then this handler will catch errors in these tags.

The following AppPage snippet shows how to catch an unexpected error from a variable-processing function. In this example, the variable $custname does not exist (it has not been created with the MIVAR tag, nor passed in from an HTML form or URL).

```
<?MIERROR>
<h2>An unexpected error has occurred.<br>
Contact <a href="mailto:webmaster@company.com"> your
Webmaster</a></h2>
<?/MIERROR>
<!-- The variable $custname has not been initialized -->
<?MIVAR >$(EVAL,$custname)<?/MIVAR>
```

When this snippet is processed by webexplode(), the following HTML is sent to the browser:

```
<h2>An unexpected error has occurred.<br>
Contact <a href="mailto:webmaster@company.com">
your Webmaster</a></h2>
```

Variable-processing Function Summary

Variable-processing functions can be conveniently split into several categories.

Functions suffixed with a "" character are available from Version 4 of the Web DataBlade only.*

Conditional Functions

These functions return true or false and allow you to make decisions in your AppPage Script.

Function	Action
`$(IF,expr,truescript)`	If `expr` evaluates to nonzero, evaluate and return `truescript`.
`$(IF,expr,truescript,falsescript)`	If `expr` evaluates to nonzero, evaluate and return `truescript`; otherwise evaluate and return `falsescript`.

Examples

```
<?MIVAR>
$(IF,$(EQ,1,2),<h1>TruePath</h1>,<h1>FalsePath</h1>)
$(IF,$(>,2,1),<b>Correct</b>,<b>Incorrect</b>)
<?/MIVAR>
```

The variable expressions above result in the following HTML output to the browser:

```
<h1>FalsePath</h1>
<b>Correct</b>
```

Remember to use the `MIVAR` *tag to delimit blocks of AppPage Script that need to be interpreted by* `webexplode()`.

Arithmetic Functions

Funtion	Action
`$(+,var1,var2,...varn)`	Returns the sum of the numbers `var1..varn`.

`$(-,val1,val2,...valn)`	Returns the result of subtracting the numbers `val2` through `valn` from `val1`, right to left.
`$(*,val1,val2,...valn)`	Returns the result of multiplying the numbers `val1`, `val2` through `valn`, left to right.
`$(/,var1,var2,...varn)`	Returns the result of dividing the number `var1` by `var2` through `varn`, left to right.
`$(MOD,value1,value2)` *	Divides `value1` by `value2` and returns the remainder, or *modulus*.

Arithmetic functions accept decimal or integer arguments and perform all calculations in decimal arithmetic (from Version 3.32 of the Web DataBlade onward). Arithmetic functions that allow more than two arguments allow a maximum of ten.

Examples

```
<?MIVAR name=six>$(+,1,2,3)<?/MIVAR>
<?MIVAR name=eighteen>$(-,24,$six)<?/MIVAR>
<?MIVAR name=sixteen>$(*,4,2,2)<?/MIVAR>
<?MIVAR name=answer>$(/,$sixteen,2,2)<?/MIVAR>
<?MIVAR>The result is $answer<?/MIVAR>
```

The variable expressions above result in the following output to the browser:

```
The result is 4
```

From Version 4 of the Web DataBlade:

```
<?MIVAR>The answer is $(MOD,11,3)<?/MIVAR>
```

resulting in:

```
The answer is 2
```

Number Conversion Functions

Number conversion functions allow you to truncate and round a number.

Function	Action
`$(FIX,value)`	Truncates the real number value to an integer; *discards* any fractional part.
`$(ROUND,value,digit)`	Rounds the numeric value to `digit` number of digits and returns this value.
`$(TRUNC,value,digit)`	Truncates the numeric value to `digit` number of digits and returns this value.

Examples

```
<?MIVAR>
$(FIX,99.9)<br>
$(ROUND,100.568,2)<br>
$(TRUNC,100.568,2)
<?/MIVAR>
```

The variable expressions above yield the following HTML:

```
99<br>
100.57<br>
100.56
```

Number Comparison Functions

These functions allow you to compare two numbers and test whether a value is an integer or whether it is numeric at all.

Function	Action
`$(=,val1,val2)`	Return true if `val1` and `val2` are equal, else return false; both operands should be numbers.
`$(<,val1,val2)`	Return true if `val1` is less than `val2`, else false; both operands should be numbers.
`$(>,val1,val2)`	True if `val1` is greater than `val2`; false otherwise.
`$(!=,val1,val2)`	True if `val1` does not equal `val2`; false otherwise.

$(<=,val1,val2)	True if val1 is less than or equal to val2; false otherwise.
$(>=,val1,val2)	True if val1 is greater than or equal to val2; false otherwise.
$(ISINT,value)	True if value is an integer; false otherwise. If a decimal value such as 1.0 is used, true is returned because it evaluates to an integer.
$(ISNUM,value)	True if value is numeric; false otherwise.

Examples

Listing 15-10 contains the number comparison examples. Listing 15-11 contains the resulting HTML.

Listing 15-10. Number comparison examples.

```
<?MIVAR cond=$(=,99,99.0)>
Correct: 99 = 99.0<br>
<?/MIVAR>

<?MIVAR cond=$(<,99.9,100)>
Correct: 99 < 100<br>
<?/MIVAR>

<?MIVAR cond=$(!=,5.45,5.46)>
Correct: 5.45 != 5.46<br>
<?/MIVAR>

<?MIVAR>
$(IF,$(>,99.99,99.98),Correct: 99.99 > 99.98<br>,Incorrect)
$(IF,$(>=,20,21),Incorrect,Correct: 20 not > 21<br>)
$(IF,$(<=,20,21),Correct: 20 < 21<br>,Incorrect)
$(IF,$(ISINT,99.9),Incorrect,Correct: 99 is not an integer<br>)
$(IF,$(ISINT,99.0),Correct: 99.0 is treated as an
integer<br>,Incorrect)
$(IF,$(ISNUM,99.9), Correct: 99.9 is a number,Incorrect)<br>
$(IF,$(ISNUM,NinetyNine),Incorrect,Correct: <i>Text correctly
rejected</i><br>)
<?/MIVAR>
```

Listing 15-11.   The HTML output from List. 15-10.

```
Correct: 99 = 99.0<br>
Correct: 99 < 100<br>
Correct: 5.45 != 5.46<br>
Correct: 99.99 > 99.98<br>
Correct: 20 not > 21<br>
Correct: 20 < 21<br>
Correct: 99 is not an integer<br>
Correct: 99.0 is treated as an integer<br>
Correct: 99.9 is a number<br>
Correct: <i>Text correctly rejected</i><br>
```

Vector and Argument Selection

These functions work with lists. A list can either be a vector (array) or a string that contains a delimited list of items.

Function	Action
`$(INDEX,which,string)`	Extracts a substring from a delimited list of strings. The delimited list of strings should contain one or more values delimited by a comma. The `which` parameter identifies the appropriate substring by position. Note that positions start at 0.
`$(NTH,index,arg0,arg1,..argn)`	Similar to `INDEX`. Selects the argument at position `index`, starting at 0. Once the argument is selected, it is evaluated and then returned.
`$(VECSIZE,$vecname)*`	Returns the number of elements in vector `$vecname`.
`$(VECAPPEND,$vecname,value)*`	Appends `value` to the end of vector `$vecname`.

Examples

For the following variable expressions:

```
<?MIVAR >$(INDEX,2,"1,2,3,4,5")<br><?/MIVAR>
<?MIVAR name=myString>One,Two,3.3,Four<?/MIVAR>
<?MIVAR >$(INDEX,2,$myString)<?/MIVAR>
```

the following results are output:

```
3<br>
3.3
```

See the SEPARATE *and* REPLACE *functions later to see how to work with variable vectors returned from form fields such as Select lists and checkboxes.*

For the following variable expressions:

```
<?MIVAR>
$(NTH,2,one,two,<b>three</b>,four)
<?/MIVAR>
<?MIVAR
   cond=$(EQ,$(NTH,2,one,two,three,four),three)>
Success
<?/MIVAR>
```

the following results are output:

```
<b>three</b>
Success
```

Using VECSIZE and VECAPPEND

From Version 4 of the Web DataBlade, the VECSIZE and VECAPPEND functions are available.

For example, List. 15-12 shows a simple form that contains a select list from which multiple options can be selected. The selected data from this list is passed to webdriver as a variable vector. The size of the variable vector is then obtained when the AppPage processes the received form data (see Chap. 17, "Dynamic Web Forms Programming," for an explanation of forms with the Web DataBlade).

If the user selects two options from the select list, then the AppPage output is as follows when the AppPage is reinvoked on submission:

```
Number of elements selected is: 2<br>
```

The VECAPPEND function adds a new element to the vector. Assuming that we are processing the variable vector from List. 15-12, we can add a new element as follows:

```
<!-- Delimit the block using MIVAR; can use MIBLOCK also -->
<?MIVAR cond=$(NXST,$myList)>
<form method=post action=$WEB_HOME>
<select name=myList multiple size=4>
<option value=one>One
<option value=two>Two
<option value=three>Three
<option value=four>Four
<option value=five>Five
<option value=six>Six
</select>
<input type=hidden name=MIval value=$MIval>
<input type=submit value="Go">
</form>
<?/MIVAR>



<?MIVAR cond=$(XST,$myList)>Number of elements selected is:
$(VECSIZE,$myList)<br><?/MIVAR>
```

```
<?MIVAR cond=$(XST,$myList)>
$(VECAPPEND,$myList,"NewValue")
Number of elements now is: $(VECSIZE,$myList)<br>
<?/MIVAR>
```

If the user selected two items from the `select` list in List. 15-12 then the previous snippet for `VECAPPEND` would result in the following output:

```
Number of elements now is: 3<br>
```

String Comparison

String comparison functions compare two strings for equality, with or without lettercase sensitivity.

Function	Action
$(EC,str1,str2)	True if str1 is identical to str2 regardless of case; false otherwise.
$(EQ,str1,str2)	True if str1 is identical to str2, including case; false otherwise.
$(NC,str1,str2)	True if str1 and str2 are *not* identical, regardless of case; false otherwise.
$(NE,str1,str2)	True if str1 and str2 are *not* identical including case; false otherwise.

Spaces are significant in the evaluation of variable expressions. For example, the variable expression $(EQ,abc,abc) is not equivalent to $(EQ, abc, abc) because the last expression has a space before the string abc.

Listing 15-13 contains examples of string comparison.

The AppPage Script in List. 15-13 will result in the following HTML output:

```
True:Strings match regardless of case<br>
True:Strings don't match regardless of case<br>
False:Strings don't match on case<br>
True:Strings match including case<br>
True:Strings don't match on case<br>
False:Strings match including case<br>
```

Listing 15-13.   *Examples of string comparison.*

```
<?MIVAR>
$(IF,$(EC,abc,ABC),True:Strings match regardless of case<br>,)
$(IF,$(NC,abc,ABD),True:Strings don't match regardless of case<br>,)
$(IF,$(EQ,abc,ABC),,False:Strings don't match on case<br>)
$(IF,$(EQ,ABC.DEF,ABC.DEF),True:Strings match including case<br>)
$(IF,$(NE,abc,ABC),True:Strings don't match on case<br>,)
$(IF,$(NE,ABC.DEF,ABC.DEF),,False:Strings match including case<br>)
<?/MIVAR>
```

String IO Functions

The `TRACEMSG` function is used to write a string to the output file denoted by `MI_WEBEXPLOG`. If `MI_WEBEXPLOG` is not set, the function does nothing.

`$(TRACEMSG,string)`	Writes string to a trace file.

Examples

For example:

```
<?MIVAR>$(TRACEMSG,$MIval called)<?/MIVAR>
```

If the AppPage containing the above function was called `mypage`, then the trace file would contain the following output

```
17:22:28  MSG          mypage called
```

String Properties Functions

String properties functions interrogate strings for content and size.

Function	Action
`$(POSITION,string1,string2)`	Returns the starting position of `string2` in `string1`; otherwise 0 if `string2` is not found. The first character in `string1` is 1 (not 0).
`$(STRLEN,string)`	Returns the length of the string.
`$(SUBSTR,string,start,length)`	Extracts the substring of `string`, starting at `start`, for `length` characters. Characters are numbered from 1. The `length` is optional; if omitted, the whole string from the `start` parameter to the end of the `string` is returned.

Listing 15-14. *String properties functions.*

```
<?MIVAR>
$(POSITION,Hello World,World)<br>
$(STRLEN,Hello World) <br>
$(SUBSTR,Hello World,1)<br>
$(SUBSTR,Hello World,7)<br>
$(SUBSTR,World Wide Web,7,4)<br>
$(SUBSTR,$(SUBSTR,World Wide Web,7),6)
<?/MIVAR>
```

Examples

Listing 15-14 contains examples of using string properties functions. The following output is returned to the HTML page from List. 15-14.

```
7<br>
11 <br>
Hello World<br>
World<br>
Wide<br>
Web
```

String Conversion Functions

String conversion functions transform their arguments in various ways to produce a string result.

Function	Action
$(LOWER,string)	Returns string in lowercase.
$(REPLACE,string1,string2,string3)	Replaces all occurrences of string2 with string3 within string1.
$(SEPARATE,vector,stringval)	Separates items in the variable vector vector with the string value stringval.

`$(STRFILL,string,numcopies)`	Concatenates `numcopies` of `string` and returns the result.
`$(TRIM,string)`	Removes leading and trailing whitespace from `string`.
`$(UPPER,string)`	Converts the `string` to uppercase and returns it.

Listing 15-15. *String conversion functions.*

```
<?MIVAR>
$(LOWER,This was MIXED CASE)<br>
$(UPPER,This was MIXED CASE)<br>
$(REPLACE,This is a string, ,<br>) <br>
$(STRFILL,"<b>World Wide Web<b><br>",4)
$(STRLEN,"    Web    ")<br>
$(STRLEN,$(TRIM,"    Web    "))<br>
<?/MIVAR>
```

Examples

Listing 15-15 contains examples of using string conversion functions. The variable expressions in List. 15-15 will produce the HTML output below:

```
this was mixed case<br>
THIS WAS MIXED CASE<br>
This<br>is<br>a<br>string <br>
<b>World Wide Web<b><br><b>World Wide
Web<b><br><b>World Wide Web<b><br><b>World Wide
Web<b><br>
11<br>
3<br>
```

HTML- and URL-related Functions

These functions apply specifically to HTML-encoded strings and content and are used to create items such as cookies or to transform characters to and from their entity references.

Function	Action
$(HTTPHEADER,name,value)	Adds the HTTP header name with the value to an AppPage.
$(UNHTML,string)	Replaces special HTML characters with their corresponding entity references.
$(URLDECODE,string)	Converts all hexadecimal values in string to their nonalphanumeric ASCII characters.
$(URLENCODE,string)	Converts nonalphanumeric characters to hexadecimal codes, and returns the resulting string.

Displaying Raw HTML Using UNHTML

The UNHTML function can be used to display raw HTML, instead of having the browser interpret the HTML. For example, the function

```
$(UNHTML,<html><body></body></html>)
```

will return the following characters:

```
&lt;html&gt;&lt;body&gt;&lt;/body&gt;&lt;/html&gt;
```

When the browser renders these characters, they will be displayed as

```
<html><body></body></html>
```

You can also use the HTTPHEADER function to instruct the browser to display an HTML page in raw form. See the examples later in this section.

Encoding Strings Using URLENCODE and URLDECODE

The URLENCODE function enables you to encode strings so that white-space and control characters are replaced by URL control codes. For example, the following snippet takes the string

```
This is my parameter string
```

and encodes it for use in the ANCHOR tag:

```
<?MIVAR>
<a href=
http://theale2/webdriver?MIval=myPage&myParameter=
$(URLENCODE,This is my parameter string)
>Go</a>
<?/MIVAR>
```

The resulting output that is written to the HTML page is as follows:

```
<a href=
http://theale2/webdriver?MIval=myPage&myParameter=This
+is+my+parameter+string
>Go</a>
```

The URLDECODE function takes a URLENCODED string and replaces the URL control characters with their textual equivalents. For example,

```
$(URLDECODE,$(URLENCODE,This is my parameter string))
```

will return

```
This is my parameter string
```

Using HTTPHEADER for Cookies and Content

The HTTPHEADER function places HTTP headers in your AppPages so that you can download pages that are not HTML pages. You can also use the HTTPHEADER function to set cookies.

The first example sets the HTTP content-type header for the browser so as to state that the incoming information is to be displayed as plain text. The second example sets a cookie on the browser client, appUserName, to the value of an AppPage variable.

```
$(HTTPHEADER,content-type,text/plain)
$(HTTPHEADER,set-cookie,appUserName=$userID)
```

AppPage-variable-based Variable Functions

Variable functions take parameters that are AppPage variables, and create, destroy, expand or test for their existence.

Function	Action
$(EVAL,varname)	Evaluates the AppPage variable varname and returns the string result. On failure, an exception is returned.
$(NXST,variablename)	True if variablename has *not* been assigned a numeric or string value; false otherwise.
$(SETVAR,varname,value)	Sets the AppPage variable varname to the value value.
$(UNSETVAR,varname)	Unsets the variable varname if set; otherwise do nothing.
$(XST,varname)	Return true if varname exists (has been assigned a numeric or string value); false otherwise.

Examples

Listing 15-16 contains examples of these functions.
The functions in List. 15-16 produce the following output.

```
Evaluated String<br>
Correct: variable does not exist<br>
Correct: variable does not exist<br>
Correct: variable is set to World Wide Web<br>
Correct: variable has been unset<br>
```

Logical Functions

These functions operate in a manner similar to the logical functions in other languages.

Function	Action
$(AND,val1,val2,...valn)	Returns the logical AND of integers val1 through valn. Processing stops when a false condition is reached.
$(NOT,value)	Returns the logical negation of value.
$(OR,val1,val2,...valn)	Returns the logical OR of the integers val1 through valn. Processing stops when condition is true.
$(XOR,var1,var2,...varn)	Returns the logically exclusive OR of the integers var1 through varn.

Listing 15-16. AppPage fragment for AppPage-based variable functions.

```
<?MIVAR name=textVariable>Evaluated String<?/MIVAR>
<?MIVAR>
$(EVAL,$textVariable)<br>
$(IF,$(NXST,$notAVariable),Correct: variable does not exist,
incorrect)<br>
$(IF,$(XST,$notAVariable),incorrect,Correct: variable does not
exist)<br>
$(SETVAR,aVariable,World Wide Web)
$(IF,$(XST,$aVariable),Correct: variable is set to $aVariable,)<br>
$(UNSETVAR,$aVariable)
$(IF,$(XST,$aVariable),incorrect,Correct: variable has been
unset)<br>
<?/MIVAR>
```

Examples

Listing 15-17 contains examples of logical functions.
Listing 15-17 will produce the following output.

```
1<br>
0<br>
1<br>
0<br>
0<br>
1
```

Listing 15-17. Logical functions.

```
<?MIVAR>
$(AND,$(EQ,ABC,ABC),$(NE,ABC,DEF))<br>
$(NOT,$(EQ,abc,abc))<br>
$(OR,$(EQ,12,11),$(NE,A,B))<br>
$(XOR,$(EQ,abc,abc),$(EQ,abc,abc))<br>
$(XOR,$(EQ,abcd,abc),$(EQ,abcd,abc))<br>
$(XOR,$(EQ,abcd,abc),$(EQ,abc,abc))
<?/MIVAR>
```

Navigating Websites

There are two basic methods for navigating between web pages. You can use hidden fields in forms, or you can specify the target page and parameters through a hyperlink.

Using Forms

If you use a form to navigate the website, then `webdriver` will be called to process the form data when you submit the form. This will include the nominated AppPage that you want to have process the form data.

Using forms to navigate between AppPages is useful when you need to transfer parameters. For example, you can create hidden form fields to contain these parameter values, and send them along with the form to the next AppPage.

However, you don't have to include any form data other than the name of the target AppPage. For example, the following form states that the AppPage `targetAppPage` will be processed when the user clicks the `Next Page` button.

```
<form method=post action=<?MIVAR>$WEB_HOME<?/MIVAR>>
<input type=hidden name=MIval value=targetAppPage>
<input type=submit value="Next Page">
<form>
```

Using Hyperlinks

You can also use hyperlinks to navigate between AppPages. If you are passing parameters, then you will need to `URLENCODE` them.

For example, the following URL is designed to call the `targetAppPage` when the `Home` hyperlink is clicked. When the `targetAppPage` is processed by `webexplode()`, the `$param1` AppPage variable will be set to `Hello World`. To get there, however, it must be URL encoded to retain the whitespace.

```
<?MIVAR>
<a href="$WEB_HOME?MIval=targetAppPage&param1=$
(URLENCODE,Hello World)">
Home</a>
<?/MIVAR>
```

Summary

In this chapter, we have covered the fundamentals of using AppPage tags, AppPage variables, and variable-processing functions to create dynamic web pages from AppPage templates stored in the database. You can use this chapter as a reference to look up the tags and functions, with examples, that you require. We have also learned the options available for navigating AppPages. We have extended the basic "Hello World" application to include the listing of web server variables on the client by using AppPage Script on the server to write them to an HTML page.

You can now approach the wider issues of selecting data from the database and working with forms knowing that you have the flexibility of the AppPage tags and functions to help you capture and render information dynamically.

Web Database Programming with AppPages

In this chapter:

- Selecting data from the database using AppPage Script
- Basic searching and drill down
- Managing volume data with data windows
- Maintaining data in the database
- Using SQL-related system variables
- Two-pass query processing
- Displaying error diagnostics with the MIERROR tag
- Calling SQL procedures from the web page

This chapter shows how to use AppPage Script to create dynamic web pages that maintain data in the Informix database. Data maintenance includes adding, retrieving, and modifying data over the intranet or Internet. Using the simple examples in this part of the book, you can learn to create a dynamic database-driven website.

This chapter is mainly concerned with the interface to the database from an AppPage; other chapters focus on managing forms dynamically or using AppPage variable functions to render content dynamically. See Chaps. 17 and 15, respectively for a detailed treatment of these topics.

Selecting Data from the Database Using AppPage Script

To build web pages dynamically from the contents of a database, we need to learn first how to select the data from the database. Then we need to understand how to format that data for presentation in an HTML page.

Building a Select Statement Using the MISQL Tag

Use the MISQL tag to perform any valid query that your version of the Informix database server supports. This includes SELECT, INSERT, UPDATE, DELETE, and EXECUTE PROCEDURE. You use the SQL-related system variables (detailed later in this chapter) to enhance the reporting of the results, especially if an error is encountered.

For example, the following MISQL tag selects all the columns from the stock table where the description contains the string 'ball':

```
<?MISQL SQL="SELECT
    stock.stock_num, stock.manu_code,
    stock.description, stock.unit_price,
    stock.unit, stock.unit_descr
FROM stock WHERE description like '%ball%';">
```

Using Variables in the MISQL Tag

You can use AppPage variables to parameterize the query or even to substitute for the whole query. The webexplode() function will substitute the variable reference for the variable value before submitting the SQL statement to the database server. The following two examples show how to do this.

```
<?MISQL SQL="SELECT * FROM $table WHERE
$where_clause">
...
<?/MISQL>
<?MISQL SQL="$sqlQuery">
...
<?/MISQL>
```

The first example contains two variables, `$table` and `$where_clause`. Assuming that they are set as follows:

```
$table : customer
$where_clause: customer_num = 121
```

then the `MISQL` tag becomes

```
<?MISQL SQL="SELECT * FROM customer WHERE customer_num
= 121">
```

The second example places the whole SQL statement in a variable. Assuming that `$sqlQuery` is set as follows:

```
select fname, lname from customer order by 2 desc
```

then the `MISQL` tag becomes

```
<?MISQL SQL="select fname, lname from customer order
by 2 desc">
```

Handling Errors

You can nominate an `MIERROR` tag to handle errors encountered while processing the SQL statement or any errors with the `MISQL` tag itself that `webexplode` encounters. To do this, you use the `ERR` attribute of the `MISQL` tag. For example:

```
<?MIERROR ERR=sqlError>
    An error has occurred: $MI_ERRORCODE
<?/MIERROR>
<?MISQL ERR=sqlError SQL="select * from
stock">..<?/MISQL>
```

If the SQL statement fails, then the SQL query in the `MISQL` tag, along with any other queries executed on that page or any nested pages, are rolled back and discarded. The `webexplode()` function then uses the contents of the nominated error handler, in this case `sqlError`, to render the appropriate HTML.

To nominate means to refer to the label of an `MIERROR` tag that is to handle errors for that tag. See the section, "Using SQL-related System Variables" for the details of how to handle errors and report the specifics by using SQL-related system variables.

It is good practice always to nominate an MIERROR *tag to handle errors from the* MISQL *tag. You do this by naming an* MIERROR *tag in the* ERR *attribute of the* MISQL *tag. You can then apply error-handling behavior at the* MISQL *tag-specific level or implement group error handling for a set of* MISQL *tags by nominating the same* MIERROR *handler for each.*

Conditional Execution of the MISQL Tag

You can use the COND attribute of the MISQL tag to determine whether to process that MISQL tag. For example, you can use the COND attribute to determine whether or not you are inserting data or retrieving data:

```
<?MISQL COND=$(EQ,$state,POST) SQL="insert into cus-
tomer....">
<?MISQL COND=$(EQ,$state,GET) SQL="select * from cus-
tomer">
```

Formatting the Result Set

When the SQL in an MISQL tag is executed successfully, a result set is generated. For SELECT statements, this contains the column values for every row retrieved. Whatever appears between the start and end MISQL tags is considered formatting information for the values returned in the query and is referred to as the MISQL body. It is this body that is iterated for every row in the result set.

```
<?MISQL SQL="..">
    formatting directives
<?/MISQL>
```

You can place any HTML in the MISQL body. The webexplode() method does not validate HTML. You can refer to AppPage variables in the MISQL body without delimiting them with the MIVAR tag. You can also set the values of variables. In this sense, MISQL operates like the MIVAR tag. For example:

```
<?MISQL SQL="select * from stock">
    $myCustomer : required stock number is $1
    $(SETVAR,$stock_num,$1)
<?/MISQL>
```

When selecting data from the database, you should remember that the MISQL body is written to the resulting AppPage *once for every row returned in the query.*

Using Column Values

Column values are returned in special variables that denote the column position in the SELECT statement. They start at 1, and continue in increments until all columns are identifed. For example, the following query places the values of the four columns in four variables:

```
<?MISQL SQL="select fname, lname, company, phone from
customer">
First Name: $1<br>
Last Name: $2<br>
Company: $3<br>
Phone: $4<br>
<?/MISQL>
```

As the MISQL body iterates around the result set, the variables $1 through $4 are refreshed with the column values for the current row.

Using HTML Tables to Format the Result Set

You don't have to use tables to format the result set, but it helps. Listing 16-1 shows how to format the result set by using a simple HTML table to list the column values. The AppPage contains a query that selects stock details from the stock table and formats the results.

Note that the MISQL body contains only those HTML tags to format one table row. If you placed the TABLE inside the MISQL body, then you would create a table for each row returned in the result set.

Figure 16-1 shows the browser display of List. 16-1.

Listing 16-1. *Using* `select1.html` *to format a Result Set via an HTML table.*

```
<h2>Selecting Stock Details</h2>
<TABLE BORDER=0 CELL_PADDING=0>
<TR>
        <TH> stock_num </TH>
        <TH> manu_code </TH>
        <TH> description </TH>
        <TH> unit_price </TH>
        <TH> unit </TH>
        <TH> unit_descr </TH>
```

Listing 16-1.   (continued)

```
</TR>
<?MISQL SQL="SELECT
       stock.stock_num,
       stock.manu_code,
       stock.description,
       stock.unit_price,
       stock.unit,
       stock.unit_descr
FROM stock WHERE description like '%ball%';">

<TR>
       <TD> $1 </TD>
       <TD> $2 </TD>
       <TD> $3 </TD>
       <TD> $4 </TD>
       <TD> $5 </TD>
       <TD> $6 </TD>
</TR><?/MISQL>
</TABLE>
```

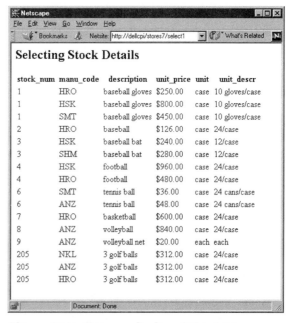

Figure 16-1. *Browser display of List. 16-1*
after webexplode().

Listing 16-2 shows an alternative method of formatting the result set. We still use tables to control the formatting, but the column names are adjacent to the column values. Figure 16-2 shows the browser result. The best way of controlling this format is by using a walking window approach, described in the next section.

Version 4 Enhancements

From version 4 of the Web DataBlade, there are two enhancements to the MISQL tag. The first is the introduction of the RESULTS attribute to the tag, and the second is the ability to nest MISQL tags.

Listing 16-2. *Using* `select2.html` *as an alternative table format.*

```
<h2>Selecting Stock Details</h2>
<TABLE BORDER=0 CELL_PADDING=0>
<?MISQL SQL="SELECT
       stock.stock_num,
       stock.manu_code,
       stock.description,
       stock.unit_price,
       stock.unit,
       stock.unit_descr
FROM stock WHERE description like '%ball%';">

<TR>
       <TD> <B>stock_num:</B> </TD><TD> $1 </TD>
</TR>
<TR>
       <TD> <B>manu_code:</B> </TD><TD> $2 </TD>
</TR>
<TR>
       <TD> <B>description:</B> </TD><TD> $3 </TD>
</TR>
<TR>
       <TD> <B>unit_price:</B> </TD><TD> $4 </TD>
</TR>
<TR>
       <TD> <B>unit:</B> </TD><TD> $5 </TD>
</TR>
<TR>
       <TD> <B>unit_descr:</B> </TD><TD> $6 </TD>
</TR><?/MISQL>
</TABLE>
```

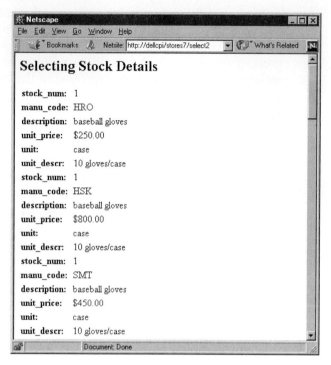

Figure 16-2. *Browser display of List. 16-2 after*
`webexplode()`.

Using the `RESULTS` Attribute for Master-Detail Queries

The `RESULTS` attribute names a variable that will contain the
`ResultSet` of the query; `RESULTS` specifies the name of a container
whose attributes are the column values. These values are addressed
by position. To access the results value, cite the column number, dot
(.), `RESULTS` attribute.

Typically, you would use a results set to parameterize one query
by the contents of another; the second query is performed in its
entirety for every row retrieved from the first. In other words, the
second query is nested.

Listing 16-3 shows the results of a simple Master-Detail query to
look up all orders for all customers in the `stores7` database.

In this example, all order items are listed for all customers in the
`customer` table. To do this, the `customer_num` column of the
`customer` table is used to perform a key lookup against the `orders`
table for all order items for the current `customer_num`. Note that we
can use namespace values in the nested query.

Listing 16-3. `resultSet.html`, *a Master-Detail query using* RESULTS.

```
<HTML>
<BODY>
<?MISQL
SQL="select trim(fname) || ' ' || trim(lname),
customer_num from customer order by 1;" RESULTS=master>
<h2>CustomerName:  $master.1</h2>
<TABLE BORDER=3>
<TH>Order Num</TH><TH>Order
Date</TH><TH>Shipment</TH><TH>Payment</TH>
<?MISQL
SQL="select order_num, order_date, ship_instruct,
paid_date from orders
where customer_num=$master.2 order by 2;"
RESULTS=detail>
<TR>
<TD>$detail.1</TD>
<TD>$detail.2</TD>
<TD>$detail.3</TD>
<TD>$detail.4</TD>
</TR>
<?/MISQL>
<BR>
</TABLE>

<?/MISQL>
</BODY>
</HTML>
```

Figure 16-3 shows the browser display of the resulting HTML page.

tip

Nesting two or more queries for the sake of formatting a collected result set is not always the best option if you can join the tables. For each master record, a set of detail records are selected; even though the detail records may be retrieved on key value, however, you are advised to compare the results of merging two or more queries into one by running the query in dbaccess *and using* SET EXPLAIN *to check the query plans.*

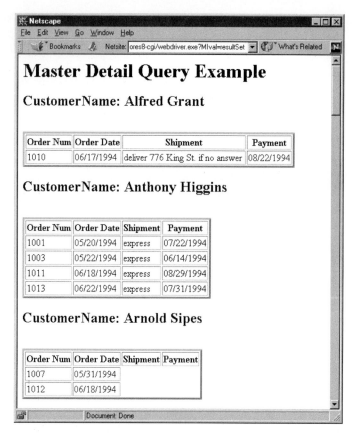

Figure 16-3. *Browser display of* `resultSet.html` *after* `webexplode()`.

Basic Searching and Drill Down

This section shows how to perform simple search and drill-down functions using SQL queries and parameterized hyperlinks. The example dynamically creates a web page to show selected contents of the customer table. For the purposes of the example, let's assume that we are an intranet user browsing our customer database. These are the requirements:

- We would like to see a list of customers and the companies they work for.
- We want to be able to select customers using exact or wildcard matches against customer name.

Accordingly, the example performs the following:

- Displays an HTML form for allowing the user to select a customer by way of customer name.
- Allows the user to type in the exact or partial customer name.
- Sends the form data to the database where the customer details are selected.
- Formats the results of the query into an HTML page that is then displayed to the user.

This example introduces the following key features:

- working with forms,
- passing form data to the web server and then to the Informix Web DataBlade,
- processing form data as parameters to a web page that is created on the database server,
- using form data to parameterize an SQL statement to fetch data from the database,
- formatting the results of the SQL statement in HTML.

Using a Selection Screen

In List. 16-4, we create a form to allow the customer name to be entered and sent to the web server. This AppPage is stored in the Informix database.

Listing 16-4. Select the customerName AppPage.

```
<html>
<head>
<title>Select Customer</title>
</head>
<body>

<p> </p>

<p align="center"><strong><big><big><big>
Select Customer List
</big></big></big></strong></p>
```

Listing 16-4. *(continued)*

```
<form method="POST"
      name="selectionForm"
      action="<?MIVAR>$WEB_HOME<?/MIVAR>">

  <input type="hidden" name="MIval" value="HelloWorld4">
  <div align="center"><center>
  <table border="0" width="45%" height="77">
    <tr>
      <td width="30%" height="1" valign="top">
          <div align="right"><p><font color="#000000">
          <big><strong>Customer: 
          </strong></big></font>
      </td>
      <td width="70%" valign="top" height="1"
align="left">
          <input type="text" name="customerName"
size="30">
      </td>
    </tr>
    <tr>
      <td width="30%" height="27"></td>
      <td width="70%" height="27">
          <input type="submit" value="Select"
name="submitButton">
          <input type="reset" value="Reset" name="B2">
      </td>
    </tr>
  </table>
  </center></div>

</form>
</body>
</html>
```

To summarize List. 16-4, this is a simple HTML form. However, there are two key features that differentiate it from the standard HTML form

- The form `action` is a string that contains an AppPage Script tag. This tag delimits a variable called $WEB_HOME (the "$" is

part of the syntax). The contents of $WEB_HOME refer to the
webdriver program.

- A hidden form field is defined with a specific name, MIval. The
  value of this form field is the name of the AppPage that will
  process the form data. In our example, the AppPage is called
  HelloWorld4.

In List. 16-5, the AppPage Scripting tags have been replaced by
the generated strings. The Web DataBlade replaces the AppPage
tags with the values of variables defined in the webdriver configuration file.

The HTML page in List. 16-5 is not stored in the database. It is
output by the webdriver program, which acts like a standard CGI
program sending standard output to the web server and, from there,
back to the browser.

**Listing 16-5. Listing 16-4 after being processed by the
Web DataBlade and sent to the browser.**

```
<html>
<head>
<title>Select Customer</title>
</head>

<body>

<p> </p>

<p align="center"><strong><big><big><big>
Select Customer List
</big></big></big></strong></p>

<form method="POST"
      name="selectionForm"
      action="/stores7-cgi/webdriver.exe">

  <input type="hidden" name="MIval" value="HelloWorld4">
  <div align="center"><center>
  <table border="0" width="45%" height="77">
    <tr>
      <td width="30%" height="1" valign="top">
        <div align="right"><p><font color="#000000">
        <big><strong>Customer: 
```

Listing 16-5.   (continued)

```
            </strong></big></font>
        </td>
        <td width="70%" valign="top" height="1"
align="left">
            <input type="text" name="customerName"
size="30">
        </td>
    </tr>
    <tr>
        <td width="30%" height="27"></td>
        <td width="70%" height="27">
            <input type="submit" value="Select"
name="submitButton">
            <input type="reset" value="Reset" name="B2">
        </td>
    </tr>
  </table>
  </center></div>

</form>
</body>
</html>
```

To summarize List. 16-5, the AppPage Scripting tags have been replaced by contents of webdriver variables.

- The $WEB_HOME has been replaced by /stores7-cgi/ webdriver.exe. This is the CGI program that will control dynamic page generation by calling Web DataBlade functions in SQL statements. The contents of the $WEB_HOME variable are defined in the Web DataBlade configuration file, discussed in a later chapter.
- The URL /stores7-cgi/ refers to a directory on the web server host that has been registered as a CGI directory by the web server software
- The hidden form field, MIval, does not change. There were no AppPage Scripting tags surrounding it that may have directed the Web DataBlade to perform some operation on it

note

On NT systems, the `webdriver` *program is called* `webdriver.exe` *and should be invoked with the* `.exe` *suffix. On UNIX systems, the* `webdriver` *program is simply called* `webdriver` *and does not need to have a suffix.*

Figure 16-4 shows the browser display of List. 16-5.

What Happens Next

So far, we have typed in the URL (for example, `http://dellcpi/stores7-cgi/webdriver.exe?Mival=HelloWorld3`). An AppPage has been extracted from the Informix database, the AppPage Script tags expanded, and the final HTML page sent to the browser. The user can now type in the customer selection.

When the user enters the customer name (exact or wildcard), and clicks the `Select` button:

- the form contents are processed as defined in the `action` property of the form declaration;
- the AppPage called `HelloWorld4` is retrieved from the Informix database, the AppPage Script tags are processed, and the output HTML page is sent first to the web server and then to the browser.

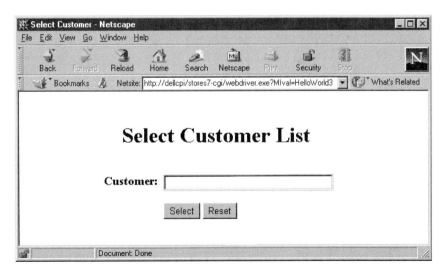

Figure 16-4. *Selection screen display.*

It is the second bullet that is described in the next two listings. This is where the customer data is selected and formatted dynamically within the web page.

What Are Wildcard and Exact Matches?

A wildcard match refers to the selection of data that is not exact. The part of the data that is not exact is defined with a character called a 'wildcard'. For example, to select customers whose surnames begin with "Ha" from a customer database, the actual string to match against the surname would be "Ha%." The "%" is the wildcard character. This character is understood by the SQL parser inside the Informix database server, and tells the database server to match any surnames that begin with "Ha." This would include Harrison, Harris, and Harridan. In contrast, an exact match tells the server to match the search string exactly with the customer surname. For example, the search string "Pauli" must match exactly, character for character, against a surname of Pauli in the customer table.

Selecting and Displaying Data

Listing 16-6 shows the AppPage source that contains AppPage Script tags to select and format customer information from the Informix database.

Listing 16-6. *AppPage to select and display the customer details (`helloworld4`).*

```
<html>
<head>
<title>Display Customers</title>
</head>

<body>

<p> </p>

<p align="center">
<big><big><big>
<strong>Display Customer List</strong>
</big></big></big>
</p>
```

Listing 16-6. *(continued)*

```
<p align="center">
<big><strong>Database:
<?MIVAR>$MI_DATABASE<?/MIVAR></strong></big>
</p>

<table border="0" width="100%">
    <tr>
      <td width="34%" align="center" bgcolor="#5E5E5E">
          <big><strong>
          <font color="#FFFFFF">Name</font></strong>
          </big>
      </td>
      <td width="47%" align="center" bgcolor="#5E5E5E">
          <big><strong>
          <font color="#FFFFFF">Company</font>
          </strong></big>
      </td>
      <td width="19%" align="center" bgcolor="#5E5E5E">
          <big><strong>
          <font color="#FFFFFF">Zipcode</font>
          </strong></big>
      </td>
      </tr>
<?MISQL
    SQL="select
              fname || ' ' || lname,
                company,
              zipcode
            from customer
          where lname like '$customerName';">
      <tr>
        <td width="34%" bgcolor="#C0C0C0">$1</td>
        <td width="47%" bgcolor="#C0C0C0">$2</td>
        <td width="19%" bgcolor="#C0C0C0">$3</td>
      </tr>
<?/MISQL>
</table>
<p> </p>
</body>
</html>
```

Listing 16-6 contains a number of interesting features that make working with a database from a web page straightforward.

- The `MISQL` AppPage Script tag is used for specifying the SQL to be executed.
- The `$1`, `$2`, `$3` variables between the `<?MISQL>` and `<?/MISQL>` tag delimiters are the three columns selected from the `customer` table.
- `$customerName` is the name of the form text field in the selection screen that has been transformed into an AppPage variable by the `webdriver` program.
- `$customerName` is used to parameterize the `where` clause of the `select` statement.

In summary, the form data in the text field, called `customerName`, is used as a variable in the AppPage. When the Web DataBlade processes the AppPage, it will substitute the value inside the variable for the variable in the AppPage.

The Web DataBlade will then execute the SQL. For each row returned by the SQL query, the HTML inside the `<?MISQL>` and `<?/MISQL>` tags is executed. The `$1`, `$2`, and `$3` variables represent the column values selected; they will change for every row returned. Assuming the string "`P%`" is entered into the text field on the selection screen, the resulting output is shown in List. 16-7.

Extended Tag Syntax

AppPage Script tags are called `extended` tags. They conform to the SGML (standardized general markup language) syntax of which HTML is a derivative. The Web DataBlade can identify AppPage Scripting tags because of the "`?`" character. If the "`?`" was removed, the Web DataBlade would ignore them, and they would be sent to the browser. The browser ignores them, too, so the tags will be displayed on the browser screen.

Listing 16-7 contains the HTML produced after the AppPage in List. 16-6 has been processed by the Web DataBlade. The AppPage Scripting tags have been interpreted; the SQL tag has resulted in a database query that produced a list of customers; and, for each customer returned, the customer details have been formatted in an HTML table.

Listing 16-7 shows three HTML table rows formatted identically. This is coded as one table row in the source AppPage in List. 16-6.

```
<html>
<head>
<title>Display Customers</title>
</head>
<body>

<p> </p>

<p align="center">
<big><big><big>
<strong>Display Customer List</strong>
</big></big></big>
</p>

<p align="center">
<big><strong>Database: stores7</strong></big>
</p>

<table border="0" width="100%">
    <tr>
      <td width="34%" align="center" bgcolor="#5E5E5E">
              <big><strong>
              <fontcolor="#FFFFFF">Name</font>
              </strong>
              </big>
      </td>
      <td width="47%" align="center" bgcolor="#5E5E5E">
              <big><strong>
              <font color="#FFFFFF">Company</font>
              </strong></big>
      </td>
      <td width="19%" align="center" bgcolor="#5E5E5E">
              <big><strong>
              <font color="#FFFFFF">Zipcode</font>
              </strong></big>
      </td>
      </tr>
```

Listing 16-7.   (continued)

```
    <tr>
      <td width="34%" bgcolor="#C0C0C0">Ludwig
Pauli              </td>

      <td width="47%" bgcolor="#C0C0C0">All Sports
Supplies </td>
      <td width="19%" bgcolor="#C0C0C0">94086</td>
      </tr>

    <tr>
      <td width="34%" bgcolor="#C0C0C0">Jean
Parmelee          </td>
      <td width="47%" bgcolor="#C0C0C0">Olympic City
</td>
      <td width="19%" bgcolor="#C0C0C0">94040</td>
      </tr>

    <tr>
      <td width="34%" bgcolor="#C0C0C0">Chris
Putnum            </td>
      <td width="47%" bgcolor="#C0C0C0">Putnum's Putters
</td>
      <td width="19%" bgcolor="#C0C0C0">74006</td>
      </tr>

</table>
<p> </p>
</body>
</html>
```

Listing 16-7 shows spaces between the forename and surname. These spaces are part of the values of the names retrieved from the database. The browser will ignore all but one space between the forename and surname. They are included in the listing to show the actual result, but you can trim away the spaces using the SQL trim *function.*

It is useful to show the query that will be executed by the Web DataBlade, in dbaccess first. Now, dbaccess is a character-based interface to the Informix database server, provided as part of the server deliverable. You can perform various database administrative tasks and well as run queries in dbaccess.

The following two `dbaccess` screen shots show the query that will be processed by the Web DataBlade, as well as the results of that query.

Figure 16-5 shows the same query entered into `dbaccess`.

Figure 16-6 shows the `dbaccess` output for that query.

The next screen shows the query output as sent to the browser by `webdriver.exe`. Figure 16-7 shows the rendering of List. 16-7 in the browser window.

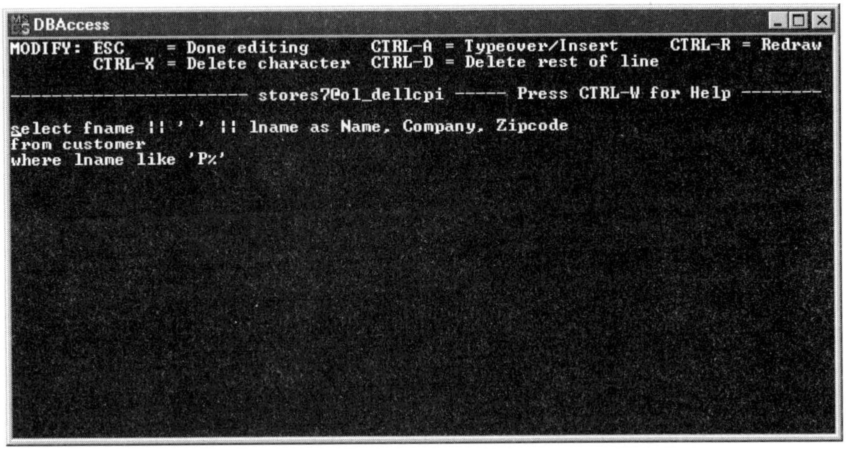

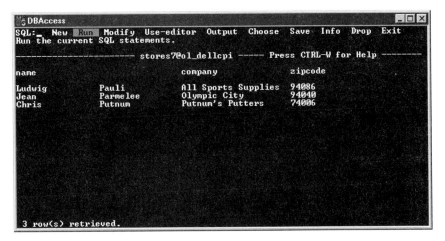

Figure 16-5. *The* dbaccess *listing of the query processed by the AppPage.*

Figure 16-6. *The* dbaccess *listing of the query results.*

Display Customers - Netscape
File Edit View Go Window Help
Back Forward Reload Home Search Netscape Print Security Stop
Bookmarks Netsite: http://dellcpi/stores7-cgi/webdriver.exe What's Related
Display Customer List
Database: stores7
Name Company Zipcode
Ludwig Pauli All Sports Supplies 94086
Jean Parmelee Olympic City 94040
Chris Putnum Putnum's Putters 74006
Document: Done

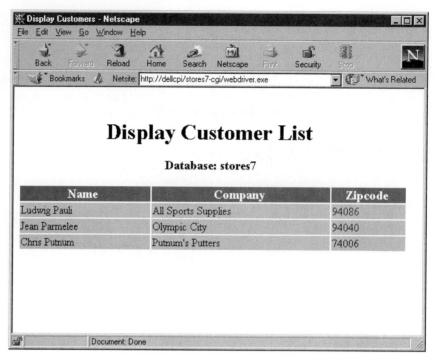

Figure 16-7. Results of the SQL query are displayed.

The next few screens show a different query against the same data (Figs. 16-8, 16-9 and 16-10, 16-11, and 16-12 and 16-13).

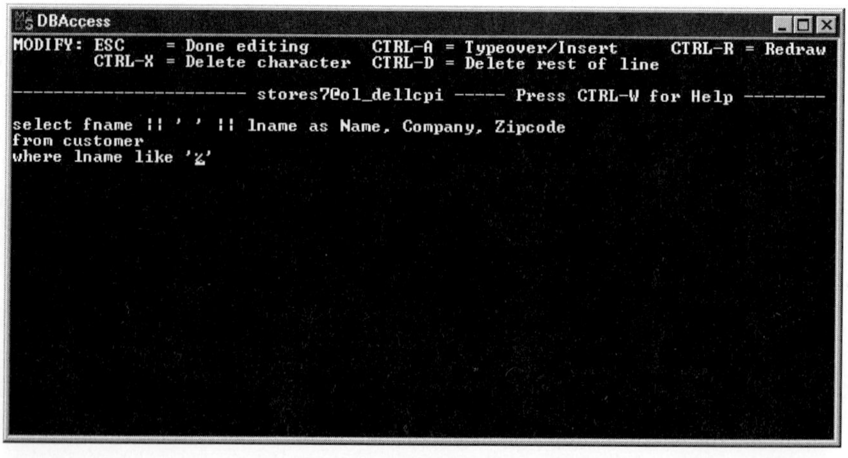

DBAccess
MODIFY: ESC = Done editing CTRL-A = Typeover/Insert CTRL-R = Redraw
CTRL-X = Delete character CTRL-D = Delete rest of line
stores7@ol_dellcpi ----- Press CTRL-W for Help
select fname || ' ' || lname as Name, Company, Zipcode
from customer
where lname like '%'

Figure 16-8. The `dbaccess` *query for all customers.*

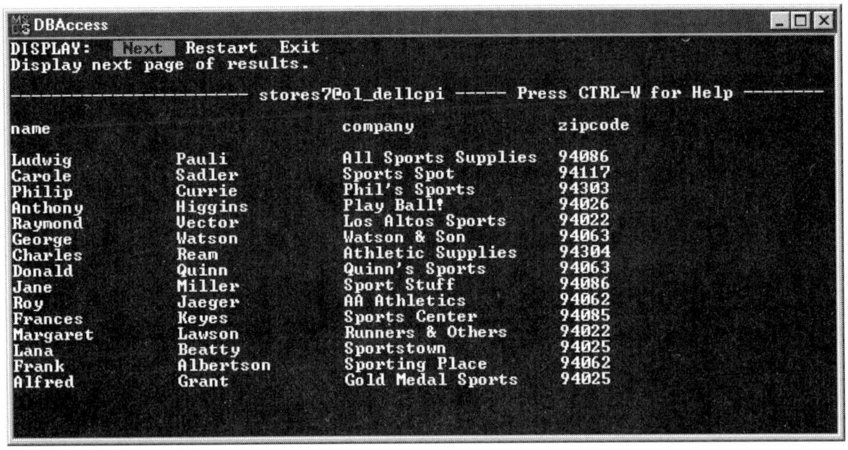

Figure 16-9. The `dbaccess` *output for the 'all customers' query.*

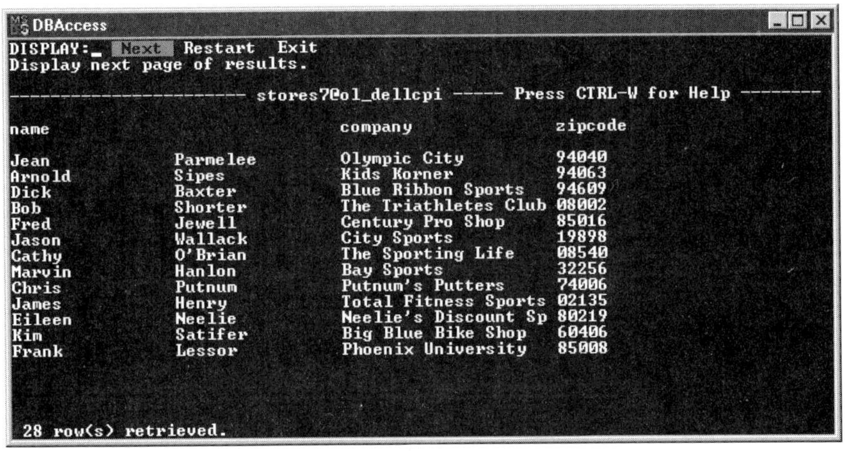

Figure 16-10. *Fig. 16-9 (continued).*

Drilling Down to the Customer Details

It is useful in web applications to provide a *drill-down* feature, which allows navigation from summary data to a more detailed break-down of that data. Often, the database schema is designed to support these drill-down requirements by providing data split between tables containing summary data and tables containing details for a specific summary item.

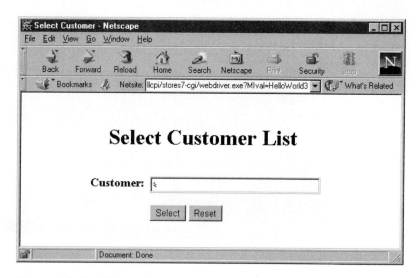

Figure 16-11. *"Select Customer List" selection screen with wildcard selection.*

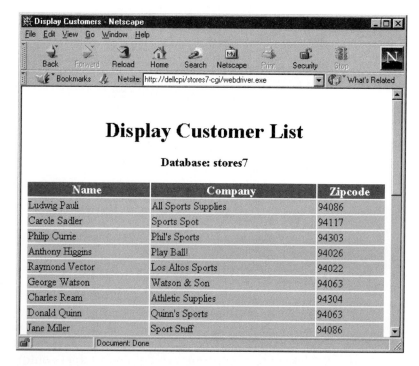

Figure 16-12. *All customers displayed.*

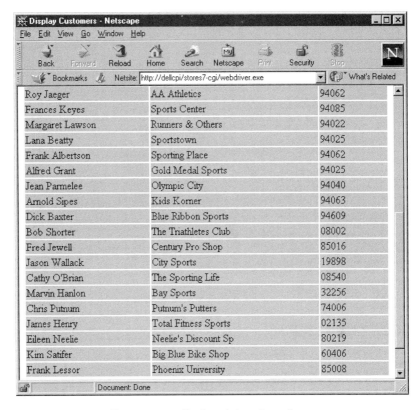

Roy Jaeger	AA Athletics	94062
Frances Keyes	Sports Center	94085
Margaret Lawson	Runners & Others	94022
Lana Beatty	Sportstown	94025
Frank Albertson	Sporting Place	94062
Alfred Grant	Gold Medal Sports	94025
Jean Parmelee	Olympic City	94040
Arnold Sipes	Kids Korner	94063
Dick Baxter	Blue Ribbon Sports	94609
Bob Shorter	The Triathletes Club	08002
Fred Jewell	Century Pro Shop	85016
Jason Wallack	City Sports	19898
Cathy O'Brian	The Sporting Life	08540
Marvin Hanlon	Bay Sports	32256
Chris Putnum	Putnum's Putters	74006
James Henry	Total Fitness Sports	02135
Eileen Neelie	Neelie's Discount Sp	80219
Kim Satifer	Big Blue Bike Shop	60406
Frank Lessor	Phoenix University	85008

Figure 16-13. *All customers displayed (continued).*

What Is a Database Schema?

The database schema is the definition of database tables, columns, column datatypes, table indices, and the relations between tables. It is physically represented by DDL (data definition language) statements, which create tables, indexes, referential constraints, and stored procedures.

For this example, we will extend the customer query from the preceding section. These are the new requirements:

- From the customer list, drill down to the customer detail by selecting a customer from the list.

Changes to the Existing AppPages

The only change to the customer selection screen is the name of the AppPage that will process the form data and run the database query. Since this is defined by the hidden field called `MIval`, we change the value of that field:

```
<input type="hidden" name="MIval" value="HelloWorld5">
```

There are a number of interesting changes to the customer list display.

- The AppPage that will process the query results is changed.
- The customer name is changed into an anchor using the `<A>` and `</A>` HTML tag delimiters.
- Notice that between the `<?MISQL>` and `<?/MISQL>` tags, Web DataBlade variables do not need to be delimited with the `<?MIVAR>` tag.
- The AppPage that will process the drill-down request is referred to inside the anchor for the customer name, instead of in a hidden form field.

The last bullet above is important. Up to now we have used a hidden form field to identify the next web page to be displayed. Now, the hyperlink for customer name refers to `webdriver` directly, and the hyperlink also contains the customer ID of the selected customer.

Listing 16-8 shows the AppPage source for the new customer list display.

Listing 16-8. Revised customer list display.

```
<html>
<head>
<title>Display Customers</title>
</head>
<body>
<p> </p>

<p align="center">
<big><big><big>
<strong>Display Customer List</strong>
</big></big></big>
</p>

<p align="center">
<big><strong>Database:
<?MIVAR>$MI_DATABASE<?/MIVAR></strong></big>
</p>
```

Listing 16-8.   (continued)

```
<table border="0" width="100%">
    <tr>
      <td width="34%" align="center" bgcolor="#5E5E5E">
         <big><strong>
         <font color="#FFFFFF">Name</font></strong>
         </big>
      </td>
      <td width="47%" align="center" bgcolor="#5E5E5E">
         <big><strong>
         <font color="#FFFFFF">Company</font>
         </strong></big>
      </td>
      <td width="19%" align="center" bgcolor="#5E5E5E">
         <big><strong>
         <font color="#FFFFFF">Zipcode</font>
         </strong></big>
      </td>
      </tr>

<?MISQL
    SQL="select
            fname || ' ' || lname,
          company,
           zipcode,
          customer_num
      from customer
        where lname like '$customerName';">
    <tr>
      <td width="34%" bgcolor="#C0C0C0">
         <a href='$WEB_HOME?MIval=
               HelloWorld6&selectedCustomer=$4'
onMouseOver='status="Display Details for Customer $4";
return true;'>$1</a>
      </td>
      <td width="47%" bgcolor="#C0C0C0">$2</td>
      <td width="19%" bgcolor="#C0C0C0">$3</td>
    </tr>
<?/MISQL>

</table>
  <p> </p>
</body>
</html>
```

In summary, this example will parameterize the drill-down link on customer name with the customer ID. Note the `onMouseover` event handler for the customer name hyperlink. When the mouse passes over the hyperlink, the browser status bar will display a message containing the actual customer ID that the link is for.

Listing 16-9 shows the HTML output when the user enters "P%" into the browser text field on the selection screen.

Listing 16-9.   The HTML output for customers matching "P%."

```
<html>
<head>
<title>Display Customers</title>
</head>
<body>

<p> </p>

<p align="center">
<big><big><big>
<strong>Display Customer List</strong>
</big></big></big>
</p>

<p align="center">
<big><strong>Database: stores7</strong></big>
</p>

<table border="0" width="100%">
    <tr>
      <td width="34%" align="center" bgcolor="#5E5E5E">
            <big><strong>
            <font color="#FFFFFF">Name</font></strong>
            </big>
      </td>
      <td width="47%" align="center" bgcolor="#5E5E5E">
            <big><strong>
            <font color="#FFFFFF">Company</font>
            </strong></big>
      </td>
      <td width="19%" align="center" bgcolor="#5E5E5E">
            <big><strong>
            <font color="#FFFFFF">Zipcode</font>
            </strong></big>
```

Listing 16-9. (continued)

```
    </td>
    </tr>

    <tr>
      <td width="34%" bgcolor="#C0C0C0">
          <a href='/stores7-cgi/webdriver.exe?MIval=
          HelloWorld6&selectedCustomer=101' onMouseOver=
          'status="Display Details for Customer 101";
          return
true;'>Ludwig          Pauli          </a></td>
      <td width="47%" bgcolor="#C0C0C0">All Sports
      Supplies </td>
      <td width="19%" bgcolor="#C0C0C0">94086</td>
    </tr>

    <tr>
      <td width="34%" bgcolor="#C0C0C0">
          <a href='/stores7-cgi/webdriver.exe?MIval=
          HelloWorld6&selectedCustomer=116' onMouseOver=
          'status="Display Details for Customer
          116";return true;'>
          Jean          Parmelee          </a></td>
      <td width="47%" bgcolor="#C0C0C0">Olympic City
      </td>
      <td width="19%" bgcolor="#C0C0C0">94040</td>
    </tr>

    <tr>
      <td width="34%" bgcolor="#C0C0C0">
          <a href='/stores7-cgi/webdriver.exe?MIval=
          HelloWorld6&selectedCustomer=124' onMouseOver=
          'status="Display Details for Customer
          124";return true;'>
          Chris          Putnum          </a></td>
      <td width="47%" bgcolor="#C0C0C0">Putnum's Putters
      </td>
      <td width="19%" bgcolor="#C0C0C0">74006</td>
    </tr>

</table>
<p> </p>
</body>
</html>
```

The interesting feature of this HTML page is that, when a customer name is clicked, the hyperlink asks the web server to execute a CGI program, in our case, `webdriver.exe`. In addition, we parameterize this call to `webdriver` by passing in some parameters in standard URL encoded format.

Figure 16-14 shows the query results shown in the browser window. The customer name is hyperlinked to drill down to the details for that customer.

Why Use CGI in a Hyperlink?

Often, hyperlinks in web pages refer to HTML pages and image objects on a host computer. When the link is clicked, the page and its associated elements are downloaded. However, because the AppPage is stored in the database and needs to be processed by the Web DataBlade, we ask the web server to execute the CGI program called `webdriver` *to perform this task. However, an AppPage can contain links to HTML pages and objects that are not stored in the Informix database.*

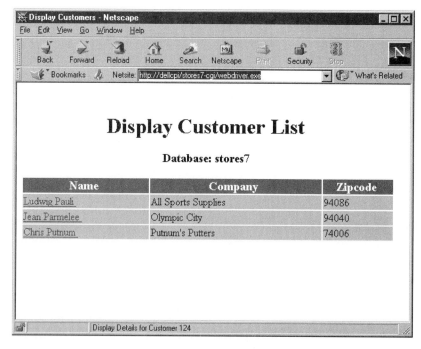

Figure 16-14. *Customer list display with hyperlinks.*

Displaying Customer Detail

Once the customer list is displayed, the user can *drill down* to the customer detail by clicking a customer name. The details for that customer are then selected from the database, formatted into HTML, and returned to the browser.

Note that on the *Display Customer List* screen, the browser status bar will display a message containing the customer ID of the customer the mouse has focus on; for example:

```
Display Customer Details for Customer 116
```

Listing 16-10 shows the AppPage source for the customer detail screen.

Listing 16-10.   Customer detail AppPage source.

```
<html>
<head>
<title>Home Page</title>
</head>

<body>

<p> </p>

<p align="center"><big><big><big><strong>Display
Customer</strong></big></big></big></p>

<p align="center"><strong>Customer Number Selected is:
<?MIVAR>$selectedCustomer<?/MIVAR></strong></p>
<div align="center"><?MIVAR NAME="$MI_NULL">
<?/MIVAR>
<?MISQL
    SQL="select fname, lname, company, address1, address2,
        city, state, zipcode, phone from customer where
        customer_num=$selectedCustomer;">
<div align="center"><center>

<table border="0" width="95%">
  <tr>
```

Listing 16-10.   (continued)

```
    <td width="27%" align="right"><strong>Forname: </strong></td>
    <td width="73%" bgcolor="#C0C0C0"><strong>$1</strong></td>
  </tr>
  <tr>
    <td width="27%" align="right"><strong>Surname: </strong></td>
    <td width="73%" bgcolor="#C0C0C0"><strong>$2</strong></td>
  </tr>
  <tr>
    <td width="27%" align="right"><strong>Company: </strong></td>
    <td width="73%" bgcolor="#C0C0C0"><strong>$3</strong></td>
  </tr>
  <tr>
    <td width="27%" align="right"><strong>Address: </strong></td>
    <td width="73%" bgcolor="#C0C0C0"><strong>$4</strong></td>
  </tr>
  <tr>
    <td width="27%" align="right"></td>
    <td width="73%" bgcolor="#C0C0C0"><strong>$5</strong></td>
  </tr>
  <tr>
    <td width="27%" align="right"><strong>City: </strong></td>
    <td width="73%" bgcolor="#C0C0C0"><strong>$6</strong></td>
  </tr>
  <tr>
    <td width="27%" align="right"><strong>State: </strong></td>
    <td width="73%" bgcolor="#C0C0C0"><strong>$7</strong></td>
  </tr>
  <tr>
    <td width="27%" align="right"><strong>Zipcode: </strong></td>
    <td width="73%" bgcolor="#C0C0C0"><strong>$8</strong></td>
  </tr>
</table>
</center></div><?/MISQL>
</div>
</body>
</html>
```

The variable that is set to the customer ID is called
$selectedCustomer. This is set in the hyperlink that was created in
the customer list page.

```
http://dellcpi/stores7-cgi/webdriver.exe?MIval=
HelloWorld6&selectedCustomer=124
```

The `webdriver.exe` program uses the parameters from the hyperlink to extract the relevant web page from the database and parameterize the SQL statement in the extracted web page. In the hyperlink above, the parameters are `MIval` and `selectedCustomer`. The details of parameter passing are discussed in a later chapter.

Listing 16-11 shows the HTML output that is sent to the browser after being processed by the Web DataBlade, assuming that the user selected customer `124`, as in the hyperlink above.

Figure 16-15 shows the browser display. The customer detail is rendered from the HTML page output by the Web DataBlade.

Listing 16-11.   The HTML output from List. 16-10.

```
<html>
<head>
<title>Home Page</title>
</head>

<body>

<p> </p>

<p align="center"><big><big><big><strong>Display
Customer</strong></big></big></big></p>

<p align="center"><strong>Customer Number Selected is:
124</strong></p>
<div align="center">

<div align="center"><center>

<table border="0" width="95%">
  <tr>
    <td width="27%" align="right"><strong>Forname: </strong></td>
    <td width="73%" bgcolor="#C0C0C0"><strong>Chris
</strong></td>
  </tr>
  <tr>
    <td width="27%" align="right"><strong>Surname: </strong></td>
    <td width="73%" bgcolor="#C0C0C0"><strong>Putnum
</strong></td>
  </tr>
```

Listing 16-11. *(continued)*

```
<tr>
  <td width="27%" align="right"><strong>Company: </strong></td>
  <td width="73%" bgcolor="#C0C0C0"><strong>Putnum's Putters
</strong></td>
</tr>
<tr>
  <td width="27%" align="right"><strong>Address: </strong></td>
  <td width="73%" bgcolor="#C0C0C0"><strong>4715 S.E. Adams
Blvd</strong></td>
</tr>
<tr>
  <td width="27%" align="right"></td>
  <td width="73%" bgcolor="#C0C0C0"><strong>Suite 909C
</strong></td>
</tr>
<tr>
  <td width="27%" align="right"><strong>City: </strong></td>
  <td width="73%" bgcolor="#C0C0C0"><strong>Bartlesville
</strong></td>
</tr>
<tr>
  <td width="27%" align="right"><strong>State: </strong></td>
  <td width="73%" bgcolor="#C0C0C0"><strong>OK</strong></td>
</tr>
<tr>
  <td width="27%" align="right"><strong>Zipcode: </strong></td>
  <td width="73%" bgcolor="#C0C0C0"><strong>74006</strong></td>
</tr>
</table>
</center></div>
</div>
</body>
</html>
```

Managing Volume Data with Data Windows

When you use the MISQL tag to select data from the database, the number of rows returned is called the *result set*. The body of the MISQL tag is processed once per row. So, if the MISQL query returns

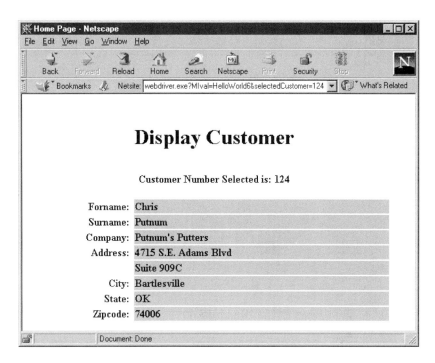

Figure 16-15. *Browser display of customer detail.*

100 rows, then the `MISQL` body is processed 100 times. If the `MISQL` body displays an HTML table row, then 100 table rows will be created. In some cases, you want control over how many rows to display on the screen at any one time. In addition, you may also want to scroll backward and forward in the result set. This section shows you how to do this.

Customizing the number of rows returned is an important topic because it allows you to control the amount of data sent over the network. For example, suppose a mobile car mechanic needed a breakdown of car components for a specific car. He dials in from the laptop in the field and selects a make and model of car. Unless he filters that data in some way, the details of potentially many hundreds of components will be downloaded in an HTML page. It would be better if we had a window on that data and could perhaps allow the user to select the window size.

Chapter 17 contains detailed working examples of using data windows, including how to dynamically alter the size of the data window.

What are Data Windows

Using the data windows feature of AppPage Script, you can display a subset of the rows in the result set instead of displaying the whole result set at once. The result set is the total number of rows returned from a query after all the filters have been applied. You scroll through the result set using the data window. If the data window is four rows long, then you can scroll forward and backward four rows at a time.

How do Data Windows Work

When the MISQL tag is processed, the database server executes the SQL query. Once all the rows are returned from the query, webexplode() extracts the rows that are in the data window. These rows are then processed in the body of the MISQL tag. Note that each time you scroll the data window, the query is executed again in its entirety.

Creating Data Windows by Using the MISQL Tag

The MISQL tag has the following two attributes set:

- WINSTART—this is the first record in the result set to begin with
- WINSIZE—this is the number of rows to process (the window) including the first record.

For example, if WINSTART is 1 and WINSIZE is 4, then we will process records 1 through 4 inclusive.

Listing 16-12 shows how to create a basic data window using the MISQL tag. The example selects the first and last names of customers from the customer table. Figures 16-16 and 16-17 show the browser display of the resulting HTML. Listing 16-12 displays four rows at any one time. You can scroll forward and backward in the result set. If you are at the start of the result set, you can only scroll forward. The scroll request is contained in the Next and Previous hyper-links, which are calls to webdriver parameterized by the winstart and winsize value required.

An extension to the basic data window model is the use of *subscripted fields*. If we change the example as follows:

```
<tr><td>$1 $2</td><td>$1[2] $2[2]</td></tr>
```

then for each row in the data window, we get two records back. This may be useful if you want summary data in a small window size

Listing 16-12. Using `dataWindow.html`—*a basic data window AppPage.*

```
<html>
<body>
<h2>Data Windows Example</h2>

<?MIVAR cond=$(NXST,$winstart) name=winstart>1<?/MIVAR>
<?MIVAR cond=$(NXST,$winsize) name=winsize>4<?/MIVAR>
<table border=1>
<?MISQL sql="select fname, lname from customer"
        winstart=$winstart winsize=$winsize>
<tr><td>$1 $2</td></tr>
<?/MISQL>
</table>
<br>
<?MIVAR cond=$(!=,$winstart,1)>
<a
href=$WEB_HOME?MIval=$MIval&winstart=$(+,$winstart,
$winsize)&winsize=4>Next 4</a>
<a href=$WEB_HOME?MIval=$MIval&winstart=$(-
,$winstart,$winsize)&winsize=4>Previous 4</a>
<?/MIVAR>
<?MIVAR cond=$(=,$winstart,1)>
<a
href=$WEB_HOME?MIval=$MIval&winstart=$(+,$winstart,
$winsize)&winsize=4>Next 4</a>
<?/MIVAR>
</body>
</html>
```

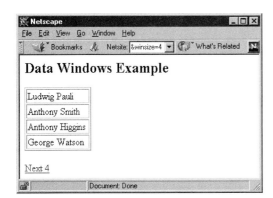

Figure 16-16. First four rows in the data window.

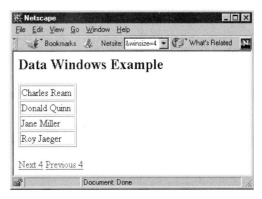

Figure 16-17. Second four rows in the data window.

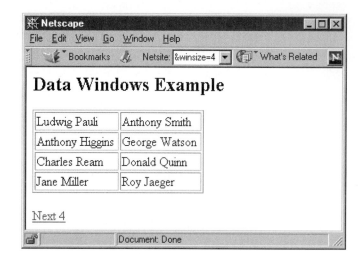

Figure 16-18. *Using subscripted fields in the data window.*

but don't want to keep clicking through multiple windows. Figure 16-18 shows the browser rendering; the four rows in the window are displayed, but with two result set rows to one display row.

Maintaining Data in the Database

This section shows how to *update, delete,* and *insert* data into the database from the browser. In most cases, you will use HTML forms to capture the data to insert into a table or to update a table. Chapter 17, "Dynamic Forms Programming," details the specifics of forms programming, so in this chapter we will concentrate on the essentials of managing the data.

Inserting Data into the Database

You can insert data into the database using HTML forms to capture the data and the MISQL tag to post that data into a database table. You may also want to validate the data before it is inserted into the database table.

As a web developer, you have the choice of using the same AppPage to capture and insert the data into the database or using one AppPage to capture the data and another to validate and insert into the database. It depends on your preference. However, if you wish to validate the data entered by the user and redisplay the form on error, you are better off using one AppPage to contain the form and the validations.

Listing 16-13. Processing an INSERT query.

```
<?MIERROR name=handleError>Error $MI_ERRORMSG Occurred
<?/MIERROR>

<?MISQL err=handleError sql="
   INSERT INTO customer (
        customer_num, fname, lname, company, address1,
        address2, city, state, zipcode, phone)
   VALUES (
        0, '$fname', '$lname', '$company',
        '$address1', '$address2', '$city', '$state',
        '$zipcode', '$phone');">
<?/MISQL>
```

Listing 16-13 shows an INSERT statement. The AppPage variables have been created beforehand or passed in via a form.

Updating Data in the Database

Listing 16-14 contains an UPDATE statement. If one or more rows are successfully updated, the Success message is output.

Listing 16-14.   The UPDATE statement.

```
<?MIERROR name=handleError>Error $MI_ERRORMSG Occurred
<?/MIERROR>

<?MISQL err=handleError sql="UPDATE customer SET
      fname = '$fname' ,
      lname = '$lname' ,
      company = '$company' ,
      address1 = '$address1' ,
      address2 = '$address2' ,
      city = '$city' ,
      state = '$state' ,
      zipcode = '$zipcode' ,
      phone = '$phone'
      WHERE customer_num = '$customer_num' ;">
   <h2>Success! Customer $customer_num updated</h2>
<?/MISQL>
```

Listing 16-15.   The DELETE *statement.*

```
<?MIERROR name=handleError>Error $MI_ERRORMSG Occurred
<?/MIERROR>

<?MISQL err=handleError sql="delete from customer where
customer_num = '$customer_num';">
<?/MISQL>

<?MIVAR cond=$(!=,$MI_ROWCOUNT,0)>
<h2>Success! Customer $customer_num_deleted. </h2>
<?/MIVAR>
```

Deleting Data in the Database

Listing 16-15 contains the DELETE statement. If the DELETE query
deletes a row, $MI_ROWCOUNT will be nonzero and we can output a
Success message.

Preprocessing Data Before Query Execution

For INSERT and UPDATE statements, there are two basic validations
you should perform:

- escape single quotes
- validate numeric fields

Escaping Single Quotes

You should preprocess any string-based variables to escape single
quotes. When webexplode() expands the variables as part of the
SQL statement for the MISQL tag, any unescaped single quotes will
result in a syntax error returned from the database server when the
query is processed.

Listing 16-16 shows the REPLACE function applied to form data to
change every occurrence of the ' character to '' (escaped ' character).

Validating Numeric Fields

You should also make sure that numeric fields are actually numeric;
otherwise a syntax error will be generated by the database server.
Listing 16-17 shows an example.

Listing 16-16.   Escaping single quotes.

```
<?MIVAR name="fname" default="" >
$(REPLACE,$form_fname,','')<?/MIVAR>
<?MIVAR name="lname" default=""
>$(REPLACE,$form_lname,','')<?/MIVAR>
<?MIVAR name="company" default="" >
  $(REPLACE,$form_company,','')<?/MIVAR>
<?MIVAR name="address1" default=""
  >$(REPLACE,$form_address1,','')<?/MIVAR>
<?MIVAR name="address2" default=""
  >$(REPLACE,$form_address2,','')<?/MIVAR>
<?MIVAR name="city" default=""
>$(REPLACE,$form_city,','')<?/MIVAR>
<?MIVAR name="state" default=""
>$(REPLACE,$form_state,','')<?/MIVAR>
<?MIVAR name="zipcode" default="" >
  $(REPLACE,$form_zipcode,','')<?/MIVAR>
<?MIVAR name="phone" default=""
>$(REPLACE,$form_phone,','')
<?/MIVAR>
```

Listing 16-17.   Validating numeric fields.

```
<?MIVAR name=errorText
cond=$(NOT,$(ISNUM,$customer_num))>
Field "customer_num" was an invalid numeric.
<?/MIVAR>
```

An AppPage, and any AppPages exploded within it, are executed within one transaction. If an error is encountered by webexplode()*, all the SQL statements executed for the current transaction will be rolled back. If possible, try to create separate pages for* INSERT*s,* UPDATE*s and* SELECT*s. Since each page is contained within one transaction, you can manage the commitment control more easily.*

Using SQL-related System Variables

There are several system variables that are set by webdriver when you execute a query, and you can access them like any another variable. Accordingly, the system variables adhere to the syntax of

Table 16-1.   SQL-related system variables.

Variable	When set	Description
MI_COLUMNCOUNT	on execution	Number of columns retrieved.
MI_CURRENTROW	start of current row	Currently formatting row.
MI_ERRORCODE	on error	SQL error code returned.
MI_ERRORMSG	on error	Error message returned.
MI_ERRORSTATE	on error	SQLSTATE returned from the query.
MI_ROWCOUNT	after execution	Total number of rows retrieved in the query.
MI_SQL	on execution	The SQL statement executed.

other AppPage variables; they are preceded by the dollar ($) sign, and are lettercase sensitive.

The values of these variables are lost between AppPages unless the webexplode() function is called recursively to explode AppPages in a nested sequence. If you attempt to use these system variables in an AppPage before the first MISQL tag has been processed, webdriver will report an error because, until the MISQL tag is executed, these variables are undefined. If you need to access the values of these variables between AppPages that are not exploded together, then you can assign the values to hidden form fields or write them to tables in the database. Table 16-1 lists these variables.

MI_COLUMNCOUNT

This variable contains the number of columns retrieved in the query. It can be accessed in every iteration of the MISQL body but will be set to the same value in each iteration. It remains set for the remainder of the AppPage, or until the next MISQL statement. For example, MI_COLUMNCOUNT is useful in a query where the number of columns is unknown. For example:

```
select * from customer where ...
```

However, this variable is especially useful for dynamically formatting the output of queries when the query detail is hidden elsewhere (in a dynamic tag, for example).

MI_CURRENTROW

This variable contains the number of the row currently being formatted from the result set. It is set at the start of the MISQL body iteration before the text in the MISQL body is processed. For example, if a SELECT query returns ten rows (in whatever order), for each iteration of the MISQL body, MI_CURRENTROW will be set from one and incremented at the start of each iteration, until we have processed all ten rows. Then MI_CURRENTROW will remain set at ten after the MISQL tag ends until the end of the AppPage or until the next MISQL tag is processed.

MI_ERRORCODE

This variable is set to the error code returned by the SQL statement. The Informix database server will set a variable called SQLCODE when executing an SQL statement. On error, the code is posted to this variable.

If webexplode() encounters an error while processing an AppPage tag (e.g., bad syntax), then webexplode() will return "–937" in this variable; otherwise the SQL error code will be returned in this variable.

This is an Informix-specific error code and maps onto the same error messages that you will find if you perform finderr <errorcode> at the command line, unless the error is –937, in which case the MI_ERRORMSG is defined by the Web DataBlade. In both cases, MI_ERRORMSG contains the details you require.

MI_ERRORMSG

This variable contains the error text that accompanies the error code, and it is set by the database server. As mentioned in the MI_ERRORCODE section, this message maps onto the message that is given by finderr for the returned error code.

MI_ERRORSTATE

This is the SQLSTATE value returned from the SQL statement, and it is only set when an error occurs. When an SQL statement executes, the database server sets a status code into a variable called SQLSTATE. The status encoded breaks down as success, warning, no rows, no more rows, or error. On error, the database server will return a code to indicate that the SQL statement did not execute successfully.

MI_ROWCOUNT

This variable contains the number of rows retrieved in the SQL statement. Typically, after an INSERT or execute procedure, MI_ROWCOUNT will be 1; for an UPDATE, SELECT, or DELETE, the MI_ROWCOUNT will be set to the number of rows affected.

For example, if you were to select 10 rows from a table with 100 rows, then MI_ROWCOUNT will be set to 10, even if the table was scanned to filter the 10 result rows.

This variable contains the correct value *after* the query has been processed; you cannot rely on the value of MI_ROWCOUNT when it is referenced in the body of the current MISQL tag.

MI_SQL

This variable contains the text of the current or last SQL statement. It is set on execution of the MISQL tag, and it is set to the same value for every iteration of the MISQL body. It remains set until the end of the AppPage or the next MISQL tag.

You may want to use this variable for writing an audit log of your critical queries after they are executed and for displaying error diagnostics to the user in the browser.

Using and Displaying Query Information

You can use the system variables to make decisions which direction page generation should go or to display query information to the user. Note that some variables have values that remain constant throughout the execution of the MISQL tag, some are set upon completion of the MISQL tag, and some change with each iteration of the MISQL formatting body.

Listing 16-18 shows how to use these system variables when implementing a simple select. The aim is to provide a running display of when these variables are set and when they change. Figure 16-19 shows the output of List. 16-18

Listing 16-18. The systemVariablesSel.html, *which illustrates the settings of SQL system variables.*

```
<h2>SQL Related System Variables</h2>
<b><font size=+1>Variables Set During Execution of</font>
<pre>"select  fname, lname from customer where city like
'Sunny%'"</font></pre>
```

Listing 16-18. *(continued)*

```
<table border=1>
<tr>
       <th><small>MI_CURRENTROW</th>
       <th><small>First Name</th>
       <th><small>Last Name</th>
       <th><small>MI_COLUMNCOUNT</th>
       <th><small>MI_SQL</th>
</tr>
<?MISQL sql="select   fname, lname from customer where city
like 'Sunny%'">
<tr>
       <td>$MI_CURRENTROW</td>
       <td>$1</td>
       <td>$2</td>
       <td>$MI_COLUMNCOUNT</td>
       <td><small>$MI_SQL</td>
</tr>
<?/MISQL>
</table>

<h3>Variables Set After Execution or Persisting:</h3>
<?MIVAR>
<table border=1>
<tr>
       <td align=center><b><small>MI_COLUMNCOUNT</td>
       <td align=center><b><small>MI_CURRENTROW</td>
       <td align=center><b><small>MI_ROWCOUNT</td>
</tr>
<tr>
       <td>$MI_COLUMNCOUNT</td>
       <td>$MI_CURRENTROW</td>
       <td>$MI_ROWCOUNT</td>
</tr>
<tr>
       <td colspan=3 align=center><b><small>MI_SQL</td>
</tr>
<tr>
       <td colspan=3 align=center><small>$MI_SQL</td>
</tr>
</table>
<?/MIVAR>
```

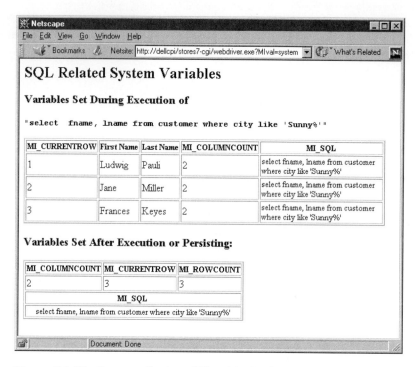

Figure 16-19. *Browser display of List. 16-18 after* `webexplode()`.

The same system variables are set whether you use a SELECT or a query such as INSERT or EXECUTE PROCEDURE. Listing 16-19 shows the setting for these variables when the MISQL query is EXECUTE PROCEDURE. This example shows the calling of an SQL procedure from an AppPage. The procedure returns two snippets of HTML, which are positioned accordingly in the HTML page. Figure 16-20 shows the browser display of List. 16-19.

In passing, it is useful to look at the stored procedure, `exampleProcedure()`, that is used in List. 16-19. This procedure returns two values, both of type HTML. These values are coded as strings, but need to be cast to the HTML datatype using the ":: " operator, since HTML is the return type. The two return values contain the HTML tags to render some text in bold and small italic.

```
create procedure exampleprocedure()
returning html, html
return
    "<b><i><small>Result text 1"::html,
    "<b><i><small>Result Text 2"::html;
end procedure;
```

```
<h2>SQL Related System Variables</h2>
<b><font size=+1>Variables Set During Execution of</font>
<pre>"execute procedure exampleProcedure()"</font></pre>
<table border=1>
<tr>
       <th><small>MI_CURRENTROW</th>
       <th><small>Result 1</th>
       <th><small>Result 2</th>
       <th><small>MI_COLUMNCOUNT</th>
       <th><small>MI_SQL</th>
</tr>
<?misql sql="execute procedure exampleProcedure()">
<tr>
       <td>$MI_CURRENTROW</td>
       <td>$1</td>
       <td>$2</td>
       <td>$MI_COLUMNCOUNT</td>
       <td><small>$MI_SQL</td>
</tr>
<?/misql>
</table>

<h3>Variables Set After Execution or Persisting:</h3>
<?mivar>
<table border=1>
<tr>
       <td align=center><b><small>MI_COLUMNCOUNT</td>
       <td align=center><b><small>MI_CURRENTROW</td>
       <td align=center><b><small>MI_ROWCOUNT</td>
</tr>
<tr>
       <td>$MI_COLUMNCOUNT</td>
       <td>$MI_CURRENTROW</td>
       <td>$MI_ROWCOUNT</td>
</tr>
<tr>
       <td colspan=3 align=center><b><small>MI_SQL</td>
</tr>
<tr>
       <td colspan=3 align=center><small>$MI_SQL</td>
</tr>
</table>
<?/mivar>
```

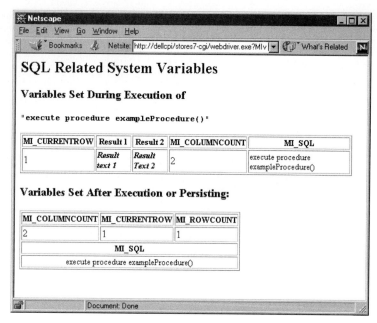

Figure 16-20. Browser display of List. 16-19.

Because the procedure returns two values, MISQL can deal with $1 and $2 as if two columns were retrieved from a table. The returning HTML strings are placed unchanged in the two table columns, Result 1 and Result 2. Because the text consists of HTML formatting tags, the resulting text is formatted accordingly.

Why Use HTML Return Types?

We could have returned two VARCHAR strings instead of two HTML types, in which case, we would not need to cast them. However, it is useful to know that you can use HTML as shown; you can then use functions such as weblint and webexplode() on your HTML fragments, which you cannot do with VARCHAR strings. Decide on the treatment that best suits your required functionality.

Two-pass Query Processing

If an AppPage contains an MISQL tag that attempts to update the table from which the AppPage is selected (wbPages or webPages) then the Informix database server returns an error.

It is illegal to issue a DDL statement inside a user-defined routine, because the user-defined routine is executed as part of a DML (data manipulation language) statement. Therefore, if your AppPage contains any `MISQL` tags that perform DDL statements such as `DROP TABLE`, then the database server will return an error.

Setting the `MIqry2pass` Variable

To get around this anomaly, you can set a variable in `web.cnf`, or in a URL, to tell `webdriver` that it must use a two-pass method to execute the query.

For example, in `web.cnf`, set the variable for all AppPages as follows:

```
MIqry2pass  on
```

or set the parameter for a single AppPage:

```
http://theale2/stores-cgi/webdriver?MIval
=myPage&MIqry2pass=on
```

How `MIqry2pass` Works

When `MIqry2Pass` is set to on:

- `webdriver` selects the AppPage requested:

  ```
  select object from wbPages where ID='mypage';
  ```

- `webdriver` then executes the `webexplode()` function as follows:

  ```
  execute function
  webexplode(object,'var1=value&var2=value2');
  ```

AppPage Builder uses this technique to allow inserts into the table from which it selects AppPages.

The two-pass method has a performance penalty, so only set the `MIqry2pass` *variable on when it is unavoidable.*

Displaying Error Diagnostics with the MIERROR Tag

If an SQL error is encountered or an error occurs when webexplode() processes an AppPage tag, the current AppPage explosion is stopped and any updates to the database are rolled back. The generated HTML page will contain the HTML specified by your MIERROR tag if present. If no MIERROR tag can be found, webdriver will write default error diagnostic text to the HTML page. For production-level web applications, you should trap all errors and help the user past them.

SQL Error Diagnostics

Listing 16-20 contains the AppPage source to display error diagnostic information when an error is encountered; it is listed to show the use of the system variables that are set. The listing contains a deliberate error: the table customer is written as customers. The default, unhandled message looks something like the following:

```
Exception from Informix: X42000:-206:Base table not
found
```

We should make this information more helpful to the user, so we trap the error by using an MIERROR tag. When the AppPage is exploded, the MIERROR tag will be actioned when the MISQL tag is processed, and the contents of the system variables output. The user can mail the webmaster with the appropriate error code and text. Figure 16-21 shows the results.

If the SQL statement was changed to the following:

```
select f_name from customer
```

then the browser output would be as shown in Fig. 16-22.

Tracing Queries on the Web Server

Your best strategy is to handle all errors (SQL and scripting) using MIERROR. Nevertheless, for a detailed examination of all queries that are executed on the server for a particular URL, you can set the tracing variable MI_WEBEXPLEVEL in the webdriver configuration file, web.cnf. You can then trace the query that is actually sent to the database server by looking at the trace file. This feature is useful when your queries are constructed dynamically and you can't see

Listing 16-20. *The* `errorVariables.html` *AppPage source.*

```
<html>
<body>

<?MIERROR err=sqlErrorHandler>
<h1>Error encountered!</h1>
<hr>
<table>
      <tr><td align=right><b>SQL Statement:</td><td>$MI_SQL</td></tr>
      <tr><td align=right><b>Error code: </td><td>
$MI_ERRORCODE<td></tr>
      <tr><td align=right><b>Error Message: </td><td>
$MI_ERRORMSG</td></tr>
      <tr><td align=right><b>SQLSTATE: </td><td>
$MI_ERRORSTATE</td></tr>
</table>
<hr>
Contact the <a href="mailto:webmaster@mysite.com?subject=
$MI_ERRORCODE?text='$MI_ERRORMSG'">Webmaster</a>
to report this error.
<?/MIERROR>

<?MISQL err=sqlErrorHandler sql="select * from customers"><?/MISQL>

</body>
</html>
```

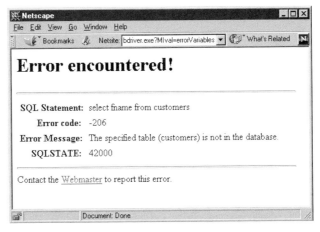

Figure 16-21. *Browser display of List. 16-20.*

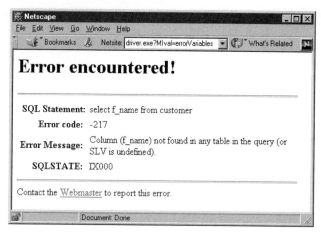

Figure 16-22. Browser display for bad column name.

---

from the AppPage what the query will be, or if there is no MIERROR handler
implemented and you have an urgent need to fix the problem. However, you
should avoid turning this feature on in the live environment too often and if you
do, only for a short time. Tracing webdriver activity to a file will visibly
degrade performance.

---

webdriver **Error Diagnostics**

If webexplode() encounters an error in the AppPage, MI_ERRORCODE
is set to -937. Examples of webdriver errors include undefined
variables in an AppPage or bad syntax in an AppPage tag. The
default error diagnostic information displayed in the browser looks
something like the following:

```
Exception from Informix: XUWEB1:-937:Undefined vari-
able:$my_var
```

We should make this information more helpful to the user. We now
use the same listing (errorVariables.html) but change the SQL
statement to illustrate this point. We change the SQL statement to:

```
<?MISQL sql="select fname from customer"> $my_var
<?/MISQL>
```

where $my_var has not been created or initialized. Requesting the
AppPage returns the screen in Fig. 16-23 to the browser:

Figure 16-23. Undefined variable error.

Beware that $MI_SQL is correctly set only after the appropriate MISQL tag has executed. You can get undefined variable errors anywhere in an AppPage that references an undefined variable, not just in the MISQL tag. Consequently, you should nominate a separate MIERROR handler for MISQL tags when the content of $MI_SQL is to be displayed.

Using MIERROR Effectively

You can customize the behavior of the MIERROR tag. The default behavior of the MIERROR tag is to behave like an MIVAR tag. You can, however, make MIERROR behave like MISQL or like a dynamic tag that you have created to handle errors generically.

MISQL Tag Substitution

You can transform the MIERROR tag into an MISQL tag easily. You add the tag attribute to mierror as follows:

```
<?mierror err=myError tag=misql
        sql="select description from appErrors
            where id=$MI_ERRORCODE">
Error in $MIval: $1
<?/mierror>
```

When this MIERROR tag traps an exception from webexplode(), the tag behaves like an MISQL tag from that point on. In the example, the value of $MI_ERRORCODE is used to look up a custom error message, whose description is output to the HTML page.

Dynamic Tag Substitution

See Chap. 19, "Creating and Using Dynamic Tags," for instructions on how to create a generic error handler using dynamic tags.

Calling SQL Procedures from the Web Page

You can invoke User Defined Routines (UDRs) from an AppPage using the EXECUTE PROCEDURE command in the MISQL tag. The UDRs include the DataBlade functions, such as webexplode(), and your own stored procedures. From Version 4 of the Web DataBlade, you can invoke UDRs directly by using a syntax that looks like the syntax for dynamic tags.

Using the Power of Stored Procedures

If you are web-enabling an existing application, your business logic may be stored in the database in stored procedure language (SPL) routines and functions. Instead of rewriting this logic, you want to reuse it instead.

You can use the MISQL tag to invoke the stored procedure in the database. If the stored procedure returns multiple values, you can capture them in AppPage Script. For example, assume the following procedure is created:

```
create procedure multipleData() returning
varchar(20), integer;
return 'Return Value 1', 101;
end procedure;
```

The procedure is invoked using the MISQL tag, and the return values are interpreted as follows:

```
<?MISQL sql="execute procedure multipleData()">
$1, $2
<?/MISQL>
```

You can also invoke procedures that RETURN WITH RESUME, which will iterate the MISQL tag.

Calling Procedures Directly from Version 4

From Version 4 of the Web DataBlade, you can invoke a stored procedure directly from the AppPage. This is quicker than using EXECUTE PROCEDURE with the MISQL tag.

To invoke a UDR directly from the AppPage, you need to create the UDR in the database mapped by web.cnf (if it has not already been created), register the UDR, and invoke the UDR from the AppPage.

Registering UDRs

Information about the UDRs that we can invoke directly is stored in a table called webudrs, which is installed with AppPage Builder from Version 4 of the Web DataBlade. You can register your own UDRs as well as the existing UDRs supplied by the Web DataBlade product (webexplode() for example).

You can also use Data Director for Web to invoke UDRs directly. Register the UDR as shown in this section, and then invoke the UDR from the AppPage as shown in the next section. Even though the web content is stored in the Data Director for Web schema, webexplode() will still use the webudrs table to map onto the callable UDR.

Assume that we have created the following stored procedure in the database:

```
create procedure formatData ( str lvarchar ) returning
lvarchar;
return '<h1>' || str || '</h1>';
end procedure;
```

This procedure takes an input string and returns the string in HTML format (as a level-one heading).

To register this stored procedure, perform the following:

- in AppPage Builder, select Add Object.
- select the Routine option; the Add a User Defined Routine screen should appear (see Fig. 16-24).
- select formatData from the Routine/Signature pull-down list and click Continue.
- the screen will refresh, populated with the function metadata; enter a Description (optional).
- enter a Class (optional). You can enter any class name that is meaningful to your project; if you enter system, you will not be able to delete the UDR from the webudrs table.
- click Save.

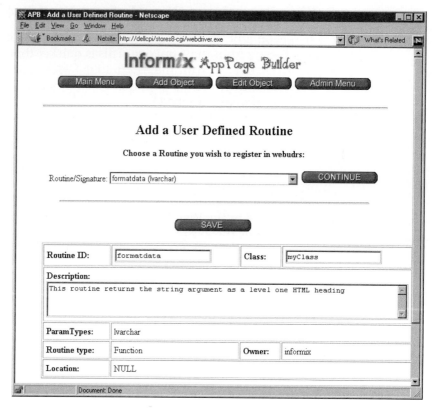

Figure 16-24. *Add a UDR to the* `webudrs` *table.*

Calling UDRs

Once the UDR is registered, you call it from the AppPage. For example:

```
<?formatdata name=resultVar 1="Hello Procedure">
<?MIVAR>$resultVar<?/MIVAR>
```

When `$resultVar` is expanded, the HTML page will contain:

```
<h1>Hello Procedure</h1>
```

Listing 16-21 shows an AppPage that invokes the `webexplode()` function to explode a string. For this example, `webexplode()` was registered in the `webudrs` table as described previously. The resulting HTML is:

```
<html><body>
<h1>Hello Cortez of WebWorld</h1>
</body></html>
```

Generating Files Instead of Web Pages

You can use stored procedures to generate a comma delimited file on the web server (in contrast to generating a comma delimited file in AppPage Script for the client). The following example was developed for UNIX.

- Create a control procedure to interface to the operating system.
- Create a shell script to produce the comma delimited output file.
- Create the MISQL tags to invoke and parameterize the control procedure and shell script.

Create a Control Procedure

The following procedure invokes a shell script called runRep.sh and passes a string parameter, which is the WHERE clause of the query.

tip

You can extend this example to include the passing of the whole *query.*

```
create procedure  callScript(
      where_clause lvarchar);
system 'sh runRep.sh ' || '"' || where_clause
      || '"';
end procedure;
```

Listing 16-21. Using `directUDR.html` to explode a string.

```
<html><body>
<?webexplode
    name=pageFragment
    1="<h1>Hello <?MIVAR>$userName of
$company<?/MIVAR></h1>"
    2="userName=Cortez&company=WebWorld">
<?MIVAR>
$pageFragment
<?/MIVAR>
</body></html>
```

Create a Shell Script to Produce the Comma Delimited File

The following script (`runrep.sh`) reads the `webpages` table and writes comma separated fields to the output file.

```
dbaccess myDatabase << !
unload to '/tmp/myFile.out'
select id || ',' || read_level
from webpages
$1
!
```

Invoke and Parameterize Using AppPage Script

To filter the query, use the following in the AppPage. For example, assume you want the details for the `apb_edit` AppPage:

```
<?MIVAR name=clause>where ID = "apb_edit"<?/MIVAR>
<?MISQL sql="execute procedure
             callScript('$(EVAL,$clause)')">
$1
<?/MISQL>
```

To select all rows:

```
<?MISQL sql="execute procedure callScript('')">
```

Summary

In this chapter we have learned the essentials of maintaining data in the Informix database by using AppPage Scripting tags. In particular, we learned how to create windows on the data that we select so that we can manage the volume of data transferred to the browser. We also learned how to use SQL-related AppPage variables for reporting errors to the user at the browser and how to use the MIERROR tag to control the reporting of error diagnostics. In addition, we learned how to call stored procedures from the AppPage, including the direct calling of registered UDRs.

Dynamic Web Forms Programming

In this chapter:

- HTML form properties
- How the Web DataBlade processes forms
- Creating a basic form
- Handling user events in JavaScript
- Validating form data
- Example: a database browser using dynamic forms

If HTML forms provide the web application developer with a flexible tool for interacting with the user, the Web DataBlade allows the forms developer to capture and render database content easily using AppPage Script and SQL. In addition, JavaScript allows the forms developer to create highly interactive dialogs with the user. You can combine these technologies to create dynamic database-driven web forms.

This chapter is concerned with using AppPage Script, JavaScript, and HTML to create interactive forms, together with the client- and server-side processing of form data. From a practical standpoint, HTML forms and JavaScript forms programming go together, and you can use both with AppPage Script to create dynamic web forms at both the client and the server. To underline the main points of the chapter, a database browser application is listed that pulls together the interactive JavaScript, SQL, and AppPage Scripting elements in order to render the contents of the database dynamically.

If you are creating web forms for the Internet, you must aim for the broadest useability platform, which amounts to creative use of HTML forms (and basic JavaScript), with the server implementing some business logic. If you have a controlled user base, such as an intranet platform where everyone uses (or is supposed to use) the same browser and plug-ins, then you have more flexibility with the deployment technology; you can use Java forms if you want to create a bona fide GUI look and feel to the web forms.

HTML Form Properties

This section describes the essential properties of the form tag and form fields. Table 17-1 lists the attributes of the FORM tag. The aim of this section is to fasttrack through the FORM syntax and basic JavaScript form event handling so that you can code an interactive event-driven form very quickly.

Table 17-1. Attributes of the FORM tag.

Attribute	Description
NAME	Optional. Labels the form so that you can use the label in JavaScript code.
METHOD	Mandatory. GET or POST.
ACTION	Mandatory. Names the URL of the application to process the form data. Can also be a mailto: URL
ENCTYPE	Optional. Defines the encoding method of the form data when it is passed to the web server.
onEvent	Optional. Defines an event handler for the form.
TARGET	Optional. Identifies the target frame for form results after the form has been processed.

The FORM Tag

```
<FORM
    [NAME=<formlabel>]
    METHOD=<method>
    ACTION=<url>
    [ENCTYPE=<enctype>]
    [OnEvent=<eventhandler>]
    [TARGET=<targetframe>]
</FORM>
```

You can type in the tag and attributes in any case. If you define an event handler, then the lettercase of the event handler reference must match the lettercase of the actual event handler definition in the code.

The NAME Attribute

This attribute associates a label with the form and is used mostly by JavaScript event handlers. In any HTML page containing a form, you can use JavaScript to address the form by name or position in an array of forms for that page. For example, if the HTML page contains three forms and the third is called myForm, then the following are equivalent:

- document.forms[2] will yield a reference to the third form object in a web page, starting from zero.
- document.forms["myform"] will yield the form object with the name attribute set to myform.
- document.myform will yield the same form object.

The METHOD Attribute

There are two methods that the browser can use to send the form data to the web server, POST and GET, as shown in Table 17-2. You can use either of these options in your form.

Table 17-2. **The POST and GET methods.**

Method	Description
POST	Form values are created as environment variables for the web server ACTION program.
GET	The browser sends form values in the QUERY_STRING variable, which acts as a command line parameter to the program specified in the ACTION attribute of the form.

The ACTION Attribute

This attribute specifies the application to process the form result. Typically, this is a server-side program. If webdriver is processing the form data, this value is set to the contents of $WEB_HOME, which translates to a call to the CGI or API version of webdriver. You can also set this attribute to the value mailto:e-mail_address, and the form data will be sent to the e-mail address specified in URL-encoded form. For example:

```
<form action="http://theale2/stores7-cgi/webdriver"
method=post>
<form action=<?MIVAR>$WEB_HOME<?/MIVAR>method=post>
<form action=mailto:webmaster@mywebsite.com
method=post>
```

When the first form is submitted, the browser will connect to the web server at port 80 on the theale2 machine, and then the web server will invoke the webdriver program in the directory known to the web server as stores7-cgi. The second example is an AppPage Script version of the first, where $WEB_HOME translates to http://stores7-cgi/webdriver. The third example is an example of the mailto URL format.

The ENCTYPE Attribute

The browser *encodes* the form data before the data is sent to the web server. The web server will then pass the parameters to the receiver defined by the ACTION property.

The default, standard encoding format is application/x-www-form-urlencoded. You can override the default encoding with the ENCTYPE property.

The encoding converts spaces to a plus sign (+) and nonalphanumeric characters to a percent sign (%) followed by two hexadecimal digits, which represent the ASCII code for the character.

then you must URLENCODE *variables that may contain spaces or non-alphanumeric characters. If you use an AppPage variable in a URL specification and the variable contains any special characters, your web server will report an error. It is wise to act defensively and* URLENCODE *any variables that are passed as part of a URL in the* ANCHOR *tag. See the* contentDetail.html *AppPage at the end of this chapter for a working example of using* URLENCODE *to pass parameters in a URL that are otherwise passed in a form.*

You only want to change ENCTYPE *if you are using the* FILE *form element type. To upload files from the client to the web server using the* FILE *type form element, set* ENCTYPE *to* multipart/form-data.

onEvent

This attribute specifies a form-level JavaScript *event handler* that will be called when the event occurs. Typically, this is the *submit* event that is triggered when the user clicks the form Submit button. For example,

```
<form action=<?MIVAR>$WEB_HOME<?/MIVAR>
      method=post
      onSubmit="return doSubmitHandler(this);">
```

The event handler returns a boolean result, which tells the browser either to execute the submit event (true) or cancel the event and return focus to the form (false).

TARGET

This attribute identifies the target frame to display the form results, if any. The default is the current frame or window. The following example will display the resulting AppPage in the frame with the name mainPanel:

```
<form method=post action=<?MIVAR>$WEB_HOME<?/MIVAR>
target="mainPanel">
```

Form Fields

The types of form field are listed in Table 17-3. Each form field can have a name so that you can reference the form field in JavaScript. Additionally, each form field can have one or more events handled by JavaScript event handlers.

Table 17-3. **Types of form field.**

Element	Description
BUTTON	A button used to trigger events explicitly.
CHECKBOX	Single or multiple checkbox items, from which one or more can be selected.
FILE	Specifies the local path for a file that is to be uploaded to the web server when the form is submitted.
RADIO	Single or multiple radio button items from which only one can be selected.
RESET	Resets the form fields to the values initially displayed, which are set using the VALUE form field attribute.
SELECT	A list of options from which one or more can be selected.
SUBMIT	Submits a form to the server when clicked.
TEXT	A single line of text.
TEXTAREA	Multiple lines of text.

The BUTTON Element

The following tag creates a button with the name myButton. The button label is Click Me. When clicked, the browser pops up a JavaScript alert box with a message.

```
<input type=button name=myButton value="Click Me"
        onClick="alert(this.value + '-Well Done!');">
```

When the form is submitted, the target AppPage will receive a variable called myButton initialized to the contents of the value attribute.

The CHECKBOX Element

The following tags create two checkbox items with the same name. Checkbox items with the same name are called checkbox groups, and they are referenced as variable vectors in AppPages. You can check more than one checkbox.

The checked attribute of the first tag tells the browser to display that element as checked. If the form is reset using the Reset button, or by the reset() JavaScript method, the checkbox is rechecked.

```
<input type=checkbox   name=myCheck value="One" checked
    onClick="var x=this.value; alert(x + ' Clicked');">

<input type=checkbox   name=myCheck value="Two" checked
    onClick="var x=this.value; alert(x + 'Clicked');">
```

Each variable vector element will contain the value of a checked item, taken from the `value` attribute of a `checkbox` item. When either of these `checkboxes` are clicked, the browser will popup a box to display the `value` selected.

This example shows the JavaScript `onClick` *event handler being used as a group of statements, in contrast to a function call.*

When the form is submitted, the target AppPage will receive a variable called `myCheck`, which is a variable vector whose elements are set to the values of the checked items in the checkbox group.

The `FILE` Element

The `file` element creates a textbox whose value is set from a `filedialog` box. This tag is used to upload files from the browser client to the web server.

```
<input type=file name=myFile value="Unsupported"
size=20 onChange="confirm('Do you want\n' + this.value
+ '?');">
```

AppPage Script can process these `files` after they have been uploaded. For example, you may want to upload a thumbnail image to the database. This form field allows you to specify the image file. You then write AppPage Script to insert the transmitted image into the database.

A `filedialog` box is a selection box implemented with the look and feel native to the installed browser platform (for example, it will look like a windows file dialog on windows, and an X-Windows file dialog under X-Windows). A file dialog allows you to select one file from a folder on the client. The browser initiates the file dialog display. The web programmer has no control over it in HTML or JavaScript.

You cannot set the contents of the `FILE` *input field in JavaScript or HTML. This is considered a security risk by the browser, since to do so would allow the JavaScript programmer to interpret or address the local disk drive content. Only the user can set the contents of this field.*

The RADIO Element

The following tags create two `radio` elements with the same name. As with the checkbox element, `radio` elements with the name in the same form are grouped together. For Radio buttons in the same group, you can only select *one* Radio button.

```
<input type=radio name=myRadio value="Option One"
checked onClick="alert(this.value + ' selected');">
<input type=radio name=myRadio value="Option Two"
onClick="alert(this.value + ' selected');">
```

In this example, when either of the Radio buttons are clicked, the `onClick()` JavaScript event handler is invoked to display a message.

The RESET Element

The `reset` element resets the form. The `reset` element is rendered as a button by the browser. When the button is clicked, the form elements are reset to their default values. You also can reset the form using the `form.reset()` method in JavaScript.

The following example shows the creation of a `reset` field that, when clicked, prompts the user to confirm that the form should be reset; if the user affirms, the form is reset, otherwise it is not.

```
<input type=reset name=myReset value="Reset Form"
onClick="if (confirm('Really Reset?'))
            return true;
        else {
            alert('Nothing Reset');
            return false;
        }">
```

Note the use of inline event handling code in the `onClick` event handler. You don't have to create a separate function that will process the event, you can code a specific behavior inline.

The SELECT Element

This element allows you to create a list of items from which one or more can be selected.

The `SIZE` attribute allows you to specify the display size of the list. If `SIZE` is omitted or set to one, the list is rendered as a pull-down list. If `SIZE` is set to a value greater than one, then a scrolling list is rendered.

If the MULTIPLE attribute is set, more than one item in the list can be selected. When the form field value is sent to the web server, the Web DataBlade will interpret the form field as a variable vector, with each element corresponding to a chosen item.

Each item in the list is defined using an OPTION attribute as follows:

```
<OPTION VALUE=myValue>Label for Value
```

The Label is displayed in the browser. The Value is submitted as form data if the OPTION is chosen by the user.

Listing 17-1 shows pull-down and scrolling list versions of the SELECT element.

The example in List. 17-1 contains an event handler that displays a popup box to confirm the value of the selection.

The SUBMIT Element

The submit element is a button that when clicked performs the form ACTION that in most cases involves calling a program on the web server to handle the form data passed to it. If you want an AppPage to handle the form data, the web server will invoke webdriver

Listing 17-1. The SELECT element.

```
<select name='mySelect'
           onChange= "alert(this.options
                      [this.selectedIndex].value +
                      ' Selected');">
           <option value='One'>Option One
           <option value='Two' selected>Option Two
</select>
<select name='multipleSelect '
     size=4 multiple
     onChange =
     "alert(this.options[this.selectedIndex].value +
     ' Selected') ;">
     <option value='One'>Option One
     <option value='Two' >Option Two
     <option value='Three'>Option Three
     <option value='Four' selected>Option Four
</select>
```

(as long as you have specified this in the ACTION attribute of the FORM tag).

```
<input type=submit name=submitButton value="Send"
onClick="return confirm('Really Send?');";
```

The example above shows the definition of a Submit button. Associated with this button is an onClick event handler. When the Submit Button is clicked, this event handler will be triggered, and will popup a JavaScript dialog that will return true or false depending on the user response. If the user clicks Cancel in the dialog, then false will be returned to the event handler, which will abort the submit event, and the form data will not be submitted.

The TEXT Element

This element is a single-line text input area. You can specify the size with the SIZE attribute.

```
<input type=text name=myText value="Default Value"
size=20
onChange="this.value+=prompt('Add text to ' +
this.value);">
```

In this example, when the user changes any character in the text field and loses focus from the field (by tabbing out or clicking another part of the screen), the onChange event handler is called to prompt the user to add some text to the existing field value. This text is then appended to the text field.

The TEXTAREA Element

This element allows you to create a textarea on the form for entering strings of text over multiple lines. In the example below, if the value of the textarea changes, then the JavaScript event handler will confirm the new value.

```
<textarea name=myTextArea cols=40 rows=3 wrap=virtual
onChange="alert('New Text is\n' +this.value);">
Default Value
</textarea>
```

The wrap attribute affects the way the text is displayed on screen, as well as how the text is transmitted to the web server. Table 17-4 shows the values for the wrap attribute.

Table 17-4.   The wrap attribute values.

Wrap attribute Value	Description
Virtual	The text will wrap at the column boundry, called a soft wrap. Only the screen field wraps; the text is sent to the server as typed.
Physical	If the screen field wraps, a hard linebreak is sent to the server as if it were typed.
Off	No soft linebreak will occur.

tip

You can use dynamic tags to format your form and form fields. If you implement a standard set of events in form fields across one or more websites that contain forms, then you should implement those standard events in dynamic tags that create an instance of the form field. You can use the SELECTLIST, RADIOLIST, *and* CHECKBOXLIST *dynamic tags as starting points for this. See Chap. 19, "Creating and Using Dynamic Tags," for the details on using these form-related dynamic tags.*

How the Web DataBlade Processes Forms

Forms are useful for capturing data that is to be stored in the database and for capturing the filters for a database query.

When we submit a form to the web server, the form data needs to be processed. The form data may consist of a set of filters for performing a query. For example, we may have entered the customer name into a text field, and when we submit the form, we want the list of customers that match the selection criteria displayed.

To do this, we need to understand how the Web DataBlade processes the form data.

Minimum Information Required

When the form is submitted, the ACTION attribute of the FORM tag will nominate a server-side program to process the form data. This program will be webdriver. It doesn't matter whether the URL to invoke webdriver is a CGI or API call, or whether it is a basic or secure URL. The process is the same. (For information on CGI, API, basic and secure URLs, see Chap. 23, "Web Server Integration").

The minimum required information is the URL for the `webdriver` program and the ID of the page to process the form data. For example:

```
<FORM NAME=myForm
      METHOD=POST
      ACTION="<?Mivar>$WEB_HOME<?/MIvar>">
  <INPUT TYPE=HIDDEN NAME=MIval
         VALUE=targetProcessingForm>
(form fields....)
</FORM>
```

The ACTION URL

The URL to invoke on submission of the form is defined in the ACTION attribute of the FORM tag. This attribute is set to $WEB_HOME, which is initialized in the web.cnf file. For example, assume $WEB_HOME is set in web.cnf as follows:

```
WEB_HOME   /myCgi/webdriver.exe
```

Also, assume the AppPage that contains the form has the ACTION attribute set as follows:

```
ACTION="<?Mivar>$WEB_HOME<?/Mivar>"
```

Then the exploded HTML will look like this:

```
ACTION=/mycgi/webdriver.exe
```

Specifying the URL is not enough, however. We also need to specify the target AppPage that will process the form data and generate the HTML for the next page.

The Target AppPage

To specify the target AppPage that is invoked via the ACTION URL, use a hidden input field with the name of MIval.

When you specify this AppPage, what we are specifying is the next page to explode from the database. The target AppPage does not have to use all of the form data that is passed to it.

For example, to specify that the validateForm AppPage is to receive and process form data, enter the following:

```
<INPUT TYPE=HIDDEN
       NAME="MIval" VALUE="validateForm">
```

If you do not specify a form field called MIval, webdriver *will use the value of* MIval *in the* web.cnf *file. However, it is good programming practice to set* MIval *in the form.*

The Final Result

When the form is submitted to the web server, the data will be encoded, and the web server will invoke webdriver via the URL in the ACTION attribute, and POST the unencoded data to the webdriver program.

webdriver will then use the value of the MIval form field to select the AppPage from the table containing the AppPages (wbPages or webpages, for example). The form data is passed into the webexplode() function along with all the other variables from the web server and webdriver environment.

How do AppPages Use Form Data?

The form fields that you submit to webdriver are turned into AppPage variables with the name that you assigned to the field in the form. These variables can then be manipulated just like any other AppPage variable. Therefore, it is essential that you name the form fields using the NAME attribute.

Creating a Basic Form

The example in List. 17-2 (ExampleForm1.html) is a form that contains an example form field for each type of element except the FILE element. When the Submit button is clicked, the AppPage ExampleForm2 is invoked to process the form data.

The ACTION URL is defined as follows:

```
<form name=myForm method=POST
      action="<?mivar>$WEB_HOME<?/mivar>">
```

The target AppPage is initialized in the form as follows:

```
<input type=hidden name="MIval"
      value="ExampleForm2">
```

Note also that we can pass the name of the currently exploded AppPage as form data. This is achieved by referencing the $MIval variable, which contains the name of the AppPage being exploded:

```
<input type=hidden name="callingForm"
      value="<?mivar>$MIval<?/mivar>">
```

Figure 17-1 shows the browser output of the form, with some values selected.

Listing 17-2. `ExampleForm1.html`.

```
<html>
<body>
<h2>Example Form</h2>
<form name=myForm method=POST
        action="<?mivar>$WEB_HOME<?/mivar>">
<table border=2>
<tr><td><h3>Checkbox</h3></td>
<td>
<input type=checkbox  name=myCheck value="One Checked" checked>
<input type=checkbox  name=myCheck value="Two Checked">
<td></tr>
<tr><td><h3>Radio</h3></td>
<td>
<input type=radio name=myRadio value="Option One" checked>
<input type=radio name=myRadio value="Option Two">
</td></tr><tr>
<td><h3>Select</h3></td>
<td>
<select name='mySelect'>
<option value='Option One Selected'>Option One
<option value='Option Two Selected' selected>Option Two
</select>
</td></tr><tr>
<td><h3>Select</h3></td>
<td>
<select name='myMultipleSelect'  size=4 multiple>
<option value='Option One Selected'>Option One
<option value='Option Two Selected' >Option Two
<option value='Option Three Selected'>Option Three
<option value='Option Four Selected' selected>Option Four
</select>
</td></tr><tr>
<td><h3>Text</h3></td>
<td>
<input  type=text name=myText value="Default Value" size=20>
</td></tr><tr>
<td><h3>TextArea</h3></td>
<td>
<textarea name=myTextArea cols=40 rows=3 wrap=virtual>
Default Value
</textarea>
</td></tr><tr>
```

Listing 17-2. *(continued)*

```
<td><h3>Reset</h3></td>
<td>
<input type=reset name=myReset value="Reset Form">
</td></tr><tr>
<td><h3>Submit</h3></td>
<td>
<input type=submit name=mySubmitButton value="Send">
</td>
</tr>
</table>
<input type=hidden name="MIval" value="ExampleForm2">
<input type=hidden name="callingForm"
       value="<?mivar>$MIval<?/mivar>">
</form>
</body>
</html>
```

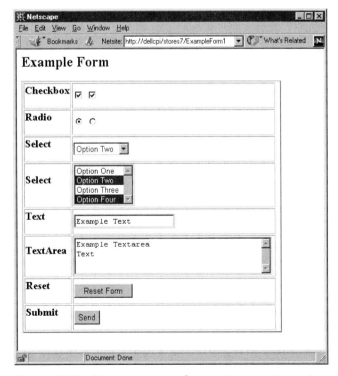

Figure 17-1. *Browser output of* `ExampleForm1.html`.

Listing 17-3 shows the `ExampleForm2.html` AppPage, which
accepts the form field data from `ExampleForm1.html` and displays it
on the screen.

Figure 17-2 shows the browser display of `ExampleForm2.html` after
it has been exploded to process the form data. Note the display of
the checked items and the items selected from the `MultipleSelect`
list. Note also the use of the `SEPARATE` variable-processing function

Listing 17-3. *The* `ExampleForm2.html` *AppPage.*

```
<html>
<body>

<?mivar>
<h2>Results of $callingForm</h2>
<?/mivar>
<?mivar name=displaySelected>$(SEPARATE,$myMultipleSelect, AND )<?/mivar>
<?mivar name=displayChecked>$(SEPARATE,$myCheck, AND )<?/mivar>

<?mivar>
<table>
<tr>
<td align=right>
<b>Checkbox value:</td><td>$displayChecked</td></tr>
<tr><td align=right>
<b>Radio value:</td><td>$myRadio</td></tr>
<tr><td align=right>
<b>Single Select Value:</td><td>$mySelect</td></tr>
<tr><td align=right>
<b>Multiple Select Value:</td><td>$displaySelected</td></tr>
<tr><td align=right>
<b>Text Value:</td><td>$myText</td></tr>
<tr><td align=right>
<b>TextArea Value:</td><td>$myTextArea</td></tr>
<tr><td align=right>
<b>Submit Button Value:</td><td>$mySubmitButton</td></tr>
</table>

<?/mivar>
</body>
</html>
```

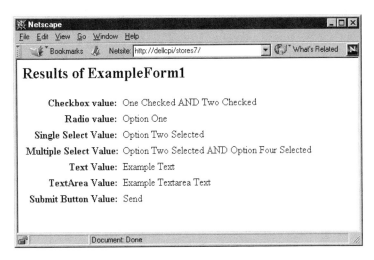

Figure 17-2. Browser display of the `ExampleForm2.html` *AppPage.*

in `ExampleForm2.html`. These features will be explained in the next section.

Interpreting Multiple Values in SELECT Lists and CHECKBOX Items

`ExampleForm1.html` contains a `checkbox` group, called `myCheck`, and two `select` lists, called `mySelect` and `myMultipleSelect`. The form field `mySelect` can only select one item. The forms fields `myCheck` and `myMultipleSelect` can have multiple items selected. How do we interpret multiple values if we have only one variable name?

The `checkbox` group `myCheck` and the multiple `select` list `myMultipleSelect` are passed to the target AppPage as *variable vectors*. A variable vector is a special variable that contains multiple values, called elements. The variable vector name is the same as the name of the form field variable. You can however identify individual elements of the vector by position.

Formatting Variable Vector Values

The AppPage `ExampleForm2.html` contains the following code to format the variable vectors:

```
<?mivar name=displaySelected>
$(SEPARATE,$myMultipleSelect, AND )<?/mivar>
<?mivar name=displayChecked>
$(SEPARATE,$myCheck, AND )<?/mivar>
```

First the SEPARATE function inserts the string " AND " between elements. The results are assigned to new AppPage Script variables, and they are subsequently displayed in the browser.

Retrieving Elements from Variable Vectors

You retrieve elements from variable vectors by position. You can use the INDEX variable-processing function to access an element by its position in the variable vector.

When the variable vector is initialized, the elements are not delimited. To use the INDEX function, you need to delimit the elements with a comma.

The following snippet shows how to extract the first element from the variable vector $myMultipleSelect. The positions start from zero.

```
<?mivar name=formattedString>
$(SEPARATE,$myMultipleSelect,",")<?/mivar>
<?mivar>$formattedString<?/mivar>
<?mivar>$(INDEX,0,$formattedString)<?/mivar>
```

We use the SEPARATE function first to delimit the variable vector elements with a comma, and then to assign the result to a variable called formattedString. We then use the INDEX function on the formatted string to extract the first element.

From Version 4 of the Web DataBlade, you can use the VECSIZE function to return the number of elements in the variable vector. You use the VECSIZE variable-processing function as follows:

```
<?mivar>$(VECSIZE,$myMultipleSelect)<?/mivar>
```

Handling Nonexistent Data

The user may decide not to enter any data into a form field. The user may decide not to select an option from a select list. If the form field has been assigned a default value, then the user may just delete it.

An AppPage variable will only be created for the target AppPage if the form field in the browser has been set to a value, including spaces. If the form field has no value, then any reference to that form field using the form field name in the target AppPage will result in an error.

You can handle the absence of variables by using the NXST variable-processing function. For example, you would insert the following at the top of the AppPage:

```
<?mivar cond=$(NXST,$myText)
        name=myText>Default Value<?/mivar>
```

This snippet tests for the existence of a variable called $myText. If the variable does not exist, then a new variable called $myText is created, and the value is set to the string Default Value. You can then refer to the $myText variable in the remainder of the AppPage (see Chap. 12 for a full listing of the properties of the MIVAR tag).

Handling User Events in JavaScript

You can use JavaScript in forms if you need to handle user events, such as mouseclicks, and perform client-side processing before the form is submitted. In addition, you use JavaScript to set the values of form fields on the client, depending on what the user types in.

JavaScript has access to the internal properties of forms and form elements in the browser. The attributes that you set in a form or form element can be addressed and in most cases changed by JavaScript, giving you a layer of control not available in HTML. You can use event handlers with forms to create a dynamic interaction with the user.

Chapter 5 contains examples how to connect JavaScript to Java in the browser, which will allow you to present form data to Java methods without submitting the form. For example, you can send form data back to the database via a hidden Java applet that connects to the database via JDBC, either directly or via remote methods on the web server host.

What Are Events in Forms?

When the user interacts with a form, such as entering data into form fields, changing data in a form field, or clicking a button, an event is generated. An event is a signal that JavaScript can trap and react to. Table 17-5 lists the events that we are interested in.

What Are Event Handlers?

An event handler consists of one or more JavaScript commands that are executed when an event occurs. The command can be a call to a JavaScript function, or one or more commands outside of a JavaScript function.

The basic syntax of an event handler in a form is:

```
<TAG ATTRIBUTES eventHandler="JavaScript">
```

Table 17-5. JavaScript events.

Event	When actioned
blur	When input focus is removed from a form element.
click	When the user clicks on a link or form element.
change	When the user changes the value of a form element.
focus	When input focus is given to a form element.
load	When a page is loaded.
mouseover	When the user moves the pointer over a hyperlink.
mouseout	When the user moves the pointer off a hyperlink.
reset	When a form is reset.
select	When the user selects the data in a form field.
submit	When a form is submitted.
unload	When the user leaves the page.

For example:

```
<input type=text name=myText value="Default Value"
size=20
onChange="this.value+=prompt('Add text to ' +
this.value);">
```

In this example, when the user changes the value of the form field, the onChange event will be triggered, and the JavaScript between the quotes will be executed.

Strictly speaking, an event handler such as onChange does nothing by itself. If a change event occurs, and no onChange event handling code exists, then nothing will be done. The onChange event handler is a placeholder for your code; the onChange handler passes control to any JavaScript that is defined for it.

What Is this ?

The keyword this *refers to the JavaScript object currently in scope. In the example above,* this *refers to the text form field.*

Available Event Handlers

Table 17-6 lists the event handlers that you can use in your forms, browser documents, and windows.

Table 17-6.   Event handlers applied to browser objects.

Object	Event handlers
BUTTON element	onClick
Browser window	onLoad, onUnload, onBlur, onFocus
CHECKBOX	onClick
FILE element	onBlur, onChange, onFocus
FORM	onSubmit, onReset
HTML Document	onLoad, onUnload
Hyperlink	onClick, onMouseOver, onMouseOut
RADIO button	onClick
RESET button	onClick
SELECT list	onBlur, onChange, onFocus
SUBMIT button	onClick
TEXT element	onBlur, onChange, onFocus
TEXTAREA element	onBlur, onChange, onFocus

Generating Events

Instead of waiting for the user to generate an event, you can generate an event using JavaScript. If defined, the event handler for the component you have generated the event for will pick up the event.

For example, if you wanted to submit the form using JavaScript instead of waiting for the user to press the Submit button, you could perform the following:

```
<input type=button value='Click to Submit'
    onClick='this.form.submit()'>
```

In a lot of cases, you invoke event handlers such as form.submit() after validating the data on the form when the user clicks the Submit button.

Notice that in this example, the form.submit() method is invoked by using the reference to the form from the form field. Every form field has a reference to the form that it belongs to. You can refer to the form by using this.form when the form field object is in scope.

For example, in the following snippet, when the user tabs or clicks into the text field, the `select()` method is called to highlight all the text in the text field.

```
<input type=text size=20 onFocus="select();">
```

You can also generate events for other form fields. For example, the next snippet will highlight the text in a form field called `otherField` when focus is given to the `myField` text field:

```
<input type=text name=myField
    onFocus="this.form.otherField="select();">
```

You can have multiple `submit` *buttons on a form, each with a different event handler to customize the behavior of the validation. For example, you could have a* `submit` *button that performed validation, and another that did not. The difference is that each* `submit` *button is defined with separate event-handling code.*

Table 17-7 lists a summary of events that you can generate in JavaScript. See Table 17-6 for the objects you can apply them to.

Validating Form Data

When the user enters data into a form for inserting into or updating a table, you will in most cases want to validate the data. You can validate the data on the client using JavaScript, on the server using SQL or AppPage Script or both.

Table 17-7. *Events that can be generated using JavaScript.*

Event	Description
`blur()`	Removes focus from the form field.
`click()`	Generates a click event for the hyperlink or form field.
`focus()`	Gives input focus to the form field.
`select()`	Selects (highlights the text) in the form field.
`reset()`	Resets the form.
`submit()`	Submits the form.

Performing Validation on the Client

The advantage of validating the form data on the client is that you are not taking up the bandwidth required to send the form data to the server, have it validated, and then display the error output back on the browser client. If you want to validate data on the client, you use JavaScript to do this. This involves trapping an event, such as the `submit` event, and validating the form fields accordingly.

You can validate the form fields when the user submits the form, or as the user navigates around the form.

If the validation contains dependencies between form fields, then it may be worth waiting until the user submits the form.

If the user has a lot of form fields, it may be worth performing the validation when the user submits the form. In contrast, the user may require that the validation is performed on a field-by-field basis as the form data is entered.

It is worth prototyping this part of the user interface if you are developing a commercial website. If you decide that you will perform validation on a field-by-field basis, beware that some users may object to the popup boxes that are reported on a field-by-field basis. Some users like to see the error report listed at the top of the form.

Performing Validation on the Server

You can validate the form fields on the server, where the server is defined as the web server invoking `webdriver` to explode an AppPage that contains the validation rules. There is no client-side validation of form field data in this scenario.

You can perform server-side validation of client data using hidden frames or applets on the browser client. See Chap. 5 for instructions on how to do this.

Instead, in this scenario the form fields are validated by an AppPage, which writes the error report to the resulting HTML page, which is then downloaded to the browser, together with the form, for re-entry of data. The same AppPage that contains the form usually performs the validation, although it can be any nominated AppPage. Other programs, such as CGI programs, can also perform the server-side validation.

If you are web enabling existing business logic lodged in the database as SPL validation routines, you can pass the form data to these routines using the `MISQL` tag, and interpret the result in AppPage Script.

Client-side Validation Using JavaScript

You can validate the format and content of form fields on the client using JavaScript.

Validating Text Fields

The JavaScript below validates a text field for the following properties:

- can only contain letters and digits (no whitespace),
- must be a minimum of 10 characters and no more than 40 characters.

When the Submit button is clicked, a JavaScript function is called to validate the text field. If the field fails validation, then a popup box is displayed to inform the user of the error. The following snippet shows the form declaration and the text element:

```
<form method="POST"
      action="<?mivar>$WEB_HOME<?/mivar>
      onsubmit=
"return validateTextField(this)">
<input type="text" name="mytextField"
size="20" maxlength="40">
```

If the validation fails, then false is returned by the validateTextField() function. If false is returned, then the submit event is abandoned; otherwise the submit event proceeds, and the form data is sent to the web server.

Listing 17-4 shows the JavaScript validation function. Figure 17-3 shows the popup box if the text field contains whitespace, and

Listing 17-4.   JavaScript validation of text form fields.

```
function validateTextField(theForm)
{

  if (theForm.mytextField.value == "")
  {
    alert("Please enter a value for the \"mytextField\" field.");
    theForm.mytextField.focus();
    return (false);
  }
```

Table 17-4. *(continued)*

```
  if (theForm.mytextField.value.length < 10)
  {
    alert("Please enter at least 10 characters in the \"mytextField\"
field.");
    theForm.mytextField.focus();
    return (false);
  }

  if (theForm.mytextField.value.length > 40)
  {
    alert("Please enter at most 40 characters in the \"mytextField\"
field.");
    theForm.mytextField.focus();
    return (false);
  }

  var checkOK =
"ABCDEFGHIJKLMNOPQRSTUVWXYZabcdefghijklmnopqrstuvwxyz0123456789-";
  var checkStr = theForm.mytextField.value;
  var allValid = true;
  for (i = 0;  i < checkStr.length;  i++)
  {
    ch = checkStr.charAt(i);
    for (j = 0;  j < checkOK.length;  j++)
      if (ch == checkOK.charAt(j))
        break;
    if (j == checkOK.length)
    {
      allValid = false;
      break;
    }
  }
  if (!allValid)
  {
    alert("Please enter only letter and digit characters in the
\"mytextField\" field.");
    theForm.mytextField.focus();
    return (false);
  }
  return (true);
}
```

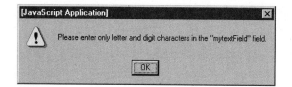

Figure 17-3. *Invalid alphanumeric characters entered.*

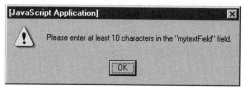

Figure 17-4. *Not enough characters entered.*

Fig. 17-4 shows the popup box if the text field does not contain the minimum number of characters.

Validating Numeric Fields

Listing 17-5 contains a JavaScript function that validates a text field for a number that can only contain a comma and a period separator (for example, 1,999.99) and that must be greater than 100.99. A value entered of 100.98 will fail validation, as will entering any character that is not a digit. Figure 17-5 shows the popup box if the number is less than 100.99.

Listing 17-5. *Numeric validation using JavaScript.*

```
function Form1_Validator(theForm)
{

   var checkOK = "0123456789-.,";
   var checkStr = theForm.myNumber.value;
   var allValid = true;
   var decPoints = 0;
   var allNum = "";
   for (i = 0;  i < checkStr.length;  i++)
   {
     ch = checkStr.charAt(i);
     for (j = 0;  j < checkOK.length;  j++)
       if (ch == checkOK.charAt(j))
         break;
     if (j == checkOK.length)
     {
       allValid = false;
       break;
     }
   }
```

Listing 17-5. *(continued)*

```
      if (ch == ".")
      {
        allNum += ".";
        decPoints++;
      }
      else if (ch != ",")
        allNum += ch;
    }
    if (!allValid)
    {
      alert("Please enter only digit characters in the
\"myNumber\" field.");
      theForm.myNumber.focus();
      return (false);
    }

    if (decPoints > 1)
    {
      alert("Please enter a valid number in the
\"myNumber\" field.");
      theForm.myNumber.focus();
      return (false);
    }

    var chkVal = allNum;
    var prsVal = parseFloat(allNum);
    if (chkVal != "" && !(prsVal >= "100.99"))
    {
      alert("Please enter a value greater than or equal
to \"100.99\" in the \"myNumber\" field.");
      theForm.myNumber.focus();
      return (false);
    }
    return (true);
  }
```

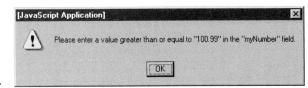

Figure 17-5. *Numeric validation alert.*

If you want to validate the form fields for a business-related dependency, then you should implement the business rule on the server. This can be achieved using stored procedures, for example, that the target AppPage can invoke. Implementing this rule on the server will allow the rule to be shared among cooperating applications.

Server-Side Validation Using AppPage Script

You can validate form fields using AppPage Script. The validation is part of the `webexplode()` of the target AppPage that receives the form data.

The target AppPage that receives the form data can be the same AppPage that captures the form data, or it can be another page. In most cases it is easier if the same AppPage captures and validates the data, so that the form can be redisplayed along with the error messages that direct the user to re-enter the form data.

Structure of the Validation Page

When you use the same AppPage to capture form data and validate that data, you can structure your AppPage into two sections:

- a section that captures form data;
- a section that validates the data, displays any error messages, redisplays the form, or accepts and processes the correctly validated data.

Once the data has been validated successfully, you can then apply the data as appropriate. For example, you may want to insert the form data as a record into a database table, or update table columns with the form data.

The example in Listing 17-6 shows the validation applied to a form that is used to capture data for a new stock record in the `stores7` database. The AppPage is called `captureStock.html`. The AppPage has the following characteristics:

- The form is split into two segments, GET and POST.
- The variable `$apb_state_` controls which segment is processed using the `MIBLOCK` tag with the `COND` attribute.
- In the GET segment, `MIval` is set to `captureStock.html`, and `$apb_state_` is set to POST.
- The GET segment captures the form data. On submission of the form, the AppPage is reinvoked to process the form data.
- When the form is reinvoked, the POST segment is processed.

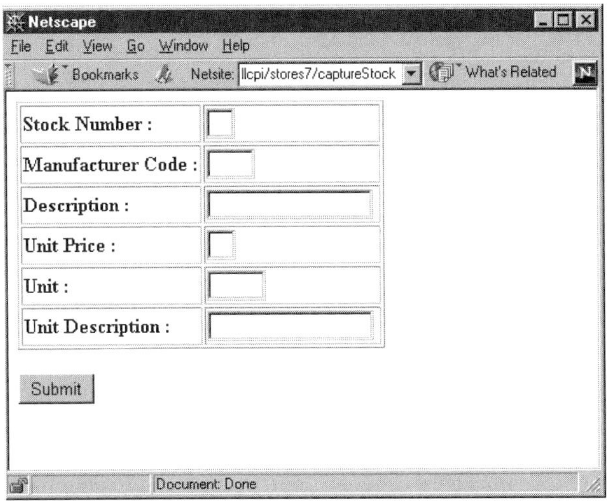

Figure 17-6. Capture the form data (the GET Phase).

- If any of the form field values are mandatory and have not been entered, error text is output to the HTML page.
- If any numeric form fields, such as `stock_number` are not numeric, error text is output to the HTML page.

If any errors are encountered, error text is displayed in the HTML output, and the user must re-enter the data. If all the form fields pass the validation rules, the new stock record is inserted into the database. Listing 17-6 shows the AppPage to process form data capture and validation.

Figure 17-6 shows the form in the browser.

Listing 17-6. *The* `captureStock.html` *AppPage.*

```
<html>
<body>
<?mivar name="apb_state_"  default="GET">$apb_state_<?/mivar>
<?mivar name="apb_error_"><?/mivar>

<?miblock cond=$(EQ,$apb_state_,POST)>
    <?mivar name="apb_state_"
        cond=$(NXST,$apb_stock_num)>ERROR<?/mivar>
    <?mivar name="apb_error_"
        cond=$(NXST,$apb_stock_num)>$apb_error_<BR>Field "Stock
```

Listing 17-6.   (continued)

```
Number" is mandatory.<?/mivar>
    <?mivar name="apb_state_"
        cond=$(NXST,$apb_manu_code)>ERROR<?/mivar>
    <?mivar name="apb_error_"
        cond=$(NXST,$apb_manu_code)>$apb_error_<BR>Field
"Manufacturer Code" is mandatory.<?/mivar>
    <?mivar name="apb_state_"
        cond=$(NXST,$apb_description)>ERROR<?/mivar>
    <?mivar name="apb_error_"
        cond=$(NXST,$apb_description)>$apb_error_<BR>Field
"Description" is mandatory.<?/mivar>
    <?mivar name="apb_state_"
        cond=$(NXST,$apb_unit_price)>ERROR<?/mivar>
    <?mivar name="apb_error_"
        cond=$(NXST,$apb_unit_price)>$apb_error_<BR>Field "Unit
Price" is mandatory.<?/mivar>
    <?mivar name="apb_state_"
        cond=$(NXST,$apb_unit)>ERROR<?/mivar>
    <?mivar name="apb_error_"
        cond=$(NXST,$apb_unit)>$apb_error_<BR>Field "Unit" is
mandatory.<?/mivar>
    <?mivar name="apb_state_"
        cond=$(NXST,$apb_unit_descr)>ERROR<?/mivar>
    <?mivar name="apb_error_"
        cond=$(NXST,$apb_unit_descr)>$apb_error_<BR>Field "Unit
Descr" is mandatory.<?/mivar>

<?miblock cond=$(EQ,$apb_state_,POST)>

    <?mivar name="apb_state_"
      cond=$(NOT,$(ISNUM,$apb_stock_num))>ERROR<?/mivar>
    <?mivar name="apb_error_"
      cond=$(NOT,$(ISNUM,$apb_stock_num))>$apb_error_<BR>Field "Stock
Number" was an invalid numeric.<?/mivar>
    <?mivar
name="apb_stock_num">$(REPLACE,$apb_stock_num,',")<?/mivar>
    <?mivar
name="apb_manu_code">$(REPLACE,$apb_manu_code,',")<?/mivar>
    <?mivar
name="apb_description">$(REPLACE,$apb_description,',")<?/mivar>
    <?mivar
```

Listing 17-6.   (continued)

```
name="apb_unit_price">$(REPLACE,$apb_unit_price,',")<?/mivar>
    <?mivar name="apb_unit">$(REPLACE,$apb_unit,',")<?/mivar>
    <?mivar
name="apb_unit_descr">$(REPLACE,$apb_unit_descr,',")<?/mivar>

    <?mivar name="apb_sql")>INSERT INTO stock (
            stock_num, manu_code, description, unit_price,
            unit, unit_descr) VALUES (
            $apb_stock_num, '$apb_manu_code',
            '$apb_description', $apb_unit_price, '$apb_unit',
            '$apb_unit_descr');
    <?/mivar>

    <?misql cond=$(EQ,$apb_state_,POST)
      sql="$apb_sql">Success! $MI_ROWCOUNT rows inserted.
    <?/misql>
    <?/miblock>
    <?mivar cond=$(EQ,$apb_state_,ERROR)>$apb_error_<?/mivar>

<?mivar name="apb_state_"
        cond=$(EQ,$apb_state_,ERROR)>GET<?/mivar>
<?/miblock>

<?mivar name=apb_state_ default="GET">$apb_state_<?/mivar>
<?miblock cond=$(EQ,$apb_state_,GET)>
<FORM METHOD=POST ACTION=<?mivar>$WEB_HOME<?/mivar>>

    <INPUT TYPE=hidden NAME=MIval
        VALUE="<?mivar>$MIval<?/mivar>">
    <INPUT TYPE=hidden NAME=apb_state_ VALUE="POST">
    <TABLE BORDER=1>
      <?mivar name="apb_stock_num"
        default="">$apb_stock_num<?/mivar>
      <?mivar name="apb_manu_code"
        default="">$apb_manu_code<?/mivar>
      <?mivar name="apb_description"
        default="">$apb_description<?/mivar>
      <?mivar name="apb_unit_price"
        default="">$apb_unit_price<?/mivar>
      <?mivar name="apb_unit" default="">$apb_unit<?/mivar>
      <?mivar name="apb_unit_descr"
        default="">$apb_unit_descr<?/mivar>
```

Listing 17-6. (continued)

```
      <?mivar>
        <tr>
          <td><b> Stock Number <b>:</td>
          <td><input type=text name="apb_stock_num"
                    value="$apb_stock_num" size="0"><BR></td>
        </tr>
        <tr>
          <td><b> Manufacturer Code <b>:</td>
          <td><input type=text name="apb_manu_code"
                    value="$apb_manu_code" size="3"><BR></td>
        </tr>
        <tr>
          <td><b> Description <b>:</td>
          <td><input type=text name="apb_description"
                    value="$apb_description" size="15">
       <BR></td>
        </tr>
        <tr>
        <td><b> Unit Price <b>:</td>
          <td><input type=text name="apb_unit_price"
                    value="$apb_unit_price" size="0">
       <BR></td>
        </tr>
        <tr>
          <td><b> Unit <b>:</td>
          <td><input type=text name="apb_unit"
       value="$apb_unit" size="4">   <BR></td>
        </tr>
        <tr>
          <td><b> Unit Description <b>:</td>
          <td><input type=text name="apb_unit_descr"
       value="$apb_unit_descr" size="15">  <BR></td>
        </tr>
<?/mivar>
</TABLE><P>

<input type="submit" value="Submit">
</FORM>
<?/miblock>
</body>
</html>
```

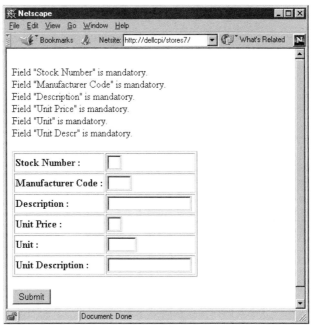

Figure 17-7. *Validate and display the error messages (The POST phase).*

Figure 17-7 shows the validation output when some of the mandatory fields are left blank.

If you use Data Director for Web, you can use the properties of the input and update form wizards to generate basic validation conditions, such as making sure that form fields are not blank and that numeric values are numeric.

Example: A Database Browser Using Dynamic Web Forms

You can leverage the power of dynamic web forms to create a simple but very sophisticated database browser. In this section is a complete example of a database browser that is run over the web. The example allows you to select a table from a list of tables in the database, select the columns from the table, and then view the data in the order you choose within a walking window that you can configure (see Chap. 16 for an introduction to walking data windows). The example pulls together all the major topics that we have discussed in previous chapters by combining AppPage Scripting, HTML forms, and JavaScript into a practical and highly useable application.

This example is a practical demonstration of the following:

- dynamic constructing of queries via JavaScript, and using these queries to fetch data from the database via a form,
- using JavaScript to set and unset form data in response to user events,
- using a form to parameterize the sort order of a query result set,
- using form values as parameters,
- using hyperlinks for form navigation,
- using the `separate` and `replace` variable-processing functions for walking windows,
- dynamically constructing select lists, radio buttons, and check-boxes,
- using variable expressions to render a page dynamically,
- using frames and forms.

Database Browser Functionality

The database browser functionality can be listed as follows:

- Choose a table that you want to query.
- Select the columns from that table that you want to view.
- Select the number of rows (the *window*) to display.
- Choose the column to order the result set; decide whether ascending or descending order.
- Query the First, Next, Previous and Last set of rows.
- Reorder the query by a different column and sort sequence.

The database browser is a two-frame frameset, with the top frame used to select a database table to browse, and the bottom frame used to select the columns for the selected table, and display the results of walking the table.

Selecting a Table and Columns

The top-level frameset is called `DBrowser.html` and can be called using the CGI or API `webdriver`. For example:

```
http://dellcpi/your-URL-prefix/
webdriver.exe?MIval=DBrowser
```

Replace the URL prefix `your-cgi-path` with your own CGI URL prefix.

The Top-level Frameset

Listing 17-7 shows the first page in the application, `DBrowser.html`. This AppPage describes the frameset of the application, with the `viewHeader.html` AppPage displayed in the top frame and a blank page of results in the bottom frame. The header frame is called `Header` and is always visible, allowing you to select another table at any point. The frame that displays all of the results is called `main`.

The `Blank.html` page is very simple:

```
<html><body></body></html>
```

Once the top-level frameset is displayed you can select a table from the pull-down list and click the Select button. A list of columns from the selected table is displayed in the main frame.

Listing 17-7. *The* `DBrowser.html` *AppPage.*

```
<html>
<head>
<title>Database Browser</title>
</head>
<frameset framespacing="0" border="false" rows="30%,*" frameborder="0">
  <frame name="Header"
         scrolling="no"
         noresize
         src="<?MIVAR>$WEB_HOME?MIval=viewHeader<?/MIVAR>">
    <frame name="main" scrolling="auto"
src="<?MIVAR>$WEB_HOME?MIval=Blank<?/MIVAR>">
  </frameset>
  <noframes>
  <body>
  <p>This page uses frames, but your browser doesn't support them.</p>
  </body>
  </noframes>
</frameset>
</html>
```

Displaying the List of Tables

Listing 17-8 shows the `viewHeader.html` AppPage. This AppPage creates the `SELECT` list of tables from the database, and, once the table is selected, submits the form to the web server, instructing `webdriver` to explode the `columnList` AppPage, which contains the columns the user may select.

Listing 17-8. *The* `viewHeader.html` *AppPage.*

```
<html>
<head>
<title>Database Browser</title>
<base target=main>
</head>
<body>
<script Language="JavaScript">
function Form1_Validator(theForm)
{
  if (theForm.selectedTable.selectedIndex < 0)
  {
    alert("Please select one of the \"selectedTable\" options.");
    theForm.selectedTable.focus();
    return (false);
  }
  return (true);
}
</script>
<form method="POST"
      action="<?MIVAR>$WEB_HOME<?/MIVAR>"
      onsubmit="return Form1_Validator(this)"
      name="Form1">

<input type=hidden name=MIval value=columnList>

<table border="0" width="100%">
    <tr>
      <td valign="top">
        <?wbImg name="book" path="/" ext="gif">
      </td>
      <td valign="middle"><div align="right"><p>
        <font face="Arial"><big><strong>Select Table :
```

Listing 17-8. *(continued)*

```
        </strong></big></font>
      </td>
      <td valign="middle"><font face="Arial">
        <select name="selectedTable" size="1">
            <?MISQL SQL="select tabid, tabname
                        from systables order by 2;">
              <option value="$1">$2</option>
            <?/MISQL>
      </select></font></td>

    </tr>
    <tr>
      <td width="6%"><small>
        <font face="Arial"></font></small></td>
      <td width="20%"><div align="right"><p>
        <font face="Arial"><strong> </strong></font>
      </td>
      <td width="24%"><small><font face="Arial">
        <input type="submit" value="Select" name="B1">
        <input type="reset" value="Reset"
                    name="B2"></font></small>
      </td>
      <td width="16%">
        <small><font face="Arial"></font></small>
      </td>
    </tr>
  </table>
</form>
</body>
</html>
```

The key segment of List. 17-8 is the SELECT list, which is formed by interrogating the systables table using the MISQL tag to obtain a list of tables in the database:

```
<select name="selectedTable" size="1">
    <?MISQL SQL="select tabid, tabname
            from systables order by 2;">
          <option value="$1">$2</option>
    <?/MISQL>
    </select>
```

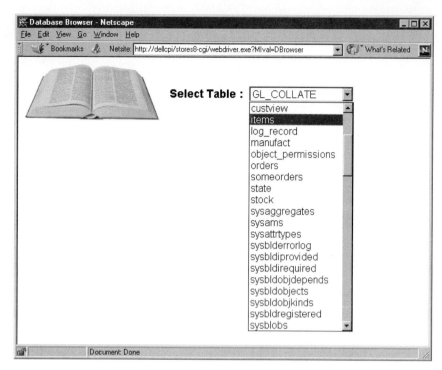

Figure 17-8. *Select tables—browser display.*

Figure 17-8 shows the browser display of Lists. 17-7 and 17-8. Once the user selects a table, the main frame is populated with a list of columns that the user can select.

Displaying the Columns for the Selected Table

Listing 17-9 shows `columnList.html`, which displays all the columns for the table selected in the `viewHeader.html` AppPage. The user can select one or more columns. The user can also select the number of rows to display in the walking data window. Once the user has selected her columns and the number of rows to display, the form is submitted, and the `contentDetail` AppPage is displayed in the main frame to show the data for the selected columns.

In List. 17-9, the variable `$selectedTable` is passed from the form in the `Header` frame, and used to select the column names for the selected table from the system catalogs.

Listing 17-9. *The* `columnList.html` *AppPage.*

```
<html>
<head>
<title>Database Browser</title>
<!-- Parameters in are:
$selectedTable: Table ID if the table in systables.
-->

<script>
// Check all the columns as selected
function checkAll( colForm ) {
    with (colForm)  {
        for (var i=0; i <= selectedColumn.length-1; i++) {
           selectedColumn[i].checked=true;
        }
    }
}

// Uncheck all the columns
function uncheckAll ( colForm ) {
    with ( colForm )  {
        for (var i=0; i <= selectedColumn.length-1; i++) {
           selectedColumn[i].checked=false;
        }
    }
}

// Submit processing
function doSubmit( colForm ) {
    with ( colForm ) {
        for (var i=0; i <= selectedColumn.length-1; i++) {
            if ( selectedColumn[i].checked == true ) {
                orderClause.value +=
                   "<OPTION value=" + selectedColumn[i].value +
                   ">" + selectedColumn[i].value;
            }
        }
    }
    return true;
}

</script>
```

Listing 17-9. (continued)

```
<?MIERROR ERR=NOVARIABLES>
No table selected.
<?/MIERROR>

<?MIERROR ERR=SELECTERROR>
An error has occurred while retrieving column information.
<?/MIERROR>
</head>
<body>
<form method="POST" action="<?MIVAR>$WEB_HOME<?/MIVAR>"
      onSubmit="return doSubmit(this);">

<strong>
<font face="Arial">Select the Number of Rows to Display:
<input type="text" name=WINSIZE value=5 size=3></font> </strong><br>
<strong><font face="Arial">
Select the Columns you would like to display:</font>
</strong></p>


<!-- MIval contains the name of the AppPage that will process
     the results
     winsize is set to the number of rows to display
     selectedTable needs to be passed in also
-->
  <input TYPE="hidden" NAME="MIval" VALUE="contentDetail">
  <input type="hidden" NAME="orderClause" VALUE="">
  <input TYPE="hidden" NAME="selectedTable"
         VALUE=<?MIVAR>$selectedTable<?/MIVAR>
  <table border="0" width="100%">
    <tr>
      <td width="33%" align="center" bgcolor="#D3D3D3">
        <font face="Arial">
          <strong>Column Name</strong>
        </font>
      </td>
      <td width="33%" align="center" bgcolor="#D3D3D3">
        <font face="Arial"><strong>Choose</strong></font>
      </td>
    </tr>
<?MISQL SQL="select colname from syscolumns
            where tabid = $selectedTable;">
```

Listing 17-9. *(continued)*

```
    <tr>
      <td width="33%">
        <font face="Arial">$(UPPER,$1)</font>
      </td>
      <td width="33%">
        <div align="center"><center><p><font face="Arial">
        <input type="checkbox" name="selectedColumn"
               value="$1"></font>
      </td>
    </tr>
<?/MISQL>
</table>
<table border="0" width="100%">
    <tr>
      <td width="33%">
        <div align="center"><center><p><small>
        <font face="Arial">
        <input type="button" value="Choose All"
               name="chooseall"
               onClick="checkAll(this.form);">
        <input type="button" value="Choose None"
               name="choosenone"
               onClick="uncheckAll(this.form);">
        <input type="submit" value="Select"
               name="submit">
        </font></small>
      </td>
    </tr>
 </table>
</form>
</body>
</html>
```

Figure 17-9 shows the browser display of Listing 17-9 when the user selects the `stock` table.

There are two interesting features of Listing 17-9.

First, if the user clicks the Choose All button, a JavaScript function (`checkAll`) is called to check all the checkboxes. If the Choose None button is clicked, a JavaScript function (`uncheckAll`) is run to uncheck all the checkboxes.

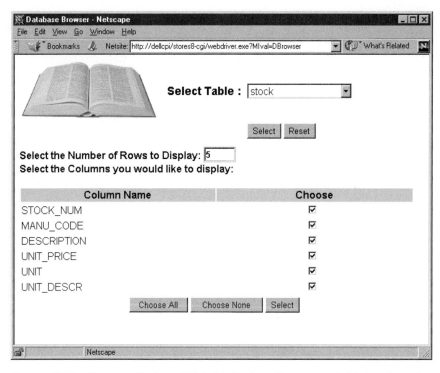

Figure 17-9. Browser display of List. 17-9 when the `stock` table is selected.

Second, when the form is submitted, the selected columns are used to dynamically format part of a SELECT list that will be constructed by the target AppPage for the form. This SELECT list contains a list of columns the user can select from to request a reordering of the query results. The JavaScript function doSubmit() is called to create this string and assign it to one of the hidden form variables.

Selecting Data Using the Column Specifications

Listing 17-10 shows the contentDetail.html AppPage. This is the AppPage that selects and formats the data from the selected table and columns, within a data window of the selected size. You can reorder the result set in ascending or descending mode by selecting a column to reorder with, and clicking the Reselect button. When the frame is refreshed, the column selected as the sort column is rendered in *italics*. Only the displayed columns are contained in the pull-down list; this is because the columnList AppPage in List. 17-9 passed the OPTION list for the SELECT tag that is rendered here.

Listing 17-10. *The* `contentDetail.html` *AppPage.*

```
<html>

<head>
<title>Top Page 1</title>

<!--
Parameters:
$selectedColumn - this is a variable vector, with a list of
column names to be used in the SELECT clause.
$orderClause    - this is the list of ORDER fields if
specified.
$displayFormat  - 0: simple fields, 1: table field
-->

<?MIERROR ERR=LISTERR>
Error selecting values from table.
<?/MIERROR>
<?MIERROR ERR=noTable>
No table selected with $selectedTable.
<?/MIERROR>

</head>
<body>

<?MIVAR COND=$(NXST,$WINSTART)   NAME=WINSTART>0<?/MIVAR>
<?MIVAR COND=$(<,$WINSTART,0)    NAME=WINSTART>0<?/MIVAR>

<?MIVAR NAME=ascdesc DEFAULT="">$ascdesc<?/MIVAR>
<?MIVAR COND=$(NXST,$orderList) NAME=ascdesc> <?/MIVAR>
<?MIVAR COND=$(XST,$orderList)  NAME=orderSpec>
ORDER BY $(SEPARATE,$orderList,",")<?/MIVAR>
<?MIVAR COND=$(NXST,$orderList) NAME=orderList><?/MIVAR>
<?MIVAR COND=$(NXST,$orderSpec) NAME=orderSpec
  DEFAULT="">$orderList<?/MIVAR>
<?MIVAR COND=$(AND,$(XST,$selectedColumn),$(NXST,$selectList))
NAME=selectList>$(SEPARATE,$selectedColumn,",")<?/MIVAR>


<?MISQL ERR=noTable
        SQL="select tabname from systables
            where tabid = $selectedTable;">
```

Listing 17-10. *(continued)*

```
    $(SETVAR,$selectedTableName,$1)
<?/MISQL>
<?MISQL ERR=noTable
        SQL="select count(*) from $selectedTableName;">
    $(SETVAR,$recordCount,$1)
<?/MISQL>



<?MIBLOCK>
<form NAME=listForm ACTION=<?MIVAR>$WEB_HOME<?/MIVAR>>
<?MIVAR>
    <input type=hidden name=MIval value=$MIval>
    <input type=hidden name=selectedTable
            value=$selectedTable>
    <input type=hidden name=selectList value="$selectList">
    <input type=hidden name=selectedColumn
            value="$selectedColumn">
    <input type=hidden name=orderClause value="$orderClause">
    <input type=hidden name=WINSIZE value="$WINSIZE">
    <input type=hidden name=WINSTART value="$WINSTART">
<?/MIVAR>


<?MIVAR>
<font face="Arial" size=2>
<strong>Select the column to re-order the display: </strong>
<select name=orderList>>
  $orderClause
</select>
Ascending
<input type=radio name=ascdesc value="ASC"
$(IF,$(OR,$(EQ,$ascdesc,),$(EQ,$ascdesc,ASC)),CHECKED)>
Descending
<input type=radio name=ascdesc value="DESC"
$(IF,$(EQ,$ascdesc,DESC),CHECKED)>
<input type=submit value='Reselect'>
</font>
<?/MIVAR>

<table border="1" width="100%">
  <?MIVAR NAME=headers>
  $(REPLACE,$selectList,",",</font></strong></td>
```

Listing 17-10. *(continued)*

```
  <td bgcolor='#D3D3D3'><strong>
    <font face=Arial size=2>)<?/MIVAR>
  <?MIVAR COND=$(XST,$orderList) NAME=headers>
    $(REPLACE,$headers,$orderList,<I>$orderList</I>)
  <?/MIVAR>
  <tr><td bgcolor="#D3D3D3"><strong><font face="Arial" size=2>
      <?MIVAR>$(UPPER,$headers)<?/MIVAR>
                </font></strong></td>
  </tr>
<?MISQL
    WINSIZE=$WINSIZE
    WINSTART=$WINSTART
    SQL="select $selectList
         from $selectedTableName $orderSpec $ascdesc;">
        <tr>
           {<td><font face="Arial" size=2>$*</font></td>}
        </tr>
<?/MISQL>
</table>

<?MIVAR>
<table border="0" width="100%">
  <tr>
    <td align="center"><strong><font face="Arial">
      <a
href="$WEB_HOME?MIval=$MIval&orderList=$orderList&orderClause=
|$(URLENCODE,$orderClause)&ascdesc=$ascdesc&selectList=$(URLENCODE,
$selectList)&orderSpec=$(URLENCODE,$orderSpec)&selectedTable=
$selectedTable&selectedColumn=$(URLENCODE,$selectedColumn)&WINSIZE=
$WINSIZE&WINSTART=0">First $WINSIZE Rows</a></font></strong>
    </td>
    <td align="center"><strong><font face="Arial">
      <a
href="$WEB_HOME?MIval=$MIval&orderList=$orderList&orderClause=
$(URLENCODE,$orderClause)&ascdesc=$ascdesc&selectList=$(URLENCODE,
$selectList)&orderSpec=$(URLENCODE,$orderSpec)&selectedTable=
$selectedTable&selectedColumn=$(URLENCODE,$selectedColumn)&WINSIZE=
$WINSIZE&WINSTART=$(-,$WINSTART,$WINSIZE)">Previous $WINSIZE
Rows</a></font></strong>
    </td>
    <td align="center"><strong><font face="Arial">
```

Listing 17-10. *(continued)*

```
        <a
href="$WEB_HOME?MIval=$MIval&orderList=$orderList&orderClause=
$(URLENCODE,$orderClause)&ascdesc=$ascdesc&selectList=$(URLENCODE,
$selectList)&orderSpec=$(URLENCODE,$orderSpec)&selectedTable=
$selectedTable&selectedColumn=$(URLENCODE,$selectedColumn)&WINSIZE=
$WINSIZE&WINSTART=$(+,$WINSTART,$WINSIZE)">Next $WINSIZE
Rows</a></font></strong>
    </td>
    <td align="center"><strong><font face="Arial">
        <a
href="$WEB_HOME?MIval=$MIval&orderList=$orderList&orderClause=
$(URLENCODE,$orderClause)&ascdesc=$ascdesc&selectList=$(URLENCODE,
$selectList)&orderSpec=$(URLENCODE,$orderSpec)&selectedTable=
$selectedTable&selectedColumn=$(URLENCODE,$selectedColumn)&WINSIZE=
$WINSIZE&WINSTART=$(-,$recordCount,$WINSIZE)">Last $WINSIZE
Rows</a></font></strong>
    </td>
  </tr>
</table>
<?/MIVAR>

</form>
<?/MIBLOCK>

</body>
</html>
```

By clicking the appropriate link at the foot of the page, you can navigate to the first or last rows in the result set, or the next and previous row. The sort order of the columns is maintained when walking the result set.

Figure 17-10 shows the rows from the `stock` table listed in ascending order of the `stock_num` column. Figure 17-11 shows the rows from the `stock` table listed in descending order of `unit_price`.

Note that if you reorder the query in the middle of walking the result set, then the reordered set of rows are displayed with the same `WINSTART` and `WINSIZE` settings; so, if you reorder while viewing rows 6 to 10, then you will see rows 6 to 10 of the reordered result set when the frame is redisplayed. You can change this by using JavaScript to set the hidden form fields accordingly when the reselect is requested.

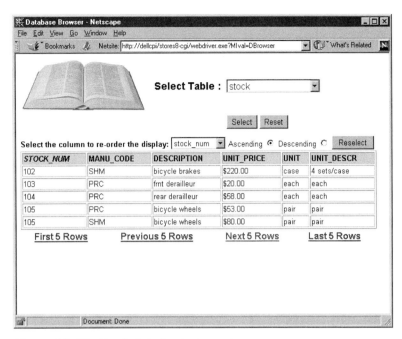

Figure 17-10. *Stock data in stock number sequence.*

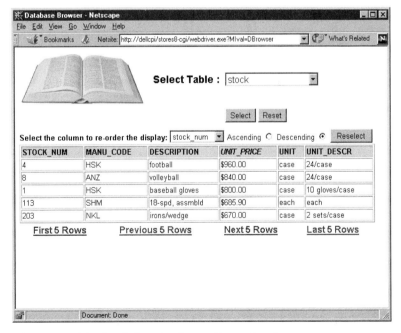

Figure 17-11. *Stock data in descending unit price sequence.*

The essential form state is maintained between submissions of the form. That is, the sort order, the sort sequence (ascending or descending Radio button selection), and the current position in the data window. The variables passed into the `contentDetail` AppPage are stored in hidden form fields, so that when the form in the page is submitted, the data persists.

For example, the `MISQL` query that selects the data from the `stock` table is fully parameterised by AppPage parameters that derive from previous form submissions:

```
select $selectList from $selectedTableName
       $orderSpec $ascdesc;
```

The hyperlinks that control the walking of the result set need to include the form variables in the URL, since we are not using the form to pass them. Because the variable values are contained in a URL, we need to `URLENCODE` them to ensure that any control characters are replaced by URL-friendly characters. For example:

```
<a href= "$WEB_HOME?MIval=$MIval&orderList=$orderList
&orderClause=$(URLENCODE,$orderClause)&ascdesc=
$ascdesc&selectList=$(URLENCODE,$selectList)
&orderSpec=$(URLENCODE,$orderSpec)&selectedTable=
$selectedTable&selectedColumn=$(URLENCODE,
$selectedColumn)&WINSIZE=$WINSIZE&WINSTART= $(+,
$WINSTART,$WINSIZE)">Next $WINSIZE Rows</a>
```

Summary

In this chapter we have seen how you can use JavaScript and AppPage Script to create interactive forms. We learned how the Web DataBlade processes form data. The essentials of handling user events in JavaScript were also covered. We also saw how to validate form data on the browser client using JavaScript, and on the database server using AppPage Script. In addition, the technique for uploading client files to the database server was demonstrated. Finally, we put most of these techniques together to create an interactive database browser that combined client-side JavaScript event handling with SQL and AppPage Script to render selected contents of the database dynamically.

Managing Documents in the Information Repository

In this chapter:

- The intranet information repository revisited
- Content items and content metadata
- Example MIME types
- Uploading client files using forms
- Changing content-types dynamically
- Example: a simple document repository

You can store all kinds of documents in the Informix database. For example, you can store word-processing documents, spreadsheets, presentations, PDF documents, project plans, and all kinds of documents that you use in your desktop environment. Chapter 3 discussed the digital value chain, and the customer solution cycle. Part of this cycle is the intranet information repository that stores the media asset base. This chapter is concerned with managing the document base in such a way that we can use the browser to upload documents into the database as well as retrieve the documents from the database. To this end, we elaborate a practical application that you can extend to suit your own specific requirements.

The Intranet Information Repository Revisited

Increasingly, intranets are used to manage the corporate asset base. If a company can manage all of its documentation and content items by way of a browser and content repository database, then a layer of complexity is removed from the internal business process.

Suppose, for example, that a company wants to publish a brochure hailing the latest products and services. Before the Internet, the company would have contracted a printing house to publish the brochure. Now, using a browser-based content repository application, the company can submit the document in PDF format to the database and publish this document to the website. Instead of printing the brochure in a batch of possibly hundreds, an Internet user can download the PDF document from the Informix database via the web interface to the content repository that stores the brochure and other related documents.

Content Items and Content Metadata

We define *content* as the media asset, for example, a GIF file or a Microsoft PowerPoint presentation. This is the object that is stored in the blobspace or smart blobspace of the Informix database. Content *metadata* is information about the object: the document name, description, file system path, and author, to name a few. This metadata is stored in a table in the database. You can also store a pointer to the object in the blobspace or smart blobspace with the metadata for the object.

The following `create table` statement contains columns for document object metadata and for the document object itself. The table stores information on the MIME type of the document, a description of the document, the author of the document, and a column called `object` that is used to contain a pointer (the large object handle) to the actual object in the smart blobspace, `sbspace2`.

```
create table myAppDocuments
    (
        id varchar(40) not null ,
        mime_type varchar(40) not null ,
        description varchar(250,20),
        author varchar(40),
        object blob
    )
        put object in (sbspace2);
```

As you can see, metadata is really another way of describing attributes for objects stored in the database. The metadata requirements for applications vary. Essentially, however complicated the metadata schema looks, it will map down to a content item and a list of attributes that describe it.

The example in this chapter captures document objects plus metadata for the object, so you will see how it fits together later.

Example MIME Types

Because we are delivering content items from the repository to the browser client, we need to be able to tell the browser what type of document the browser will receive so that the browser can handle the document itself, using a plug-in or a helper application. The HTTP header attribute `content-type` is used by the browser to obtain the MIME type of the information being downloaded.

You can set the `content-type` *attribute in AppPage Script dynamically using the* `HTTPHEADER` *variable-processing function. There is more information on this topic later in the chapter.*

Plug-Ins and Helper Applications

The difference between a plug-in and a helper application is that the plug-in runs inside the browser and is called via the browser API. A helper application is a separate application that runs outside the browser. Some desktop programs have plug-ins that allow you to use desktop documents inside the browser.

The browser uses the MIME type of the information it received to decide whether the browser software can render the data, or whether it must pass control to the plug-in or invoke the helper application. Netscape Navigator, for example, allows you to define MIME types and associate the plug-in or helper application for the MIME type.

Document Types and Extensions

Anyone familiar with Data Director for Web or AppPage Builder knows that, when you create objects such as AppPages and import objects such as image files, a MIME type is associated with that content. In Data Director for Web, for example, you use or add to the extension mappings that associate an object extension (such as DOC) with a MIME type (such as `application/ms-word`). When the HTML page is generated by `webexplode()`, the resulting HTML will contain tags that reference the content items that are stored in the database. However, a MIME type is also associated with the content item in the HTML. See Chap. 20, "Working with Large Objects," and Chap. 13, "Creating and Managing Websites with Data Director for Web," for a detailed explanation of how `webdriver` works with large objects and extension mappings.

Table 18-1 lists some example documents that you can store in the database.

If you use Data Director for Web, then you can list the extension mappings by using `Tools/Extensions` *in Site Manager to see a comprehensive list of MIME types associated with document extensions.*

Table 18-1.   Example document types.

Document type	Extension	MIME type in browser
Word-processing document	DOC	application/ms-word
Spreadsheet document	XLS	application/ms-excel
Plain text	TXT	text/plain
QuickTime movie	QT	video/quicktime
Video clip	AVI	video/avi
Audio file	WAV	audio/x-wav
PDF document	PDF	audio/x-wav
Zip compressed data	ZIP	application/x-zip-compressed

Uploading Client Files Using Forms

If you use a web browser that supports client file upload, you can use `webdriver` to upload files from your client machine. You can set the `MI_WEBUPLOADDIR` file variable in your `web.cnf` file to specify the directory on the web server machine in which uploaded files are placed. This variable is not mandatory. If it is not specified, the client file will be placed in the default temporary location, `/tmp`, for example.

Related AppPage Variables

When the form is submitted, you can access the variables listed in Table 18-2 in the AppPage that processes the form.

In Table 18-2, the "Variable name" column item is to be replaced by the name assigned to the form field variable. For example, if your form field is called `myDocument`, then:

- `input_file` is `myDocument`
- `input_file_name` is `myDocument_name`
- `input_file_type` is `myDocument_type`

`webdriver` creates the variables `myDocument_name` and `myDocument_type` and makes them visible to the AppPage.

An Upload Example

Listing 18-1 shows the AppPage `uploadDocs.html`. This AppPage allows you to select files from the client so that you can upload them to the web server for processing, which usually involves inserting them into the Informix database on the database server

Table 18-2. AppPage variable available for client file upload.

Variable name	Description
input_file	Absolute pathname of the uploaded file on the web server machine.
input_file_name	Absolute pathname of the client file.
input_file_type	MIME type of the uploaded file.

Listing 18-1. *The* `uploadDocs.html` *AppPage.*

```
<html>
<body>
<?mivar cond=$(NXST,$form_state) name=form_state>GET<?/mivar>

<?miblock COND=$(EQ,$form_state,POST)>
<?mivar>
    Input File on server is: $myDocument1<br>
    Input File on client is: $myDocument1_name<br>
    Input File type is: $myDocument1_type<br><hr>

    Input File on server is: $myDocument2<br>
    Input File on client is: $myDocument2_name<br>
    Input File type is: $myDocument2_type<br><hr>

    Input File on server is: $myDocument3<br>
    Input File on client is: $myDocument3_name<br>
    Input File type is: $myDocument3_type<br><hr>

    Input File on server is: $myDocument4<br>
    Input File on client is: $myDocument4_name<br>
    Input File type is: $myDocument4_type<br><hr>
<?/mivar>
<?/miblock>

<?miblock COND=$(EQ,$form_state,GET)>
<form ENCTYPE=multipart/form-data name=docsForm
action=<?mivar>$WEB_HOME<?/mivar> method=POST>
<h2>Enter Document Paths:</h2><br>
<input type=file size=40 name=myDocument1><br>
<input type=file size=40 name=myDocument2><br>
<input type=file size=40 name=myDocument3><br>
<input type=file size=40 name=myDocument4><br>

<input type=hidden name=MIval value=<?MIvar>$MIval<?/MIvar>
<input type=hidden name=form_state value=POST>
<input type=submit value='Upload'>
</form>
<?/miblock>
</body>
</html>
```

machine. The AppPage `uploadDocs.html` allows you to select four client files, and when you submit the form using the Upload button, the documents are uploaded to the web server directory specified by the `webdriver` variable `MI_WEBUPLOADDIR`.

The example assumes the `web.cnf` contains the following setting:

```
MI_WEBUPLOADDIR d:\stores7
```

The AppPage `uploadDocs.html` contains two sections delimited with the `MIBLOCK` tag. The first displays the confirmatory output of the `FILE` input form field variables as converted by `webdriver`. The second captures the files to upload.

The form fields that capture the files to upload range from `myDocument1` through `myDocument4`. `webdriver` creates two new variables for each file, `myDocument1_name` and `myDocument1_type` through `myDocument4_name` and `myDocument4_type`, respectively. The contents of the variables are output to the browser.

The `myDocument` variable that is displayed is a combination of the `MI_WEBUPLOADDIR` directory, the form field name, and the process ID of the `webdriver` process. Note that, in the browser output, documents with the same form field name accepted by the same `webdriver` process are uniquely identified.

Figure 18-1 shows an example Windows client `filedialog` that allows you to select a file whose path is imported into the relevant form field. Figure 18-2 shows browser output of `uploadDocs.html` and the capture of the client filename paths. Figure 18-3 shows the result of processing the client files after the form is submitted. No client file is imported into the database in this example.

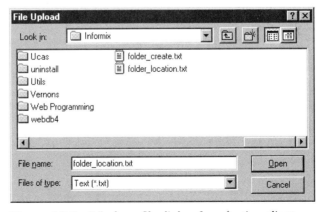

Figure 18-1. *Windows file dialog for selecting client files to upload.*

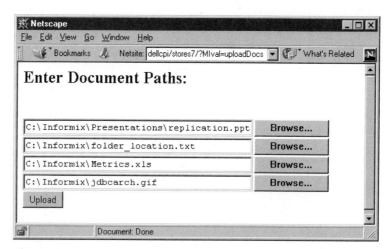

Figure 18-2. *Browser output of* `uploadDocs.html` *with client files selected.*

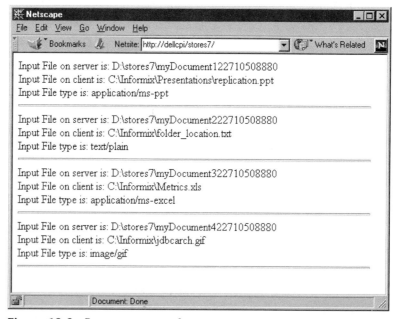

Figure 18-3. *Browser output after* `uploadDocs.html` *uploads the client files to the web server.*

Referencing Documents on the Filesystem

Instead of storing the document object in the database, you can store the path of the document as metadata. In this case, when you render the document name in the browser, you provide a FILE *URL as the hyperlink to the document, in contrast to a* webdriver *URL.*

Changing Content Types Dynamically

You can change the content type of the AppPage that you are downloading using the HTTPHEADER function to set the content-type header that is interpreted by the client browser.

What Is an HTTP Header?

The client browser requires two pieces of information to process the downloaded information.

- The *status* header tells the client browser about the status of its request.
- The *content-type* header tells the browser the MIME type of the content that is being downloaded.

For example, a status code of 200 tells the browser that the HTTP request was successful, and the data is being sent. A status code of 401 will instruct the browser to pop up an authentication dialog. For example, if you are using a secure URL prefix, status 401 will instruct the browser to pop up the authentication dialog to capture the username and password for NSAPI or ISAPI authentication (see Chap. 23, "Web Server Integration," for more information on this topic).

The content-type header tells the browser what type of data to expect so that the browser can render it correctly by using internal software or by using a plug-in or helper application. For example, if the content-type was defined as application-msword and your browser has the Microsoft Word plug-in installed, or Microsoft Word defined as a helper application, then the downloaded data would be passed to an instance of the Microsoft Word application.

As long as the browser is instructed to manage the content-type *in a specific way, the* content-type *can be any string that you define. For example, if you added Microsoft Word as a helper application for*

the MIME type `application/myType`, *then setting* `content-type` *to* `myType` *via the* `HTTPHEADER` *function will result in the browser invoking Microsoft Word. You can set helper applications in Navigator 4.05, for example, using* `Edit/Preferences/Navigator/Applications`.

Using HTTPHEADER to Change the Content Type Dynamically

The AppPage in List. 18-2 will result in the text in List. 18-3 being output by `webexplode()`. The browser will render this text as plain text, not HTML. The browser will display the text as shown in Fig. 18-4.

You can trace the HTTP output using the CGI version of `webdriver`. *Go to the directory where the CGI* `webdriver` *resides, set* `MIval` *in the environment, and type* `webdriver`. *The* `webdriver` *will write the exploded AppPage to the screen, including the* `content-type` *setting.*

Listing 18-2. *AppPage containing the* HTTPHEADER *function to change the* content-type *as understood by the browser.*

```
<html>
<body>
<h1>This example will be displayed as plain text in the browser</h1>
</body>
</html>
<?mivar>$(HTTPHEADER,content-type,text/plain)<?/mivar>
```

Listing 18-3. *The* webdriver *output sent to the browser.*

```
content-type: text/plain
content-length: 99

<html>
<body>
<h1>This example will be displayed as plain text in the browser</h1>
</body>
</html>
```

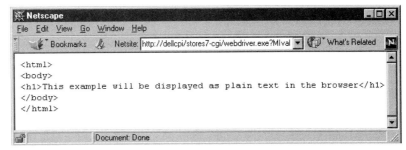

Figure 18-4. Browser display of List. 18-3.

Selecting Content Types

In the next example a form is presented to the user, who can select how to view the AppPage. The user has three choices: HTML, plain text, or edit the page using Microsoft Word. When the form is submitted, the AppPage will return the exploded version of itself as the nominated content-type.

Listing 18-4 shows the AppPage source.

Listing 18-4. *The* `httpHeaderForm.html` *AppPage source.*

```
<html>
<body>
<h2>Choose How to Display This Page</h2>
<?mivar>
<form method=post actioon=$WEB_HOME>
<input type=hidden name=MIval value=$MIval>
<select name=param1 size=3>
<option selected value="text/html">HTML
<option value="text/plain">Plain Text
<option value="application/ms-word">MS Word
</select>
<input type=submit value=Go>
</form>
<?/mivar>
</body>
</html>

<?mivar cond=$(XST,$param1)>
$(HTTPHEADER,content-type,$param1)
<?/mivar>
```

Figure 18-5 shows the plain text browser display. Figure 18-6 shows the HTML display; Fig. 18-7 shows the dialog that is popped up when the Microsoft Word option is selected, and it is followed by Fig. 18-8, which shows the exploded AppPage displayed in Microsoft Word.

Exporting Tables as Formatted Files for Downloading to the Client

There may be instances where you want to export the contents of one or more database tables to a formatted file for input to another program, perhaps on another machine. Often, the export file consists of a comma-delimited set of columns for each record in a table.

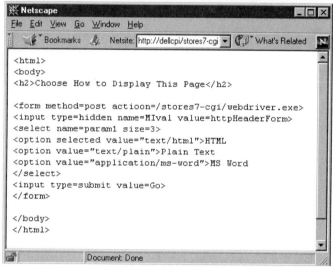

Figure 18-5. *Plain text display selected.*

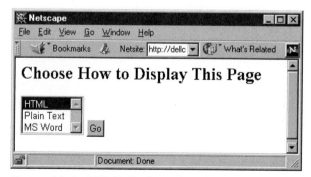

Figure 18-6. *HTML display selected.*

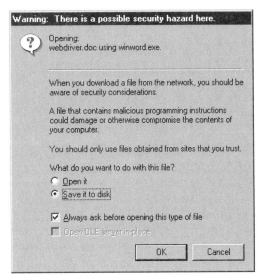

Figure 18-7. Confirm open or save of Microsoft Word document.

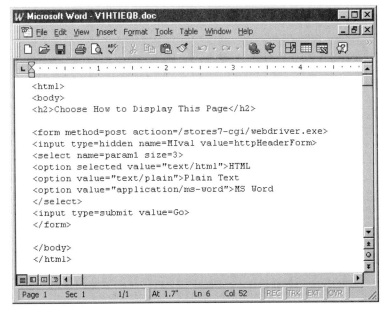

Figure 18-8. Editing the exploded AppPage in Microsoft Word.

Listing 18-5.   AppPage to generate comma-delimited output.

```
<?MISQL sql="select trim(fname) || ',', trim(lname) || ',',
                 trim(company) || ',', trim(state)
           from customer">
$1$2$3$4
<?/MISQL>
<?mivar>
$(HTTPHEADER,content-type,application/myDownloadType)<?/mivar>
```

Sometimes you have to write a CGI script to take the export request and create the export file on the web or database server. You then have to provide a link to the new file so that you can download it—unless you are happy to move the file manually using FTP (file transfer protocol).

You can use AppPage Script and the HTTPHEADER function to create a comma-delimited file, download it, and save it—all without CGI or FTP.

Listing 18-5 shows a simple AppPage that selects and delimits four columns from the customer table. The result is specified as content type myDownloadType. You can specify your own content type: If you are using a non-Windows client, you can create a new helper application type in the Navigator Preferences dialogs, and set this to Save File.

The following sample output is generated:

```
Ludwig,Pauli,All Sports Supplies,MI
Anthony,Smith,Play Ball!,AK
Anthony,Higgins,Play Ball!,CA
George,Watson,Watson & Son,CA
Charles,Ream,Athletic Supplies,CA
Donald,Quinn,Quinn's Sports,CA
```

Example: A Simple Document Repository

This example shows how to

- add documents to the database,
- update the document metadata and, optionally, the document that is stored in the database,

- delete documents from the database,
- view documents using hyperlinks that map onto `webdriver` URLs to extract the document object from the database.

A document is a content item. A content item can be any kind of object: an image, audio sample, video sample, or Microsoft Word document, for example.

You should use large object caching to speed up the retrieval of your documents when you have selected an individual document to download. See Chap. 25, "Performance Tuning Essentials," for details of how to cache large objects.

Functions Included

There are four functions included with this example:

- View documents in the repository.
- Add a document to the repository.
- Edit document metadata and update the document object in the repository.
- Delete a document from the repository.

View Documents

The View Documents screen allows you to view the complete list of documents in the repository. You can also select a document to be downloaded from the database to the browser for viewing.

Add Document

The Add Document screen allows you to add a document to the repository. You assign a name, description, and document type (MIME type) and specify the client path from which the document will be taken to be stored in the database.

Edit Document

The Edit Documents screen allows you to change the metadata for an object. If you don't specify a new document to upload, then the existing document stored in the database remains attached to this metadata. If you decide to upload a new document to replace an existing document, then the new object LO handle is stored with the metadata.

Delete Document

You delete documents from the View Documents screen. When the Delete option is selected, the View Documents screen is refreshed, and in the process, the document is deleted from the database.

Content Schema

Listing 18-6 contains the very simple content repository schema.

Listing 18-7 shows the unloaded contents of the appmimetypes table.

Viewing Documents

Listing 18-8 shows the viewDocuments.html AppPage. The user can download a document for viewing, or choose to edit or delete the document.

The complete list of documents in the repository is displayed. The user clicks the Name column, or clicks the Radio button to select or deselect one item for editing or deleting.

Listing 18-6.   Content repository schema.

```
create table appdocuments
    (
        export_id serial not null ,
        id varchar(40) not null ,
        mime_type varchar(40) not null ,
        description varchar(250,20),
        object blob
    );

create table appmimetypes
    (
        mime_name varchar(40) not null ,
        mime_type varchar(40) not null ,
        extension varchar(14) not null ,
        object_type varchar(40) not null
    );
```

Listing 18-7. *The* UNLOAD *of the* appmimetypes *table.*

```
HTML,text/html,text/html,Document,
Microsoft Word,application/msword,doc,Document,
Microsoft PowerPoint,application/ppt,ppt,Document,
Microsoft Excel,application/xls,xls,Document,
Microsoft Project,application/mpp,mpp,Document,
Adobe PDF,application/pdf,pdf,Document,
Plain Text,text/plain,txt,Document,
Image (GIF),image/gif,gif,Image,
```

Listing 18-8. *The* viewDocuments.html *AppPage.*

```html
<html>
<head>
<title>View Documents</title>

<script language=javascript>
function setAddLink( pForm, linkPage ) {
      pForm.MIval.value = linkPage;
      pForm.submit();
}

var selectedDocument=null;
function selectDocument( documentName ) {
    selectedDocument = documentName;
}

function docSelected( pForm, linkPage ) {
    if (selectedDocument==null) {
      alert("No Document Selected");
      return false;
    }
    pForm.id.value = selectedDocument;
    setAddLink( pForm, linkPage );
}
```

Listing 18-8.   (continued)

```
function docDelete( pForm ) {
    if (selectedDocument==null) {
      alert("No Document Selected");
      return false;
    }
    if (confirm("Confirm delete of " + selectedDocument)) {
      pForm.delAction.value="DELETE";
      pForm.id.value = selectedDocument;
      setAddLink( pForm, <?MIVAR>"$MIval"<?/MIVAR> );
    }
}
function doReset(pform) {
    selectedDocument=null;
    pform.reset();
}
</script>
</head>

<body bgcolor="#FFFFFF" text="#000000" link="#660066"
      vlink="#996699" alink="#6699FF">


<CENTER><h2>View Documents</h2></CENTER>

<?MIBLOCK COND=$(AND,$(XST,$delAction),$(EQ,$delAction,DELETE))>
<?MISQL SQL="delete from appDocuments where id = '$id';"><?/MISQL>
<?/MIBLOCK>

<?MIVAR>
<form method="POST" action="$WEB_HOME">
<INPUT TYPE=HIDDEN NAME=MIval VALUE=viewhelp>
<INPUT TYPE=HIDDEN NAME=id>
<INPUT TYPE=HIDDEN NAME=delAction>


  <table border="0" width="100%">
    <tr>
      <td width="28%" align=left><font face="arial, helvetica">
          <small><u><strong>Name</strong></u></small></font></td>
      <td width="5%" align=left><font face="arial, helvetica">
          <small><u><strong></strong></u></small></font></td>
```

Listing 18-8. *(continued)*

```
        <td width="37%" align=left><font face="arial, helvetica">
            <small><u><strong>Description</strong></u></small>
            </font></td>
        <td width="30%" align=left><font face="arial, helvetica">
            <small><u><strong>Document Type</strong>
            </u></small></font></td>
    </tr>
<?/MIVAR>

<?MIERROR NAME=HANDLEERR>
Error selecting Help Documents
<?/MIERROR>

<?MISQL
  ERR=HANDLEERR
  SQL="SELECT h.id, m.mime_name, h.description, h.object, h.mime_type
     FROM appDocuments h, appmimetypes m
      where h.mime_type = m.mime_type">
    <tr>
      <td width="28%"><font face="arial, helvetica">
          <small><A HREF="$WEB_HOME?LO=$4&type=$5"
          onMouseOver="window.status='Click to View'; return
          true;">$1</A></small></font></td>
      <td width="5%"><font face="arial, helvetica">
          <small></small><input type="radio" value="$1"
          name="selectedHelp" onClick="selectDocument(this.value);">
          <small></small></font></td>
      <td width="37%"><font face="arial,
helvetica"><small>$3</small></font></td>
      <td width="30%"><font face="arial,
helvetica"><small>$2</small></font></td>
    </tr>
<?/MISQL>

  </table><font face="arial, helvetica"><small>

<CENTER>
  <p>
      <input type="reset" value="Reset" name="B2"
          onClick="doReset(this.form);">
```

Listing 18-8.   (continued)

```
          <input type="submit" value="Add" name="addDocument"
                 onClick="setAddLink(this.form,this.name);">
          <input type="button" value="Edit" name="editDocument"
                 onClick="docSelected(this.form,this.name);">
          <input type="button" value="Delete" name="deletedocument"
                 onClick="docDelete(this.form);"></p>

</CENTER>
</form>
</font></body>
</html>
```

Downloading Documents

You download a document by clicking the Name link. When clicked,
the webdriver URL is actioned by the web server, and webdriver is
invoked to fetch the large object and construct the HTTP header for
the browser. The content-type attribute of the HTTP header will be
set to the document_type of the document (which is the same as the
MIME type).

For example, clicking the Book Image link will result in a GIF
image being extracted from the Informix database and displayed
on its own in the browser window. Figure 18-9 illustrates this. The
browser handles MIME types of type image/gif.

Figure 18-9. *Viewing the* Book Image *content item.*

Suppose that the browser has no plug-in for the document being downloaded. For example, assuming that the browser does not have an Microsoft Word plug-in. When an Microsoft Word document is selected for downloading, a dialog similar to Fig. 18-10 may be displayed.

If you decide to open the document, then Microsoft Word is invoked on the browser client, and the downloaded document is passed to it. If you want to save the document back to the repository, save the document locally, and then use the Edit Documents screen to reload the file from the client.

End-to-End MIME Type Mappings

Figure 18-11 shows the Data Director for Web extension mappings for large objects that were imported into the Data Director for Web schema with an extension of DOC.

Using Netscape Navigator, for example, you can set new helper application preferences that use the HTTP header attribute content-type to map onto the browser handling of that content. Figure 18-12 shows the details for handling Microsoft Word documents.

When an Microsoft Word document is extracted from the database and downloaded to the browser, the browser will map the

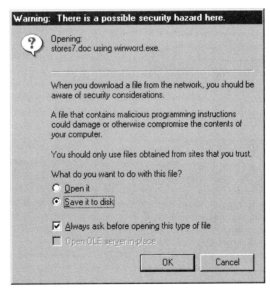

Figure 18-10. *Downloading a Microsoft Word document.*

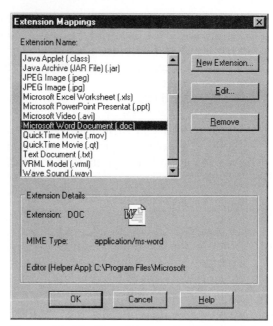

Figure 18-11. *Data Director for Web extension mapping for Microsoft Word documents.*

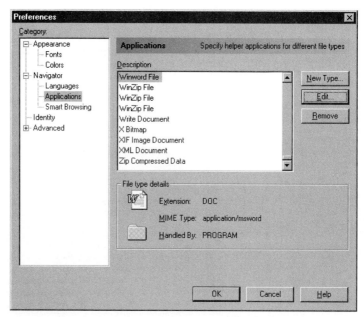

Figure 18-12. *Netscape Navigator application preferences for Microsoft Word.*

content-type `application/msword` with the configured helper application, and pass the document to the helper.

Data Director for Web stores large object references in its own schema (table `wbBinaries`). When `webdriver` retrieves a large object, it knows from `web.cnf` that, unless otherwise directed, it will take the LO handle and the MIME type for the object from the `wbBinaries` table entry for that object.

In our example, we store object references in the `appDocuments` table. Data Director for Web objects and our objects will reside in the same default smart blobspace, but in our example, the LO handle is stored in the `appDocuments` table. The `viewDocuments.html` AppPage retrieves the LO handle from the `appDocuments` table and parameterizes the `Name` hyperlink with it.

AppPage Script to Create the `webdriver` URL

If large object caching is enabled and the document is in cache, the large object will be retrieved from cache.

The document information is taken from the `appDocuments` table as follows:

```
SELECT h.id, m.mime_name, h.description,
       h.object, h.mime_type
FROM appDocuments h, appmimetypes m
WHERE h.mime_type = m.mime_type
```

A `webdriver` hyperlink is specified in the AppPage that is formed from the data extracted in the above query:

```
<A HREF="$WEB_HOME?LO=$4&type=$5"
        onMouseOver="window.status='Click to View';
        return true;">$1</A>
```

The object column, $4, contains the LO handle of the document. The `mime_type` column, $5, contains the MIME type of the document. The link text is the name of the document.

The View Documents AppPage

Listing 18-8 shows the `viewDocuments.html` AppPage. Figure 18-13 following shows the View Documents screen.

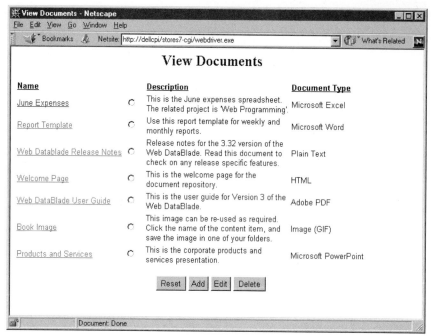

Figure 18-13. *The AppPage* `viewDocuments.html` *rendered in the browser.*

Adding Documents to the Content Repository

Listing 18-9 shows the `addDocument.html` AppPage. This AppPage contains a form that captures the document metadata and the document object and inserts this information into the database. The AppPage is broken down into two sections: form data capture on the client, and form data processing on the database server.

Using ENCTYPE for Document Upload

Because the form will be uploading documents from the client, the encoding of the form is set explicitly as follows:

```
<form method="POST" action="$WEB_HOME"
     ENCTYPE="multipart/form-data"
   onsubmit="return Form1_Validator(this)"
   name="Form1">
```

Listing 18-9. *The* `addDocument.html` *AppPage.*

```
<html>
<head>
<title>Add Document</title>
</head>

<?MIERROR ERR=HANDLEERR>
Error in Select from appmimetypes
<?/MIERROR>

<?MIERROR ERR=INSERTERROR>
Error in insert into appDocuments
<?/MIERROR>

<?contentHeader link="Add Document">
<?jsValidation>

<?MIVAR>
<form method="POST" action="$WEB_HOME" ENCTYPE="multipart/form-data"
      onsubmit="return Form1_Validator(this)"
name="Form1">
<?/MIVAR>
<input TYPE="hidden" NAME="MIval" VALUE="addDocument">
<input TYPE="hidden" NAME="action" VALUE="on">

</font>
<table border="0" width="101%">
    <tr>
      <td valign="middle" align="right"><font face="arial,
      helvetica"><small><strong>Name: </strong></small></font></td>
      <td valign="middle"><font face="arial, helvetica">
          <input type="text" name="id" size="20"
          maxlength="40"></font></td>
      <td valign="middle"><font face="arial, helvetica"></font></td>
    </tr>
    <tr>
      <td valign="middle" align="right"><font face="arial,
      helvetica"><small><strong>Document Type:
      </strong></small></font></td>
```

Listing 18-9.   (continued)

```
      <td valign="middle"><font face="arial, helvetica"><small>
        <select name="mime_type" size="1">
          <?MISQL ERR=HANDLEERR SQL="select mime_name, mime_type
          from appmimetypes">
            <OPTION VALUE='$2'>$1
          <?/MISQL>
      </select></small></font></td>
      <td valign="middle"><font face="arial, helvetica"></font></td>
    </tr>
    <tr>
      <td align="right"><font face="arial, helvetica">
      <small><strong>Description:</strong></small></font></td>
      <td ><font face="arial, helvetica"><textarea rows="4"
      name="description" cols="30"></textarea></font></td>
    </tr>
    <tr>
      <td  align="right"><font face="arial,
      helvetica"><strong><small>Document
      Location:</small></strong></font></td>
      <td ><font face="arial, helvetica"><input type="file"
      name="object" size="30"></font></td>
    </tr>
    <tr>
      <td  align="right"><font face="arial, helvetica">
       </font></td>
      <td >
       <font face="arial, helvetica"><small>
       <input type="submit" value="Add Document" name="add">
       <input type="reset" value="Reset" name="B2">
       <input type=submit value="Show Documents" name="showDocs"
       onClick="this.form.MIval.value='viewDocuments';return
       true;"></small>
       </font></td>
    </tr>
  </table><font face="arial, helvetica">
</form>


<?MIBLOCK COND=$(NXST,$description)>
<?MIVAR NAME=$description><?/MIVAR>
<?/MIBLOCK>
```

Listing 18-9. *(continued)*

```
<?MIBLOCK COND=$(XST,$action)>

    <?MISQL   ERR=INSERTERR
       SQL="insert into appDocuments
             values (0, '$(REPLACE,$id,',''')',
             '$(REPLACE,$mime_type,',''')',
             '$(REPLACE,$description,',''')', filetoblob(
             '$object','client','appDocuments','object'));">
    <?/MiSQL>
    <strong>The Document <?MIVAR>$id<?/MIVAR> was added to the
    database.</strong>
<?/MIBLOCK>
</font></body>
</html>
```

We can then specify the form field to accept the client document path:

```
<input type="file" name="object" size="30">
```

Selecting the Document Type

The list of document types, or MIME types, is held in the
appmimetypes table. You can use a table like this to control the accepted types of content for your repository, or you can use the
wbExtensions table if you use Data Director for Web and want to use
all the predefined content-types. The purpose of the appmimetypes
table is to map the MIME type of the document we will add with the
document metadata, so that when we want to download this document, webdriver can transfer the MIME type as part of HTTP header
for the document (the content-type attribute of the HTTP header).
The MIME types are rendered in a select list as follows:

```
<select name="mime_type" size="1">
      <?MISQL ERR=HANDLEERR
             SQL="select mime_name, mime_type
                   from appmimetypes">
          <OPTION VALUE='$2'>$1
      <?/MISQL>
</select>
```

Inserting the Document

When the form is submitted, the form fields are added to the document repository, which in our case is the `appDocuments` table. The metadata is processed with the `REPLACE` function to escape any single quotes. The document object is also stored in the database.

The `filetoblob()` function is used to take the file that has been transferred from the client to the web server and insert it into the `appDocuments` table. The value of the `$object` variable is set to the path of the object that has been transferred to the web server, which may include `MI_WEBUPLOADDIR` if this `webdriver` variable has been set. The following snippet shows the `insert` statement that adds the document to the database:

```
<?MISQL   ERR=INSERTERR
   SQL="insert into appDocuments  values (
        0, '$(REPLACE,$id,','')',
        '$(REPLACE,$mime_type,','')',
        '$(REPLACE,$description,','')',
        filetoblob('$object','client',
                  'appDocuments','object'));">
<?/MISQL>
```

The Add Document AppPage

Listing 18-9 shows the `addDocument.html` AppPage.

Figure 18-14 shows `addDocument.html` rendered as the Add Document Screen

Figure 18-15 shows the Add Document screen *after* a document has been inserted into the database.

Editing Content Metadata and Replacing the Document

You enter the Edit Document screen by clicking one of the radio buttons on the View Documents screen, and then clicking the `Edit` button. You can change the content metadata in the Edit Document screen. You can also replace the document reference that was held in the repository by uploading another document. The `Document Type` of the edited document is selected by default.

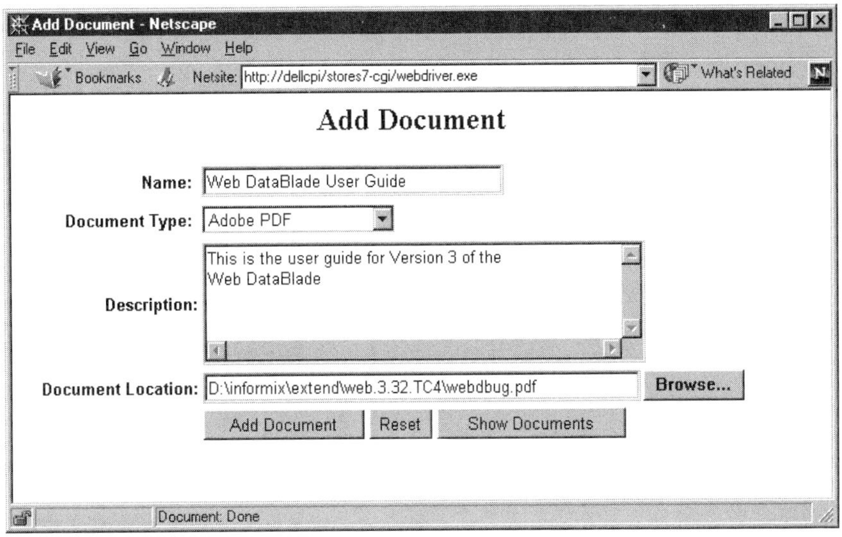

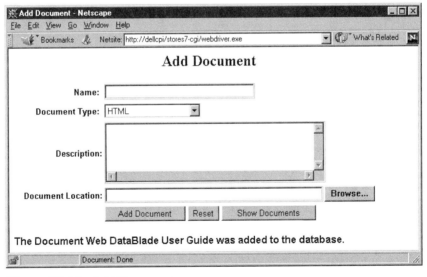

Figure 18-14. *Add Document screen.*

Figure 18-15. *Add Document screen.*

When `editDocument.html` is processed by `webexplode()`, the document metadata is selected from the `appDocuments` table as follows:

```
<?MISQL  COND=$(NXST,$action)
    SQL="select unique id, mime_type, description
         from appDocuments where id = '$id';">
         $(SETVAR,$oldid,$1)
         $(SETVAR,$mime_type,$2)
         $(SETVAR,$description,$3)
<?/MISQL>
```

The `$id` variable is passed as a form field from `viewDocuments.html`. The `$oldid` variable set in the above snippet is used to update the original record. The form fields are populated with the contents of the database as follows (using the `description` field as an example):

```
<textarea rows="4"
name="description" cols="30">$description</textarea>
```

Updating the `appDocuments` Table

The metadata and, optionally, the client file, are used to update the `appDocuments` table when the user clicks the Apply button. The following snippet shows the `update` statement:

```
<?MISQL  ERR=UPDATEERR
   SQL="update appDocuments
        set id = '$(REPLACE,$id,',''')',
        mime_type =  '$(REPLACE,$mime_type,',''')',
        description = '$(REPLACE,$description,',''')',
        object = filetoblob('$object',
                 'client','appDocuments','object')
        where id = '$old_id';">
<?/MISQL>
```

The `filetoblob()` function will create a new large object and assign the object's new handle to the `appDocuments.object` column. If the user did not specify a new file to upload, another UPDATE statement is used to exclude the update of the object column. Using the following test, the AppPage can detect if the object has or has not been uploaded:

```
<?MIBLOCK COND=$(XST,$object)>
```

The Edit Document AppPage

Listing 18-10 shows the `editDocument.html` AppPage. Figure 18-16 shows the Edit Document screen after changes have been applied.

Listing 18-10. *The* `editDocument.html` *AppPage.*

```
<html>
<head>
<title>Edit Document</title>
</head>

<?MIERROR ERR=UPDATEERR>
Error in Update into appDocuments: $MI_ERRORMSG
<?/MIERROR>

<?MIERROR ERR=SELECTERR>
Error in Select from appDocuments: $MI_ERRORMSG
<?/MIERROR>

<?contentHeader title="Edit Document">
<?jsValidation>

<?MISQL  COND=$(NXST,$action) SQL="select unique id, mime_type,
             description from appDocuments where id = '$id';">
     $(SETVAR,$oldid,$1)
     $(SETVAR,$mime_type,$2)
     $(SETVAR,$description,$3)
<?/MISQL>

<?MIVAR>
<form name="form1" method="POST" action="$WEB_HOME"
     ENCTYPE="multipart/form-data"
     onsubmit="return Form1_Validator(this)"
     name="FrontPage_Form1">
<?/MIVAR>
<input TYPE="hidden" NAME="MIval" VALUE="editDocument">
<input TYPE="hidden" NAME="action" VALUE="on">
<input TYPE="hidden" NAME="old_id"
<?MIBLOCK COND=$(NXST,$action)>
     VALUE=<?MIVAR>"$oldid"<?/MIVAR>
<?/MIBLOCK>
<?MIBLOCK COND=$(XST,$action)>
     VALUE=<?MIVAR>"$id"<?/MIVAR>
<?/MIBLOCK>
</font>
<?MIVAR>
<table border="0" width="101%">
```

Listing 18-10.   (continued)

```
   <tr>
     <td valign="middle" align="right">
        <font face="arial, helvetica"><small><strong>Name:
        </strong></small></font></td>
     <td valign="middle"><font face="arial, helvetica">
        <input type="text" name="id" size="20" maxlength="40"
              value="$id"></font></td>
     <td valign="middle"><font face="arial, helvetica">
                          </font></td>
   </tr>
   <tr>
     <td valign="middle" align="right">
     <font face="arial, helvetica"><small>
        <strong>Document Type: </strong></small></font></td>
     <td valign="middle">
        <font face="arial, helvetica"><small>
<?/MIVAR>
     <select name="mime_type" size="1">
       <?MISQL  SQL="select mime_name, mime_type
                  from appmimetypes
                    where mime_type = '$mime_type'">
        <OPTION VALUE='$2' SELECTED>$1
       <?/MISQL>
       <?MISQL  SQL="select mime_name, mime_type
                  from appmimetypes
                    where mime_type != '$mime_type'">
        <OPTION VALUE='$2'>$1
       <?/MISQL>
     </select></small></font></td>
<?MIVAR>
     <td valign="middle">
        <font face="arial, helvetica"></font></td>
   </tr>
   <tr>
     <td align="right"><font face="arial, helvetica"><small>
        <strong>Description:</strong></small></font></td>
     <td ><font face="arial, helvetica">
       <textarea rows="4" name="description" cols="30">
          $description
       </textarea></font></td>
   </tr>
```

Listing 18-10.   (continued)

```
<tr>
  <td  align="right">
     <font face="arial, helvetica"><strong>
     <small>Document Location:</small></strong></font>
  </td>
  <td ><font face="arial, helvetica">
     <input type="file" name="object"
            size="30"></font></td>
</tr>
<tr>
  <td  align="right">
  <td >
    <input type="submit" value="Apply" name="add">
    <input type="reset" value="Reset" name="B2">
    <input type=submit value="Show Documents"
            name="showDocs"
            onClick="this.form.MIval.value='viewDocuments';
                     return true;">
  </td>
</tr>
</table><font face="arial, helvetica">
</form>
<?/MIVAR>

<?MIBLOCK COND=$(NXST,$description)>
<?MIVAR NAME=$description><?/MIVAR>
<?/MIBLOCK>
<?MIBLOCK COND=$(XST,$action)>

  <?MIBLOCK COND=$(XST,$object)>
  <?MISQL  ERR=UPDATEERR
    SQL="update appDocuments
        set id = '$(REPLACE,$id,',''')',
            mime_type =  '$(REPLACE,$mime_type,',''')',
            description =  '$(REPLACE,$description,',''')',
            object = filetoblob('$object','client',
                     'appDocuments','object')
        where id = '$old_id';">
  <?/MiSQL>
  <?/MIBLOCK>
```

Listing 18-10.   (continued)

```
    <?MIBLOCK COND=$(NXST,$object)>
    <?MISQL   ERR=UPDATEERR
      SQL="update appDocuments
           set id = '$(REPLACE,$id,',''')',
               mime_type =  '$(REPLACE,$mime_type,',''')',
               description =  '$(REPLACE,$description,',''')'
           where id = '$old_id';">
    <?/MiSQL>
    <?/MIBLOCK>
    <strong>The Document <?MIVAR> $old_id has been updated.
<?/MIVAR></strong>
<?/MIBLOCK>
</font></body>
</html>
```

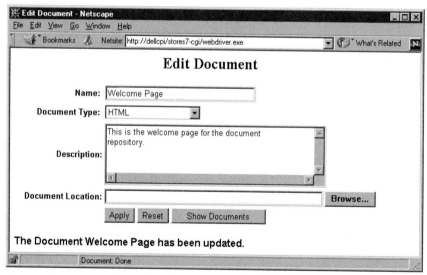

Figure 18-16. The Edit Document screen after changes have been applied.

Figure 18-17. Confirmatory prompt for delete document.

Deleting a Document

From the View Documents screen, the user can delete a document by selecting one of the Radio buttons next to the document name, and then clicking the Delete button. A confirmatory dialog is displayed that allows the user to cancel or proceed. For example, if the user selected to delete the Web DataBlade User Guide, the dialog in Figure 18-17 would appear.

If OK is clicked, `viewDocuments.html` is reinvoked and the deletion is performed, as follows:

```
<?MISQL SQL="delete from appDocuments
        where id = '$id';"><?/MISQL>
```

The contents of the `appDocuments` table are then reselected.

Summary

This chapter has implemented a basic content repository, which allows you to store any kind of object in the Informix database and then select the object for viewing in the browser. The concept of content metadata was developed. In order to view objects in the browser, we learned how to store the content-type of the data in the repository so that we can tell the browser how to render it on demand. The chapter has also shown how to upload client files via forms and how to change the content-type of objects dynamically according to how we want to view the information. At the start of the chapter, we also saw how relevant the chapter example is to the intranet information repository element of the customer solution cycle outlined in Chap. 3. In summary, you now have a simple but effective working application to interface your desktop with the database.

Creating and Using Dynamic Tags

In this chapter:

Maintaining websites can be a costly business. To start with, the website has to be created. The site should have a common look and feel. Then you need to manage the rendering of dynamic content within that look and feel. Once the site is live, you will need to apply changes to the site; new pages, changes due to user feedback, a new company logo; a new product attribute in the product table that needs to be displayed to the user. The cost of maintaining a website is often overlooked. Every web page has a cost to create, and a cost to maintain. The trouble with building web page applications is that it is all too easy to go your own way and reinvent the wheel. This chapter will show you how, using the *dynamic tag* facilities of the Web DataBlade, you can reduce the maintenance requirements of your website substantially, and allow your web projects to create and maintain websites using a common code repository.

What Are Dynamic Tags?

A dynamic tag is an AppPage Scripting tag that you can create yourself as if it were an HTML or standard AppPage Scripting tag. Dynamic tags allow AppPage segments to be shared among multiple AppPages. This reduces maintenance requirements and centralizes the source of updates to web applications.

Dynamic tags can be created using any text editor, but they are registered in the Informix database using AppPage Builder or Data Director for Web. The dynamic tag is stored in the AppPage Builder or Data Director for Web schema. You can also manually insert the dynamic tag into the appropriate table from an `.sql` script using SQL Editor or `dbaccess`.

Dynamic tags allow you to specify standard components that appear on every AppPage, such as headers and footers. Since dynamic tags are expanded along with the AppPage tags by the `webexplode` function, changes made to a dynamic tag are automatically applied to all AppPages that include that dynamic tag. Informix products, such as Data Director for Web and AppPage Builder, provide several *system dynamic tags,* as well as the ability to create your own *user dynamic tags.*

When you install the Data Director for Web product or the AppPage Builder product that comes with the Web DataBlade, you are given several useful dynamic tags.

Why Use Dynamic Tags?

Using dynamic tags allows you to realize several benefits.

- At the simplest level, you can use a dynamic tag as an AppPage fragment to include in another AppPage.
- You can then add parameters to the dynamic tag to customize its behavior by using standard AppPage Scripting tags or other dynamic tags.
- AppPage segments can be shared among multiple AppPages.
- AppPage maintenance requirements are reduced.
- Updates to web applications become centralized.
- You are able to specify standard components that appear on every AppPage in your web application.
- The need for HTML programmers to know how to write SQL queries is eliminated, since the tag can perform the query.

Varieties of Dynamic Tag Applications

Dynamic tags can be created for a variety of uses. The list below is by no means exhaustive. The idea is to reuse code in a variety of contexts.

Web Page Headers

A dynamic tag can be created to render a standard header for every web page in the website. You can also parameterize this header tag to create links depending on the content of the web page.

Web Page Footers

A dynamic tag can also be used to render a standard footer for every web page in the website. You can, for example, create a footer that contains the webmaster mail address and some copyright information.

Web Page Look and Feel

You can use a dynamic tag to create a standard look and feel for the web page by creating a tag that contains information about the background image, link color, text color, and fonts.

JavaScript Form Validation and Error Handling

Dynamic tags can be created to implement JavaScript form field validation, for example, JavaScript date validation, text size validation, lettercase sensitivity, mandatory attribute requirements, and so forth. The JavaScript is defined once in the tag and is instantiated in every AppPage that requires this validation. A dynamic tag can also be created that implements JavaScript error handling, especially when using forms. If an error occurs when processing a form on the browser client, JavaScript can take control to display a popup alert box or fetch another web page from the server. The JavaScript is defined once in the tag and is instantiated in every AppPage that requires this error handling.

AppPage Generic Error Handling

A dynamic tag can be used in every AppPage that requires a generic error handler. This error handler is created once but is reused again and again in different web pages, thus enabling consistent error-handling behavior across a website.

Customized Option Lists with JavaScript Event Handlers

You can use a dynamic tag to create a select list, checkbox list, or radio button list with common JavaScript event-handling behavior. For example, you may want to define common behavior when changing the values of these form fields. Data Director for Web and AppPage Builder come with dynamic tags to create these option lists, but you can extend these or create your own to provide a more event-based treatment of the form fields.

Common Forms and Forms Results Processing

You may want to create a number of forms that can be reused across your site, thus giving a standard interface to table data, which preempts the inconsistent table treatment inevitable with a variety of coders.

Standard SQL Filters

You may have an installation where some SQL queries in the application require a standard filter. For example, a user will log into a web application in the corporate intranet. Each user may be able to see only database content specific to his or her department. There-fore, most queries may involve specifying a department filter in the WHERE clause of the SQL. You can use a dynamic tag to create this functionality once so that the functionality can be reused across the site. Using SQL filters like this allows you to create arbitrarily complex SQL expressions that implement application rules. You can make SQL parameterization as simple or complicated as you like; the trick is to identify reusable functionality.

Schema Encapsulation

It is possible to define an interface for every application table in the database. This interface would handle selection, insertion, deletion, and updates to the table. The dynamic tag would be parameterized in such a way as to accept the relevant data and perform the associated operation to the table. By defining a standard interface to the database schema, you are *encapsulating* the database schema and the operations to manipulate the tables in that schema, thus virtually eliminating the requirement for a web programmer to understand SQL. The definition of such an interface would take place in the design phase of a web project.

While dynamic tags will eliminate the need for most users of the tags to write SQL, it does not eliminate their need to understand the concepts behind relational databases.

Dynamic Menus

You can use dynamic tags to create dynamic menus. Suppose you needed to create a menu navigation panel in one frame that changed as you navigated your way through a site, and the menu options were stored in the database. Instead of hardcoding the menu options or hardcoding the SQL to render the menu options, you would create a dynamic tag to contain the SQL and to format the menu option results. You would implement the dynamic tag in each frame that required it.

Context-sensitive Help

You can implement context-sensitive help with HTML and Java-Script using dynamic tags. For example, if every form field contained a Tip or Help hyperlink (or button), then a dynamic tag could define the behavior and context of the help by accepting parameters from the link. Using AppPage Script, the form field details are passed to the relevant dynamic tag as parameters, and the generated code is defined accordingly.

It is better to create dynamic tags than to code inline on the web page. You only need to change the tag, not the web page. If the tag is used throughout the website, you have also avoided changes to individual pages in multiple locations.

Structure of a Dynamic Tag

Every dynamic tag has the components listed in Table 19-1.

Specifying Dynamic Tag Parameters

Parameters and tag attributes are synonymous when using dynamic tags. Parameters allow you to modify the behavior of a dynamic tag depending on parameter values. Remember that, when you use AppPage Scripting tags, each tag has a set of attributes that you can set; some are mandatory, some are optional. When you use HTML tags, you specify attributes and values in the same way (for example, the ACTION attribute of the FORM tag). These attributes for the dynamic tag are called parameters, and when you instantiate a dynamic tag in an AppPage, you pass parameters to the tag as if they were attributes to the tag.

Table 19-1. *Fundamental dynamic tag components.*

Tag component	Description
ID	Mandatory. Identifies the tag.
description	Optional. Describes the tag.
parameters	Optional. Describes the parameter specification.
tag body	Can contain HTML, JavaScript, and AppPage Script.
class	Optional. A code that can be used by a custom retrieval mechanism to categorize different types of dynamic tags.

Syntax of Dynamic Tag Parameters

Parameters in the parameters column are separated by an ampersand (&). You can assign a default value to a parameter by specifying the parameter and its value as a name/value pair. A parameter that does not need a default value is specified by the parameter followed by an equal sign (=) with no value following.

Parameters are delimited by a commercial at (@) before *and* after the parameter name within the body of the dynamic tag.

When a dynamic tag is encountered in an AppPage, the tag is verified to check that all parameters requiring a value are assigned a value. Following the definition of the dynamic tag, the tag can be invoked in any AppPage.

Passing AppPage Variables to Dynamic Tags

All attributes are passed as literal text into the dynamic tag. If you want to pass a variable into a dynamic tag and then use the value, then you must use the dynamic tag parameter only where variables are evaluated in the body of the dynamic tag. For example, if you wanted to display the value of `$emp_name` in the `display_image` tag, you would have to put `MIVAR` tags around it. Given the dynamic tag

```
<?doSql SQL_CODE=$sql_statement>
```

then the parameter `$sql_statement` needs to be coded as follows in the `doSql` dynamic tag body:

```
<?MIVAR>@SQL_CODE@<?/MIVAR>
```

which evaluates to

```
<?MIVAR>$sql_statement<?/MIVAR>
```

> **tip**
>
> *If you use a parameter in the body of the dynamic tag but have not defined it in the parameter section, then the parameter is classed as mandatory. If you do not pass a value to this parameter,* webexplode *will report an error. You can avoid this by adding the parameter name in the parameter section of the dynamic tag declaration and giving it no value. For example,* &myParam=&myOtherParam=.

Dynamic tags accept variables, variable expressions, and constants as parameter values. The `COND` attribute to AppPage tags is also a valid attribute for a dynamic tag. The `COND` attribute specifies a condition that is evaluated before the tag is processed. If the condition is true, the tag is processed. The COND attribute can also involve variable expressions.

The COND attribute of a dynamic tag is evaluated once, when the tag is encountered in an AppPage. This means that the subsequent state of any variables used will not affect the outcome of the COND attribute.

Escaping Special Characters

In order to place a commercial "@" symbol in a dynamic tag, you must use a special parameter.

For example, enter the following in your parameter field:

```
&ATSIGN=@
```

Enter the following in the dynamic tag field:

```
<HR>
<A HREF="mailto:webmaster@ATSIGN@yourcompany.com">
webmaster@ATSIGN@yourcompany.com</A>
```

In the snippet above, @ATSIGN@ has been assigned the value of "@" via a static parameter.

Example with Parameters

The following example shows how to use parameters in various ways. The example creates a dynamic tag called parameterExample, and an AppPage called tagParameters.html that will instantiate the dynamic tag by parameterizing a reference to it, in order to render sections of a web page.

Listing 19-1 shows the dynamic tag body, and List. 19-2 shows the AppPage that references the parameterExample dynamic tag. Listing 19-3 shows the HTML sent back to the browser by webexplode, and Fig. 19-1 shows the browser display of List. 19-3.

Listing 19-1. *The* parameterExample *dynamic tag.*

```
<br><h3>
<?MIVAR>
Parameter 1 has been set to: @param1@<br>
Parameter 2 has been set to: @param2@<br></h3>
<?/MIVAR>
```

```
<h1>Parameter Passing with Dynamic Tags</h1>
<h2>Example to show Parameter Passing</h2>
<LI>No Parameters passed.
<?parameterExample>

<LI>Both Parameters passed.
<?parameterExample param1="This is Parameter One"
                   param2="This is Parameter Two">

<LI>The next example shows how to pass variables as parameters.
<?MIVAR NAME=paramString1>This is the content of a variable<?/MIVAR>
<?MIVAR NAME=paramString2>$paramString1 for parameter 2<?/MIVAR>
<?parameterExample param1=$paramString1
                   param2=$paramString2>

<LI>The next tag will never be evaluated.
<?parameterExample COND=$(=,1,0)>
```

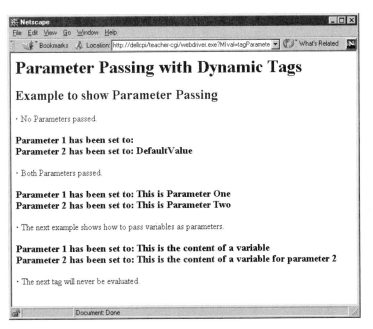

Figure 19-1. *Browser display of List. 19-3.*

Listing 19-3.   HTML sent back to the browser.

```
<h1>Parameter Passing with Dynamic Tags</h1>
<h2>Example to show Parameter Passing</h2>
<LI>No Parameters passed.
<br><h3>

Parameter 1 has been set to: <br>
Parameter 2 has been set to: DefaultValue<br></h3>

<LI>Both Parameters passed.
<br><h3>

Parameter 1 has been set to: This is Parameter One<br>
Parameter 2 has been set to: This is Parameter Two<br></h3>

<LI>The next example shows how to pass variables as parameters.

<br><h3>

Parameter 1 has been set to: This is the content of a
variable<br>
Parameter 2 has been set to: This is the content of a variable
for parameter 2<br></h3>

<LI>The next tag will never be evaluated.
```

What the Example Does

Using `tagParameters.html` (List. 19-2), the example shows the following:

- The first invocation of `parameterExample` uses the defaults assigned to the tag parameters.
- The second invocation sets both parameter values.
- The third invocation sets the two parameters to the contents of AppPage variables. Note that the variables are expanded within the tag using `<?MIVAR>`.
- The fourth example shows how to code a tag with the COND attribute. This example will never result in the tag being evaluated, since the condition will always evaluate to false.

Defining the `parameterExample` Tag in Data Director for Web

If you use Data Director for Web, then you can edit the properties of the dynamic tag. If you select the property sheet for the dynamic tag in the Site Manager window, then you can modify the tag properties. Figure 19-2 shows the parameter definition for `parameterExample`. Figure 19-3 shows the tag body definition for `parameterExample`.

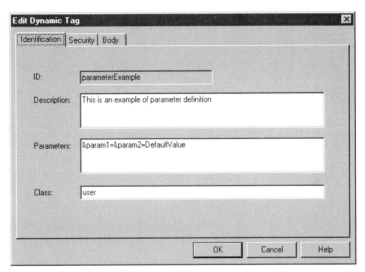

Figure 19-2. Data Director for Web dynamic tag parameter definition.

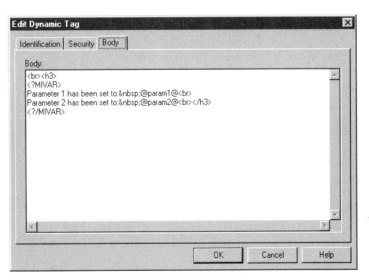

Figure 19-3. Data Director for Web dynamic tag body definition.

Where Are Dynamic Tags Stored?

Dynamic tag definitions are stored in the Informix database in a table that is dedicated to them. Depending on the client application you are using, the name of the table differs. Table 19-2 shows the differences.

The schema definition for the dynamic tag table is different for AppPage Builder and Data Director for Web. AppPage Builder requires a minimal set of attributes to define a tag. Data Director for Web requires more attributes to realize the extra functionality that Data Director for Web allows, such as item locking and dynamic tag versioning (which is not available with AppPage Builder).

Tables 19-3 and 19-4 describe the table attributes for each product table.

In both schemas, the dynamic tag is stored in a column of type HTML, which is a Web DataBlade object type. In addition, the extra Data Director for Web attributes are used to store the values that Data Director for Web uses for repository control. Interestingly, the `wizData` attribute is a `BLOB`. This is used to store the values of the tag when the Data Director for Web dynamic tag wizard is used to create the dynamic tag.

Table 19-2. Dynamic tag master tables.

Product	Table
App Page Builder	`webTags`
Data Director for Web	`wbTags`

Table 19-3. Attributes of the APB `webTags` table.

Attribute	Description
`ID`	The tag name.
`parameters`	The parameters passed to the tag.
`class`	The class of the tag.
`description`	Description of the tag.
`content`	The content of the tag as an HTML object type.

Table 19-4. **Attributes of the Data Director for Web** `wbTags` **table.**

Attribute	Description
ID	The tag name.
parameters	The parameters passed to the tag.
class	The class of the tag.
description	Description of the tag.
object	The content of the tag as an HTML object type.
current_version	The current version of the tag.
last_changed	When the tag was last modified.
last_changed_by	The user who last changed the tag.
last_locked	When the tag was last locked.
last_locked_by	The user that locked the tag.
wizData	The properties of the tag; only for tags generated by Data Director for Web wizard.

When Are Dynamic Tags Processed?

When `webexplode` encounters a dynamic tag in an AppPage, the body of the dynamic tag is substituted for the tag identifier. If you specify a tag within your AppPage that is not defined in the relevant tags table, no error is generated and the tag is returned unaffected in the `webexplode` function output as if it were text.

Note that the names of system defined AppPage tags (such as `MIVAR`) take precedence over the names of dynamic tags.

System Dynamic Tags

System dynamic tags are provided when you install Data Director for Web or AppPage Builder. They are stored in the `wbTags` or `webTags` table, respectively.

AppPage Builder Dynamic Tags

These tags are installed with APB, and are listed in Table 19-5. They are a useful introduction to using dynamic tags if you use APB as the development environment.

Table 19-5.   Tags specific to AppPage Builder.

System dynamic tag	Description
APB_ERROR	Displays error diagnostics on the web page. Use this tag to display error codes and diagnostic text returned from the Informix database server.
APB_IMG	Generates an IMG tag for an image in the webImages table, using the image ID as the key. The tag will fetch the height, width, and MIME type if defined, and, will use the LO handle for the image from the object column in the webImages table.
APB_IMG_URL	Generates a URL for an image in the webImages table using the image ID as the key.
APB_INPUT_IMG	Generate an INPUT tag with TYPE=image for an image in the webImages table, using the image ID as the key.
APB_PAGE_URL	Generates a URL for an AppPage in the webPages table, using the page ID as the key.

Essential Dynamic Tags For Forms

There are three essential system dynamic tags that both APB and Data Director for Web use, and they are listed in Table 19-6.

The CHECKBOXLIST Tag

The CHECKBOXLIST system dynamic tag simplifies the creation of an HTML checkbox list based on the attributes you specify. The CHECKBOXLIST has the tag attributes listed in Table 19-7.

Using the CHECKBOXLIST Dynamic Tag

The next example, in List. 19-4, shows how to use the CHECKBOXLIST dynamic tag. The example uses the CHECKBOXLIST dynamic tag to

Table 19-6.   Essential dynamic tags for forms.

System dynamic tag	Description
CHECKBOXLIST	Creates an HTML checkbox list.
RADIOLIST	Creates an HTML radio list.
SELECTLIST	Creates an HTML select list.

Table 19-7. The CHECKBOXLIST tag attributes.

Attribute	Mandatory?	Description
NAME	Yes	Specifies the form name of the checkbox.
SQL	Yes	The SQL statement that will return a list of items that will form the set of checkboxes.
CHECKED	No	The SQL statement that will return a list of items that are initially checked.
CHECKONE	No	Specifies the value of an item that is initially checked.
PRE	No	The text that precedes every checkbox field.
POST	No	The text that follows every checkbox field.

Listing 19-4. AppPage to select states with at least one customer and to check those states with more than one customer.

```
<h1>States with Customers</h1>
<form name=MyForm
   method=POST action=<?MIVAR>$WEB_HOME<?/MIVAR>

<?mivar>
  <input type=hidden name="MIval" value="$MIval">
<?/mivar>

<?CHECKBOXLIST
   NAME="myCheckBox"
   SQL="select distinct sname from state s, customer c
      where s.code=c.state "
   PRE="State: " POST="<BR>"
   CHECKED="select sname from state s,customer c
         where s.code=c.state and s.code in (
select state from customer group by 1 having count(*) > 1)")

<br>
* Checked states contain more than one customer

</form>
```

select all states from the `state` table (in the `stores7` database) that
have at least one customer, and then it sets the `CHECKED` attribute for
those states that have more than one customer.

Figure 19-4 shows the browser output for List. 19-4.

The `RADIOLIST` Tag

The `RADIOLIST` system dynamic tag simplifies the creation of an
HTML form radio button list based on the attributes you specify. The
`RADIOLIST` has the tag attributes listed in Table 19-8.

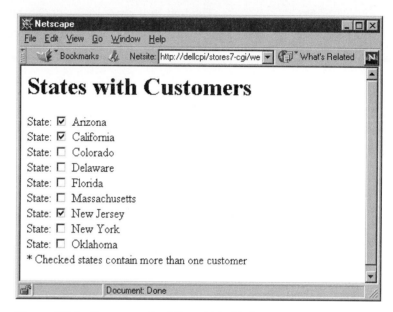

Figure 19-4. *Browser output from List. 19-4.*

Table 19-8. *The* `RADIOLIST` *tag attributes.*

Attribute	Mandatory?	Description
NAME	Yes	Specifies the Form name of the radio button list.
SQL	Yes	The SQL statement that will return a list of items to form the radio button list.
CHECKED	No	The SQL statement that will return a list of items that are initially selected; for a radio list, you require a singleton select.

Table 19-8. *(continued)*

CHECKONE	No	Specifies the value of an item that is initially selected.
PRE	No	The text that precedes every checkbox field.
POST	No	The text that follows every checkbox field.

Listing 19-5. *AppPage source to select all manufacturers.*

```
<h1>Select a Manufacturer</h1>
<FORM name=MyForm method=POST action=<?MIVAR>$WEB_HOME<?/MIVAR>

<?RADIOLIST
   NAME="myCheckBox"
   SQL="select manu_name from manufact order by 1"
   PRE="<b>" POST="</b><BR>"
   CHECKED="select manu_name from manufact where lead_time in
            (select min(lead_time) from manufact)">
<br>
<h4>* Selected manufacturer has shortest lead time</h4>
</form>
```

Using the RADIOLIST Dynamic Tag

The next example, List. 19-5, shows how to use `RADIOLIST` to render a radio button list. The example selects all the manufacturers from the `manufact` table (in the `stores7` database), and chooses by default the manufacturer with the smallest lead-time for delivery. Figure 19-5 shows the browser output.

The `SELECTLIST` Tag

The `SELECTLIST` system dynamic tag simplifies the creation of an HTML selection list based on the attributes you specify. The `SELECTLIST` has tag attributes as shown in Table 19-9.

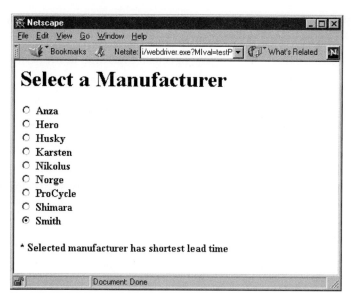

Figure 19-5. *Browser output of List. 19-5.*

Using the SELECTLIST Dynamic Tag

The following example in List. 19-6 performs the same query as the RADIOLIST example, but uses instead two variants of the SELECTLIST tag. The first SELECTLIST displays a SELECT form field that displays selected items in a window that allows five of them

Listing 19-6. *AppPage with different styles of* SELECTLIST *dynamic tag.*

```
<h1>Select a Manufacturer</h1>
<FORM name=MyForm method=POST action=<?MIVAR>$WEB_HOME<?/MIVAR>
<br>
<?SELECTLIST NAME="mySelectList"
     SQL="select manu_name from manufact order by 1"
     SELECTED="select manu_name from manufact where
     lead_time in ( select min(lead_time)
                    from manufact)"
     SIZE="5"
     MULTIPLE>
<h4>* Selected manufacturer has shortest lead time</h4>
<?SELECTLIST NAME="mySelectList"
     SQL="select manu_name from manufact order by 1"
     SELECTED="select manu_name from manufact where
        lead_time in ( select min(lead_time)
                       from manufact)"
     SIZE="1">
</form>
```

to be displayed at once. This is achieved by stating the SIZE attribute to be greater than one and by also setting the MULTIPLE attribute. The second SELECTLIST shows how to create a drop-down select list, from which you can select one item. The second SELECTLIST has no MULTIPLE attribute and has SIZE defined as 1, which enables the drop-down feature. Figure 19-6 shows the browser output.

Using WebBuilder Class Tags in Data Director for Web to Include Database Web Content

Data Director for Web contains extra dynamic tags that are not present in AppPage Builder. These tags are defined as belonging to the webBuilder class, and are used by Data Director for Web to refer to other resources within the Data Director for Web schema. Table 19-10 lists these tags.

You will use these tags as a quick way to generate HTML tags to link and embed web content when that content is stored in the Informix database. For example, you may want to include a link to

Figure 19-6. *Browser output of List. 19-6.*

Dynamic tag	Description
wbEmbed	Embeds a resource in an AppPage using the EMBED tag.
wbImg	Embeds an image in an AppPage using the IMG tag.
wbInclude	Embeds an AppPage in another AppPage using webexplode recursively.
wbLink	Creates an anchor for an AppPage with an optional image link.

a PDF document, or a video file with an avi format. Alternatively, you may want to embed objects such as PDF, audio, and video documents in your web page and use a browser plug-in to work with that content inside the web browser.

Data Director for Web provides wizards to let you put the WebBuilder class dynamic tags together, and these are available in the AppPage editor.

tip   *You can get and set the attributes of all dynamic tags (whether system, WebBuilder, or user) using the Edit Tag menu option for the dynamic tag. Select the dynamic tag in AppPage Editor, right-click, and select Edit Tag.*

tip   *You can get and set the properties of all dynamic tags using the Properties sheet for the dynamic tag. In Site Manager, right-click on the dynamic tag and select Properties. You can set properties such as parameters, description, and the code for the tag body. Alternatively, you can use AppPage Editor to edit the tag body, where you will have access to AppPage Editor wizards.*

The wbEmbed Tag

You use this tag to embed a resource, such as an audio or video object, in an AppPage using the HTML EMBED tag. When the HTML page is downloaded to the browser, the embedded object will be handled by an application or plug-in. Table 19-11 lists the attributes.

Using the wbEmbed Tag to Include Audio Content from the Database

This example will show how to generate the HTML to embed audio links in the web page using the wbEmbed dynamic tag. We want to create an AppPage that embeds an audio object, so that the object will be handled, in the browser window, by a plug-in. In our case, we will use the Netscape LiveAudio plug-in.

We have used Data Director for Web to store the audio document in the Informix database, using the Add Resource option. Figure 19-7 shows the Site Manager view of this document.

We now want to deliver this audio object to the Web. We therefore need to create an AppPage to include a reference to this object so that webdriver will extract it from the database. Once we have

Table 19-11.   *The wbEmbed tag attributes.*

Attribute	Mandatory?	Description
NAME	Yes	Name of object
PATH	No	Path of object, default is "/"
EXT	No	Object extension, e.g., gif
HEIGHT	No	Height of embedded object in HTML page
WIDTH	No	Width of object in HTML page

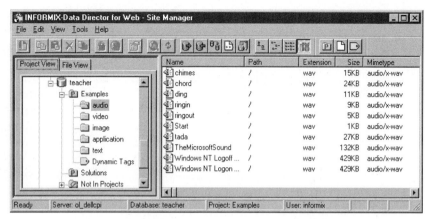

Figure 19-7. *The audio objects stored in the Informix database, showing the* path *and* extension *attributes.*

created the AppPage as a new resource, we edit the page using AppPage Editor. We then use the appropriate Insert Resource wizard in AppPage Editor to create the dynamic tag we require. Later in this chapter, we learn how to use the Insert Resource wizard; for now, we will just look at the resulting dynamic tag.

The following snippet shows the use of this tag:

```
<?wbEmbed name="TheMicrosoftSound" path="/" ext="wav"
width="145" height="60">
```

When the browser receives the HTML page to display, the tag has been converted to the following text.

```
<EMBED SRC="/teacher-cgi/webdriver.exe?MIval=/
TheMicrosoftSound.wav"  WIDTH=145 HEIGHT=60 >
```

Figure 19-8 displays the resulting HTML page.

You may want to extend the webBuilder *tags to* URLENCODE *the name of the object used to eliminate embedded whitespace; otherwise you may receive an error when the links are clicked.*

The wbImg Tag

You use this tag to generate an HTML IMG tag. The default IMG tag properties, such as WIDTH and HEIGHT, come from the wbBinaries table, but you can override this information by setting the tag parameters for HEIGHT, WIDTH, BORDER, ALT and ALIGN. See Table 19-12.

Figure 19-8. *Linked and embedded audio using* `wbLink` *and* `wbEmbed`.

Table 19-12. **The `wbImg` tag attributes.**

Attribute	Mandatory?	Description
NAME	Yes	Name of the image
PATH	No	Path of the image, default is "/"
EXT	No	Extension, e.g., `gif`, `jpeg`, default is `gif`
HEIGHT	No	Image height
WIDTH	No	Image width
BORDER	No	Specifies whether the image has a border
ALT	No	Specifies the popup label for the image
ALIGN	No	Image alignment

Using the `wbImg` Tag to Deliver Image Content from the Database

This example uses the `wbImg` tag to generate the HTML for an `IMG` tag, with the `SRC` attribute pointing to an object in the Informix database. The `wbImg` tag for the globe image is as follows:

```
<?wbImg name="globe" path="/" ext="gif" ALT="This is a
globe.">
```

The HTML delivered to the browser is as follows:

```
<IMG SRC=/teacher-
cgi/webdriver.exe?LO=56a2c988d9c8b7a602000000020000002e
020000b210e0360000000001000000000000006f626a656374520c5
719440090205b0cf8b3520cc338480090205b0c0cb4520c01000000
&MItypeObj=image/gif ALT="This is a globe.">
```

Figure 19-9 renders this object.

You should use the large object (LO) reference where possible to take advantage of server caching of images.

By using a dynamic tag, you can reset content properties in the generated HTML page without changing the AppPage source code. For example, you can change the image description in Site Manager (using the Properties sheet), and the wbImg *tag will yield the correct* ALT *attribute for the* IMG *tag, which is taken from the image description.*

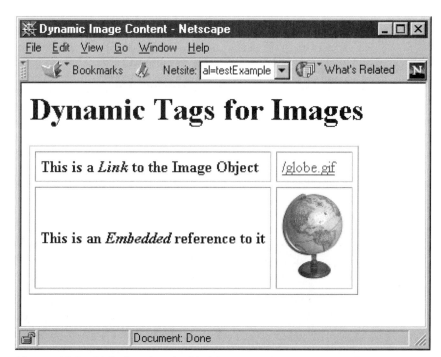

Figure 19-9. *Linked and embedded images using* wbLink *and* wbEmbed.

tip

You can edit the generated tag in AppPage Editor by selecting the dynamic tag and then right-clicking the mouse. You can set extra tag attribute values, and override the generated attribute values, whose defaults are taken from the content metadata. For example, you can use wbImg *to embed an* IMG *tag in the HTML page, which will include any descriptive text for the image in the* ALT *attribute for the* IMG *tag. The descriptive text is taken from the description field for the image in the Informix database. By setting the tag parameters in AppPage Editor at the point of call, you can override the* ALT *text by setting your own descriptive text for that one instance of the dynamic tag.*

The wbInclude Tag

You use the wbInclude tag (see Table 19-13 for attributes) to explode an AppPage within another AppPage. For example, your error handling may require that a standard error page be displayed to the user; in the MIERROR tag you would request that the error-handling page be exploded using the wbInclude dynamic tag. The wbInclude dynamic tag calls the webexplode function to fetch the page you specify with the parameters to the tag.

Using the wbInclude Tag to Explode AppPages and AppPage Fragments

The next example shows how to explode the contents of an AppPage at a certain point in the AppPage being currently being processed by webexplode. The wbInclude dynamic tag calls webexplode to process an AppPage, and the results are inserted into the AppPage at the point where wbInclude is referenced.

The example inserts the contents of an AppPage, called includedPage, into an HTML table cell. The includedPage itself contains two dynamic tags to render an image and an audio object.

Table 19-13. The wbInclude *tag attributes.*

Attribute	Mandatory?	Description
NAME	Yes	Name of the AppPage.
PATH	No	Path of the AppPage.
EXT	No	Extension of the AppPage.

In one of the table cells, a link to the AppPage `includedPage` is also shown.

You can call `webexplode` *without calling* `wbInclude`. *You may want to do this if you need to pass extra parameters to the AppPage requested. Alternatively, you can modify the* `wbInclude` *tag to accept an attribute that defines the extra parameters.*

Listing 19-7 shows the contents of `includedPage`. The `includedPage` code is not a complete HTML page. Rather, it is a reuseable fragment that can be utilized elsewhere. By defining its own table context, it can be easily inserted into other tables, as the example shows.

Listing 19-8 shows the contents of the calling AppPage, with `wbInclude` shown, as well as the `wbLink` tag for comparison.

Figure 19-10 shows the browser output of the AppPage in List. 19-8.

Figure 19-11 shows the browser output after the link in Fig. 19-10 is clicked. This shows the AppPage fragment in its own page.

The `wbLink` Tag

You use the `wbLink` tag to create a hyperlink to a resource, such as an HTML page, an image file, audio file, or video file. The parameter values are converted to attributes of the HTML anchor tag, `<A>`. See Table 19-14.

To specify an image that forms the link, populate the `IMGNAME`, `IMGPATH`, and `IMGEXT` attributes. If `IMGNAME` is specified, then `TEXT` is not displayed.

Listing 19-7. *The* `includedPage` *AppPage.*

```
<TABLE BORDER=0>
<TR>
<TD COLSPAN=2><h2>This cell is an included page</h2></TD>
</TR><TR>
<TD ALIGN=center>
<?wbImg name="globe" path="/" ext="gif">
</TD>
<TD ALIGN=center>
<?wbEmbed name="TheMicrosoftSound" path="/" ext="wav" width="145"
          height="60"  >
</TD>
</TR></TABLE>
```

```
<HTML>
<HEAD><TITLE>Embedding Pages Using Tags</TITLE></HEAD>
<BODY>
<h1>Embedding Pages Using Tags</h1>

<TABLE BORDER=1 CELLPADDING=5 CELLSPACING=5>
<TR><TD><b>This is a <i>Link</i> to the AppPage</TD>
<TD>
<?wbLink name="includedPage" path="/" ext="html">
</TD></TR>
<TR>
<TD><b>This is an <i>Embedded</i> reference to it</TD>
<TD>
<?wbInclude name="includedPage" path="/" ext="html">
</TD></TR></TABLE>
</BODY>
</HTML>
```

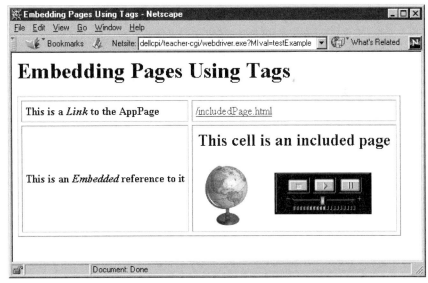

Figure 19-10. *Browser output of the AppPage in List. 19-8.*

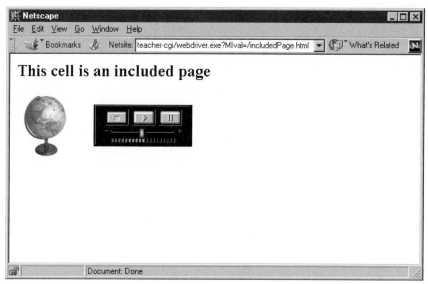

Figure 19-11. Browser output from the hyperlink in Fig. 19-10.

Table 19-14. The `wbLink` tag attributes.

Attribute	Mandatory?	Description
NAME	Yes	Name of the resource being linked to.
PATH	No	Path of the resource being linked to.
EXT	No	Extension of the resource being linked to.
TARGET	No	Anchor, or bookmark, in the linked document to append to the hyperlink (not to be confused with the target frame—see `WINDOW`).
TEXT	No	Link text.
WINDOW	No	The target window or frame to contain the rendering of the link.
IMGNAME	No	Name of the image that will action the link if clicked.
IMGPATH	No	Path of the image.
IMGEXT	No	Extension of the image.

note

Using Data Director for Web, you can set all of the attributes of the wbLink *tag by editing the tag in AppPage Editor. The Insert Resource wizard does not itself populate all of the available attributes.*

Using the wbLink Tag with Images

We have already seen how you can use the wbLink tag in AppPages. This example shows how you can use an image in the wbLink tag to action the hyperlink when clicked.

The snippet below shows that we want to use the globe.gif image to action the link to the AppPage includedPage.html when the globe is clicked.

```
<?wbLink NAME="includedPage" PATH="/" ext="html"
IMGNAME="globe" IMGEXT="gif" IMGPATH="/">
```

Figure 19-12 shows the browser output after webexplode has processed the AppPage containing the wbLink tag.

Figure 19-12. Using wbLink *to link to an AppPage using an image.*

Inserting Database Resources into AppPages Using the Insert Resource Tag Wizard

You can insert references to database resources (e.g., PDF documents, images, MS-Office documents, audio, and video) using a wizard in Data Director for Web called the Insert Resource wizard. This wizard helps you generate a dynamic tag reference automatically, with the relevant attributes set to the appropriate values. This saves the developer the trouble of hand coding a reference to a database object. The wizard is available in AppPage Editor.

The aim is to insert a reference in an AppPage to a database object, ideally using a `webBuilder` class dynamic tag. You can extend these tags to provide even more functionality, depending on your project requirements.

In AppPage Editor, you select the type of resource you want to insert. These resources are stored in the database. They include images, audio, video, VRML, AppPages, MS-Office documents, and any type of content for which you have defined an extension above and beyond the defaults installed with the Data Director for Web product.

You can choose to generate a `webBuilder` class dynamic tag—or no dynamic tag, in which case HTML is generated.

You can choose to generate a *link* to the resource from the current AppPage; alternatively, you can choose to generate the code to *embed* the resource in the AppPage.

For either of these options, you can then choose to use a dynamic tag or to generate HTML code directly into the AppPage instead of using a dynamic tag.

Table 19-15 lists the insertion options, and Table 19-16 lists the insertion methods.

Table 19-15. Resource insertion options.

Option	Description
Embed	Resource is inserted directly into the AppPage with the appropriate HTML tag, e.g., EMBED, IMG.
Link	Resource is linked to from the AppPage.

Table 19-16.   **Resource insertion methods.**

Method	Description
Dynamic Tag	Either `wbLink` or the appropriate dynamic tag, such as `wbEmbed` or `wbImg`, is inserted into the AppPage.
Static HTML	If the resource is linked, an anchor tag is inserted into the HTML page. If the resource is embedded, an `EMBED` or `IMG` tag, for example, is inserted.

You can modify the dynamic tags provided as options in the Insert Resource wizard. In this way, you can extend and reuse this extended functionality in your AppPages. If you choose not to use the dynamic tags provided by this dialog, then you cannot reuse any functional extension that you have defined.

Embedding Resources

The type of resource that you include will determine the `webBuilder` class dynamic tag that is generated, or, if you require HTML, the HTML tag that is generated.

Table 19-17 lists the dynamic tags generated for the default resource types in Data Director for Web. For example, if you want to insert an Image using the wizard, the dynamic tag generated is `wbImage`.

Table 19-17.   **Dynamic tags used by default resources.**

Resource type	Dynamic tag generated
Image	`wbImage`
Video	`wbEmbed`
Audio	`wbEmbed`
AppPage	`wbInclude`
VRML	`wbEmbed`
Application documents (e.g., PDF, MS-Office)	`wbEmbed`

Linking Resources

If you choose to generate a link to the resource on the AppPage, then the dynamic tag generated is `wbLink`. This tag will be parameterized by the resource metadata, such as name and extension. This information is taken from the Data Director for Web system catalogs.

For all the resource types in Table 19-17, you can generate a `wbLink` tag to link the resource on the AppPage instead.

Generating HTML instead of a Dynamic Tag

The HTML generated by the Insert Resource wizard depends on whether you want to link or embed the resource.

Using HTML to Link the Resource in an AppPage

An HTML `anchor` tag is generated to link the resource. The hyper reference itself is a call to `webdriver` to extract the object from the Informix database. Figure 19-13 shows the HTML generated in the Insert Resource wizard for an HTML link to an image stored in the database.

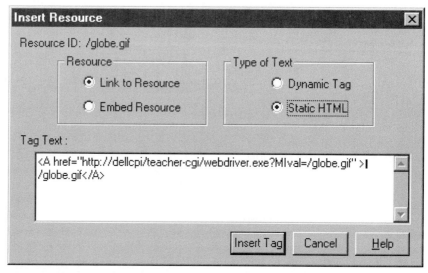

Figure 19-13. An HTML anchor for an image in the database.

Using HTML to Embed the Resource in an AppPage

An HTML tag is generated to embed the resource in the database. For images, the IMG tag is generated and the large object handle (LO handle) is included in the `webdriver` URL (see Fig. 19-14). For documents such as spreadsheet documents, the EMBED tag specifies the `webdriver` URL to extract the document from the database (see Fig. 19-15).

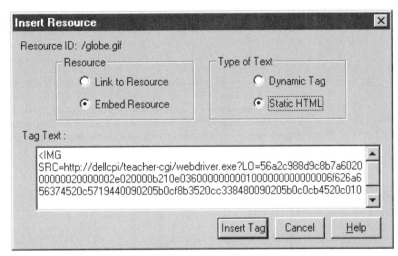

Figure 19-14. The IMG *tag with large object handle generated for an image stored in the database.*

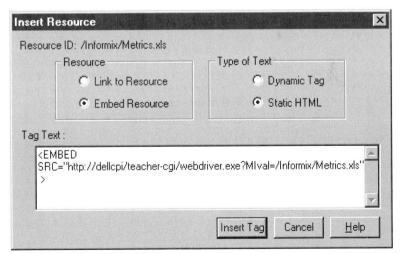

Figure 19-15. The embed *tag generated for a spreadsheet stored in the database.*

Using the Insert Resource Wizard Step by Step

To illustrate how to insert a resource into an AppPage using AppPage Editor, we will select a PDF document from the content repository and insert a reference to it in the AppPage.

What Is a Content Repository?

As discussed in Chap. 3, a content repository stores all the media assets that you or your company holds. This includes media objects of all types stored in the filesystem or database. Database objects are binary objects (BLOBs), but each object has one or more metadata attributes that describe the content in some way; for example, date created, MIME type, size, rendering characteristics, content owner. In a departmental setting, content may be organized into departmental folders, using a content management web application running against the Informix database to manage the folder heirarchy. In a business information context, the repository may be split into folders for press cuttings, contacts, product information, and so forth. The Data Director for Web content repository is the Data Director for Web schema; the content is AppPages, images, audio, video, and other objects; and the metadata is viewed in Site Manager and AppPage Editor. See Chapter 18 for a practical application.

Selecting the Insert Resource Wizard

In AppPage Editor, there are icons to select the resource you want to insert, and in most cases the same dialog appears with the type field defaulted to the type of resource you have selected to insert.

Choose a Resource

In AppPage editor, select the Insert Document wizard. You are presented with the dialog in Fig. 19-16, with the resource type of the document to choose selected by default (in our case, `application`). Select the document from the list, and click OK.

Link or Embed the Document in the AppPage

There are four ways to insert the PDF document we have selected (see Figs. 19-17 through 19-20). Data Director for Web provides four options at the next stage of the Insert Resource wizard. We can generate a hyperlink to the PDF document, or embed the PDF document reference in the web page. Whether we link or embed, we

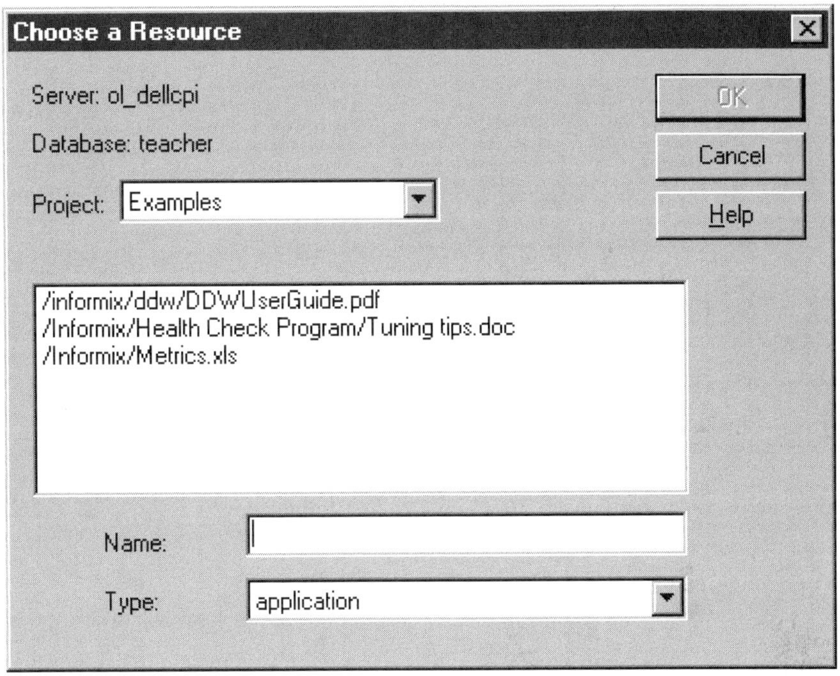

Figure 19-16. Choose a resource to include in an AppPage.

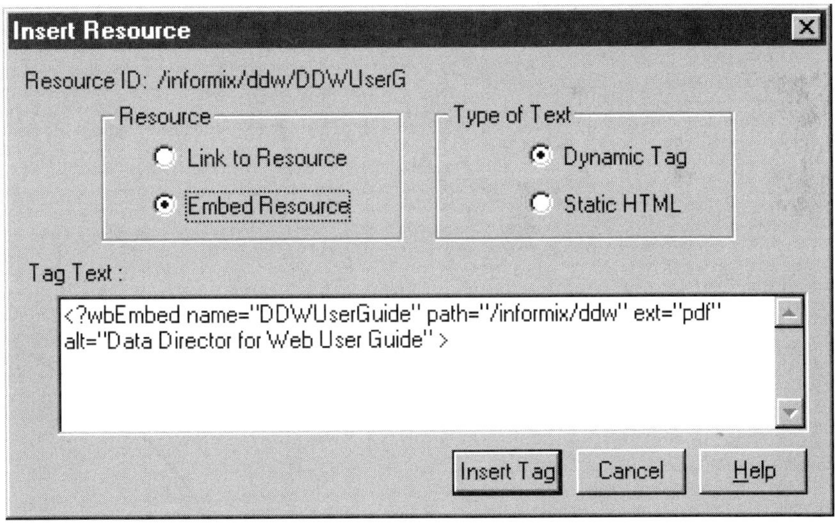

Figure 19-17. Insert Resource options: Embed the resource using a dynamic tag.

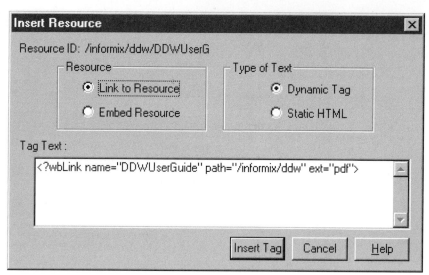

Figure 19-18. Insert Resource options: Link the resource using a dynamic tag.

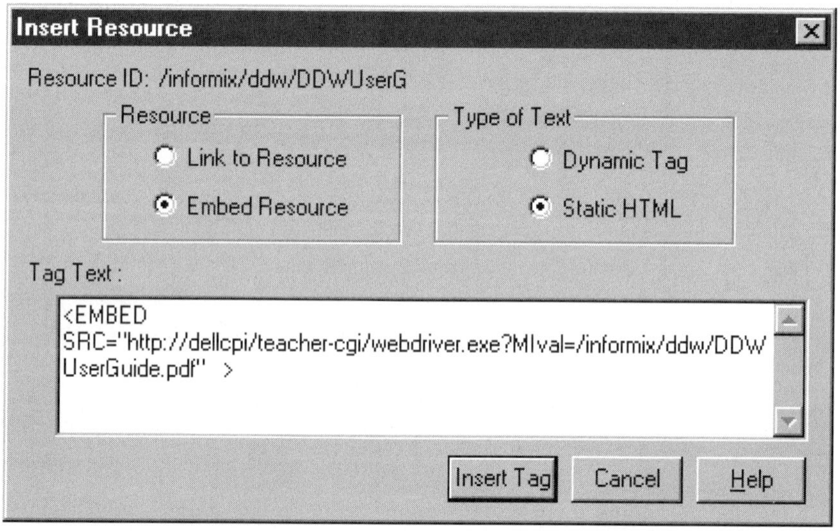

Insert Resource

Resource ID: /informix/ddw/DDWUserG

Resource
- ○ Link to Resource
- ● Embed Resource

Type of Text
- ○ Dynamic Tag
- ● Static HTML

Tag Text :

```
<EMBED
SRC="http://dellcpi/teacher-cgi/webdriver.exe?MIval=/informix/ddw/DDW
UserGuide.pdf"  >
```

[Insert Tag] [Cancel] [Help]

Figure 19-19. Insert Resource options: Embed the resource using HTML.

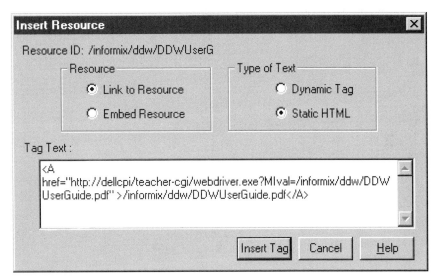

Figure 19-20. Insert Resource options: Link the resource using HTML.

have the option to use a dynamic tag or generate HTML without a dynamic tag.

The tag textbox will refresh for each option you choose, to show the text that will be inserted into the AppPage. Once you have selected the option you require, click the Insert Tag button, and the code displayed in the tag textbox will be exported to the AppPage currently being edited.

Displaying the Results in the Browser

Using the generated dynamic tag or inline HTML code, the PDF document is displayed by the browser plug-in when the AppPage is requested (see Fig. 19-21).

You need to have the ADOBE ACROBAT plug-in installed in your browser configuration for this to work. The advantage of using a plug-in is that the plug-in application runs in the browser window, not as a separate application.

In order to generate the correct value for WEB_HOME *in the tag textbox using the HTML option, you need to set the value of* WEB_HOME *in the Site Manager Preview Settings. In Site Manager, select Tools/Preview*

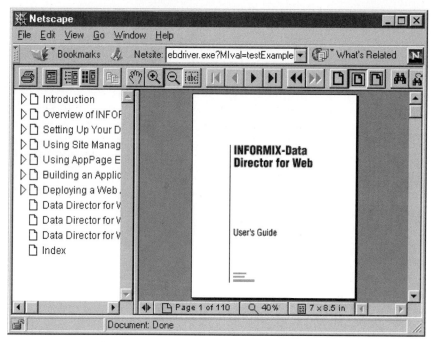

Figure 19-21. *The PDF document displayed in the browser using the Adobe PDF Plug-In.*

Settings from the Site Manager menu bar. Select the Preview Configuration for the project you are using (or the Default configuration if a project configuration is not specified). In the Preview Settings window, edit the Preview Configuration, and set WEB_HOME *to the value that exists in the* server *file* web.cnf.

Creating User Dynamic Tags

As a web application developer, you will want to create your own dynamic tags for your web applications. You can declare parameters and assign default values to them. You code the body of the dynamic tag, which can include references to other user or system dynamic tags, (e.g., wbImage) or to AppPage tags (e.g., MISQL).

Why Create User Dynamic Tags?

System dynamic tags are useful but will not provide for all the different requirements of a function-rich web application. The Web DataBlade allows you to extend the system dynamic tags by creating new dynamic tags based on them, and also to create dynamic tags to perform virtually any set of functions that AppPage Script allows.

Later in this chapter, we will show how to create an *auditing footer* for a web page, which keeps track of the users that have accessed the page and creates a hit counter to register how many times the page has been accessed. This is implemented in a *user* dynamic tag, and it is the kind of functionality best achieved with dynamic tags: website-wide functionality, created and maintained in one place, implemented in many AppPages.

Creating User Dynamic Tags

You can create a user dynamic tag in one of three ways:

1. Use `dbaccess` to add a row to the `wbTags` or `webTags` table.
2. Use the Create Dynamic Tag function in Site Manager within Data Director for Web.
3. Use the Add Dynamic Tag page within AppPage Builder.

You will almost certainly use the second or third option. The installation scripts for Data Director for Web and AppPage Builder use the first.

The five essential elements of a dynamic tag are listed in Table 19-18.

Table 19-18. Essential elements of a dynamic tag.

Element	Description
ID	The dynamic tag name.
Description	The dynamic tag description.
Parameters	A list of parameters for the dynamic tag separated by "&," with optional default values for the parameters.
Class	A code that can be used by a custom retrieval mechanism to group related tags.
Body	The dynamic tag code.

Data Director for Web and AppPage Builder will allow you to set this data accordingly.

Scope of User Dynamic Tags

When you create a dynamic tag, you assign it to a project. In Data Director for Web, if you have not selected a project, the tag is created in the Not in Projects folder.

The ID of a tag identifies the tag in the `wbTags` or `webTags` table. The project in which the tag resides is not part of the tag *identity*. You cannot create two dynamic tags with the same name in the same database, even if you want the tags to belong to different projects.

Creating a Web Page Header with User-defined Dynamic Tags

The example in List. 19-9 shows how to create a web page header using a header dynamic tag. The tag will create for the web page a header that includes an image. The image is a link to another AppPage. The link is a parameter to the tag.

The parameter definition is simple: `link=` (see Fig. 19-22 for browser output).

The following tag is inserted at the top of the AppPage.

```
<?header LINK=Home>
```

Listing 19-9. *Dynamic tag source.*

```
<html>
<head><title>Global Wholesalers</title></head>

<body bgcolor="#FFFFFF">

<a href="<?mivar>$WEB_HOME<?/mivar>?MIval=@link@">
<img src="<?mivar>$WEB_HOME<?/mivar>?MIvalObj=globe&MItypeObj
          =image/gif" border=0></a>
<font size=+3 face="arial" color="#003300"><b>Global Wholesalers, Inc.
          </b></font>
<br clear=all>
<hr>
```

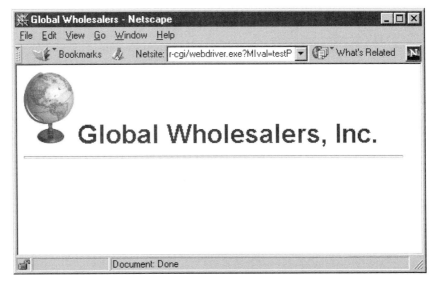

Figure 19-22. Browser output for the header tag in List. 19-9.

Auditing Your Website and Creating Web Page Hit Counters

It is useful to see who has accessed a web page, and, in some cases, what his/her IP address was at the time. In other words, you may want to *audit* your website access. This can be more than a web server IP address log. You may want to *personalize* your site for a one-to-one marketing edge in the presentation of web content; if so, using dynamic tags to track the user navigation path in the Informix database is ideal.

You can create an audit trail and hit counter for the AppPage referenced process very easily without CGI scripting. This example shows how to implement an audit trail and a web page hit counter in a footer dynamic tag. The following functions are supported:

- Include a standard e-mail link (showing how to use the "@" character).
- Display the most recently changed details for the page using information from the database.
- Add an entry to an `audit` table in the database to say who accessed the page and what his/her IP address was.
- Display a message if this is the first time the page has been accessed.
- Maintain a hit counter for the page in the database.

The user dynamic tag to do this, `auditFooter`, is shown in List. 19-10. The AppPage source is shown in List. 19-11.

If you want to use the $REMOTE_USER variable, you will need to use the API `webdriver`, *such as the NSAPI* `webdriver`, *to perform user authentication. Otherwise, the* $REMOTE_USER *variable is set to the value of* REMOTE_USER *in the* `web.cnf` *file. If your web application code controls user access, then you can use your own variable. For example, you can use an HTTP cookie to store the username and then use the cookie variable instead.*

The dynamic tag name and the actual parameter names are not letter case sensitive.

Listing 19-10. *The* `auditFooter` *dynamic tag.*

```
<hr>
<!- Include a standard mailto link ->
<center>Questions? Email me at
<a href="mailto:webmaster@ATSIGN@mysite.com">
   webmaster@ATSIGN@mysite.com</a>
<br>
</center>

<!- Display Last Changed Details ->
<?misql sql="select author, last_changed, last_changed_by from
        wbPages where id='@page@';">
Created by: $1<br>
Last Modified: $2<br>
Last Modified by: $3<br>
<?/misql>

<!- Add an entry to the audit table to say who accessed the page  ->
<?misql sql="insert into audit (access_tm, page_id, remote_user, com-
        ment) values ( current, '@page@','$REMOTE_USER','HOST:
        $REMOTE_HOST');">
<font size=-1 color=red>Access logged.<br></font>
<?/misql>

<!- The more traditional 'hit counter' might go something like this
... ->
<?misql sql="update hits set (num_hits)=(num_hits + 1) where
page_id='@page@' and log_date=today;">
<?/misql>
<!- Find out how many rows were updated using dbinfo and store it in
    a variable ->
<?misql sql="select unique dbinfo('sqlca.sqlerrd2') from systables;">
   $(SETVAR,num_rows,$1)
<?/misql>
<?misql cond=$(EQ,$num_rows,0) sql="insert into hits
(page_id,log_date,num_hits) values ('@page@', today, 1 );"><font
size=-1 color=red>First access to the page!<br>
</font>
<?/misql>

</body>
</html>
```

Listing 19-11.   The AppPage source for the page rendered in Fig. 19-23.

```
<?header LINK=Home>
Thank you for calling.
<?auditfooter PAGE="$MIval">
```

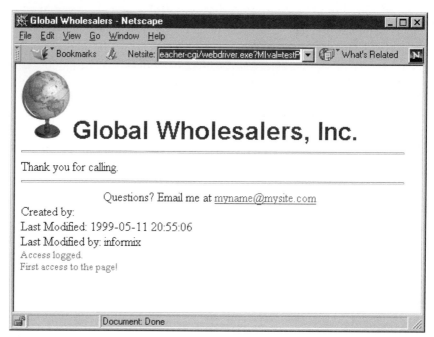

Figure 19-23. Browser output for the auditFooter *tag.*

Creating an AppPage Generic Error Handler with User Dynamic Tags

You can use a dynamic tag to create a generic error handler that hides the details of error handling from the AppPage developer.

For example, you may want to implement a generic error handler that will catch all uncaught errors arising from MISQL commands (plus any other uncaught errors in AppPage tags). An uncaught error is an error in an AppPage tag or database SQL that does not have an MIERROR error-handling tag nominated.

Listing 19-12. *The* `sqlErrorHandler` *dynamic tag source.*

```
<TITLE>Error Report</TITLE>
Executing page "<?MIVAR><EM>$MIval</EM><?/MIVAR>" failed:
<H4>
    Error Code: <?MIVAR>$MI_ERRORCODE<?/MiVAR><br>

<?MIVAR>$(IF,$(XST,$MI_ERRORMSG),Error Message:
$MI_ERRORMSG)<?/MIVAR>
</H4>
```

```
<?MIERROR tag=sqlErrorHandler>
<?/MIERROR>
<?MISQL SQL="select good from bad"><?/MISQL>
```

The scope of the generic error handler is the AppPage being processed, including all dynamic tags and AppPage fragments exploded within that AppPage (for example, if `webexplode` is called recursively).

This example uses the error handling defined in a dynamic tag. The `MIERROR` tag is specified in such a way that, if the `MIERROR` tag is actioned in the event of an uncaught error, then the dynamic tag called `sqlErrorHandler` is substituted for it.

Listing 19-12 shows the dynamic tag source for the `sqlErrorhandler` dynamic tag. Listing 19-13 shows the AppPage source that references the tag. Figure 19-24 shows the browser display when the SQL error in List. 19-13 is handled by the `MIERROR` tag.

tip

You may want to place the generic `MIERROR` *handlers such as this in the header tags you specify.*

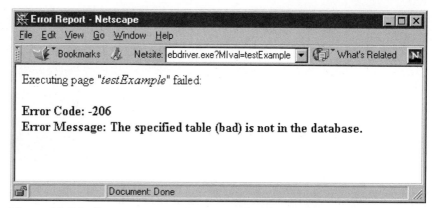

Figure 19-24. *Browser output after processing the AppPage shown in List. 19-13.*

Summary

In this chapter, we have learned what dynamic tags are, how they are structured, and how they work to deliver code reuse in dynamic web applications.

We have also looked at some of the uses of dynamic tags in real world situations, such as tracking and auditing web page access.

Data Director for Web was used to illustrate how to use system and webBuilder class tags to rapidly deploy dynamic tag functionality in AppPages.

The lessons learned here will allow you to apply code reuse in all your Web DataBlade applications to reduce the maintenance overhead of those applications in all phases of the web project lifecycle.

Working with Large Objects

In this chapter:

- What is a large object?
- Retrieving large objects by name
- Utilize caching by retrieving large objects by large object handle
- Customizing large object retrieval using query strings
- Using images in a basic online shopping catalog

Think of a news website, such as `http://www.bbc.co.uk/news`. When the latest story breaks, the reporter has to write her story. The story is submitted to an editor, who organizes the story and begins to marshal all the appropriate material. This material includes related news items from the news archive, audio and video links from the televised version of the story, and also pictures to bring home the story's immediacy: The editor may need to search a picture archive for just the right image (person or thing) to accompany the story. Within this publishing cycle, properly managing the storage, maintenance, and retrieval of these objects (images, audio, and video) is crucial for delivering content to the editor for composition and presentation on the Web. Therefore, it is important to understand the fundamentals of what website objects are and how they are accessed, especially when those objects reside in a database. As the urgency of news production helps emphasize, the efficacy of website content repositories depends on flexible and efficient access to stored large objects. This chapter will help you understand how to access these objects in the Informix database for web delivery to the client browser. This knowledge will help you grasp some essentials of delivering sophisticated multimedia content over the Web from a database.

What Is a Large Object?

A *large object* (LO) is data that, in most cases, is greater than 255 bytes in length or contains non-ASCII character representations. Examples of large object data are

- images (GIF or JPEG, for example),
- documents (such as MS-Office documents),
- sound (for example, WAV files),
- video (such as AVI files),
- image maps.

Apart from the HTML datatype, the Web DataBlade uses two other types of large objects, BLOB and CLOB, as shown in Table 20-1.

Table 20-1. **The BLOB and CLOB datatypes.**

Datatype	Description
BLOB (binary large object)	Undifferentiated byte stream to store binary data (e.g., images, video, application programs) with a size of up to 2 GB.
CLOB (character large object)	Byte stream that can be used to store printable characters; size up to 2 GB.

What Is a BLOB?

A *binary large object* datatype is designed to hold data that a program can generate. These data include graphic images, satellite images, video clips, audio clips, or formatted documents such as those produced by MS-Office. Informix Dynamic Server with Universal Data Option and Informix Dynamic Server.2000 permits any kind of data in a BLOB column.

What Is a CLOB?

The *character large object* datatype stores a block of text. It is designed to store ASCII text data, including formatted text such as HTML or PostScript. Although you can store any data in a CLOB object, Informix tools expect a CLOB object to be printable, so restrict this datatype to printable ASCII text.

Retrieving Large Objects

The Web DataBlade module provides built-in support for objects typically found in web applications, such as images, audio, and video. New object types can also be added. These objects are stored in database tables as *large objects* so that webdriver can be used to manipulate them.

If you use Data Director for Web or AppPage Builder to maintain your website, large objects are stored in a predefined schema. Table 20-2 lists the default tables that store the large objects.

Large objects stored in these tables are sometimes referred to as *static* large objects. *Static* does not mean that the object cannot change; rather, the table structure makes it possible to retrieve large objects by name.

tip

You don't have to store your web content in the predefined Data Director for Web or AppPage Builder schema. You can use different

Table 20-2. Large object tables by product.	
Table	**Product**
wbBinaries	Data Director for Web
webImages	AppPage Builder

tables, as long as you set the schema variables in `web.cnf` *correctly. You may want to set separate tables if you inherit a content base that is already stored in a separate schema.*

You can use AppPage Builder or Data Director for Web to store large objects in the database. You can also use `dbaccess` if you want to write SQL yourself. Once the object is in the database, your web application will want to retrieve it for downloading to the browser.
There are three essential methods for retrieving large objects:

- by object name,
- by large object handle,
- by query string (Version 4 onward).

Retrieving Large Objects by Name

You can use `webdriver` to retrieve a large object from a table in the database by specifying the `webdriver` variables that uniquely identify the object. This method of retrieval is most likely used when retrieving a single object.
In order for `webdriver` to fetch the object, `webdriver` needs to know which table and table column the object is stored in (see List. 20-1). This information is not fixed, because your application requirements may differ from the schema that is used by the AppPage Builder and Data Director for Web products.
Retrieving large objects by name means that `webdriver` must know the following:

- the name of the database table in which the large object is stored,
- the name of the `BLOB` columns storing the large object,
- the name of the `VARCHAR` column that identifies the appropriate row where the object is stored,
- the value to check against the `VARCHAR` column to identify the row you want to retrieve from the database table,
- the MIME type and subtype that are used to export the large object and that the browser uses to render the object appropriately.

tip

Retrieval of large objects by name always requires a database connection; therefore, it may be slower than retrieval by LO handle. Retrieving large objects by LO handle may not require a database connection if large object caching is enabled.

```
# web.cnf file
INFORMIXDIR D:\informix
INFORMIXSERVER ol_dellcpi
MI_USER informix
MI_PASSWORD informix
MI_DATABASE stores

# Retrieve large objects by name
MInamObj ID
MIcolObj object
MItabObj? wbBinaries
MItypeObj? image/gif
```

In List. 20-1, the wbBinaries table, specified by MItabObj, contains images stored as large objects. The ID column (MInamObj) contains a unique identifier for each row of the wbBinaries table. The object column (MIcolObj) contains the large object. The MIvalObj value, specified in the URL, identifies the unique value to determine which row to retrieve.

Based on these variables, webdriver builds the following SELECT statement to retrieve the large object:

```
SELECT $MIcolObj from $MItabObj where
$MInamObj='$MIvalObj'
```

You can override the default values for the webdriver variables in the URL to retrieve a large object.

If MIvalObj *is set in a URL, all other* webdriver *environment variables (*MItab, MIcol, MInam, MIval*) are ignored and the specified large object is extracted. Therefore, do* not *set* MIvalObj *in your* web.cnf *file.*

Example—Retrieving Large Objects by Name

In the following example, the AppPage in List. 20-2 retrieves image objects from the wbBinaries table. In this case, you know the exact name of the objects you wish to display to the client.

Listing 20-2. Retrieving large objects by name.

```
<html>
<head><title>OnLine Shopping Mall</title></head>

<body bgcolor="#FFFFFF">
<img src="<?mivar>$WEB_HOME<?/mivar>?MIvalObj=
globe&MItypeObj=image/gif" border=0>

<font size=+3 face="arial" color="#002200"><b>OnLine
Shopping Mall</b></font>
<br clear=all>
<hr>
<center>
<h3>Welcome to the OnLine Shopping Mall</h3>
<p>

<center>
<h2>Under Construction</h2>
<img src="<?mivar>$WEB_HOME<?/mivar>?MIvalObj=
menatwork&MItypeObj=image/gif" border=0>
</center>

<p>
<hr>
Questions? Contact <a href="mailto:webmaster@yoursite.com">
                          webmaster@yoursite.com</a>
</body>
</html>
```

*For all examples in this section, we assume the Data Director for Web
schema, not the AppPage Builder schema, is being used.*

The images we retrieve are called `globe` and `menatwork`. We
could have easily used AppPage variables to specify the large object
names.

Listing 20-2 illustrates the use of retrieval by name, and List. 20-3
shows the HTML sent to the browser (see browser display in Fig. 20-1).

In List. 20-3, the `img` URL takes the form:

Listing 20-3. **The HTML output for the AppPage**
in List. 20-2.

```
<html>
<head><title>OnLine Shopping Mall</title></head>

<body bgcolor="#FFFFFF">
<img src="/stores7-cgi/webdriver.exe?MIvalObj=globe" border=0>

<font size=+3 face="arial" color="#002200"><b>OnLine Shopping
Mall</b></font>
<br clear=all>
<hr>
<center>
<h3>Welcome to the OnLine Shopping Mall</h3>
<p>

<center>
<h2>Under Construction</h2>
<img src="/stores7-cgi/webdriver.exe?MIvalObj=menatwork"
border=0>
</center>

<p>
<hr>
Questions? Contact <a href="mailto:webmaster@yoursite.com">
                        webmaster@yoursite.com</a>
</body>
</html>
```

```
<img src="/stores7-cgi/webdriver.exe?MIvalObj=
menatwork" border=0>
```

What this denotes is that `webdriver` will be used to extract the large object from the database. `webdriver` will look at the `wbBinaries` table, using `ID` as the key and `menatwork` as the key

Figure 20-1. *Browser display of List. 20-3.*

value, and will extract the LO handle. The LO handle will specify a location in a blobspace or smart blobspace in which the BLOB resides, and will then extract the BLOB.

In order to do this, webdriver will need the remaining large object variables set. Since they are defined in web.cnf, we don't have to supply them in the URL. If any of the web.cnf variables should refer to different tables and/or columns, then the variables need to be overridden in the URL specification.

Schema-based Variables to Define Object Locations

The webdriver configuration file, web.cnf, needs to know where to find the objects you request by name. These variables are described in Table 20-3. You can override the contents of one or more of these variables in your application at any time.

Table 20-3.   Schema-based variables to request objects by name.

Variable	Mandatory?	Description
MItabObj	Yes	Name of the table that stores large objects.
MIcolObj	Yes	Name of the column that stores LO handles in table MItabObj (BLOB).
MInamObj	Yes	Name of the column that identifies the object (varchar). Each value in this column is unique.
MIvalObj	Yes	Similar to MIval. Its value to check against the MInamObj column to identify the row you want to retrieve from the table designated to contain web application large objects.
MItypeObj	Yes	MIME type and subtype used to export the large object. Example valid MIME type and subtype: image/gif.

Version 4

You can use the Web DataBlade administration tool with Version 4 of the Web DataBlade to define the contents of these variables without editing web.cnf directly.

Table 20-4 lists the defaults for each of AppPage Builder and Data Director for Web. Up to and including Version 3.3 of the Web DataBlade, you will edit the web.cnf file.

Table 20-4.   The LO variable values for AppPage Builder and Data Director for Web.

Variable	AppPage Builder value	Data Director for Web value
MitabObj	webImages	wbBinaries
MicolObj	object	object
MinamObj	ID	ID
MItypeObj	image/gif	image/gif

Translation of Large Object Variables by `webdriver`

Given the `img` URL in List. 20-3, we can show what the SQL initiated by `webdriver` will be.

This is the `img` URL:

```
<img src="/stores7-cgi/webdriver.exe?MIvalObj=menatwork"
border=0>
```

The SQL statement will vary according to the configuration in use, which determines the tables that `webdriver` will query.

Using the AppPage Builder Configuration

Assuming the defaults in Table 20-4, the SQL call to retrieve the large object with the AppPage Builder schema becomes:

```
select object from webImages where ID = 'menatwork'
```

Using Data Director for Web Configuration

Assuming the defaults in Table 20-4, the SQL call to retrieve the large object with the Data Director for Web schema becomes:

```
select object from wbBinaries where ID = 'menatwork'
```

Overriding Large Object Attributes

If we look closely at the URL for the `IMG` tag in List. 20-2, we find that the only parameter specified is `MIvalObj`. We could have specified `MItypeObj`, which defines the MIME type of the object. We did not, however, because `MItypeObj` is already defaulted in the `web.cnf` file.

If the object type was JPEG, then we would need to override the default value of the `web.cnf` variable so that the resulting HTML would define the correct rendering of the object in the browser. We can do this in the `img` URL as follows:

```
<img src="/stores7-cgi/webdriver.exe?MIvalObj=
menatwork&MItypeObj=image/jpeg" border=0>
```

Note the following:

- `MIvalObj` denotes the value of the `ID` column in the `wbBinaries` table and is declared as a parameter to the (CGI) `webdriver` program.
- `MItypeObj` denotes the MIME type of the object and is also defined as a parameter to the (CGI) `webdriver` program.
- the parameters are separated by the standard "`&`" operator.

You can override all of the schema parameters for objects in a URL specification. As might be expected, you can also use AppPage variables to define the variable name, the variable value, or both.

Utilize Caching by Retrieving Large Objects by Large Object (LO) Handle

When a large object is stored in the Informix database, it is stored in a *blobspace*, or *smart blobspace*. This space consists of a special chunk designed to handle large objects. The description of the location of the large object is called a *large object handle*—LO handle for short.

When an object is inserted into the database from the filesystem (using the `fileToBlob` function, for example), an LO handle is returned from that function. This value is stored in the database column that refers to the large object in the `wbBinaries` or `webImages` table.

When you wish to extract the large object by name, `webdriver` must first look up the ID of the object in `wbBinaries` or `webImages` using the `ID=value` column/value pair. Once the object has been found in the table, `webdriver` extracts the LO handle and then retrieves the object from the blobspace.

tip

Retrieving objects by LO handle is the only method that takes advantage of large object caching.

You can retrieve large objects by LO handle when you dynamically retrieve the results of a SELECT statement. You can set webdriver variables to specify large object handles and their output MIME type, as shown in Table 20-5. The variables in Table 20-4 are passed in the URL to webdriver in name/value pairs.

If the LO and MItypeObj variables are set, then all the other webdriver environment variables are ignored. Therefore, *do not* specify LO in your web.cnf file. The variable LO is the LO handle taken from the object column in the wbBinaries or webImages table; realistically, then, you can set it only by selecting the appropriate object from the database.

tip

To retrieve LO handles, select them from the table that stores the large objects. This method of retrieving large objects is useful when you are retrieving many objects that satisfy a query.

Listing 20-4 shows how to retrieve an object by LO handle. In this example, we are selecting the menatwork image metadata from the wbBinaries table, as well as the LO handle from the wbBinaries.object column. The actual URL will contain the LO handle, which webdriver will use to address the image directly when the browser renders the page. Listing 20-5 shows the resulting HTML.

Note that in List. 20-5, the LO handle is a long stream of digits. Note also that the ALT attribute of the IMG tag takes its data from the metadata for the image, which you can set in the Properties sheet for the image in the Data Director for Web Site Manager (you can also set this directly using dbaccess if you wish).

Table 20-5.   The webdriver LO handle variables.

Variable	Value
LO	Large object handle as a string of digits.
MItypeObj	Mime type and subtype used in the generated HTML for rendering the object in the browser.

Listing 20-4.   *Retrieving large objects by LO
handle, with metadata.*

```
<?misql sql="SELECT a.object, b.super_type || '/' ||
 b.sub_type, a.width, a.height, a.description
       FROM wbBinaries a, wbExtensions b
       WHERE a.ID='menatwork'
       AND a.path='/'
       AND a.extension='gif'
       AND a.extension=b.extension;">
<IMG SRC=$WEB_HOME?LO=$1&MItypeObj=$2 WIDTH=$3 HEIGHT=$4
 ALT="$5">
<?/misql>
```

```
IMG SRC=/stores7-
cgi/webdriver.exe?LO=50a2c988d9c8b7a602000000020000003e0
20000b310e0360000000001000000000000006f626a656374620c571
9440090806e0cf853620cc338480090806e0c0c54620c01000000&MI
typeObj=image/gif
WIDTH=0 HEIGHT=0 ALT="Under Construction Sign">
```

Customizing Large Object Retrieval Using Query Strings

The preceding two methods for retrieving large objects did not apply any filters to the operation of extracting an object from the database, apart from using the unique ID or LO handle for the object. Retrieval by *query string* is similar to retrieving large objects by name, but it uses a customized query to override the default query constructed by webdriver. You can therefore deploy a more granular, secure schema-specific approach to extracting large objects from your application database.

In the previous two methods, you can set the values of schema variables dynamically to extract objects that may reside in a schema other than the one used by AppPage Builder or Data

Table 20-6.   Query string Variables in `web.cnf`**.**

Variable	Mandatory?	Description
`lo_query_string`	Yes	A parameterized SQL statement to extract the large object from the database.
`lo_query_params`	Yes	A list of parameters substituted for the parameters in the `lo_query_string`.
`lo_error_zerorows`	Yes	The integer error number that should be be returned if the SQL statement in `lo_query_string` returned zero rows.
`lo_error_sql`	Yes	The integer error number that should be returned if an SQL error occurs when retrieving a large object using the SQL in `lo_query_string`.

Director for Web, but the emphasis here is on customization to implement application-specific filters.

You define variables in `web.cnf` (using the Web DataBlade Administration Tool) to control large object retrieval by query string (see Table 20-6).

important

Retrieving large objects by query string overrides the default query built by `webdriver`*. You need therefore to consider creating two* `webdriver` *mappings and two* `webdriver` *configurations, one for each mapping. The first can use the query string method, the second can use the default* `webdriver` *query. If you have defined many user variables in your old configuration, you can base your new configuration on the old configuration, but remember: You may have to keep them in step.*

How Customization Works

If you have defined the `lo_query_string` and `lo_query_params` variables in `web.cnf`, then `webdriver` will perform large object retrieval by query string, *regardless* of whether you have defined the remaining schema variables for large object retrieval (such as `MItabObj`).

`webdriver` will then take the query in `lo_query_string`, and replace all formal parameters in the string left to right with actual parameters taken from the variables defined in `lo_query_params`. The operation is conceptually similar to `sprintf` in C, where the `%s` parameter is replaced by the actual string value passed to the `sprintf` function.

Then `webdriver` executes the query. Remember that the end result is an LO handle to an object in a blobspace. Any custom query in `lo_query_string` that does not return an LO handle should consider the results to be undefined.

The number of `%s` placeholders in `lo_query_string` must equal the number of parameters in `lo_query_params`.

When retrieving large objects by LO handle, we do not incur a database read if the required object is in cache. Retrieval by query string will incur the same overhead as retrieval by name, since we are using `MIvalObj` to obtain the LO handle of the object. You must evaluate the priorities specific to your project. Securing objects may not be high on the list; on the other hand, if these objects are scanned images of top secret documents, it makes sense to filter the users (although you would be wiser in this case to secure the URL using NSAPI, for example, rather than applying security at object level). Nevertheless, there are situations where one AppPage may render images selectively based on attributes of the user profile, and it may be easier to use a customised object query than code the specific query throughout the application.

Handling Errors When Using Query Strings

You can catch errors that occur when executing the query in `lo_query_string`. There are two events that can be interpreted using `webdriver` variables:

- The query in `lo_query_string` returns no rows.
- The query in `lo_query_string` returns an error.

Using `lo_error_zerorows` to Handle No Rows Returned

If no rows are returned from the query in `lo_query_string`, then use `lo_error_zerorows` to specify the integer error number that should be returned to `webdriver`. This error number is then exported to the relevant `webdriver` variables that can be displayed back in the browser, via an `MIERROR` tag if defined. If no error handler is defined, then `webdriver` will display the standard error report, with the error number specified by `lo_error_zerorows` and the matching error message for that error number.

Using `lo_error_sql` to Handle SQL Errors

If the SQL statement in `lo_query_string` encounters an SQL error (such as *syntax error*), then you can set the variable `lo_error_sql` to return a specific error number back to `webdriver`. `webdriver` will then report the error back to the browser, via an `MIERROR` tag if defined. If no error handler is defined, then `webdriver` will display the standard error report, with the error number defined by `lo_error_sql` and the matching error message for that error number.

Using Images in a Basic Online Shopping Catalog

This section will show how to use images in an Online Shopping Catalog application that is delivered over the Internet. The application may be rendered in the desktop browser or in a special browsing kiosk in a shopping mall. We will also see how to retrieve objects from a schema that does not use the `webImages` or `wbBinaries` tables.

Example Functionality

The aim is to display a list of products that satisfy a product category and then allow the user to select a product from that list for detailed rendering of the product information.

In most applications of this type, at least two types of image are created—thumbnail and full size. Thumbnail images are created so that the best quality image can be produced for the thumbnail size. The original images are collected from their source(s) (scanned or otherwise) and transferred to the production shop. Usually at this stage, thumbnail images are created from the full-size images. Both are then stored in the content repository, which may be the filesystem or a database such as Informix Dynamic Server.

In this example, we use thumbnail images to display a small picture of the product in a listing of products for a product category called *computers and peripherals*. We then want to select a particular product from the list and display the full-size image in a product detail screen. This means that we store two images for every product image—a thumbnail version and a full-size version. The thumbnail image is rendered in the product list screen, and the full-size image in the product detail screen.

Basic Image Schema

There are two main tables in the example. The `catalog_smart` table is used to store large object data for a product. The `cat_descr` column is used to store descriptive text, and the `cat_picture` is used to store the full-size image.

```
create table catalog_smart (
    catalog_num integer,
    stock_num smallint,
    manu_code char(3),
    unit char(4),
    cat_descr clob,
    cat_picture blob,
    cat_advert varchar(255,65),
    prod_type char(10),
    primary key (catalog_num)
);
```

The second table of interest is the `catalog_thumbnail` table. This links to the `catalog_smart` table on `catalog_num` and is used to store the thumbnail version of the image in the `catalog_smart.cat_picture` column.

```
create table catalog_thumbnail (
    catalog_num integer,
    thumbnail blob,
    primary key (catalog_num)
);
```

Import of Descriptive Text (CLOB) Data

The long description of the product in the `catalog_smart` table is a CLOB column. The description is imported from a text file, which is stored in the filesystem. The text file is imported into the database using the `filetoclob()` function:

```
filetoclob( 'd:\text\portable computer.txt',
            'client'),
```

Import of Image (BLOB) Data

The function `filetoblob()` is used to import an image from a file in the filesystem to a BLOB column in the database. For example, to import the GIF image of a laptop computer into the BLOB column of the `catalog_thumbnail` table, the following code was used:

```
insert into catalog_thumbnail
values (
2199, 3199,filetoblob(
'd:\Images\thumbnail\portable computer 2.gif',
'client' )
)
```

The `filetoblob()` function returns a large object (LO) handle, and this value is stored in the table column.

Display List of Products—AppPage

The AppPage in List. 20-6 displays the list of product items in a selected category. We are not concerned with the selection screen here. When the user clicks either the thumbnail image or the text link, the product detail screen is displayed.

Parameters Passed to the AppPage

The single parameter passed in from the selection screen is $category. This is the category code for the products requested. In our case, the category selected is *computers,* which is a short code for *computers and peripherals.* The table `prod_types` maintains this category code and description information. You could call this page using the following URL:

```
http://dellcpi/teacher-cgi/webdriver.exe?MIval=
category_list&category=computers
```

Category List AppPage Source

Listing 20-6 shows the AppPage source to display the products in the category *computers and peripherals.* This AppPage is called with the URL shown above, designed to show how to extract the large object handle for the thumbnail image from the database, and use it in an IMG tag.

Listing 20-6. **The** `categoryList.html` *AppPage Source.*

```
<?header link=welcome function="Browse Products">
<center>
<h2>Products of type:
<?misql sql="select type_desc from prod_types where prod_type=
'$category'">
$1
<?/misql><br></h2>

<table border=1 cellspacing=2>
<tr><th>Catalog #</th><th>Stock #<br>Manu
CD</th><th>Product</th><th>Information</th></tr>
<?misql
  sql="select unique c.catalog_num, c.stock_num, c.manu_code,
             s.description, c.cat_advert, d.thumbnail
      from catalog_smart c, stock s, catalog_thumbnail d
      where c.stock_num=s.stock_num and
            c.manu_code=s.manu_code and c.unit=s.unit and
            c.prod_type='$category'
            and c.catalog_num = d.catalog_num
      order by 1;">
<tr><td>$1</td><td align=center>$2<br>$3</td><td>$4</td>
<td><table border=0 width="100%"><tr>
<td width="25%">
<a href=$WEB_HOME?MIval=m9_prod_dtl&catalog_num=$1>
    <img src="$WEB_HOME?LO=$6&MItypeObj=image/gif"
        align=left  border=no>
   </a>
</td>
<td><a href=$WEB_HOME?MIval=m9_prod_dtl&catalog_num=$1>$5</a>
</td>
</tr></table></td>
</tr>
<?/misql>
</table>
</center>
<p>
<?footer page="$MIval">
```

Listing 20-7.   Section of HTML page generated from List. 20-6.

```
<tr><td>2199</td><td align=center>3199<br>ANZ</td><td>Laptop
Computer</td>

<td><table border=0 width="100%"><tr>
<td width="25%"><a href=/teacher-
cgi/webdriver.exe?MIval=m9_prod_dtl&catalog_num=2199>
    <img src="/teacher-
cgi/webdriver.exe?LO=c86f1e0cd9c8b7a602000000020000043020000b510e036
000000000100000000000000007468756d626e61696c19440090a0670cc494690cc3384
80090a0670cd894690c01000000&MItypeObj=image/gif" align=left
border=no>
    </a>
</td>
<td><a href=/teacher-
cgi/webdriver.exe?MIval=m9_prod_dtl&catalog_num=2199>Laptop
Computer.</a>
</td>
</tr></table></td>
</tr>
```

The first `misql` tag selects the long description for the category code using the `$category` parameter. The second `misql` tag selects the thumbnail product images from the `catalog_thumbnail` table. The large object handle is stored in the `thumbnail` column, and is used to parameterize the `src` attribute of the HTML `img` tag. Since we are only dealing with GIF images, the MIME type is not parameterized in the database. We could store the MIME type of the image in the `catalog_thumbnail` table if we had wanted and used this value in the `img` tag.

Listing 20-7 shows a section of the HTML page generated from the AppPage source in List. 20-6. Note that the LO handle is a parameter to the `webdriver` CGI program.

note

Images are not extracted from the database when the LO handle is read from the appropriate image table by webexplode. *The LO handle is used to parameterize the* SRC *attribute of the* IMG *tag. When the HTML page is sent to the browser, the* IMG *tag directs the browser to send a request to the web server to run* webdriver *(as a CGI program or an API interface, depending on the configuration) to extract the object with the nominated LO handle for downloading. If the image is in* `webdriver` *cache on the web server machine, the image is taken from cache instead.*

Using `Header` and `Footer` Tags

The `header` dynamic tag is used to parameterize the header of the displayed page. We pass in the page title and a link back to the `welcome` page. The `header` tag is shown in List. 20-8.

The `footer` dynamic tag displays information about the AppPage itself, and inserts the name and IP address of the user into an audit table to register the user who requested the page. A separate hits table is used to record the number of hits for that AppPage. There is more on this topic in Chap. 19, "Creating and Using Dynamic Tags." For now, List. 20-9 displays the source of the `footer` tag.

note

If you use a secure URL prefix with NSAPI or ISAPI, for example, then the value of `$REMOTE_USER` *is set to the user ID entered at authentication login.*

Browser Display of Category Items

Figure 20-2 shows the browser output of the category list.

Listing 20-8. *The* `header` *dynamic tag.*

```
<html>
<head><title>Global Wholesalers</title></head>

<body bgcolor="#FFFFFF">

<a href="<?mivar>$WEB_HOME<?/mivar>?MIval=@link@">
<img src="<?mivar>$WEB_HOME<?/mivar>?MIvalObj=globe&MItypeObj=image
/gif" border=0 alt="New Query"></a>
<font size=+3 face="arial" color="#003300"><b>@function@</b></font>
<br clear=all>
<hr>
```

Listing 20-9. *The* `footer` *dynamic tag.*

```
<hr>
<center>Questions? Email me at
<a
href="mailto:myname@ATSIGN@mysite.com">myname@ATSIGN@mysite.com</a>
<br>
</center>

<?misql sql="select author, last_changed, last_changed_by from
wbPages where id='@page@';">
Created by: $1<br>
Last Modified: $2<br>
Last Modified by: $3<br>
<?/misql>

<?misql sql="insert into audit (access_tm, page_id, remote_user,
            comment) values ( current, '@page@','$REMOTE_USER','HOST:
            $REMOTE_HOST');">
<font size=-1 color=red>Access logged.<br></font>
<?/misql>

<?misql sql="update hits set (num_hits)=(num_hits + 1) where
page_id='@page@' and log_date=today;">
<?/misql>

<?misql sql="select unique dbinfo('sqlca.sqlerrd2') from systables;">
   $(SETVAR,num_rows,$1)
<?/misql>
<?misql cond=$(EQ,$num_rows,0) sql="insert into hits
(page_id,log_date,num_hits)
        values ('@page@', today, 1 );"><font size=-1 color=red>First
access to the page!<br>
</font>
<?/misql>

</body>
</html>
```

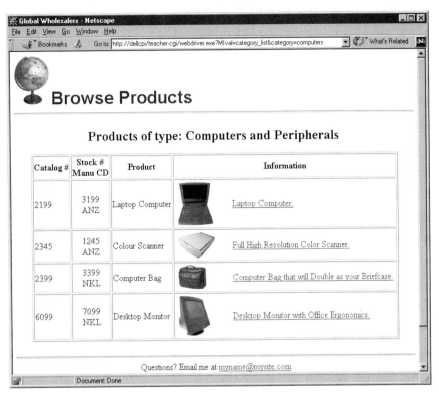

Figure 20-2. Browser display of the category items.

Display Product Detail—AppPage

When the user has selected a product to browse in more detail, the user can click the thumbnail or the short text link beside it. The product detail page is downloaded to the browser and the product detail displayed, including the full-size image of the product.

Parameters Passed

The product category number is passed in the link from the category list page. For example, the AppPage for the category list page contains the lines:

```
<a href=$WEB_HOME?MIval=prod_dtl&catalog_num=$1>
<img src="$WEB_HOME?LO=$7&MItypeObj=image/gif"
    align=left  border=no></a>
```

When the use clicks the image in this link, the AppPage prod_dtl is exploded. The `catalog_num` of the product item is passed as a parameter in the URL. The `catalog_num` is taken from the query that selects the list of catalog items from the database. The `prod_detail` page will use the parameter `$catalog_num` to select the product details from the database.

Product Detail—AppPage

Listing 20-10 shows the AppPage source for the product detail page. Note that the `header` tag is now parameterized with a new title for the displayed page.

This AppPage tests whether the `catalog_num` parameter has been passed in. If not, the user is directed to another page. Then the product detail is selected from the `stock` and `catalog_smart` tables. The full-size image is taken from the `cat_picture` column of the `catalog_smart` table. The information is then rendered in the HTML table. Listing 20-11 shows a section of the resulting HTML Page generated by `webexplode` to retrieve and format the full-size image and product detail.

Listing 20-10. *The* `prod_dtl.html` *AppPage source.*

```
<?header link=welcome function="Browse Product Detail">
<center>

<?miblock cond="$(NXST,$catalog_num)">
 You did not enter this page correctly from the product summary page,
please go
   <a href=<?mivar>$WEB_HOME<?/mivar>?MIval=categoryList>
back</a> and try again.
<?/miblock>
<?miblock cond="$(XST,$catalog_num)">
<H3>Product Detail for Catalog Number:
<?mivar>$catalog_num<?/mivar><br>
</H3><center>
<table border=1>
<?misql sql="select c.stock_num,c.manu_code,c.unit,c.cat_descr,
   cat_picture,unit_price, qty_on_hand, cat_advert
   from catalog_smart c, stock s
  where c.stock_num=s.stock_num and c.manu_code=s.manu_code and
c.unit=s.unit
   and c.catalog_num=$catalog_num">
```

Listing 20-10.   (continued)

```
<tr><td><b>Catalog #:</b> $catalog_num</td>
    <td rowspan=4> <img src="$WEB_HOME?LO=$5&MItypeObj=image/gif"></td>
</tr>
<tr><td><b>Stock #:</b> $1<br><b>Mfg:</b> $2</td></tr>
<tr><td><b>Price/Unit:</b> $6 <b>/</b> $3</td></tr>
<tr><td><b>Qty On Hand: </b> $7</td></tr>
<tr><td colspan=2>$8<p>$4</td></tr>
<?/misql>
</table>

<?miblock cond="$(=,$MI_ROWCOUNT,0)"><font size=+2>Sorry, we were unable
to find the information for product code <?mivar>$catalog_num<?/mivar><br>
<?/miblock>
</center>
<?/miblock>

<?footer page="$MIval">
```

Listing 20-11.   Section of HTML page generated from List. 20-10.

```
<H3>Product Detail for Catalog Number: 6099<br>
</H3><center>
<table border=1>

<tr><td><b>Catalog #:</b> 6099</td>
    <td rowspan=4> <img src="/teacher-
cgi/webdriver.exe?LO=747c1e0cd9c8b7a60700000007000000ac000000d43af51b
0100000001000000000000006361745f70696374757265002821770ce0e6610cc3384
8002821770cf4e6610c01000000&MItypeObj=image/gif"></td>
</tr>
<tr><td><b>Stock #:</b> 7099<br><b>Mfg:</b> NKL</td></tr>
<tr><td><b>Price/Unit:</b> $699.00 <b>/</b> each</td></tr>
<tr><td><b>Qty On Hand: </b> 1</td></tr>
<tr><td colspan=2>Desktop Monitor with Office Ergonomics.<p>Desktop
monitor with all the features that the office ergonomics enthusiast
will enjoy. Especially useful for CAD applications.
</td></tr>
</table>
```

Browser Display of the Product Detail

Figures 20-3 through 20-6 show the browser display of the product detail for some of the products in the *Computers and Peripherals* Category after they have been selected from the category list page.

Figure 20-3. *Example product item display, cat. no. 2199: laptop.*

Figure 20-4. *Example product item display, cat. no. 6099: monitor.*

Figure 20-5. Example product item display, cat. no. 2345: scanner.

Figure 20-6. Example product item display, cat. no. 2399: computer bag.

Summary

In this chapter we have learned how to use large objects, such as images and audio files, in a web application. Since these objects are stored in the database, we have also learned how to retrieve large objects from the database in a variety of ways, each with its own advantages.

In addition, we have learned how to use thumbnail and full-size images in a simple Online Catalog application.

The examples presented in this chapter differ in degree, not in kind, from functionally rich and complex web applications that use a sophisticated content repository to store multimedia objects. This chapter has shown you how to retrieve those large objects as part of creating a dynamic web page.

A Customer Maintenance Application

In this chapter:

- Selecting customers and building dynamic queries
- Viewing and scrolling customer details
- Editing customer details
- Adding customer details
- Deleting customer details
- Screen navigation using JavaScript and forms
- Dynamic headers and footers

This chapter presents a complete example of a browser application that maintains customer details in the Informix database using HTML forms, AppPage Script, and JavaScript. The example application is an end-to-end development exercise: HTML forms are deployed on the client to capture data, JavaScript is used to add interactivity to the client and generate SQL queries dynamically, and AppPage Script is used to process form data on the database server. This is the vertical view of the application. The horizontal view of the application covers screen navigation: This example uses HTML forms on the client and AppPage Script on the database server to navigate between screens.

Application Functionality

The functionality of the application is very simple.

- Select one or more customers from the database by specifying an optional number of basic string filters.
- Scroll the result set produced from the query.
- Edit the details for a selected customer.
- Delete the details for a selected customer.

Table 21-1 lists the application components.

Selecting Customers and Building Dynamic Queries

From this screen you can

- select one or more customers using basic filters,
- build dynamic queries,
- display the current state of the dynamic query,
- choose to add a new customer.

The user can enter basic substrings into each of the form fields to filter the SQL query that is sent to the database. For the `State` form field, you can select the state description from the pull-down select list, and the state code is written to the `State` form field.

The user can display the current form of the query string at any time by clicking the Show Query button.

The user can also request to add a new customer from this screen.

Table 21-1. AppPages by function.	
Screen function	**AppPage source**
Select Customer	`selectCustomer.html`
View Customer	`viewCustomer.html`
Edit Customer	`editCustomer.html`
Delete Customer	`deleteCustomer.html`
Header	`header` dynamic tag
Footer	`footer` dynamic tag

Entering Query Filters

If you enter a string into a form field, that string is used in an SQL `like` clause to perform a match on that column for any row that contains that string. For example, Fig. 21-1 shows the Select Customer screen when two filters have been entered: `Ath` in the Company field, and `California` in the State field.

The resulting query sent to the database server is:

```
select customer_num, fname,lname,
       company,address1,address2,city,
       state,zipcode,phone
from customer
where company like '%Ath%' and state like '%CA%'
```

Each filter you enter is added onto the end of the `where` clause. If you don't enter any filters, then no `where` clause is generated.

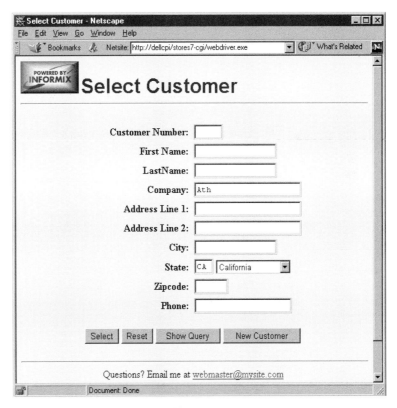

Figure 21-1. *Entering query filters.*

Showing the Current Query

You display the current query string by clicking the Show Query button. For the filter in the section above, the JavaScript dialog in Fig. 21-2 is displayed.

In response to the Show Query request, a JavaScript function is invoked to dynamically build the SELECT statement. The following snippet shows how:

```
var whereClause = "";

with (pForm) {
      if (customer_num.value != "") {
           whereClause += " customer_num = " +
                customer_num.value;
      }
      if (fname.value != "") {
        if (whereClause != "") whereClause += " and ";
          whereClause += " fname like '%" +
                fname.value + "%'";
```

The pForm variable is the FORM object that is passed to the JavaScript function. If the appropriate form fields are not blank, then the form field value is appended to the whereClause.

Submitting the Query

Click the Select button, and the query that has been built dynamically is submitted to webdriver as form data. The viewCustomer.html AppPage is then processed, and the query is executed. The resulting display looks like Fig. 21-3.

In Fig. 21-3, there were two rows that matched the query filters. If the query found no rows, then the screen in Fig. 21-4 is displayed.

The SELECT statement is built when the user submits the form using the Select button. A JavaScript function is used to build the statement dynamically using the form data. In addition, a second

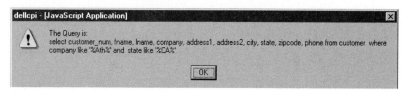

Figure 21-2. Show Query.

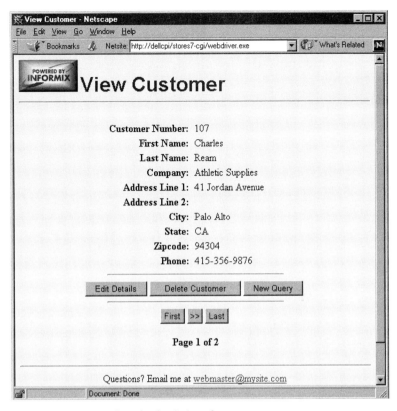

Figure 21-3. Results of submitting the query.

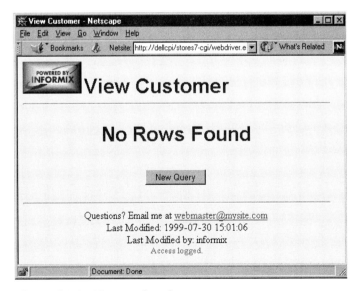

Figure 21-4. No rows found.

`select` statement is built to select the `count` of rows that match the query criteria. This statement also has the query filters applied using the same dynamically built `whereClause`, as shown in the following snippet.

```
sqlStatement += (whereClause != "") ? " where " +
whereClause : "";

// set the form field value to be the
// dynamically created query
pForm.sqlQuery.value = sqlStatement;
pForm.sqlCount.value = "select count(*) from customer " +
        ((whereClause != "") ? " where " + whereClause
                        : "");
```

Two hidden form fields are created to hold the two queries.

```
<INPUT TYPE=hidden NAME=sqlQuery VALUE="">
<input type=hidden name=sqlCount VALUE="">
```

The following JavaScript statement assigns the dynamically built SQL statement to the `sqlQuery` form field.

```
pForm.sqlQuery.value = sqlStatement;
```

Select Customer AppPage Source

Listing 21-1 shows the `selectCustomer.html` AppPage.

Listing 21-1. The `selectCustomer.html` AppPage.

```
<?header link=selectCustomer title="Select Customer">

<?mierror tag=mivar> An Error occurred in processing the insert
form:<BR><B>
<PRE>$MI_ERRORMSG</PRE></B>Please go Back and try again.<?/mierror>

<script language="javascript">
function showQuery(pForm, pDisplay) {
var sqlStatement = "select customer_num, fname, lname, company,
address1, address2, city, state, zipcode, phone from customer ";
var whereClause = "";
```

Listing 21-1. (continued)

```
with (pForm) {
    if (customer_num.value != "") {
        whereClause += " customer_num = " +
                        customer_num.value;
    }
    if (fname.value != "") {
     if (whereClause != "") whereClause += " and ";
     whereClause += " fname like '%" +
            fname.value + "%'";
    }
    if (lname.value != "") {
     if (whereClause != "") whereClause += " and ";
     whereClause += " lname like '%" +
            lname.value + "%'";
    }
    if (company.value != "") {
     if (whereClause != "") whereClause += " and ";
     whereClause += " company like '%" +
            company.value + "%'";
    }
    if (address1.value != "") {
     if (whereClause != "") whereClause += " and ";
     whereClause += " address1 like '%" +
            address1.value + "%'";
    }
    if (address2.valuc != "") {
     if (whereClause != "") whereClause += " and ";
     whereClause += " address2 like '%" +
            address2.value + "%'";
    }
    if (city.value != "") {
     if (whereClause != "") whereClause += " and ";
     whereClause += " city like '%" +
            city.value + "%'";
    }
    if (state.value != "") {
     if (whereClause != "") whereClause += " and ";
     whereClause += " state like '%" +
            state.value + "%'";
    }
    if (zipcode.value != "") {
```

Listing 21-1. (continued)

```
              if (whereClause != "") whereClause += " and ";
              whereClause += " zipcode like '%" +
                    zipcode.value + "%'";
          }
          if (phone.value != "") {
              if (whereClause != "") whereClause += " and ";
              whereClause += " phone like '%" +
                    phone.value + "%'";
          }
      } // end with

      sqlStatement += (whereClause != "") ? " where " +
                          whereClause : "";
      if (pDisplay == true) alert("The Query is:\n" +
                    sqlStatement);
      //
      // set the form field value to be the dynamically
      // created query
      //
      pForm.sqlQuery.value = sqlStatement;
      pForm.sqlCount.value =
    "select count(*) from customer " +
    ((whereClause != "") ? " where " + whereClause : "");
      return true;
}
</script>

      <!-- Select form -->
      <center>
      <FORM METHOD=POST
            ACTION="<?mivar>$WEB_HOME<?/mivar>"
            onSubmit="return showQuery(this,false);">
      <INPUT TYPE=hidden NAME=MIval
    VALUE="<?mivar>viewCustomer<?/mivar>">
      <INPUT TYPE=hidden NAME=sqlQuery VALUE="">
      <INPUT type=hidden name=sqlCount value="">
      <TABLE BORDER=0 width=100%>

      <?mivar>
      <tr>
      <td align=right width=50%><b> Customer Number: <b></td>
```

Listing 21-1. (continued)

```
        <td><input type=text name="customer_num"  size="4">
    <BR></td>
        </tr>
        <tr>
        <td align=right><b> First Name: <b></td>
        <td><input type=text name="fname"  size="15" maxsize=15>
    <BR></td>
        </tr>
        <tr>
        <td align=right><b> LastName: <b></td>
        <td><input type=text name="lname"  size="15">  <BR></td>
        </tr>
        <tr>
        <td align=right><b> Company: <b></td>
        <td><input type=text name="company"  size="20">
    <BR></td>
        </tr>
        <tr>
        <td align=right><b> Address Line 1: <b></td>
        <td><input type=text name="address1"  size="20">
    <BR></td>
        </tr>
        <tr>
        <td align=right><b> Address Line 2: <b></td>
        <td><input type=text name="address2"  size="20">
    <BR></td>
        </tr>
        <tr>
        <td align=right><b> City: <b></td>
        <td><input type=text name="city"  size="15" >  <BR></td>
        </tr>
        <tr>
        <td align=right><b> State: <b></td>
        <td><input type=text name="state"  size="2">
<?/mivar>
<select name="state_select" size=1
onChange=
"this.form.state.value=this.options[this.selectedIndex].value;
">
<?misql sql="select code, sname from state order by 1">
<option value="$1">$2
```

Listing 21-1. *(continued)*

```
<?/misql>
<option value="" selected>
</select><?mivar>   <BR></td>
      </tr>
      <tr>
      <td align=right><b> Zipcode: <b></td>
      <td><input type=text name="zipcode"  size="5">
      <BR></td>
      </tr>
      <tr>
      <td align=right><b> Phone: <b></td>
      <td><input type=text name="phone"  size="18">  <BR></td>
      </tr>
      <?/mivar>
      </TABLE><P>
      <!--  Submit button for form -->
      <input type="submit" value="Select">
      <input type="reset" value="Reset">
      <input type="button" value="Show Query"
            onClick="showQuery(this.form,true);">
      <input type="submit" value="New Customer"
            onClick="this.form.MIval.value='newCustomer';
        return true;">
      </FORM>
      </center>
<?/miblock>

<?footer  page="$MIval" audit="Select Customer: From: $REMOTE_HOST">
```

Viewing and Scrolling Customer Details

From this screen, the user can

- edit the details for the currently displayed customer,
- delete the details for the currently displayed customer,
- requery the database using a new set of filters,
- display the first, last, next, or previous customer records.

When the user clicks the Select button on the Select Customer screen, the query that is constructed dynamically on the browser is posted to `webdriver` as just another form field data value.

The View Customer AppPage takes this query and executes it using the `MISQL` tag. The result set returned from the query is displayed in a data window with a size of one row.

The data window is managed in such a way that the user can select the first, last, next, and previous customers in the result set. If the user is on the first or last row, the Next and Previous buttons are displayed accordingly.

Figure 21-5 shows the first record in the result set displayed.

Figure 21-6 shows the next record displayed after the `>>` button is clicked. Note that the result set navigation button bar has *changed* to accommodate the ability to scroll backward and forward in the result set.

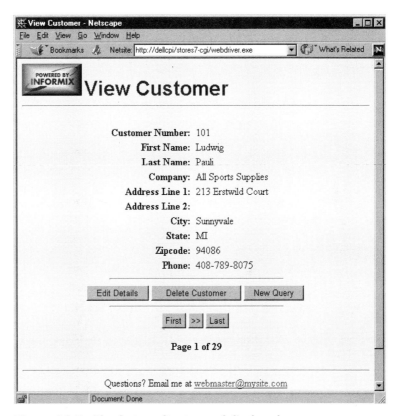

Figure 21-5. *The first result set record displayed.*

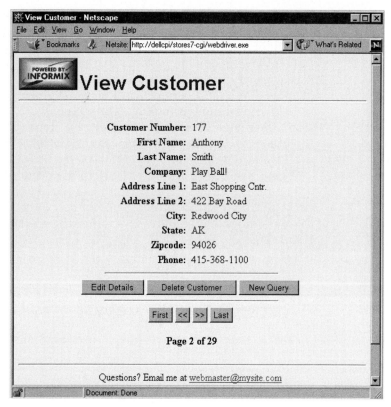

Figure 21-6. The second result set record displayed.

Figure 21-7 shows the last record displayed after the Last button has been clicked. Note that the result set navigation button bar has changed to accommodate the position of the record; we can only go backward from here.

Scrolling Through the Result Set

Suppose the user did not enter any filters in the Select Customer screen. When the Select button is clicked on that screen, the View Customer screen is displayed, which is the `webdriver` output from processing the `viewCustomer.html` AppPage.

The query that the `viewCustomer.html` AppPage executes yields a result set. The View Customer screen displays the rows in that result set *one at a time.* It is able to do this by using the walking window technique of AppPage Script. When the walking window form navigation buttons are clicked, the form data is set in such a way as

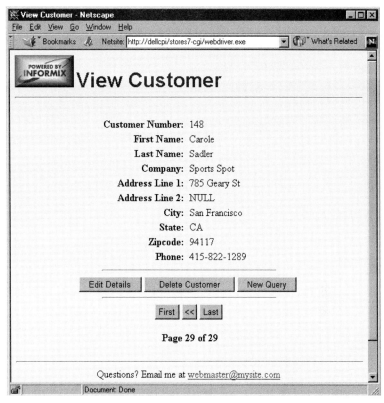

Figure 21-7. The last result set record displayed.

to parameterize the logic of the `viewCustomer.html` AppPage, in particular, the `WINSIZE` and `WINSTART` attributes of the `MISQL` tag.

The following snippet shows how two form fields, called `winstart` and `previous`, are set by using AppPage variable-processing functions to increment or decrement the result set position.

```
<input type-"hidden" name=winstart
       value=<?mivar>$(+,$winstart,1)<?/mivar>>
<input type="hidden" name=previous
       value=<?mivar>$(-,$winstart,1)<?/mivar>>
```

If another user adds a row to the customer table while we are navigating it, then the number of rows in the result set that we can view will increase dynamically, provided the newly added row matches the query filter. As we scroll through the result set, we will see the number of pages increase—or decrease if other users delete customers!

Rendering the Result Set Navigation Path

When the browser user clicks the appropriate button to fetch the first, next, last, or previous customer record that matches the filter criteria, a JavaScript event handler is used to set the value of WINSTART for the subsequent invocation of the AppPage. A form field exists called winstart, and, depending on which way we want to scroll, winstart.value is set accordingly. For example, this snippet sets the value of the winstart form field to 1 if the user clicks the First button:

```
<input type=submit value="First"
       onClick="this.form.winstart.value=1;
       return true;">
```

The following snippet sets the value of winstart to the last record in the result set if the Last button is clicked.

```
<?mivar cond=$(!=,$NUM_ROWS,1)>
    <input type=submit value="Last"
  onClick="this.form.winstart.value=$NUM_ROWS">
<?/mivar>
```

When the viewCustomer AppPage is requested again, the value of the winsize form field set by JavaScript is used in the MISQL query to control the record that is displayed:

```
<?misql sql="$sqlQuery"
    winstart=$winstart winsize=1>
```

Listing 21-2 shows the relevant AppPage source that dynamically generates the navigation buttons to scroll through the query result set.

We are scrolling the query result set, not *the records in the customer table. Even so, for every invocation of the* MISQL *tag, the query is applied in its entirety. The* webexplode() *function will return the window on the data after it has reselected the data according to the filters you have specified.*

Displaying the Number of 'Pages'

The number of *pages* is the same as the number of *rows* that match the query filter criteria, of which only one is returned in the data window by webexplode().

Listing 21-2. Conditional output of result set navigation buttons.

```
<?mivar cond=$(!=,$NUM_ROWS,1)>
        <input type=submit value="First"
      onClick="this.form.winstart.value=1; return true;">
<?/mivar>
<?mivar cond=$(!=,$winstart,1)>
        <input type=submit value="<<"
              onClick="with (this.form) {
              winstart.value=previous.value;
              }
          return true;">
<?/mivar>
<?mivar cond=$(!=,$winstart,$NUM_ROWS)>
        <input type=submit value=">>">
<?/mivar>
<?mivar cond=$(!=,$NUM_ROWS,1)>
        <input type=submit value="Last"
      onClick="this.form.winstart.value=$NUM_ROWS">
<?/mivar>
```

The number of rows (pages) that match the filter criteria is obtained at the start of the AppPage as follows:

```
<?misql sql="$sqlCount">
  $(SETVAR,$NUM_ROWS,$(FIX,$1))
<?/misql>
```

The AppPage variable $NUM_ROWS is set to the value of

```
select count(*) from customer $where_clause
```

where $where_clause is set by JavaScript in the Select Customer form. In essence, two queries are sent as form data by the Select Customer and View Customer forms: the query to select the data, and the query to select the number of rows that are to be returned with that data. The View Customer form has to resend this data to itself as we scroll the result set.

Later in the AppPage, we display the current page information as follows:

```
<?mivar>
<h4>Page $winstart of $NUM_ROWS</h4>
<?/mivar>
```

View Customer AppPage Source

Listing 21-3 contains the complete AppPage source of
`viewCustomer.html`.

Listing 21-3. *The* `viewCustomer.html` *AppPage source.*

```
<?header link=selectCustomer title="View Customer">

<script language=javaScript>
function deleteConfirm(pForm) {
        with (pForm) {
            if (confirm("Really Delete Customer: " +
                    customer_num_input.value + " " +
                    fname.value + " " + lname.value + " ?")) {
            MIval.value='deleteCustomer';
            return true;
            }
        }
        return false;
}
</script>
<?mivar name=winstart default=1>$winstart<?/mivar>
<?mivar name=MI_NULL> <?/mivar>
<?mivar name=MI_NOVALUE> <?/mivar>

<center>

<FORM NAME=viewForm METHOD=POST
   ACTION=<?mivar>$WEB_HOME<?/MIVAR>>
<input type="hidden" name=MIval
     value="<?mivar>$MIval<?/mivar>">
<input type="hidden" name=winstart
     value=<?mivar>$(+,$winstart,1)<?/mivar>>
<input type="hidden" name=previous
     value=<?mivar>$(-,$winstart,1)<?/mivar>>
<input type="hidden" name="sqlQuery"
     value="<?mivar>$sqlQuery"<?/mivar>>
<input type="hidden" name="sqlCount"
      value="<?mivar>$sqlCount"<?/mivar>>
```

Listing 21-3. *(continued)*

```
<!--
For simplicity, select the number of rows in the table to illustrate the
feature
-->
<?misql sql="$sqlCount">$(SETVAR,$NUM_ROWS,$(FIX,$1))<?/misql>
<TABLE BORDER=0 cellpadding=1  width=100%>
<?misql sql="$sqlQuery" winstart=$winstart winsize=1>

<!-- Include some fields for confirmatory output on delete screen
-->
$(SETVAR,$CUSTOMER,$1)
<input type="hidden" name="customer_num_input" value=$1>
<input type="hidden" name="fname" value="$(TRIM,$2)">
<input type="hidden" name="lname" value="$(TRIM,$3)">

<TR>
        <TD align=right width=50% > <B>Customer Number:</B> </TD><TD >
$1 </TD>
</TR>
<TR>
        <TD align=right> <B>First Name:</B> </TD><TD > $2 </TD>
</TR>
<TR>
        <TD align=right> <B>Last Name:</B> </TD><TD > $3 </TD>
</TR>
<TR>
        <TD align=right> <B>Company:</B> </TD><TD > $4 </TD>
</TR>
<TR>
        <TD align=right> <B>Address Line 1:</B> </TD><TD> $5 </TD>
</TR>
<TR>
        <TD align=right> <B>Address Line 2:</B> </TD><TD> $6 </TD>
</TR>
<TR>
        <TD align=right> <B>City:</B> </TD><TD> $7 </TD>
</TR>
<TR>
          <TD align=right> <B>State:</B> </TD><TD> $8 </TD>
```

Listing 21-3.   (continued)

```
</TR>
<TR>
          <TD align=right> <B>Zipcode:</B> </TD><TD> $9 </TD>
</TR>
<TR>
          <TD align=right> <B>Phone:</B> </TD><TD> $10 </TD>
</TR>
<?/misql>
</TABLE>
<?miblock cond=$(!=,$MI_ROWCOUNT,0)>
<hr width=50%>
<input type=submit value="Edit Details" onClick=
          "this.form.MIval.value='editCustomer'; return true;">
<input type=submit value="Delete Customer" onClick="return
     deleteConfirm(this.form);">
<input type=submit value="New Query"
     onClick="this.form.MIval.value='selectCustomer';
     return true;">

<hr width=50%>
<?mivar cond=$(!=,$NUM_ROWS,1)>
        <input type=submit value="First"
        onClick="this.form.winstart.value=1;
             return true;">
<?/mivar>
<?mivar cond=$(!=,$winstart,1)>
        <input type=submit value="<<"
        onClick="with (this.form) {
             winstart.value=previous.value;
                          }
             return true;">
<?/mivar>
<?mivar cond=$(!=,$winstart,$NUM_ROWS)>
        <input type=submit value=">>">
<?/mivar>
<?mivar cond=$(!=,$NUM_ROWS,1)>
        <input type=submit value="Last" onClick=
"this.form.winstart.value=$NUM_ROWS">
<?/mivar>
```

Listing 21-3. *(continued)*

```
<br>
<?mivar><h4>Page $winstart of $NUM_ROWS</h4><?/mivar>
<?/miblock>
<?miblock cond=$(=,$MI_ROWCOUNT,0)>
<font size=+3 face="arial" color="#003300">
<b>No Rows Found</b></font><br><br>
<input type=submit value="New Query">
<script language=JavaScript>
    document.viewForm.MIval.value='selectCustomer';
</script>
<?/miblock>
</FORM>
</center>
<?footer page="$MIval" audit="View Customer From: $REMOTE_HOST">
```

Editing Customer Details

From this screen, the user can

- change the selected customer details and save the changes to the database,
- choose to requery the database,
- choose to add a new customer to the database.

When the user clicks the Edit Details button in the View Customer screen, the details for the currently displayed customer are reselected from the database and displayed in a form that is used for updating the customer. Each column value is written to a corresponding form field so that the user can change them if required (except the key value).

When the user has completed her updates, the user clicks the Save button to update the selected customer in the customer table from the data in the form.

Figure 21-8 shows the Edit Customer screen when customer 106 has been selected for edit.

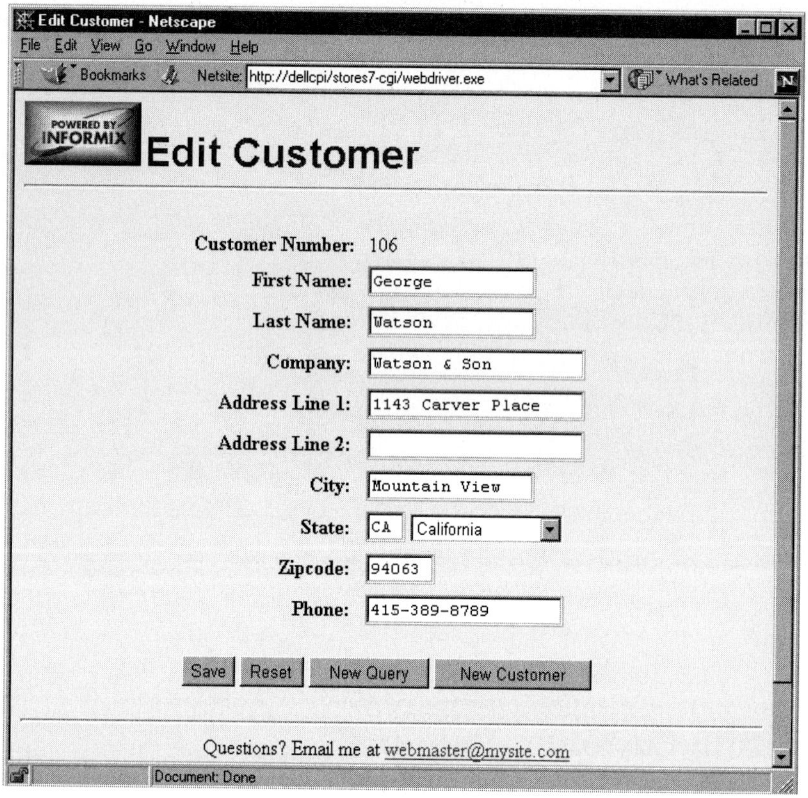

Figure 21-8. *Edit Customer screen.*

Setting the `State` Form Field

When the customer details are first displayed, the `State` form field
is set to the state code that is taken from the selected customer
record. This code is used to lookup the state description in the `state`
table. The complete set of state codes and descriptions are retrieved
from the database and used to populate a `select` list so that the
user can change the customer's state entry. In addition, when a state
is selected from the list, JavaScript traps this event and writes the
state code for the selected state to the `state` form field.

The initial state of the `select` list is set to the description of the
state code currently stored for this customer. The following snippet
shows these features:

```
<select name=apb_state_change size=1
        onChange=
"this.form.apb_state.value=
```

```
this.options[this.selectedIndex].value;">
  <?misql sql="select code, sname from state order
              by 1">
    <option value="$1"
    $(IF,$(EQ,$apb_state,$1),selected)>$2
  <?/misql>
</select>
```

The default `selected` option is set when the customer state code equals the state code currently being processed in the result set of the `MISQL` tag.

JavaScript is able to set the value of the `apb_state` form field by mapping to the containing form and then referencing the target form field by name. Each form field contains an object handle to its containing form, so it is easy to address and set form fields when handling events among them.

See Chap. 19, "Creating and Using Dynamic Tags," for a description of how to use the SELECTLIST *dynamic tag with forms.*

Saving the Changes to the Database

When the customer clicks the Save button, a confirmatory dialog is output by JavaScript which asks the user to confirm the changes before they are saved. This dialog is shown in Fig. 21-9.

If the user selects Cancel, the update is cancelled, otherwise the form is submitted. The following snippet shows the `onClick` event handler for the `submit` form field, and the JavaScript function that is called when the Submit button is clicked.

```
<INPUT type=submit value="Save"
       onClick="return updateConfirm(this.form);">
<script language=javaScript>
function updateConfirm (pForm) {
```

Figure 21-9. Save Changes confirmatory dialog.

```
        return confirm ("Confirm the updates for Customer " +
                        pForm.apb_customer_num.value + " ?");
    }
</script>
```

You can trap submit *events at the form level by using the* onSubmit *event handler in the declaration of the FORM.*

The SQL to update the customer table is shown in the following snippet. The AppPage variables contain the validated and escaped strings from the input form. The AppPage variable $apb_customer_num is used as the key to update the customer record with the new values. In our example, apb_customer_num contains the value 106.

```
<?mivar name="apb_sql_">
UPDATE customer SET
    fname = '$apb_fname' ,
    lname = '$apb_lname' ,
    company = '$apb_company' ,
    address1 = '$apb_address1' ,
    address2 = '$apb_address2' ,
    city = '$apb_city' ,
    state = '$apb_state' ,
    zipcode = '$apb_zipcode' ,
    phone = '$apb_phone'
WHERE customer_num = $apb_customer_num;<?/mivar>
```

If the UPDATE is successful, a confirmatory message is output to the HTML page and is eventually displayed in the browser, as shown in Fig. 21-10.

Edit Customer AppPage Source

Listing 21-4 contains the AppPage source for editCustomer.html.

Adding Customer Details

From this screen, the user can

- enter the details for a new customer and add them to the database,
- choose to requery the database.

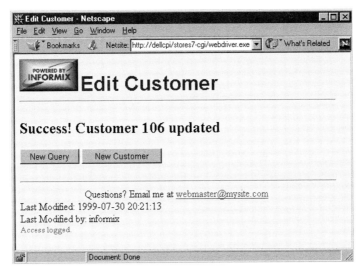

Figure 21-10. *Successful update confirmed.*

Listing 21-4. *The* `editCustomer.html` *AppPage source.*

```
<?header link=selectCustomer title="Edit Customer">

<?mierror TAG=MIVAR><B>Error in update page:</B><BR>
Code: $MI_ERRORCODE<BR>
Msg: $MI_ERRORMSG<BR>
<?/mierror>

<script language=javaScript>
function updateConfirm (pForm) {
    return confirm ("Confirm the updates for Customer " +
                pForm.apb_customer_num.value + " ?");
}
</script>
<!-- Database update form for the customer table -->
<?mivar name="apb_state_" default="GET">$apb_state_<?/mivar>
<?mivar name="apb_error_"><?/mivar>
<!-- POST state: process the update to the table -->
<?miblock cond=$(EQ,$apb_state_,POST)>

        <!-- replace ' with double " so sql will not fail -->
        <?mivar name="apb_fname" default="" >
        $(REPLACE,$apb_fname,',")<?/mivar>
```

Listing 21-4.   (continued)

```
        <?mivar name="apb_lname" default="" >
        $(REPLACE,$apb_lname,',")<?/mivar>
        <?mivar name="apb_company" default="" >
        $(REPLACE,$apb_company,',")<?/mivar>
        <?mivar name="apb_address1" default="">
        $(REPLACE,$apb_address1,',")<?/mivar>
        <?mivar name="apb_address2" default="">
        $(REPLACE,$apb_address2,',")<?/mivar>
        <?mivar name="apb_city" default="">
        $(REPLACE,$apb_city,',")<?/mivar>
        <?mivar name="apb_state" default="">
        $(REPLACE,$apb_state,',")<?/mivar>
        <?mivar name="apb_zipcode" default="" >
        $(REPLACE,$apb_zipcode,',")<?/mivar>
        <?mivar name="apb_phone" default="">
        $(REPLACE,$apb_phone,',")<?/mivar>
        <!--   Build SQL for update statement -->
        <?mivar name="apb_sql_"> UPDATE customer SET
        fname = '$apb_fname' ,
        lname = '$apb_lname' ,
        company = '$apb_company' ,
        address1 = '$apb_address1' ,
        address2 = '$apb_address2' ,
        city = '$apb_city' ,
        state = '$apb_state' ,
        zipcode = '$apb_zipcode' ,
        phone = '$apb_phone'
        WHERE customer_num = '$apb_customer_num' ;<?/mivar>

        <!--  Process Update SQL -->
        <?misql cond=$(EQ,$apb_state_,POST) sql="$apb_sql_">
           <h2>Success! Customer $customer_num_input updated</h2>
        <?/misql>
        <form method=post action="<?mivar>$WEB_HOME<?/mivar>">
            <input type=hidden name=MIval value="selectCustomer">
            <input type=submit value="New Query">
            <input type=submit value="New Customer"
onClick="this.form.MIval.value='newCustomer'; return true;">
        </form>
<?/miblock>
```

Listing 21-4.   (continued)

```
<!-- Database update form for the customer table. -->
<!-- Setup state variable -->
<?mivar name="apb_state_" default="GET">$apb_state_<?/mivar>
<!-- GET state: display the HTML form for the table -->
<?miblock cond=$(EQ,$apb_state_,GET)>
<center>
        <!--- update form -->
        <FORM METHOD=POST ACTION=<?mivar>$WEB_HOME<?/mivar>
        <!-- Hidden variables -->
        <INPUT TYPE=hidden NAME=MIval VALUE="<?mivar>$MIval<?/mivar>">
        <INPUT TYPE=hidden NAME=apb_state_ VALUE="POST">
        <INPUT TYPE=hidden NAME=customer_num_input
        VALUE="<?mivar>$customer_num_input<?/mivar>">

        <!-- Load Values for current row -->
        <?misql sql="SELECT customer_num, fname, lname, company,
address1, address2, city, state, zipcode, phone FROM customer
        WHERE customer_num = '$customer_num_input';"><?/misql>
        <?mivar name="apb_customer_num" default="$1">$apb_customer_num
        <?/mivar>
        <?mivar name="apb_fname" default="$2">$apb_fname<?/mivar>
        <?mivar name="apb_lname" default="$3">$apb_lname<?/mivar>
        <?mivar name="apb_company" default="$4">$apb_company<?/mivar>
        <?mivar name="apb_address1" default="$5">$apb_address1
        <?/mivar>
        <?mivar name="apb_address2" default="$6">$apb_address2
        <?/mivar>
        <?mivar name="apb_city" default="$7">$apb_city<?/mivar>
        <?mivar name="apb_state" default="$8">$apb_state<?/mivar>
        <?mivar name="apb_zipcode" default="$9">$apb_zipcode<?/mivar>
        <?mivar name="apb_phone" default="$10">$apb_phone<?/mivar>

        <?mivar>
        <TABLE>
        <tr>
            <td align=right><b> Customer Number: </b> </td>
            <td>$apb_customer_num  <INPUT type=hidden name=
"apb_customer_num" value="$apb_customer_num"></td>-
        </tr>
        <tr>
```

Listing 21-4. (continued)

```
            <td align=right><b> First Name: </b> </td>
            <td> <input type=text name="apb_fname" value="$apb_fname"
                size="15">  </td>
      </tr>
      <tr>
            <td align=right><b> Last Name: </b> </td>
            <td> <input type=text name="apb_lname" value="$apb_lname"
                size="15">  </td>
      </tr>
      <tr>
            <td align=right><b> Company: </b> </td>
            <td> <input type=text name="apb_company"
                value="$apb_company" size="20">  </td>
      </tr>
      <tr>
            <td align=right><b> Address Line 1: </b> </td>
            <td> <input type=text name="apb_address1"
                value="$apb_address1" size="20">  </td>
      </tr>
      <tr>
            <td align=right><b> Address Line 2: </b> </td>
            <td> <input type=text name="apb_address2"
                value="$apb_address2" size="20">  </td>
      </tr>
      <tr>
            <td align=right><b> City: </b> </td>
            <td> <input type=text name="apb_city" value="$apb_city"
                size="15">  </td>
      </tr>
      <tr>
            <td align=right><b> State: </b> </td>
            <td> <input type=text name="apb_state" value="$apb_state"
                size="2">
<?/mivar><select name=apb_state_change size=1
     onChange="this.form.apb_state.value=this.options
[this.selectedIndex].value;">
<?misql sql="select code, sname from state order by 1">
<option value="$1" $(IF,$(EQ,$apb_state,$1),selected)>$2
<?/misql>
</select><?mivar>
```

Listing 21-4.   (continued)

```
    </td>
      </tr>
      <tr>
         <td align=right><b> Zipcode: </b> </td>
         <td> <input type=text name="apb_zipcode" value=
              "$apb_zipcode" size="5">  </td>
      </tr>
      <tr>
         <td align=right><b> Phone: </b> </td>
         <td> <input type=text name="apb_phone" value="$apb_phone"
              size="18">  </td>
      </tr>
      </TABLE>
      <?/mivar>    <P>
      <!-- Submit button for form -->
      <INPUT type=submit value="Save" onClick="return
updateConfirm(this.form);">
      <input type=reset value="Reset">
      <input type=submit value="New Query"
onClick="this.form.MIval.value='selectCustomer'; return true;">
      <input type=submit value="New Customer"
      onClick="with (this.form) {
                    MIval.value='newCustomer';
                    apb_state_.value='GET';
                    return true;} ">
      </FORM>
</center>
<?/miblock>
<?footer page="$MIval"
audit="Edit Customer: $customer_num_input From: $REMOTE_HOST">
```

When the user chooses to add a new customer from the Select Customer or Edit Customer screens, the Add Customer screen is displayed. When the user has completed the data entry form, as shown in Fig. 21-11, clicking the Insert Customer button will insert the new customer record into the database. A confirmatory screen is then displayed, as shown in Fig. 21-12, that shows the new customer number created.

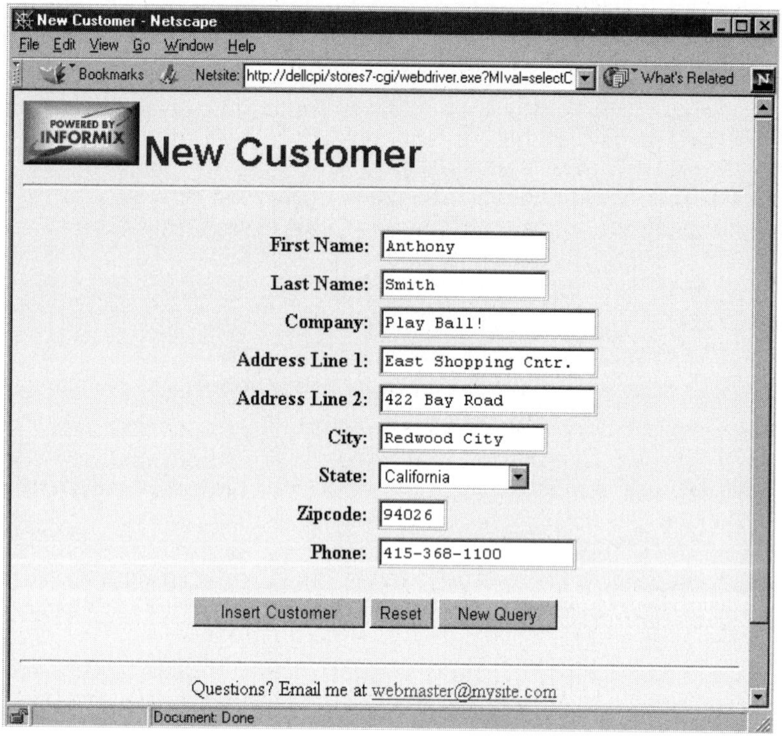

Figure 21-11. New Customer screen.

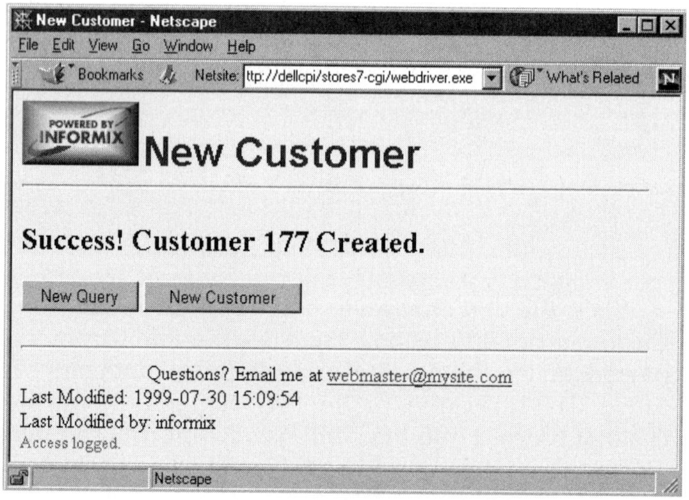

Figure 21-12. New Customer confirmatory screen.

Form Input Validation

Validation is limited to making sure that mandatory fields have been entered and that numeric fields are numeric. Because validation is performed in AppPage Script, it takes place on the database server after the form is submitted. All form fields are declared as mandatory. To check whether a form field has been entered, the following AppPage Script is used:

```
<?mivar name="apb_error_" cond=$(NXST,$apb_company)>
(Error Message)
<?/mivar>
```

The `apb_error_` variable is set if the `Company` form field (named `apb_company` in the form) had no data entered into it, which means that the variable will not be created by `webdriver` on form submission.

Preprocessing of Data

Character fields are passed through the `REPLACE` function to escape single quotes. If the single quotes are not escaped, the SQL will fail with a syntax error. The resulting string is assigned to a variable, which is used in the `INSERT` statement.

```
<?mivar name="apb_company">
$(REPLACE,$apb_company,',")
<?/mivar>
```

Inserting a New Customer Record

Once the form fields have been successfully validated, an `INSERT` statement is created as a string expression and assigned to an AppPage variable, `apb_sql`. This variable is then used in the `MISQL` tag.

```
<?mivar name="apb_sql")>
INSERT INTO customer (
    customer_num, (other fields) phone)
VALUES (
            0, (other fields) '$apb_phone');
<?/mivar>
<!-- Process Insert SQL if no errors -->
<?misql cond=$(EQ,$apb_state_,POST)
        sql="$apb_sql"><?/misql>
```

The customer table has a `serial` column, called `customer_num`, whose value is automatically incremented by the database server when a new record is inserted into the customer table. This is the value displayed in Fig. 21-12.

New Customer AppPage Source

Listing 21-5 shows the `newCustomer.html` AppPage.

Listing 21-5. The `newCustomer.html` AppPage.

```
<?header link=selectCustomer title="New Customer">
<?mierror tag=mivar>
An Error occurred in processing the insert form:<BR><B>
<PRE>$MI_ERRORMSG</PRE></B>Please go Back and try again.
<?/mierror>

<?mivar name="apb_state_"  default="GET">$apb_state_<?/mivar>
<?mivar name="apb_error_"><?/mivar>

<?miblock cond=$(EQ,$apb_state_,POST)>

        <!-- validate mandatory fields -->
        <?mivar name="apb_state_"
        cond=$(NXST,$apb_fname)>ERROR<?/mivar>
        <?mivar name="apb_error_"
        cond=$(NXST,$apb_fname)>$apb_error_<BR>* Field
"fname" was mandatory but was not entered.<?/mivar>
        <?mivar name="apb_state_"
        cond=$(NXST,$apb_lname)>ERROR<?/mivar>
        <?mivar name="apb_error_"
        cond=$(NXST,$apb_lname)>$apb_error_<BR>* Field "lname" was
mandatory but was not entered.<?/mivar>
        <?mivar name="apb_state_"
        cond=$(NXST,$apb_company)>ERROR<?/mivar>
        <?mivar name="apb_error_"
        cond=$(NXST,$apb_company)>$apb_error_<BR>* Field "company"
was mandatory but was not entered.<?/mivar>
        <?mivar name="apb_state_"
        cond=$(NXST,$apb_address1)>ERROR<?/mivar>
        <?mivar name="apb_error_"
```

Listing 21-5. (continued)

```
        cond=$(NXST,$apb_address1)>$apb_error_<BR>* Field "address1"
was mandatory but was not entered.<?/mivar>
        <?mivar name="apb_state_"
        cond=$(NXST,$apb_address2)>ERROR<?/mivar>
        <?mivar name="apb_error_"
cond=$(NXST,$apb_address2)>$apb_error_<BR>* Field "address2" was
mandatory but was not entered.<?/mivar>
        <?mivar name="apb_state_"
        cond=$(NXST,$apb_city)>ERROR<?/mivar>
        <?mivar name="apb_error_"
        cond=$(NXST,$apb_city)>$apb_error_<BR>* Field "city" was
mandatory but was not entered.<?/mivar>
        <?mivar name="apb_state_"
        cond=$(NXST,$apb_state)>ERROR<?/mivar>
        <?mivar name="apb_error_"
        cond=$(NXST,$apb_state)>$apb_error_<BR>* Field "state" was
mandatory but was not entered.<?/mivar>
        <?mivar name="apb_state_"
        cond=$(NXST,$apb_zipcode)>ERROR<?/mivar>
        <?mivar name="apb_error_"
        cond=$(NXST,$apb_zipcode)>$apb_error_<BR>* Field "zipcode"
was mandatory but was not entered.<?/mivar>
        <?mivar name="apb_state_"
        cond=$(NXST,$apb_phone)>ERROR<?/mivar>
        <?mivar name="apb_error_"
        cond=$(NXST,$apb_phone)>$apb_error_<BR>* Field "phone" was
mandatory but was not entered.<?/mivar>

        <?miblock cond=$(EQ,$apb_state_,POST)>
        <!-- assign default values -->
         <!-- validate that integers are integers -->
         <!-- replace ' with double " so sql will not fail -->
        <?mivar name="apb_fname">$(REPLACE,$apb_fname,',")<?/mivar>
        <?mivar name="apb_lname">$(REPLACE,$apb_lname,',")<?/mivar>
        <?mivar name="apb_company">$(REPLACE,$apb_company,',")
        <?/mivar>
        <?mivar name="apb_address1">$(REPLACE,$apb_address1,',")
        <?/mivar>
        <?mivar name="apb_address2">$(REPLACE,$apb_address2,',")
        <?/mivar>
        <?mivar name="apb_city">$(REPLACE,$apb_city,',")<?/mivar>
```

Listing 21-5. (continued)

```
<?mivar name="apb_state">$(REPLACE,$apb_state,',")<?/mivar>
<?mivar name="apb_zipcode">$(REPLACE,$apb_zipcode,',")
<?/mivar>
<?mivar name="apb_phone">$(REPLACE,$apb_phone,',")<?/mivar>

<!-- Build SQL for insert statement -->
<?mivar name="apb_sql")>
INSERT INTO customer (
  customer_num, fname, lname, company, address1,
  address2, city, state, zipcode, phone)
VALUES (
  0, '$apb_fname', '$apb_lname', '$apb_company',
  '$apb_address1', '$apb_address2', '$apb_city',
  '$apb_state', '$apb_zipcode',
  '$apb_phone');
<?/mivar>
<!-- Process Insert SQL if no errors -->
<?misql cond=$(EQ,$apb_state_,POST) sql="$apb_sql">
<?/misql>
<?misql cond=$(EQ,$apb_state_,POST)
sql="select DBINFO('sqlca.sqlerrd1')
  from systables
  where tabname = 'systables'">
  <h2>Success! Customer $1 Created.</h2>
  $(SETVAR,$NEWCUST,$1)
<?/misql>

<form method=post action="<?mivar>$WEB_HOME<?/mivar>">
  <input type=hidden
         name=MIval value="selectCustomer">
  <input type=submit value="New Query">
  <input type=submit value="New Customer"
onClick="this.form.MIval.value='newCustomer'; return true;">
</form>

<?/miblock>
<!-- Display error message if we got an error -->
<?mivar cond=
$(EQ,$apb_state_,ERROR)>$apb_error_<?/mivar>
```

Listing 21-5. *(continued)*

```
        <?footer cond=$(NE,$apb_state_,ERROR)
        page="$MIval"
        audit="New Customer: $NEWCUST created From: $REMOTE_HOST">

        <!-- Reset State so form is redisplayed for errors -->
        <?mivar name="apb_state_"
        cond=$(EQ,$apb_state_,ERROR)>GET<?/mivar>
<?/miblock>

<!-- Database insert form for the customer table.
<!-- Setup state variable -->
<?mivar name=apb_state_ default="GET">$apb_state_<?/mivar>
<!-- GET State: display the HTML form for the table -->
<?miblock cond=$(EQ,$apb_state_,GET)>
        <!-- input form -->
        <center>
        <FORM METHOD=POST ACTION=<?mivar>$WEB_HOME<?/mivar>
        <!-- hidden variables -->
        <INPUT TYPE=hidden NAME=MIval
     VALUE="<?mivar>$MIval<?/mivar>">
        <INPUT TYPE=hidden NAME=apb_state_ VALUE="POST">
        <TABLE BORDER=0 WIDTH=100%>

        <?mivar name="apb_fname" default="">$apb_fname<?/mivar>
        <?mivar name="apb_lname" default="">$apb_lname<?/mivar>
        <?mivar name="apb_company"
        default="">$apb_company<?/mivar>
        <?mivar name="apb_address1"
        default="">$apb_address1<?/mivar>
        <?mivar name="apb_address2"
        default="">$apb_address2<?/mivar>
        <?mivar name="apb_city" default="">$apb_city<?/mivar>
        <?mivar name="apb_state" default="">$apb_state<?/mivar>
        <?mivar name="apb_zipcode"
        default="">$apb_zipcode<?/mivar>
        <?mivar name="apb_phone" default="">$apb_phone<?/mivar>

        <?mivar>
        <tr>
        <td align=right width=50%><b> First Name: <b></td>
```

Listing 21-5.   (continued)

```
   <td><input type=text name="apb_fname"
      value="$apb_fname" size="15">  <BR></td>
   </tr>
   <tr>
   <td align=right><b> Last Name: <b></td>
   <td><input type=text name="apb_lname"
      value="$apb_lname" size="15">  <BR></td>
   </tr>
   <tr>
   <td align=right><b> Company: <b></td>
   <td><input type=text name="apb_company"
      value="$apb_company" size="20">  <BR></td>
   </tr>
   <tr>
   <td align=right><b> Address Line 1: <b></td>
   <td><input type=text name="apb_address1"
      value="$apb_address1" size="20">  <BR></td>
   </tr>
   <tr>
   <td align=right><b> Address Line 2: <b></td>
   <td><input type=text name="apb_address2"
      value="$apb_address2" size="20">  <BR></td>
   </tr>
   <tr>
   <td align=right><b> City: <b></td>
   <td><input type=text name="apb_city" value="$apb_city"
      size="15">  <BR></td>
   </tr>
   <tr>
   <td align=right><b> State: <b></td>
   <td><?/mivar>
<select name="apb_state" sizc=1>
   <?misql sql="select code, sname
          from state order by 1">
      <option value="$1">$2
   <?/misql>
</select><?mivar>
   </td>
   </tr>
   <tr>
   <td align=right><b> Zipcode: <b></td>
```

Listing 21-5. *(continued)*

```
        <td><input type=text name="apb_zipcode"
            value="$apb_zipcode" size="5">  <BR></td>
        </tr>
        <tr>
        <td align=right><b> Phone: <b></td>
        <td><input type=text name="apb_phone"
            value="$apb_phone" size="18">  <BR></td>
        </tr>
        <?/mivar>
        </TABLE><P>
        <!-- Submit button for form -->
        <input type="submit" value="Insert Customer">
        <input type="reset" value="Reset">
        <input type="submit" value="New Query"
     onClick="this.form.MIval.value='selectCustomer';
             return true;">
        </center>
        </FORM>
<?footer page="$MIval" audit="" From: $REMOTE_HOST">
<?/miblock>
```

Deleting Customer Details

In the View Customer screen, the user can choose to delete the currently displayed customer from the database. When the Delete Customer button is clicked, the user confirms deletion before the customer is deleted from the database.

For example, assume we want to delete customer 176. We select the customer from the Select Customer screen by entering 176 into the Customer Number field and clicking Select. The View Customer screen is displayed as shown in Fig. 21-13.

We then click the Delete Customer button. JavaScript traps this event, and displays a confirmatory prompt asking the user whether he would like to continue, as shown in Fig. 21-14.

If the user clicks Cancel, the delete request is cancelled, otherwise the deleteCustomer AppPage is invoked to delete the customer from the customer table. When the customer has been deleted successfully, the browser displays the page shown in Fig. 21-15.

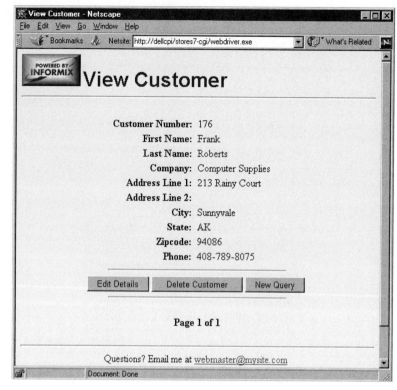

Figure 21-13. *View Customer 176 to delete.*

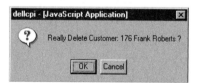

Figure 21-14. *JavaScript dialog to confirm deletion.*

If the customer had already been deleted by another user after the first user selected the customer but before he chose to delete, then the deleteCustomer AppPage traps this and generates the response as shown in Fig. 21-16.

Delete Customer AppPage Source

Listing 21-6 shows the deleteCustomer.html AppPage.

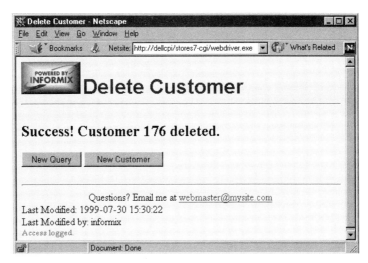

Figure 21-15. *Delete Customer confirmation page.*

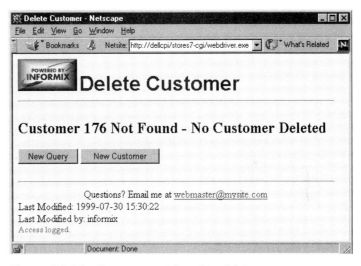

Figure 21-16. *Customer not found to delete.*

Screen Navigation Using JavaScript and Forms

Forms are used to navigate between screens, in contrast to hyperlinks. The default page selected is usually the current AppPage, `$MIval`. This can be overridden in JavaScript, depending on the button the user clicks. For example, in `deleteCustomer.html`, if the user clicks the New Customer button, the `onClick` JavaScript event

Listing 21-6. *The* `deleteCustomer.html` *AppPage.*

```
<?header link=selectCustomer title="Delete Customer">

<!-- Error Handling for this Page -->
<?mierror tag=mivar>
An Error occurred in processing the Delete request:<BR><B>
<PRE>$MI_ERRORMSG</PRE></B>
Please go Back and try again.<?/mierror>

<!-- Delete the Customer -->
<?misql sql="delete from customer
        where customer_num = '$customer_num_input';">
<?/misql>

<!-- Check if customer was deleted -->
<?mivar cond=$(!=,$MI_ROWCOUNT,0)>
<h2>Success! Customer $customer_num_input  deleted. </h2>
<?/mivar>
<?mivar cond=$(=,$MI_ROWCOUNT,0)>
<h2>Customer $customer_num_input Not Found -
  No Customer Deleted</h2>
<?/mivar>

<!-- Navigation -->
<form method=post action="<?mivar>$WEB_HOME<?/mivar>">
        <input type=hidden name=MIval value="selectCustomer">
        <input type=submit value="New Query">
        <input type=submit value="New Customer"
      onClick="this.form.MIval.value='newCustomer';
             return true;">
</form>

<?footer page="$MIval" audit="Delete Customer:
$customer_num_input From: $REMOTE_HOST">
```

handler is actioned to change the value of the form field `MIval` to
the name of the New Customer AppPage, `newCustomer`. The event
handler returns `true` so that the form can be submitted and the
`newCustomer` AppPage exploded. The coding is shown below.

```
<!-- Navigation -->
<form method=post
```

```
            action="<?mivar>$WEB_HOME<?/mivar>">
        <input type=hidden
                name=MIval value="selectCustomer">
        <input type=submit value="New Query">
        <input type=submit value="New Customer"
            onClick =
    "this.form.MIval.value='newCustomer';
            return true;">
    </form>
```

This example uses forms to navigate screens, even though in some cases there is no input data other than the button values. You may decide to use forms for navigation if you have a number of variables to pass between screens that would make using hyperlinks too cumbersome. For example, you should use the URLENCODE *variable-processing function when passing parameters via hyperlinks. If you use a form, the browser will automatically encode the data, making the coding overhead simpler.*

The Edit Customer AppPage, editCustomer.html, has a variant on the above. From the Edit Customer screen, the user can click the New Customer button to navigate to the newCustomer.html AppPage. However, newCustomer.html is a two-stage AppPage: (1) form data capture; (2) form data processing. The value of the form variable to control the initial state of the newCustomer AppPage is set to GET, and the target AppPage is set to newCustomer, as shown in the following snippet.

```
<input type=submit value="New Customer"
onClick="with (this.form) {

    MIval.value='newCustomer';

    apb_state_.value='GET';

    return true;}">
```

Extending the Application

It is reasonably simple to implement some extensions in this application. For example, the user may not want to view all the columns for the selected customer. Additionally, the user may want to order the selected rows based on one or more columns in ascending or descending sequence. For either of these cases, you can implement the column and order selection logic as shown in the final section of Chap. 17 dealing with the database browser.

Dynamic Headers and Footers

The AppPages in this chapter use the same dynamic tags to render both the header and footer of the HTML page. This is a simple but useful example of code reuse. In addition, each instance of the dynamic tag in an AppPage is parameterized to yield specific behavior in the dynamic tag for that particular AppPage.

Creating Headers

Each AppPage header uses the `header` dynamic tag. This tag takes two parameters:

- a link to a home page,
- a string as title of the page.

The header displays an image as an IMG hyperlink. The page title is displayed next to it. For example, the New Customer AppPage, `newCustomer.html`, contains the following reference to the `header` dynamic tag.

```
<?header link=selectCustomer title="New Customer">
```

When the HTML page is constructed, the logo will be created as a hyperlink that, when clicked in the browser, will invoke the `selectCustomer.html` AppPage.

Listing 21-7 shows the `header` dynamic tag.

Listing 21-7.   The `header` dynamic tag.

```
<html>
<head><title>@title@</title></head>

<body bgcolor="#F7F7F7">

<a href="<?mivar>$WEB_HOME<?/mivar>?MIval=@link@">
<img src=
"<?mivar>
$WEB_HOME<?/mivar>?MIvalObj=informix_button&MItypeObj=image/gif"
border=0 alt="New Query"></a>
<font size=+3 face="arial" color="#003300"><b>@title@</b></font>
<br clear=all>
<hr>
```

note

See Chap. 19, "Creating and Using Dynamic Tags," for detailed information on dynamic tags. See Chap. 20, "Working with Large Objects," for instructions how to retrieve large objects (e.g., images) from the database.

Creating Footers

Each AppPage uses the `footer` dynamic tag, which takes two parameters:

- the current AppPage ID,
- the IP address of the browser client.

For example:

```
<?footer page="$MIval" audit="" From: $REMOTE_HOST">
```

The `$MIval` variable will be set to the ID of the currently exploding AppPage.

The `footer` tag selects the AppPage metadata information, such as the most recently changed date, and writes it to the HTML page.

It then creates an audit log entry in the `audit` table for the AppPage. The tag then increments the hit count for the calling AppPage.

Note that if you are using the API `webdriver`, the `REMOTE_HOST` variable may not be available to you.

Listing 21-8 contains the `footer` dynamic tag.

Listing 21-8. The `footer` *dynamic tag*.

```
<hr>
<center>Questions? Email me at
<a
href="mailto:webmaster@ATSIGN@mysite.com">webmaster@ATSIGN@mysite.com</a>
<br>

</center>
<?misql sql="select last_changed, last_changed_by from wbPages where
id='@page@';">
Last Modified: $1<br>
```

Listing 21-8. *(continued)*

```
Last Modified by: $2<br>
<?/misql>

<?misql sql="insert into audit (access_tm, page_id, remote_user,
comment) values ( current, '@page@','$REMOTE_USER','@audit@');">
<font size=-1 color=red>Access logged.<br></font>
<?/misql>

<?misql sql="update hits set (num_hits)=(num_hits + 1) where
page_id='@page@' and log_date=today;">
<?/misql>
<!-- Find out how many rows were updated using dbinfo and store it in
a variable -->
<?misql sql="select unique dbinfo('sqlca.sqlerrd2') from systables;">
   $(SETVAR,num_rows,$1)
<?/misql>
<?misql cond=$(EQ,$num_rows,0) sql="insert into hits
(page_id,log_date,num_hits) values ('@page@', today, 1 );"><font
size=-1 color=red>First access to the page!<br>
</font>
<?/misql>

</body>
</html>
```

Summary

In this chapter we have a simple end-to-end working example that shows how to maintain data in the database using HTML forms, AppPage Script, JavaScript, and dynamic tags. We have also seen how to create dynamic SQL queries on the browser client using JavaScript, as well as how to execute these queries on the database server using HTML forms and AppPage Script.

Even though AppPage Script executes on the server and JavaScript on the client, we have seen how easy it is to integrate these technologies to produce a functional browser interface to the database. Larger production-level applications that you develop will differ in degree, not in kind, from this example.

Part

4

Advanced Configuration and Performance

Understanding webdriver Configuration

In this chapter:

- The webdriver program
- The Web DataBlade Module Administration Tool
- webdriver configurations
- webdriver variables
- webdriver configuration file format from Version 4
- Configuring webdriver—The basics
- Example: Creating a webdriver configuration for a catalog application (Versions 3 and 4)
- Converting web.cnf from Version 3 to Version 4
- Overwriting webdriver variables
- Managing application characteristics
- Connecting to multiple databases

The `webdriver` Program

The term `webdriver` is used to refer to one of the following:

- the CGI program used with CGI URLs,
- the NSAPI DLL or shared object used with Netscape web servers,
- the ISAPI DLL used with Microsoft Internet Informix Server,
- the Apache DLL or shared object used with the Apache web server.

It is convenient to use the term `webdriver` when talking about configuration, since the essential configuration issues are the same for each type of `webdriver` program.

The `webdriver` configuration file is called `web.cnf`. This file stores all the information required to connect to the Informix database, retrieve web content, and process AppPage templates. In Version 3 of the Web DataBlade, a single `web.cnf` file maps to one URL prefix and one database.

In Version 4, there is only one `web.cnf`, denoted by the environment variable `MI_WEBCONFIG`. This single `web.cnf` contains mappings for each URL prefix.

See Chap. 12, "Web DataBlade Architecture," for details on how `webdriver` fits into the Web DataBlade architecture.

See Chap. 23, "Web Server Integration," for details on the different types of `webdriver` program.

The Web DataBlade Module Administration Tool

The Web DataBlade Module Administration Tool is a browser application that is introduced with Version 4. This tool is the interface to the `web.cnf` file for creating new `webdriver` mappings and for creating and updating `webdriver` configurations.

When Version 4 is installed, the administration tool is installed into its own schema, and is created with a URL prefix such as `dbname-admin`, which you need to add to the web server so that you can invoke the administration tool from the browser. In this chapter you will see examples of how to use this tool. Note that you can edit the `web.cnf` file yourself if you need to.

note

The Web DataBlade Module Administration Tool needs to be installed in each database that will contain the Web DataBlade. When you install Version 4 of the Web DataBlade, you will also install the Web DataBlade Module Administration Tool.

`webdriver` Configurations

A Web DataBlade module application needs a number of variables defined for it. Up to Version 4, all of these variables were defined in the `web.cnf` file associated with a particular URL prefix. Therefore, the `webdriver` configuration was wholly contained in the `web.cnf` file.

If you are using a version of the Web DataBlade before Version 4 (for example, Version 3.32) then, to access multiple databases with different `webdriver` configurations, you need to create multiple `web.cnf` files, one for each database.

From Version 4, most of these variables are defined in a table called `webconfigs`. A collection of variables stored in the `webconfigs` table is called a `webdriver` configuration. All `webdriver` configurations are stored in the `webconfigs` table. You identify a set of variables for a particular configuration by the value of a column called `config_name`.

We can define a `webdriver` *configuration* for Version 3 of the Web DataBlade as the `web.cnf` file, in contrast to the Version 4 implementation, which is the web mappings in `web.cnf` plus the variables defined in the `webconfigs` table.

tip

From Version 4, you can include disabled variables in a `webdriver` *configuration. Even though the Web DataBlade Module Administration Tool lists the* `webdriver` *variable as part of the* `webdriver` *configuration, the* `webdriver` *variable does not affect the way* `webdriver` *behaves. This feature is useful when you develop applications and need to disable and enable* `webdriver` *functionality many times but you do not want to keep adding and deleting the variable from the* `webdriver` *configuration. In Version 3 of the Web DataBlade, you need to comment out the variable in* `web.cnf` *using the "#" character.*

`webdriver` Variables

Different types of variables are required by `webdriver`. Some tell `webdriver` which tables to read to retrieve AppPages from; others alter the behavior of `webdriver`; still others are application specific as created and named by the application developer. Whether you are using Version 3 or Version 4, you can define three types of variable:

- schema-related variables,
- feature-related variables,
- user-created (application) variables.

Schema-related Variables

The *schema-related* `webdriver` variables identify where the App-Pages for a particular configuration are stored. If you use AppPage Builder for application development, then these variables must be set. If you use Data Director for Web, then you do not have to set these variables. This is because you can set the `MI_WEBSCHEMADEF` variable to the value "wb", which tells `webdriver` to use the predefined Data Director for Web schema.

The schema-related variables are the minimum set of `webdriver` variables that you must set to be able to use the Web DataBlade. These variables are set when you initially create a `webdriver` configuration based on either the AppPage Builder or Data Director for Web configurations.

You can create your own set of tables to hold AppPages and large objects. In this case, since you would create your new configuration based on the AppPage Builder schema, you would change the values of the variables such as `MInam` and `MItab`. Nevertheless, if you use your own schema, the schema-related *variables* must be set to point to your schema.

Table 22-1 describes the schema-related `webdriver` variables. Realistically, you will be using large objects such as GIF images and

Table 22-1. Mandatory schema-related variables.

Variable	Description
MItab	The name of the table where the AppPages are stored for all applications in this configuration.
MIcol	The name of the column in the `MItab` table that contains the AppPage as an HTML object.
MInam	The name of the column that contains the identity of the AppPage. This is a VARCHAR column.
MIval	The value stored in the `MInam` column. This identifies the *default* AppPage we need to fetch from the table denoted by `MItab` if `MIval` is not set in a URL or form.

Table 22-2. Large object schema-related variables.

Variable	Description
MItabObj	The name of the table where the large objects are stored for all applications (`webimages` or `wbBinaries`, for example).
MIcolObj	The name of the column in the `MItabObj` table that contains the large object reference (`object`, for example).
MInamObj	The name of the column that contains the identity of the large object (`ID`, for example).
MIvalObj	The value stored in the `MInam` column. This is set dynamically when retrieving large objects by name, and it identifies the value in the `MInamObj` column.

perhaps office documents such as MS-Excel spreadsheets. You therefore need to define more variables that nominate the *large object schema*. These are listed in Table 22-2.

Schema-related Variables in Version 4

The schema-related variables are defaulted in the three configurations that are installed with Version 4 of the Web DataBlade.

Default Settings for Schema-related Variables

The default settings for the schema-related variables depend on the configuration they belong to. There are three default configurations.

- APB. This configuration sets the schema-related variables to refer to the APB schema.
- DDW. This configuration sets the schema-related variables to refer to the DDW schema.
- ADMIN. This configuration sets the schema-related variables to refer to the ADMIN schema, on which the Web DataBlade Module Administration Tool operates.

Table 22-3 lists the default settings for the different configurations. Because the AppPages for Data Director for Web are managed by a windows client application, MIval only has meaning when set for running applications, in contrast to AppPage Builder, which is a browser application.

Table 22-3. Schema-related variable settings.		
Variable	**Configuration**	**Value**
MItab	APB	webpages
MItab	DDW	wbpages
MItab	ADMIN	webcmpages
MIcol	APB	object
MIcol	DDW	object
MIcol	ADMIN	object
MInam	APB	ID
MInam	DDW	ID
MInam	ADMIN	ID
MIval	APB	Apb
MIval	DDW	Application specific
MIval	ADMIN	Cm

The Data Director for Web configuration needs only to have the schema_version *or* MI_WEBSCHEMADEF *variable set to the value "*wb*" for* webdriver *to map the Data Director for Web schema correctly.*

How the webexplode Function Uses the Schema-related Variables

When webdriver processes a webdriver URL (for example, http://dellcpi/catalog/HelloCatalog), webdriver will put together an SQL statement from the following template:

```
SELECT webexplode($MIcol,'ENVIRONMENT')
FROM $MItab
WHERE $MInam = '$MIval';
```

If you are using the Data Director for Web configuration or a configuration based on it, then the following SQL statement is produced for the URL http://dellcpi/catalog/HelloCatalog:

```
SELECT
webexplode(object,'variable=val&variable=val&..') FROM
wbpages WHERE ID = 'HelloCatalog'
```

If you are using the AppPage Builder configuration or a configuration based on it, then the following SQL statement is produced for the same URL:

```
SELECT
webexplode(object,'variable=val&variable=val&..') FROM
webpages WHERE ID = 'HelloCatalog'
```

The ENVIRONMENT parameter is a string of variable assignments in URL-encoded form. These are the variables that are created in the configuration and that you add to the configuration.

You have control over how many variables you pass to webexplode. *You may want to stop variables from being passed to* webexplode *for both performance and security reasons. As a general rule, you should pass only variables that affect the behavior of the AppPage, not variables that affect the behavior of* webdriver. *See Chap. 24, "Securing Your Web Applications," for more details on this topic.*

Feature-related Variables

The feature-related webdriver variables enable specific webdriver features, such as AppPage caching or large object support. You do not have to include these webdriver variables in a webdriver configuration; you only add and set them when you want to enable a particular feature. An example would be MI_WEBDRVLEVEL and MI_WEBDRVLOG, which set the webdriver tracing level and trace output file.

User-related (Application) Variables

These variables are used by AppPage Script. You can set variables to control the behavior of your AppPage Script applications. An example would be specialOffer, which can be set to a string, including HTML formatting, that describes a special offer. For example:

```
specialOffer    <I>One Hundred Floppy Disks</I>
```

webdriver Configuration File Format, Version 4

From Version 4, you create one web.cnf file for each Informix server instance.

The `web.cnf` file format can be briefly listed as follows:

- `global` section,
- `setvar` section,
- `map` section.

Global **Section**

The `global` section of the `web.cnf` file describes the `webdriver` variables that are global to the client connection to the database. These variables will have the same values whichever URL prefix you use. For example:

```
<global>
debug_file /tmp/driver.log
debug_level 2
anchorvar WEB_HOME/webdriver.exe
</global>
<map path=/stores7-cgi>
</map>
```

The Version 3.x equivalent would be:

```
MI_WEBDRVLOG        /tmp/driver.log
MI_WEBDRVLEVEL    2
WEB_HOME    /stores7-cgi/webdriver.exe
```

The WEB_HOME *variable in Version 3 is set to include the URL prefix. From Version 4, the URL prefix is defined in the* map *section of* web.cnf.

Table 22-4 lists the set of variables you can initialize in the `global` section.

You can map these variables onto Version 3 equivalents using Appendix A, "Variable Mappings."

Setvar **Section**

The `setvar` section of the `web.cnf` file describes environment variables, or variables that you can also set in your UNIX or Windows environment. In particular, the `setvar` section describes the Informix environment variables such as INFORMIXDIR, INFORMIXSERVER, and DBDATE.

```
<setvar>
INFORMIXDIR D:\informix
INFORMIXSERVER ol_dellcpi
</setvar>
```

Table 22-4.   Variables you can set in the global section of
               web.cnf.

Variable	Description
dbconnmax	Maximum number of connections to the database.
anchorvar	Always set to WEB_HOME; translates to a URL prefix written to the exploded HTML file.
driverdir	Apache and CGI webdriver only; used by webdriver to coordinate the interaction with the web server.
debug_file	Log file for webdriver tracing.
debug_level	Level of webdriver tracing.
maxcharsize	If you are using a multibyte character set, set this value greater than 1 to force URL-encoding of every character sent to webexplode().
config_user	Name of the Web DataBlade Module Administration Tool user.
config_password	Password of the config_user user.

The Version 3.x equivalent is:

```
INFORMIXDIR      D:\informix
INFORMIXSERVER   ol_dellcpi
```

Map **Section**

The map section of the web.cnf file describes the mapping between a URL prefix on the web server and a webdriver configuration stored in a database. The variables in the map section describe how webdriver connects to a particular database. The collection of variables that make up a single map section in the web.cnf file is called a webdriver mapping. For example:

```
<map path=/stores7-wb4-cgi>
database stores74
user informix
password 86520153fd81d8940fb742b4fabba23a
password_key informix
config_name ddw
</map>
```

The `map` section assigns variables to values that are used to connect to a database for that URL.

The `database`, `user`, and `config_name` variables are mandatory, since they nominate the database to connect to, the user to connect as, and the variables settings (schema, feature, and user related) to use, which are in the configuration defined with the `config_name` variable.

The equivalent Version 3 settings in `web.cnf` would be:

```
MI_DATABASE        stores74
MI_USER            informix
MI_PASSWORD        86520153fd81d8940fb742b4fabba23a
MI_PASSWORD_KEY    informix
```

Table 22-5 lists the variables that you can set in the `map` section of `web.cnf`.

`webdriver` Environment Settings

The `webdriver` program needs to locate the `web.cnf` file to read the mapping information so that it can connect to the database. To locate the `web.cnf` file, `webdriver` requires an environment

Table 22-5. *Variables that you can set in the* `map` *section of* `web.cnf`.

Variable	Description
database	Informix database to connect to.
user	Name of the user to connect to the database with.
password	Encrypted password for user.
password key	Decryption key for password.
server	Informix server to connect to; if not set, the value of INFORMIXSERVER (in the setvar section) is used.
config_name	The webdriver configuration to use, e.g., apb, ddw, catalog.
config_security	Only the user specified in the config_user variable in the global section can use this particular webdriver mapping.

variable called `MI_WEBCONFIG` to be set to the full pathname of the `web.cnf` file. For example, if the `web.cnf` file is located in `D:\catalog\configs`, then set `MI_WEBCONFIG` to:

```
D:\catalog\configs\web.cnf
```

Use the following sections to locate your web server and `webdriver` usage so that you can set `MI_WEBCONFIG` in the environment properly.

CGI `webdriver`

The CGI `webdriver` ignores the environment variable `MI_WEBCONFIG` and always looks for the `web.cnf` file in the same directory as the CGI `webdriver` program.

NSAPI `webdriver`

Set the variable in the Netscape web server startup file and in the environment of the user who starts the Netscape web server processes.

ISAPI `webdriver`

Set `MI_WEBCONFIG` as a system variable using the Start\Settings\Control Panel and the System icon. Set in the first List box in the Environment tab.

Apache `webdriver`

Set the variable in the Apache web server startup file (usually a shell script) or in the environment of the user who starts the Apache web server.

Configuring `webdriver`—the Basics

This section shows how to create a basic `webdriver` configuration in Version 3 and Version 4 of the Web DataBlade. The example uses the CGI version of `webdriver`. For information on how to use NSAPI, ISAPI, or (from Version 4) the Apache API, see Chap. 23, "Web Server Integration."

The example illustrates how to connect the URL prefix /shopper with the Informix database via the webdriver program and the webdriver configuration file. The following steps are covered:

- What is the basic configuration?
- connecting to the database,
- configuring WEB_HOME as an anchor variable,
- configuring the web schema,
- adding feature-related variables,
- adding user (Application) variables,
- the result: a basic web.cnf in Version 3 and Version 4.

Once the basics work, you can then extend your configuration in areas such as the following:

- password encryption (see Chap. 24),
- basic and secure URL prefixes for NSAPI, ISAPI, and Apache API (see Chap. 23)
- performance optimizations, such as caching AppPages and large objects (see Chap. 25)

What Is the Basic Configuration?

The basic webdriver configuration allows webdriver to connect to the Informix database to call the webexplode() function to explode an AppPage. You don't need a web server to do this; you can call the CGI webdriver from the command line and have the exploded AppPage written to the screen.

If the AppPage contains hyperlinks that reference other AppPages or large object content such as images that reside in the Informix database, then the webdriver reference WEB_HOME needs to be included also. In short, you need to configure the Informix connectivity settings, as well as the web content schema where the AppPages reside.

Connecting to the Database

The webdriver needs to connect to the database to explode AppPages and retrieve web content. The web.cnf file must contain the basic connectivity information to allow webdriver to do this.

Communication between webdriver and the Informix Server

The Informix server instance can be local (on the web server machine with webdriver) or remote. If the Informix server instance is remote, then the appropriate settings must exist in the registry (NT4), or SQLHOSTS *(UNIX) so that the Informix server mappings in* web.cnf *can be resolved. Remember that* webdriver *uses these settings to connect to the Informix server and database to read AppPages and extract large objects, so in this sense,* webdriver *is a client program and therefore needs the Informix connectivity layer on the machine where it runs (the web server).*

Assume that we want to connect to the catalog database as the user cortez. We need to specify

- the database that webdriver will connect to,
- the user that webdriver will connect as,
- the password for the user,
- the value of INFORMIXDIR,
- the INFORMIXSERVER to connect to.

Version 3

The connectivity requirements are implemented in the web.cnf file as shown in List. 22-1.

See Chap. 24 for details of how to encrypt the password in web.cnf.

Version 4

The connectivity requirements are implemented in the web.cnf file as shown in List. 22-2. Note that the password and password_key variables are set differently. If you use the Web DataBlade Module Administration Tool or the webconfig utility to add a mapping, then the password is encrypted.

Listing 22-1. Connectivity in Version 3.

```
MI_DATABASE          catalog
MI_USER              cortez
MI_PASSWORD          cOrtez
REMOTE_USER?         default

INFORMIXDIR          d:\informix
INFORMIXSERVER       ol_dellcpi
```

Listing 22-2. **Connectivity variables in Version 4.**

```
<setvar>
INFORMIXDIR D:\informix
INFORMIXSERVER ol_dellcpi
</setvar>
<map path=/shopper>
database catalog
user cortez
password 2deda0277c0bd8cd59b97024d1a907be
password_key 37b5790f
</map>
```

You can override the INFORMIXSERVER *setting in the* map *section to connect to a different Informix server by including the* server *variable.*

Configuring WEB_HOME as an Anchor Variable

We need to set the WEB_HOME variable so that it can be used throughout the application as an anchor variable. This allows you to use the $WEB_HOME variable in an AppPage, and the URL prefix will be substituted for it. For example:

```
<FORM METHOD=POST ACTION=<?mivar>$WEB_HOME<?/mivar>
```

becomes

```
<FORM METHOD=POST ACTION=/shopper/webdriver.exe>
```

Version 3

For the CGI URL prefix /shopper, set the WEB_HOME variable in web.cnf as follows:

```
WEB_HOME /shopper/webdriver.exe # for CGI
```

If the /shopper URL prefix was an NSAPI or ISAPI URL, for example, then WEB_HOME would be:

```
WEB_HOME /shopper/              # for NSAPI
WEB_HOME /shopper/drvisapi.dll  # for ISAPI
```

Version 4

You use `WEB_HOME` as the `anchorvar` (you can call it what you want, but `WEB_HOME` is the standard). You edit the `web.cnf` file and place `WEB_HOME` in the `global` section.

This is an example for the CGI `/shopper` URL prefix:

```
<global>
anchorvar WEB_HOME/webdriver.exe
</global>
```

See Chap. 23 for `anchorvar` examples in NSAPI, ISAPI, and Apache API.

The CGI `web.cnf` file must reside in the same directory as the CGI `webdriver` program. In an installation where you have an API `webdriver` (e.g., NSAPI) and a CGI `webdriver` in use, you need two `web.cnf` files. The first is for the CGI mapping that resides in the CGI `webdriver` directory, and the second is the mapping for the NSAPI (or ISAPI or Apache API) `webdriver`. This second `web.cnf` file is the file mapped by the `MI_WEBCONFIG` system environment variable that is passed to the API version of `webdriver`. The CGI `webdriver` does not need `MI_WEBCONFIG` set.

Configuring the Web Schema

The web schema is the schema that stores the web content such as AppPages, image files, audio files, and office documents. The variables in `web.cnf` that define the schema are called the schema-related variables.

Version 3

If you use AppPage Builder, then you need to set the list of mandatory schema-related variables in `web.cnf`. If you are using a different set of tables to store web content, then you need to set the values of these variables to the names and columns of the approriate tables. For example:

```
# AppPage storage
MInam?          ID
Micol?          object
MItab?          webpages
```

```
# Large Object storage, e.g., audio, documents, graphics
MItabObj?  webimages
MIcolObj?  object
MInamObj?  ID
MItypeObj? image/gif
MIval      apb
```

Note that `MIval` is defaulted to `apb`; if we invoke the `/shopper/ webdriver.exe` URL without setting `MIval` on the command line, the AppPage Builder application will be displayed.

If you use Data Director for Web, then you just need to set the following variables:

```
MI_WEBSCHEMADEF  wb
MI_WEBTAGSSQL    SELECT parameters,object FROM wbTags
WHERE webupper(ID)=webupper('$MI_WEBTAGSID');
```

You can also set the other schema variables, such as `MInam`, `MItab`, and so forth explicitly, but you still need to set `MI_WEBTAGSSQL`:

```
MInam                ID
MIcol                object
MItab                wbPages
MItabObj?  wbBinaries
MIcolObj?  object
MInamObj?  ID
MItypeObj? image/gif
MI_WEBTAGSSQL    SELECT parameters,object FROM wbTags
WHERE webupper(ID)=webupper('$MI_WEBTAGSID');
```

Version 4

The web schema is stored in a configuration. The configuration is identified by name, and the set of configuration settings are stored in the `webconfigs` table.

If you use AppPage builder, you can use the `apb` configuration that comes with Version 4. If you use Data Director for Web, you can use the Data Director for Web configuration that also comes with Version 4.

Assuming that we use the AppPage Builder configuration, then the `map` entry for the `/shopper` URL becomes:

```
<map path=/shopper>
database catalog
```

```
user cortez
password c0rtez
config_name apb
</map>
```

Realistically, we will want to add variables to this configuration, so create a new configuration, called shoppers, from the apb configuration; then assign the configuration name as shown in the next snippet:

```
<map path=/shopper>
database catalog
user cortez
password c0rtez
config_name shoppers
</map>
```

In most circumstances, you will create the configuration first and then add the webdriver mapping. See the example at the end of this chapter for the step-by-step details.

Figure 22-1 shows the basic shopper configuration in the Web DataBlade Module Administration Tool before we have added any other variables.

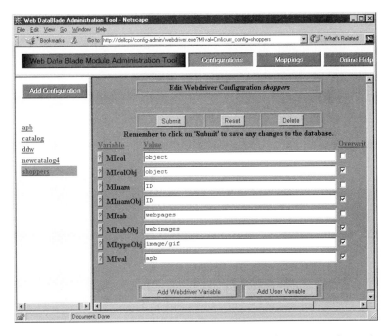

Figure 22-1. The shopper *configuration based on the* apb *configuration.*

tip

It is worth creating a new configuration based on the AppPage Builder or Data Director for Web configuration so that you never need to adjust these template configurations.

Setting Feature-related Variables

At this point, we can use the settings in `web.cnf` to connect `webdriver` to the Informix database.

You can also add feature-related variables at this point. These variables control `webdriver` behavior.

Version 3

Variables in `web.cnf` are global to all applications that use it. The following variables specify a `webdriver` trace and trace output file.

```
MI_WEBDRVLEVEL 64
MI_WEBDRVLOG   d:\catalog\log\webdrvlog.log
```

Version 4

You can add variables to the `web.cnf` file directly, or you can add them to the configuration that you have created for your application. See the example later in this chapter to learn how to add variables to the configuration. The snippet below shows the Version 4 equivalents of the `MI_WEBDRVLOG` and `MI_WEBDRVLEVEL` variables added to the `global` section so that they are available to all mappings.

```
<global>
debug_file      d:\catalog\logs\webdriver.log
debug_level     64
anchorvar       WEB_HOME/webdriver.exe
</global>
```

Setting User (Application) Variables

You may want to add variables that an application may use. For example, you may want to use a Java applet that connects to the Informix database directly using the Informix JDBC Type 4 driver.

Using Version 3, you may therefore store the `driver` classname, JDBC URL, and JDBC driver `jar` archive name in `web.cnf` as follows:

```
JAVACLASS       viewCustomer.class
APPARCHIVE      viewCustomerJdbc.jar
JDBCARCHIVE     ifxjdbc.jar
JDBCDRIVER      com.informix.jdbc.IfxDriver
```

Using Version 4, you use the Add User Variable screen in the Admistration Tool to add a variable and variable value to the configuration. See the example later in this chapter for more information on how to do this.

tip

See Chap. 9, "Integrating Java Applets with the Database," for more details on integrating JDBC, Java, and AppPages.

Final web.cnf in Version 3 and Version 4

The basic webdriver configuration for Version 3 of /shopper is shown in List. 22-3. The basic webdriver configuration of /shopper for Version 4 is shown in List. 22-4. Figure 22-2 shows the shoppers configuration after the user variables have been entered.

Listing 22-3.   Basic Version 3 web.cnf.

```
#
# web.cnf: /shopper CGI URL
#
# connectivity
MI_DATABASE                     catalog
MI_USER              cortez
MI_PASSWORD                     c0rtez
REMOTE_USER?         default
INFORMIXDIR          d:\informix
INFORMIXSERVER       ol_dellcpi


# anchorvar

WEB_HOME /shopper/webdriver.exe # for CGI

# AppPage storage

MInam?      ID
Micol?      object
MItab?      webpages

# Large Object storage, e.g., audio, documents, graphics

MItabObj?   webimages
MIcolObj?   object
MInamObj?   ID
```

Listing 22-3. *(continued)*

```
MItypeObj? image/gif
Mival?          apb

#
# Note: you can use the following two variables for the
# Data Director for Web schema
#
# MI_WEBSCHEMADEF  wb
# MI_WEBTAGSSQL    SELECT parameters,object FROM wbTags
WHERE webupper(ID)=webupper('$MI_WEBTAGSID');


#
# the following variables are not essential for connecting webdriver
# to the database for retrieving web content

# feature related - optional

MI_WEBDRVLEVEL      64
MI_WEBDRVLOG        d:\catalog\log\webdrvlog.log


# user (application) related - optional


JAVACLASS       viewCustomer.class
APPARCHIVE      viewCustomerJdbc.jar
JDBCARCHIVE     ifxjdbc.jar
JDBCDRIVER      com.informix.jdbc.IfxDriver
```

Listing 22-4. `web.cnf` *in Version 4.*

```
# With this configuration file you define webdriver specific
# variables that allow a connection to the database where the full
# configuration will be extracted by the webconfigs table



# Global: variables defined here are webdriver global variables that
#    are used for sizing and diagnostics.
```

Listing 22-4.   (continued)

```
#     (dbconnmax, maxcharsize, driverdir, debug_file, debug_level,
#      anchorvar)
<global>
debug_file          d:\catalog\log\webdriver.log
debug_level         64
anchorvar           WEB_HOME/webdriver.exe
</global>


# Setvar: variables defined here are variables that would usually be
# set in the environment before executing the client program,
# INFORMIXDIR and INFORMIXSERVER should be set here if they are not
# set before starting the appropriate webserver
<setvar>
INFORMIXDIR         D:\informix
INFORMIXSERVER      ol_dellcpi
</setvar>


# Map path=/virtual: variables set here are used to map a URL
# into a connection request, each map will require:
#   (mandatory)     database, user, config_name
#   (optional)      server, password, password_key
#
<map path=/catalog-admin>
database catalog
user informix
password 12afc2e9bd17b772b544811adbf3e8cc
password_key 37175268
</map>




<map path=/shopper>
database catalog
user cortez
password 2deda0277c0bd8cd59b97024d1a907be
password_key 37b5790f
config_name shoppers
</map>
```

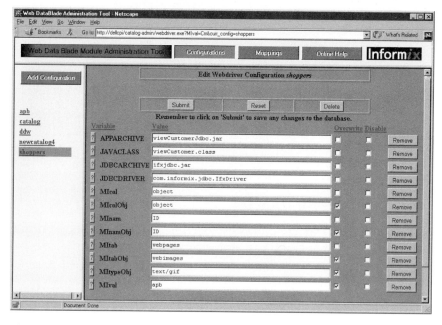

Figure 22-2. *The* `shoppers` *configuration.*

Example: Creating a `webdriver` Configuration for a Catalog Application—Version 4

This example takes you through the steps necessary to create a basic `webdriver` configuration for a Version 4 application.

- Add the application URL prefixes to the web server.
- Perform the preliminary configuration to set up the Web DataBlade Module Administration Tool.
- Create a configuration.
- Add feature-related variables to the configuration.
- Add user-related (application) variables to the configuration.
- Add the URL mappings that will use the configuration to `web.cnf`.
- Ensure that `MI_WEBCONFIG` is set in the web server environment.
- Create the AppPages.
- Invoke the AppPages.

Add the Application URL Prefixes to the Web Server

The application will use the following URL:

- `/catalog-admin`—this invokes the Web DataBlade Module Administration Tool.
- `/catalog`—this is a basic unauthenticated NSAPI URL.

See Chap. 23, "Web Server Integration," for details on how to set up basic NSAPI URL prefixes.

Preliminaries

To get to the stage where we can create `webdriver` configurations and mappings for the application, the following must be performed:

- Create the `catalog` database.
- Register the web DataBlade in the `catalog` database.
- Set the `MI_WEBCONFIG` variable.
- Use the `webconfig` tool to create the `/catalog-admin` mapping and configuration in the `catalog` database.

The final result should be a database called `catalog` that contains the schema and web pages for the Web DataBlade Module Administration Tool application. A `web.cnf` file will be created with the path `MI_WEBCONFIG`. This `web.cnf` file will contain the mapping for the `/catalog-admin` URL.

Create a Configuration

We want to be able to use the Data Director for Web schema but add more variables to the `webdriver` configuration above and beyond the schema-related variables that you get with the standard Data Director for Web schema. So, we create a new configuration based on the Data Director for Web configuration. We can then add more variables without impacting the Data Director for Web configuration that was installed with the Web DataBlade Module Administration Tool.

Invoke the Web DataBlade Module Administration Tool using `/catalog-admin`, and choose to add a new configuration called `catalog`. A screen similar to Fig. 22-3 will be displayed. Enter `catalog` in Configuration Name, and base the new configuration on `ddw` (Data Director for Web).

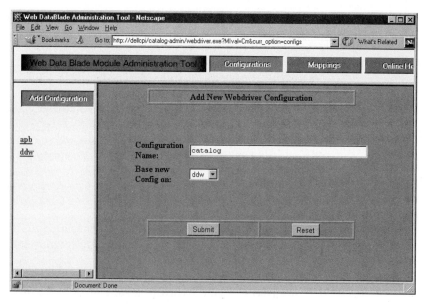

Figure 22-3. *Add the* `catalog` *configuration.*

When submitting this form, a new configuration called `catalog` will be created in the `catalog` database. We can then edit this configuration and add variables to it.

Add Feature-related Variables

As an example, we will add three variables:

- `raw_password`—this will enable us to list the `webdriver` environment in the browser;
- `upload_directory`—this will specify on the web server the directory that will contain uploaded client files;
- `show_exceptions`—this will allow us to display error messages from the database server (including `webexplode()` errors) instead of the status 500 HTTP error.

From the `/catalog-admin` URL, select Configurations, and then click the `catalog` configuration. The list of variables defined for the Data Director for Web configuration should be displayed, similar to Fig. 22-4.

To add feature-related variables, click the Add Webdriver Variable button. The frame should refresh with the Add Webdriver Variable to *catalog* screen. This screen lets you add settings to your configuration that alter the behavior of `webdriver` in some way.

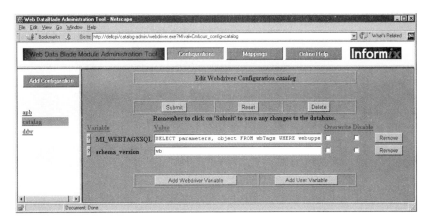

Figure 22-4. Basic `catalog` *configuration for Edit.*

The Variable Name pull-down list contains the list of `webdriver` variables that you can set. Choose the `show_exceptions` variable. Note that the Value textarea is set to the default value for that variable. For `show_exceptions`, the default value is `on`. Figure 22-5 shows the browser display at this point.

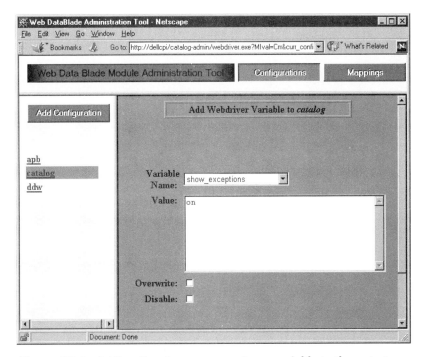

Figure 22-5. Adding the `show_exceptions` *variable to the* `catalog` *configuration.*

Click the Add button. The screen refreshes with the variable added to the Edit Webdriver Configuration *catalog* screen.

Repeat the same procedure for the `upload_directory` and `raw_password` configurations. For example, set `upload_directory` to `/informix/clientfiles` or `d:\temp`, and `raw_password` to `raw`.

Add Application Variables

We will now add two application, or user, variables to the `catalog` configuration. These variables are

- `shopper`—a generic name for the user;
- `specialOffer`—the current special offer for the online catalog.

To add these variables: from the Edit Webdriver Configuration *catalog* screen, click the Add Add User Variable button. The Add User Variable to *catalog* screen will be displayed. From the Add User Variable to *catalog* screen, type the variable name and value, and click the Add button. Figure 22-6 shows the screen for the `specialOffer` variable.

Once the user variables have been added, click the Submit button on the Edit screen to save the configuration change to the database. Figure 22-7 shows the configuration that is saved.

Using the AppPage Builder or Data Director for Web configuration has no effect on the creation of variables as described here.

Add the URL Mappings

We now need to add a mapping to `web.cnf`. this mapping will link a web server URL prefix with an Informix database server, database, and configuration. For this example, we will create the `/catalog` mapping.

At some point you will have to create the `/config` URL prefix in the web server. You can do this before or after this step.

From the Web DataBlade Module Administration Tool, select *Mappings*.

A list of existing mappings will be displayed, together with the Add New Webdriver Mapping frame. In this frame:

- type `catalog` in the URL prefix textbox,
- select `catalog` from the Configuration Name SELECT list,
- type the username of the user that will connect to the Informix database server,
- type the password of this user,
- retype the password.

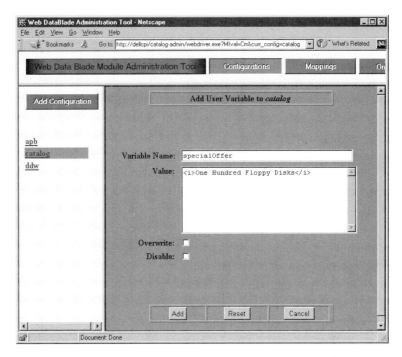

Figure 22-6. *Adding the* `specialOffer` *variable to the* `catalog` *configuration.*

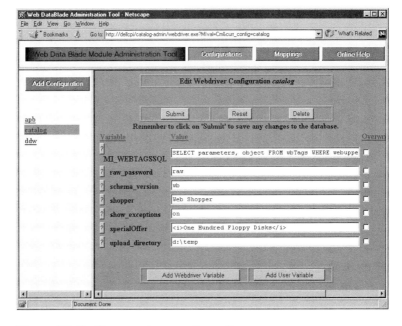

Figure 22-7. *The* `catalog` *configuration.*

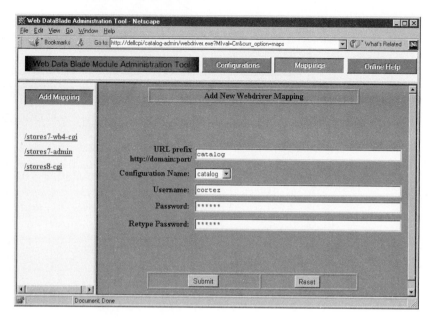

Figure 22-8. *Add the* /catalog *mapping.*

Figure 22-8 shows an example.

Once the mapping has been saved to the database, we have in place the mapping of a web server URL prefix to a web.cnf entry, which maps onto a set of variables (a configuration) stored in the database under the name catalog.

The following snippet from the web.cnf file shows the mapping created.

```
<map path=/catalog>
database stores74
user cortez
password 34d5888e59380124f6056ff430a07523
password_key 37b3f2bd
config_name catalog
</map>
```

Add and Verify Mappings Using the webconfig Utility

When you use the Web DataBlade Module Administration Tool to add a mapping, the database that the mapping connects to is set to the database that the Web DataBlade Module Administration Tool is currently being delivered from. For example, if you install the Web

DataBlade Module Administration Tool in the `catalog` database, then when you create the `/catalog` mapping from the Web DataBlade Module Administration Tool, the database for the mapping is set to `catalog`.

What if you want to target a different database or database server? You can edit the `web.cnf` file manually, or—better—you can use the `webconfig` utility that comes with the Web DataBlade Version 4.

Add a Mapping

You can use the `webconfig` utility to add a mapping section to `web.cnf`. Using this utility, you can set the database name and database server directly. Listing 22-5 shows an example command line dialog. This example shows a new mapping called `/catalog-secure` that uses the catalog configuration in the `catalog` database; the connecting user is `cortez`. Remember to set the environment variable `MI_WEBCONFIG` before running the `webconfig` utility. Listing 22-6 shows the results written to `web.cnf` from the `webconfig` command entered in List. 22-5.

Listing 22-5.   Run the `webconfig` utility to create a mapping between the `web.cnf` file and entries in the `webconfigs` table.

```
D:\>webconfig -addmap -p /catalog-secure -n catalog -d
catalog -u cortez
Using $MI_WEBCONFIG=d:\catalog\configs\web.cnf
Enter password for user 'cortez': ******
Enter password again: ******
Enter password key [37b3f64a]: special
'd:\stores7\wb4\cgi-bin\web.cnf' updated
D:\informix\extend\web.4.00.TC1B1\utils>
```

Listing 22-6.   The map configuration from the `webconfig` data in List. 22.5.

```
<map path=/catalog-secure>
database catalog
user cortez
password a4f2f5b079efbe0c24dde42034900fa8
password_key special
config_name catalog
</map>
```

Verify a Mapping

You can use `webconfig` to verify a mapping that you have created with the Web DataBlade Module Administration Tool or created manually using the `webconfig` tool. When a mapping is verified, the `webconfig` utility will attempt to connect to the nominated database (using `INFORMIXSERVER` or the overrding server variable), check the configuration in the `webconfigs` table, and check the schema.

For example, List. 22-7 shows the `/catalog` mapping verified by the `webconfig` utility.

Create the AppPages

We can create an AppPage that uses the variable settings we have just created. Listing 22-8 shows a simple AppPage that uses the two variables we have created.

Listing 22-7.   Verify the `/catalog` mapping using `webconfig`.

```
D:\>webconfig -verify -p /catalog
Using $MI_WEBCONFIG=d:\catalog\configs\web.cnf
Checking: /catalog
         : database=catalog
         : user=cortez
         : password=<encrypted>
         : config_name=catalog
Connect : Success
Config  : 7 variables found
Schema  : ddw (source_table=wbPages, content_column=object, id_column=ID)
AppPages: 68
```

Listing 22-8.   The `HelloCatalog.html` AppPage.

```
<html>
<body>
<h1>
   <?mivar>Hello $shopper<?/mivar>
</h1>
<h2><?mivar>Todays Special Offer is
$specialOffer<?/mivar></h2>
</body>
</html>
```

This AppPage can be stored in the AppPage Builder or Data Director for Web schema. The `catalog` configuration is based on the Data Director for Web schema, so the schema variables will be mapped onto the Data Director for Web tables that store the web content, including this AppPage. We could have used the AppPage Builder configuration instead if we did not have Data Director for Web.

Invoke the AppPages

At the browser, you can type `http://dellcpi/catalog/HelloCatalog`, and the screen listed in Fig. 22-9 should appear.

The user variables were created without the Overwrite checkbox being checked. The following URL will have no effect: `http://dellcpi/catalog/HelloCatalog&shopper=wanderer`. *To allow the setting of AppPage variables dynamically via URLs, hyperlinks, and forms, set the Overwrite checkbox in the Edit Webdriver Configuration screen.*

If we define the `shopper` variable as overwritable in the Edit Configuration screen, then we can type in the following URL:

`http://dellcpi/catalog/HelloCatalog&shopper=and+Welcome`

The screen in Fig. 22-10 will be displayed.

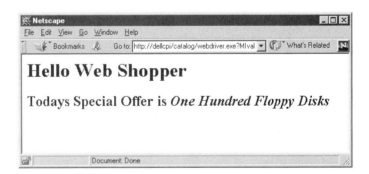

Figure 22-9. Add the `/catalog` mapping.

Figure 22-10. Dynamically changing a variable when the Overwrite checkbox is selected.

Example: Creating a `webdriver` Configuration for a Catalog Application—Version 3.x

This section shows how to create the catalog application described above in Version 3.x of the Web DataBlade.

The steps to follow are the same, except for the `web.cnf` variables:

- preliminaries,
- add the application URL prefixes to the web server,
- add connection-related variables to the `web.cnf` file,
- add schema-related variables to the `web.cnf` file,
- add feature-related variables to the `web.cnf` file,
- add user-related (application) variables to the `web.cnf` file,
- create the AppPages.

Preliminaries

Ensure that the Web DataBlade has been registered in the `catalog` database. Register the AppPage Builder application or the Data Director for Web schema, depending on which product you wish to use.

Note that you don't have to set `MI_WEBCONFIG` unless you are using the ISAPI version of `webdriver`. You should, however, take a copy of `web.cnf` from the Web DataBlade installation directories and place it in a folder that has restricted access to prevent unauthorized editing.

Add the Application URL Prefixes to the Web Server

Add the `/catalog` prefix to the web server. See Chap. 23, "Web Server Integration," for details on how to add URL prefixes to the web server.

You cannot use Version 3.x and Version 4 `webdrivers` *together, unless you are using the CGI version of* `webdriver`. *You should upgrade from Version 3.x to Version 4 instead and change the web server mappings accordingly.*

Add Connection-, Schema-, and Feature-related Variables to `web.cnf`

Manually edit `web.cnf`. Add the entries shown in List. 22-9.

The `shopper` *variable is defined with the* `?` *suffix; this allows us to assign values to the variable dynamically.*

```
# connection information
MI_DATABASE   catalog_dev
MI_USER       cortez
MI_PASSWORD   cortez
REMOTE_USER?  default

INFORMIXSERVER        ol_dellcpi
INFORMIXDIR           d:\informix

# anchor variable
WEB_HOME      /catalog/

# schema related variables
# Data Director for Web schema is used with all the defaults
# include the Dynamic Tag query for
MI_WEBSCHEMADEF    wb
MI_WEBTAGSSQL      SELECT parameters,object FROM wbTags
WHERE webupper(ID)=webupper('$MI_WEBTAGSID');

# feature related
MI_WEBRAWPASSWORD         raw
MI_WEBUPLOADDIR           d:\temp
MI_WEBSHOWEXCEPTIONS      on

# user related variables
shopper?           Web Shopper
specialOffer       <i>One Hundred Floppy Disks</i>
```

You can call the HelloCatalog AppPage as follows, assuming
that the /catalog URL prefix has been set up in the web server:

```
http://dellcpi/catalog/HelloCatalog
```

Converting web.cnf from Version 3 to Version 4

You can take your existing web.cnf files and convert them to the
Version 4 format very easily using the webconfig utility.

For example:

```
webconfig -convert -p /catalog4 -n newcatalog4 -f
d:\catalog\version3\web.cnf
```

This command will perform the following:

- Convert the Version 3 `web.cnf` in the `d:\catalog\Version3` directory into a new mapping and configuration.
- The new mapping will be called `/catalog4`.
- The new configuration will be called `newcatalog4`.
- The `newcatalog4` configuration will contain all the feature and user variables defined in the Version 3 `web.cnf` file.

Note that if you have started with a fresh installation of the Version 4 Web DataBlade in another database, then you will have to change the `MI_DATABASE` variable in the Version 3 `web.cnf` to refer to the new database, since the `webconfig` utility with the `-convert` option needs to know the target database in order to create the new configuration.

Assume that the connection variables in the Version 3 `web.cnf` are as follows:

```
MI_DATABASE        catalog
MI_USER            informix
MI_PASSWORD        informix
REMOTE_USER?       default
```

After the `webconfig` utility has completed, the Version 4 `web.cnf` contains the following mapping:

```
<map path=/catalog4>
database catalog
user informix
password informix
server ol_dellcpi
config_name newcatalog4
</map>
```

You can use the Web DataBlade Module Administration Tool to edit the new configuration, `newcatalog4`.

Overwriting `webdriver` Variables in a URL

You can assign default values to `webdriver` variables. You can also overwrite the values of variables if `webdriver` will let you. The `webdriver` will let you overwrite the value of a variable if you have created the variable yourself, or if the variable is feature related and is defined as overwritable in the product.

If you define your own variables, you can overwrite these variables if you mark the variables as overwritable.

To overwrite a `webdriver` variable means that you can assign a value to the variable in a URL or a form that has a transient application. For example, if you do not specify a value for `MIval` in a call to `webdriver`, then the default value is assumed as defined in the `webdriver` configuration. You can, however, set the value of `MIval` in a URL or in a form; this new value will be discarded after the AppPage has been exploded.

From Version 4, you use the Web DataBlade Module Administration Tool to check the Overwrite checkbox next to the variable declaration in the Edit Configuration screen, and then submit the changes to the database.

In Version 3, you suffix the variable in `web.cnf` with a question mark. For example:

```
MIval?      StartPage
```

User-defined variables can be overwritten dynamically. However, only a small number of schema- and feature-related variables can be overwritten. These are listed below.

```
MIval
MInam
MItab
MIcol
MIvalObj
MInamObj
MItabObj
MicolObj
MIqry2pass
MI_WEBACCESSLEVEL
MI_WEBGROUPLEVEL
```

In Version 4, the Web DataBlade Module Administration Tool will ignore the Overwrite checkbox for any other schema- or feature-related variables.

Managing Application Characteristics

Each Web DataBlade application has different characteristics. Some applications may want to use Java and JDBC to connect a Java applet from the browser to the Informix database directly. In this case, you may want to store the JDBC URL and JAR file paths in the `web.cnf` file so that all applications mapped by the URL prefix will share the values of these variables.

For example, the following three URLs define the entry points to three different applications in the same database and schema. The URL prefix is `/shopper`.

```
http://theale2/shopper/BuyersHome.html
http://theale2/shopper/SellersHome.html
http://theale2/catalog/productsHome.html
```

If the `Buyers` application had an authenticating view of the application as well as an unauthenticated view:

```
http://theale2/shopper-secure/BuyersHome.html
http://theale2/shopper/BuyersHome.html
```

then `/shopper-secure` is a different URL prefix. Even so, the `buyers` application may need variables that are used by both the authenticated and unauthenticated applications.

Version 3

You set application variables in all the `web.cnf` files that have a URL mapping for the application. If you have a basic and an authenticated URL prefix, then you need two `web.cnf` files. Potentially, each file will have the same application variables set within it. If you use ISAPI, then you can define a master `web.cnf` file that maps a URL to a specific `web.cnf` file for that URL prefix (see Chap. 23 for more information). You still need to duplicate the application variables across the `web.cnf` files.

Version 4

The one `web.cnf` file will contain multiple URL prefix mappings. If you have a basic URL and an authenticating URL, then each mapping can share the same configuration. This configuration will contain the application variable settings that were formerly duplicated under Version 3.

important

From Version 4, you can use only one NSAPI, ISAPI, or Apache API web.cnf file with one web server. This is because you need to set the anchorvar variable appropriately. You can have multiple web servers on the same machine, but you still need to set MI_WEBCONFIG in the environment of the web server to point to the different web.cnf file if the operating environment will allow you to do this.

Connecting to Multiple Databases

You can use one database to store the *web content* for multiple applications. The application data may be spread over several databases. For example, if you use Data Director for Web, the Data Director for Web configuration and schema may exist on the `catalog` database, but the pricing and product information, which is fed from other data sources, may exist in two separate databases; called `pricing`, and `product`. This doesn't mean that you don't want to import this data onto one database if it is not practical to have data spread over multiple remote locations. However, from an architectural perspective, your application data can reside on a remote database server and database separate from the AppPages and large objects.

You can also use multiple databases to store web content for multiple applications. For example, you may want to deploy a development and production version of an online catalog, in which case:

- Two databases exist, `catalog_dev` and `catalog_prod`, possibly on different Informix servers;
- Data Director for Web (or AppPage Builder) schema is installed on both;
- One `web.cnf` exists on the development web server, and it maps to `catalog_dev`;
- One `web.cnf` exists in the production web server, and it maps to `catalog_prod`.

Using Data Director for Web, you can deploy web content from one database to another database on a different Informix server. In this example, we deploy applications from `catalog_dev` to `catalog_prod`.

For more information about deploying web applications using Data Director for Web, see Chap. 13, "Creating and Managing Websites with Data Director for Web."

You can use the server variable in the `map` *section to override* `INFORMIXSERVER` *in the* `setvar` *section. This feature allows you to connect to multiple database servers from the same* `web.cnf` *file, which is not possible before Version 4. Before Version 4, one* `web.cnf` *file maps one URL prefix to one database by default.*

Summary

In this chapter we have seen the essential differences between the webdriver configurations of Versions 3 and 4 of the Web Data-Blade. We learned what a webdriver configuration is and how webdriver uses it. We learned about the different types of webdriver variable and how they are implemented. The Web DataBlade Module Administration Tool was introduced as a tool to manage mappings and configurations. We also configured a simple application under Version 3 and Version 4.

Web Server Integration

In this chapter:

- Web server interfaces
- CGI process architecture
- API process architecture
- Configuring the CGI webdriver
- Configuring the NSAPI webdriver
- Configuring and using the ISAPI webdriver
- Configuring the Apache API webdriver
- Version 4 change summary
- Web server mapping of distributed applications

Integration of your web applications with the web server is a crucial topic. By planning your web server integration correctly, you can realize benefits in the areas of web application performance and security. To do this, you need to understand the ways in which the webdriver program is integrated with the web server.

This chapter covers two essential areas. The first is an overview of the two architectures, CGI and API, to show how they differ and why. The second area is a summary how to configure webdriver for CGI, NSAPI, ISAPI, and the Apache API, as well as a summary of specific similarities between the configurations.

Most of the examples in this chapter have been run under Microsoft Windows NT4 Server. Where a UNIX implementation exists and differs in functionality, a note will be given of any differences.

Web Server Interfaces

There are four essential interfaces to the web server for the Web DataBlade webdriver program.

- CGI: This is the default out-of-the-box implementation of webdriver. The webdriver executable is called as a CGI program.
- Netscape API (NSAPI): Integration of a webdriver shared object or DLL with the Netscape Web Server (UNIX and NT).
- Microsoft IIS API (ISAPI): Integration of a webdriver DLL with the Microsoft Internet Information Server (NT and 95).
- Apache API: Integration of the webdriver with the Apache Web Server (available in Version 4 of the Web DataBlade only).

There is one program for the CGI connection to the database, called webdriver. There is a separate DLL for each of the APIs. For each API implementation, there are two configurations, called *basic* and *secure*. The basic API configuration is the first step up from CGI; it uses the shared object or DLL to connect to the database. The secure configuration uses the same shared object or DLL, but it requires the user to log into the URL for the user ID and password to be authenticated against user entries in the database.

Each interface is explained in detail in the following sections.

The webdriver executable and DLLs need to be visible to the web server software; in most cases this means moving the relevant objects to a directory on the web server machine. You can load these objects from a shared directory on the network, but performance may suffer.

You don't need to host the web server software and the Informix database server on the same machine. The web server software and the webdriver objects can reside on the web server machine (say, under Microsoft Windows NT 4.0 Server), and the Informix database server can reside on a different machine on the network (under AIX or HP-UX, for example). In this case, the client connectivity libraries must be installed on the web server machine so that the webdriver objects can communicate with the remote Informix database server.

CGI Process Architecture

CGI is the default out-of-the-box configuration of webdriver. If you use the CGI version of webdriver, it should run with any web server that supports CGI.

In contrast, API integration means that the web server loads a special version of webdriver when the web server starts. This involves configuration tasks specific to the web server you are using.

Figure 23-1 is a diagrammatic representation of the CGI process architecture in relation to the Web DataBlade.

Table 23-1 lists the components with a summary description.

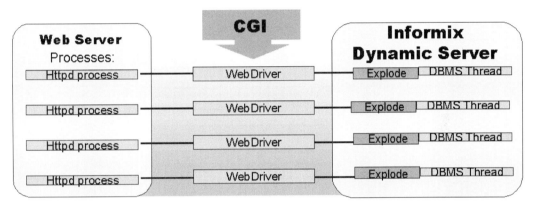

Figure 23-1. *CGI process architecture.*

Table 23-1. CGI process architecture (Web DataBlade) summary.

Component	Description
Web server	The machine with the web server software installed.
HTTPD process	Web server thread running the HTTPD program, e.g., Netscape Enterprise Server.
webdriver	CGI version of the webdriver executable.
Informix Dynamic Server	The Informix database server. This can reside on the same machine as the web server, or on a different machine.
Explode	This is the webexplode() function of the Web DataBlade. It is executed as a DataBlade function inside the Informix server.
DBMS thread	This is a sqlexec thread created when webdriver connects to the database to run the webexplode() function.

The web server process is *multithreaded;* it will service many HTTP requests simultaneously. Each HTTP request will be a separate thread, which will spawn the CGI call to the `webdriver` program to access a web page from the database.

An example URL for a CGI implementation under NT would be:

```
http://dellcpi/stores7-cgi/webdriver.exe?Mival=homePage
```

An example URL for a CGI implementation on UNIX would be:

```
http://theale2/stores7-cgi/webdriver?Mival=homePage
```

For NT, the only difference is the `.exe` after the `webdriver` name.

The web server thread knows that the `stores7-cgi` directory is a CGI directory, since this mapping was established before the URL was invoked (see later on how to specify *URL prefixes*). The web server will then attempt to spawn the `webdriver` program as a separate process. This process will act as a client to access the Informix database. Once `webdriver` has the database connection, the Informix server considers it a DBMS (`sqlexec`) thread. `webdriver` will then call the `webexplode()` function to expand the selected AppPage.

Under CGI, a `webdriver` *process will be started for each HTTP request. This means that the operating system will have to start a new copy of* `webdriver` *every time. For a site with many users, or even a site with a small number of users but many requests to the database to fetch an AppPage, this overhead is unnecessary. You are advised to use the basic API implementation in place of CGI if your web server will support it.*

What Is Multithreaded?

A single-threaded process is a process that can only service one thread—its own. The process (e.g., a program executable) is started by the operating system (e.g., UNIX or NT). The process consists of program instructions and data. The operating system starts the program at the first program instruction, the program continues until the end, then stops. In contrast, a multithreaded program can have many client threads of execution. A thread is a schedulable entity that can start, be interrupted (suspended), resume, and stop at or before the end of the program. It contains the state of thread execution, a copy of variable data, a stack for processing data and instructions, and a program counter, which is the position of this thread in the program. A multithreaded program can therefore run many client threads one at a time. In other words, only one copy of the program is running, but it is shared by many client threads that proceed as if they are running the program alone. Each client takes its turn to have some program code executed; this is called multitasking. *When a thread is suspended and another is resumed, this is called* context-switching. *The context-switching software will save the state of a thread in a process control block. Sometimes an application (such as the Java Virtual Machine, or JVM) swaps threads from running to suspended; sometimes the operating system acts as switchboard. The program code for a multithreaded process does not have to manage this itself. A multithreaded Java application, for example, will create threads that are managed by the JVM. In fact, the JVM is itself a collection of threads that manage, among other things, the AWT and garbage collection, which are system (or* daemon) *threads. A running Java applet or application is a* user *thread inside the JVM. Even with JVM-style assistance, though, a multithreaded application should know how to suspend itself (be cooperative) and be thread safe (by serializing access to shared data).* Cooperative multitasking *is when a thread will voluntarily yield for another thread.* Pre-emptive multitasking *is when the operating system or an application suspends a running thread and puts it in a waiting queue. The web server (e.g., Netscape Enterprise Server) and the Informix Dynamic Server Virtual Processes are multithreaded.*

To configure your Web DataBlade application for CGI, you need to create a `webdriver` configuration to service CGI requests, and you must create the URL prefixes in the web server that will allow you to identify a CGI request. This is described in the section, "Configuring the CGI `webdriver`."

Note that using the `webdriver` CGI model does not allow you to use the web server to authenticate access to the Informix database.

API Process Architecture

The `webdriver` API (application program interface) process architecture is designed to allow developers to write their own functions and have them called by a running web server in such a way that the code is treated as if it were part of the web server runtime, which enables the web developer to use the web server as an authentication platform.

If a user-written function conforms to an API, this means that the function will accept parameters of a certain type and in a certain order and that it will pass a result back that conforms to a specific type.

There are four versions of `webdriver` (three in Version 3)—CGI, NSAPI, ISAPI, and Apache API (Version 4 only). The CGI runs stand-alone; NSAPI conforms to the interface defined by Netscape; ISAPI conforms to the interface defined by Microsoft; Apache API conforms to the interface defined for Apache. Each API version will consist of a set of functions to call the `webexplode()` function and, optionally, to authenticate user access to an AppPage.

The API version of `webdriver` consists of a special library of functions that are callable by the web server. These functions are built into a shared-object library that is loaded by the web server when a URL is requested. This library is accessed as a DLL (dynamic link library) on NT and as a shared object on UNIX.

You can write your own functions in a language such as C, and the web server can call them in the same way. The C functions must conform to the published API for the web server; the API version of `webdriver` conforms in the same way.

Why Integrate Using an API?

Although the setup of the relevant API libraries can look complicated, it is worth doing. This is because the `webdriver` functions are integrated with the running web server and offer both a performance increase over CGI and the ability to use the web server as an authentication platform outside of the web application code.

Figure 23-2 illustrates the integration of `webdriver` with the web server to access the Informix database.

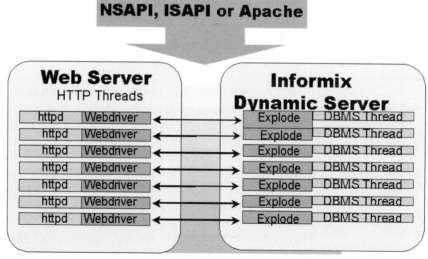

Figure 23-2. API process architecture.

Table 23-2.	The API component summary.
Component	Description
webdriver	The functions that are part of the `webdriver` shared-object library. Each web server has a specific version of the `webdriver` shared object it must use.
DBMS thread	This is a `sqlexec` thread created when the API `webdriver` connects to the database to run the `webexplode()` function. Unlike CGI, this connection is maintained.

Figure 23-2 shows how the `webdriver` code is integrated with the executing web server. Most of the components in Fig. 23-2 have the same description listed in Table 23-1; the components that differ in the API implementation are summarized in Table 23-2.

Informix provides `webdriver` versions for Netscape, Microsoft, and Apache web servers. Although the steps you take to configure them are different, the configuration of each `webdriver` relies on the same type of information. To configure your Web DataBlade application to use the web server API, you must create a `webdriver` configuration to service API requests, and you must create the URL prefixes in the web server that will allow you to identify API requests. Using the API option, you can create *basic* and *secure* URL prefixes to allow you to use the basic (unauthenticated) or secure (authenticated) `webdriver`.

tip

When using the API `webdriver`*, you have a limited set of web server variables available to AppPage Script. Appendix B lists these variables.*

Configuring the CGI `webdriver`

The aim of configuring a CGI `webdriver` is to allow the web server to find the `webdriver` program when it is referenced in a URL and to allow the `webdriver` program to access the Informix database, as well as to provide the variables from the web server environment and the requesting URL.

Summary Configuration

You should install `webdriver` on the machine that has the web
server software installed. The steps to follow are:

1. Create a CGI directory (e.g., `stores7-cgi`). You need to create
   this directory before registering it with the web server.
2. Register the CGI directory with the web server.
3. Copy the CGI version of `webdriver` and the `web.cnf.example`
   file to the CGI directory. Rename `web.cnf.example` to
   `web.cnf`.
4. Use BladeManager to register the Web DataBlade in the database you will be using to store web content (see Chap. 12).
5. Install the AppPage Builder schema in the same database.
   This will ensure from the outset that you have a working web
   application to manage web content.
6. Change the variables in `web.cnf` to point at the correct
   Informix server and database.

CGI Setup Components

The `webdriver` Configuration File (`web.cnf`)

The CGI `webdriver` will use the information in this file to connect to
the Informix server and database. It must reside in the same directory
as the CGI `webdriver` executable. All Web DataBlade applications
use a variable called `$WEB_HOME` to make the `webdriver` call transparent, removing the need to know whether you are using CGI or
API. For CGI, the `$WEB_HOME` `webdriver` variable is defined in
Version 3 as follows:

```
WEB_HOME/url_prefix/webdriver
```

In Version 4:

```
anchorvar WEB_HOME/webdriver
```

You cannot use the same `web.cnf` for CGI *and* API options, unless
you are using the secure URLs with the Microsoft IIS web server and
the `MI_WEBCONFIG` variable has been set in the web server environment. In this case, you have to refer to the CGI mapping in the
master `web.cnf` (see the section on ISAPI later).

The `webdriver` Executable

The CGI `webdriver` executable should be moved from the Web DataBlade installation directory to the `cgi-bin` directory that will contain the `web.cnf` file.

URL Prefixes

The URL prefixes are used to instruct the web server that the URL is a request to invoke a CGI program, not a URL request for a document (e.g., an HTML page). A URL prefix is a logical name declared to the web server that maps down to a physical directory on the filesystem addressable by the web server. The web server will recognize the *URL prefix* in a URL and will spawn the `webdriver` process, passing parameters from `web.cnf`, from the web server environment, and from within the URL itself (such as `MIval`), to the `webdriver` program.

For example, in the following URL,

```
http://theale2/stores7-cgi/webdriver?MIval=Start
```

the *URL prefix* is `stores7-cgi`. This is the prefix declared to the web server.

Although you can configure multiple CGI URL prefixes that map to the same folder and hence the same `web.cnf` and `webdriver` program, there is no advantage in doing this.

Configuring the Web Server for CGI

A web server that supports CGI can run the CGI version of `webdriver` to connect to the database. Each web server will have a method for registering a CGI URL prefix. For completeness, however, this section briefly lists the steps required to register the CGI `webdriver` for the three web servers addressed in this book.

Using Netscape FastTrack and Enterprise Servers

The web server needs to have a mapping between a URL prefix and a CGI directory that is visible to the web server. The URL `stores7-cgi` needs to be mapped onto the directory `D:\stores7\cgi-bin`.

The name we give to the web server is a logical name which maps down to a folder.

The example that follows is for Netscape Enterprise Server 3.6 running under Microsoft Windows NT 4.0 Server.

Log in to the Netscape Server Administration. The Netscape Systems Administrator will have set the Server Administration to run on a particular port. In the browser, enter the URL for the Server Administration (e.g., `http://dellcpi:81`). Enter a user ID and password if requested.

The screen should resemble Fig. 23-3.

For the particular server you wish to configure, click the relevant link or button. Once in the Administration screen for that server, click the Programs button.

Add a CGI directory. Figure 23-4 shows the Programs screen to add a CGI directory. From this screen, you need to enter the fields shown in Table 23-3.

Figure 23-5 shows the logical and physical mapping entries that you need to type. Click the OK button. Figure 23-6 is displayed.

Click the Save and Apply button. Once the changes have been saved, you can view the list of CGI-registered CGI directories on the screen, as Fig. 23-7 shows.

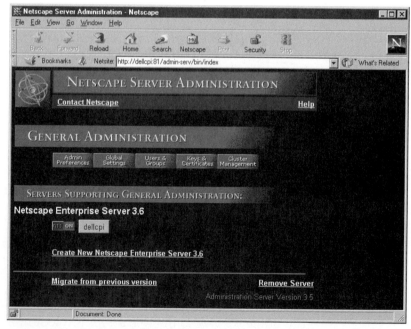

Figure 23-3. *Netscape Administration Server main screen.*

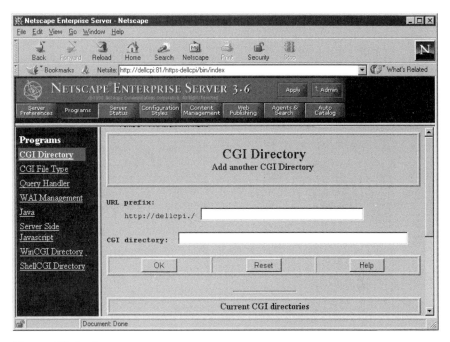

Figure 23-4. Programs screen.

Table 23-3.	The CGI mapping fields.

Field	Description
URL prefix	This is the logical name of the URL that the user will type (e.g., `stores7-cgi`).
CGI directory	This is the physical directory in which the `webdriver` program and the `web.cnf` file reside.

You can become confused on what is a document *directory and what is a* program *or cgi directory. A document directory is a filesystem directory that contains HTML pages and content such as GIF images. A program directory contains executable content, such as* webdriver. *If you mistakenly create a document directory for* webdriver, *the* webdriver *program will not be found as a CGI program.*

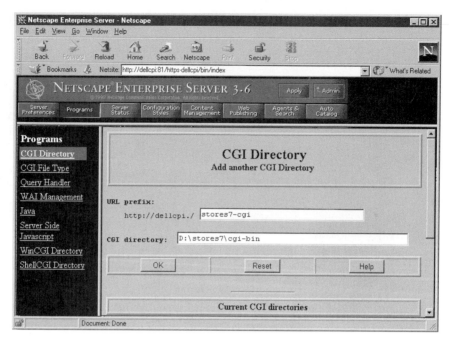

Figure 23-5. *Creating the* `stores7-cgi` *mapping.*

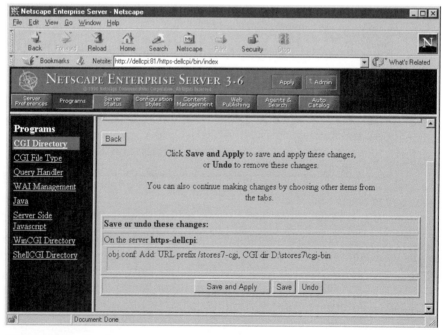

Figure 23-6. *Confirmatory screen for CGI mapping.*

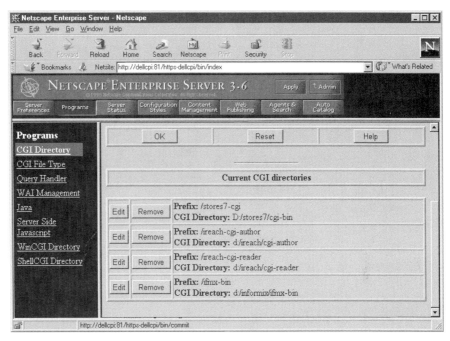

Figure 23-7. *Viewing the list of registered CGI directories.*

Using Microsoft Internet Information Server Version 4 for CGI

Start the Microsoft Internet Services Manager. This is usually found under Windows NT4 Option Pack\Microsoft Internet Information Server. The Microsoft Management Console will be displayed, which should look similar to Fig. 23-8. Select the website for which the CGI directory is to be mapped.

We now want to add a Virtual Directory to the site. Right-click the site and select New\Virtual Directory, or select Action\New\Virtual Site from the menu bar. The New Virtual Directory wizard will be displayed. Enter the URL prefix that you wish to assign to the CGI directory, as shown in Fig. 23-9, and click Next. For example, enter `stores7` for a URL of the following form:

```
http://dellcpi/stores7/webdriver.exe?MIval=Start
```

The next screen of the wizard allows you to specify the actual folder that contains the `webdriver` executable and the `web.cnf` configuration for it. Enter the folder details as shown in Fig. 23-10, and click Next.

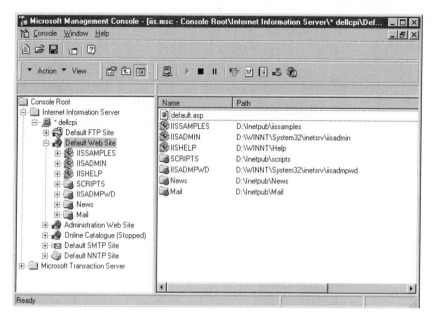

Figure 23-8. *Using Microsoft Management Console with a selected website to add a new CGI mapping.*

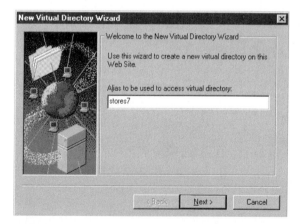

Figure 23-9. *Specify the CGI URL prefix.*

If you will be hosting a CGI webdriver *and an ISAPI* webdriver *on the same IIS web server (you have set* MI_WEBCONFIG *in the system environment), you will need to create a master* web.cnf *that controls the mappings for the different configurations. In this case, the master* web.cnf *will refer to the* web.cnf *in the* stores7\cgi-bin *directory. See the section, "Configuring and Using the ISAPI webdriver," later in this chapter.*

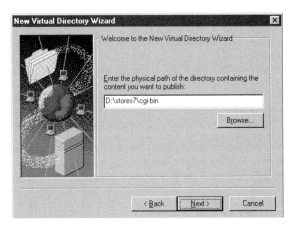

Figure 23-10. *Specify the physical path of the CGI components.*

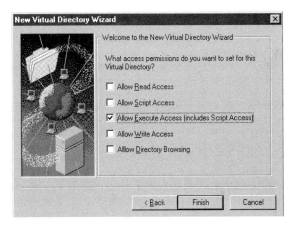

Figure 23-11. *Specify the CGI directory permissions.*

The next screen of the wizard allows you to set directory permissions. Check the Allow Execute box, as shown in Fig. 23-11, and click Finish. A new mapping will appear under the selected website.

Apache Web Server

Copy the `web.cnf` file and the CGI `webdriver` executable into the `cgi-bin` directory defined to the Apache web server.

The `httpd.conf` file in the Apache `conf` directory is the file you need to edit to declare your CGI directories using the `ScriptAlias` command.

For example, to declare the `cgi-bin` directory under NT in the `httpd.conf` file, add the following `ScriptAlias` directive.

```
ScriptAlias /cgi-bin/ "D:/Program Files/Apache
Group/Apache/cgi-bin/"
```

You can define multiple CGI directories to Apache in this way. You can also create under one CGI directory subdirectories that contain different `web.cnf` files that access different databases or contain different application profiles.

For example, we can define a `stores7`-only CGI `webdriver` configuration by creating a subfolder under `cgi-bin` called `stores7`, placing `webdriver` and `web.cnf` in that directory, and invoking the CGI `webdriver` as follows:

```
http://dellcpi/cgi-bin/stores7/webdriver.exe?MIval=Start
```

In this way you can create subdirectories for mapping several databases or for many specific `webdriver` configurations for one database.

For more information on the Apache web server, look at `http://www.apache.org`.

Configuring the NSAPI `webdriver`

The aim of configuring the NSAPI `webdriver` is to allow the Netscape web server to load the Netscape-specific `webdriver` shared-object library, and to optionally define any authentication mappings for users who are connecting to the Informix database.

NSAPI Setup Components

The `webdriver` Configuration File (`web.cnf`)

The NSAPI `webdriver` will use the information in this file to connect to the Informix server and database.

The `webdriver` Shared-object Library

The NSAPI `webdriver` comprises a set of functions to invoke the `webexplode()` DataBlade function and authenticate user access to the Informix database. The shared object does not have to be in the

Table 23-4.	The webdriver DLLs installed for Version 3 of the Web DataBlade on NT4.

Shared Object	Description
drvnsapi35.dll	webdriver for Netscape Enterprise Server 3.5
drvnsapi30.dll	webdriver for Netscape Enterprise Server 3.0
drvnsapi20.dll	webdriver for Netscape Enterprise Server 2.0

Table 23-5.	The webdriver DLLs installed for Version 4 of the Web DataBlade on NT4.

Shared Object	Description
drivernsapi36.dll	webdriver for Netscape Enterprise Server 3.6
drivernsapi35.dll	webdriver for Netscape Enterprise Server 3.5

same directory as the `web.cnf` file, but moving the correct shared object for the appropriate Netscape web server from the installation directory to an application directory is recommended.

The Web DataBlade is provided with a shared object that targets a specific Netscape web server. You use the shared object that applies to your web server. These objects are found in the installation directory for the Web DataBlade, usually `$INFORMIXDIR/extend`.

For example, under Microsoft Windows NT 4.0 Server and Web DataBlade 3.32.TC4, Tables 23-4 and 23-5, respectively, list the shared objects that are installed in the `$INFORMIXDIR/extend/web.3.32.TC4/webdriver/netscape` folder.

URL Prefixes

The URL prefixes are used to instruct the Netscape web server that the URL denotes a call to an *NSAPI function* in the `webdriver` shared object. The API URL prefixes are essentially called *basic* and *secure;* the basic prefix invokes the `informix_explode` NSAPI function to `webexplode()` the AppPage, and the secure prefix invokes the `informix_explode` function after performing authentication of the user requesting the secure URL prefix.

For example, in the following URL:

```
http://theale2/stores7-basic/?MIval=Start
```

the *URL prefix* is `stores7-basic`. This is the prefix declared to the web server.

You can configure multiple URL prefixes to the same Informix database from the web server. In Version 3, multiple basic URL prefixes could use the same `web.cnf` and multiple secure URL prefixes could use the same `web.cnf`, but you could not mix the two; the URL prefixes for basic and secure resulted in two `web.cnf` files. In Version 4, there is only one `web.cnf` for NSAPI; this file contains the mappings for all the URL prefixes.

Object Configuration File (`obj.conf`)

This file contains the mappings between CGI and NSAPI URL prefixes and physical directory names, together with the actions that should be taken when the web server encounters a URL prefix. An NSAPI URL prefix will have a *translation* directive, which maps the URL prefix to a web server *object,* and a list of NSAPI `webdriver` *functions* that are defined for this object. These functions do all the work of user authentication and dynamic web page generation. Instead of `webdriver.exe` parameterizing and calling `webexplode()`, it is the NSAPI function `informix_explode`, that is part of the shared object on NT.

You can define multiple URL prefixes in the `obj.conf` file.

The `obj.conf` file is stored in the `config` directory of the Netscape server instance that has been created on the web server computer. Each server instance will have its own `config` directory, and therefore, its own set of URL prefix mappings.

Summary Configuration

The NSAPI `webdriver` obtains configuration information about the Web application environment from `web.cnf` and the `obj.conf` Netscape Web server configuration file.

Version 4 of the Web DataBlade also uses information from the `webdriver` configuration stored in the database.

Version 4 Only

If you used the `websetup` utility initially to configure the Web DataBlade module for your database, the utility might have automatically performed some of the steps in this section.

- Create a directory to contain the `web.cnf` configuration file that will be used by an NSAPI-mapped URL.
- Stop the Netscape web server.
- Register the basic `webdriver` shared object in the Netscape configuration file, `obj.conf`.
- Optionally, register the secure `webdriver` shared object in `obj.conf`.
- Add authentication variables to `web.cnf`.
- Restart the Netscape web server.

Version 4 Only

You can run the `webconfig` *utility at the operating system command prompt to add the special* `webdriver` *mapping, called* `/dbname/admin`, *to the* `web.cnf` *file that invokes the Web DataBlade Module Administration Tool.*

Creating a `webdriver` NSAPI Directory

Create a directory on the web server host, for example:

```
D:\stores7\nsapi\
```

Copy the sample `webdriver` configuration file, `web.cnf.example`, to this directory and rename it `web.cnf`. You then need to change the variable definitions in `web.cnf` to access the Informix database (see Chap. 22). In particular, you must remember to set `WEB_HOME` correctly.

For example, if we have an NSAPI URL mapping called `stores7-basic`, then `WEB_HOME` will be set as follows:

```
WEB_HOME        /stores7-basic/
```

The `web.cnf.example` *file is located in the directory* `$INFORMIXDIR/extend/web.version/install`, *where* `$INFORMIXDIR` *refers to the main Informix directory and* `version` *refers to the current version of the Web DataBlade module installed on your computer.*

Registering the NSAPI `webdriver` with the Netscape Web Server

Copy the appropriate shared object to the directory containing the `web.cnf` file, and optionally rename the object to `drvnsapi.dll` or `drvnsapi.so`, depending on whether you are using NT or UNIX.

Listing 23-1.   The NSAPI object directives in `obj.conf.`

```
Init fn="load-modules" \
shlib="D:/informix/extend/WEB.3.32.TC1/netscape/drvnsapi.dll"\
funcs="informix_auth,informix_explode,informix_init"
Init fn="informix_init"
```

Edit the `obj.conf` file that the Netscape web server uses to control URL prefix mapping and NSAPI shared-object references. Listing 23-1 shows an example of this file.

For Version 4 of the Web DataBlade, the `funcs` parameter above is changed:

```
funcs="informix_auth,informix_require_auth,
informix_explode,informix_init"
```

The `Init` directives of the `obj.conf` file register Web server application functions with the Netscape web server and point to the location of the shared object that contains the functions. The `Init` directives must fit on a single line.

The first `Init` directive registers the functions used by the NSAPI `webdriver` and points to the shared object that contains the functions specified by the `shlib` parameter. The full pathname must be specified.

The second `Init` directive indicates that the web server initializes the NSAPI `webdriver` with the `informix_init` NSAPI function when the web server starts.

Adding URL Prefix Translation to the `obj.conf` File

We need to map a URL to an NSAPI `webdriver` function and, optionally, we want to enable permissions against the URL.

You add a *URL prefix* to the `obj.conf` file by adding a `NameTrans` directive. The `NameTrans` directives in the `obj.conf` file specify the Netscape *object* that is called to manage the next step when a user specifies the URL prefix in a browser.

A URL prefix can be seen in the following URL.

```
http://dellcpi/stores7-nsapi/?Mival=Start
```

The URL prefix that is configured in `obj.conf` is `stores7-nsapi`. This prefix will map down to a physical directory that stores the `web.cnf` file—in our case, `D:\stores7\nsapi`.

The web server uses the `NameTrans` directive to map a URL prefix to an action that the web server has to perform, such as invoking a function that conforms to the NSAPI interface. These actions are defined within `object` tags in the `obj.conf` file.

For the `stores7` database, we want to create two NSAPI URLs, one that is authenticated and one that is not. Authenticated URLs are defined as *secure* `webdriver` objects, and unauthenticated URLs are called *basic* `webdriver` objects.

Creating the URL Prefixes

Put the name translation directives in the default object, as shown below in List. 23-2.

Listing 23-2.   *Creating basic and secure URL prefix mappings.*

```
<Object name=default>
NameTrans fn="pfx2dir" from="stores7-nsapi" dir="D:/stores7/nsapi"
name="stores7_basic"
NameTrans fn="pfx2dir" from="stores7-secure" dir="D:/stores7/nsapi"
name="stores7_secure"
</Object>

<Object name="stores7-basic ">
Service method=(GET|POST) fn="informix_explode"
filename="D:/stores7/nsapi/web.cnf"
</Object>

<Object name="stores7-secure">
AuthTrans fn="basic-auth" auth-type="basic"
userdb=" D:/stores7/nsapi/web.cnf" userfn="informix_auth"
PathCheck fn="require-auth" auth-type="basic" realm="Secure"
Service method=(GET|POST) fn="informix_explode"
filename="D:/stores7/nsapi/web.cnf"
</Object>
```

Version 4 Only

The AuthTrans *directive has the* userdb *parameter set to the mapping information in the* web.cnf *file defined by* MI_WEBCONFIG. *The* PathCheck *parameter is set to the following:*

```
PathCheck fn="informix_require_auth" auth-type=
"basic" realm="Secure"
```

The PathCheck directive indicates that authorization is required. The AuthTrans directive indicates that the informix_auth NSAPI function performs the authorization based on the user access information from the web.cnf file specified in the userdb parameter. The web.cnf file should be the same as the one specified in the filename parameter of the Service directive.

You can have multiple basic and secure URLs for the same database. You may want to do this to enable part of your website to be secure. The protected URLs would be mapped as Secure *objects.*

Basic webdriver Object Definition

Listing 23-2 shows the basic webdriver object, named stores7-basic. The Service directive indicates the call to the informix_explode NSAPI function, which in turn makes the call to the Informix webexplode() function. The filename parameter is the web.cnf file used by this webdriver object.

Version 4 Only

The filename *parameter of the* Service *function is not required. The path to* web.cnf *is specified in the web server environment variable* MI_WEBCONFIG.

When the following URL is entered, the Start AppPage will be fetched from the database and exploded using the informix_explode NSAPI function without asking for a username and password.

```
http://dellcpi/stores7-basic/?Mival=Start
```

Secure `webdriver` Object Definition

Listing 23-2 shows the `stores7-secure` object. The `PathCheck` directive indicates that authorization is required. The `AuthTrans` directive indicates that the `informix_auth` NSAPI function performs the authorization. The `filename` parameter of the `Service` directive is the `web.cnf` file used by this `webdriver` object. Note that this `webdriver` object is different from the basic `webdriver` object.

When the following URL is entered, the browser will pop up a dialog box to ask for a user ID and password. This information will be authenticated by the NSAPI authentication functions, which take information from `web.cnf` configuration and user information in the database. If the user authenticates, then the `Start` AppPage will be fetched from the database and exploded using the `informix_explode` NSAPI function.

```
http://dellcpi/stores7-secure/?Mival=Start
```

important

To ensure that the correct URL mapping is chosen, the NSAPI `webdriver` *NameTrans directives should precede other* `NameTrans` *directives. This is because the web server evaluates the directives in sequential order.*

Setting Authentication Variables

In the `web.cnf` for your secure URL prefix, you need to set the variables that tell the methods in `webdriver` which database tables contain user information. For example:

```
MIpagelevel     read_level
MIuserpasswd    password
MIuserlevel     security_level
MIusertable     webusers
MIusername      name
```

Table 23-6 explains the meaning of these values.

Version 4 Only

You only need to manually add the first NameTrans *directive for a particular database to the* `obj.conf` *file, usually a file whose URL prefix points to the special* webdriver *mapping that invokes the Web DataBlade Module Administration Tool. Use the Netscape Administration Server to add any subsequent* NameTrans *directives.*

Table 23-6.   Authentication variables in `web.cnf`.

Value	Description
`webusers`	Table that contains user information to validate against.
`name`	The `varchar` column in the `webusers` table that contains the name of a valid user.
`security_level`	The `integer` that is used to validate against the AppPage `read_level` as the user navigates the site.
`password`	The `varchar` column in the `webusers` table that contains the password for name.
`read_level`	In the table specified by the `MItab` variable, the `integer` column that contains the read level for an AppPage.

You can register only one NSAPI `webdriver` *with a particular Netscape web server. This is because the names of the modules registered in the Netscape web server are always the same for any version of the Web DataBlade Module, and you cannot register more than one module with the same name with the Netscape web server.*

Before version 4, the basic and secure URL prefixes could map to different directories, each containing a different `web.cnf`. *This* `web.cnf` *could map to a completely separate database or Informix server. Because the Netscape objects are separate* `webdriver` *objects, you can treat them as mapping down to totally separate configurations of* `webdriver`.

Before running NSAPI `webdriver` *via Netscape Server, run the command line CGI* `webdriver` *to make sure the connection to the Informix database is good. If the connection is not good, use the* `SetNet32` *utility to set correct registry values on Windows platforms, or set the correct entries in the* `SQLHOSTS` *file on UNIX; also check the settings in* `web.cnf`.

Configuring and Using the ISAPI `webdriver`

The ISAPI `webdriver` is a dynamic link library (DLL), called `drvisapi.dll`. Microsoft's Internet Information Server loads the DLL the first time a URL pointing to the ISAPI `webdriver` is encountered.

ISAPI Setup Components

The `webdriver` Configuration File (web.cnf)

The ISAPI `webdriver` will use the information in this file to connect to the Informix server and database. The variable `MI_WEBCONFIG` is used by the web server to identify `web.cnf` in the filesystem.

The `webdriver` Shared-object Library

The ISAPI `webdriver` comprises a set of functions to invoke the `webexplode()` DataBlade function and authenticate user access to the Informix database. The shared object does not have to be in the same directory as the `web.cnf` file, but moving the correct shared object from the `installation` directory to an `application` directory on the web server is recommended.

URL Prefixes

The URL prefixes are used to instruct the IIS web server that the URL denotes a call to a *function* in the ISAPI `webdriver` shared object.

Summary Configuration

1. Create a directory on the web server to contain the `web.cnf` file (for example, `D:\stores7\isapi`).
2. Copy the sample `webdriver` configuration file, called `web.cnf.example`, from the Microsoft directory where the Web DataBlade was installed to the directory created in Step 1 and rename it `web.cnf`. Update the `web.cnf` file with the minimum required information, including secure authentication variables for secure URLs.
3. If the system variable `MI_WEBCONFIG` is set, update the `web.cnf` file pointed to the `MI_WEBCONFIG` to include a mapping between the new URL prefix and the path to the new `web.cnf` file.
4. Copy the `drvisapi.dll` file from the directory where the Web DataBlade module is installed to the directory created in Step 1. You can copy this file to another directory if required.
5. Add basic and secure URL prefix mapping information to the Microsoft Internet Information Server so that the web server calls the ISAPI `webdriver` module when you specify a URL prefix that has a mapping definition.
6. Add an ISAPI authentication filter to the secure URL prefix.
7. Add an authenticating NT user.

note

To register a URL prefix for Version 4 of the Web DataBlade, you must use the instructions for IIS Version 4 below.

Creating a Basic and Secure URL Prefix in Version 4 of Microsoft IIS

To create a URL prefix in IIS for both basic and secure URLs, you follow the same procedure that is described in the subsection, "Using Microsoft Internet Information Server Version 4 for CGI," to set up a Virtual Directory.

For example, suppose we want to create a basic unauthenticated URL prefix called `stores7-basic` to replace the need for the CGI `webdriver` under IIS. Follow the procedure for creating a Virtual Directory as described previously, but map `stores7-basic` to a directory called, for example, `D:\stores7\isapi\basic`. Place the `web.cnf` file for this specific URL in this directory. If you are using more than one ISAPI URL prefix, update the `web.cnf` file pointed to by the system variable `MI_WEBCONFIG` to map the new URL prefix with the new `web.cnf`.

We can invoke the ISAPI `webdriver` now, without going on to register the DLL as a filter for authentication. For example, you can now invoke the following URL:

```
http://dellcpi/stores7-basic/drvisapi.dll/HelloWorld
```

To create a secure URL prefix called `stores7-secure`, map the Virtual Directory to a directory called, for example, `D:\stores7\isapi\secure`. Place the `web.cnf` file for this specific URL in this directory. If you placed a copy of `drvisapi.dll` in this directory, you could call it just like the basic URL prefix (but using `/stores7-secure/drvisapi.dll`) instead, but there is no point in doing that. We need to apply the security filter to the secure URL prefix to enable authentication when any URL containing this prefix is invoked from this web server.

Creating a Basic and Secure URL Prefix in Version 3 of Microsoft IIS

You use the Microsoft Internet Service Manager to create a directory mapping to the directory that contains the `drvisapi.dll` shared object.

Start the Microsoft Internet Services Manager. Double-click the icon of the WWW Service. Click the Directories tab in the WWW Service Properties window. Click the Add button. Enter the full directory path for the directory that contains the `drvisapi.dll` shared object in the Directory field of the Directory Properties window, for example, `D:\stores7\isapi\basic`. Enter the URL prefix in the Alias field under Virtual Directory, for example, `/stores7-basic`. Under the Directory page, click the Edit Properties button, highlight `D:\stores7\isapi\basic`, and select the Execution checkbox. Click OK to save the new URL prefix and close the Directory Properties window. Click OK to close the WWW Service Properties window.

Adding the ISAPI Authentication Filter to the Secure URL Prefix

With all the API `webdrivers`, there is a basic URL prefix and a secure URL prefix. A secure URL prefix demands that the web server know which shared object to invoke to authenticate the user making the HTTP request.

Setting Authentication Variables

This task is the same as it is for the NSAPI `webdriver`. See the sub-section, "Setting Authentication Variables," which closes the NSAPI section.

Specifying an Authenticating NT User

Under NT, authentication involves not only validating the user ID and password of the user at the browser, but also *validating a nominated NT user at the web server.* This user is specified in the `web.cnf` mapped to the secure URL and must be a valid user on the web server machine. The NT administrator needs to create a dummy NT user with ordinary user privileges if an existing user cannot be included. You must then specify the user's logon name and password in two variables in the `web.cnf`. The `drvisapi.dll` authentication methods use these values to check against the NT user registry.

For example, if the dummy (or existing) NT user name is `isapi_user` and the user password is `isapi_password`, add to the Version 3 `web.cnf` file:

```
MI_WEBNTUSER       isapi_user
MI_WEBNTPASSWORD   isapi_password
```

for Version 4:

```
iis_nt_user        isapi_user
iis_nt_password    isapi_password
```

tip

For Version 4 of the Web DataBlade, use the Web DataBlade Module Administration Tool to add these variables.

Setting the ISAPI Filter DLL

To enable ISAPI authentication, you need to attach the ISAPI filter DLL to verify the user ID and password that the user enters to the browser dialog when the secure URL is requested. This is the same file as the ISAPI `webdriver`, `drivisapi.dll`. For IIS, Version 3 filter registration differs from Version 4.

Using Microsoft Internet Information Server Version 4.   From the Internet Services Manager (or the Microsoft Management Console), select the website for which you want to add the authenticating filter. Select the Properties sheet for that site, select the ISAPI Filters tab, then click the Add button.

Enter the filter properties into the Filter Properties dialog. For example, if the `drvisapi.dll` resides in the `d:\stores7\isapi\secure` directory, enter this path into the Executable box. Enter a descriptive name into the Filter Name box. Figure 23-12 shows an example of this dialog, and Fig. 23-13 shows the ISAPI Filters Property sheet once the filter has been added.

What Is an ISAPI Filter?

An ISAPI filter is a program that responds to events during the processing of an HTTP request. In our case, the ISAPI `webdriver` operates as both the `webdriver` that sends `webexplode()` requests to the Informix database server and as the authentication filter that validates the user ID and password with the values in the table specified by the authenticating variables in `web.cnf`. An ISAPI filter is always loaded into the memory allocated to the website in IIS 4. You can specify more than one filter to process the incoming data. The filters are processed in the order they appear in the ISAPI Filters Property sheet.

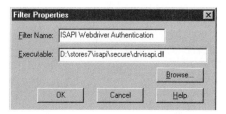

Figure 23-12. Register the ISAPI
authenticating filter in IIS.

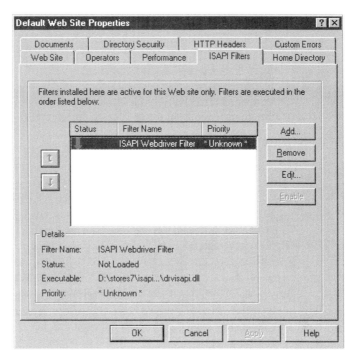

Figure 23-13. ISAPI Filters Property sheet.

IIS Version 3. You need to add the ISAPI filter to the registry with NT's Registry Editor. The Registry key and value is as follows:

```
HKEY_LOCAL_MACHINE
    /SYSTEM
        /CurrentControlSet
            /Services
                /W3SVC
                    /Parameters
                        /Filter DLLs
```

Filter DLLs is the value name where filter DLLs reside. Because IIS 3.0 uses the filter sspifilt.dll, that entry will already exist.

Add a comma and the full path and the name of the drvisapi.dll after the "sspifilt.dll" (the IIS 3.0 filter). Commas separate multiple entries.

Enabling Basic Authentication for the Secure URL Prefix

Internet Information Server Version 4 allows you to enable authentication at the URL level, which means that you can use ISAPI for unauthenticated URLs as well as for URLs that will require a user ID and password to access. This allows you to take advantage of the performance improvements over CGI without requiring the user to authenticate unnecessarily just because you have one secure URL on the site.

Even though the filter may have been added, it is only used if basic authentication is enabled for the virtual directory that represents the secure URL prefix. To add basic authentication, select the properties sheet for the virtual directory, and select the Directory Security tab. Assuming the secure URL prefix is mapped to the IIS virtual directory `stores7-secure`, the display should look something like Fig. 23-14.

In the Anonymous Access and Authentication Control box, click the Edit button. The Authentication Methods dialog should appear. Check Basic Authentication, and uncheck Allow Anonymous Authentication and Windows NT Challenge/Response. Figure 23-15 shows this setting. Click OK.

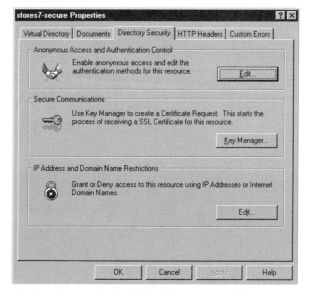

Figure 23-14. *Secure URL properties display.*

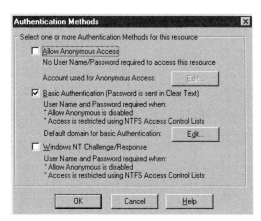

Figure 23-15. Enabling basic authentication.

When entered in the browser, the secure URL should now result in a dialog that asks for the username and password the first time the secure URL is invoked.

There is a difference in user authentication between Versions 3 and 4 of IIS. In Version 3 you can choose to have no authentication on a URL prefix (the default), or you can enable authentication and it will apply to all URL prefixes. In Version 4 you can set authentication options for a distinct URL prefix.

Single and Multiple ISAPI Configurations

Until Version 4 of the Web DataBlade, you had to create multiple `web.cnf` files if your web applications were spread across more than one database. The `web.cnf` file nominated the `INFORMIXSERVER` and database; accordingly, if a URL prefix required web pages from a database that was not configured in an existing `web.cnf` file, you had to create another `web.cnf` and associate it with the URL prefix.

Version 4 of the Web DataBlade uses one `web.cnf` file that contains multiple URL prefix mappings that can nominate a separate database and `webdriver` configuration.

This section shows you how to manage single and multiple ISAPI URLs for Version 3 of the Web DataBlade, using the `stores7` ISAPI directory as an example.

The aim is to tell the ISAPI `webdriver` where to find the `web.cnf` file that it must use. This is achieved by setting a variable in the IIS environment called `MI_WEBCONFIG` (this variable is also used in

Version 4 of the Web DataBlade). The contents of `web.cnf` will differ according to whether the ISAPI `webdriver` is to service *single* or *multiple* `webdriver` configurations.

Single `webdriver` ISAPI Configuration

This section applies to a single ISAPI configuration for a basic or secure URL prefix. An example directory `D:\stores7\isapi` can be used. Ensure that a `web.cnf` file and `drvisapi.dll` is placed in the `D:\stores7\isapi` directory.

Optionally, set the Windows NT system environment variable `MI_WEBCONFIG` to the full path of `web.cnf` using Control Panel\System\Environment. For example:

```
MI_WEBCONFIG=d:\stores7\isapi\web.cnf
```

Figure 23-16 shows the Environment tab for entering this system variable.

Be sure your `<drive>:\informix\bin` directory is included in the system environment `PATH` variable. Otherwise, you will receive errors when IIS tries to load the ISAPI shared object.

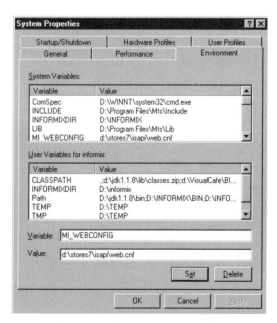

Figure 23-16. *Adding* `MI_WEBCONFIG` *to the NT system environment.*

You must then reboot the Windows NT machine so that the new system environment `MI_WEBCONFIG` will be effective in the IIS Service.

Multiple `webdriver` ISAPI Configurations

If you want to create three URL prefixes with three different `webdriver` configurations, then you must change the `web.cnf` file specified by the variable `MI_WEBCONFIG`. If you don't need multiple configurations, then you don't need to set `MI_WEBCONFIG`. However, once this variable is set, you need to use it to control all your `web.cnf` settings, including the CGI setting. This section shows you how to do this.

The example in this section creates three different `webdriver` configurations for ISAPI. Table 23-7 lists the URLs that we will configure.

Example URLs include:

```
http://dellcpi/stores7/webdriver.exe?MIval=HelloWorld
http://dellcpi/stores7-basic/drvisapi.dll/HelloWorld
http://dellcpi/stores7-secure/drvisapi.dll/HelloWorld
```

The first is the CGI call to `webdriver`. The second is a basic unauthenticated call to the `webdriver` shared object. This call is the first step up to integrate `webdriver` with the web server to eliminate CGI overhead. The third example URL is a secure call to the `webdriver` shared object. This URL is configured with basic authentication, so that the first time a URL containing `/stores7-secure` is invoked, the user must enter username and password details.

For example, you could have deployed a Web DataBlade application in three databases. In contrast, you may be using a single database for web content, but you require multiple views on the application pages that are organized by department: one view for the administrator, one view for the employees and another view for the managers.

Each view will have a different configuration, possibly using a different set of tables to store the web pages or perhaps an application-

Table 23-7. Example URLs.

URL prefix	Purpose
stores7	Used for the CGI `webdriver` URL.
stores7-basic	Basic unauthenticated ISAPI `webdriver` URL.
stores7-secure	Secure authenticated ISAPI `webdriver` URL.

specific set of variables initialized to different values (e.g., JDBC URLs that differ in user and password values), or maybe one or more of the URL prefixes are authenticated.

Whatever the reason, the steps to follow are:

- Create the `web.cnf` files for each URL prefix.
- Create a controlling, and add the path to this file to the NT system variable `MI_WEBCONFIG`.
- Add the URL prefix mapping for each URL prefix to the controlling `web.cnf` denoted by `MI_WEBCONFIG`.

What we do is this: Set the NT system variable `MI_WEBCONFIG` to a *general* configuration file, which will refer to a *specific* `web.cnf` file for each URL prefix. Use Control Panel\System\Environment. For example:

```
MI_WEBCONFIG=D:\stores7\isapi\web.cnf
```

Figure 23-16 (on page 854) shows the display of the Environment tab of the System Properties dialog.

Listing 23-3 shows the contents of the file pointed to by `MI_WEBCONFIG`. This is the controlling `web.cnf` file.

Listing 23-4 shows the contents of the `web.cnf` file for the `stores7` URL, which is a CGI URL.

Listing 23-3. *The* `web.cnf` *file referenced by* `MI_WEBCONFIG`, *mapping all the* `web.cnf` *files.*

```
#
# This is the controlling web.cnf which maps the
# configuration files for each URL prefix.
#
# You don't need this file if the system variable
# MI_WEBCONFIG isn't set
#
# In this file, we have three URL prefixes:
#
# stores7           : CGI webdriver
# stores7-basic     : basic ISAPI URL prefix
# stores7-secure    : secure, authenticated URL prefix
#
```

Listing 23-3. *(continued)*

MI_WEBCONFIG mapping

```
/stores7/webdriver.exe          d:\stores7\cgi-bin\web.cnf
/stores7-basic/drvisapi.dll     d:\stores7\isapi\basic\web.cnf
/stores7-secure/drvisapi.dll    d:\stores7\isapi\secure\web.cnf


#
# Note: you can call the individual web.cnf files by
# different names.
# For example:
#/stores7/webdriver.exe          d:\stores7\cgi-bin\cgi.cnf
#/stores7-basic/drvisapi.dl     d:\stores7\isapi\basic\basic.cnf
#/stores7-secure/drvisapi.dll d:\stores7\isapi\secure\sec.cnf
#
```

The value of WEB_HOME for /stores7-basic is

```
WEB_HOME                /stores7-basic/drvisapi.dll
```

The value of WEB_HOME for /stores7-secure is

```
WEB_HOME                /stores7-secure/drvisapi.dll
```

Listing 23-4. *The* stores7 *version of* web.cnf.

```
# Connection variables

     MI_DATABASE        stores7
     MI_USER            Informix
     MI_PASSWORD        informix
     REMOTE_USER? default

# If you are using the CGI Webdriver, include the following:
     WEB_HOME           /stores7/webdriver.exe
     INFORMIXDIR  d:\informix
     INFORMIXSERVER     ol_dellcpi

# AppPage table variables
```

Listing 23-4. (continued)

```
    MInam           ID
    MIcol           object
    MItab           wbPages

    MItabObj?       wbBinaries
    MIcolObj?       object
    MInamObj?       ID
    MItypeObj?      image/gif


    MI_WEBMAXHTMLSIZE       90000

# Data Director for Web Environment Variables

    MI_WEBSCHEMADEF         wb
    MI_WEBTAGSSQL           SELECT parameters,object FROM wbTags
WHERE webupper(ID)=webupper('$MI_WEBTAGSID');
    .OPTOFC                 1
```

Configuring and Using the Apache API `webdriver`

Informix provides shared-object libraries for integrating `webdriver` with the Apache web server program, `HTTPD`. You need to rebuild the Apache web server to integrate these shared objects with the `HTTPD` binary executable. This section lists the main configuration tasks for Apache `webdriver` integration.

Apache API Setup Components

The `webdriver` Configuration File (`web.cnf`)

The Apache `webdriver` will use the information in this file to connect to the Informix server and database. The variable `MI_WEBCONFIG` is used by the web server to identify `web.cnf` in the filesystem to the `webdriver` object.

The `webdriver` Shared-object Library

There are two shared objects for Apache, `explode` and `explode_ssi`. The former is used for basic and secure URL prefixes, and the latter allows you to include server-side includes (SSI) in your AppPages. The

Apache `webdriver` comprises a set of functions to invoke the `webexplode()` DataBlade function and authenticate user access to the Informix database. The shared object used does not have to be in the same directory as the `web.cnf` file, but moving the correct shared object for the Apache web server is recommended.

What Are Server-side Includes?

Server-side includes (SSI) are web server directives that are stored in the HTML source file. The web server will process the directives before the page is sent to the browser, executing the SSI directives in sequence. In this respect, SSI directives are similar to AppPage Scripting tags, except that AppPage tags are processed by `webexplode()`. *If an AppPage contains SSI directives, they will be processed by the web server after the AppPage Scripting tags have been processed by* `webexplode()`, *which ignores SSI. An example of an SSI directive would be to include the last-changed timestamp for a web page, include a hit count, or include page header and footer information.*

URL Prefixes

The URL prefixes are used to instruct the Apache web server that the URL denotes a call to a *function* in the Apache `webdriver` shared object.

Apache Web Server Configuration File (`httpd.conf`)

The file `httpd.conf` resides in the `conf` directory where the Apache web server is installed. This file enables Apache to map URL prefixes, CGI directories, and `webdriver` shared objects. You update this file to include nondefault CGI directory locations (using the `ScriptAlias` directive as discussed previously), and `webdriver` shared-object locations, using the `Location` directive (shown in this section).

Apache Web Server Build Configuration (`Configuration`)

The `Configuration` file is located in the `src` directory beneath the main Apache installation directory. This file contains the information required to build the `HTTPD` executable file. In our case, we need to edit this file in order to specify the Informix `webdriver` shared objects that will be linked into the `HTTPD` executable. We also need to specify the Informix directory paths so that the utility that rebuilds the `HTTPD` executable can resolve the symbolic names referred to in the shared objects and link in the relevant binary objects in the Informix libraries contained in the Client Software Developers Kit.

Summary Configuration

1. Create a directory on the web server to contain `web.cnf`. Copy the sample `webdriver` configuration file, called `web.cnf.example`, from the `install` directory where the Web DataBlade was installed to a directory on the Web server computer and rename it `web.cnf`. Update the `web.cnf` file with the minimum required information.

2. Copy the `explode` or `explode_ssi` objects from the directory where the Web DataBlade module is installed to the directory created in Step 1. You can copy the object file to another directory if required.

3. Register the Apache `webdriver` module with the Apache Web server by editing the Apache Web server configuration file called `Configuration`, located in the `src` directory under the main Apache web server directory.

4. Configure the Apache web server for your operating system by running the `Configure` program located in the `src` directory under the main Apache web server directory.

5. Recreate the `HTTPD` binary.

6. Add URL prefix information to the Apache web server configuration file `httpd.conf` so that the web server calls the Apache `webdriver` module when you specify a URL prefix that maps to `webdriver`.

7. In the Apache web server environment, set the `MI_WEBCONFIG` and `LD_LIBRARY_PATH` environment variables to point to the full pathname of the `web.cnf` file and the Informix libraries, respectively.

For information on how to rebuild the Apache web server, look at `http://www.apache.org`. The Informix product documentation also contains a detailed breakdown how to rebuild the Apache web server.

Registering the Apache `webdriver` with the Apache Web Server

The Apache `webdriver` (`explode` or `explode_ssi`) is built into the `HTTPD` executable, and the module specification is stored in the Apache `Configuration` file. Once the configuration information has been entered into this file, a `make` utility is run to rebuild the `HTTPD` executable, linking in the `webdriver` shared object and also resolving any symbolic names to the Informix libraries contained in the installed Client SDK directories.

Adding URL Prefix Translation to the `httpd.conf` File

You can register basic and secure URL prefixes with the Apache web server by adding entries to the `httpd.conf` file.

Each `webdriver` mapping in the `web.cnf` file has a corresponding `Location` directive in the `httpd.conf` file, which defines the URL prefix.

You define separate `Location` directives for basic and secure URL prefixes. Listing 23-5 shows both types of directive using `stores7` as an example.

In List. 23-5, the first `Location` directive specifies a basic URL prefix. The `informix_explode` function resides in the `explode` or `explode_ssi` shared object, which has already been linked into the `HTTPD` executable. When the web server receives the following HTTP request

```
http://dellcpi/stores7-basic/Start
```

then the Apache web server will call the `informix_explode` function, which in turn will call the `webexplode()` DataBlade function to expand the AppPage called `Start`.

The second `Location` directive in List. 23-5 specifies a secure URL prefix. When the Apache web server receives the following HTTP request

```
http://dellcpi/stores7-secure/Start
```

then Apache will use `webdriver` to authenticate the HTTP request by asking for a user ID and password combination to be validated against the tables defined in the `webdriver` configuration for that URL prefix. Once the user has been authenticated, `informix_explode` is called to expand the AppPage called `Start`.

Listing 23-5.   Basic and secure URL mappings in `httpd.conf`.

```
<Location /stores7-basic>
SetHandler informix_explode
</Location>

<Location /stores7-secure>
SetHandler informix_explode
AuthType Basic
AuthName /stores7-secure
require valid-user
</Location>
```

The Apache web server environment must have the variable MI_WEBCONFIG *set to point to the* web.cnf *file that the Apache* webdriver *requires. This* web.cnf *file will contain the mapping and configuration information for the* /stores7-basic *and* /stores7-secure *URL prefixes.*

The URL prefix in the Location *directive in* httpd.conf *must match a URL mapping in the* webdriver *configuration file specified with* MI_WEBCONFIG.

Version 4 Change Summary

webdriver **Configuration**

Cleverly, Informix have extended the way MI_WEBCONFIG was used in Version 3 of the Web DataBlade to create a webdriver configuration model that eliminates the requirement to maintain multiple web.cnf files.

The variable MI_WEBCONFIG is defined in the web server environment to identify the path to the web.cnf file (it can be named anything, but web.cnf is descriptive). If you are using CGI, MI_WEBCONFIG is ignored, since the CGI webdriver requires web.cnf to be in the same directory as the webdriver executable.

You will need a separate web.cnf for each of the Netscape, Microsoft, and Apache web servers that you use.

Using WEB_HOME

The following subsections show how to define WEB_HOME for Version 3 and Version 4 of the Web DataBlade.

Version 3 for Netscape.
```
WEB_HOME /stores7/webdriver.exe # CGI mapping
WEB_HOME /stores7-basic/ # NSAPI mapping
WEB_HOME /stores7-secure/ # NSAPI mapping
```

Version 4 for Netscape.
```
anchorvar WEB_HOME/webdriver  # CGI
anchorvar WEB_HOME # NSAPI does not require a shared
                   # object reference
```

Version 3 for Microsoft.

```
WEB_HOME /stores7/webdriver.exe # CGI
WEB_HOME /stores7-basic/drvisapi.dll # ISAPI
WEB_HOME /stores7-secure/drvisapi.dll # ISAPI
```

Version 4 for Microsoft.

```
anchorvar WEB_HOME/stores7/webdriver # CGI
anchorvar WEB_HOME/drvisapi.dll # ISAPI
```

Version 4 for Apache (There Is No Supported Version 3 of the Web DataBlade for Apache).

```
anchorvar WEB_HOME # Apache API and CGI
```

Ensure that the system environment variable PATH *includes the directory that contains the Informix executables.*

Version 4

You should create a URL prefix for the Web DataBlade Administration Tool, for example, /stores7-admin. *You can use the* webconfig *utility to do this. You should also add the URL prefix to IIS as described in this chapter.*

Web Server Mapping of Distributed Applications

In the world of distributed web content delivery, you will have to manage web content in multiple locations. This includes multiple web server machines, multiple databases on the same web server machine, or databases located on a remote machine that may be dedicated to the Informix server. For the Informix Web DataBlade, this essentially maps down to the management of multiple webdriver configurations as part of the web server setup.

Figure 23-17 shows configuration of multiple files and multiple databases for Versions 3 and 4 of the Web DataBlade. Table 23-8 lists the items in Fig. 23-17.

Web Server Platforms

The Version 4 web server platform uses one web.cnf file for each running web server, and this web.cnf file is denoted by the MI_WEBCONFIG environment variable.

You should create one web.cnf file for each web server that runs on your web server machine if they are different web server products.

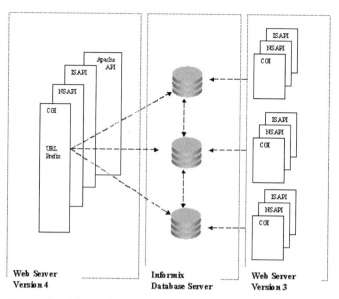

Figure 23-17. Multiple web configurations and databases for Versions 3 and 4 of the Web DataBlade.

Table 23-8.   Components listed in Fig. 23-17.

Component	Description
Web Server Version 3	The web server platform for Version 3 of the Web DataBlade; to show the `webdriver` configuration limitations.
Web Server Version 4	The web server platform for Version 4 of the Web DataBlade; to show addressing of multiple configurations from a single `webdriver` configuration.
Informix Database Server	Informix Dynamic Server.2000 or Universal Data Option, containing 3 example databases.
CGI	The CGI `webdriver` configuration.
NSAPI	The NSAPI `webdriver` configuration.
ISAPI	The ISAPI `webdriver` configuration.
Apache API	The Apachi API `webdriver` configuration.

In summary, the `web.cnf` file contains the URL prefix mapping that the web server identifies. Each mapping identifies a `webdriver` configuration. Multiple URL prefixes can be written in the `web.cnf` file in Version 4 of the Web DataBlade. Therefore, you do not have to create multiple versions of the `web.cnf` file.

Figure 23-17 shows the Version 3 web server platform. It shows that for each web server product you need a separate `webdriver` configuration file. You also need multiple `web.cnf` files for each configuration of an application.

Figure 23-17 shows the two `web.cnf` DataBlade versions communicating with the same database. This is for illustration only; you should only run Version 4 of the `webdriver` configuration against Version 4 of the Web DataBlade.

Clearly, the Version 4 `webdriver` configuration has reduced this administrative overhead from the web server setup.

Distributing the Web Server and Informix Database Server

The horizontal and diagonal lines in Fig. 23-17 represent the distributed connectivity layer between the Web Server and the Informix database that stores the `webdriver` configurations and web content. The Informix database includes access to application and legacy data, in contrast to web-content-specific data such as AppPages, images, and audio objects.

For example, you may have an NT4 Server machine running IIS or Netscape Enterprise Server that requires web content from the Informix Dynamic Server database, which resides on an AIX machine across the LAN. `webdriver` can access the remote database to extract AppPages as long as the registry settings in `setnet` have been configured for the remote Informix server. If the web server host is UNIX, then the target Informix servers will need to be registered in the `sqlhosts` file in `$INFORMIXDIR/etc`.

By carefully managing the `webdriver` configuration files through URL prefix mapping, one web server can be configured to access multiple databases.

If the web server and the Informix database server are on separate machines, you should install the Informix Client Software Development Kit (CSDK) on the web server. `webdriver` needs two components of the CSDK to be installed: LIBDMI Client Interface and Informix-Connect for runtime.

Distributing Database Access

Intranet sites that deploy multiple applications may opt to use one database per application, therefore one web server has to provide access for multiple databases. Some installations may need to present a special view of data to the intranet platform for the management tier of the organization to interrogate, such as a Data Mart.

This Data Mart presents an aggregated summary of transactions that is calculated overnight from a larger database of transaction data. The intranet application to view this data has no access to the wider set of transaction data, which may even reside in a non-Informix database.

Informix Dynamic Server will allow you to address multiple databases within the same Informix server instance, or databases served by other Informix server instances distributed across a network. These are the vertical lines in Fig. 23-17. You can either address the target database table in longhand or create a synonym on the web-enabled database (the one addressed by `web.cnf`) that translates to the remote Informix server, database, and table.

You may, however, find that not all of your data can be accessed in this way; for example, you may not be able to access certain DataBlade datatypes from another database. You are advised to map the URL prefix to the database that has web content such as AppPages, images, and other complex objects; if the dynamic content is derived from data that is distributed across several databases, you will have to test the remote access in `dbaccess` first.

Summary

This chapter has shown how to integrate the web server with the middleware webdriver. You can now implement CGI for Netscape, Microsoft IIS, and Apache. You can also implement NSAPI, ISAPI, and the Apache API. Clearly, the first step after CGI is to use the API for your web server. We learned how to authenticate URLs and how to differentiate a secure URL from a basic unauthenticated URL. We also learned how to manage multiple configurations of URLs for different web application requirements. Using the techniques in this chapter, you are now in a position to integrate your web server with `webdriver`, as well as manage multiple secure and nonsecure URL mappings to different databases from a single web server.

Securing Your Web Applications

In this chapter:

- Implementing security in the `webdriver` configuration file
- Implementing security in the web server
- Restricting access to AppPages
- Distributed web server security
- Integrating dynamic web applications with the secure sockets layer (SSL)

With increasing urgency, the expanding universe of Internet commerce confronts the need to capture and store confidential information in a secure manner via open technologies. The Web DataBlade allows you to secure the application layer by using the techniques described in this chapter; particularly important for the security of your e-commerce applications is the secure sockets layer, or SSL. In this chapter, you will learn how to secure your Web DataBlade applications at the application and web server level, including SSL.

Security Components

For the Web DataBlade, three main components constitute the means to implement greater security:

- the `webdriver web.cnf` file (password and username security),
- the web server (username security and secure sockets layer encryption),
- the AppPage (AppPage-level security)

Secure sockets layer (SSL) security is transparent to the Web DataBlade and is important when delivering e-commerce applications over the web. A special section is devoted to this later in the chapter.

Implementing Security in the `webdriver` Configuration File

The following tasks are necessary to ensure security using the `web.cnf` file:

- password protect web server database connections,
- encrypt the password,
- establish selective passing of variables to `webexplode()`,
- set `MI_USER` to a user with less privilege,
- set `MI_WEBRAWPASSWORD` to a value other than one.

Password Protect Web Server Connections

The web server process is started under a user account on the web server machine. When a URL is requested that maps onto a `webdriver` request, the web server will connect to the database via CGI or an API such as NSAPI or ISAPI.

When the web server connects to the database, it connects as a database client on behalf of a nominated database user.

The nominated database user is specified in the `MI_USER` variable in `web.cnf` as follows:

```
MI_DATABASE       catalog
MI_USER           cortez
```

If the web server runs as `MI_USER`, then no password is required; otherwise a password is required.

For example, assuming that the web server is run as the three users listed in Table 24-1 against the specified `MI_USER`, the password requirements are as shown in the table.

It is common for web servers to run as the `nobody` user, so unless your `MI_USER` is nobody (not recommended), then you will need to implement a password.

The password of the nominated database user is specified in the `MI_PASSWORD` variable in `web.cnf` as follows:

```
MI_DATABASE       catalog
MI_USER           cortez
MI_PASSWORD       sw0rd
```

One of the problems in setting `MI_PASSWORD` in the `web.cnf` file is that other users on the web server machine can potentially view the file. The webmaster should set the file-level permissions for the `web.cnf` file accordingly. For almost every URL prefix that you create, there is a corresponding `web.cnf` file up to Version 4 of the Web DataBlade; from Version 4, there is one `web.cnf` nominated in the variable `MI_WEBCONFIG`; however, multiple web servers can have the environment variable `MI_WEBCONFIG` set to different `web.cnf` files.

`MI_USER` must at least have connection privileges to `MI_DATABASE`.

If you wish not only to secure the `web.cnf` file itself using filesystem permissions but to encrypt `MI_PASSWORD` as well, then you should encrypt the password for `MI_USER` so that only `webdriver` can decrypt it. This is explained in the next section.

Table 24-1. *Password requirement for web server database connections via a nominated user.*

Web server user	Value of MI_USER	Password required?
cortez	cortez	No
cortez	randall	Yes
nobody	cortez	Yes

note

When using secure URL prefixes, the actual database connection is against MI_USER. *For example, if* MI_USER *is set to* Informix *and you connect via NSAPI, entering* randall *for the username and* myPassword *for the password, then the user connection as shown by* onstat-u *is* Informix, *not* randall.

Encrypting Passwords

You use the webpwcrypt program to encrypt a password. The webpwcrypt program resides in the utils subdirectory of the Web DataBlade installation directory, which can be found under $INFORMIXDIR/extend. You can either run webpwcrypt from that directory or place the utils directory in the PATH environment variable.

You store the encrypted password and a chosen password key in the web.cnf file. Only webdriver can decrypt the password using the password key.

The webpwcrypt program takes three parameters, which are listed in Table 24-2.

For example, to encrypt the password for the user cortez using the key myKeyString for database catalog, perform the following:

- Invoke the webpwcrypt program:

    webpwcrypt catalog cortez mykeystring

- You will be prompted for the password for the user cortez. Enter the password.
- You will be asked to verify the password. Enter it again.

The webpwcrypt program will then display the values of MI_PASSWORD and MI_PASSWORD_KEY to the screen. These are the variables and values you need to set in web.cnf.

Listing 24-1 shows this example run under NT4.

Table 24-2.   The webpwcrypt **parameters.**

Parameter	Description
database	Value of MI_DATABASE.
user	Value of MI_USER.
key	User-supplied string.

```
D:\informix\extend\web.3.32.TC4\utils>webpwcrypt catalog
cortez myKeyString
Enter password for user 'cortez': *****
Enter password again: *****
MI_PASSWORD 09ed6f3ad83d0c42bf320cd66fe7f84a
MI_PASSWORD_KEY myKeyString
```

Put the output from webpwcrypt into web.cnf as follows:

```
MI_DATABASE          catalog
MI_USER              cortez
MI_PASSWORD          09ed6f3ad83d0c42bf320cd66fe7f84a
MI_PASSWORD_KEY      myKeyString
```

The variables MI_PASSWORD *and* MI_PASSWORD_KEY *are not passed to* webexplode(). *They cannot be viewed in RAW mode.*

Selective Passing of Variables to webexplode()

When the webdriver program or shared object executes, it collects every variable from the following sources:

- the web.cnf file,
- the web server environment,
- the query string (the URL, with variables separated by "&").

The variable values are then *URL-encoded* before being passed to the webexplode() function.

Passing all of these variables into webexplode() is an overhead we can reduce by nominating selected variables to *push* into the webexplode() function. The associated benefit is that we can reduce the visibility of these variables in the browser. For confirmation, setting MI_WEBRAWMODE in the URL will bring back only the selected, or *pushed,* variables.

Note that

- pushing selected variables reduces execution time for webdriver and webexplode();
- the number of instances of each AppPage in cache is reduced by reducing the number of possible sets of variables that can be exploded.

Most of the time, `webdriver` configuration variables do not need to be exploded. Variables that are used in your application should always be pushed.

By default, the CGI `webdriver` passes every variable extracted from the web server environment. These environment variables are specific to the web server used.

Setting `MI_WEBPUSHVARS`

The `webdriver` variable `MI_WEBPUSHVARS` is used to flag the requirement to push selected variables to `webexplode()`. You set it to the value `select` as follows:

```
MI_WEBPUSHVARS    select
```

Use `MI_WEBPUSHVARS` to include only those variables that affect the web application logic.

When `MI_WEBPUSHVARS` is set to `select`, the syntax extensions listed in Table 24-3 are enabled in `web.cnf`. In the following example, `MI_WEBEXPLOG` will *not* be passed to `webexplode()`:

```
MI_WEBPUSHVARS    select
!MI_WEBEXPLOG     d:\stores7\nsapi\basic\webexplog.log
```

In the next example, `MI_WEBEXPLOG` *will* be passed to `webexplode()`:

```
MI_WEBPUSHVARS    select
MI_WEBEXPLOG d:\stores7\nsapi\basic\webexplog.log
```

Table 24-3. *Syntax extension for* `MI_WEBPUSHVARS`.

Prefix	Result
!	The variable is not passed to `webexplode()`.
No Prefix	The variable is passed to `webexplode()` if it is initialized in `web.cnf`.
+	If the variable is a web server variable, then pass it to `webexplode()`; otherwise do not pass it.

In the next example, the `HTTP_USER_AGENT` web server variable *will* be passed to `webexplode()`:

```
MI_WEBPUSHVARS    select
+HTTP_USER_AGENT
```

Note that you do not have to specify

```
!HTTP_USER_AGENT
```

in order to stop `HTTP_USER_AGENT` being passed to `webexplode()`. If `MI_WEBPUSHVARS` is set to `select`, then web server variables will only be passed if preceeded by the "+" character.

Selective Variable Passing from Version 4

You cannot set `MI_WEBPUSHVARS` from Version 4 of the Web DataBlade. From Version 4, user variables are passed into the `webexplode()` function. These are variables that you create in the Web DataBlade Module Administration Tool. If you want to pass web server variables to `webexplode()`, then you create the variable as a user variable in the Web DataBlade Module Administration Tool and assign the value "+" to it.

You can use a `webdriver` *trace to see what variables are passed to* `webexplode()`. *This is useful for debugging purposes. It is also useful if you need to check which variables are being set by a particular web server product. In* `web.cnf`, *you can set the following two variables:* `MI_WEBDRVLEVEL` *(to* `0xFFFF`*) and* `MI_WEBDRVLOG` *(to the absolute path of the trace file). If you are using an API* `webdriver`, *such as NSAPI, then restart the web server if you introduce these variable settings. The output will differ depending on whether you are using the API* `webdriver` *shared object or the CGI* `webdriver` *program.*

Implementing Security in the Web Server

Fundamentally, you want to be able to stop some users from retrieving a web page from the web server. A hyperlink that the user clicks, or a URL that the user types into the browser, should contain a URL prefix mapping that can be secured at the web server level and that will stop the page being sent to the client if the user is not authorized to view it.

Using the Secure Web Server API

The security that you can implement from the web server will vary with the web server product. For example:

- with Netscape, you can implement NSAPI;
- with Microsoft Internet Information Server, you can use ISAPI;
- with Apache, you can use the Apache API from Version 4 of the Web DataBlade.

See Chap. 23, "Web Server Integration," for details on how to create *secure URL prefixes* that require a username and password combination to access.

By using a secure URL prefix, you can restrict access to a whole website or just a part of the site.

If you can't use a web-server-assisted security method (for example, you only have CGI access), then you can do the following:

- maintain a table that contains a list of users and passwords,
- create an AppPage to contain a form that requests the username and password,
- create an AppPage to process the submitted form and check that the username and password exist in the `user` table.

In a CGI-only implementation, you can maintain user information and preferences using HTTP *cookies,* which you can set for all the user data using the `HTTPHEADER` AppPage function. Alternatively, you can create one cookie for the username, and then use a dynamic tag that selects the user information from the database at the head of each AppPage, parameterizing the dynamic tag with the username stored in the cookie. Selecting user preferences from the database is more secure than using HTTP cookies, since the client never sees the preferences if they are used to render a web page dynamically.

URL Prefix Mappings

When creating CGI or API URL prefix mappings, you should hide the physical paths from the URL. For example, the physical directory

```
/theale2/website/stores7/cgi-bin
```

should be mapped as a URL prefix in the web server as follows:

```
/theale2/stores7-cgi
```

Checking Password Validity

When using the API `webdriver` (for example NSAPI), you require a username and password combination to access a secure URL prefix. The username and passwords are by default cached in the webserver memory. If users are deleted from the Informix database table that stored the combinations or the passwords are changed, then the cached information is wrong.

To get around this, you can specify how the API `webdriver` works with username and password combinations.

You set the `MI_WEBAUTHCACHE` variable in `web.cnf` to reset username and password combinations. You can use one of three settings, as shown in Table 24-4.

An example setting would be:

```
MI_WEBAUTHCACHE    check
```

Setting `MI_WEBAUTHCACHE` to `on` is the fastest. This is the default if not set. Ultimately, setting this variable depends on how well you are in control of your Informix database and the user table that the API `webdriver` uses for authentication. Performance is critical, so try to avoid anything that would involve a database request for each instance of a secure URL invocation.

Forcing Reauthentication

You may want an authenticated user to log in again at some point. For example, if the user goes home and leaves the authenticated browser session open all night, this is a security risk, especially if *another* user sits at the same desk the following morning, however briefly. Normally, once you have authenticated, you stay that way

Table 24-4. *Settings for* `MI_WEBAUTHCACHE`.

Setting	Description
on	Use the cached password, which is the default behavior if `MI_WEBAUTHCACHE` is not set.
off	Use the password stored in the database.
check	check if the cached password is the same as the database value. If different, store the new password from the database in cache.

until you close the last instance of your browser down. You may want to specify an amount of time before the user must reauthenticate.

If you are using NSAPI, then you configure an *authentication timeout*. The authentication timeout works like this: If the timeout is set at 60 seconds, for example, then a 60-second delay between requests for any secure URL means that you will be asked to log in again when you next request a secure URL from that browser session.

There are three essential variables that control this feature, as shown in Table 24-5.

An example configuration would be

```
MI_WEBAUTHTIMEOUT        5
MI_WEBAUTHCOOKIE         APITIMEOUT
MI_WEBAUTHHOME  http://theale2/stores-
cgi/webdriver?MIval=userInfo
```

Forcing Remote User Connections to the Database with NSAPI

When using NSAPI, the value of the REMOTE_USER webdriver variable is set to the value of the username that the user entered when authenticating. However, this is not the database user that the web server connects to the database with; that user is defined in the MI_USER webdriver variable.

If you want the database connection to run as the REMOTE_USER, you need to set another variable in web.cnf. From release web.3.32.TC4 of the Web DataBlade, there is an additional authorization method for the NSAPI webdriver. If MI_USER_REMOTE is set to on in the web.cnf file, all database requests connect as the REMOTE_USER user instead of the MI_USER user. The REMOTE_USER

Table 24-5. Variables for authentication timeout.	
Variable	***Purpose***
MI_WEBAUTHTIMEOUT	Number of seconds before the username/ password pair times out.
MI_WEBAUTHCOOKIE	Name to give to a cookie that will be used to maintain the encoded timestamp.
MI_WEBAUTHHOME	If a cookie cannot be set, redirect the user to the page specified by the value of this variable.

user must be added to the user access table identified by the `MIusertable` variable (typically the `webUsers` table) to enable `MI_USER_REMOTE` authorization.

Due to Informix database user requirements, if you set `MI_USER_REMOTE` to `on`, the `REMOTE_USER` user must be a valid operating-system user with database connection privileges. Therefore, this authentication method should be restricted to intranet rather than Internet applications.

Restricting Access to AppPages

Although you can use secure URL prefixes to restrict access to any URL that contains the prefix, you may want to restrict access to AppPages also. Historically, this facility was provided for those users who could not use NSAPI, but it is nevertheless a useful feature to know. For authenticating users (using NSAPI, ISAPI, or Apache API), it is the `webdriver` shared object that validates the AppPage permissions against the user. For CGI users, the value of `MI_WEBACCESSLEVEL` is used.

The table that stores the AppPages contains a column called `read_level` (depending on your schema, this is either `wbPages` or `webpages`). This value is set when the AppPage is created, and defaults to zero. You use this column to test whether the user at the browser can access the AppPage or is prevented from doing so. To do this, you can either set a variable called `MI_WEBACCESSLEVEL` or, for secure URLs using NSAPI, ISAPI, or Apache API, set `MIuserlevel`.

Entries for CGI

The following four entries state that the `read_level` column in the `wbPages` table stores the read level for the AppPage requested. All users connecting to the database via the `web.cnf` containing these lines have an access level of `2`. If `wbPages.read_level` has a value greater than `2`, the HTML page `http://dellcpi/noAccess.html` will be downloaded instead. This page is located in the web server *document root* directory.

```
MItab                 wbPages
MIpagelevel           read_level
MI_WEBACCESSLEVEL     2
MI_WEBREDIRECT     http://dellcpi/noAccess.html
```

For example, AppPage `HelloWorld.html` has `read_level` set to 3 in the `wbPages` table. If this AppPage is requested by a user whose URL maps onto the `web.cnf` file containing the above four lines, then the `noAccess.html` page will be retrieved instead. You can specify an AppPage in the database for `MI_WEBREDIRECT`, provided that the `read_level` is set to 0.

Secure URL Settings

When using NSAPI, ISAPI, or Apache API with secure URLs, you should *not* define `MI_WEBACCESSLEVEL` if you want to allow each authenticating user that uses the same `web.cnf` file to have a different access level; otherwise all authenticating users will have the same AppPage-level permissions.

For example, if you define `MI_WEBACCESSLEVEL`, users `cortez` and `sales` will have the same AppPage-level security, even though these users have different AppPage permission levels defined in the table that stores user authentication information (when using the API `webdriver`).

Instead, use the `MIuserlevel` variable in `web.cnf` to nominate the column in a table that is used to authenticate the username and password entered at the browser.

Read Chap. 23, "Web Server Integration," for an understanding of how to configure `web.cnf` for use with *secure URL prefixes*.

For example, the following extract from a `web.cnf` file is a set of variables that are used to nominate the authenticating table and column in the Informix database, as described in Chap. 23. The relevant variable at the moment is `MIuserlevel`, which is set to the value `security_level`; `security_level` is the name of a column in the `webusers` table that stores the equivalent of `MI_WEBACCESSLEVEL` for the user authenticating at the browser:

```
MIusertable        webusers
MIusername         name
MIuserpasswd       password
MIuserlevel        security_level
MIpagelevel        read_level
```

If you want *all* of your authenticating users to share the same AppPage-level permissions, then set the `security_level` column to the same value for all users. If you use `MI_WEBACCESSLEVEL` instead, the chances are that you will encounter a user with a slightly different requirement, and you will need to reconfigure.

If `MIpagelevel` *is not set in* `web.cnf`, *no AppPage checking is performed.*

Basic URL Settings

If you are using NSAPI, ISAPI, or Apache API *without* authentication, then use `MI_WEBACCESSLEVEL`, because users will not be logging on and therefore we cannot fetch the AppPage permissions level from the database.

Restricting Schema Permissions

The database administrator should also protect the tables that store the website. For example:

- grant `SELECT` access to `public` on tables that store AppPages;
- restrict `UPDATE` access to tables in the Data Director for Web or AppPage Builder schema.

Restricting Access to Large Objects

You can restrict access to media content such as office documents, audio, video, and any media type that you store in the database. From Version 4 of the Web DataBlade, you can retrieve large objects by *query string*. The latter option allows you to specify a custom query that can include an authorization table to validate the requesting user against a set of permissions for that user.

For instructions on how to retrieve large objects using custom queries, see Chap. 20, "Working with Large Objects."

Distributed Web Server Security

Figure 13-16 in Chap. 13, "Creating and Managing Websites with Data Director for Web," shows an example website *deployment* architecture across the firewall. The live web server accesses the Informix database located in front of the firewall.

Running anything on a system directly accessible via the Internet is inherently insecure to a degree. To access the Informix database server located on a machine accessible on the Internet, though, the intruder would need to have:

- the IP address of the database server machine;
- the IP port number that the database server is listening on;

- the `dbservername` of the database server;
- a valid username and password combination for the machine where the database server is running;
- access to an Informix-enabled client application, for example, an Informix-enabled ODBC driver plus an ODBC application; or
- detailed knowledge of the Informix SQLI protocol, and the ability to code a program to fool the database server into believing that it is talking to a genuine Informix client by emulating the necessary ASF and SQLI dialogue, which is extremely unlikely.

If you feel that the Informix database server should be behind the firewall with the web server in front of the firewall, this is no problem as long as the `sqlhosts` (UNIX) or `registry` (NT) settings on the web server nominate a named port through the firewall, the target database server machine, and the Informix server name, service, and protocol.

Integrating Dynamic Web Applications with the Secure Sockets Layer (SSL)

In the expanding universe of e-commerce, a question frequently asked is, How can you integrate Web DataBlade applications with secure e-commerce transactions? The answer: Use a secure web server that implements the secure sockets layer protocol. Configuring a secure web server using *secure sockets layer* (SSL) is *transparent* to Web DataBlade applications.

While you can use NSAPI or ISAPI to ensure authenticated access to your URLs, once the user has logged on, web content is not sent securely over the network.

The Web DataBlade operates behind the components that *encrypt* and *decrypt* all the web content transferred to and from network clients, such as the browser when using a secure web server. For example, suppose you want to capture a customer's credit card details using an HTML form and then store these details in the Informix database. The HTML form is an AppPage that is taken from the database and passed through the SSL protocol by the web server to the browser as *encrypted* data. The browser understands SSL, so when the user enters his credit card details and clicks the `Submit` button, the form data is encrypted and sent back to the web server using SSL.

Why Use a Secure Web Server?

A *secure web server* is useful when sensitive data is being transferred between the browser and the web server, for example when a credit card number is entered on a form that is posted to the website. If you need to stop people from snooping on data that you receive or send or if you need to verify that the web server you are talking to really is the web server that you think it is, then you need a secure web server.

There are essentially three reasons for using a secure web server: *confidentiality, integrity,* and *authenticity.* For e-commerce applications, you need all three.

- Confidential information needs to stay confidential. Someone may be snooping the data that you are sending and receiving: You may be sending your credit card details or viewing your private bank account details.
- Information may be modified in transit, but you will not know anything about it. For example, you may submit a transfer of funds between your bank accounts; someone captures the message, changes the target bank account, and replays the message.
- You may be sending information to an impersonator. For example, you may send your credit card details to a company that is pretending to be someone else.

Even if you don't use the Web DataBlade as an e-commerce platform, you may still want to secure your web transactions. For example, if you have reports stored as word processor documents or spreadsheets in the database, you may want to send them in a secure manner over the network; in addition, you may want to use an HTML form to upload a sensitive spreadsheet or word processor document.

What Is a Secure Web Server?

A *secure web server* is designed to guarantee confidentiality, integrity, and authenticity by using a combination of encryption and certification. If a web server implements the SSL protocol, you can use it as a secure web server.

A secure web server differs from the normal web server in that it is configured to use the SSL protocol, `https://`, instead of `http://`. You communicate with a secure web server using `https://`. If you use `http://`, you will not receive any data.

For example, you can use Netscape Enterprise Server (NES) as a secure web server. If you have NES already installed and running for `http://` requests (on port 80, for example), then you use the Netscape Administration Server to create another instance of NES on a different port. You then configure this new web server to use SSL, as described later.

To interact with a secure web server, you also need a browser client than implements the SSL protocol, for example, Netscape Navigator.

A Brief Overview of SSL

A basic understanding of the components in SSL is worth obtaining, since the overall architecture is surprisingly simple and elegant. The components can be listed as:

- *public key* encryption, for encrypting data sent over the network between web servers and browser clients;
- *symmetric* encryption, which allows a web server and a browser to encrypt at the level of the *browser session;*
- *certification,* which allows web servers and browsers to verify that they are who they say they are through a third party, called a certification authority;
- a *certification authority* (CA) that digitally signs a certificate verifying that the holder of the certificate sent to you is who they say they are;
- a *digital signature,* which is encrypted text attached to a message, such as a certificate; the signature is based on the contents of the message and is used to verify that the message has not been tampered with.

Public Key Encryption

When data is sent over the Internet or intranet using SSL, it is scrambled so that it looks like a random stream of bytes. One end of the communication link scrambles, (*encrypts*) the data and the other end unscrambles (*decrypts*) the data.

Encrypted text is called *ciphertext,* because the algorithm used to encrypt the data is called a *cipher.* Ciphers vary in strength and therefore vary in elapsed time to encrypt. Generally, when a web server and a browser start an SSL dialog (called a *handshake*), both agree on the strongest cipher that they can both use. The stronger the cipher, the harder it is to crack. Ciphers are installed by default when you install the web server and the browser.

To encrypt data using a cipher, an *encryption key* is used. If the same key is used to encrypt and decrypt data, then the key is called a *symmetric* key. Using symmetric keys opens up the risk that one end of the communication link has obtained the encryption key and can therefore impersonate someone else. To get around this, a technique is used called *public key encryption.*

Public key encryption involves the use of two keys to encrypt data, a *private key* and a *public key.* This is called a *key-pair,* and is usually generated by a web server program. If the private key encrypts, the public key decrypts and vice versa. The private key is known *only* to the web server. The public key is sent to any client that requests a secure transaction. Therefore, data encrypted by the private key must be from one source—the web server that has the private key.

The public key is the key that is sent by the web server to anyone that wants to perform an encrypted transaction with the web server. For example, if you want to perform an encrypted transaction with a secure web server to send your credit card details, the web server must send you a public key so that you can decrypt the messages that the web server will send encrypted with its private key. If you then encrypt a message with the public key, only the web server can decrypt the message you send using its private key; you can't use the public key to encrypt data and decrypt data; you need the key-pair. Since only the secure web server has the private key, any message your browser sends encrypted with the public key can only be decrypted by the web server.

The file that contains the key-pair should be secured in the web server filesystem. If this file is ever copied, you must regenerate the key-pair and introduce the new pair to the secure web server.

Symmetric Encryption

Symmetric encryption means that the same encryption key is used to encrypt and decrypt data. Both ends of the communication link share the same encryption key. This is faster than public key encryption, but less secure.

Certification

Certification provides the required level of authentication for web servers and clients. A certificate is a message that contains the public key of a web server and the digital signature of a certification authority (CA). The CA verifies that the holder of the certificate is genuine. The client must have some degree of trust in the CA for this to work.

Certification Authority

A certification authority (CA) may be an internal certification server on the intranet or a public authority such as VeriSign (`http://www.verisign.com`). A CA is a trusted third party. The company or individual that owns the secure web server will send a public key as well as company or private details to the CA; in due course the certificate is returned with a digital signature of the CA.

Digital Signatures

A digital signature is attached to a message and verifies that the message has not been tampered with. For example, a secure web server certificate can be passed unencrypted to the browser; appended to this certificate is a block of encrypted text—the digital signature. To produce this signature, the message content (in this case, the certificate) is run through an encryption algorithm. If the message has been tampered with at even the smallest level, the signature and the message will not match when the signature is decrypted at the browser.

The Secure Web Server SSL Cycle

Symmetric encryption runs the risk of exposing the encryption key to an impersonator, and public key encryption is slower than symmetric encryption. Cleverly, a secure web server such as Netscape Enterprise Server gets around both of these problems by combining them to take advantage of both.

The web server sends the public key to the browser embedded in a digitally signed certificate. If the browser authenticates the certificate, it then generates its own private key, called a *session key,* and encrypts it using the public key it received from the web server. The encrypted session key is then sent to the web server. The web server decrypts this session key using the web server private key.

For the remainder of the transaction, the session key is used to encrypt data at one end and decrypt data at the other.

In this scenario, we have symmetric encryption embedded within public key encryption, with authentication by certification. Confidentiality, integrity, and authenticity are therefore realized.

Figure 24-1 shows this cycle in more detail.

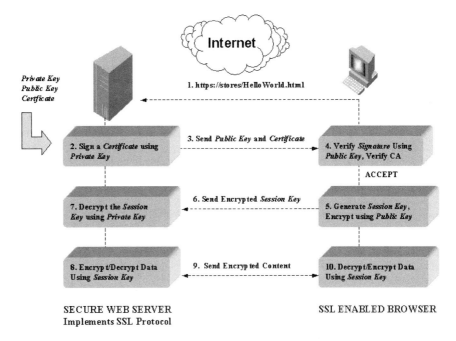

Figure 24-1. *Secure web server SSL cycle.*

In Fig. 24-1, the web server receives an `https://` request from the browser. The web server responds with a signed certificate of authenticity that also contains the public key from the key-pair stored on the web server. Once the web browser accepts this certificate, the web browser and web server agree on the strongest cipher they can both use to encrypt data. On agreement, the browser generates a session key, and encrypts it with the public key contained in the certificate. This encrypted key is sent to the web server, which then decrypts it using the web-server-based private key.

From this point, both the web server and the browser will use the same session key to encrypt and decrypt data either way. For example, the web server can send an encrypted spreadsheet, and the browser will decrypt it; both the encryption and the decryption will use the same session key. Similarly, if the browser wanted to submit credit card details in an HTML form, the browser would encrypt the form data using the session key, submit the data, and the web server would decrypt the form data and then invoke the appropriate AppPage to store the form data in the database.

There is some additional overhead in this secure communication, so it is usually best to reserve it only for pages that require this level of security. For example, some of your hyperlinks can use `http://`, *and the*

SSL hyperinks can use `https://`. *Remember, though, that the* `https://` *server operates on a different port.*

You may want to extend the metadata for AppPages to flag whether the AppPage is secure. For example, you may want to maintain a lookup table keyed by AppPage ID to contain all the secure AppPages. You would prefix `$WEB_HOME` *with* `https://` *in a calling AppPage. You can then include this logic in a dynamic tag, parameterizing the tag with the ID of the AppPage to encapsulate your secure web server handling across your applications.*

Where Does the Web DataBlade Fit In?

Web DataBlade applications are transparent to secure web servers. You can use the `https://` protocol to connect to a secure web server that will send you encrypted web content that is retrieved from the Informix database. Figure 24-2 outlines this architecture.

Different web servers can connect via `webdriver` to the same database. Therefore, you can have a secure web server (`https://`) and a nonsecure web server (`http://`) connecting to the same Informix database. Either can use NSAPI, ISAPI, Apache API (Version 4), or the CGI `webdriver`.

For example, suppose you wanted to download a sensitive word processor document that is stored as a `BLOB` in the Informix database using the Data Director for Web schema. Let's assume that the URL to fetch this document is:

```
http://theale2/secure/?MIvalObj=securedoc&type
=application/ms-word
```

If you did not want to encrypt this information, you could use `http://` as shown above. Entering this URL would connect the browser to port 80 on the `theale2` machine.

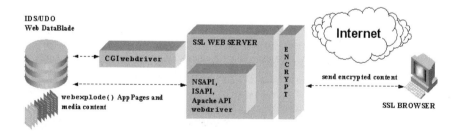

Figure 24-2. *Web DataBlade and SSL.*

If you wanted to encrypt this information, then you would type

```
https://theale2:90/secure/?MIvalObj=securedoc&type
=application/ms-word
```

There are two differences in these URLs: The first is that `https://` is used instead of `http://`; the second, that the secure web server is on port 90 instead of port 80. The default web server uses port 80; port 90 is used by the secure instance of the web server.

The `webdriver` URL does not change. The document is retrieved by name in both examples. However, in the second example, when the document is passed through the web server, the resulting message will be encrypted. Therefore, the document will need to be decrypted at the browser.

If the client submits form data in a secure manner using `https://`, the data will be written to the database *after* it has been decrypted by the web server.

Configuring a Secure Web Server

To set up a Web DataBlade installation using both nonsecure and secure communication, you will need to set up two web servers, using a different port number for each.

Create the appropriate URL prefixes in the new web server (see Chap. 23, "Web Server Integration," for instructions how to do this).

You don't have to change the `web.cnf` file, but you do have to prefix `$WEB_HOME` with `https://`.

The steps to follow generally are as follows:

- generate a key-pair file for public key encryption,
- generate a certificate request,
- request a certificate,
- install the certificate,
- enable SSL in the web server.

Generate a Key-Pair File

First, it is necessary to generate key-pair file that contains the public and private keys. Generating the key-pair file is specific to the web server, but it usually means that you have to run a program that accepts one or more parameters, including a password and an alias name to identify the file. Make sure that the resulting key-pair file is secure on the web server machine.

Generate a Certificate Request

You need to generate a request for a security certificate. The procedure will differ depending on your web server, but the result is a certificate-signing request that contains all the relevant details, including the web server's host name and key-pair file details.

Request and Install the Certificate

You request the actual certificate from a certificate authority such as VeriSign. You submit the certificate-signing request to the CA. In due course, you will receive the certificate by email. Some CAs offer trial certificates with a limited lifespan, so that you can test before you buy. Once you have received the certificate from the CA, you install it on your web server.

Enable SSL

Finally, you must enable SSL on the web server by using the appropriate administration interface to switch SSL on. There is more than one level of SSL. Your web server will tell you which levels are available for you to select, but generally select as many as you can.

Summary

In this chapter, we have learned how to secure a Web DataBlade application by implementing passwords, password encryption, and web server integration techniques such as NSAPI and ISAPI. We have also learned how to enable AppPage permission settings. These two skill sets combined will enable you to structure hierarchical website permissions with considerable granularity.

We also learned how to configure a secure sockets layer (SSL) connection to the web server, using `https://` and security certificates. This technique will prove an especially valuable guarantee of secure e-commerce transactions for your Web DataBlade application.

Performance-tuning Essentials

In this chapter:

- Performance-tuning objectives
- Areas for performance tuning
- Tuning the web server
- Tuning the database server
- Tuning the network
- Single- and multiple-server architectures
- Tuning the application queries
- Web DataBlade tuning
- Caching large objects
- Full and partial caching of AppPages

Effective performance tuning of your web application and application platform is essential. You may need to deliver an e-commerce, mission-critical website to the customer as quickly as possible without compromising functionality. Not only do you have AppPages to explode, multimedia content to deliver, and application business rules to trigger; you also need to manage the load on the web server, the database server, and the hosting machines on which they reside. This chapter is a guide to the essentials of performance tuning the different components in a Web DataBlade application. You can use the material contained in this chapter as a pointer to the more detailed treatment in the appropriate documentation set you are using for your platform.

Performance-tuning Objectives

Performance tuning needs to address specific objectives. For web applications, where we have the complexities of the network, web servers, firewalls, web applications, and databases, we should measure performance by one particular objective: the quickest response time for the user at the browser—not the quickest batch run or the most effective algorithm or the best method for rendering graphics— the quickest response time for the user at the browser.

For business websites this is crucial; studies have shown that after ten seconds waiting for a response, the user will press the Stop button and you've lost a sale—potentially many repeat sales. It really is that important, because the hype factor in the Internet commerce space makes potential customers feel cheated if they can't get what they consider acceptable response times.

Think about your own personal response when you phone a customer call center: If you have to wait more than ten seconds for a voice at the other end, if you are given the music of the spheres, on and on, you put the phone down. You had wanted to make an order; now probably not. It's no different on the Internet. In fact, the customer is increasingly in charge. What media guru Marshall McLuhan called the Global Village has become the Global Market. The most inconsequential customer will have at his disposal the most basic, pointillist technique for restricting your cash flow—the Stop button.

We can use a set of traditional approaches to tuning the components in the web architecture for performance. We need to understand the cost/benefit of tuning each area.

Areas for Performance Tuning

The total response time in a web application is the sum of the elapsed time to service network, web server, database and web application functions. When developing web applications, it is easy to forget about the performance of each of these components. After all, performance can be left to the webmaster and database administrator. It's what you pay consultants for. It's hard enough delivering your own component on time, let alone worry about the performance of the system as a whole.

Unfortunately, the webmaster and database administrator can only do so much. The bottleneck in most business systems—web or otherwise—is the application. This comes down to poor application design and poor query design.

Sixties media guru Marshall McLuhan thought that the printing press brought linear perspective to mankind but that the electronic age was eroding it—or improving it—through montage. He was not a systems consultant brought in to review an application. Linear perspective rules in the world of applications.

While you can tune the performance of components in each of your system tiers, some tuning areas yield more benefit than others.

Figure 25-1 lists a general form of cost/benefit assessment as to which components can yield high performance gains with low overhead.

The table columns in Fig. 25-1 can be summarized as follows:

- *Area.* This is the architecture component as a discrete, tunable entity.
- *Tuning Improvement.* How much you can tune the performance of each *area.*

Area	Tuning Improvement	Implementation Effort	Application Impact
Database Configuration	High	Low	None
Database Hardware	High	Low	None
Web DataBlade Configuration	High	Low	None
Database Indexes	High	Medium	None
Operating System	Low	Low	None
Web Server	Low	Low	None
Network	Low	Medium	None
Hardware Architecture	Medium	Low	None
Database Disk Utilization	Medium	Medium	None
AppPage Embedded SQL	Medium	Medium	Low
AppPage Construction	Low	Medium	Medium
Database Schema	High	High	High

Figure 25-1. *Tuning areas.*

- *Implementation Effort.* How much effort goes into implementing the level of *tuning improvement.*
- *Application Impact.* Impact on the Web DataBlade application in terms of required code changes.

For example, you can achieve a high performance gain by tuning the database server configuration. To do this requires one or two days working out the correct Informix ONCONFIG parameters and then implementing the required configuration, usually in two or three iterations of the overall tuning exercise. This task should not negatively impact—or *regress*—the web application.

In contrast, if the database schema is badly designed so that a set of queries perform poorly, then it takes a lot of time and effort to put it right. This is because the database design is fundamental to the whole application that uses it. At best tuning the database schema is merely a form of denormalization; at worst it is a significant redesign. Almost any change you make to the database schema can result in a change to application code. Note that the Data Director for Web and AppPage Builder schemas are logically separate from the application schema, which contains application rules and data. The web content stored in the Data Director for Web schema, for example, may be much larger in volume than the application data expressed through it. On the other hand, the application data may be a Data Mart that delivers millions of records through a very thin application surface, with a small number of AppPages and graphics unwinding from a small set of dynamic tags.

Between these extremes, you have a tradeoff between tuning improvement and implementation effort.

Tuning the Web Server

Every web server product has its own procedures for performance tuning, and some are based on specific characteristics of the product itself. This section lists some important topics that you may want to locate in your web server documentation.

Essentially, we hope that tuning the web server will help us manage HTTP requests coming in over the network so that we can process them as quickly as possible. In our case, the HTTP requests will involve a call to webdriver to explode an AppPage, retrieve a document from the database, retrieve an object or web page from cache, or retrieve an AppPage from cache for a *deferred* `webexplode()` (see section, "Partial AppPage Caching," later in this chapter). As a result, tuning the web-server-specific parameters also involves `webdriver` tuning to ensure that we manage the interface between the web server and the Web DataBlade efficiently (see "Web DataBlade Tuning" later in this chapter).

You should ensure where possible that you use the NSAPI, ISAPI, or Apache API `webdriver` shared object.

Persistent Connection Timeouts

Web servers that support HTTP 1.1 onward can maintain persistent connections to the browser. However, if the browser is inactive, the connection should be timed out. You may be able to set a persistent connection timeout to forcibly time out idle sessions. However, if you set this value too high, you risk consuming resources for browser sessions that are idle.

Tuning the Number of Simultaneous Requests

The web server can process a number of HTTP requests simultaneously using multiple threads. These are called *active requests*. When the browser sends an HTTP request to the web server, the web server will process the request if it has not exceeded the configured number of active requests. If it is already processing the maximum number of active requests, then the browser has to wait until a slot is free. The HTTP requests themselves have short duration. If the HTTP request maps onto a `webdriver` request, though, it may take longer to process the database part of the request.

As a basic metric, you can expect around 200 HTTP requests per second to be processed by one thread. Accordingly, you can scale this up by setting what in some web servers is a default of 128 simultaneous requests. You should consider increasing the number of simultaneous requests if many HTTP requests are taking many seconds to complete.

Tuning Domain Name System (DNS) Lookups

Some web servers allow you to enable or disable DNS lookup. If enabled, then the web server will look up the hostname for the *every* client using the IP address of the client.

In some web servers, DNS lookup serializes multiple threads, which means that lookup is performed on behalf of one active request at a time. To get around this, your web server may allow you to enable asynchronous DNS.

Turning DNS Off

If you disable DNS to eliminate a potential bottleneck in the web server, you may not be able to restrict access to resources based on the hostname of the client. Additionally, the web server log files will contain only the IP address of the client, not the hostname.

Caching DNS

If you need to use DNS to resolve hostnames for restricting access to resources, then it is important that some web servers allow you to cache DNS entries. In this case, the hostname and IP address pair are cached. You can set an elapsed time for expiry of cached entries.

Tuning the Database Server

An iterative approach to performance tuning will allow you to tune the Informix configuration parameters one at a time (see Fig. 25-2). In summary, the essential tasks include:

- Take regular measurements of resource utilization and database activity.

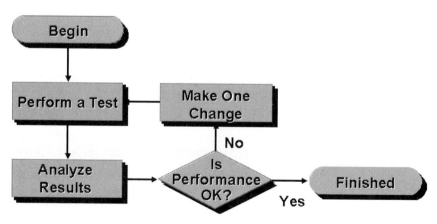

Figure 25-2. *Basic tuning methodology.*

- Identify symptoms of performance problems, for example, inordinate utilization of CPU, memory, or disks.
- Tune the Informix database server configuration one parameter at a time.
- Optimize the chunk and `dbspace` configuration.
- Optimize table placement, the sizing of extents, and fragmentation.
- Optimize and manage your table indexes.
- Optimize the background I/O activities: logging, checkpoints, page cleaning.
- Optimize the application and SQL.

Browser clients can be considered OLTP (on-line transaction processing) users. Typically, OLTP environments have a large number of users performing a high volume of short transactions (e.g., `INSERT`, `UPDATE`, `DELETE`). In our case, each AppPage—and any AppPage exploded recursively—is one transaction.

The remainder of this section covers some essential points about OLTP tuning and assumes that you are familiar with the parameter settings in the `ONCONFIG` server configuration file.

Critical Success Factors in OLTP Server Tuning

Specific targets in a tuning exercise will be:

- to obtain high read and write buffer cache rates,
- to obtain fast checkpoints,
- to maximize I/O throughput.

Buffer Cache Rates

The buffer cache is part of the Informix server resident memory segment. When reading and writing data, the data pages are placed in cache. Therefore, when we want to read and write data, it is best if the pages containing that data are in cache, since we are then reducing disk I/O. If they are on disk, the server has to fetch them, involving a potentially slow disk read. The read cache rate is the most important statistic. The write cache rate is based on physical and logical log writes plus the writing of dirty pages to disk between and during checkpoints.

Read cache rates should be greater than 95 percent. Write cache rates should be greater than 85 percent. Cache rates are displayed using `onstat -p`.

Increasing the Cache Rate

If you have lower cache rates than expected, try increasing the number of BUFFERS in the ONCONFIG file. This increases the amount of buffers in memory so that, when data pages are brought into memory, older pages are not aged out (written to disk or discarded) as quickly.

If you have very low LRU_MAX_DIRTY and LRU_MIN_DIRTY values, then you may not reach optimal write cache rate, since buffers are being flushed to disk often. These parameters are usually set low to reduce the time it takes to perform a checkpoint.

Fast Checkpoints

In an OLTP environment, it is critical to have short checkpoint durations. Ideally, this means that a checkpoint should take no more than one or two seconds.

During a checkpoint, all pages that have been modified in shared memory buffers are written to disk. During this operation, all user sessions in critical sections of code are suspended. Any attempt to modify pages is blocked during the checkpoint. Therefore, we need a checkpoint to complete as quickly as possible. We can configure checkpoint writes, checkpoint durations, and the interval between checkpoints to achieve this.

Checkpoint Writes

It is worth listing checkpoint write activity in summary form:

- Data pages are written to disk by page cleaners.
- A page cleaner thread is assigned to each chunk in the system.
- During a checkpoint, a page cleaner will locate all dirty pages in cache for its chunk, and make a request to the AIO (aysynchronous I/O) or KIO (kernel I/O) threads to write them to disk.

As a basic metric, configure one page cleaner thread per LRU queue. However, if the page cleaner threads are always busy, then add more page cleaner threads. You can monitor page cleaner activity states with the onstat -F command.

Checkpoint Durations

You decrease checkpoint durations by reducing the amount of work performed within a checkpoint; essentially, this means that there are less dirty pages to write to disk during the checkpoint. We would like these pages to be written to disk *between* checkpoints.

You can lower the LRU_MAX_DIRTY and LRU_MIN_DIRTY parameters in the ONCONFIG file to achieve this. For example, assume LRU_MIN_DIRTY is five and LRU_MAX_DIRTY is ten. When any queue pair has ten percent of the buffers in the modified queue, the page cleaner threads will begin requesting writes of pages to disk until only five percent remain. In general, the more buffers you have, the lower the setting for these parameters; even down to one and two.

Checkpoint Intervals

Checkpoints occur when either of the following is true:

- number of seconds specified by the CKPINTVL parameter has elapsed;
- physical log file is 75 percent full.

Increasing CKPINTVL and the physical logfile size in the ONCONFIG file will ensure that you do not initiate checkpoints too often, but make sure that the checkpoint duration is down to one or two seconds by reducing LRU_MIN_DIRTY and LRU_MAX_DIRTY. You can use onstat -m to see when checkpoints occurred and how long they took.

Maximizing I/O Throughput

We can maximize I/O throughput by

- removing I/O bottlenecks,
- implementing and optimizing a fragmentation strategy,
- optimizing the utilization of indexes.

The key to laying out data effectively is to distribute the data and indexes to eliminate I/O bottlenecks and maximize I/O throughput. For example:

- Use a volume manager (LVM) to stripe the data across the disks, or fragment the data (not the indexes) by round robin.
- Create expression-based fragmented indexes for large tables that receive a large percentage of activity. This will reduce the number of index pages that must be searched.
- Limit the number of index fragments to reduce the overhead of expression evaluation.

tip

Some LVM's place a header at the start of each disk device. If this is the case, use an offset for each chunk to avoid using this area.

Configuring Shared Memory

Configuring the shared memory used by the database server is important because this is where the buffer cache resides. As a guideline, you can use the *initial* settings for shared memory as shown in Table 25-1.

In an OLTP environment, there are typically a larger number of locks required than in a decision support (DSS) environment. It is best to overestimate this figure, since the memory overhead of locks is small. The number of locks is also influenced by the lock mode of the tables accessed.

Tables with *row*-level locking can increase concurrency but require more locks; in contrast, tables with *page*-level locking can potentially reduce concurrency, but they require fewer locks. The lock mode of a table is determined by application requirements; you need to bear in mind, however, that if your table row size is fairly small, then in a selective OLTP setting you will be locking more rows than you need if the lock mode for the table is page.

Table 25-1. *Initial settings for shared memory in an OLTP environment.*

Parameter	Initial setting
BUFFERS	Set to 50–75% of available memory.
LOCKS	1000 × number of users.
PHYSBUFF	Pages per I/O should be around 75% of the buffer size.
LOGBUFF	Pages per I/O should be around 75% of the buffer size.
LRUS	Start with four LRU pairs per CPU VP.
CLEANERS	One page cleaner thread per LRU pair.
SHMVIRTSIZE	32000 + (expected number of users × 800)
CKPTINTVL	Set to 9999. Let the physical log initiate checkpoints to start with.
LRU_MAX_DIRTY	Set to 10.
LRU_MIN_DIRTY	Set to 5.
RA_PAGES	Set to 32.
RA_THRESHOLD	Set to 30.

While OLTP environments do not require as much virtual memory as DSS environments, it is important to ensure that enough virtual memory exists for various operations, such as sorts resulting from an ORDER BY statement. You can monitor the shared use of the virtual segment of memory using the onstat -g seg command.

When using this command, look for large values in the blkfree column of the virtual segment. Each block represents 8 K, so you can reduce the amount of virtual shared memory by 8 times blkfree, which can be reused elsewhere, such as in the BUFFERS parameter.

Increasing the amount of shared memory allocated to the database server may force paging at the operating-system level. Especially on a platform that hosts both the web server and the database server, you need to monitor this using vmstat *(UNIX) or* perfmon *(NT).*

Physical and logical log *buffers* improve performance by reducing the number of writes to the physical log and logical logs on disk. Essentially, the ideal is to reduce the number of disk I/Os required to write the buffer contents to disk. This can be achieved by altering the values of LOGBUFF and PHYSBUFF until the buffer sizes are as close as possible to the *pages per I/O* reported in the output from the onstat -l command. The output from onstat -l contains a column, pages/io, that provides this value. By aligning the sizes of the physical and logical log buffers in this way, we can avoid performing unnecessary disk operations from these log buffers.

Don't spend too much time configuring RA_PAGES and RA_THRESHOLD for OLTP-based systems. These parameters control the number of read-ahead pages that you can bring into shared memory, which is only valid if there is some *locality* in the query result set that is also present on disk. If you set RA_PAGES too high and you don't really need most of the pages that are fetched in from disk, then you may be unnecessarily forcing out pages that are required. Typically, OLTP queries require filtered subsets of data. However, you should still perform a check to see whether you have configured these parameters correctly.

You can monitor read-ahead using the onstat -p command. This command will display the columns ixda-RA, idx-RA and da-RA; the sum of these columns should be close to the RA-pgused column. If the sum is much higher, then read-ahead pages are not being used; in addition, the read-cache rate may decrease since pages are being read into the buffer pool but never used.

You may need more buffers if the server has performed *foreground writes*. Foreground writes are synchronous writes of dirty pages to disk to accommodate new pages read from disk. You can check if foreground writes have occurred using onstat -F.

Locating Static and Dynamic Web Content

In terms of volatility within the database, AppPages and large objects can be considered *static*. Although they are created and updated in the development environment, once put live, they are static (see Chap. 13 "Creating and Managing Web-sites Using Data Director for Web," for an overview of the development and deployment paths available).

Dynamic database content refers to tables that are regularly added to, updated, or both. For example, an order_items table in a database that supports an online catalog will be added to regularly.

Ideally, you should try to locate on disk devices separate from dynamic content the following: the tables in the Data Director for Web or AppPage Builder schema, or any of the static tables that support your web content. You can do this by

- creating chunks with path mappings to specific disks,
- assigning these chunks to dbspaces,
- locating a table to a dbspace when you create the table.

If you want to make sure that the tables in a dbspace reside on one device, then create one or more chunks for that device and assign these chunks to the dbspace in which you locate the tables.

Just because you can store multimedia content in the database doesn't mean that you should do so without qualification. For example, think twice before storing large video objects in the server: This effectively turns the server into a glorified filesystem, since we are not articulating the behavior of the content, which is the domain of the DataBlade. What you should store are the video metadata, including the filesystem path. Since we should cache large objects, then we will abuse the cache by storing content such as large video objects in the database.

Resourcing Other DataBlades

Some Web DataBlade applications need to coexist with other DataBlades that have disk and blobspace requirements crucial to their operation, such as the Excalibur Text Blade. The Excalibur Blade has requirements for logged and unlogged smart blobspaces. For example, the user may enter a search string into a form in the browser; when the form is submitted, a text search is performed against the Excalibur-created indexes in the database server.

When using other Blades, you need to include their specific requirements into the performance-tuning exercise. The documentation that comes with the DataBlade will tell you how to configure the Informix server to operate with the new Blade. You need to assess the impact of these extra Blades early so that you can include their dependencies in your tuning exercise.

Tuning the Network

The network is a significant kink in the content delivery chain. If the network performance is not optimal, then no matter how we tune the database, operating system, and web server, the critical success factor of quick response time for the browser user will be compromised.

Aside from the physical implementation of the network (which is out of scope for this book), there are a number of practical approaches you can take to improve the use of the network by the web application. In summary:

- Optimize the client/server dialog between webdriver and the database server using the OPTOFC variable setting.
- Configure the database connectivity.
- Limit the result set returned from SQL queries.

Using the OPTOFC Variable

You can optimize the SQLI protocol dialog between the webdriver client and the database server by setting a variable called OPTOFC. Set the OPTOFC variable in the webdriver configuration file, web.cnf. For example:

```
.OPTOFC      1
```

The term OPTOFC means *optimize open fetch close*. It is a feature designed to change the way prepared cursors work. The net result is that client/server traffic can be reduced (some have suggested by around 40 percent). The client/server traffic is a product of the client and server implementing the SQLI protocol, which is the protocol that allows an Informix client program to talk directly (or, *natively*) to an Informix server. This is the protocol that the JDBC Type 4 driver uses. The webdriver program (CGI or API) is a database client with a native connection to the database.

Because the sequencing of the SQLI dialog is changed when OPTOFC is set, error-handing logic in programs such as ESQL/C programs may not work as expected (for example, OPEN CURSOR errors may be encountered in the FETCH statement).

Database Connectivity

If the web server and the database server are on the same machine, it is worth considering the use of a shared memory or stream/named-pipe connection between the webdriver thread in the web server and the Informix database server. This is called a *local* connection, but it does have drawbacks. Table 25-2 summarizes the networking protocols available to you on UNIX and NT for local and remote connections.

Using Local Connections

The essential aim is to make the connection between webdriver and the database as fast as possible when both are on the same machine. You may opt to use stream or named pipes over a network-based connection.

A *shared-memory* connection uses an area of shared memory through which the webdriver client and the Informix server communicate. Shared memory provides very fast access to the database server, but it can pose security risks, especially if the web server is an Internet-visible machine. For example,

- an erroneous or untrusted application could view or destroy message buffers;
- if the client application performs explicit memory addressing, over-indexing could write all over the message portion of shared memory.

Table 25-2.   Networking protocols.

Connect type	UNIX	NT	Informix protocol
Sockets (TCP/IP)	Supported	Supported	onsoctcp
TLI (TCP/IP)	Supported	Not supported	ontlitcp
TLI (IPX/SPX)	Supported	Not supported	ontlispx
Shared memory	Supported	Not supported	onipcshm
Stream pipe	Supported	Not supported	onipcstr
Named pipe	Not supported	Supported	onipcnmp

A *stream pipe* connection allows interprocess communication between processes running on the same computer. In this case, `webdriver` has a stream pipe connection with the Informix server. Stream pipes don't have the security risks associated with shared-memory connections, but they might be slower than shared memory connections on some machines.

A *named pipe* is an API for two-way interprocess communication on Windows NT. Named pipes store data in memory and retrieve it when requested, in a way similar to reading and writing from the filesystem.

Associated problems you can encounter when the web and database servers are on the same machine are:

- The memory requirements of the web server software and the database server may slow everyone down, because memory is being paged out by the operating system as each component demands its own allocation.
- Network-based connections between `webdriver` and the database server have to coexist with the network connections being made by other Internet or intranet users.

It may be best to use stream or named pipes in the latter case. However, you need to change, test, and change again until you obtain the best result for your system.

> **tip**
>
> *If you find that you are running out of database server connections, try adding extra* DBSERVERALIAS *entries to the* ONCONFIG *file. This will result in starting up additional TCP listener threads. You will have to change the value of* INFORMIXSERVER *in* web.cnf, *and create multiple mappings from the web server to multiple* web.cnf *files that contain the different* INFORMIXSERVER *values (this is easier in Version 4). This process is easier if you have multiple web servers since, simplistically, each web server can map onto a specific alias.*

Distributed Web Server and Database Server

If the web server and the database server are on different machines, then `webdriver` can only make a network connection to the database server, so you may encounter bandwidth issues when transferring a large amount of graphical and other large object content from the database server to the web server.

If the web server is hosted on a machine accessible from the Internet, then it is likely that some web content that resides on a database server behind a firewall will be transferred outside of the firewall, on the web server, by `webdriver`. The web content being transferred from the database machine may start to saturate the available bandwidth that the firewall connection provides.

The essential requirement in this case is that you implement AppPage and large object caching in *secure* directories on the web server machine that is outside the firewall.

Limiting SQL Result Sets

You should limit the result set sent back to the client when using the `MISQL` AppPage tag. Try to perform most of the filtering in the SQL statement, rather than in the AppPage tag itself.

The aim is to reduce the amount of data sent between the web server and the browser client. The SQL statement should be as restrictive as possible in the `WHERE` clause. In addition, use the `WINSTART` and `WINSIZE` directives to limit the actual number of rows that are formatted by `webexplode()` and sent back to the browser. You can extend this walking window approach by implementing a stored procedure that *returns with resume*, as explained in Chap. 16.

Restrictive SQL is applicable to Java applets that use JDBC, as well as AppPages. For JDBC performance tuning, see Chap. 8, "Essential JDBC Programming."

Single- and Multiple-server Architectures

You can locate the web server and database server on different machines or on the same machine. What drives the final architecture is usually one or more of the following issues (or variants of them):

- Is high-availability failover required?
- Is there a requirement to replicate application data across multiple database servers and across a firewall?
- Can a single machine handle the expected volume of Internet or intranet requests, as well as service those requests using the local database server?

For example, an online catalog may have a critical requirement that the customer must be able to place an order online; even if the web server goes down or the database server goes down, the customer must not be prevented from placing an order. To ensure this you need a high-availability web server that will source web content from a high-availability database. This requires multiple web server machines that contain a local installation of the Informix server with the appropriate `product` and `order` databases, which are replicated from the backend product capture system and between the failover web servers.

We can summarize the options as single platform and multiple platform.

Single Platform

In this model, one machine hosts the web server, the Informix database server, and databases. When using a single machine, it is better to use multiple processors so that you can spread applications across them.

If your machine has multiple applications as well as the web server and database server, you may run into trouble at some point. For example, if you have a four-CPU machine, then you are wise to devote three of them to the Informix server, leaving the fourth to the operating system and web server.

This is easier to manage than the multiple-platform architecture but may suffer from overloading of the CPU and memory.

If you need to share the load of site hits across multiple web servers, then multiple platforms are the best alternative. There is a chance that in the single-platform configuration you may not have enough CPUs to service the web server and database server, plus any other applications that the machine hosts.

Multiple Platform

Multiple web servers can connect to a single database. Multiple web servers can also connect to multiple databases (see Chap. 23, "Web Server Integration," for instruction how to configure this architecture).

In this model, multiple machines host web servers that connect to a separate machine that hosts the Informix database. The advantage of this platform is that you can spread the availability of the web servers across multiple machines, eliminating the single point of failure that is implicit in the single-platform model. You can, however, install the web server and the Informix database server on multiple machines.

There are distinct advantages when using multiple web server connections to the Informix database:

- It is a better way to utilize nonoptimal server hardware.
- You can locate nondatabase web activity away from the database server. For example, you can place streaming video and audio content away from the Informix database server.

- It allows the database to make the best use of CPU resources.
- It allows load sharing among web servers.

Tuning the Application Queries

However much the database server and the web server are tuned, if the web application contains very poorly designed queries, performance will degrade. By the same token, if the database design is poor, the ability to write optimal queries will suffer accordingly.

Application tuning, together with AppPage and large object caching, is the most important factor in performance tuning for Web DataBlade applications.

Supporting Different Types of Online Query

It is important that the database schema is properly constructed to support the different types of query that the user may request. For a large corporate intranet with a controlled user base, the query requirements can be well-defined in advance, since they may well be driven by the higher-level management tier of the organization who have specific online reporting requirements.

The query characteristics therefore differ for each application. Think about how you would design the database for an Internet bookshop where thousands of users can search on part of a book title across possibly millions of books. Compare that with the financial directors who want information on sales year to date and same time last year. The essential point is that *the database must support the online query requirements*.

General SQL Query Guidelines

Again, assuming that the web application is based on the OLTP model, the following general guide will help:

- Try to use prepared SQL statements in Java applets and applications.
- Ensure that `insert` cursors are used where appropriate in stored procedures.
- Set the isolation level to dirty read or cursor stability in `web.cnf`.

- Rewrite correlated subqueries as a `join` if possible. A subquery is correlated when the value it produces depends on the value produced by the outer `SELECT` statement. Because the result of a subquery may be different for each row, the subquery is executed again for every row in the outer query if the correlation values differ between iterations of the outer query. This process takes time.
- Fetch only the required number of rows and columns.
- Update only changed columns. This can reduce lock contention by not locking index entries for columns updated redundantly.
- Use `SET EXPLAIN` to check that the query plan is as expected. This will show the effect of statistics, data distributions, indexes, fragmentation, and SQL statement structure on query performance.

By default, a logged database has an ISOLATION LEVEL *of* COMMITED READ *and a* LOCK MODE *of* NOT WAIT. *At least the lock mode should be changed to wait some number of seconds for all* webdriver *sessions. The choice of isolation level needs to be determined by the application developers, but it should not be allowed simply to default. Configure the* MI_WEBINITIALSQL *variable in the* web.cnf *file to set the* LOCK MODE *to wait a number of seconds. Consider explicitly setting the session* ISOLATION LEVEL *with this configuration parameter even if the application developers state that* COMMITTED READ *is an appropriate isolation level for this application.*

Using the WINSTART *and* WINSIZE *attributes of the* MISQL *tag does not reduce the generated result set in the database server. See Chap. 16 for more information.*

To support the queries you perform, you need to make sure that data distribution statistics are kept on appropriate columns that are used in your queries. The next section describes how to gather the relevant statistics.

Gathering Data Distribution Statistics

Your testing and production databases should contain data distribution statistics so that the query optimizer in the database server can produce the best query plan to execute the query. The best query plan is the one with the lowest-cost access path to the data.

Without appropriate statistics, the optimizer may interpret what you think is a lean and well-structured query as a worst-case table scan of all tables in the query.

The command to gather statistics is called UPDATE STATISTICS. The essential aim of running the UPDATE STATISTICS command is to gather as much information about the distributions of values in a column as possible. This will directly assist the query optimizer to create a query execution plan to retrieve the data you require.

Web Application and Large Object Schema

The Data Director for Web or AppPage Builder schemas can be included in the UPDATE STATISTICS job. The average count-per-value of key columns in these tables is almost unique, so in almost every case we are expecting a key lookup on the data. For example, when we select an AppPage we use the ID column in the wbPages table. Browser clients will not request a set of AppPages, only a single page at a time. Similarly, there will be no requirement to scan the wbBinaries table for a few large objects.

You are advised to configure AppPage and large object caching if you want to realize visible performance benefits in your web application.

Application Data Schema

This schema contains the application data. For example, an Online Catalog will contain database tables that support pricing and product availability. Users will be querying product information and placing orders via the pages and objects that come from the web content schema (for example, Data Director for Web), but the pricing and product data will reside in tables created for the Online Catalog application domain. These tables could be legacy tables that have been web enabled; they may be used by other applications that are not web based. Accordingly, these application tables need to be included in the UPDATE STATISTICS job.

Types of UPDATE STATISTICS

There are three basic settings for UPDATE STATISTICS, as shown in Table 25-3.

Table 25-3.   Basic settings of UPDATE STATISTICS.

Setting	Description
HIGH	Create distribution cells for each distinct value in a column.
MEDIUM	Create distributions that represent an 85% to 99% accurate sampling of the values in a column.
LOW	Update statistics for the systables, syscolumns, and sysindexes tables only.

Guidelines for UPDATE STATISTICS

- UPDATE STATISTICS HIGH for all columns that head an index, all columns in queries with equality filters (such as "="), and all join columns.
- For the remaining columns in the table, UPDATE STATISTICS MEDIUM.
- UPDATE STATISTICS LOW for each column in a multicolumn index for which UPDATE STATISTICS HIGH was not run.
- UPDATE STATISTICS for stored procedures.

Optimizing UPDATE STATISTICS

- For very large tables, run UPDATE STATISTICS HIGH at the column level, *not* the table level.
- For tables with no indexes, run UPDATE STATISTICS MEDIUM for the entire table.
- Run multiple UPDATE STATISTICS commands for different tables in parallel. A basic metric you can use is three UPDATE STATISTICS sessions per physical CPU.

Using SET EXPLAIN in Web DataBlade Applications to Check the Query Plan

Database query performance is critical in database-driven websites. Accordingly, it is important that the correct *indexes* are used for queries that are expected to use them.

tip

An approach to monitoring query performance should be built into your project from the start. Don't wait until the application is live to test query performance. Ensure that you implement a volume-testing phase that will run the application against a database created with the expected volume of data. Some projects also use the expected volumes in the application design phase to ensure that the correct schema is designed to support the types of query expected.

You can use the database server to monitor long-running queries, whether or not `webdriver` or a 4GL application issues the query.

You can use `onstat -g sql` and `onstat -g sql <session_id>` to look at the SQL being executed for all connected sessions or a particular session.

For long-running queries, you can use `SET EXPLAIN` to trace the query path that the server uses. Normally, you set this in the application code, such as 4GL. Using the Web DataBlade, you can specify `SET EXPLAIN` in the `web.cnf` file as follows:

```
MI_WEBINITIALSQL set explain on;
```

The `MI_WEBINITIALSQL` variable is used to set the database session characteristics for the database connection.

The output file from `SET EXPLAIN ON` is stored in a directory on the *database server* machine. Under NT4, a folder called `sqexpln` is created. In this folder, the `SET EXPLAIN` output is stored as separate files based on the username of the user that has connected to the database server. For example, if `MI_USER` is set to `cortez`, then a file is created called `cortez.out`.

note

You should only use `SET EXPLAIN ON` *for testing. Turn it off for the live environment and whenever you need to time the application.*

Web DataBlade Tuning

The main method of improving the performance of Web DataBlade module applications is to enable caching of both AppPages and large objects (such as image files). However, you should check the configuration parameters of your Web DataBlade application to make sure that any optimizations that can be performed are performed.

Web DataBlade Tuning Checklist

The following is a quick checklist for Web DataBlade performance tuning. Each item is covered in more detail in subsequent sections.

- Use the web server API `webdriver`.
- Set and monitor the peak number of connections from `webdriver` to the database server.
- Release and refresh database connections from `webdriver` in a controlled manner.
- Interrupt long-running queries that will consume server resources.
- Interrupt queries when the browser user requests them to be stopped.
- Optimize dynamic tag lookups.
- Set the `LOCK MODE` for applications that contain update and insert queries.
- Reduce the number of variables passed to `webexplode()`.
- Implement AppPage and large object caching.

The first and last of these are the most important and give the greatest performance benefits when configured correctly. Chapter 23 on web server integration shows how to integrate `webdriver` with NSAPI, ISAPI, and Apache. Later in this chapter, large object and AppPage caching are explained in detail.

Using the Web Server API

If you are serious about creating a high-performance web application, then don't use CGI when you can use NSAPI, ISAPI, or the Apache API. The Web DataBlade installation notes will tell you which web server versions your `webdriver` shared objects will work with, but you will receive at least the NSAPI and ISAPI shared objects and, from Version 4 of the Web DataBlade, a shared object that works with Apache. The basic metric is this: If you use a Netscape, Microsoft, or Apache server that will run the API `webdriver` shared object, don't use CGI.

There are two distinct advantages in using the API:

- elimination of CGI process overhead,
- reuse of database connections.

Set the Peak Number of Connections

You can establish the maximum number of connections to the database using the variable `MI_WEBDBCONNMAX`. You should set it to the same value as the number of web server threads—128, for example.

Monitoring the Connection Pool

This section is applicable only to the NSAPI `webdriver`. The *connection pool* is a set of `webdriver` connections to the database from the web server, up to `MI_WEBDBCONNMAX`. As HTTP requests arrive at the web server, connections are opened to the database, up to the value of `MI_WEBDBCONNMAX`. These connections remain open and are given to any web server thread that needs a database connection.

You may find that the number of HTTP requests exceeds the number of available connections in the connection pool. In this case, the web server thread requesting the `webdriver` connection will wait. You can monitor the connection pool using a trace from `webdriver` by setting the following variables in `web.cnf`:

```
MI_WEBDRVLEVEL 1024
MI_WEBDRVLOG   /usr/informix/stores/logs/webdrvlog.log
```

The first variable sets the tracing level, the second sets the trace output file. You should look for `WAITING` in the trace output, which means that there is connection pool saturation. You should set `MI_WEBDBCONNMAX` to the number of web server threads to avoid this situation.

Releasing Database Connections

When using the API `webdriver`, you can specify how many times a single connected `webdriver` thread will be requested to perform a database operation before it is dropped and recreated. Restarting a connection will consume time, so we can try to increase the elapsed time of the active connection by setting the following variable in `web.cnf`:

```
MI_WEBRECONNECT 500
```

The default for `MI_WEBRECONNECT` is 20.

The advantage of larger numbers is that there are fewer requests to open and close database connections.

If you suspect that memory is not being freed properly from the connected database sessions, then set a lower value for `MI_WEBRECONNECT`*; when the database connection is closed, memory should be freed.*

Interrupting Long-Running Queries

We don't want to allow the user at the browser to request an AppPage that fires off a query that may take forever to complete. For example, suppose that the web application allows you to look up the *name* of all homeowners by geographical area. You select the area code and enter a search string, called `surname`. If you enter `SMITH`, you will almost certainly get a long-running query and, if the relevant tables have not been indexed correctly with the appropriate granularity of statistics, the chances are that the user will press the Stop button after a few minutes. This type of query exists in the real world.

Another example would be the lack of proper filtering in the AppPage that captures the selection criteria. If the data volumes suggest that the user must enter some default value to narrow down the search, but the AppPage does not implement this rule, then you may end up scanning very large tables.

Clearly, we need a mechanism to stop long-running queries. Since `webdriver` is the database client, we implement the `MI_WEBQRYTIMEOUT` variable in `web.cnf` as follows:

```
MI_WEBQRYTIMEOUT     30
```

This setting tells `webdriver` to interrupt a running query if it has not completed in 30 seconds.

Remember to use the `MIERROR` tag with all of your queries to capture unexpected errors or aborts.

Interrupting Queries if the Stop Button Is Used

The user at the browser may press the Stop button at any time. If a database query is being executed on behalf of that user via the API `webdriver`, then the query will carry on regardless, even though the connection between the browser and the web server has been cancelled. This has two impacts: First, the query is consuming resources in the database server; second, the API thread that has sent the query cannot service another query if any are waiting to be serviced.

What we want is the query to be stopped if the user presses the Stop button. You can set the variable `MI_WEBKEEPALIVE` to specify the number of seconds after which `webdriver` will check the browser connection. For example:

```
MI_WEBKEEPALIVE     5
```

This example tells `webdriver` that the browser connection must be checked every five seconds.

The `MI_WEBKEEPALIVE` variable is only available for NSAPI and ISAPI, and for the Apache API from Version 4 of the Web DataBlade.

Waiting for a Database Connection

When a `webdriver` thread tries to obtain a database connection, you can specify the amount of time (in milliseconds) that it will wait by using `MI_WEBDBCONNWAIT` as follows:

```
MI_WEBDBCONNWAIT      0.5
```

When the thread yields, it allows any waiting threads to be serviced.

Optimizing Dynamic Tag Access

If you use the Data Director for Web schema, then you can optimize the way dynamic tags are accessed. On a page with many dynamic tags, or even if dynamic tags are used frequently across the application, you should consider changing the value of `MI_WEBTAGSSQL` in `web.cnf` to remove the `webupper()` function. For example, the default value of `MI_WEBTAGSSQL` is

```
MI_WEBTAGSSQL   SELECT parameters,object FROM wbTags
WHERE webupper(ID)=webupper('$MI_WEBTAGSID');
```

You can change this to be

```
MI_WEBTAGSSQL   SELECT parameters,object FROM wbTags
WHERE ID='$MI_WEBTAGSID';
```

If you do this, make sure that the instance of the dynamic tag in the AppPage matches the value of the `wbTags.ID` column exactly.

Setting the LOCK MODE for INSERT and UPDATE Queries

If you have an application with INSERT or UPDATE queries, configure SET LOCK MODE in the `web.cnf` file, which will force the database server to wait on behalf of `webdriver` if it cannot acquire a lock. Otherwise, `webdriver` will return with an error. The following snippet shows how to configure SET LOCK MODE in the `web.cnf` file:

```
MI_WEBINITIALSQL SET LOCK MODE TO WAIT 20;
```

Remember, all sessions that request a URL that maps onto the `web.cnf` file containing this setting will have LOCK MODE set to WAIT 20 seconds.

Selective Variable Passing

You can reduce the number of variables passed to `webexplode()` from the web server and `webdriver` environment if you set MI_WEBPUSHVARS to the value `select` and manually specify which variables are pushed into the `webexplode()` function. See Chap. 24, "Securing Your Web DataBlade Applications," for more information on this topic.

Optimizing API Cache

Chapter 23 contains a full description of the security settings for variables in the `web.cnf` file. The associated performance impact is described here.

Setting MI_WEBAUTHCACHE

If you set this variable to `check`, then the web server will only go to the database if the browser and the web server have different values for a user's password, or if the web server is not caching the password. This allows the user to change his password on a screen and then not be forced to immediately relogin to the database. An administrator will not be able to lock a user out of the system by changing his or her password, since the authenticated password is stored in the web server. Generally `check` is the quickest throughput for secure URL connections.

Caching Web Content for Performance

In an e-commerce environment, managing your server objects is vital to making sure that you implement the optimal web content delivery architecture. Using a *cache* on the web server to store objects such as AppPages, images, audio, and other documents will reduce the load on the database server. Caching is covered in more detail in later sections of this chapter. This subsection summarizes what object caching is for the Web DataBlade.

Retrieving data from the disk is always much faster than retrieving data from the database, which is why caching improves the performance of web applications.

Why Use Caching?

You cache AppPages and large objects on the web server machine. This will allow you to take advantage of faster filesystem access of web content. If the web and database servers are on different machines, then caching these objects on the web server will allow you to take advantage of the resources of the web server and leave the database server to service query requests and business logic implemented in the database.

When a URL requests an AppPage, `webdriver` will extract the AppPage from the Informix database and that page will be exploded by the `webexplode()` function. When the resulting HTML page is sent to the browser, it may contain references to objects such as GIF images, audio files, or QuickTime video files. For example, the following snippet of HTML will result in `webdriver` being called via CGI to extract the `menatwork` image from the Informix database so that it can be downloaded to the browser:

```
<IMG SRC=http://dellcpi/stores7-
cgi/webdriver.exe?MIvalObj=menatwork>
```

If we had implemented object caching and `menatwork` had previously been extracted from the Informix database, then we could have taken this object from the large object cache *instead* of the Informix database. Taking the object from cache would have been faster than taking it from the database. In the snippet above, we would, however, need to use the LO handle to take advantage of large object caching. This is because accessing an object by name always involves a database access to retrieve the LO handle from the appropriate column, in order to then extract the object from the blobspace using the LO handle as an address.

Most browsers are able to cache locally the web pages and the content items that are downloaded. The browser may not use its cache to render a page that is the product of a function such as `webdriver`. However, this has no real effect on the caching strategy for a large e-commerce website, because the site may have many hundreds of clients accessing pages and images, and each new client will want to download the data it does not have in cache. Therefore, e-commerce sites need to implement a caching strategy to ensure that repeatedly accessed content items are available as quickly as possible.

Using the Web DataBlade doesn't stop you from referring to content stored in the filesystem. You can include filesystem URLs that map onto objects stored in a filesystem directory without invoking webdriver. *It depends on the specifics of the application. Even so, you can store the URL itself in the database as metadata for the web content that you deliver from the filesystem. This will allow you to search for the content using an HTML FORMS interface.*

Examples of frequently accessed content items include banner ads, company logos, buttons, button bars, and graphical menus. These items are frequently in the header or footer of a web page. They may be cached at the browser client but, with many hundreds of users, we need to cache them on the server for *everyone*.

It is important that we cache objects on the database server in order to increase response time at this point in the content delivery chain. What we are trying to do is reduce the overhead on the database server (where the content resides) by caching as many frequently accessed objects as possible outside of the database. This is not because the database is slow at performing the extraction; rather, in a fast and dynamic e-commerce environment, we want the Informix server to perform queries to resolve business rules rather than fetch objects.

What Is AppPage Caching?

Although an AppPage is passed through the webexplode() function, if the page content is not dynamically created, it may as well be a static AppPage and placed in cache. If only a portion of the AppPage is static, then that portion is a candidate for caching, also.

In AppPage caching, static AppPages are stored on *disk* after they have been initially passed through the webexplode() function. For subsequent references to the AppPage, webdriver uses the (exploded) cached AppPage instead of requesting the AppPage from the database and passing it through webexplode().

You can use *partial* AppPage caching for AppPages that include some dynamic content. The *static* portion of the AppPage is cached, and only the dynamic content is passed through the webexplode() function.

What Is Large Object Caching?

Large object caching is similar to AppPage caching, except large objects are cached to disk after they have been extracted from the *blobspace* in which they reside. If you update a large object, a new LO (large object) handle is generated, and this LO handle is stored in the object column of the `wbBinaries` table (or their equivalents).

tip

Retrieving large objects by LO handle will allow `webdriver` *to use the cached version of the large object. If you update the source of the large object, such as updating an image resource with another image file, then a new LO handle is generated and stored in the database. You are advised to use a dynamic tag to fetch the LO handle for a large object resource when the page is exploded. When the AppPage is rendered in the browser, the up-to-date LO handle will be used to fetch the object from cache after the initial load from the database.*

What Is the Cache?

The cache directories reside on the same machine as the web server. The server cache is a special set of one or more directories created by the website administrator or Informix DBA to hold all cached objects. Large objects are the multimedia items (such as images, audio, and video) that reside in a blobspace managed by the Informix database server. When these objects are cached, a copy of the object is stored in a cache directory in the filesystem.

Large objects are stored with a filename that is a compressed version of the LO handle for the object. These files are stored in a directory whose name is formed from the name of the database where the object comes from.

AppPages are stored in a directory that is formed from the database name plus the AppPage name. In this directory are stored all the variants of the AppPage encountered to date. The variants are formed from the different set of variable values passed into the `webexplode()` function for that AppPage.

Caching Large Objects for Performance

To enable large object caching of database objects, set the variables in your `web.cnf` file shown in Tables 25-4 and 25-5. The variables are described in the next few subsections.

Table 25-4. Large object caching variables.

Variable (up to Version 3.3)	Version 4 plus
MI_WEBCACHEDIR	cache_directory
MI_WEBCACHEADMIN	cache_admin
MI_WEBCACHEPASSWORD	cache_admin_password
MI_WEBCACHESUB	cache_buckets
MI_WEBCACHEPAGE	cache_page
MI_WEBCACHEMAXLO	cache_maxsize
MI_WEBPAGELIFE	cache_page_life

Table 25-5. Variables introduced in Version 4.

Variable	Description
cache_page_debug	When set to ON, enables AppPage cache debugging; default value is OFF.
cache_page_buckets	The number of subdirectories to create under the cache directory when using AppPage caching.

MI_WEBCACHEDIR/cache_directory

This variable specifies the directory on the Web server computer in which cached large objects and AppPages are placed. If this variable is not set, then no caching of either large objects or AppPages is possible.

MI_WEBCACHEPASSWORD / cache_admin_password

The password for the cache administration web page that gives the user the ability to maintain cache entries in the cache directories.

MI_WEBCACHEADMIN / cache_admin

The name of the cache administration web page that gives the user the ability to maintain cache entries in the cache directories. For example, you can add, delete, purge, or view them.

MI_WEBCACHESUB / cache_buckets

Number of subdirectories per database created under the directory-specified MI_WEBCACHEDIR. Default is one subdirectory per database.

If you expect many large objects to be cached, you can create more than one subdirectory per database under the MI_WEBCACHEDIR directory by specifying a higher number of MI_WEBCACHESUB. The subdirectories created are named database_name0, database_name1, and so forth. There is no limit to the number of large objects that can be placed in these subdirectories, other than any operating system limitations.

If you modify the setting for MI_WEBCACHESUB, *the algorithm used to locate large objects in the database subdirectories changes. Therefore, you should remove all large objects from the subdirectories if you change the value for* MI_WEBCACHESUB.

MI_WEBCACHEPAGE / cache_page

The variable MI_WEBCACHEPAGE enables AppPage caching. The default is OFF. To enable, set the variable to ON.

MI_WEBCACHEMAXLO / cache_maxsize

Maximum size in bytes of large objects to be cached. Default is 64 K. Realistically, you may want to increase this figure to take account of the typical web content that is delivered from the database. For example, a staff manual in PDF format may be more than 500 K.

When you set the MI_WEBCACHEDIR variable, webdriver places a large object in its disk cache the first time the large object is retrieved. Subsequent retrievals of that large object are made from this disk cache.

MI_WEBPAGELIFE / cache_page_life

This variable specifies the length of time after which an AppPage is refreshed from the database. The unit specification is shown in Table 25-6.

For example:

```
MI_WEBPAGELIFE 12h
```

This setting ensures that the AppPages cached by this web.cnf will reside in cache for 12 hours before being refreshed by webdriver.

Table 25-6. **Time units for** MI_WEBPAGELIFE.

Qualifier	Anticipated age of cached object
h,H	hours
d,D	days
s,S	seconds

Example Cache Configuration

Listing 25-1 shows an example web.cnf configuration. If you are using Version 4 of the Web DataBlade, it is easy to translate the Version 3 variable names into Version 4 variable names.

The configuration in List. 25-1 has the following settings:

- Caching is enabled for large objects and AppPages, and the cache directory for MI_DATABASE is D:\stores\cache.
- There are five cache subdirectories for the stores database.
- Large objects up to 1 Mb can be cached.
- AppPage caching is turned on.
- AppPages are refreshed from the database if the cached version is two elapsed days old.

Listing 25-1. **Example cache configuration section in** web.cnf.

```
#
MI_DATABASE                    stores
#
# General Caching profile for Large Objects and AppPages
MI_WEBCACHEDIR                 D:\stores\cache
MI_WEBCACHESUB                 5
#
# Large Object Caching Profile
MI_WEBCACHEMAXLO               1024000
#
# AppPage Caching profile
MI_WEBCACHEPAGE                on
MI_WEBPAGELIFE                 2d
```

Managing Large Object Caching

In some environments, you may want to vary the caching strategy. For example, some content may not require aging as frequently as others. A spreadsheet may be updated once a week and stored inside the database for intranet delivery. The spreadsheet is cached once at start of week and remains in cache for the remainder of the week. A PDF document is created once and may never be changed. You need to be able to identify the volatility of web content in such as way that you are not aging the cache prematurely.

A simple way to address this is to nominate a separate web configuration and manage the cache variables by URL. Up to Version 4, you create a separate `web.cnf` file. From Version 4, you create a separate configuration (see Chap. 22, "Understanding `webdriver` Configuration," for more details on the differences between Web DataBlade versions). For example, the `spreadsheet` objects may be aged after 72 hours. The online catalog images may be aged seasonally. It depends on your application requirements. The risk with distributing URLs across an object base is that you may end up caching an object in multiple places if it is used by more than one page. So, you need to ensure that the objects are bound to a specific URL prefix if tight cache management is important.

Housekeeping the Large Object Cache

Listing 25-2 shows a sample `find` command for UNIX that can be used to clean out the large object cache. In most cases, you would want to put this into a `cron` script to be run nightly. If you notice your cache filling too quickly, you can run it more frequently. The frequency is application specific.

You need to run this command as the owner of the files in the cache directory or as the superuser. Replace `/stores` with the name of the cache directory as specified in `MI_WEBCACHEDIR`. Modify the `+7` to be the value (in days) that you want files monitored.

Up to Version 4 of the Web DataBlade, two variables existed to perform housekeeping of large objects: `MI_WEBCACHECRON` *and* `MI_WEBCACHELIFE`. *Because some users encountered problems when using these variables, they were quickly superseded by this* `find` *method of housekeeping the large object cache, which is totally under user control.*

The first `find` will delete files based on the modification time of the file. The second `find` will delete files based on the last access time of the file. Choose the one that best fits your needs.

Listing 25-2. Housekeeping the large object cache.

```
#
# delete all files under /stores that have not been
# modified for 7 days
find /stores -depth -mtime +7 -exec rm {} \;

# delete all files under /stores that have not been
# accessed for 7 days
find /stores -depth -atime +7 -exec rm {} \;
```

Alternatively, you can write your own `find` command based on these examples.

Note that AppPages are cached in the `MI_WEBCACHEDIR` directory and so are subject to this housekeeping, regardless of the setting of the AppPage cache refresh variable, `MI_WEBPAGELIFE`. If you want to exclude AppPages from this housekeeping method, identify the large object subdirectories in `MI_WEBCACHEDIR` that you will use in the `find` command, and issue as many `find` commands as there are large object subdirectories. Remember that `webdriver` will, by default, create one subdirectory in `MI_WEBCACHEDIR` named after the database specified in `web.cnf`. If you set `MI_WEBCACHESUB` to 5, for example, then up to five subdirectories will be created for that database. Nominate all of these in the `find` command.

If you don't want to complicate things and have enough disk space to accommodate a lot of cached content, then you can let `MI_WEBPAGELIFE` refresh the AppPages, and run the `find` command script manually.

Caching AppPages for Performance

We know that, if your application contains many static AppPages, you can improve performance by eliminating some database requests and retrieving AppPages directly from the disk cache used by `webdriver`.

If an AppPage is cached, then all or part of the AppPage is defined as *static*. If the whole AppPage is static, then, without caching, `webexplode()` will repeatedly generate the same HTML every time the AppPage is referenced. You need to identify which AppPages are candidates for AppPage caching early on, so that you can prepare your caching configuration for the system and acceptance test phases you have defined and, ultimately, for the live environment.

Full and Partial AppPage Caching

You can cache AppPages in parts: a *static* part and a *dynamic* part. The *static* part of the AppPage does not change with each invocation, including the variables passed into the AppPage. The *dynamic* part may change with each invocation, including AppPage variables.

The dynamic part is always exploded by webexplode().

The ability to identify static and dynamic parts to an AppPage gives you the ability to reduce the *key size* of the AppPage in cache, which is formed from the variable values that are passed into the AppPage by webexplode(), and therefore reduce the number of AppPage variants held in cache as well. You also have more flexibility in identifying AppPages for caching, since you can identify parts of AppPages that can be exploded once per *season* (for example, AppPages for an online catalog) and parts that need to be exploded at all times.

Partial AppPage caching is explained later, in the section, "Partial AppPage Caching."

important

webdriver *checks all of the variables passed into the AppPage and creates an instance of the exploded AppPage for each possible set of these variable assignments when they are encountered. In order to optimize AppPage caching, use the* MI_WEBPUSHVARS *variable described in Chap. 24, "Securing Your Web Applications." Using this variable will limit the number of instances of an AppPage to those variable assignments that affect the web application logic. From Version 4 of the Web DataBlade, only user variables in the configuration are passed to* webexplode().

important

Changes to the underlying data in the database do not mean that the cached AppPage will be refreshed from the database automatically. webdriver *cannot know when the underlying data has changed; it can only track changes to the variables passed into the AppPage. For example, if you add a new* customer *record to the database,* webdriver *cannot detect this and will use the cached AppPage that reads the* customer *table if the* MI_WEBPAGELIFE *of the page has not expired. For this reason, you need to combine the speed of filesystem retrieval with the strengths of dynamic page generation by understanding the volatility of your AppPages and then nominating the AppPages for caching and setting the value of* `MI_WEBPAGELIFE`, *accordingly.*

There are different levels of volatility for different types of AppPages. These are described in Table 25-7. You can use this table to map out the page volatility for each of your AppPages so that you can nominate the AppPages most suitable for caching.

Single-instance AppPage Caching

A single instance of an AppPage is an AppPage that never changes, no matter how many variables are passed into the AppPage. The variable values may differ, but they have no effect on the *behavior* of the AppPage Script, so the HTML output is unchanged for each `webexplode()` of the AppPage.

Multiple-instance AppPage Caching and Volatility

A multiple instance of an AppPage is an AppPage whose HTML output from `webexplode` varies according to the variables passed into the AppPage, including the underlying data. If AppPage explosion varies, then we need to know how frequently it will vary. For example, data selected by an AppPage may vary every hour, day, week, quarter, or year. These intervals will give us our frequency, and hence *volatility*.

If the frequency, or interval, is known, the volatility can be described as *low*. If the AppPage can vary at any time (for example, using real-time data), the volatility is *high*.

Table 25-7.   AppPage instance and volatility.

AppPage instance	Volatility	Description
Single	Zero	AppPage does not change when exploded.
Multiple	Low	The underlying data changes at known intervals, so the AppPage changes at known intervals when exploded.
Multiple	High	Changes to AppPages when exploded cannot be determined.

If an AppPage refers to large objects, such as images, by name, then, as long as the rest of the page is static, the AppPage is considered static even if the large object changes in the database. This is because object retrieval by name will always involve a lookup of the large object (LO) handle in the database; it is the URL for the object that is static. If the AppPage refers to a large object by LO handle, then a change in the object in the database results in a new LO handle, so you should not consider the AppPage to be wholly static.

Implementing AppPage Caching

To implement AppPage caching, there are two basic steps:

- Configure AppPage caching in the `webdriver web.cnf` file.
- Register one or more AppPages for caching.

The first step involves setting variables in `web.cnf` to tell `webdriver` that AppPage caching is required and to specify housekeeping parameters. The second step involves registering specific AppPages for caching by using a special page that you invoke from the browser.

Configuring AppPage Caching

To configure AppPage caching in `web.cnf`, set variables listed in Table 25-8.

Using `cache_page_buckets` to Manage Multiple AppPage Instances

As a basic metric, if you have an AppPage that may have over 1000 exploded variations, then set `cache_page_buckets`. This creates a separate subdirectory under `cache_directory` for *every* exploded variant of an AppPage. The reason for this extra functionality is that it is easier for `webdriver` to fetch the exploded AppPage in cache when it is qualified by a subdirectory path, rather than extracting it from a list of exploded variants of the one AppPage in a single directory.

note

If you modify the setting for `cache_page_buckets`, *the algorithm used to locate the different versions of the AppPage in the subdirectories changes. Remove all AppPages from the subdirectories if you change the value for* `cache_page_buckets`. *You can use the* `find` *script listed previously to do this.*

Table 25-8.   AppPage caching variables.

Variable/Version 4	*Description*
MI_WEBCACHEPAGE/ cache_page	Set to ON to enable AppPage caching; OFF to disable it. Default is OFF.
MI_WEBCACHEDIR/ cache_directory	Full pathname of the web server directory in which to place cached AppPages and large objects.
cache_page_buckets (Version 4 onwards only)	Number of subdirectories for an AppPage under cache_directory. Default is 1 per AppPage.
MI_WEBPAGELIFE/ cache_page_life	If the timestamp of the cached AppPage exceeds this value, then refresh the AppPage from the database.
MI_WEBCACHEADMIN/ cache_admin	Name of the cacheadmin page if the default is not used (optional).
MI_WEBCACHEPASSWORD/ /cache_admin_password	Password used to perform operations from the MI_WEBCACHEADMIN page (optional).

Housekeeping the AppPage Cache using cache_page_life

You can specify an interval of time after which the AppPage will be refreshed from the database at the next webexplode(). This interval is defined using cache_page_life (MI_WEBCACHELIFE). Each time an AppPage is retrieved from cache, if the timestamp indicates that the AppPage is older than the value of cache_page_life, the AppPage is refreshed from the database.

You need to set both MT_WEBCACHEPAGE *and* MI_WEBCACHEDIR *to enable AppPage caching. If either is not set, caching of AppPages is not enabled. If* MI_WEBCACHEDIR *is not set, caching of large objects is not enabled either.*

Administering AppPages for Caching

Once the webdriver variables have been set up, you need to register AppPages for caching.

webdriver outputs a special page for use with administering AppPages in cache. The default name of this page is cacheadmin. You can change the name of this page and assign a password for all operations from this page using two webdriver variables. For example:

```
MI_WEBCACHEADMIN        webcacheadmin
MI_WEBCACHEPASSWORD     mypassword
```

If neither are set, the default page is called `cacheadmin` with no password.

If `MI_WEBCACHEADMIN` is set to `webcacheadmin`, or any other value, the same cache administration page is delivered to the browser by `webdriver`, except that you can't access it using the default name `cacheadmin`; you have to specify `webcacheadmin` in the URL. If you specify `cacheadmin` instead, `webdriver` will not find the page. This enables a basic form of security for administering AppPage cache.

For example, if `MI_WEBCACHEADMIN` is not set:

```
http://theale2/stores-cgi/webdriver.exe?MIval=
cacheadmin
```

If `MI_WEBCACHEADMIN` is set to `webcacheadmin`:

```
http://theale2/stores7-cgi/webdriver.exe?MIval=
webcacheadmin
```

You can invoke the cache administration page via CGI or the API `webdriver`.

Invoking the Cache Administration Page

The cache administration page is invoked from the browser. For example:

```
http://dellcpi/stores7/cacheadmin
```

A screen similar to Fig. 25-3 should be displayed.
The screen fields have the following functions:

- Directory: This shows the value of `MI_WEBCACHEDIR`.
- AppPage: This takes the name of the AppPage to perform the action against.
- Password: Enter the value of `MI_WEBCACHEPASSWORD` for any operation you perform if this variable is set.
- Action: Check the type of action you want to perform.
- Check Database: When registering an AppPage, check or don't check whether the AppPage is in the table nominated by `MItab`.

Registering an AppPage for Caching

To register an AppPage for caching:

- enter the name of the AppPage in the AppPage textbox,
- click the Enable radio button,
- click Submit.

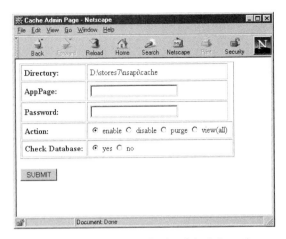

Figure 25-3. *AppPage Cache Administration.*

A directory will be created under `$MI_WEBCACHEDIR\`
`databasename\apppagename`. Cached AppPage variants will be
stored in this directory.

For example, suppose `MI_DATABASE` in `web.cnf` was set to the value
`stores`, the AppPage was called `HelloWorld`, and `MI_WEBCACHEDIR`
was set to `D:\stores\nsapi\cache`. Then the following directory
would be created if `HelloWorld` was registered from this screen:

```
D:\stores\nsapi\cache\stores.HelloWorld
```

Inside this directory, a separate file would be created for each
invocation of the AppPage that contained a difference in parameter
values passed into `webexplode()`.

Unregistering an AppPage for Caching

To disable AppPage caching for an AppPage:

- enter the name of the AppPage in the AppPage textbox,
- click the Disable radio button,
- click Submit.

Purging AppPage Cache Entries

To remove AppPages from cache:

- enter the name of the AppPage in the AppPage textbox,
- click the Purge radio button,
- click Submit.

Listing AppPage Cache Entries

To list all the AppPages registered for caching (enabled or otherwise):

- click the View radio button,
- click Submit.

If `MI_WEBCACHEPASSWORD` *has been set, then make sure you enter the value of this variable into the Password box in the cache administration screen.*

Optimizing AppPage Caching

If you add, change, or remove a variable in `web.cnf`, then the AppPages registered for cache will have another variant cached when you next request them, unless you are using `MI_WEBPUSHVARS` correctly. Remember that the variant is based on the variables passed into `webexplode()`, and these include those from the web server and `webdriver` environments. Cut down the number and relevance of these variables by using `MI_WEBPUSHVARS` to push only those variables that directly affect AppPage behavior.

Integrating AppPage Caching in Your Project Lifecycle

You can implement AppPage caching in the development environment, but this should not be for performance or stress testing of the application. Rather, this should be a confidence measure to ensure that your application works as expected against a caching surface. The Informix DBA and/or the project Technical Design Authority (Technical Lead) should monitor the cache wherever it is implemented. For example, we should be able to trace whether an AppPage is cached and prove that the following are implemented correctly:

- caching of AppPages (full or part),
- caching of large objects,
- cache cleanup.

The Technical Lead needs to have a good understanding of which AppPages are candidates for caching based on an understanding of the dynamic content rendered when the page is exploded. For example, a weekly report delivered to the intranet can be cached for the whole week before it is aged or cleaned. This also applies to large objects. For example, a quarterly report saved in PDF format is managed in the Informix database, but it ought to be cached until it is refreshed.

If you are using NSAPI to access a secure URL for an AppPage that is registered for caching, then be careful if you use MI_WEBAUTHTIMEOUT *and* MI_WEBAUTHCOOKIE *also, since a variable called* MIAUTH_ID *can be set that will change as you access the AppPage repeatedly, caching each invocation. You can see this variable set at the top of the cached AppPage. Ensure that you test the complete application with all the* webdriver *variables set to monitor this kind of behavior.*

Partial AppPage Caching

Partial AppPage caching allows you to use a special tag, called MIDEFFERED to delimit a block of AppPage source that is *always* exploded by webexplode(), even if the AppPage is in cache.

Partial AppPage caching allows you to reuse a page in cache while parameterizing that page with variable values. Without the MIDEFFERED *tag, each variable value you passed in would result in a newly cached page that may never be used again.*

Using the MIDEFERRED Tag

The cached AppPage contains the exploded contents of the original AppPage. Normally, all of the cached page would be returned to the browser without any further action. However, if the cached AppPage contains one or more sections whose explosion is *deferred*, then the cached AppPage is passed through webexplode() *again*, together with all the variables, so that the deferred content can be exploded into HTML to be sent back to the browser. webdriver knows that the cached page needs to be passed through webexplode() again because the suffix of the cached page is .def.

Deferred content is a section of an AppPage that is delimited by the MIDEFFERED tag, which is similar to the MIBLOCK tag.

When webdriver is passed a page from cache, the first tag it should encounter is MIDEFERRED, since the outer tags have previously been exploded. The MIDEFERRED tag is similar to MIBLOCK in that it defined a block of text that is to be expanded by webdriver. This block of text can contain Web DataBlade tags and variables that are expanded when encountered. The resulting output is sent back to the browser with the rest of the web page; it is *not* written to a file in cache. The next time the AppPage is invoked with the same variable values, this process is repeated.

Using the `MIDEF`/`defer` Variable Prefix

The variable values passed into the AppPage form a key that is used to look up the AppPage in the cache directory. If any one variable value changes, then another instance of the exploded AppPage is stored in cache. If you want to optimize the caching of AppPages, then reduce the number of AppPage variables from the cached AppPage key. You do this by prefixing the AppPage variable with the prefix `defer`. Before Version 4 of the Web DataBlade, you used the `MIDEF` prefix.

If you try to use AppPage variables in the `MIDEFFERED` section that are initialized outside that section, the variable will not be recognized by `webexplode()` because the AppPage script that initialized the variable has been exploded, not deferred. In this case, pass the variable as a parameter using the `defer` (or `MIDEF`) prefix.

`webdriver` will reuse AppPages in cache if all but the deferred variables are the same. If the deferred variables are identical across invocations, `webdriver` will still `webexplode` the cached page to resolve the deferred variable values. This is because the deferred variable value is not part of the cached page key and the deferred section has not been exploded.

Registering AppPages That Are Partially Cached

See the subsection, "Registering an AppPage for Caching," in this chapter.

Invoking and Viewing Partially Cached AppPages

To view a cached AppPage, look in the directory specified by `MI_WEBCACHEDIR`. A folder will be created with the name of `MI_DATABASE.AppPagename`.

For example, List. 25-3 shows the AppPage source of `HelloWorld.html`. Assuming that the value of `MI_DATABASE` is `stores`, when this AppPage is registered for AppPage caching using the Cache Administration tool, a directory will be created on the web server called `stores.HelloWorld` in the `$MI_WEBCACHEDIR` directory.

Assume that the AppPage is invoked as follows:

```
http://dellcpi/stores/HelloWorld&Param1=
World&defer.param2=Test3
```

`Param1` will form part of the key to look up the AppPage in cache. The variable `param2` is prefixed with the keyword `defer`, so

Listing 25-3. AppPage source of HelloWorld.html.

```
<html>
<body>
<h1>
   <?mivar>Hello $Param1<?/mivar>
</h1>
<?mideferred>
   <h2><?mivar>This is the value of
$defer.param2<?/mivar></h2>
<?/mideferred>
</body>
</html>
```

Listing 25-4.   "Hello World" AppPage in cache.

```
access=0;
MI_WEBTAGSSQL=SELECT+parameters%2c+object+FROM+wbTags+WHERE+
webupper%28ID%29%3dwebupper%28%27%24MI%5fWEBTAGSID%27%29%3b&MIval=
HelloWorld&Param1=World&WEB_HOME=%2fstores8%2dcgi%2fwebdriver%2eexe
<html>
<body>
<h1>
   Hello World
</h1>

   <h2><?mivar>This is the value of $defer.param2<?/mivar></h2>

</body>
</html>
```

the value of param2 will not form part of the key. The value will be written dynamically to the HTML page for each invocation of the AppPage.

Listing 25-4 shows the cached AppPage in List. 25-3.

Listing 25-5 shows the HTML sent to the browser, which is the cached AppPage in List. 25-4 after being exploded a second time.

Note that the cached AppPage in List. 25-4 contains mivar tags that have not been exploded. This is because the MIDEFERRED tag delimits them.

Listing 25-5.   HTML output of List. 25-4.

```
<html>
<body>
<h1>
   Hello World
</h1>

   <h2>This is the value of Test3</h2>

</body>
</html>
```

 Up to Version 4 of the Web DataBlade, use the MIDEF_ *prefix instead of the* defer. *prefix.*

The text at the top of List. 25-4 is the list of AppPage variables passed to webexplode. The remainder of the document is the cached AppPage, including the deferred section.

Each time the AppPage is invoked with the same set of variable values, the cached version is put through webexplode() so that the remaining AppPage tags can be exploded.

Summary

In this chapter, we have seen how, when approaching performance issues, we need to focus on the end users. Total performance is the sum of all the cooperating components. We have looked at a basic tuning methodology for performing incremental changes to the way any component is configured.

We have listed some guidelines for tuning the web server, the network, and the database server.

We have seen that the largest potential gains come from tuning the Web DataBlade configuration, application, and database.

AppPage and large object caching, together with optimal SQL queries, are seen as the best way of improving web application performance.

Debugging Web DataBlade Applications

In this chapter:

- A problem scenario
- Isolating problems
- Testing the web server
- Running `webdriver` interactively
- Checking the web server configuration
- Checking database server availability
- Debugging with Raw mode
- Tracing the `webexplode()` function
- Tracing `webdriver`
- Checking AppPage Script with `WebLint`

As you build a Web DataBlade application, from time to time you will need to debug your own and other people's code. You may also have to check the workings and interaction of all the components in the end-to-end architecture, such as the web server, `webdriver`, and the database server.

This chapter is concerned with debugging Web DataBlade applications as well as tracking down problems in an end-to-end context. Superficially, you can separate debugging applications from troubleshooting incidents in a live application but, realistically, you may need to trace a problem end to end in a development context as well as a live context. It is therefore useful to have a checklist of information that you can use in either case.

If you need to debug Java applets or applications, Chap. 8 contains the details of how to debug and tune the performance of Java applets and applications that use the JDBC Type 4 driver from Informix. Chapter 25 details the performance-tuning tasks that you may want to follow to manage your live environment optimally.

A Problem Scenario

Suppose an intranet user complains of slow response at the browser from your site. You wrote the code; all the bugs were removed and it worked fine, until now. What's the problem? Is it a bug in the SQL of an `MISQL` tag, or is it a problem with the configuration of the database server? Could it be the web server or the network that is slow?

This example highlights some of the overlap between debugging and performance tuning. In this scenario, the web server or the database server may be down. However, the problem may be that the database has not been optimized; for example, the development schema may have been deployed to the production machine without indexes applied to the tables, or `UPDATE STATISTICS` may not have been run.

When trying to solve a problem such as this, you can follow a few simple steps to *isolate the problem area.*

Isolating Problems

You can follow a simple methodology to isolate the component that is failing.

1. Make sure the browser can retrieve a simple page from the web server; if the web server returns a simple page, then try test 2.
2. Run `webdriver` interactively; if `webdriver` returns a page successfully, then test 3.

3. Check the web server configuration, including the API `webdriver` configuration.

If test 1 fails, then you need to correct the problem in the web server. If test 2 fails, then you need to check the connectivity settings from the web server to the database server, check the database server availability, and check the CGI `webdriver` configuration.

Test 3 is used to identify problems connecting the API `webdriver` to the Informix server and maintaining that connection.

These tests are explained in the following sections.

Testing the Web Server

We need to test the browser connection to the web server. First we make sure that the web server can retrieve files from the filesystem. Most web servers are configured to have a default page displayed when the URL does not specify a page. For example, assuming that the web server on the `theale2` machine listens on port 80, enter the following URL:

```
http://theale2/
```

The default home page for the web server should be displayed. If this has not been configured, ask the webmaster for a web page in the web server document directories that you can use to test with. If you can't get a response from the web server, the web server may be down or you have a network problem.

If everything works fine, run `webdriver` interactively.

Running `webdriver` Interactively

You can run `webdriver` interactively to check the `webdriver` connection to the database. Log onto the web server machine and run the CGI `webdriver` from the command line. You will need to locate the directory in which the CGI `webdriver` has been placed.

It is a good idea to configure a CGI `webdriver` *even if you use NSAPI, ISAPI, or Apache API, so that you can perform this basic test. Remember to place the* `web.cnf` *file in the same directory as the* `webdriver` *program.*

If `MIval` is not set in the `web.cnf` file (or the appropriate configuration in Version 4), then set `MIval` in the shell environment. For example, under UNIX:

```
setenv MIval=HelloWorld
export MIval
```

or, under NT

```
set MIval=HelloWorld
```

You can set other variables in the shell environment if they are not present in `web.cnf`. When all the relevant variables have been set, run `webdriver`, as shown in List. 26-1.

The output in List. 26-1 shows the content type (`MIME` type), content length and the exploded AppPage. This proves that `webdriver` can connect to the database server, and that the `webexplode()` function is working as expected against the configured schema.

If you are using the NSAPI, ISAPI, or Apache API `webdriver` shared object, then the connection from the web server to the database may have hung. This may indicate long-running queries in the database server with all the `webdriver` threads active, resulting in `webdriver` HTTP requests being delayed in the web server.

Listing 26-1.   Running `webdriver` ***interactively.***

```
D:\stores7\cgi-bin>webdriver
content-type: text/html
content-length: 142

<HTML>
<HEAD>
    <TITLE>Hello World</TITLE>
</HEAD>

<BODY>
    <CENTER>

        <H1> Hello World</H1>
    </CENTER>
</BODY>
</HTML>
D:\stores7\cgi-bin>
```

See Chap. 25 for information on how to approach tuning the web server and the `webdriver` configuration to manage problems in web server and `webdriver` connectivity.

To check the NSAPI, ISAPI, or Apache API `webdriver` configuration, see Chap. 23, "Web Server Integration," for details on these `webdriver` settings.

If `webdriver` will *not* output the exploded page, then one of the following may be true:

- The `web.cnf` settings may be corrupt.
- The database server may be down.
- The connection settings on the web server may be incorrect.

For example, if the connectivity settings in `web.cnf` specify a database that does not exist, then `webdriver` returns the following to the screen:

```
Status: 500 Couldn't connect to database!
```

Checking the Web Server Configuration

There are three essential checks to perform.

- Check the connectivity settings from the web server to the database server.
- Check the URL prefix mappings in the web server.
- Check the `webdriver` configuration.

Checking Connectivity Settings

The `webdriver` program runs on the web server, so it must be able to connect to the Informix server and database as a client program whether the database server is local or remote.

The following pointers may help you diagnose the problem:

- Check that you have the correct version of the client connectivity libraries installed on the web server machine.
- Check that the value of `INFORMIXSERVER` in `web.cnf` is a valid server name; check the `ONCONFIG` file on the database server machine for the list of valid server names under `DBSERVERNAME` and `DBSERVERALIASES`.
- If the web server is an NT machine, check the registry settings by using the `setnet` program and run the `ILogin` program to

connect to the Informix server and database named in the `web.cnf` file, taking the defaults from the registry; if this fails, check that the `INFORMIXSERVER` name, protocol, hostname, and listener port are correct for the target database server.

- If the web server is a UNIX machine, check the `SQLHOSTS` entries for the target database server; make sure that the `INFORMIXSERVER`, protocol, hostname, and service correctly map onto the database server machine and Informix instance; check that the port setting of the named service in the web server services file correctly maps onto the configured listener port on the database server.

Check the URL Prefix Mappings in the Web Server

The web server must be able to invoke `webdriver` either as a CGI program or through the NSAPI, ISAPI, or the Apache API `webdriver`.

If you can run the CGI `webdriver` from the command line but you normally use the API version, then check the web server URL prefix mapping and the `webdriver` configuration.

If you can run the CGI program from the command line but not when invoked as a CGI program from the web server, then check the URL prefix mapping for the CGI `webdriver` in the web server configuration.

See Chap. 23, "Web Server Integration," for details on configuring `webdriver` for different web servers and creating URL prefixes.

Check the `webdriver` Configuration

Apart from checking the connection variables such as `INFORMIXSERVER`, `MI_DATABASE`, and `MI_USER`, you can check whether any of the following variables have been set:

- `MI_WEBRECONNECT`: If set too low, `webdriver` may attempt to refresh the database connection too often; the default is 20, so use the default unless reconnection is visibly slowing the system.
- `MI_WEBQRYTIMEOUT`: If set too low, `webdriver` may prematurely stop a query that was issued to the database.
- `MI_WEBKEEPALIVE`: If set too high, any broken connection between the browser and the web server may not be trapped quickly enough by `webdriver` to stop any queries being executed on behalf of the broken session from taking up web server and database server resources.

- MI_WEBDBCONNMAX: If `webdriver` threads in the server are WAITING, consider increasing this value to the number of HTTP web server threads.

See Chap. 25, "Performance-tuning Essentials," for more information on these topics.

Monitoring the Connection Pool for the NSAPI `webdriver`

You may want to check the status of the `webdriver` connections to the Informix database server. You can monitor the status of the NSAPI `webdriver` connections to the database as follows:

- set `MI_WEBDRVLEVEL` to `1024`,
- set `MI_WEBDRVLOG` to point to the `webdriver` trace output file.

See the section on tracing `webdriver` later in this chapter for more information about setting the `webdriver` trace variables.

When the trace variables are set, the following sample output will be written to the trace output file. Listing 26-2 shows an example trace.

The CGI `webdriver` will also cause similar output to be written to the trace output file if the `webdriver` trace level is set to 1024, but in this case the CGI connection is not persistent and has no real meaning in the trace.

Listing 26-2. Connection pool trace.

```
(173-a9a168,1) DEBUG: Sun Aug 22 23:52:19 1999
     thread   conn     sessid   status rqs max database      user    qt
qd  ka

001 00101100 00abd298    24        run  10  20  catalog  cortez   30
0   2
002 00079ac0 000eb478    27        run   5  20  catalog  cortez   30
0   2
003 000aa9d0 00105990    28        run   2  20  catalog  cortez   30
0   2
004 00079890 00100548    35        sleep    2 20 catalog    cortez   30
0   2
```

Table 26-1. Connection pool trace description.

Column	Description
thread	`webdriver` thread ID
conn	database connection ID
sessid	session ID as shown by `onstat -u`
status	connection status
rqs	number of requests on this connection
max	maximum number of requests for the connection before the connection is reopened; set by `MI_WEBRECONNECT`
database	name of database being accessed
user	name of the user that `webdriver` is connecting to the database as
qt	query timeout interval, set by `MI_WEBQRYTIMEOUT`
qd	how long the query has been running in `ka` amounts
ka	interval in seconds between checking if the connection is still alive

Table 26-1 lists the meaning of the columns from the trace in List. 26-2. Using the trace values, you may want to check the following information:

- Are any `webdriver` threads overloaded with connection requests (the `rqs` column)?
- Are there any slow-running queries (check the `qd` column)?
- Is the query timeout set too high? (Check the `qt` column, but timeout may need to vary depending on the application requirements.)
- Run `onstat -g ses <sessid>` and `onstat -g sql <sessid>` to monitor the SQL being run from a particular `webdriver` thread.

Connections are shut down and recreated after `MI_WEBRECONNECT` number of requests. If you reach the maximum number of connections set by `MI_WEBDBCONNMAX` (default is 16) and all threads are processing queries, you will notice a `WAITING` message to the right of the `ka` column. If you see the `WAITING` message frequently, consider raising the value of `MI_WEBDBCONNMAX`.

Checking Database Server Availability

Log onto the database server machine. You can run the `onstat -m` command to check if the Informix server is online. For example, if the database server is on the `theale2` machine:

```
theale2 4% onstat -m
shared memory not initialized for INFORMIXSERVER
'online_pln'
```

This output shows that the database server is down. If the database server was online, then the first line of output will resemble the following snippet:

```
theale2 2% onstat -m | more
INFORMIX-Universal Server Version 9.13.UC2   --
On-Line -- Up 20 days 03:10:48 -
-- 20800 Kbytes
```

You should check the messages output from `onstat -m` to see what may be holding up clients such as `webdriver` (for example, long checkpoint durations). The output from `onstat -m` will also show you if there were any loading errors when the Web DataBlade functions were loaded into the Informix server environment (see Chap. 12, "Web DataBlade Architecture," for an example listing that shows the loading of DataBlade functions confirmed to the message file).

You may also want to run some diagnostic commands on the database server machine, such as:

- `onstat -g seg`: shared memory allocations.
- `onstat -g sql`: who is running SQL?
- `onstat -g sql <session id>`: detailed SQL listing for a particular session.
- `onstat -K`: locks held.

Debugging with RAW Mode

You can use the *RAW mode* feature of `webdriver` to debug your web application. Raw mode enables you to

- display the variables that are passed to the `webexplode()` function, including web server variables and variables in `web.cnf`, and identify where variable assignments are made;
- display the AppPage source stored in the database without exploding the AppPage tags.

In most cases, you will use RAW mode to debug AppPages in a development context, but you may want to use RAW mode in a live production environment when you need to check the values of variables passed from the browser, web server, and `webdriver` configurations.

Enabling RAW Mode

To enable RAW mode to debug output, you need to perform the following:

- Set `MI_WEBRAWPASSWORD` in the `web.cnf` file; if you are using Version 4 or later, set `raw_password` in the `webdriver` configuration.
- Specify `MI_WEBRAWMODE` in the URL for the AppPage you wish to trace.

You set this variable in `web.cnf` as follows:

```
MI_WEBRAWPASSWORD        myPassWord
```

You can retrieve the unexpanded AppPage by specifying, in a URL:

```
MI_WEBRAWMODE=myPassWord
```

`webdriver` returns the unexpanded AppPage as stored in the database, including the AppPage module tags. RAW mode also displays all variables and where they were assigned.

Figures 26-1 and 26-2 show example output for the very simple "`HelloWorld`" AppPage.

Tracing Variable Assignments

Table 26-2 lists the columns under which information about variables is displayed.

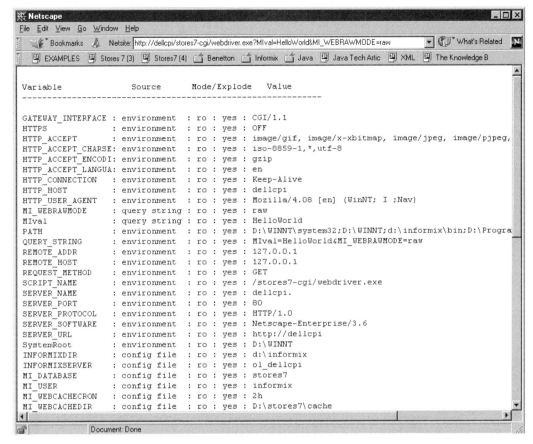

```
Variable            Source      Mode/Explode   Value
------------------------------------------------------------
GATEWAY_INTERFACE  : environment : ro : yes : CGI/1.1
HTTPS              : environment : ro : yes : OFF
HTTP_ACCEPT        : environment : ro : yes : image/gif, image/x-xbitmap, image/jpeg, image/pjpeg,
HTTP_ACCEPT_CHARSE : environment : ro : yes : iso-8859-1,*,utf-8
HTTP_ACCEPT_ENCODI : environment : ro : yes : gzip
HTTP_ACCEPT_LANGUA : environment : ro : yes : en
HTTP_CONNECTION    : environment : ro : yes : Keep-Alive
HTTP_HOST          : environment : ro : yes : dellcpi
HTTP_USER_AGENT    : environment : ro : yes : Mozilla/4.08 [en] (WinNT; I ;Nav)
MI_WEBRAWMODE      : query string : ro : yes : raw
MIval              : query string : ro : yes : HelloWorld
PATH               : environment : ro : yes : D:\WINNT\system32;D:\WINNT;d:\informix\bin;D:\Progra
QUERY_STRING       : environment : ro : yes : MIval=HelloWorld&MI_WEBRAWMODE=raw
REMOTE_ADDR        : environment : ro : yes : 127.0.0.1
REMOTE_HOST        : environment : ro : yes : 127.0.0.1
REQUEST_METHOD     : environment : ro : yes : GET
SCRIPT_NAME        : environment : ro : yes : /stores7-cgi/webdriver.exe
SERVER_NAME        : environment : ro : yes : dellcpi.
SERVER_PORT        : environment : ro : yes : 80
SERVER_PROTOCOL    : environment : ro : yes : HTTP/1.0
SERVER_SOFTWARE    : environment : ro : yes : Netscape-Enterprise/3.6
SERVER_URL         : environment : ro : yes : http://dellcpi
SystemRoot         : environment : ro : yes : D:\WINNT
INFORMIXDIR        : config file : ro : yes : d:\informix
INFORMIXSERVER     : config file : ro : yes : ol_dellcpi
MI_DATABASE        : config file : ro : yes : stores7
MI_USER            : config file : ro : yes : informix
MI_WEBCACHECRON    : config file : ro : yes : 2h
MI_WEBCACHEDIR     : config file : ro : yes : D:\stores7\cache
```

Figure 26-1. *RAW Mode output from the* "HelloWorld" *AppPage invocation.*

The *variable* can be a variable set by the web server, set by a cookie from the browser, or set by the webdriver configuration. This is the variable that you can use in AppPage Script, by prefixing the variable name with the "$" character.

The *source* value indicates who set the variable value. Table 26-3 lists the meaning of the variables as displayed in both Version 3 and Version 4 of webdriver under the *source* column.

The *mode* field shows the mode of the variable, which can have one of the following values:

- rw—the variable can be overriden
- ro—the variable is read only

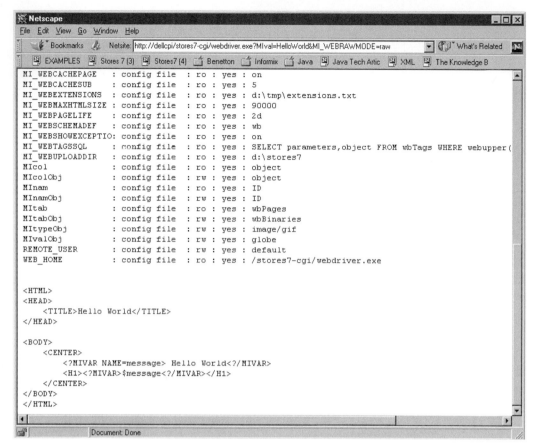

Figure 26-2. *RAW Mode output from the "HelloWorld" AppPage invocation.*

Table 26-2.	**Columns in the RAW mode trace of variables.**
Trace column	**Description**
Variable	The name of the variable.
Source	Indicates where the variable has been set.
Mode	`ro` (read only) or `rw` (read/write).
Explode	Is the variable passed to `webexplode()`? (yes or no)
Value	The current value of the variable.

Table 26-3. Source column values displayed in RAW mode.

Environment setting	Where set
config file	web.cnf
config table	webconfigs table
query string	QUERY_STRING environment variable
path info	PATH_INFO environment variable
cookie	web browser cookie
post	METHOD=POST in the calling HTML form
uri	NSAPI URL (NSAPI only)
environment	web server environment (CGI only)
rq->vars	web server environment (NSAPI only)
rq->headers	web server environment (NSAPI only)
rq->reqpb	web server environment (NSAPI only)
sn->client	web server environment (NSAPI only)
iis cblock	web server environment (ISAPI only)
iis filter	web server environment (ISAPI only)
session	session variable
driver_err	MI_DRIVER_ERROR
apache hdrs	web server environment (Apache only)
apache req	web server environment (Apache only)

The *explode* file indicates whether the variable is passed to webexplode() by webdriver.

The *value* column shows the current value of the variable.

Tracing the webexplode() Function

You can trace webexplode() activity by setting the MI_WEBEXPLEVEL and MI_WEBEXPLOG variables in the webdriver configuration. For Version 3, set the variables in web.cnf; for Version 4, set the variables using the Web DataBlade Module Administration Tool.

The `MI_WEBEXPLEVEL` variable is a setting for `webexplode()` tracing. The `MI_WEBEXPLOG` variable is the full pathname of the file to contain the trace output. For example:

```
/webapps/logs/webexplode.log
```

Version 3 Settings for `MI_WEBEXPLEVEL`

Table 26-4 lists the available settings for `MI_WEBEXPLEVEL` before Version 4 of the Web DataBlade.

Setting `MI_WEBEXPLEVEL` Correctly

To enable a feature, set `MI_WEBEXPLEVEL` to the value for that feature. If you want to enable more features, add the value for that feature to `MI_WEBEXPLEVEL`. Table 26-5 lists an example.

Table 26-4.   Version 3 settings for `MI_WEBEXPLEVEL`***.***

Setting	Feature
1	Writes trace output as comments to the HTML page.
2	Conditional information.
4	Tag attribute information.
8	Variable information.
16	Results of processing dynamic tags.
32	Logs the SQL statements executed from the `MISQL` tag.

Table 26-5.   Setting `MI_WEBEXPLEVEL`***.***

Settings	Result
32	Traces SQL queries from `MISQL`, and sends the output to `MI_WEBEXPLOG`.
33	Add 1 to 32 and you get SQL tracing sent as comments to the HTML page that is sent to the browser.
40	32 plus 8: SQL and variable information sent to `MI_WEBEXPLOG`.
41	32 plus 8 plus 1: SQL and variable information sent as HTML comments to the page that is sent to the browser.

tip

Be careful when sending output to the HTML page; you may swamp the network with your debug output! However, you may want to send output to the browser to isolate your trace information from someone else's. Tracing to MI_WEBEXPLOG *will capture all traces for all users browsing the URL prefix that maps onto the* webdriver *configuration containing the trace setting.*

Tracing webexplode—Example

Listing 26-3 shows an example AppPage, which contains a variable reference and an MISQL tag.

We set MI_WEBEXPLEVEL to 41 in the webdriver configuration. The URL we invoke is:

```
http://dellcpi/stores7-
cgi/webdriver.exe?Mival=trace&shopper=cortez
```

Listing 26-4 shows the HTML sent to the browser.

Listing 26-3. *The* trace.html *example.*

```
<html>
<body>
<h2>Hello <?mivar>$shopper<?/mivar></h2>
<?misql sql="select manu_code, manu_name from manufact">
$1,$2<br>
<?/misql>
</body>
</html>
```

Listing 26-4. *The HTML output of* trace.html *with* MI_WEBEXPLOG *set to 41.*

```
<!--- WebDebug:* START $MI_WEBEXPLEVEL : 41--->
<!--- WebDebug:set VAR:$MI_WEBEXPLEVEL=41---><!--- WebDebug:set
VAR:$MI_WEBEXPLOG=d:\stores7\cgi-bin\webexplog.log--->
<!--- WebDebug:set VAR:$MI_WEBEXTENSIONS=d:\tmp\extensions.txt--->

<html>

<html>
<body>
<h2>Hello <!--- WebDebug:?MIVAR---><!--- WebDebug:get VAR:$+ERROR
            =NULL---><!--- WebDebug:$shopper<?/mivar></h2>
```

Listing 26-4. *(continued)*

```
<?misql sql="select manu_code, manu_name from manufact">
$1,$2<br>
<?/misql>


</body>
</html>---><!--- WebDebug:get VAR:$shopper=cortez--->cortez</h2>
<!--- WebDebug:?MISQL---><!--- WebDebug:get VAR:$+ERROR=NULL--->
<!--- WebDebug:
$1,$2<br>
<?/misql>


</body>
</html>---><!--- WebDebug:set VAR:$MI_ROWCOUNT=0---><!---
WebDebug:set VAR:$MI_COLUMNCOUNT=0---><!--- WebDebug:set
VAR:$MI_SQL=select manu_code, manu_name from manufact--->
<!--- WebDebug:select manu_code, manu_name from manufact--->
<!--- WebDebug:set VAR:$MI_COLUMNCOUNT=2---><!--- WebDebug:set
VAR:$MI_CURRENTROW=1--->
SMT,Smith          <br>
<!--- WebDebug:set VAR:$MI_CURRENTROW=2--->
ANZ,Anza           <br>
<!--- WebDebug:set VAR:$MI_CURRENTROW=3--->
NRG,Norge          <br>
<!--- WebDebug:set VAR:$MI_CURRENTROW=4--->
HSK,Husky          <br>
<!--- WebDebug:set VAR:$MI_CURRENTROW=5--->
HRO,Hero           <br>
<!--- WebDebug:set VAR:$MI_CURRENTROW=6--->
SHM,Shimara        <br>
<!--- WebDebug:set VAR:$MI_CURRENTROW=7--->
KAR,Karsten        <br>
<!--- WebDebug:set VAR:$MI_CURRENTROW=8--->
NKL,Nikolus        <br>
<!--- WebDebug:set VAR:$MI_CURRENTROW=9--->
PRC,ProCycle       <br>
<!--- WebDebug:set VAR:$MI_ROWCOUNT=9--->


</body>
</html>
```

You can see that the variables passed into `webexplode()` are set as AppPage variables at the top of the listing (for clarity, most of the variable settings have been removed from the listing). The `webexplode()` function preprocesses the page (the page format is contained in comments) before generating the HTML output. Note also that you can see variables set by `webexplode()`, such as `MI_CURRENTROW`.

If we set `MI_WEBEXPLEVEL` to 33 (SQL tracing to HTML comments), then the debug output is very simple:

```
<!--- WebDebug:select manu_code, manu_name from
manufact--->
SMT,Smith          <br>
ANZ,Anza           <br>
```

and so on.

Version 4 Settings

From Version 4 of the Web DataBlade, there are more settings to play with. You have a finer level of output displayed to the HTML page or `MI_WEBEXPLOG` than in Version 3. Table 26-6 lists the granularity for displaying messages, and Table 26-7 lists the trace settings.

To set features, you add feature settings together (see the example for Version 3). For example, if you want to trace the SQL from `MISQL` tags, monitor variable access, and write the output as HTML comments, set `MI_WEBEXPLEVEL` to 73 (64 plus 8 plus 1) in the Web DataBlade Module Administration Tool.

Table 26-6. *The* `MI_WEBEXPLEVEL` *trace output granularity settings.*

Setting	Result
1	Trace output is sent to the HTML page as comments.
2	Messages are output on entry to all functions.
4	Messages are output for internal loops.

Table 26-7. *The* `MI_WEBEXPLEVEL` *trace settings.*

Setting	Feature
8	Watches variable access.
16	Traces extended variable-processing functions.
32	Usage details for user-defined tags and cache hits.
64	Shows SQL statements processed in the SQL attribute of the `MISQL` tag.
128	Messages communicated to `webdriver`.
256	Reserved.
1024	Watches the usage of `MIDEFFERED` and deferred variables.
2048	Traces direct calls to UDRs.
4096	Traces `MIEXEC`.

Tracing `webexplode`—Version 4 Example

Listing 26-5 shows the `trace.html` AppPage shown previously in List. 26-3 after it has been exploded and returned to the browser.

For production environments, you should not *set* `webexplode()` *or* `webdriver` *tracing in order to ensure that performance is optimal. If you set tracing ON, remember to housekeep the log files, since trace output is always added to the end of an existing file.*

Tracing `webdriver`

You can trace `webdriver` activity by setting variables in the `webdriver` configuration that determine the trace level and trace output file.

Version 3 Settings

The two variables that you set in `web.cnf` are as follows:

- `MI_WEBDRVLEVEL` sets the trace level.
- `MI_WEBDRVLOG` is the full pathname of the trace output file.

```
<!--- WebDebug:158      * START $MI_WEBEXPLEVEL : 73--->
<html>
<body>
<h2>Hello <!--- WebDebug:158        VAR (VarTag) enter
>$shopper<?/mivar></h2>
<?misql sql="select manu_c--->cortez<!--- WebDebug:158        VAR
(VarTag) exiting---></h2>
<!--- WebDebug:158        Sql Tag: orig:<?MISQL  sql="select manu_code,
manu_name from manufact">
$1,$2<br>
<?/misql>
</body>
</html>---><!--- WebDebug:158            Sql Tag exec :  select
manu_code, manu_name from manufact--->
SMT,Smith          <br>
ANZ,Anza           <br>
NRG,Norge          <br>
HSK,Husky          <br>
HRO,Hero           <br>
SHM,Shimara        <br>
KAR,Karsten        <br>
NKL,Nikolus        <br>
PRC,ProCycle       <br>
<!--- WebDebug:158            Sql Tag: exiting--->
</body>
</html>
```

Table 26-8 lists the available settings for the `MI_WEBDRVLEVEL` variable.

Version 4 Settings

You set the following variables either in the `global` section of `web.cnf`, or in the configuration for our mapping, using the Web DataBlade Module Administration Tool.

- `debug_level`: `webdriver` **trace setting** (was `MI_WEBDRVLEVEL`)
- `debug_file`: `webdriver` **trace output file** (was `MI_WEBDRVLOG`)

Table 26-8. *The* MI_WEBDRVLEVEL webdriver *tracing settings.*

Trace value	*Feature*
1	Logs name/value pairs passed from the browser to the web server as pblocks (NSAPI only).
2	Logs callbacks from the database server.
4	Logs webdriver query requests to the database server, such as calls to the webexplode() function or authorization requests.
8	Logs large object requests.
16	Logs AppPage headers.
32	Logs large object headers.
64	Logs client file upload information.
128	Reserved.
256	Logs session variables.
512	Logs information similar to NSAPI (CGI only).
1024	Logs connection pool information.

Table 26-9 lists the available settings for the debug_level variable.

These settings are additive; to set multiple features, add the feature settings together and set debug_level to that value.

See the subsection, "Monitoring the Connection Pool for the NSAPI webdriver" earlier in this chapter for a practical example of using webdriver tracing.

Checking AppPage Script with WebLint

The WebLint() function is a Web DataBlade utility you can use to find syntax errors within AppPage tags.

You set a checking level for WebLint, which alters the error-reporting behavior of the utility. You then nominate one or more AppPages to pass through the WebLint() function. These AppPages are validated against the checking level set for WebLint.

You can still invoke AppPages if the AppPage contains syntax errors. A syntax error may result in a runtime *error when the tag that contains the error is processed by the* webexplode() *function.*

Table 26-9. *The* `debug_level` `webdriver` *tracing settings.*

Trace value	Feature
1	Logs name/value pairs passed from the browser to the web server as `pblocks` (NSAPI only).
2	Logs callbacks from the database server.
4	Logs `webdriver` query requests to the database server, such as calls to the `webexplode()` function or authorization requests.
8	Logs large object requests.
16	Logs AppPage headers.
32	Logs large object headers.
64	Logs client file upload information.
128	Logs information as AppPages are added and retrieved from the AppPage cache.
256	Logs request variables.
512	Logs information similar to NSAPI (CGI only).
1024	Logs connection pool information.
2048	Logs `session` management information.
4096	Logs parameters to `webexplode()` in decoded format.
8192	Logs parameters to `webexplode()` in encoded format.
16384	Timestamps each request of `webdriver`.

`WebLint` Syntax-checking Levels

The `WebLint()` function performs checks at the levels shown in Table 26-10.

Table 26-10. *The* `WebLint` *syntax-checking levels.*

Level	Description
0	Returns *pass* or *fail*. Checking stops as soon as an error is encountered.
1	Returns *pass* or *error text,* which describes the first error encountered.
2	Returns *pass* or *error text* for every error encountered.
3	Same processing as level 2, with additional checks on variables; a warning is issued if a value is not assigned to a variable within the AppPage.

Invoking the `WebLint` Function

You can invoke the `WebLint` utility in a number of ways.

- using AppPage Builder,
- using Data Director for Web,
- as an SQL function,
- from the command line.

Using `WebLint` with AppPage Builder

You can set the level of `WebLint` checking, called `WebLint` parsing, in AppPage Builder from the Edit User screen, which is accessed from the Admin Menu or from the Administration footer of an AppPage Builder page.

When you add or edit an AppPage, `WebLint` checking will be applied in accordance with the user preference you have set. The `WebLint` output is written to a textarea at the foot of the Add or Edit AppPage screen.

Using `WebLint` with Data Director for Web

You invoke `WebLint` from AppPage Editor. The advantage of using `WebLint` from AppPage Editor is that you can click on an error reported by `WebLint`, and it will take you to that point in the AppPage source so that you can correct it.

To invoke `WebLint()` from AppPage Editor, perform the following:

- select `Tools/Syntax Check(WebLint)` from the AppPage Editor Menu
- select the checking level from the list of radio buttons
- click the `Execute WebLint` button.

Figure 26-3 shows an example.

Using `WebLint` in an SQL Statement

You can invoke the `WebLint()` function in an SQL expression. When you call `WebLint()` in this way, you need to pass two arguments to the `WebLint()` function:

- an HTML object, or a string that will cast to an HTML object;
- the checking level.

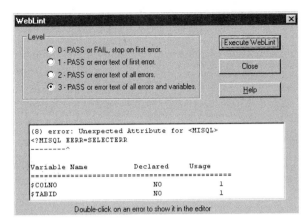

Figure 26-3. *Running* `WebLint` *in AppPage Editor.*

For example,

```
select ID, WebLint(object,3) from wbPages
```

The `WebLint` *utility does not evaluate dynamic tags within the AppPage. You can perform a degree of syntax checking on dynamic tags by checking the object column in the table that stores dynamic tags; for example:* `select WebLint(object,3) from wbTags`.

Invoking `WebLint` from the Command Line

A utility *program* called `WebLint` is provided with the Web DataBlade and you call this program from the command line. The utility is installed in the `$INFORMIXDIR/extend/web*/utils` directory, where `web*` is the version of the Web DataBlade you have installed.

To use `WebLint` from the command line, change to the `utils` directory or set the `utils` directory into the `PATH` environment variable and enter the following command:

```
WebLint <level> < <AppPage source>
```

For example:

```
WebLint 3 < sample.html
cat sample.html | WebLint 3
type sample.html | WebLint 3
```

The `WebLint` utility will write the results to standard output, which you can redirect to a file for convenience.

Summary

This chapter has shown how to debug Web DataBlade applications in a development context, as well as how to troubleshoot live system problems in an end-to-end context. We have learned how to run `webdriver` interactively, check the web server configuration, use RAW mode to list variables available to `webdriver` and `webexplode()`, and how to trace `webexplode()` and `webdriver` activity. In summary, we have a checklist that can be used by developers as problems arise when building, deploying, and supporting a Web DataBlade application.

Appendix

A

Variable Mappings

This Appendix lists the `webdriver` variables whose names have changed between Versions 3 and 4 of the Web DataBlade. The aim of this list is to help you use a variable name from Version 3 and map it onto the equivalent from Version 4, or vice versa.

Version 3 variable	Version 4 equivalent
MI_WEBACCEPTCKI	accept_cookie
MI_WEBAUTHCACHE	auth_cache
MI_WEBCACHEADMIN	cache_admin
MI_WEBCACHEPASSWORD	cache_admin_password
MI_WEBCACHESUB	cache_buckets
MI_WEBCACHEDIR	cache_directory
MI_WEBCACHEMAXLO	cache_maxsize
MI_WEBCACHEPAGE	cache_page
MI_WEBPAGELIFE	cache_page_life
MI_USER_REMOTE	connect_as_user
MI_USER_DBCONNMAX	connect_user_max
MI_WEBRECONNECT	connection_life
MI_WEBDBCONNWAIT	connection_wait
MI_WEBDRVLEVEL	debug_level
MI_WEBDRVLOG	debug_file
MI_WEBERRORPAGE	error_page
MI_WEBERRORGLSPOST	error_gls_post
MI_WEBEXTENSIONS	extensions
MI_WEBNTPASSWORD	iis_nt_password
MI_WEBNTUSER	iis_nt_user
MI_WEBINITIALSQL	init_sql
MI_WEBKEEPALIVE	keepalive
MI_WEBLOBUFSIZE	lo_buffer_size
MI_WEBLOSQLERROR	lo_error_sql
MI_WEBLOZEROROWS	lo_error_zerorows
MI_WEBLOPARAMS	lo_query_params
MI_WEBLOQUERY	lo_query
MI_WEBMAXHTMLSIZE	max_html_size
MI_WEBSSITMPDIR	parse_html_directory
MI_WEBQUERYTIMEOUT	query_timeout
MI_WEBREDIRECT	redirect_url
MI_WEBRAWPASSWORD	raw_password
MI_WEBSCHEMADEF	schema_version
MI_WEBSESSION	session
MI_WEBSESSIONSUB	session_buckets
MI_WEBSESSIONHOME	session_home
MI_WEBSESSIONLIFE	session_life
MI_WEBSESSIONLOC	session_location
MI_WEBSHOWEXCEPTIONS	show_exceptions
MI_WEBUPLOADDIR	upload_directory

B

The **webdriver** Variables

This Appendix lists webdriver variables according to function:

- Retrieving AppPages (schema-related webdriver variables)
- Data Director for Web specific
- Enabling NSAPI, ISAPI, and Apache security
- Enabling basic AppPage-level security
- Enabling AppPage caching
- Enabling Large Object caching
- Interrupting queries
- Enabling webdriver tracing
- Enabling webexplode() tracing
- Defining the SQL environment
- Retrieving large objects by name
- Retrieving large objects by query string
- Retrieving large objects by LO handle
- Enabling Use of Session Variables in AppPages
- Handling errors with the MI_DRIVER_ERROR variable
- Uploading client files

- Passing image map coordinates
- Using RAW mode with `webdriver`
- Web Server Variables Available with NSAPI, ISAPI, and Apache API
- Managing connections
- Customizing `webexplode()`

This appendix describes the `webdriver` variables that you can set for a `webdriver` configuration. If you are using Version 4 of the Web DataBlade, you can use the Web DataBlade Module Administration Tool to set the variables as part of a *configuration*. If you are using Version 3 of the Web DataBlade, you can set the Version 3 equivalents manually in the `web.cnf` file. Both schema-and feature-related variables are included in this appendix. To map a Version 4 variable onto an existing Version 3 equivalent, see *Appendix A*.

Retrieving AppPages
(Schema-related `webdriver` Variables)

The following table describes the schema-related `webdriver` variables; you must set all of these variables when you create a `webdriver` configuration that is not based on Data Director for Web.

Variable	Mandatory?	Content
MItab	Yes	Specifies the name of the database table in which the AppPages for the web application are stored. For the AppPage Builder (APB) application, the value of this variable is "webPages."
MIcol	Yes	Specifies the name of the HTML column that contains the AppPage in the web application table. For the AppPage Builder (APB) application, the value of this variable is "object."
MInam	Yes	Specifies the name of the VARCHAR column that identifies the appropriate row of the web application table. For the AppPage Builder (APB) application, the value of this variable is "ID."
MIval	Yes	Specifies the value to check against the MInam column to identify the row you want to retrieve in the web application table. To bring up the AppPage Builder (APB) application, set this variable to the value "apb."

Data Director for Web Specific

The following table describes the `webdriver` variables used with the Data Director for Web schema.

Variable	Mandatory?	Content
schema_version	Yes	When set to "wb," specifies that the Data Director for Web schema should be used when building `webexplode()` queries.
MI_WEBTAGSSQL	Yes	Defines the table in which the dynamic tags are stored.
extensions	No	Used when the `schema_version` variable has been set to "wb" to use the Data Director for Web schema. This variable stores the name of a file on the file-system to store the results of an extension query, which is a query to find out information regarding which tables to extract data from depending on a file extension. The value of this variable should be set to "nocache" during application development when the DDW schema is being modified. The NSAPI, ISAPI, and Apache `webdrivers` are capable of caching this file. The CGI `webdriver` has to get physical file-cached data from the specified file.

Enabling NSAPI, ISAPI, and Apache Security

To use the security features of the Netscape web server, Microsoft Internet Information Server, or Apache Web Server, set the `webdriver` variables listed in the following table.

Variable	Mandatory?	Content
MIusertable	Yes	Name of the table that contains user access information. For the AppPage Builder (APB) application, the value of this variable is "webUsers," for example.
MIusername	Yes	Name of the VARCHAR column in the user access table (MIusertable) that contains the name of the database user. For the AppPage Builder (APB) application, the value of this variable is "name."

Variable	Mandatory?	Content
MIuserpasswd	Yes	Name of the VARCHAR column of the user access table (MIusertable) that contains the password of the database user. For the AppPage Builder (APB) application, the value of this variable is "password."
MIuserlevel	Yes	Name of the INTEGER column of the user access table (MIusertable) that contains the access level of the database user. For the AppPage Builder (APB) application, the value of this variable is "security_level."
MIpagelevel	Yes	Name of the INTEGER column of the AppPage table (MItab) that contains the access level of the AppPage. For the AppPage Builder (APB) application, the value of this variable is "read_level."
MIusergroup	No	Name of the INTEGER column of the user access table (MIusertable) that contains the group access level of the user. If this variable is set, the value of the group-level access of the user is passed via the variable MI_WEBGROUPLEVEL to the webexplode() function.
redirect_url	No	URL to redirect users to if they do not have access to the AppPage they attempt to retrieve.
auth_cache	No	Determines whether caching of the name/ password pairs in webdriver should be enabled. By default, caching of name/password pairs is always enabled. The check mode retests the password value when access fails because, for example, the password has changed.
iis_nt_user	Yes	Specifies the dummy account used to authenticate against when using a Microsoft Internet Information Server for authentication. A dummy account is required unless a real user account exists on the system.
iis_nt_password	Yes	Password of a valid Windows NT user. When using authentication against a Microsoft Internet Information Server (IIS), you must authenticate against a dummy account unless a real user account exists on the system. The "iis_nt_user" user refers to this dummy account.

Enabling Basic AppPage-level Security

To configure AppPage-level authorization, set the `webdriver` variables listed in the following table.

Variable	Mandatory?	Description
MIpagelevel	Yes	Specifies the name of the INTEGER column of the AppPage table (MItab) that contains the access level of the AppPage.
MI_WEBACCESSLEVEL	Yes	Specifies the access level of all users for a particular `webdriver` configuration. Contains the value of the MIuserlevel column in the MIusertable table for this user.
redirect_url	No	Specifies the URL to redirect users to if they do not have access to the AppPage they attempt to retrieve.

Enabling AppPage Caching

To set AppPage caching for your `webdriver` configuration, set the `webdriver` variables listed in the following table.

Variable	Mandatory?	Description
cache_page	Yes	Specifies whether AppPage caching is enabled or disabled. Set to ON to enable AppPage caching and OFF to disable AppPage caching. The default value is OFF.
cache_directory	Yes	Specifies the full pathname of the directory on the web server computer in which cached AppPages and large objects are placed. If this variable is not set, neither AppPages nor large objects are cached.
cache_page_buckets	No	Specifies the number of subdirectories per AppPage created under the directory specified by `cache_directory`. The default is one subdirectory per AppPage. Set this variable only if you intend on caching AppPages that might have over 1000 different versions.

cache_page_life	No	Specifies the length of time after which an AppPage is refreshed from the database. Set cache_page_life in units of seconds (s or S), hours (h or H), or days (d or D). For example, the value "5d" indicates five days.
cache_admin	No	Specifies the name of the cache administration AppPage. When MIval is set to this value, webdriver invokes this AppPage so you can add, delete, purge, or view cache entries in the cache_directory directory. The default value is cacheadmin.
cache_page_debug	No	When set to ON, enables AppPage cache debugging; default value is OFF. When enabled, allows the partial page cache mechanism to work without a cache entry— thus the developer may see the output instead of an error message.
cache_admin_password	No	Specifies that cache administration requests are processed only if the password entered in the cache administration AppPage matches this value.

Enabling Large Object Caching

To set large object caching, set the webdriver variables listed in the following table.

Variable	Mandatory?	Description
cache_directory	Yes	Specifies the directory on the Web server computer in which cached large objects are placed. If not set, large objects are not cached.
cache_buckets	No	Specifies the number of subdirectories per database created under the directory specified by cache_directory. The default is one subdirectory per database.
cache_maxsize	No	Specifies the maximum size in bytes of large objects to be cached. The default is 64 KB.

Interrupting Queries

The `webdriver` variables in the following table are used to control when a query sent from `webdriver` to Informix Dynamic Server should be interrupted.

Variable	Mandatory?	Description
`query_timeout`	Yes	Specifies the number of seconds for a query to be completed before it is interrupted.
`keepalive`	Yes	Specifies the interval in seconds at which `webdriver` checks the web browser connection. If the browser is no longer connected because a STOP or CANCEL signal has been sent by the browser, the running query is interrupted, and the web server is freed to execute the next query request. This variable applies only to the NSAPI, ISAPI, and Apache implementations of `webdriver`.

Enabling `webdriver` Tracing

The following table describes each variable for enabling `webdriver` tracing.

Variable	Description
`debug_level`	Enables `webdriver` tracing to the log file specified by the `debug_file` variable.
`debug_file`	Specifies the full pathname of the log file to which `webdriver` messages are written.

Enabling `webexplode()` Tracing

The following table describes each variable for enabling `webexplode()` tracing.

Variable	Description
MI_WEBEXPLEVEL	This `INTEGER` variable is used to turn on `webexplode()` tracing.
MI_WEBEXPLOG	When `webexplode()` tracing is enabled, the information is written to the trace file specified by the `MI_WEBEXPLOG` variable. If `MI_WEBEXPLOG` is not set, the server creates a file in the `/tmp` directory with a `.trc` file extension.

Defining the SQL Environment

The following table describes the variable you can set to customize the SQL environment for your queries.

Variable	Description
init_sql	Specifies the SQL statements that should be executed the first time a connection is made to a database. For example, this variable could be used to change the default locking strategy by using the `SET ISOLATION` SQL command.

Retrieving Large Objects by Name

You can use `webdriver` to retrieve a large object from a table in the database by specifying the `webdriver` variables that uniquely identify the object. The following table lists the `webdriver` variables used to identify a large object.

Variable	Mandatory?	Content
MItabObj	Yes	Name of the database table in which web application large objects are stored.
MicolObj	Yes	Name of the `BLOB` column that contains large objects in the table specified by the `MItabObj` variable. For the AppPage Builder (APB) application, the value of this variable is "`object`."
MInamObj	Yes	Name of the `VARCHAR` column that identifies the appropriate row of the table specified by the `MItabObj` variable. For the AppPage Page Builder (APB) application, the value of this variable is "`ID`."
MIvalObj	Yes	Value to check against the column specified by the `MInamObj` variable to identify the row you want to retrieve in the table specified by the `MItabObj` table.
MItypeObj	Yes	MIME type and subtype used to export the large object.

Retrieving Large Objects by Query String

To tailor the query constructed by `webdriver` to a specific need, use the Web DataBlade Module Administration Tool to set the following `webdriver` variables.

Variable	Mandatory?	Content
lo_query_string	Yes	Contains the SQL statement that is used to query the database for a large object.
lo_query_params	Yes	Specifies the variables that are substituted for the parameters in the SQL statement specified by the lo_query_string variable.
lo_error_zerorows	Yes	Specifies the integer error number if the SQL statement used to retrieve large objects, specified by the lo_query_string variable, returned zero rows.
lo_error_sql	Yes	Specifies the integer error number that should be returned if an SQL error occurs when you retrieve a large object using the SQL statement specified by the lo_query_string variable.

Retrieving Large Objects by LO Handle

You can retrieve large objects by large object handle (LO handle) when you dynamically retrieve the results of a SELECT statement. Set the following webdriver variables to specify LO handles and their output MIME type.

Variable	Mandatory?	Content
LO	Yes	Large object handle.
MItypeObj	Yes	MIME type and subtype used to export the large object.
lo_buffer_size	No	This variable sets the buffer size in which large object requests are serviced. By default, this buffer size is 8 KB.

Enabling Use of Session Variables in AppPages

To enable the use of session variables in your AppPages use the Web DataBlade Module Administration Tool to set the following `webdriver` variables.

Variable	Description
session	Enables the `session` variable feature. When enabled, a session ID is bound to the browser so that `session` variables, or those that are prefixed with "`session`" in an AppPage, persist for the entire user session. This variable allows you to select the method for binding a session ID to the browser. This variable can have values of "`url`," "`cookie`," or "`auto`." If set to "`url`," then the Session ID is bound to any dynamic anchor variable contained within the page. Typically, this variable would be `$WEB_HOME`. If set to "`cookie`," the session ID is tracked with a variable sent back to the browser as a cookie. If you select "`auto`," webdriver automatically determines which method is best to use.
session_home	This variable identifies which configuration file variable is used by your application to anchor `HREF` tags. For example, if your application uses `WEB_HOME` as its anchor, "`WEB_HOME`" is the value set for this variable. If multiple values are required for this variable, commas should separate them.
session_location	This variable describes how the persistent state is handled. If the session code is going to run within the same process, this variable needs to refer to the full path of the directory to create session state files. If the code is going to run as a separate process, the variable needs to refer to a port and IP-address in the form: `port@ip-address`.
session_buckets	This variable is used to define the number of subdirectories that are available to hash the session data if the site is exceptionally large. It is only required if session management is being controlled within the same process. The default is 100.

Variable	Description
session_life	This variable is used to define the amount of time a session is allowed to continue. It measures time from the last update to the session stack (if a session stack exists) or time from session creation. Granularity is in seconds (default), hours (h) or days (d), and uses the same syntax as cache_page_life.
config.compatibility	To use session management set this variable to 0; this allows "." to become a legal Web DataBlade variable character, thus allowing variables like $session.var. Set this variable to 1 to disable this feature and revert to the old behavior.

Handling Errors with the MI_DRIVER_ERROR Variable

Set the following webdriver variables with the Web DataBlade Module Administration Tool to modify the error messages seen by the browser as different types of errors are encountered.

Variable	Mandatory?	Content
show_exceptions	No	Set to ON or OFF. When on, webdriver displays the database exception returned by web-explode(). When off, webdriver displays the HTTP/1.0 500 Server error message. Default is OFF.
redirect_url	No	Set to the URL to redirect users to if they do not have access to the AppPage they attempt to retrieve.
error_page	No	Set to the value of the AppPage that contains error-handling routines. You can define a single error_page AppPage in an application to handle all MI_DRIVER_ERROR errors.

Uploading Client Files

Use the Web DataBlade Module Administration Tool to set the following `webdriver` variables to upload client files.

Variable	Mandatory?	Content
upload_directory	No	Directory on the Web server machine in which uploaded files are placed. Default is "`/tmp.`"
remove_upload_file	No	When this variable is set to FALSE, the intermediate file created during a file upload is not removed. This feature can be used to debug failures during client file upload.

Passing Image Map Coordinates

Set the `MImap` variable to enable image map coordinates to be passed to AppPages.

Variable	Mandatory?	Content
MImap	Yes	Set to ON or OFF. When on, the URL is treated as an image map, and the values are passed as x- and y-coordinates. Default is OFF.

Using RAW Mode with `webdriver`

To enable RAW mode, set the following `webdriver` configuration file variable.

Variable	Mandatory?	Content
`raw_password`	Yes	Password to enable RAW mode.

Web Server Variables Available to the API `webdriver`

Only the following web server variables are available with the NSAPI, ISAPI, and Apache API versions of `webdriver`. If you want to see the full list of variables available to your AppPages, use `MI_WEBRAWMODE` in the URL to list all the available variables (from any source). See Chap. 26, "Debugging Web DataBlade Applications," for information on how to do this.

- `AUTH_TYPE`
- `HTTP_USER_AGENT`
- `HTTP_REFERER`
- `HTTP_HOST`
- `HTTP_URI`
- `REMOTE_ADDR`
- `REQUEST_METHOD`
- `SERVER_PROTOCOL`
- `QUERY_STRING`
- `REMOTE_USER`
- `MI_WEBACCESSLEVEL`
- `MI_WEBGROUPLEVEL`

The CGI `webdriver` passes every variable gathered from the web server environment. These environment variables are specific to the web server used.

Managing Connections

Set these variables to manage `webdriver` connection to the database:

Variable	Mandatory?	Content
connect_as_user	No	When set to ON, all database requests connect as the REMOTE_USER user instead of the user defined in the web.cnf file for your webdriver mapping. In order to make use of this feature, webdriver authentication must be enabled.
connection_life	No	Maximum number of requests for the connection to the database before the connection is dropped and recreated. The default value is 100.
connection_wait	No	If the connection pool is swamped, i.e., all database connections are active, the thread yields and tries to gain a connection at a later time. This variable stores an INTEGER value that sets this wait time in milliseconds.
connect_user_max	No	When used in conjunction with the connect_as_user variable, this variable increases the number of *user* connections allowed to the value of the variable. The default value of this variable is 1.

Customizing webexplode() and webdriver

You can set these variables to work with webexplode() and the results of webexplode().

Variable	Description
MIdatatype	This variable changes the way the query that calls the webexplode() function is built by casting the column that contains the AppPages (usually MIcol) to the variable's value. By default, the datatype of the MIcol column is HTML and the standard webexplode() function assumes its first parameter is of data type HTML. By setting this variable to the name of a different datatype, you can create your own webexplode() function that expects its first parameter to be of the new datatype, and you can rely on the database server's datatype matching feature (polymorphism) to select the correct webexplode() function.
auth_crypt_udr	The name of a user-defined routine that defines a user-defined encryption program that allows the user to store encrypted passwords rather than text.
error_gls_post	This variable specifies the URL to redirect users to if they have sent an illegal character in a POST (if set to a numeric value, it will just return that as a status).
max_html_size	This variable specifies the size in bytes of the maximum returned buffer size from the webexplode() function. For example, 100,000.

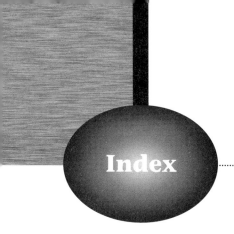

Index

Forms *(continued)*
   `mailto` URL, sending form data with, 586
   managing large objects in Java, 221–42
   navigating web sites with, 522
   passing SQL queries as form data, 744–46
   properties of. *See* `FORM` tag
   `RADIO` form field, 589–90
   `RESET` form field, 590
   reusing with dynamic tags, 670
   screen navigation using JavaScript, 777–79
   searching and drill-down, 535
   `SELECT` form field, 590–91
   `SELECTED` option, setting dynamically, 761
   server-side validation, 605
     using AppPage Script, 610–15
   setting default with `MIVAR` tag, 486
   `SUBMIT` element, 591–92
   `TEXT` form field, 592
   `TEXTAREA` form field, 592–93
   types of form field, 587–88
   uploading client files, 634–39
   using Data Windows, example, 750–59
   validating form data, 604–15
   validating text fields, 606–8
   Web DataBlade processing, 593–95
   `webdriver` URL and, 594
   wrap attributes, `TEXTAREA` form field, 593
Fragmentation
   expression-based, 897
   index fragmentation, 897
Frames, example using `DBrowser.html`, 617
`FROM` attribute, `MIBLOCK` tag, 488
FTP (File Transfer Protocol), 25, 644
`FUNCTION` attribute, `MIFUNC` tag, 493
Functional prototyping, 384

G

Generic error handling using dynamic tags, 710–12
`GET` operation, `FORM` tag, 585
`getAsciiStream` method, 220
`getBinaryStream` method, 220
`getBytes` method, 220
`getCatalogs` method, 330
`getConnection` method, 175
`getParameter` method, 264
   and the PARAM attribute, 265
   extracting parameters, 270
`getSchemas` method, 330
`getTableTypes` method, 330

Global Market, 890
Global section, `web.cnf`, 792
Global Village, 890

H

`hasMoreElements` method, 331
Header dynamic tag listing, 438, 780
`HelloCatalog.html` listing, 814
`HelloFramesWorld.html` listing, 66–67
`HelloJSWorld.html` listing, 60–61
`HelloPopupWorld.html` listing, 65
`HelloTime.html` listing, 63
HelloWorld example, AppPage, 468–80
`HelloWorld.html`, 933
`HelloWorld1.html` listing, 471–74
   exploded, 475–78
`hiddenSQL.html` listing, 104–5
Hit counters, 707–10
`home.html` listing, 443
HTML (Hyper Text Markup Language), 17, 24, 26, 32, 33
   adding SQL to web enable installed applications, 31
   and first-generation web sites, 17
   content searching, 23
   datatype, 26, 44
     casting to `LVARCHAR`, 320
   as a document type extension, 40
   programing context, 25
   searching HTML pages using JavaScript, 111–15
   static content, 19
HTML and URL related functions, AppPage Script, 517–19
HTML datatype
   memory management of, 370–71
   storage of, 370
   use in Web DataBlade, 370–71
HTTP (Hyper Text Transfer Protocol), 26, 40, 893
   definition, 40
   HTTP Headers, 639
   requests, 892, 893
   state, persistence of, 19
   tracing applet requests, 261–62
   tracing HTTP output with `webdriver`, 640
HTTP headers, 639
`HTTP_HOST` variable, 472, 974
`HTTP_REFERER` variable, 974
`HTTP_URL` variable, 974
`HTTP_USER_AGENT` variable, 474, 974
`HTTPHEADER` variable processing function, 518
   changing content types dynamically with, 639–42
   cookies, setting, 519

creating cariables in AppPages, 497
HTTP headers defined, 639
`httpHeaderForm.html` listing, 641–42
Hyperlinks, navigating with, 522

I

`IF`, variable processing function, 507
`ifx_allow_newline` procedure, 371
`IFX_AUTOFREE` environment variable
   configuring for the Statement object, 247
   definition, 190
`ifxjdbc.jar`, 167, 168, 169, 175, 176
`ifxjdbc-g.jar`. *See* JAR files
`IfxStatement`
   used with `SERIAL` and `SERIAL8`, 193
`iis_nt_password` variable, 849, 964
`iis_nt_user` variable, 849, 964
Illustra Technologies, 25
Image(s)
   gif, 45
   jpeg, 45
Image map coordinates, `webdriver` variables, 973
`IMG` tag, used with `wbImg` dynamic tag, 688
Importing and exporting content, 395–96
In-built Method, JavaScript, 74
`INDEX` attribute, `MIBLOCK` tag, 488
`INDEX`, variable processing function, 511
Informix client/server connectivity, 170. *See also* Informix SQLI protocol
   and ESQL/C, 170
   and JDBC, 170
   and ODBC, 170
Informix Dynamic Server
   Informix Dynamic Server.2000, 26, 27, 41–44, 47, 49
     web and OLTP context, 27
   Universal Data Option, 41, 42, 47
   overview, 44
   web integration products, 44
Informix Internet Foundation.2000, 27
Informix JDBC Type 4 driver, 164–65. *See also* JDBC data types
   advantages, 164
   debugging, 242–45
     tracing protocol messages, 243–44
   environment variables, 189–91
   large objects, working with, 218–20
     client storage, 220
     columns used, 218–19
     inserting and updating, 218–19
     memory configuration, 220
     retrieving, 219–20

X

PRENTICE HALL PTR
TOMORROW'S
Solutions FOR TODAY'S
Professionals.

INFORMIX GUIDE TO DESIGNING DATABASES AND DATA WAREHOUSES

INFORMIX SOFTWARE

The Informix insider's guide to database and data warehouse design.

- Provides detailed data models that illustrate each key approach to database design.
- Proven, step-by-step techniques for building your Informix-based data warehouse.

©2000, 360pgs, Paper, 0-13-016167-5

INFORMIX GUIDE TO SQL:
Reference & Syntax, Second Edition

INFORMIX SOFTWARE

The indispensable, authoritative reference to Informix SQL — fully revised for Version 8.2.

- Now includes a detailed syntax section with descriptions of all Informix SQL and SPL statements.
- Features detailed, step-by-step diagrams and a comprehensive glossary.

©2000, 900pp., Paper, 0-13-016166-7

INFORMIX GUIDE TO SQL:
Tutorial, Second Edition

INFORMIX SOFTWARE

The complete guide to mastering Informix SQL—updated for the new Version 8.2.

- Learn key SQL concepts and terms—from the basics to advanced techniques.
- Master the Informix Data Manipulation Language.

©2000, 375pp., Paper, 0-13-016165-9

VISIT US AT: WWW.PHPTR.COM OR WWW.INFORMIX.COM/IPRESS

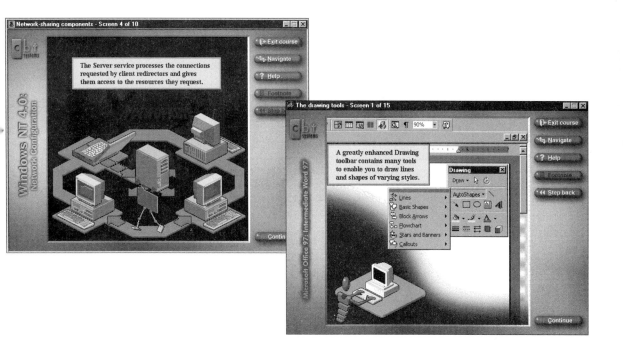

Other curricula available from CBT Systems:

- Cisco
- Informix
- Java
- Marimba
- Microsoft
- Netscape
- Novell

- Oracle
- SAP
- Sybase
- C/C++
- Centura
- Information Technology/
  Core Concepts

- Internet and Intranet
  Skills
- Internetworking
- UNIX

To order additional CBT Systems courseware today call 800.789.8590 or visit www.clbooks.com/training/cbt.htm

CBT SOFTWARE LICENSE AGREEMENT

**IF YOU DO NOT AGREE WITH THESE TERMS AND CONDITIONS,
DO NOT INSTALL THE SOFTWARE.**

This is a legal agreement you and CBT System Ltd. ("Licensor"). The licensor ("Licensor") from whom you have licensed the CBT Group PLC courseware (the "Software"). By installing, copying or otherwise using the Software, you agree to be bound by the terms of this Agreement License Agreement (the "License"). If you do not agree to the terms of this License, the Licensor is unwilling to license the Software to you. In such event, you may not use or copy the Software, and you should promptly contact the Licensor for instructions on the return of the unused Software.

1. **Use.** Licensor grants to you a non-exclusive, nontransferable license to use Licensor's software product (the "Software") the Software and accompanying documentation in accordance with the terms and conditions of this license agreement ("License") License and as specified in your agreement with Licensor (the "Governing Agreement"). In the event of any conflict between this License and the Governing Agreement, the Governing Agreement shall control.

You may:

a. (if specified as a "personal use" version) install the Software on a single stand-alone computer or a single network node from which node the Software cannot be accessed by another computer, provided that such Software shall be used by only one individual; <u>or</u>

b. (if specified as a "workstation" version) install the Software on a single stand-alone computer or a single network node from which node the Software cannot be accessed by another computer, provided that such Software shall be used by only one individual; <u>or</u>

c. (if specified as a "LAN" version) install the Software on a local area network server that provides access to multiple computers, up to the maximum number of computers or users specified in your Governing Agreement, provided that such Software shall be used only by employees of your organization; <u>or</u>

d. (if specified as an "enterprise" version) install the Software or copies of the Software on multiple local or wide area network servers, intranet servers, stand-alone computers and network nodes (and to make copies of the Software for such purpose) at one or more sites, which servers provide access to a multiple number of users, up to the maximum number of users specified in your Governing Agreement, provided that such Software shall be used only by employees of your organization.

<u>This License is not a sale. Title and copyrights to the Software, accompanying documentation and any copy made by you remain with Licensor or its suppliers or licensors.</u>

2. **Intellectual Property**. The Software is owned by Licensor or its licensors and is protected by United States and other jurisdictions' copyright laws and international treaty provisions. Therefore, you may not use, copy, or distribute the Software without the express written authorization of CBT Group PLC. This License authorizes you to use the Software for the internal training needs of your employees only, and to make one copy of the Software solely for backup or archival purposes. You may not print copies of any user documentation provided in "online" or electronic form. Licensor retains all rights not expressly granted.

3. **Restrictions**. You may not transfer, rent, lease, loan or time-share the Software or accompanying documentation. You may not reverse engineer, decompile, or disassemble the Software, except to the extent the foregoing restriction is expressly prohibited by applicable law. You may not modify, or create derivative works based upon the Software in whole or in part.

1. **Confidentiality**. The Software contains confidential trade secret information belonging to Licensor, and you may use the software only pursuant to the terms of your Governing Agreement, if any, and the license set forth herein. In addition, you may not disclose the Software to any third party.

2. **Limited Liability**. IN NO EVENT WILL THE Licensor's LIABILITY UNDER, ARISING OUT OF OR RELATING TO THIS AGREEMENT EXCEED THE AMOUNT PAID TO LICENSOR FOR THE SOFTWARE. LICENSOR SHALL NOT BE LIABLE FOR ANY SPECIAL, INCIDENTAL, INDIRECT OR CONSEQUENTIAL DAMAGES, HOWEVER CAUSED AND ON ANY THEORY OF LIABILITY., REGARDLESS OR WHETHER LICENSOR HAS BEEN ADVISED OF THE POSSIBILITY OF SUCH DAMAGES. WITHOUT LIMITING THE FOREGOING, LICENSOR WILL NOT BE LIABLE FOR LOST PROFITS, LOSS OF DATA, OR COSTS OF COVER.

3. **Limited Warranty**. LICENSOR WARRANTS THAT SOFTWARE WILL BE FREE FROM DEFECTS IN MATERIALS AND WORKMANSHIP UNDER NORMAL USE FOR A PERIOD OF THIRTY (30) DAYS FROM THE DATE OF RECEIPT. THIS LIMITED WARRANTY IS VOID IF FAILURE OF THE SOFTWARE HAS RESULTED FROM ABUSE OR MISAPPLICATION. ANY REPLACEMENT SOFTWARE WILL BE WARRANTED FOR A PERIOD OF THIRTY (30) DAYS FROM THE DATE OF RECEIPT OF SUCH REPLACEMENT SOFTWARE. THE SOFTWARE AND DOCUMENTATION ARE PROVIDED "AS IS". LICENSOR HEREBY DISCLAIMS ALL OTHER WARRANTIES, EXPRESS, IMPLIED, OR STATUTORY, INCLUDING WITHOUT LIMITATION, THE IMPLIED WARRANTIES OF MERCHANTABILITY AND FITNESS FOR A PARTICULAR PURPOSE.

4. **Exceptions**. SOME STATES DO NOT ALLOW THE LIMITATION OF INCIDENTAL DAMAGES OR LIMITATIONS ON HOW LONG AN IMPLIED WARRANTY LASTS, SO THE ABOVE LIMITATIONS OR EXCLUSIONS MAY NOT APPLY TO YOU. This agreement gives you specific legal rights, and you may also have other rights which vary from state to state.

5. **U.S. Government-Restricted Rights**. The Software and accompanying documentation are deemed to be "commercial computer Software" and "commercial computer Software documentation," respectively, pursuant to FAR Section 227.7202 and FAR Section 12.212, as applicable. Any use, modification, reproduction release, performance, display or disclosure of the Software and accompanying documentation by the U.S. Government shall be governed solely by the terms of this Agreement and shall be prohibited except to the extent expressly permitted by the terms of this Agreement.

6. **Export Restrictions**. You may not download, export, or re-export the Software (a) into, or to a national or resident of, Cuba, Iraq, Libya, Yugoslavia, North Korea, Iran, Syria or any other country to which the United States has embargoed goods, or (b) to anyone on the United States Treasury Department's list of Specially Designated Nations or the U.S. Commerce Department's Table of Deny Orders. By installing or using the Software, you are representing and warranting that you are not located in, under the control of, or a national resident of any such country or on any such list.

7. **General**. This License is governed by the laws of the United States and the State of California, without reference to conflict of laws principles. The parties agree that the United Nations Convention on Contracts for the International Sale of Goods shall not apply to this License. If any provision of this Agreement is held invalid, the remainder of this License shall continue in full force and effect.

8. **More Information**. Should you have any questions concerning this Agreement, or if you desire to contact Licensor for any reason, please contact: CBT Systems USA Ltd., 1005 Hamilton Court, Menlo Park, California 94025, Attn: Chief Legal Officer.

IF YOU DO NOT AGREE WITH THE ABOVE TERMS AND CONDITIONS, SO NOT INSTALL THE SOFTWARE AND RETURN IT TO THE LICENSOR.

of the SOFTWARE will be uninterrupted or error-free. The Company warrants that the media on which the SOFTWARE is delivered shall be free from defects in materials and workmanship under normal use for a period of thirty (30) days from the date of your purchase. Your only remedy and the Company's only obligation under these limited warranties is, at the Company's option, return of the warranted item for a refund of any amounts paid by you or replacement of the item. Any replacement of SOFTWARE or media under the warranties shall not extend the original warranty period. The limited warranty set forth above shall not apply to any SOFTWARE which the Company determines in good faith has been subject to misuse, neglect, improper installation, repair, alteration, or damage by you. EXCEPT FOR THE EXPRESSED WARRANTIES SET FORTH ABOVE, THE COMPANY DISCLAIMS ALL WARRANTIES, EXPRESS OR IMPLIED, INCLUDING WITHOUT LIMITATION, THE IMPLIED WARRANTIES OF MERCHANTABILITY AND FITNESS FOR A PARTICULAR PURPOSE. EXCEPT FOR THE EXPRESS WARRANTY SET FORTH ABOVE, THE COMPANY DOES NOT WARRANT, GUARANTEE, OR MAKE ANY REPRESENTATION REGARDING THE USE OR THE RESULTS OF THE USE OF THE SOFTWARE IN TERMS OF ITS CORRECTNESS, ACCURACY, RELIABILITY, CURRENTNESS, OR OTHERWISE.

IN NO EVENT, SHALL THE COMPANY OR ITS EMPLOYEES, AGENTS, SUPPLIERS, OR CONTRACTORS BE LIABLE FOR ANY INCIDENTAL, INDIRECT, SPECIAL, OR CONSEQUENTIAL DAMAGES ARISING OUT OF OR IN CONNECTION WITH THE LICENSE GRANTED UNDER THIS AGREEMENT, OR FOR LOSS OF USE, LOSS OF DATA, LOSS OF INCOME OR PROFIT, OR OTHER LOSSES, SUSTAINED AS A RESULT OF INJURY TO ANY PERSON, OR LOSS OF OR DAMAGE TO PROPERTY, OR CLAIMS OF THIRD PARTIES, EVEN IF THE COMPANY OR AN AUTHORIZED REPRESENTATIVE OF THE COMPANY HAS BEEN ADVISED OF THE POSSIBILITY OF SUCH DAMAGES. IN NO EVENT SHALL LIABILITY OF THE COMPANY FOR DAMAGES WITH RESPECT TO THE SOFTWARE EXCEED THE AMOUNTS ACTUALLY PAID BY YOU, IF ANY, FOR THE SOFTWARE.

SOME JURISDICTIONS DO NOT ALLOW THE LIMITATION OF IMPLIED WARRANTIES OR LIABILITY FOR INCIDENTAL, INDIRECT, SPECIAL, OR CONSEQUENTIAL DAMAGES, SO THE ABOVE LIMITATIONS MAY NOT ALWAYS APPLY. THE WARRANTIES IN THIS AGREEMENT GIVE YOU SPECIFIC LEGAL RIGHTS AND YOU MAY ALSO HAVE OTHER RIGHTS WHICH VARY IN ACCORDANCE WITH LOCAL LAW.

ACKNOWLEDGMENT

YOU ACKNOWLEDGE THAT YOU HAVE READ THIS AGREEMENT, UNDERSTAND IT, AND AGREE TO BE BOUND BY ITS TERMS AND CONDITIONS. YOU ALSO AGREE THAT THIS AGREEMENT IS THE COMPLETE AND EXCLUSIVE STATEMENT OF THE AGREEMENT BETWEEN YOU AND THE COMPANY AND SUPERSEDES ALL PROPOSALS OR PRIOR AGREEMENTS, ORAL, OR WRITTEN, AND ANY OTHER COMMUNICATIONS BETWEEN YOU AND THE COMPANY OR ANY REPRESENTATIVE OF THE COMPANY RELATING TO THE SUBJECT MATTER OF THIS AGREEMENT.

Should you have any questions concerning this Agreement or if you wish to contact the Company for any reason, please contact in writing at the address below.

Robin Short

Prentice Hall PTR

One Lake Street

Upper Saddle River, New Jersey 07458

ABOUT THE CD-ROM

The CD-ROM included with *Dynamic Web Programming* contains the following:

Informix Dynamic Server/Universal Data Option (IDS/UDO)

The latest evaluation copy for Windows NT4 can be downloaded from www.intraware.com.

Web DataBlade Version 3.32 for NT4

Readers who have IDS/UDO for Windows NT4 already can install this datablade.
   Readers who don't have IDS/UDO can download the evaluation copy, and then install the datablade.

AppPage Builder

AppPage Builder is delivered with the Web DataBlade and is installed after the Web DataBlade is installed. Read the AppPage Builder installation notes shipped with the Web DataBlade after installing the Web DataBlade.

Data Director for Web

The latest evaluation copy can be downloaded from www.intraware.com

Type 4 JDBC Driver

Download from www.intraware.com to be sure to get the latest version of the 1.x driver.

Client/SDK

Download the latest version from www.intraware.com.

CBT Module

The training module titled "Introduction to the Java Language" is included.

Source code

Most of the listings from the book are included on this CD-ROM. All of the sample applications are included.

Utilities

The Omentree Software and the JLogin utility are included. You use Omentree to create cyberspace menus's. JLogin is used to test your JDBC connections.

Platforms

The CD-ROM can be used on Microsoft Windows® 95/98/NT®.

License Agreement

Use of the software accompanying *Dynamic Web Programming* is subject to the terms of the License Agreement and Limited Warranty, found on the previous two pages.

Technical Support

Prentice Hall does not offer technical support for any of the programs on the CD-ROM. However, if the CD-ROM is damaged, you may obtain a replacement copy by sending an email that describes the problem to: disc_exchange@prenhall.com